THE BLUE GUIDES

Runestone at Kulturen, Lund, with a wolf and commemorative inscription (c 1000)

BLUE GUIDE

Sweden

Mary Alderton

A & C Black
London

WW Norton
New York

First edition 1995

Published by A & C Black (Publishers) Limited
35 Bedford Row, London WC1R 4JH

Maps by Robert Smith.

A CIP catalogue record of this book
is available from the British Library.

ISBN 0-7136-3935-0

Published in the United States of America by
WW Norton and Company, Inc
500 Fifth Avenue, New York, NY 10110

Published simultaneously in Canada by
Penquin Books Canada Limited
10 Alcorn Avenue, Toronto, Ontario M4V 3B2

ISBN 0-393-31271-2 USA

The author and the publishers have done their best to ensure the accuracy of all the
information in Blue Guide Sweden; however, they can accept no responsibility for any
loss, injury or inconvenience sustained by any traveller as a result of information or
advice contained in the guide.

After studying languages at the universities of Belfast and Tübingen, Germany, **Mary
Alderton** took a Diploma in Visual Arts in London. In both England and Sweden she
has worked as a language teacher and free-lance journalist, with emphasis on travel
features. For some years she was editor of a local history magazine. She has travelled
over 24,000km in order to write this book.

The publishers and the author welcome comments, suggestions and corrections for the next edition of Blue Guide
Sweden. Writers of the most informative letters will be
awarded a free Blue Guide of their choice.

Printed by Bath Press

PREFACE

Sweden may surprise you. Neither climate nor landscape may be quite what you expect. It is not cold all the year round—the Gulf Stream sees to that, and summertime outdoor cafés thrive north of the Arctic Circle. Nor is the whole country submerged in deep snow in the winter, since the southern tip is on a level with the England/Scotland border. The land is not covered with wild mountains as some seem to think—wild some of it certainly is, but not mountainous except in the north along the border with Norway. Some aspects of Swedish society strike the visitor as quaintly archaic, while in others it patently leads the world.

What the Swedes themselves like about Sweden is the countryside and seashore: they have a deep, almost mystical, love of nature and solitary islands, woods, meadows and lakes. Since they came comparatively late to 20C technology and wealth their roots within living memory are in the countryside. Hence the hundreds of local history museums (*hembygdsgårdar*) which collect local wooden farm buildings of the 19C and early 20C—virtually every small town has one. But also scattered about the countryside are small treasures of archaeology and art that need only to be sought out. There are medieval churches, Renaissance castles and Baroque bell-towers, 18C pastel-painted towns, runestones and Bronze Age rock carvings, Gotland picture-stones and prehistoric ship-settings, as well as folk art expressed in painted wall-hangings and decorated wooden furniture and the unique Sami (Lapp) handicraft. The wilderness in summer offers elks, orchids and shooting the rapids, in winter husky-sleds and paraskiing.

I have tried to guide the visitor into discovering the cultural gems of Sweden amid the vastness and beauty of the landscape, as well as to understand some of the industrial and social history which has made the country what it is today.

This book could not have been written without generous help from friends and others. My friend Klara Ullman, a Stockholm guide, read the Stockholm section and made very many valuable comments. The ever-helpful staff of the Stockholm Information Service were at hand to assist in every possible way, and all over the country dozens of unknown people in local tourist bureaux and museums found information for me. Liz Sinclair read the history of art section and Mary Pooley the history section and both made excellent suggestions. Gemma Davies and Judy Tither of A & C Black have always been at hand with unfailing patience, good humour and help. Most of all, thanks go to my husband Patrick who devoted his weekends and holidays to driving the length and breadth of Sweden and much of the rest of his time to encouragement and constructive discussion.

A NOTE ON BLUE GUIDES

The Blue Guide series began in 1918 when Muirhead Guide-Books Limited published Blue Guide London and its Environs. Findlay and James Muirhead already had extensive experience of guide-book publishing: before the First World War they had been the editors of the English editions of the German Baedekers, and by 1915 they had acquired the copyright of most of the famous 'Red' Handbooks from John Murray.

An agreement made with the French publishing house Hachette et Cie in 1917 led to the translation of Muirhead's London guide, which became the first 'Guide Bleu', Hachette had previously published the blue-covered 'Guides Joanne'. Subsequently, Hachette's Guide Blue 'Paris et ses Environs' was adapted and published in London by Muirhead.

In 1931 Ernest Benn Limited took over the Blue Guides, appointing Russell Muirhead, Findlay Muirhead's son, editor in 1934. The Muirheads' connection with the Blue Guides ended in 1963, when Stuart Rossiter, who had been working on the Guides since 1954, became house editor, revising and compiling several of the books himself.

The Blue Guides are now published by A & C Black, who acquired Ernest Benn in 1984, so continuing the tradition of guide-book publishing which began in 1826 with 'Black's Economical Tourist of Scotland'. The series continues to grow: there are now more than 50 titles in print, with revised editions appearing regularly, and new titles in preparation.

CONTENTS

Maps and plans

BACKGROUND INFORMATION

Geography

The area of Sweden is just under 450,000 sq km, roughly that of Spain or California. It stretches 1600km from north to south and the maximum breadth is 450km. Over half the country is covered with forest and there are 100,000 lakes.

The flat southernmost province of Skåne belongs geologically to the plains of Denmark and north Germany, and is fertile arable land. Småland to the north of it is mainly forest. The belt between Gothenburg and Stockholm is very varied, with rolling hills, lakes and farmland. Then comes the division between southern and northern Sweden, with a band of metal-rich deposits. Norrland, as the northern half of the country is called, consists of forests, lakes, rivers and mountains. The western range of mountains along the border with Norway has peaks of between 1000m and 2000m, while the great river valleys are carved out from north-west to south-east. Tens of thousands of islands fringe the coast in the archipelagos.

Forest

Since 58 per cent of Sweden is covered by forest and the visitor's impression of endless trees is the one which tends to linger, a note on forests and forestry seems appropriate. In the extreme south, in Skåne, the coast of Blekinge and up the west coast, the natural vegetation is deciduous forest, though conifers have been introduced. The deciduous trees include birch, aspen, lime, ash, maple and elm. After this the belt of mixed deciduous/coniferous trees extends to somewhat north of lake Vänern. Most of the rest of Sweden is covered with coniferous forest, virtually all Scots pine (38 per cent) and Norway spruce (46 per cent), until in the far north subarctic tundra alternates with some conifers and the birch *Betula tortuosa*. These scrubby birches can extend further into the true tundra.

In southern Sweden most of the productive forest is in private hands, but in the north the State holds most—the public forests overall amount to almost a quarter of the total. Fifty per cent is privately owned and the last quarter is worked by companies, nearly all by seven very large concerns.

The 1600km-length of Sweden from the Baltic to beyond the Arctic Circle means that growing conditions vary immensely, and the yearly growing period in the north can be half of that in the south. The average tree ready for felling in the south is 70 years old, 30m high and has a diameter of 30cm. Compare this with a tree in the north which is twice as old, half as high and two-thirds of the thickness.

Complete clearing is the preferred method of management, since this appears to be best technically, economically and environmentally. Seventy per cent of the area cut is replanted, usually in spring, and mostly with young trees grown in pots in peat.

Storm damage is naturally a hazard, but forest fires are not too much of a problem—the last big fire was in 1983 when 650 hectares were destroyed in the south-east of the country. (This is not to say that visitors must not take the utmost care with fire in the forest.)

Transport is two-thirds by road and one-third by rail. River-floating no longer takes place—the last log went down the Klarälv in 1991. Sawmills are situated in the north, near the source of supply. The fact that they tend to be on the coast reflects the old timber-floating tradition on the rivers. Paper and pulp mills are more scattered.

Animals

The most numerous and best known of Scandinavian animals is the reindeer which always belongs to a Sami owner and therefore does not count as a wild animal. The other animal perhaps associated most with Sweden is the elk ('moose' in North America). There are so many thousands of these that they have to be culled every year. The forests of Småland and of course the north are their home, and the best time to see them is at dusk when they may come to the edge of a clearing to graze. On less frequented roads they can be fatally dangerous to traffic (see end of Lappland and the Sami).

Other Scandinavian animals in order of prevalence, with possible numbers, are: beavers (many thousands), grey seals (thousands), red deer (many hundreds), wild boars (hundreds), bears (hundreds), arctic foxes (few hundreds), wolverines (under 100), a few bisons and muskoxen, and a very few porpoises and wolves.

Climate

Because of the Gulf Stream, Sweden has a warmer climate than it has a right to expect. Also, in the summer the north warms up because of the long days, and so there is little difference between north and south—the average is around 15°C in July. In the winter there is a chilling difference—the average January temperature in Karesuando is –13.8°C, in Malmö 0°C.

Midnight Sun and Aurora Borealis

The duration of the midnight sun lengthens of course as you go north of the Arctic Circle, but you do not always appreciate how much it varies according to your altitude and that of surrounding hills. It is worth climbing a local hill for a better view, and on hills south of the Arctic Circle a good view can also be enjoyed around midsummer.

In northern Sweden the aurora borealis can be seen about as often as in Scotland, perhaps 30 times a year.

Population and Administration

There are 8.7 million people in Sweden. Greater Stockholm has 1.4 million, Greater Gothenburg 700,000, Greater Malmö 450,000 and Uppsala 100,500.—the only Swedish cities with over 100,000 inhabitants. The most densely populated area lies between the three largest cities, in the southern half of the country. In the northern half of the country there are only two towns with over 50,000 people.

For administrative purposes the country is divided into 24 counties which now take the place of the old provinces. The provinces, however, retain their identity in the public mind and in tourist literature, as they often encompass a more definable geographical area, keep certain local traditions and serve local food.

The counties are subdivided into municipalities which are regions centred on towns whose names they bear. However, the population figure given here after the name of the town refers not to the municipality but to the actual built-up area, and is given for towns with more than 5000 inhabitants.

Industry and Employment

The main industries in order of importance are engineering, forestry, foodstuffs, chemicals, iron and steel, and mining. Over 90 per cent of industry is privately owned. More than one-third of those employed work in the public sector, which here includes communications and much of the energy production.

Unemployment has been low compared to the rest of Europe, but is now rising. Holidays are generous, and social benefits cover every aspect of life. Many of the services, including health-care, however, have to be partly paid for by the individual. Value-added tax is very high, but salaries are comparatively low, so there is much reliance on State help.

A Brief History of Sweden

Sweden began to emerge from the last Ice Age about 12,000 BC. Gradually the land was settled, and traces of habitation from around 6000 BC have been found in the west and south. As the climate grew milder, hunting and fishing communities were established and spread northwards and east-wards.

The **New Stone Age** period with its knowledge of agriculture reached southern Sweden about 3000 BC. People lived in long houses, farmed, mined flint and traded in Baltic amber. Their collective burials were in earth mounds, some containing stone cists, or megalithic tombs, dolmens, stone cists without mounds or passage graves. These occur in a band round western and southern Sweden and in Västergötland.

In the far north, however, hunting and fishing as a way of life—the **Arctic Stone Age**—continued as late as the Iron Age of southern regions. Tools and weapons were of slate or sometimes quartz, and elks, reindeer and bear were hunted by driving them over waterfalls.

Although the New Stone age began in Scandinavia about the same time as in Britain and Northern Europe, the beginning of the **Bronze Age** (c 1500–500 BC) was delayed because there are no metals found in southern Sweden. It was not until about 1500 BC that amber began to be traded for bronze which was worked into horns, helmets, weapons, ornaments and containers with geometrical and spiral designs. Flint was used for everyday purposes, hence favouring the southern provinces where flint was available. Most rock carvings are from the Bronze Age with some from the Late Stone Age—the change-over period lasted several centuries. Individual burial was usually in barrows or cairns, cremation became customary, and continued into the Iron Age.

The intriguing **ship-settings**, with upright boulders set in the shape of a boat, are dated to the Bronze Age or Iron Age according to the objects found in the vicinity. The largest tend to be later, though there are exceptions. The largest of all, Ales Stenar in Skåne, is said to be from the Viking period. Most are orientated north–south with the prow pointing south or at least between south-west and south-east, so the supposition is that burial in such a ship, probably after cremation, ensures the re-union of the deceased with the sun. Judgement rings of standing stones are usually dated to the Iron Age.

The **Iron Age** began in Sweden in about 500 BC, as in the rest of Europe, but is considered by Swedish historians to last until the year 1000, and includes the Viking Age. Bog ore was found in lakes and was therefore available to all, unlike bronze which had to be imported, and flint which occurred in limited areas. Trade began with the Roman Empire and Tacitus described the Suiones in AD 98 as a warrior people who had fleets of warships. They were probably the Svea who inhabited central Sweden and gradually assumed superiority over the Goths who lived to the south. Great forts were constructed, for example on the islands of Öland and Gotland.

The Old English *Beowulf* written in the 8C about events in the 5C and 6C sheds some light on society at this period since its characters can be linked with Swedish and Danish historical figures. Cremation continued to be the custom, with flat graves, and sometimes barrows, and large cemeteries of standing stones. (Since the shapes formed by these standing stones can be circles, triangles, squares or ship-shaped, I have for convenience used the Swedish-derived term 'stone-setting' to cover all of them.)

The **Roman Iron Age** (c 0–400) is a subdivision of the Iron Age, and many artefacts from the empire are found in Sweden. The **Vendel Period** (550–800) is so called because of the very rich grave-goods found in boat burials at Vendel in Uppland, which have some similarity to the finds at Sutton Hoo in England.

In arctic regions, the **Sami Iron Age** is reckoned to date from the beginning of the Christian era to around 1600. The oldest archaeological finds indentified as Sami are from the end of the first century. Trapping-pits cover a very long span, from the New Stone Age to the Middle Ages.

The **Viking Age** (c 800–1050) which overlapped into medieval times saw the three countries Sweden, Denmark and Norway beginning to carve separate destinies. (The southern provinces of Skåne, Halland, Blekinge and Bohuslän until the 17C were part of Denmark and Norway. Norway and Denmark were united until 1814.) By the Viking era the great migrations of whole peoples which had characterised earlier centuries were complete. Scandinavians set off to expand and explore. Swedish Vikings chose the east and south-east and moved along the great rivers of Russia, to which they, called 'Rus', gave their name. Similarly personal names were taken over, like 'Waldemar' which became 'Vladimir'. As indefatigable traders they penetrated to Kiev, along the Dnieper to the Black Sea and Constantinople, or they followed the Volga to the Caspian Sea, and even reached Baghdad and Bokhara, bringing back wealth and treasure. Byzantine emperors availed themselves of their fighting spirit by forming their Varangian guard. At home the Vikings established a trading town at Birka on lake Mälaren where Arabic coins have been found, among others, testifying to far-flung commercial connections.

The **Middle Ages** (c 1000–1500) can be said to begin with the baptism of king Olof Skötkonung in 1008. The ancient Asa cult of the Vikings remained remarkably tenacious, especially in Gamla (Old) Uppsala. Ansgar, a monk from Corvey, had attempted to convert the population of Birka in the 9C and other missionaries followed him, but without lasting success. Even after Olof embraced the faith, it was not until a century later that the first bishop was installed at Skara, under the archbishop of Hamburg/Bremen. The first Swedish archbishop took up his office in Old Uppsala in 1164.

Changes and upheaval in the religious and political realms abated somewhat in the 12C. New villages were established, with new churches, and monasteries were founded at Alvastra, Nydala, Varnhem and Roma. Each province had a *ting*, council, already a feature of earlier centuries, and a class of so-called *magnates* emerged from the more prosperous peasantry. At the same time forays abroad brought conquests in Finland, Russia and the Baltic countries. Meanwhile in the Danish part of southern Sweden a bishop's see was established in Dalby, and then in Lund.

Gradually society began to resemble to some extent the feudal structure of Europe. The king was elected and after his election travelled around on a royal progress, the 'Eriksgata', accepting allegiance. By the middle of the 13C Sweden had achieved a certain unity and was able from then on to assert its national identity.

The rule of **Birger Jarl** in the 13C, known as the first of the Folkung dynasty, was one of relative calm and prosperity. He encouraged the enterprises of German merchants in Sweden, fortified Stockholm, built a castle at Örebro and began the conquest of Finland. A middle class arose and new trading towns were founded. Laws were formulated, the oldest surviving provincial laws being those of Västergötland, which deal with both peasant rights and constitutional matters. The 13C was the beginning of the golden age of Gotland with Visby at its heart, where the medieval town wall still survives today.

Magnus Ladulås (1275–90) won the support of the Church and nobles, re-organised the civil service and protected the common people from exploitation. The Falun copper-mine began to yield its riches. In the following century the iron-mines of Bergslagen were being worked in an organised fashion, controlled by the State. The 14C also brought bad news, in the form of the Black Death which arrived from England, images of which are captured in Ingmar Bergman's film *The Seventh Seal*.

St. Birgitta was the most outstanding personality of the century. A noblewoman of charismatic personality and forceful character, she spent many years obtaining permission from the Pope to found the order of Brigettines at Vadstena, travelled immense distances on pilgrimage, advised the powerful and recorded her visions for posterity.

During the 13C and 14C, the **Hanse** merchants of Lübeck had increased trade with Sweden, and thereby the network's presence and power in Sweden. The town of Visby on Gotland became a vital staging-post and depot for Russian furs, English wool, Indian and West African spices, French wine and German beer, among other rich commodities. Valdemar Atterdag of Denmark attacked Sweden, conquered the southern provinces and in 1361 took Visby demanding a huge ransom. He was succeeded by his five-year-old grandson, heir to the three kingdoms of Sweden, Denmark and Norway, who died young.

But the disgruntled Swedes chose the German Albrecht of Mecklenburg to rule them for a brief interlude before **Queen Margareta** was able once more to unite the three kingdoms which she ruled with strength and wisdom (1389–96). In 1396 her great-nephew Erik of Pomerania was crowned but she continued to rule. By the **Union of Kalmar** the three countries were formally joined but each kept its own laws. When Erik took over the throne he devoted much effort and money to fighting the Hanse. Partly because of high taxes, there was a popular uprising in 1434 led by Engelbrekt Engelbrektsson of Bergslagen.

By the mid 15C the Union of Kalmar had foundered, and unrest, civil war and disorder took over. Under the regency of Sten Sture the Elder the Danes were beaten back at the Battle of Brunkeberg (Stockholm) in 1471, by a coalition of nobles and peasantry. This century also saw the establishment of the Swedish Parliament of four estates in the 1460s, and the foundation of the first university, at Uppsala in 1477.

At the beginning of the 16C Christian II of Denmark made a determined thrust to conquer Sweden once and for all and his efforts culminated in the Stockholm Bloodbath of 1520 when 82 of his opponents, including churchmen, were slaughtered on Stortorget (Main Square) in Stockholm.

The **Reformation** and **Renaissance** period was ushered in by the larger-than-life personality of **Gustav Vasa**. He led the final rebellion against the Danes and established Sweden as an independent power, helped by internal problems in Denmark and with the support of Lübeck. In 1521 he was a young fugitive, and by 1523 had become king (1523–60). Since he needed money urgently the quickest way of getting it was by sequestrating the property of the Church, so although of course other causes contributed to the Reformation in Sweden, the main motive was more financial than theological.

His sons Erik XIV, Johan III and Karl IX ruled after him until 1611—the 16C was imprinted with the Vasa stamp, with the exception of the few years when Johan's half-Polish son Sigismund reigned over Sweden and Poland together (1592–99). The power of the Hanse was broken, and Sweden became an hereditary monarchy. Lutheranism was confirmed by the Uppsala Assembly of 1593. Estonia became Swedish thus giving access to trade routes to Russia, while in the other direction settlement in the bleak northern territories was encouraged.

Gustav II Adolf, better known to European history as **Gustavus Adolphus** (1611–32), the 'Lion of the North', led Sweden into her great European adventure. At home, he reformed the administration, imported Dutch money, merchants and architects, saw to it that the resources of iron, copper and timber financed his plans, and founded Gothenburg. Abroad, the Thirty Years War, centred on the rivalries of German princes, was raging and Wallenstein the Hapsburg Commander-in-Chief invaded Jutland, so Gustavus Adolphus gathered his troops to enter the fray. He defeated Tilly, temporarily commanding the Hapsburg army, at Breitenfeld and continued south. In 1632 his army defeated Wallenstein at the battle of Lützen, but he was killed. Gustavus Adolphus was considered by Napoleon to be the equal of Hannibal, Alexander and Caesar on the battlefield, but he was also a cultured and religious man, and a statesman and politician of world stature who had made Sweden a power to be reckoned with in European politics.

Kristina, his daughter, was only six years old, but her chancellor was the brilliant Axel Oxenstierna. At the Peace of Westphalia, Sweden acquired a string of possessions along the north coast of Germany. Kristina became an intellectual and highly educated woman, and encouraged cultural contacts with Europe. The philosopher René Descartes came to Stockholm, but unfortunately did not long survive the climate. Kristina abdicated in 1654—her reasons included the fact that she had become a Catholic.

Kristina's cousin, **Karl X Gustav** (1654–60), succeeded her. During his reign the southern provinces of Halland, Blekinge, Skåne and Bohuslän became Swedish by the Treaty of Roskilde in 1658. A dramatic episode in the campaign was an epic march across the frozen Great Belt orchestrated by the gifted commander Erik Dahlberg. By 1658 Sweden was a Great Power, owning the land within her shore-line, plus west Finland, Estonia, Livonia, Pomerania and Bremen, thus ringing the Baltic. She even cast her eyes across the Atlantic, founding New Sweden, in Delaware. But still the south was rebellious, helped by Danish pique, and the Skåne War rumbled on until 1679 when yet another peace was signed.

The wars and adventures had been financed by selling land to the nobles with the result that **Karl XI** had to do something about the wealth and power of the upper classes. His drastic action is known as 'reduction', after which the aristocracy controlled only one-third of the land. He also re-organised the army and its finances, giving the officers farms and the foot-soldiers cottages.

In 1700 Russia, Poland and Denmark made a concerted attack against Sweden but **Karl XII** managed to repel them until he was defeated at the battle of Poltava in 1707. He was killed at the siege of Fredriksten in Norway in 1718. After his death peace treaties meant the loss of Sweden's Baltic provinces, and internally there was a reaction to Karl's autocratic rule. Parliament and Council were able to limit royal power and establish a species of parliamentary government.

The 18C was a time of cultural flowering inspired by France, and at the same time of trade expansion. The Swedish East India Company began operations in 1731, and efforts were again made to exploit the northern territories, this time by founding the coastal towns of Umeå, Piteå and Luleå. Under the cultivated **Gustav III** (1771–92), intellectual and artistic achievements reached a high point, but there were strong undercurrents of disaffection. The king was assassinated by an officer named Anckarström as he attended the opera-house in Stockholm.

In the Napoleonic wars Gustav IV Adolf took Britain's part and because of this lost Pomerania and Finland. The king was regarded as personally to blame and was deposed in 1809. His childless uncle took the throne, and since a successor was not to be found, Parliament invited Marshal Jean-Baptiste Bernadotte to be heir-apparent. He was eventually to reign as **Karl XIV Johan** (1818–44).

During the 19C there was a huge increase of population from 2,500,000 in 1815, to almost double that in 1900. In 1827 a thorough agricultural reform was carried through, and small parcels of land were gathered into viable units, while tight-knit groups of farms were dispersed to widely scattered more economic holdings. But increased efficiency could not contain the population. Other factors such as bad harvests, the increasing ease of transport and the wish for more personal freedom meant that from 1850 onwards emigration to America became a familiar option. In 1887 47,000 people left for America, and between 1850 and 1920 the total was over a million.

Industrial expansion gathered speed at the end of the century. Steam-powered sawmills made timber available in greater quantities, and metal industries were further developed. Industrial and trade associations were formed and free enterprise blossomed. Yet 50 per cent of the population still earned their living from agriculture.

The latter part of the 19C saw the birth of a host of popular movements. The Social Democratic movement burgeoned, together with the co-operative and the adult education movements, and organised sport. Bismarck's German Empire was admired and relations with Germany in fields of commerce and culture were enthusiastically pursued. All through the century there had been repeated disagreements with Norway which threatened the union established in 1814 and under which Norway had had self-government under a Governor General. Finally in 1905 the Union was dissolved.

After the First World War, Sweden's startling economic advance was based on her industrial products, from vacuum cleaners to ball-bearings. She suffered in the slump, not helped by the crash of Ivan Kreuger's industrial empire, and his suicide in 1932. That year also saw a new Social Democratic government under Per Albin Hansson, and the Social Democrats have now ruled Sweden for over 60 years, with only brief intermissions. This was the birth of the Swedish dream, the 'Home of the People', by which an attempt was made to create an ideal environment for living.

In 1940, Denmark and Norway were occupied by Germany, and Sweden's neutrality was strained but survived almost intact, though this time feelings in general turned against the Germans. After the Second World War the country made giant strides, since her neutrality meant her economy was relatively unscathed. The Welfare State came into its own, and for a time the national prosperity could afford it. The country welcomed immigrants to work in the factories which were the basis of its industrial wealth. There are now about half a million foreign nationals in the country.

A severe dent in the national self-esteem was caused by the assassination in 1986 of the Prime Minister Olof Palme, which has never been satisfactorily cleared up.

By 1991 more than half the population were receiving government money in one way or another. This includes those working in the public sector who made up about one-third of all employees. In recent years people have not been so ready to pay the very high income and product taxes necessary to finance State care, and at the same time demand is outstripping provision of state services.

Sweden is torn between the east, once her traditional outlet, now that the barriers are down, and the west, with the EU seeming to promise a new beginning. She was a founder member of EFTA in 1960, and now membership of the European Union, helped by the planned bridge between Malmö and Copenhagen, would make her part of Europe as never before.

Rulers of Sweden

Stenkil Dynasty	1061–1130
Dynasties of Sverker and of Erik	
Sverker I	1130–1156
Erik the Holy (St. Erik)	1156–1160
Magnus Henriksson	1160–1161
Karl Sverkersson	1161–1167
Kol and Burislev	1167–1169
Knut Eriksson	1169–1195
Sverker Karlsson	1195–1208
Erik Knutsson	1208–1216
Jon Sverkersson	1216–1222
Erik Eriksson	1222–1229
	1234–1250
Knut the Tall	1229–1234
Birger Jarl (regent)	1248–1266

Folkung Dynasty

Valdemar	1250–1275
Magnus Ladulås	1275–1290
Birger Magnusson	1290–1318
Magnus Eriksson	1319–1364
Albrecht of Mecklenburg	1364–1389

Danish Union and others

Margareta	1389–1396
Erik of Pomerania	1396–1439
Engelbrekt (regent)	1435–1436
Karl Knutsson Bonde (regent)	1438–1441
Kristofer of Bavaria	1441–1448
Karl Knutsson Bonde (regent)	1448–1457
	1464–1465
	1467–1470
Christian I	1457–1464
Sten Sture the Elder (regent)	1470–1497
	1501–1503
Hans	1497–1501
Svante Nilsson Sture (regent)	1504–1512
Sten Sture the Younger (regent)	1512–1520
Christian II	1520–1521

The Vasa Dynasty

Gustav Vasa (as regent)	1521–1523
(as king)	1523–1560
Erik XIV	1560–1568
Johan III	1568–1592
Sigismund	1592–1599
Duke Karl (regent)	1592–1604
Karl IX (Duke Karl)	1604–1611
Gustavus Adolphus (Gustav II Adolf)	1611–1632
Kristina	1632–1654

Palatinate Dynasty

Karl X Gustav	1654–1660
Karl XI	1660–1697
Karl XII	1697–1718
Ulrika Eleonora	1719–1720
Fredrik I of Hesse	1720–1751

Holstein-Gottorp Dynasty

Adolf Fredrik	1751–1771
Gustav III	1771–1792
Gustav IV Adolf	1792–1809
Karl XIII	1809–1818

Bernadotte Dynasty

Karl XIV Johan	1818–1844
Oskar I	1844–1859
Karl XV	1859–1872
Oskar II	1872–1907
Gustav V	1907–1950
Gustav VI Adolf	1950–1973
Carl XVI Gustaf	1973–

Lappland and the Sami

'Lapp' is not a Sami word. 'Sami' is their own name for themselves, or rather the English version of it which they prefer. The Swedish is (singular) *Same*, (plural) *Samer*. Their name for their land is *Sápmi*, which really ought to be used in place of Lappland, or Lapland as it is often spelt in English.

It may be confusing to see 'Lappland' on some Swedish maps, occupying approximately the western half of the modern counties of Västerbotten and Norrbotten. This was an old province now superseded as an administrative area. More generally, the word is used for the area where Sami people live and herd their reindeer—in Norway, Sweden, Finland and Russia. It may be derived from *Lappi*, the name of the Finnish region where they live. In Sweden Sami country extends over half the length of the land, down to the northern parts of Dalarna. Naturally they also move to other regions and pursue other occupations—there are 2000 Sami in Stockholm, for example.

Although their area in Sweden is far greater than in the other countries listed above, there are not so many of them—17,000—as in Norway (35,000); 4000 live in Finland and 2000 in the Kola Peninsula in Russia, giving a total of 58,000. These are official figures and the Sami themselves believe there could be up to 100,000 of them.

When the last ice-age came to an end wild reindeer roamed northwards followed by semi-nomadic hunters of unknown origin. As the ice retreated they spread across the north of the Norwegian coast and the Kola peninsula. They are of an entirely different race to the Swedes who are descended from Germanic tribes, like the English and the Germans.

Tacitus in the year 98 was the first to mention *fenni*, probably Sami. In the translation of Orosius' history, written or sponsored by King Alfred of England in the 9C, the name *finnas* occurs, linked with reindeer. Adam of Bremen (11C) mentions missionaries to the Sami and Saxo Grammaticus (13C) praises their skiing and archery. The Norse sagas contain references too, notably in Snorri Sturluson's 'Heimskringla' (13C). In the Middle Ages, the church and tax officials both became interested in the Sami, and began to gather information. From the 11C missionaries were sent out to them, but the old religion (see below) persisted until the 18C.

The Sami lived within defined areas, and survived by hunting, trapping and fishing, eating reindeer, beaver and salmon. They exchanged furs for weapons, pottery, jewellery and beer. It is thought they used domesticated reindeer for transport in the 9C and that reindeer-breeding gradually developed from this. By the 16C they were known as intensive reindeer-breeders. In 1673 a German, Johannes Schefferus, wrote 'Lapponia', a summation of what was known at that time.

With the discovery of mineral wealth in the north, Swedes took greater interest in the area: this began as early as the 17C with the discovery of silver. From 1673 Swedish 'settlers' were encouraged by concessions over taxes and military service to make a home and living for themselves in the north. They were given small parcels of land, but what was worse for the Sami was their fishing in waters which the Sami had regarded as theirs. The discovery of the great iron deposits brought Swedish money, railways, roads and towns to transform large tracts of the environment and limit grazing areas. The first reindeer-grazing law of 1886 had restricted the Sami's right to land and water to one of usage only, and when the great dams began to be built in the early 20C this reduced the traditional fishing areas also. The growth of the forestry industry also impinged on the traditional grazing areas of the reindeer, when swathes of timber were cut.

The 20C therefore saw the beginnings of a popular movement, not only among the Sami but among enlightened Scandinavians, who began to seek ways of amicable and just co-existence. One 20C problem is that of tourism. Not only are large areas devoted to catering for the tourist, but visitors encroach on the traditional way of life, can disturb reindeer herds and destroy the environment. A slight conflict of interest emerges between the Sami who are modernising reindeer-breeding and the tourist authorities who promote the picturesqueness of old Sami customs, but this is being solved in some imaginative ways.

A permanent central organisation, the Swedish Sami Association, was formed in 1950; the Nordic Sami Council was founded in 1953 to safeguard Sami interests in Scandinavia; the 1971 Reindeer Grazing Act established the rights of breeders; and various cultural bodies promote the arts, and youth activities. A flag was adopted in 1986, of red, blue, green and yellow, the colours most seen in Sami textiles. The Sami in Finland have had their own parliament since 1973, in Norway since 1989 and in Sweden since 1993.

Sami Language

The Sami language is related to Finnish. Both belong to a very small group of languages, the Finno-Ugric—also containing Hungarian—which are, oddly, not related to the great Indo-European family of languages. The Sami language can be divided into three: Southern, roughly the southern part of Swedish and Norwegian Sami areas; Central, the rest of Sweden and Norway with the Finnish Sami area; and Eastern in the Kola Peninsula in Russia. Each of these is sub-divided into respectively two, three and four sections, and some of the sub-divisions are mutually incomprehensible.

The first attempt to investigate the language was in 1557 when an English sea-captain compiled a list of 95 words. In the 17C books began to be written in Sami, but until the 20C most were on religious subjects. By looking at place-names in northern Sweden one can recognise that, for example, Jokkmokk and Svappavaara are not Swedish, but it is less easy to distinguish Sami from Finnish, and the linguistic map has great overlaps and curves. To simplify: all along the Norwegian frontier and some distance inland most names are Sami; north and east of Gällivare the non-Swedish names (the vast majority) could be Finnish, especially on the east, while south and west of it they are almost certainly Sami. On Swedish maps the Lule district version of spelling has been adopted, but it does tend to vary quite a bit.

Here for interest are some elements which can be recognised in place-names.

akka	old woman
jaure	lake
jokk, jåkka, etc.	large brook
kaise (Kebnekaise)	steep pointed mountain
kiruna	ptarmigan
loukta	creek
luspe	head of the rapids
pakte	steep cliff
sarek	little mountain
tuoddar, tunturi, Dundret	bare low fell
vare, vaara	mountain
voume	forest

The language has a very rich vocabulary in certain areas. There are eight seasons, one extra in between each pair of the usual four. One reindeer can be described in such detail that it can be picked out of a herd of several thousand, while snow in all its states can be described in several hundred ways.

In the second half of the 20C a true Sami literature has begun to develop. Besides the written and spoken language there is also a series of signs for the sun, gods, holy man, church, camp, boats, animals, holy drum and so on. These are found on holy drums, and horn jewellery and other items.

Education

In the 17C an attempt was made to educate Sami children in Swedish schools and it was hoped to train some as clergy to convert others. It was the Church which eventually established Sami schools and they often used Sami as the medium of instruction. In the first half of the 20C however Swedish was encouraged, so that the children could integrate with Swedish society. Now the families themselves choose the language they prefer.

There are some Sami pre-schools, but few Sami day-care centres. The ordinary Sami schools give the same education as Swedish schools but include instruction in Sami language and culture. In Jokkmokk there is a Sami adult college, and universities are beginning to establish departments of Sami language and culture.

Handicrafts

Lack of space in living-quarters meant that beauty in created objects had to be of use, and frequent moving meant that they had also to be tough, preferably of a rounded shape. Most families used to spend at least some time on handicrafts during slack periods of the year, and now some Sami specialise in producing work for sale to tourists. Unfortunately, there are many imitations. The label with the word 'Duodji' should ensure an article has genuinely been made by a Sami craftsman.

Reindeer skin is exquisitely soft. It is made into coats, caps, gloves and bags of all sizes from purses to rucksacks. Different parts of the skin are used for different purposes: that of the head and thighs for example is traditionally used for footwear. Reindeer sinews form the traditional sewing-thread.

Reindeer horn, preferably from the male, is used for making knife-handles and sheaths, small boxes, spoons, weaving heddles and jewellery. (Knife sheaths are also made of leather and wood, and have a characteristic bend at the end, for safety.) Sometimes elk-horn is used instead. The horn is intricately carved with Sami symbols, or geometrical or stylised floral designs. A design resembling woven ribbons is common, especially in the south. Mountain birchwood is used for carving out scoops, spoons and containers of various shapes and sizes.

Tin 'embroidery' is a particular art. Very fine threads of tin are drawn out, and one closely wrapped around another. These are laid on cloth and leather in elaborate patterns and sewn in place. The effect when several strands are laid together in curved and straight lines is both artistic and luxurious. Tin patterns are sewn on to bags, watch-straps, collars, belts and caps.

The foremost textile craft is making woven bands in brightly coloured wool which are then used to decorate clothing and to make ties and belts. Bands can be simply plaited without tools to make shoe-laces. The woven bands are made using a heddle of preferably reindeer-horn, or wood. A shuttle may be used to draw the wool through the threads but is not essential. The colours used today are the traditional red, blue, yellow and green with newer dyes as well.

Music

The Sami narrative song is called a y*oik*. It is pentatonic and has no beginning or end. Yoiking is a way of recalling history, describing nature and telling stories, and is often used for yoiking a person worthy of distinction. In the 18C and 19C it was suppressed by the missionaries, but is enjoying a revival, especially in the north.

Religion

The pre-Christian religion was closely linked with nature. A *seite*, a stone or piece of wood which stood on a holy place, was regarded as holy and offerings were made to it. Today the visitor is requested not to move anything from its position, even a set of antlers.

Every person and animal had two souls, one in the body and one outside which functioned as a protective being. The *noaidi* was the holy man or shaman who with the aid of his holy drum could enter a state of ecstasy and communicate with the dead and the gods of the dead. His first obligation was to the sick and he was believed to persuade the gods to allow the sick person to return to life on promise of certain offerings. The drums were nearly all destroyed by missionaries and there are only about 70 left. Bears were special messengers of the gods.

Reindeer-breeding

Only 15 per cent of Sami are now reindeer-breeders, with about 2500 in Sweden. There are about 275,000 reindeer in Sweden, out of a total of 750,000 in Sápmi as a whole. Until this century the southern Sami were completely nomadic, moving between forests in winter and higher pastures in summer. Others lived more or less permanently in forests, also doing some hunting and fishing. Now although some families move seasonally they have permanent homes as well.

The breeders are organised in 43 'villages' with defined rights, and only Sami may belong. Reindeer-breeding areas cover about one-third of the area of Sweden, that is, almost all of the counties of Norrbotten, Väster-botten and Jämtland, with large parts of Kopparberg and Västernorrland. The herds are gathered several times a year: in the summer, to mark the new calves; in autumn for slaughter, mainly of males; and again when snow comes—they are split into smaller groups to move to winter grazing. In the spring they return to the calving areas.

Those that move in summer eat the grass above the tree-line; in winter they graze on lichen under the snow. Lichen takes a long time to grow therefore very large areas are needed for grazing. Unfortunately the lichen absorbed large quantities of radio-active fall-out from Chernobyl in 1986, which spelt disaster for Sami exports of reindeer meat. The problems were compounded by uncertainty, conflicting advice and unexpected results from tests on animals. Now rigorous testing ensures the safety of reindeer meat.

Today radio-telephones, helicopters and snow-scooters simplify the task of herding. Reindeer may also be transported by lorry.

Homes

A reindeer-breeder may live in a tent made of birch poles fixed in a tall cone shape and covered with cloth: there is an opening at the top to let the smoke out. A central path is often marked out with stones, leading to the fireplace; around are furs on birch twigs, and utensils, tools and other possessions. The log hut is about 4m by 4m and 2m high, and usually consists of a truncated pyramid shape set on a low vertical wall. The slightly sloping top is a trap-door which can let the smoke out, and the floor is of beaten earth or concrete. The storage huts are on piles to keep out damp and animals, and some huts may be made of turf.

The Tourist in the North

Visitors are requested not to drop litter—it takes far longer to decay, possibly years, when temperatures are low for most of the year. Reindeer-herding and slaughtering are impressive to watch but spectators should try to keep well out of the way of workers. Avoid going near reindeer with calves.

Reindeer always belong to someone, so any accident must be reported. Elks do not belong to anyone but if you have an accident involving an elk it can be fatal—animals cause more than half of motoring accidents in Sweden, and 5 per cent of fatal ones. Do not move large natural objects (see under Religion above).

Art and Architecture in Sweden

Prehistoric

In Sweden, the Iron Age is reckoned to have lasted until AD 1000, so anything before that date is regarded as prehistoric. There are in any case few written records.

Rock carvings in Sweden start in the late New Stone Age period but the majority are from the Bronze Age (c 1500–500 BC). At Nämforsen they are mainly of animals, with elks predominating, but also fish, ships with crews, sun-wheels (circles containing a cross) and footprints. In Bohuslän the animals are cattle, pigs and deer, with hunters, ships, cup-marks and footprints. At Kivik there is a procession with chariots, animals, sun-wheels and ships.

During the **Roman Iron Age** (0–400) beautifully worked gold brachteates (thinly-beaten leaves) found their way to Sweden. The Vendel treasures found in boat burials in Uppland (550–800) consist of harness, weapons and armour ornamented with stylised animals with patterned bodies in gilt bronze.

The **picture-stones** of Gotland are unique. They date from the 5C to the 11C, and are adorned with spirals and interlaced patterns, horses and men, ships and dragons. A fuller description will be found in the Gotland section.

Runestones are another genre, this time common to Norway, Denmark and Sweden, used by the Germanic tribes in their native languages. The word *rune* means secret conversation or whispering. The runic alphabet was derived from or was influenced at various stages by the Greek, Latin and Etruscan alphabets. The first Primitive Norse runic alphabet had 24 letters, but about the beginning of the Viking Age these were reduced to 16, called the 'futhark' after the first six runes ('th' counts as one). Therefore one letter had to represent two or three different sounds, but even so with a knowledge of modern Swedish it is surprisingly easy to pick out words. The strokes are straight and angular, forming tall narrow letters with R and B occasionally rounded. The words are separated by small Xs.

Inscriptions have been found as far south as the Black Sea where the Vikings arrived by following the rivers. Others have been found in Scotland, the Orkneys and the Isle of Man. They serve to define the sphere of action of the Vikings, their world of commerce and their trade routes.

Runes were in use in Scandinavia as early as AD 200, carved on stone or metal objects, seldom written on paper or parchment. They were as a rule carved on tall standing stones but have also been found on metal or bone, or on wood if they are in medieval churches where occasionally they have been in Latin. The early inscriptions are difficult to decipher and appear to be magic spells. Others form poetry, with an alliterative rhyme-scheme.

In Sweden runestones are dated to between 800 and 1100, more or less coinciding with the Viking Age, with most from the 11C. There are between 3000 and 4000 and the majority are in the county of Uppland, north of Stockholm. They were placed by well-trodden paths, and tell of local inhabitants, but also of Viking sallies and commercial ventures to Russia, England and Denmark. Most are in the form of an epitaph giving the name of the dead person and the name of the one erecting the stone. Many have a religious content, or record virtues and peaceful deeds, such as building bridges or founding churches, as well as death in battle or far away. Much information has been gleaned from them about people, places, buildings, journeys, rights and boundaries. They were the first Christian monuments. Years are never given but sometimes a king is mentioned which narrows down the time span. The most famous Swedish stone at Rök, which has 800 signs, still defies complete interpretation after a hundred years of research.

Some have pictures, with crosses as well as dragons, snakes and wolves, with strapwork designs. The inscriptions themselves are usually carved on a ribbon which edges the stone, or coils itself over the surface. Traces of colour show they were painted in red, white and brown.

Romanesque (c 1000–1250)

Christianity came to Sweden in the early years of the 11C when King Olof Skötkonung was baptised at Husaby in 1008. The first churches were stave churches, such as still survive in Norway, built with upright timbers either driven into the ground or attached to a timber sill. The technique survived in Sweden's only stave church at Hedared now dated to as late as the 16C. In Lund remains of six stave churches have been found, while in the 12C Skog tapestry a stave church is shown with carved dragons' heads on the roof which give it an exotic appearance like Norwegian examples.

After this most churches were built of stone, mainly granite except in Skåne and Gotland where sandstone and limestone predominate; in forested regions wooden churches naturally continued. Brick-making was introduced to Skåne (a Danish province) in the late 12C, but did not reach Sweden until later. The oldest ground plan introduced by English missionaries in Västergötland had a simple rectangular nave and smaller rectangular chancel, then a lower round apse began to be added at the end of the 11C. The first archdiocese in Scandinavia was established at Lund, then in Denmark, in 1103, and Lund cathedral, though substantially a 19C rebuilding, is a remarkably homogenous representation of how it probably looked when first completed. Germany (the two west towers) and Lombardy (arcaded apse) have contributed to its architectural antecedents and the decorative sculpture shows Lombard and Byzantine traits in the animals and twining vegetation. This gathering of expertise in Lund benefited Skåne as skilled men went on to work in the countryside around.

The Cistercians who founded the first Swedish monastery at Alvastra in 1185 brought Burgundian traits to their churches, with straight-ended chancel and barrel-vaulted nave. Varnhem monastery church was built by monks from Alvastra and begins to show Gothic tendencies, with a round apse with ambulatory and chapels, and Roma on Gotland was another daughter foundation from Alvastra. Some churches were built for defence. A few are circular (as at Hagby), some have broad defensive towers as in south-east Skåne, and some have or had free-standing towers as at Brunflo.

There is a surprising amount of Romanesque **sculpture** in Swedish country churches. Isolated stone reliefs decorate churches inside or out and there are some carved tombs, but the number and quality of baptismal fonts is particularly impressive. Because sandstone was the preferred material, Gotland and Skåne are rich in them, and several schools can be distinguished. The school of Hegvald combined crowded figures and interlacing in a soft rounded style. One of the main workshops was that at Tryde, Skåne, also called the Majestatis workshop because the main theme was Christ in Majesty. Another is the Byzantios workshop with Byzantine and Lombardic nuances in the flat treatment and subjects of the sculptures showing stylised intricately decorated animals. The workshop of Sigraf may be that of a pupil of Byzantios.

The **wood-carvings** are another treasure. The large crucifixes of this early period tend to show Byzantine features giving the faces an Oriental look, an influence from the work of the Rhineland. (These crucifixes are known in Swedish and in the often available English leaflets as triumphal crucifixes whether the figure is in the earlier triumphal style, or of the later suffering type. This is because the chancel arch is similarly known and translated as the triumphal arch.) Figures of the Virgin or Virgin and Child also show German traits perhaps brought by Premonstratensian monks. The Cistercians brought some French influence from the Île de France with stiff monumental figures.

Wall-paintings are most common in Gotland, Skåne and Östergötland, sometimes fragmentary or faded but occasionally almost complete. They are not true frescoes but done on dry plaster. The commonest theme is Christ in Majesty in the apse, then biblical themes cover the walls, the Old Testament on the left and the New on the right. Here again Byzantine traits can be found.

Gothic (c 1250–1500)

In Linköping the cathedral was started in Romanesque style, continued in Gothic and rebuilt in High Gothic over two centuries, so it demonstrates the progression of stylistic change and also a number of foreign influences. One of these was the hall church from Germany, with aisles equal in height to the nave, a form which became increasingly common as older churches were remodelled.

Brick building started in Skåne, then went to the Mälar valley at Strängnäs and Sigtuna, and in the 13C became common all over the country. Uppsala cathedral (heavily restored) is an example of French Gothic in brick, the work of a French team of builders. The French influence is also seen in Skara, but Baltic brick Gothic became more widespread. The mendicant orders built in brick for economy's sake as in the Riddarholm church in Stockholm.

Gotland had limestone and sandstone and continued to build in stone. Here the 13C and 14C saw a flowering of ecclesiastical art in the country churches of which more remains than anywhere else in Sweden.

In 1384 the church of St. Birgitta's convent in Vadstena was begun but was not completed until 1435. It is extremely simple in plan, in accordance with St. Birgitta's instructions, of limestone with brick vaults.

In the next century, the Late Gothic period, architecture became more influenced by the German merchants living in Stockholm and other centres of commerce. Fewer churches were built except for the newly populated areas, but those from earlier periods were remodelled or extended, such as Strängnäs, Linköping, Västerås and Stockholm Storkyrka. Many churches now acquired towers, and brick vaults replaced old roofs.

Wood-carving in the area around Uppsala leaned naturally towards French styles because of the nucleus of French craftsmen, while that on Gotland tended towards German because of the influence of the Hanse merchants. One special example of Gotland carving is the calvary at Öja. As time went on and German influence spread even further both artists and finished works of art flooded in from northern Germany. The outstanding example of this is Bernt Notke's St. George and the Dragon in Stockholm (1489).

Many altarpieces were acquired in the last decades of the Gothic period and Lübeck was the most prolific supplier. In the north Haaken Gulleson of Enånger in Hälsingland was one of the most skilled wood-carvers. Towards the end of the period Flemish altarpieces began to be imported.

Murals now could spread over stone or brick vaults, but wooden roofs like that of Dädesjö were also painted. In Skåne the Vittskövle school was the main one, while in Uppland there were several excellent workshops, one of which was that of Johannes Ivan of Tierp. One especially gifted and prolific painter was known as Albertus Pictor (see Härkeberga and Härnevi in Rte 14B). In Östergötland two particular painters should be mentioned, the Risinge Master, and Amund at Södra Råda.

Medieval secular buildings which remain are mainly defensive. In most cases they were renovated and remodelled, such as at Kalmar, though the keep at Helsingborg still stands. The only complete town wall remaining surrounds Visby on Gotland, and it has the unusual advantage that building has been kept well away from it on the outside so that it can be really appreciated.

Skåne churches

The delightful white churches of the south are of course Danish. At its most basic a medieval church in these parts looks almost as if it had been put together with cubic blocks, except for the low semi-circular apse. The whole, whether brick or stone, is white-washed. The roofs are usually red tiles and finished, in the Gothic period, with stepped gables, each step on the gable having its own tiny tiled roof. However, the variations on this basic theme are innumerable, and the later additions keep to the same concept. Also of the Gothic stage are the decorative gable-ends with shallow blind lancets. Some have extra-broad towers for defence. Inside many have retained wall-paintings, fonts and crucifixes of the same era. Examples are at Falsterbo, Skanör, Everlöv, St. Olof, Maglarp, Skabersjö and Skegrie among many others, while Bosjökloster shows the idea run wild in a reconstruction as a handsome manor-house.

Renaissance (c 1530–1640)

Gustav Vasa was busy consolidating his new kingdom but found time to begin building several castles. It was his sons who completed and embellished the exteriors with rustication, arcades and ornamental gables, and the interiors with coffering and panelling, calling in German, Dutch and northern Italian masters to emulate the Renaissance style of the Continent.

The foundation stone of Gripsholm Castle was laid in 1547, Renaissance on a still medieval irregular plan. Vadstena Castle is perhaps the best example of Swedish Renaissance, and Kalmar was remodelled largely in the new fashion—both are surrounded by serviceable fortifications. Two early interiors survive, Duke Karl's Chamber at Gripsholm and the King's Chamber at Kalmar.

In Skåne the Danish nobility built themselves castles and manors, such as Torup, mainly using brick, and took over many a monastery left vacant after the Reformation, like Bosjökloster. These are for the most part unrecognisably renovated and/or not accessible to visitors.

16C secular building in the country for a time kept the old medieval traditions, but in the towns a spate of ornate German and Dutch gables and overdoors decorated the houses of wealthy merchants. Elaborate fountains also survive from this period and another rich form of sculpture was the monumental tomb. The work of Willem Boy, architect, sculptor and painter to the Vasa family, can be seen in Uppsala and Strängnäs cathedrals, and Lucas van der Werdt's tombs for Magnus Ladulås and Karl Knutsson are in the Riddarholm church in Stockholm. The four Pahr brothers, originally from Italy, worked as sculptors on several Swedish castles.

The main **painting** of this period was portraiture of which an early example of the new imported Dutch style is that of Erik XIV at Gripsholm, ascribed to Steven van der Meulen of Antwerp (1561). The important exception to the portraits is the Parhelion painting of the city in Stockholm Storkyrka (1535).

Baroque (c 1640–1730)

By the time that Queen Kristina came to the throne in 1632 Sweden was ripe for a great upsurge in the field of the arts. A type of Dutch Palladianism became a favoured style and undoubtedly the most perfect example of this is Riddarhuset in Stockholm. Kristina was a passionate art-lover and avid collector of both works of art and artists, whom she drew to her court from all over Europe. For example, her miniature painters were two Frenchmen and an Englishman, Jean Toutin, Pierre Signac and Alexander Cooper.

Soon Roman Baroque, introduced by Nicodemus Tessin the Elder and Jean de la Vallée, arrived. Tessin (1615–81) came from Germany and settled in Sweden, the first of three generations of his family to leave an indelible stamp on Swedish architecture. His two masterpieces are Kalmar cathedral in Italian Baroque, and Drottningholm Palace which is Tessin's own blend of European strands in the Baroque tradition. The interior decoration is a fitting complement to the exterior.

Jean de la Vallée (1623–96) was the son of another architect, Simon, and worked for the great private patron Magnus de la Gardie, as well as designing much of Riddarhuset in Stockholm.

After Kristina the art of the second half of the century and the first years of the next is known as Carolean Baroque, after the three Karls who reigned from 1654. The sober Skokloster Castle was built for Carl Gustav Wrangel by the German Caspar Vogel, but it is the almost complete interior that makes it an outstanding example of Swedish Baroque taste.

Nicodemus Tessin the Younger (1654–1728) followed his father as court architect and his great achievement is the Italian Baroque royal palace in Stockholm, with its elegant proportions and ingenious planning to fit the difficult site.

In the field of sculpture, Nicolaes Millich, a Classicist from Antwerp, was employed at Drottningholm, and Burchardt Precht worked closely with and for Nicodemus Tessin the Younger. Tessin also imported the two French sculptors René Chauveau and Bernard Fouquet to work on the Stockholm palace. One of the foremost stucco artists was Daniel Anckerman whose work is in Drottningholm and Strängnäs.

Similarly, many foreign painters were attracted to or summoned to Sweden. Of these the most gifted was David Klöcker Ehrenstrahl, the court painter, who produced a great quantity of work in all genres but especially portraiture. German himself, he was influenced by German and Dutch masters and used allegory freely. (He was later ennobled with 'von' before his name.) Ehrenstrahl's nephew David von Krafft (1655–1724) became court painter after his uncle and his more subdued style heralds the new feeling as Baroque begins to dissolve into Rococo.

Rococo and Gustavian (c 1730–1800)

In the 18C the main foreign influence shifted from German to French, as an affluent middle class adopted the habits and manners of French society. Swedish artists studied in France and the upper classes imported French artists. It was Carl Hårleman (1700–53) and Carl Gustav Tessin (1695–1770), the third of the Tessins, who were the chief creators of Swedish Rococo. Their first task was to finish the interior of the royal palace in Stockholm. Then Hårleman went on to decorate some of the interiors in Drottningholm. Tessin, unlike his father and grandfather, was not so much an architect as an artistically gifted administrator.

Carl Fredrik Adelcrantz was the court surveyor after Hårleman and he designed the Chinese pavilion at Drottningholm, perhaps the most representative Swedish Rococo building. He also planned Adolf Fredrik's church in Stockholm, and the palace theatres at Drottningholm and Ulriksdal.

The architect Jean Eric Rehn (1717–93) was attracted by the new Classicism he found in Italy and France, as was Erik Palmstedt (1741–1803). This Swedish neo-Classicism is known as Gustavian, since Gustav III returned from his Italian journey bubbling with enthusiasm for antiquity. The discoveries at Pompeii and Herculaneum naturally furthered the classicising tendency. The best example is probably Haga pavilion. The painter Louis Masreliez specialised in a Pompeian style.

The most important sculptor of the period was Johan Tobias Sergel (1740–1814). He studied under the court sculptor Pierre Hubert L'Archevêque, and travelled extensively in the art centres of Europe. His work is a blend of Rococo and Classicism so that he represents the Gustavian style at its best. Among his best-known works are Gustav III's statue in Stockholm and Cupid and Psyche in the National Museum there.

Rococo painting is represented by Guillaume Taraval, Johan Pasch and Domenico Francia who worked on the décor of Stockholm palace. A Swedish painter Carl Gustav Pilo went to Denmark for a time and introduced Rococo ideas there. Another Swedish artist who worked abroad was Alexander Roslin (1718–93) who found his niche in Paris, following the style of Watteau and Boucher. Elias Martin (1739–1818) was a landscape painter.

The exotic Swedish **bell-towers** reached their peak in the 18C. These are great detached wooden structures, generally taller than their churches, square in plan, with a solid heavy base, from which posts and struts carry the enclosed bell-chamber—though variants abound. The whole is finished with a decorative spire. Very often they are clad with wood shingles. From the 17C they became more and more opulent and the spires more and more bulbous, until at the end of the 18C they had distinctly Russian onion domes. From the 19C, however, bells were hung in the church's own stone tower and bell-towers were no longer built. The best bell-towers are in Norrland, the northern half of the country, where there are splendid examples at Borgsjö and Frösön (Östersund). The largest is in Skansen in Stockholm.

Classicism and Romanticism (1800–1880)

Several tendencies were at work during this period. At first mainly Classicist ideas were in the air, and these were counterpointed by a Germanic/Norse movement and nature romanticism. Karl XIV Johan, ex-Marshal Bernadotte, brought the Empire style from his native France to Sweden. His foremost architect was Fredrik Blom whose best work is the delightful little Rosendal palace in Stockholm.

As elsewhere in Europe there was a return to Gothic and Renaissance forms in various guises and combinations, led by Axel Nyström (1793–1863) and Carl Georg Brunius (1793–1863), for example Nyström's Bishop's house in Lund (1839). Fredrik Wilhelm Scholander (who worked on décor in Stockholm Palace) and Johan Fredrik Åbom (Stockholm theatre) were two influential architects in public service at this time. However, it is the work of Helgo Zetterwall (1831–1907) which the visitor seems to meet at every turn. He wished to restore all old buildings to their original form, as in Lund Cathedral, and elsewhere in his own designs used several past styles.

Much monumental **sculpture** was produced at this time, with royalty and mythology as subjects. The sculptor Niklas Byström had been a promising pupil of Sergel but did not come up to his standard. Other sculptors were Bengt Erland Fogelberg, John Börjeson, Carl Gustav Quarnström and Johan Peter Molin.

Painting turned more and more towards Romanticism. Artists portrayed Norse mythology or Swedish history in heroic poses, while nature romanticists like Edward Bergh painted the Swedish landscape and people.

Some Trends 1880–1950

National romanticism demanded a return to simplicity and natural materials and the supreme example is Ragnar Östberg's Stockholm City Hall of 1923. Other buildings in this mood are Erik Lallerstedt's Stockholm Technical College, Lars Israel Wahlmann's Tjolöholm Castle and Carl Westman's Stockholm Rådhus (town hall/courthouse).

A complete break with tradition to cope with new demands in the public building sector was heralded by such architects as Ivar Tengbom, Sigurd Lewerentz and especially Gunnar Asplund with his Stockholm City Library (1928). Asplund was the leading figure in the functionalist movement. After the Second World War the welfare state, industry and modern traffic all combined to demand new urban centres in a spate of institutional architecture.

Sculpture at the turn of the century tended towards realism, but gradually began to follow European trends. The leading sculptor was Carl Milles (1875–1955) whose home at Lidingö in Stockholm is a shrine to his prolific output. Other notable sculptors are Carl Eldh, Ivar Johnsson, Christian Berg, Stig Blomberg and Bror Marklund.

In 1937 a boost to public art came in the form of a regulation that 1 per cent of the construction costs of all new public buildings should be devoted to artistic decoration. After the war sculptors here as elsewhere began to experiment with new materials and shapes.

Many of the foremost **painters** of the last years of the 19C had formed part of the colony of Swedish plein air artists at Grez-sur-Loing, in France, who painted in water-colour and concentrated on freshness and detail. They included Carl Larsson, Nils Kreuger, Richard Bergh and Bruno Liljefors. When they came back to Sweden they were fascinated by the Swedish landscape. Larsson became one of Sweden's favourite painters with his detailed studies of everyday life. Other artists of this time were Ernst Josephson, Karl Isakson, Eugene Jansson and Carl Wilhelmson. The most gifted painter of the time, Anders Zorn (1868–1920), was to a certain extent a late Impressionist. He painted at first in water-colour and perfected the rendering of water in all its forms, then turned to oils and did many portraits, and landscapes from his own part of Sweden, Dalarna.

Fauvism was represented by Isaac Grünewald and Leander Engström, and Cubism by John Sten, among others. A few painters turned to a Swedish kind of naivism before there was a reversion to new empiricism, following André Derain, c 1920. The Halmstad group of painters were Surrealists. Then came Primitivism about 1932, with Bror Hjorth and Sven X:t Erixson. The Gothenburg Colourists were a group who explored the expressive potential of pure colour. Other trends followed those in Europe, such as Expressionism.

After the Second World War, artistic movements followed even faster on each other's heels—concretism (Olle Baertling) led to neo-Expressionism (Torsten Renqvist), then came abstract Expressionism (Öjvind Fahlström). Neo-Realism was as close as Swedish art approached to pop art, and at around the same time there was a trend towards political art. In the 1970s, among other movements, there was a return to Expressionism with Erland Cullberg, Peter Dahl and Tommy Östmar. The artistic decoration of Stockholm underground began in the 1970s, an enviable method of reaching the public.

Language

Everyone on the well-beaten tourist track in Sweden will almost certainly speak some English. After the Second World War, Sweden decided that the way to integrate with the modern world was through English, and it is now the first foreign language in schools. Most professional people speak it well.

Swedish belongs to the group of North Germanic languages, and is very closely related to Norwegian and Danish. Finnish, however, belongs to an entirely different group, and the many place-names in northern Sweden which are obviously non-Swedish are either Finnish or Sami (Lapp).

Basic vocabulary in many cases resembles English—*man, fisk, hus* and *rum* are man, fish, house and room. There are many loan-words from German and most compound words have an almost exact equivalent in German, such as the word for town hall—Swedish *rådhus*, German *Rathaus*. This, together with some quirks of German word-order, makes Swedish easy to understand if you know some German. However, German-speakers should note that almost everyone addresses everyone else with the informal *du*. Much simplification in the last century or so means that grammatical irregularities are few and far between, for example, through-out any tense the form of the verb is invariable.

For the tourist trying to string together a few basic words, one of the oddest traits is that the definite article is attached to the end of the word, so that *boken* means 'the book' and *en bok* means 'a book'. There are two genders, and 80 per cent of words are of the common gender (with *en*) and the rest are neuter (with *ett/et*). The word for 'the' is often incorporated in place-names. In the text of this book I have tried to be grammatically correct in Swedish, while not sounding too abrupt in English, with inevitable incon-sistency here and there. Again I have used illicit capital letters in certain place-names to make them more easily distinguishable to the English-speaker.

The purist may also take exception to the following very rough guide to pronunciation. If not specified, the sound is *more or less* as in English, ignoring exceptions and varying lengths. Note that the last consonant of common words is not pronounced.

Vowels

e	as in 'pay'
i	as in 'see'
o	as in 'boot' or 'pot'
y	as in French 'rue'
å	as in 'boat'
ë	as in 'pet'
ö	as in 'bird'

Consonants

g	is like 'y' in 'yes' before e, i, y, å and ö (the 'soft vowels')
j, dj, gj, hj, lj	are also like 'y'
k	is like 'ch' before the above-listed soft vowels
sch, sj, skj, stj	use a strong 'sh'
tj	is like 'ch'

Alphabet. Telephone directories can be confusing since å, ä and ö come at the end of the alphabet, v and w are grouped together since they are pronounced the same, and similarly surnames like Carlsson and Karlsson which are pronounced the same are grouped together.

The Tones. Swedish is a tonal language but the rules for using the two kinds of tone are too complex to discuss here. Fortunately most people will understand you without using the tones—they will simply be amazed and flattered that an English-speaking person should bother to make the effort to speak any Swedish.

Useful Expressions

Emergency and Medical (in emergency phone 90 000)

hjälp	help
ambulans	ambulance
läkare	doctor
brand	fire
polis	police
apotek	chemist
tandläkare	dentist
tandvärk	toothache
sjukhus	hospital
akutmottagning	casualty department
ont	pain

Sightseeing

berg	mountain
bro	bridge
dal	valley
domkyrka	cathedral
fors	rapids
gamla stan	old town
gata	street
hembygdsgård	local open-air museum
hus, huset	house, the house
kloster	monastery
konstmuseum	art museum
kyrka, kyrkan	church, the church
lilla	small
museum, museet	museum, the museum
rådhus	town hall
sjö	lake
skog	forest
slott, slottet	castle, the castle
stor, stora	big, main
torg, torget	square, the square
trädgård	garden
vattenfall	waterfall
e. Kr.	AD
f. Kr.	BC

Basic Essentials

hej, goddag	hello
ja	yes
nej, inte	no, not
tack	thank you
(there is no word for please—use 'tack' when shopping, etc.)	
ursäkta, förlåt	excuse me, pardon
var	where
när	when
jag förstår inte	I do not understand
fungerar inte	does not work
är	is, are
har	has, have

Directions

till höger	to the right
till vänster	to the left
rakt fram	straight on

Travel

färja	ferry
buss	bus
tåg	train
järnväg	railway
spår	platform
tur och retur	return
enkel	single
linbana	cable railway

Motoring

bil	car
bensin	petrol
vindruta	windscreen
däck	tyre
kassa (on petrol-pump)	(pay at) cash-desk
sedel (on petrol-pump)	(pump takes) banknotes
luft	air
vatten	water
infart	drive in
utfart	drive out

Public Places

hiss	lift
toalett	toilet
damer	ladies
herrar	gentlemen
ledig	vacant
upptagen	engaged
nyckel	key (may be kept at cash-desk)
ingång	way in
utgång	way out
stängt	closed
rea	sale
gatukök	hot snacks kiosk
gågata	pedestrian street
avgång	departure
ankomst	arrival

Accommodation

rum	room (no breakfast)
stuga	chalet
vandrarhem	youth hostel
campingplats	camp-site

Days

måndag	Monday
tisdag	Tuesday
onsdag	Wednesday
torsdag	Thursday
fredag	Friday
lördag	Saturday
söndag	Sunday
i dag	today
i morgon	tomorrow

Numbers

1	ett	20	tjugo
2	två	30	trettio
3	tre	40	fyrtio
4	fyra	50	femtio
5	fem	60	sextio
6	sex	70	sjuttio
7	sju	80	åttio
8	åtta	90	nittio
9	nio	100	hundra
10	tio		

Festivals and traditions

The Swedes punctuate the year with public festivals and gather in great crowds to celebrate together the passing of the seasons.

New Year sees fireworks and the televising of the festivities at Skansen in Stockholm, when Tennyson's 'Ring out the old, ring in the new' is recited in Swedish. Twelfth Night (6 January) is celebrated as a sort of lesser extension of Christmas, as is the feast of St. Knut on 13 January, a legacy from the 17C calendar reform. This is when the Christmas decorations are taken down.

On Shrove Tuesday, the day before Lent begins, the traditional food is a bun filled with cream and marzipan. During the weeks leading up to Easter people begin to buy or gather twigs and decorate them with coloured feathers, putting them in water to sprout new leaves. In the days before Easter Sunday, little girls dress up as old women and visit neighbours for a small gift. Eggs are painted to eat on Easter Sunday, and some places have Easter games.

The first of April is of course a day for practical jokes. On 30 April spring is formally welcomed with bonfires, songs and speeches, and in the university towns the festivities become quite a spectacle. The first of May is a holiday with political parades and speeches.

Ascension Day is a public holiday as is Whit Monday. The National Day or Flag Day is on 6 June but is not a public holiday. The Swedish flag is ceremonially flown everywhere. (The Swedish flag is displayed on every occasion for celebration, even private and family ones. Party decorations are often blue and yellow.)

Midsummer, the Saturday nearest 24 June, the feast of St. John the Baptist, is the most popular festival, with the previous day a public holiday. In the afternoon each community with due ceremony raises its maypole on some convenient green. The form of the maypole varies from district to district, but the basic shape is a cross with attached circles covered in foliage and wild flowers. All join hands around the maypole and dance and sing traditional songs. The midsummer meal consists of herring, new potatoes with dill, Sweden's favourite herb, and the first strawberries.

At the end of August and the beginning of September come the crayfish parties. (Crayfish now have to be imported due to disease and over-fishing.) Funny hats and bibs are de rigueur; the crayfish are accompanied by schnapps, and at intervals eating stops for community singing of traditional songs. In northern Sweden the crayfish are replaced by *surströmming*, fermented herring which comes in bulging tins. It is advisable to open these in the open air because of the smell.

All Saints' Day is commemorated on the Saturday after 30 October, and people put flowers and candles on the graves of family and friends. St. Martin's Day on 11 November is marked in southern Sweden with a feast of goose-blood soup and roast goose.

More Swedish people go to church on the first Sunday of Advent than at Christmas. Advent is the time for Christmas decorations in the home, not just in shops. Advent candle-holders with four candles are common, and families light one more candle on each Sunday of Advent. Candle-holders with seven candles, usually electric, feature in almost every window. There are Christmas markets and Christmas treasure-hunts, and everywhere one is offered *glögg* (mulled wine) with thin ginger biscuits. The Christmas goat (*julbock*) begins to make his appearance. Obviously of pagan origin, this goat is made of straw and comes in all sizes to suit your premises and your pocket.

The most Swedish of all festivals is that of St. Lucia on 13 December. Again misplaced because of the calendar reform, this was supposed to be the longest night of the year when people needed extra sustenance and at the same time could begin to look forward to the return of light. Every office, school and home with children has its Lucia, a girl in white with a headdress of lighted candles who brings coffee and cakes. Boys and girls in costume accompany her and they sing 'Lucia' songs, the principal one being 'Santa Lucia' sung in Swedish.

Christmas is celebrated on 24 December. Homes are decorated with Christmas curtains, table-cloths, china, place-mats and napkins, and the hostess may wear a Christmas apron. All of these may feature the Christmas gnome, dressed like a small cuddly Santa Claus, who brings the presents. The meal is a great smörgåsbord of all the favourite Swedish foods: ham, meat-balls, herring in many guises and traditional boiled dried fish, followed by rice pudding and ginger biscuits, with many accompaniments and side-dishes.

Bibliography

There are few books in English on Sweden readily available in bookshops and libraries in Britain, but the Swedes publish much in English translation. Books are expensive in Sweden—because of the high tax—but you can buy by post from the Swedish Institute catalogue (Swedish Institute, PO Box 7434, S-103 91 Stockholm) and also request more detailed book-lists on subjects which particularly interest you.

Most of the following are on their list, but those published in the USA or Britain are of course more quickly obtainable in the respective countries. The Institute also produces excellent Fact Sheets on dozens of subjects, as well as leaflets on topical issues, *Current Sweden*. Ask for order forms.

Åberg, Alf, *A Concise History of Sweden*, Stockholm, 1987

An Anthology of Modern Swedish Literature, Merrick, New York, 1989

Bronsted, Johannes, *The Vikings*, Penguin, Harmondsworth, 1983

Conforti and Walton, *Royal Treasures of Sweden*, National Gallery of Art, Washington, 1988

Elstob, Eric, *Sweden, a Traveller's History*, Boydell Press, 1979

Jansson, Sven, *Runes in Sweden*, Stockholm, 1987

Jerrolf, Mats, *A Guided Tour of Birka*, Stockholm

John, Brian, *Scandinavia, a New Geography*, Longman, London/New York 1984

Kastrup, Allan, *The Swedish Heritage in America*, Swedish Council of America, 1975

Langerlöf, Selma, *The Story of Gösta Berling*, Karlstad, 1982
   The Wonderful Adventures of Nils and *Further Adventures of Nils*, Puffin, Harmondsworth, 1990

Liman, Ingemar, *Traditional Festivities in Sweden*, Swedish Institute, 1986

Lindgren, Astrid, *Pippi Longstocking*, Penguin, Harmondsworth, 1987

Lindgren, Lyberg and Sandström, Wahlberg, *A History of Swedish Art*, Signum, 1987

Mårtensson, Jan, *Drottningholm*, Stockholm, 1985

McClean, R.J., *Teach Yourself Swedish*, Hodder and Stoughton, Sevenoaks, Kent, 1984

Millesgården, Esselte, 1983

Moberg, Vilhelm, 'Emigrant' novels, Warner Books, NY, 1983; also in Penguin, Harmondsworth

Olsson, Nils William, *Tracing Your Swedish Ancestry*, Swedish Institute, 1985

Spencer, Arthur, *Gotland*, David & Charles, 1974

Strindberg, August, *Five Plays*, New American Library, New York, 1984
   Plays (2 vols), Methuen, London, 1982

Sweden in Brief, Swedish Institute 1986

Swedish Cooking, ICA-förlaget, 1983

Swedish for Travellers, Berlitz, 1984

Treasures of Early Sweden, Gidlunds, Uppsala, 1984

Wasa, National Maritime Musuem, Stockholm, 1979

Maps

In 1991 and 1992 many road numbers were changed, so beware of using older maps. The motoring atlases, Bonniers Stora Bill & Turist Atlas, and Kak Bil Kartor (Esselte), are available in Sweden. If you wish to buy before you go, Stanfords, 12-14 Long Acre, London WC2E 9LP, supply a wide range of touring maps, city plans and large-scale maps for walkers, which are also of course available in Swedish bookshops. In towns the telephone directories have excellent local plans.

PRACTICAL INFORMATION

Planning Your Trip

When to Go. Unless you wish to ski, summer is the best time to go to Sweden. Spring is glorious in its sudden blossoming, but tourist facilities may not be open until 1 May, and some are not available until mid June, and may begin to close around mid August. (This is not so noticeable in Stockholm.) The whole of Sweden goes on holiday in July, so that holiday and tourist facilities are then fully open, but as a consequence some small cafés, restaurants, shops and businesses off the tourist track may be closed for July. If your interests include castles, churches and smaller museums then summer, i.e. June to August, is the best time to go, but to enjoy the wide open spaces May or September can be perfect.

The climate in summer is very similar to that in Britain (see Geography section) even in the far north. In other words, take a pullover and water-proof, as well as sun-cream—and a good mosquito-repellent for the north.

Passports and Formalities. Holders of British and US passports are al-lowed to stay for three months and no visa is required. Others should check with the nearest Swedish embassy or consulate.

Swedish Travel & Tourism Council. (Until April 1995 omit 1 after the first 0 in all UK numbers.) In the UK: 73 Welbeck Street, London W1M 8AN, tel. 0171-487 3135, fax 0171-935 5853; in the USA: 655 Third Avenue, 18th Floor, New York, NY 10017-5617, tel. 212-949-2333, fax 212-697-0835; in Sweden: Next Stop Sweden, PO Box 10134, 121 28 Stockholm-Globen, tel. 08-725 55 00. They will send a map, a list of hotels, and a brochure/maga-zine with addresses to help you start planning your trip.

Disabled Travellers. Sweden must be the best country in the world for the disabled traveller. The disabled are accepted into the community and catered for in a way few other countries match. Virtually every public building and place is adapted to their needs, every street-crossing has a little ramp at the kerb, and audible traffic-signals. One-third of all camp-sites are adapted with hard paths, ramps and wide sanitary areas. One-fifth of all Youth Hostels are accessible, and there are 150 allergy-free chalets available. Toilets for the disabled are everywhere, including in many tourist bureaux, and swimming-pools have shallow steps into the water. Jogging-tracks may well be accompanied by special wheelchair tracks, and some places have ski-carts for the disabled. Herb gardens may have Braille labels, and some zoos and such may allow the disabled to be driven around after hours.

Getting to Sweden

As the position changes from year to year with new routes and new airlines and, particularly, new package deals, you should obtain the latest information from the Swedish Tourist Board in your country, contained in the brochures 'Sweden' in the UK and 'Sweden Traveler' in the US, which will also give details of current package deals and offers. Below are given some indications of the services available.

By Air. From the UK: SAS (tel. 0171-734 4020) and British Airways (tel. 0181-897 4000) operate to Stockholm and Gothenburg from London. From the US there are flights by American Airlines (tel. 800-433-7300), Delta (tel. 800-241-4141), Finnair (tel. 800-950-5000), Icelandair (tel. 800-223-5500), SAS (tel. 800-221-2350) and TWA (tel. 800-438-2929).

By Rail from the UK. Dover–Ostend, Harwich–Hook of Holland and Harwich–Esbjerg are the main routes and take about 30 hours from London to Stockholm. Contact British Rail (tel. 0171-834 2345/828 0892), NSR Travel (tel. 0171-930 6666) or Eurotrain (tel. 0171-730 3402). Special rates for young people are available.

By Coach from the UK. Coaches go via Amsterdam and take nearly 48 hours to Stockholm. Contact Eurolines (tel. 0171-730 8111).

By Car from the UK. Scandinavian Seaways (tel. 01255-241234) have direct UK–Sweden ferries from Harwich (24 hours) and Newcastle (27 hours) to Gothenburg, but there are many alternative routes through France, Germany, Holland and Denmark using ferries run by Olau Line and TT-Line (tel. 01795-666666) and Sealink-Stena Line (tel. 01233-647047). At the last count there were over 30 ferry routes to Sweden from abroad, so you can always take in another country or two on the way.

No special insurance or licence is required, but contact your insurance company to verify your position.

Money. The currency is the krona, plural kronor, everyday abbreviation kr, but officially SEK, or Skr. Notes come in denominations of 10,000, 1000, 500, 100 and 50kr. Coins are 10, 5, 1 and 50 öre (half a krona). Most credit cards are accepted—you may be asked for identification. Eurocheques (use Skr when writing) are accepted and Travellers' Cheques may be changed. Many post offices as well as banks offer exchange services, while the Forex exchange offices are often more convenient.

Arriving in Sweden

There is sure to be a local tourist bureau at or near your arrival point, marked with a large 'i' on a green background. These will provide you with maps and brochures, and will usually also book rooms for you. Note that literature will sometimes not be free as in other countries, and that the booking service may also involve a fee.

Accommodation

Hotels in Sweden can be very expensive, but any kind of package deal booked from your home country will usually be good value; some packages offer accommodation linked to various activities—see the current 'Sweden' and 'Sweden Traveler' brochures. These can be complete tours, catering for different interests, or deals which the various hotel chains offer. Typically with the purchase of a card you get substantial reductions at all the hotels in the chain. Current offers will be found in the yearly hotel guide.

If, however, you wish to remain flexible and book as you go, there are several strategies. Since the hotels are catering mainly for businessmen, they offer cheap rates at weekends and during July, often half-price. The most popular alternative with the Swedes is the excellent Youth Hostel service (*vandrarhem*), happily not the prerogative of youth. Many have two-bed rooms, and good facilities for cooking. But if you favour a little more privacy you might try one of the most charming of Scandinavian inventions, the *stuga*. This is a wooden chalet of any size, and with any variation of amenities. They may be privately owned, at the bottom of someone's garden, or on a camp-site, in which case you share the facilities of the site. They may have one room and an electric ring, or have their own bathroom and room for eight people. They will often be in a lovely situation, like the camp-sites. Also available in holiday areas are flats (*lägenheter*), which can often be had for one or two nights, and where, as in the hostels and chalets, you are expected to clean up after yourself and bring your own linen and sometimes toilet paper. Camping in your own tent is also a pleasure, given the scupulous hygiene and often beautiful situations of the many camp-sites. (Bring enough Camping Gaz if you use it as it is not on sale in Sweden.)

Apart from these, there are country inns (*värdshus*) and semi-charitable institutions. Anything with a name incorporating the words *hem*, *stift*, or *gård* may have simple accommodation at very reasonable cost. A *pensionat* can be quite expensive, but a motel (*motell*) will be reasonable. New versions of the motel are springing up: the Eurostops, the Good Morning hotels, the Welcome Card hotes, and some on motorway service areas. (*Rasta* is one chain, but not all have accommodation.) A *rum* advertised along the road offers a room but no breakfast and will be the cheapest apart from camping. At tourist bureaux and hotels always ask about special deals which may be available after a certain time in the evening, and ask about cheap alternatives to hotels. Be clear about whether the price is per person or per room and whether breakfast is included in the price. It is usually possible to find reasonable lodging as you go, without booking ahead—except in Stockholm (see Rte 15). In Stockholm, Gothenburg, Lund and Uddevalla ask about student lodgings.

Restaurants

Another expensive area, but here too there are ways and means. The words to learn first are *dagens rätt*. These appear mainly at weekday lunchtimes, but are not unknown at other times, and mean the chef's dish of the day or even a choice. This can simply be a cheap and filling main course (see below under Food and Drink), with unlimited salad, a soft drink, bread and coffee usually thrown in. A *dagens* in a motorway stop or country inn will usually be good, and good value. (On Thursdays, in the winter, the *dagens* is always thick pea soup with ham, with pancakes and jam to follow.) In the towns the department stores Åhlens and Domus are highly recommended, also for coffee, snacks and light lunches. Museum cafés are usually good value, and ethnic places can be relied on—Greek, Italian or Chinese. In the evenings many restaurants cater only for expense accounts, so the obvious thing to do if on a budget is to have a *dagens* at lunchtime and do some judicious self-catering in the evening. If you want a light lunch, however, a very pleasant alternative is the *konditori*, cake-shop, which will usually have facilities for eating as well as selling food to take away. They almost always have those splendid open sandwiches, and sometimes light dishes such as salads, or warm food to order. Anything specially advertised like coffee with a certain sort of cake will be good value. If the coffee and tea are set out for you to help yourself it means you can have as much as you like for the price of perhaps 1½ cups. Most cake-shops have a queue-ticket system. A café is a more down-to-earth establishment, with more substantial meals—good value.

For a warm snack you could do worse than try a *gatukök* ('street kitchen') or *korvkiosk* (sausage kiosk) where you will get sauages, hamburgers and kebabs with imaginative garnishes and salads. Some larger ones have tables inside or out, and serve quite substantial meals. The Danish *pølse-mannen* (sausage man) and Union Jack-bedecked fish-and-chip vans can also be found.

If you try the justly famed **smörgåsbord**, the etiquette is not to heap your plate all at once with food but to go up to the buffet several times, taking a clean plate each time (your used plate will be quickly removed). Start with one of the innumerable varieties of pickled herring, then one or two of the fish dishes. The meat courses, salads and hot dishes are followed by desserts, fruit and cheese.

Meals are taken an hour or so earlier than in other countries, and you can start lunch at 11.00 and your evening meal at 18.00.

Food and Drink

Hotels and restaurants by and large serve European food. Breakfast can be a generous buffet, with bread, crispbread, sliced sausage, cheese, pickles and cereals, sometimes eggs and fruit also. Next to the yoghurt will be a jug of *filmjölk*, a sort of thin yoghurt—it is very good on cereal.

Besides European dishes you may like to try some Swedish specialities. Swedish food has of course traditionally had to keep out the cold, with lots of calories. Meatballs (*köttbullar*) with *lingonsylt*, rather like cranberry sauce, must be the favourite, followed by *pytt y panna* a fried mixture of meat and potatoes with a fried egg, and *Janssons frestelse* (Janssons temptation), baked pieces of potato, onion, eggs and cream topped with anchovies.

The glory of Swedish food is fish, and salmon must take pride of place, in steaks, smoked or *gravad* (marinated with dill). Harbour towns often have their own smoke-houses, as you can scent on arrival, and sell a mouth-watering selection of smoked fish, and fishy snacks to eat on the spot. Herring of course in all its many forms has to be tried too.

Do try the reindeer meat (*ren*), which comes smoked or plain, sliced or by the piece, frozen, fresh or dried. Elk meat (*älg*) is very good too.

Because of the price and restrictions on the sale of alcohol, much milk and virtually alcohol-free beer (*lättöl*) is drunk, as well as soft drinks (very sweet) and mineral water. Coffee is very strong (Swedes and Finns vie with one another for the highest consumption per head in the world) and tea is made continental-fashion with warm water. Both of these stand on hotplates and you usually pour out your own.

So some degree of self-catering is probably a good idea, and supermarkets make it easy to buy. Note that the green keyhole sign on packaging means something is healthy, whether low-calorie or high-fibre. Open-air markets have a good variety and good prices on fruit and vegetables, and home-grown fruit is excellent—do try the strawberries in season.

Alcohol. Alcoholic drinks are extremely expensive in bars, hotels and restaurants. Apart from the almost alcohol-free beers in supermarkets, they can otherwise be bought only in the state monopoly Systembolaget shops, still at high prices. These are open Monday to Friday, and the bottles are ranged in glass cases around the shop. You take a queue-ticket and decide what you want, then wait your turn. The queues are longest towards the end of the week—avoid late afternoon on Friday.

How to Cut Other Costs of Living

Contrary to popular belief, salaries are not higher in Sweden than elsewhere, so Swedes have made bargain-hunting into something of an artform. For foreigners not able to read the newspaper advertisements things are a little more difficult, but they have something denied to the Swedes—'Tax-free for Tourists' is the notice on almost every shop-window of any size. The shop gives you a receipt when you buy, and at your departure point you present this and your purchase at the special desk and some tax (VAT/MOMS) is refunded. Large items can be sent to your home MOMS-free. Sales (*rea*) are continually in progress. Food and other items are often marked *extrapris* on bright red labels—these are cheap offers. Some items are cheaper than in Britain—furs and leather, for example. Details of buying 'seconds' in the glass factories will be found in the text in the Kalmar to Jönköping and Skara route (Rte 5).

City cards, covering travel, parking, sightseeing and more are mentioned under Stockholm, Gothenburg and Malmö, but other areas have cards also, so be sure to ask at the tourist bureaux. Some holiday areas may have books of discount vouchers, so ask about these too. To repeat, any special offer or package deal will be worth considering. If you are retired, take some convenient identification with your birth-date, and produce it on every likely occasion. The magic word is *pensionär*.

Travelling around Sweden

By Rail. The country is covered by a network of 12,000km of railway track. Trains in Sweden are very clean and comfortable but expensive. It is usually quicker to drive than take a train. Intercity trains are not express, they simply travel between two cities. The X2000 train now cuts the time between Stockholm and Gothenburg, but you pay a supplement. There will soon also be an X2000 between Malmö and Stockholm. One way to cut costs is to buy a Scandinavian rail pass in your own country—any rail ticket bought before you go will be MOMS(VAT)-free. Alternatively, various tourist cards on sale in Sweden give cut-price travel for a certain period or area. But one of the easiest ways to travel more cheaply is to take a 'red departure' (*röd avgång*—marked with red in the time-table, at unsocial hours). Some years a special card has to be bought before you are entitled to this discount.

Be sure to *leave plenty of time* for buying tickets, and do not forget to take a queue-number ticket. Sometimes there is a faster queue for trains departing within one hour (*inom 1 timma*). It may be compulsory to have a seat-reservation. Details of Swedish rail services can be had from NSR Travel (tel. 0171-930 6666). Sleeping cabins are available on overnight services, and there are also car-trains, even to the far north. From Malmö to Kiruna it takes 26 hours, for example, and most people cut the cost of meals by taking a supply of food and drink.

If the Inland Railway has not closed down, as continually threatened, the classic trip goes from Östersund to Gällivare with stops and excursions. Write to: Inlandståget AB, Kyrkgatan 56, 831 34 Östersund.

By Bus. There are long-distance express buses between larger towns, and cheapest of all are the weekend buses (*Veckoslutsbussar*—you must book a seat), but these may not be an option for those in a hurry. Tourist bureaux should have all the information you need. Information on city bus/tram services is to be found under each city. Buses are boarded at the front, and you buy tickets from the driver. In cities plastic cards, also from the driver, are cancelled in the machine beside the driver. (For information contact Swebus/Continentbus, Gothenburg, tel. (031) 103 800.)

By Car. **Car-hire** is expensive, and the usual car-hire firms are at airports and harbours; sometimes special offers are available, depending on the season. Fly-drive deals from your own country are almost certain to be better value.

From the UK it is more economical to bring your own car, Though petrol is much more expensive than at home, motoring is overall the best option, especially for more than one person. The **roads** are excellent, well-surfaced, clearly marked and signposted, with very low traffic density, especially compared with the UK. Given the terrain and size of the country it is inevitable that many roads are unsurfaced, but these are mostly in the north and off the tourist track: some are mentioned in the text. An unmade road is marked on maps in the same way as others—it is apparently the width which counts to the map-makers.

E-lettered roads are not necessarily dual-carriageway, nor are motorways, which can be narrow with one lane in each direction. On such a two-lane road, the custom is always to move over on to the hard shoulder to allow others to pass.

Roads frequently have two numbers where routes overlap. The two numbers may have separate road-signs some distance apart, so do not panic immediately. Life is easier if you have a map published after 1992, with new road numbers. If a large town has several junctions on a motorway, the one marked with a black C leads to the centre.

Animals are a very real hazard, especially in the north, and especially elks, which cause many fatal accidents. Remember reindeer always belong to someone, and if you hit one you should report it. You must stop after an accident and give your name and address to the other party, though the police need not be called unless someone is injured. Phone 90 000 in an emergency.

Speed limits are 50kph in town, and 90kph everywhere else, with many motorways going up to 120kph. Swedish drivers in general stick to the speed limit, and in any case they try not to do more than 30kph over the limit, since at that point they are liable to lose their licences. Since the alcohol limit is very low (0.02 per cent) most do not drink and drive.

Dipped headlights are compulsory even in daylight, which means the battery is more liable to fail. Check that your interior light is out when you leave the car—this tip is from bitter personal experience and 800kr worth of taxi fares.

Toilets are frequently to be found in the lay-bys, even if not signposted. They may be closed in winter.

Picnic-sites can be truly idyllic. They are marked on maps and well signposted. Swedes are inspired picnickers and sites will often be by a lake with a stunning view, tables, benches, litter-bins and toilets. It is always a good idea to take some food and drink along with you on any journey.

It is also prudent to fill up with **petrol** before the tank gets low, as there is at least one stretch of main road in the country with no petrol or food on the roadside for 130km—places off the road with these facilities are sign-posted.

Parking is not quite as difficult as everywhere else in the modern world. Parking areas have a *P-automat* where you buy a ticket to display in your car; *P-skiva* means a parking disc which you set with the time you arrive, obtainable at police stations and town halls. Always ask every tourist bureau if they have parking concessions for tourists. It is the parking concession which makes the 'city cards' such good value (see under each city).

The unofficial pecking-order on Swedish streets is first buses, then bicycles, then cars, and *lastly, pedestrians*. **Bicycles** are a particular hazard in towns, whether there are special cycle-tracks or not. At crossroads, be cautious about turning, as cyclists will be moving with the green light across your line of travel. Avoid walking on cycle-tracks.

Virtually all **petrol stations** are self-service (*tanka själv*). *Kassa* means you pay at the cash-desk, *sedel* means the pump takes banknotes, and *konto* refers to a plastic card.

The **motoring altases** Bonniers Stora Bil & Turist Atlas, and the Kak Bil Kartor can be recommended. For other maps see under Bibliography. The **motoring organisations** are: Motormännens Riksforbund, Sturegatan 32, 114 36 Stockholm, and Kungl. Automobil Klubben, of the same address.

If you wish to bring your car in winter, you will need **winter tyres**. Hotels in the north often have car-heaters available for their guests.

By Air.   With distances as they are in Sweden it makes sense to go by air if the fares are reasonable, and sometimes there are excellent offers in high summer for students, and for stand-by passengers.

By Bicycle.   Cycling is a treat in Sweden even for those who have not tried it for years; in towns and on islands it can be the best means of transport. Harbours will have cycle-hire places, and the tourist bureaux will have addresses or may even hire out bicycles themselves. There are also cycling packages, with accommodation (Swedish Touring Club, Box 25, 101 20 Stockholm, tel. (08) 790 31 00).

By Taxi.   Taxis are expensive, and are not hailed in the street, but are available at frequent taxi ranks in the cities. Otherwise look in the yellow pages part of the telephone directory under *Taxi* and phone for one.

By Boat.   There are uncountable ferry services around the shores of Sweden, and some areas have ferry passes—ask at the tourist bureau. The Stockholm archipelago is a favourite, with a well-developed ferry system—see under Stockholm, Rte 15.

Walking.   Long-distance walking is one of the most popular holiday persuits. Trails have been marked and maps produced for hundreds of walking-tours, ranging from half-an-hour to a couple of weeks. Write to: Svenska Turistföreningen, Drottninggatan 31, 101 20 Stockholm. Local tourist bureaux have leaflets and plans, one or two even with English lists of flora and fauna to look out for.

General Information

Crime.   You are very unlikely to be attacked in Sweden. It makes sense of course to be aware of pickpockets in crowds.

Electricity.   This is 220 volts, and sockets take round two-pin plugs.

'Everyman's Right'.   This means that you can walk across anyone's property, land a boat on any shore or pick wild fruit or mushrooms anywhere, except in a nature reserve, provided you do not invade people's privacy, damage crops or disturb wild life.

Health.   The visitor to Sweden is highly unlikely to have any health problems, since hygiene and public health arrangements are of a high standard. Sweden has a reciprocal agreement for medical treatment with the UK and Form E111 can be used.

Local Customs.   You are expected to shake hands with everyone and announce your name while doing so. When invited, Swedes arrive *exactly* on time, bring flowers and sometimes make a gesture towards taking off their shoes. When drinking a toast, look round the table at everyone with your glass raised, say 'skål', drink, then look at everyone again. This happens at intervals throughout the meal or party. Be prepared for speeches even at small dinner-parties. You may find they are reserved at first, but they love to talk about Sweden to foreigners. You are never subjected to pushy sales techniques, which is refreshing, but the corollary is that you must always *ask specially* for tourist concessions and offers. The text has reminders at intervals to do this.

Newspapers. British and American newspapers can be bought in the larger towns, though often a day or so late. They can cost three times the original price.

Opening Hours. Shops and post offices open usually from 09.00 or 10.00 to 18.00 from Monday to Friday, and on Saturday morning; large department stores are sometimes open on Sunday afternoons. Petrol stations can close at 18.00. Banks are open Monday to Friday 09.30 to 15.00, but exchange offices can be found at airports, city centres and ferry terminals, with longer opening hours.

Opening hours of museums and tourist sights in Sweden are highly erratic, and change from year to year, often following a complicated pattern through the seasons and the week. They are usually closed on Mondays. **The opening hours given in the text are only a rough guide**.

Always check by phone or in person with the tourist bureau, or preferably phone the organisers, before making a long journey. As an indication, many museums and other attractions do not open until 11.00 or 12.00, and may close at 16.00. These times also vary from season to season. The many national holidays in May and June mean that many places close not only on the day but on the afternoon before. Where Swedes themselves holiday, i.e. in the country or at the seaside in July, facilities will be open. In July off the tourist track it may well be difficult to find a cup of coffee—a thermos flask is useful. Churches with recognised attractions for visitors will usually be open in the summer. The sign *vägkyrka* (way church) means a church welcomes summer travellers with enthusiastic young guides often with good English, and sometimes coffee or a small exhibition.

Public Holidays. 1 January, 6 January, Good Friday, Easter Monday, 1 May, Ascension Day, Whit Monday, Midsummer Day, All Saints' Day, Christmas Day, 26 December, 31 December. Shops, banks and offices are closed, and as mentioned above many may also be closed on the previous afternoon, including tourist bureaux. However, it is usually not too difficult to find accommodation at these times.

Public Toilets. These are not well signposted but will be in the main squares of towns and in lay-bys along country roads. Tourist bureaux very often have them (splendid idea), and country churches also have them, even if they are fairly primitive (but spotless) at the end of the churchyard. (One at least is a friendly wooden two-seater.) Some on beaches will be open only in summer. You may well have to pay, usually by a coin in the slot. You may have to ask for the key (*nyckeln till toaletten*).

Queuing Tickets. Much frustration will be saved if you always look around for a ticket-dispensing machine in such places as banks, post offices, station ticket-offices, State wine and spirit shops and chemists. Many cake-shops and flower-shops have them also.

Restricted Military Areas. Some areas are off-limits to foreigners and they are marked in various languages. Some excursions, to islands especially, may therefore not be available to foreigners.

St. Hans' Cross. This sign, ⌘ , common to Scandinavian countries, marks a site of archaeological, historical, architectural, botanical, geological interest, or a viewing point.

Sport and Leisure. There is a huge variety of sporting and leisure facilities in Sweden. The best source of current information is the local tourist bureau. Be sure to ask if there is anything unusual or special in the area—elk safaris, gold-panning, rafting, scuba-diving, veteran steam railways or any kind of festival such as 'waterfall day', when local hydro-electric dams are opened as a tourist spectacle.

Any and every winter sport is catered for, with floodlit pistes, snow scooter safaris, snow-mobiling and a host of other arrangements, including those for the not-so-energetic, like snow-sculpture exhibitions.

Cinemas show films in the original language with Swedish sub-titles and most films are English-language. There are always concerts going on, often in churches, and also out of doors in the summer. There are hundreds of small art (*konst*) and craft (*slöjd*) exhibitions all over the country in the most unexpected places.

To explore the vast almost untouched national parks consult the local tourist bureau for advice on possible hazards. See also under the individual national parks in the text.

Telephones and Postal Services. Telephones have illustrated directions for use in English. For easier foreign calls look for a *Telebutik* in the towns. To call the UK dial 009 44 then the subscriber's number, omitting the first 0. To call the USA dial 009 1, then the area code and the rest of the number. To call Sweden from the UK the code is 010 46, and from the USA 011 46. A telephone card is useful, as more and more telephones accept only cards. Notice that the telephone directories always have extremely clear town-plans, and also that the letters å, ä and ö follow z.

Use the yellow post-boxes—the blue are local, and the green are 'economy-post'. This can be worthwhile if you are posting a lot of mail—enquire in the post office. Stamps can also be bought in tobacconists' and newspaper shops. Postage for letters and post cards is the same.

Time. Sweden is one hour ahead of Britain and six hours ahead of New York.

Tipping. Service is included in all bills, except for taxis where 10 per cent is expected. In restaurants you may round up the bill.

Visiting Museums. It may be well to mention that Swedish museums are continually being rebuilt, expanded and rearranged, so that the descriptions here may no longer tally in detail, but will give an idea of scope and contents of the displays. Doors and staircases are often not labelled, so always explore in museums (and elsewhere) unless there is an obvious veto—you may come upon unsuspected gems. Always ask for English brochures: translations of information can often be borrowed, but may be stored out of sight. See also Opening Hours, above.

Besides conventional museums there are 1000 local open-air museums. (Since most old buildings are of wood, they are comparatively easy to move.) The sign usually says *hembygdsgård, forngård* or *gammelgård* but there are many variations. Skansen in Stockholm is a model for all the others, though it is in fact national in scope. Some may consist of one building (the average is six), and may date from the 17C though most are from the 19C. Some may be meticulously furnished and equipped, and larger ones have costumed inhabitants demonstrating local crafts. There are also innumerable craft and industry museums, typically consisting of an old workshop or workplace. Small local museums will have restricted opening times and seasons—always try to check at the tourist bureau—but you can often wander around the buildings even when they are not open.

1

Malmö

MALMÖ (pop. 224,000) is the third-largest city in Sweden. It lies on the west coast of Skåne, an ancient province occupying the roughly square area on the southernmost tip of the country—a flat and fertile land which is inevitably known as the granary of Sweden. Skåne gave its name to Scandinavia and was the starting point of many a Viking raid to the Continent. Because it was a Danish possession until 1658 it retains many Danish characteristics, including an accent impenetrable to northern Swedes. More interesting to the tourist, however, are the appealing medieval churches and some of the castles built or begun by Danish hands.

Malmö itself is also different from its bigger sisters Stockholm and Gothenburg. Stockholm may be more culturally vibrant and Gothenburg more commercially aware, but Malmö retains its distinctive, more homogenous character and is closer to the continent of Europe. Copenhagen is 45 minutes away by ferry, and other ferries ply to Germany.

Its pleasant and compact heart, much of it pedestrian precinct, is characterised by solid 19C buildings influenced by Dutch Renaissance style (the Renaissance reached Scandinavia largely through Holland), leavened with older buildings from medieval times onwards. Modern construction has been largely relegated beyond the old core, marked by the ring of canals. The canals go on to wind through delightful parkland and form part of the castle moat. Other green spaces lie beyond the centre, notably the very large Pildammspark.

Tourist Information: the tourist bureau is at the central station, open Mon–Fri 09.00–17.00, Sat 09.00–13.00, tel. (040) 34 12 70. *Malmö This Month*' is a free booklet with maps and information in English on transport, shopping, tourist attractions, entertainment and useful phone numbers. The **Malmö Card**, with varying duration and price, gives free or discounted travel, parking, museum-entrance, swimming, car-hire and entertainment, and can be good value depending on what you want to do. Check with the tourist bureau that opening times on specific attractions are up to date. (Opening times in this book can only be a guide.)

Public transport: a large proportion of town buses (stadsbussar) pass through Gustav Adolfs torg, with well-labelled bus-stops. County buses (Länsbussar) travel round Skåne. Bus information tel. 020-61 61 61. The mauve-painted local trains (Pågatågen) go from the 'Lokal Station' adjoining the main station. Very easy to use, tickets from machines on the platform (directions in English). Tel. as above.

Exchange: Forex, Norra Vallgatan 60, and opposite the station. Open daily 08.00–21.00.

Post office: Skeppsbron 1, just beyond the station, open Mon–Fri 08.00–18.00, Sat 09.30–13.00. Exchange.

Telephone, telegram, fax and telex: Storgatan 23, tel. (040) 25 12 32.

Emergencies: Police, Fire, Ambulance, tel. 90 000 (all over the country). **Police and lost property**, Södra Promenaden 5b, tel. (040) 20 10 00. **Doctor and dentist** on call: tel. (040) 33 35 00, 07.00–22.00, tel. (040) 33 10 00 other times. **All-night chemist**: Apoteket Gripen, Bergsgatan 48, tel. (040) 19 21 13

History. They say Malmö was built on herrings and sand. The name means 'sand-mounds', and as for the herrings, they were so plentiful they could be scooped straight out of the sea with a shovel. The first mention of the town is in a 12C document by

Bishop Eskil of Lund. It had established itself south of the present centre, probably in the area of the present Pildammspark. By 1275 the Bishop of Roskilde in Denmark was able to refer to it as a city. The centre moved to the sea-front, and commercial activity concentrated on the road now known as Adelgatan ('Nobility Street') and the two streets prolonging it at either end. In 1353 the city received a charter from Magnus Eriksson, King of Norway, Sweden and Skåne. Soon the Hanseatic League (Hanse), more particularly the city of Lübeck, was attracted by the flourishing herring harvest—the German merchants had the drive, the capital and the expertise to exploit the lucrative harbour, bringing their salt to sell in exchange for the fish. Hence the palpable German influence, most obviously in S:t Petri church.

Wave after wave of Danes, Swedes and Germans took Malmö—Valdemar Atterdag of Denmark acquired it in 1360, and in 1370 it was pawned to the Hanse for 15 years. Erik of Pomerania took it under his wing in the 15C and made it the most important city in his realm after Copenhagen. He began the building of the castle with a mint, and gave Malmö his own coat of arms with a griffin.

With the coming of the Reformation Malmö was still Danish. Two exceptional characters, Jörgen Kock, the mayor, and Claes Mortensen the clergyman, pushed Malmö into the new age. Kock obtained a printing-press on which to produce copies of Mortensen's translation of the Bible into Danish. Kock it was who entertained the Swedish King Gustav Vasa (with his 100 horses) when he and the Danish King Frederik I were negotiating an agreement called the 'Malmö Recess'. But the date engraved on every Skåne native's heart is 1658, when after all the bloodshed the province finally became Swedish. Karl X Gustav of Sweden led his army across the frozen Little and Great Belts (Denmark) to defeat the Danes and proclaim Skåne Swedish. A deliberate programme of 'Swedification' was inaugurated. However, by becoming Swedish, Malmö was reduced to the status of a provincial city in a realm whose capital was far away, instead of a more central focus of power in an important province of Denmark.

After a stagnant period, a merchant called Frans Suell (1744–1817) began to enlarge the harbour in 1775 and commercial life blossomed again. Comprehensive land-reform in the 19C led to greater prosperity in the countryside and therefore in the city also, and by the mid 19C the textile industries were thriving. Regular boats to Copenhagen were introduced in 1838, Kockums shipyard which opened as a workshop in 1840 built ships from 1870, and the first train puffed off to Lund in 1856, opening a rail-network as a fresh stimulus to commerce.

After being in the forefront of the Reformation, Malmö was also the scene of the infancy of the Social Democratic Party. August Palm, the first socialist to make his mark, delivered an historic speech here in 1881. In 1914 there took place the magnificent but ill-fated Baltic Exhibition, where all the Baltic countries including Germany and Russia presented their most advanced technology and art. In 1983 the World Maritime University, a UN foundation, was established here to give promising graduates of the developing world higher degrees in maritime studies.

Present industries include Pågens bakery, Skanska construction company and the very much slimmed-down Kockums.

The bridge to Copenhagen is scheduled to be finished in about the year 2000.

A.   The Old Town

From the many ferries or the airport, by road or rail, the signs *Centrum* are the easiest to follow. The useful C-ring is an inner ring-road provided with maps at intervals should you need to find another area than the centre. The spacious main square is **Stortorget**. In the centre stands an equestrian **statue** by John Börjeson (1896) of Karl X Gustav, the king who united Skåne with Sweden by the Treaty of Roskilde (in Denmark) in 1658. The bronze **fountain** by Stig Blomberg (1964) stands on the site of a 16C well whose reservoir is still there, marked by white stones in the pavement. The figures on the fountain represent facets of Malmö: its adopted bird, the nightingale,

S:t Petri church, hussars, an anchor, fish, witches and a blackamoor. The three top-hatted figures are the three Nordic kings who met here in 1914.

The most striking building on Stortorget is the **Rådhus** (town hall) on the W side with its dark red and grey façade. The original Late Gothic town hall was built in 1546 during Jörgen Kock's tenure as mayor; it acquired its present Dutch Renaissance appearance in the 1860s under the guidance of the architect Helgo Zettervall. The dark brick is richly ornamented with stonework scrolls and fluted pilasters, pediments and five gables with volutes. The gilded goddess over the central balcony is Themis (Justice) and the other full-length statues represent agriculture, shipping, crafts and commerce. The four busts are of the city's leading citizens: Lorenz Isac Bager, Frans Suell, Mathias Flensburg and Jörgen Kock. The undistinguished sides and the back on Kalendegatan were added in the 1950s and 1960s. At the moment the interior cannot be visited, but you could ask the tourist bureau. The Knut Banqueting Chamber is resplendent in 19C Baroque stucco, and there is a Renaissance-style council chamber and portrait-gallery of Danish monarchs. The original 15C vaulted cellars along Kalendegatan were rediscovered in 1949, but the cellars on the Stortorget side have been almost continually in use as a tavern for around 400 years, and are now a restaurant (entered from pavement level).

On the N side of the square, is the modest white **residence** of the Governor of Malmöhus County, which comprises half of Skåne. This was originally built as two houses in the 16C, which were converted to one in 1728–30 for the Governor. It has delicate stucco decoration around the windows and door, and a central gable and entrance steps which belie the fact that it was two houses. A small suite is reserved here for the royal family when they visit Malmö. Karl XV died here in 1872, and 19,000 paid their respects— when the population of Malmö was only 20,000. In 1914 the kings of Sweden, Norway and Denmark met here to declare themselves for peace and greeted the populace from the balcony. It was the first time they had met since Norway broke away from Sweden in 1905.

On an anti-clockwise circuit of the square, at the NW corner stands the **house** of the dynamic Jörgen Kock, built for him in 1522–25; only the vaulted Gothic cellars are now accessible to the tourist, used as a restaurant. The main building with its gabled façade on Västergatan has a statue of the Virgin, lions and coats-of-arms (originals in Malmö museum). The house also includes the two buildings adjoining at right-angles to each other. King Gustav Vasa stayed here in 1524 while negotiating with the king of Denmark.

Behind, in Västergatan you can look at the Rosenvingska house with a Low German inscription over the door telling us to reflect on mortality. The date of the building is given as 1534 with the coats of arms of the couple who had the house built. It has been variously a shop, soldiers' quarters, a hospital and a post office.

The cobbled **Lilla Torg** (Small Square) just off the SW corner of Stortorget is picturesquely lined on two sides with half-timbered buildings. In 1591 it was created on swampy ground to take the overflow from the market on Stortorget. From 1903 to the 1960s a covered market occupied the whole square. As a sort of replacement, the Saluhall, a complex of specialist stalls and restaurants, was built on the north-west corner.

On the west side of the square the half-timbered gable end belongs to the Ekströmska house built in the 18C for an apothecary. The half-timbered building adjoining it is a reconstruction of a building called Aspegrenska house originally in Mäster Nilsgatan.

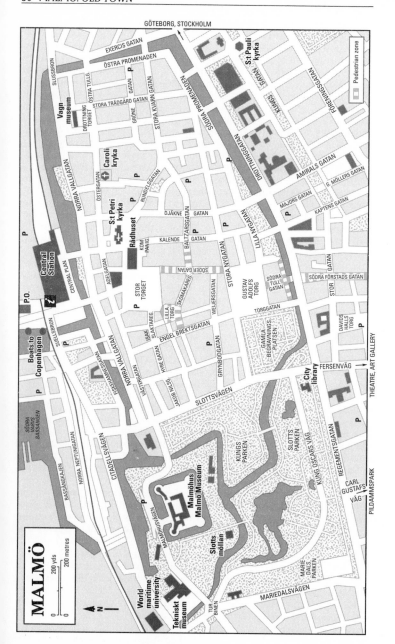

The half-timbered building on the south-west corner used as an art gallery is Faxeska house of the 1760s. It was acquired in 1842 by the Faxe family who had a wine and spirit business. Their lamp in the shape of a bunch of grapes hangs above the door.

Most of the south of the square consists of one property which was originally several. The main façade on the square is that of Niels Hammer's house (1597). The gateway was broken through into the courtyard in the 18C. Across the courtyard from the gate is Gabriel Hedmans warehouse (1852) now containing the **Form Design Center**, a permanent exhibition of Swedish design in furniture, textiles and ceramics (closed Mon). The house with the plastered walls is Pehr Malmros' house, originally half-timbered, from the early 18C. The building which faces Hjulhamnsgatan is Diedrich Sölscher's warehouse, two 18C buildings erected as utility premises for Pehr Malmros' house, with kitchen and store-rooms.

The fountain in the middle of Lilla Torg is by Thure Thörn (1973). From here take Skomakaregatan on the south-east corner. At the end on the left-hand corner is the gable-end of Flensburgska house (1590s), of brick with limestone banding, with Dutch Renaissance gables. It was owned by the Flensburg family from 1827 to 1935, and had been used among other things as a warehouse.

Almost opposite the end of Skomakaregatan, excavations have revealed an old leper hospital. This proves that the old city boundary was at least some distance to the north, since the hospital would have been situated beyond the walls. Walk up Södergatan towards Stortorget again. This street is a pedestrian precinct, and here and in the adjoining streets is one of the main shopping and eating areas of the city.

On the right just on the entrance to the square is the tall, slim and decorative **Apoteket Lejonet**, (Lion Pharmacy—all chemists in Sweden are named after animals or birds), Malmö's oldest. There has been a pharmacy on this site since 1571 when its licence was granted; its 18C wooden lion shop-sign is in the museum. The present building is from 1898. The façade is of warm red stone, with a three-storey oriel window crowned with a pinnacle and much decorative carving. One scene shows medicines in preparation. The interior still has dark panelling, wooden counters and a carved gallery displaying old flagons and bottles.

Take the narrow Kompanigatan down by the right side of the Rådhus. On the right about half-way down, somewhat obscured in a courtyard, is Kompanihuset (1520s) which was owned by the Danish Trading Company.

At the end of the lane, **S:t Petri** church, appears, whose green spire looms over the Rådhus seen from the Stortorget. There may well have been a church in the original settlement south of the town but the first church of record is a Romanesque one shown on the town's earliest seal. This was torn down as S:t Petri was built in the early 14C. By this time the Hanse merchants from Lübeck were firmly entrenched and so it is no surprise to find a North German Gothic church with more than a hint of St. Marien in Lübeck.

It is a three-aisled basilica with apse and transepts, and four chapels irregularly spaced. Flying buttresses support walls and apse. After having had a Baroque cupola, the tower acquired its present stepped gables and copper-clad 96m-high spire in 1890, so that it now matches the stepped gables on the transepts and the chapels. The brickwork of the surface is varied by string-courses, blind arcades and decorative panels of pierced burnt brick. Burnt brick banding also picks out the mouldings of the Gothic doorways. The statues on the exterior of the chapel to the left of the doorway are modern replicas. (Originals in the museum.)

Inside it is a very light building. Turn immediately left and left again to reach the **Krämare chapel** (Merchant's chapel) with its late medieval **paintings**. This was added (late 15C) as a Lady Chapel and at the Reformation was sealed off as being henceforth useless, thus happily preserving the wall and vault paintings for posterity. The rest of the church was whitewashed by zealous reformers, and during hearty 19C restoration the paintings were scraped away. At various times the chapel was used as a store, and even as the local fire-station. On the north wall there are two 'danses macabres', and below, Mary Magdalene, St. Catherine, St. Anne, Christ and St. Francis. On the west wall is another 'danse macabre', this time with the Pope, and below it the Virgin and Child. On the south wall there is Christ in the vinepress, and Church Fathers Gregory, Ambrose, Augustine and Jerome. Then comes St. Laurence and lastly St. George and a badly worn dragon. The **vault paintings** are in better condition. You can pick out amid the rampant foliage St. Veronica and her cloth with the face of Christ, St. Peter with a key, St. Paul with a sword, Christ as judge, as the Lamb of God and as the Crucified. There is also the boy Jesus with a parrot and a fig. The chapel contains a font of 1601 of sandstone and black marble with biblical illustrations. It has a chased silver basin (1919) worked in one single piece with motifs which place S:t Petri in the centre of the world. The canopy above is of oak made by Daniel Thomison who also carved the pulpit. There are two Gothic cupboards, the older from 1514. Just outside the chapel are two large bell-clappers leaning against the wall and opposite, two old chests, one of which has four coin-slots for donations to the church, the hospital, widows and children. At the back of the right aisle hangs a votive ship commemorating Malmö seamen who died in the Second World War.

The Baroque **pulpit** (1599) of sandstone and black marble is by Daniel Thomison. It is supported by a statue of Moses and surmounted by a three-tier acoustic canopy with figures of St. Peter and St. Paul. The pulpit itself has reliefs depicting the Annunciation, the Birth of Jesus, the Last Supper, the Crucifixion, Resurrection and Ascension, with Latin texts. A nice touch is the four-in-one hour-glass, sadly no longer in use. One of the glasses indicated a quarter of an hour, one half an hour, one three-quarters and one the full hour. In the floor of the nave near the pulpit lies the grave of the mayor Jorgen Kock (1555).

The 15m high **retable**, said to be largest of wood in North Europe, is dedicated to St. Nicholas, patron of seamen. It was carved by the German Hendrik Konnicke and finished on Michaelmas Day 1611. The lowest picture is the Last Supper flanked by Moses and John the Baptist with four cardinal virtues. Above it is the Crucifixion between shields which had to be swiftly changed from Danish to Swedish in 1658, but the supporters are still Danish. Above this is the Ascension with the Evangelists and caryatids representing law, faith, hope and charity, and finally 'Jahweh' in Hebrew script. The grave (1575) of Claes Mortensen, Malmö's Reformation vicar, lies within the sanctuary, and many 17C Baroque memorials hang on the walls and pillars.

The main organ above the entrance, with 5935 pipes, was made by a Danish company in 1951. The organ front and gallery are of the late 18C. The historic medieval organ, documented as early as 1500, is now in the museum and still playable. The brass chandeliers date from the 17C.

Setting off from the rear of S:t Petri north towards the canal, turn right almost immediately into Östergatan. A hundred metres or so along stands the **Caroli church**, a Greek cross in plan (1879–80) on the site of a 17C church which was built for the German population, and called after Karl XI, the reigning king. It contains a 17C carved oak font.

Opposite the Caroli church is **S:t Gertrud**, a well-restored complex of buildings covering 10,000 sq m. Östergatan, the continuation of Adelgatan, was once the main thoroughfare, and here stand three merchants' houses and 19 other buildings dating from the 1530s onwards, with most from the 19C. It is used for education and leisure, and is not generally open to tourists, though the courtyards provide a quiet retreat from Östergatan. The first house of the block (coming from the centre of town) dates from the 18C and the second is Niels Kuntze's house of the 1530s with a 19C façade. The second house on the left in the first courtyard is a 17C warehouse and adjoining this along its rear is an 18C half-timbered house.

On the other side of Östergatan opposite the end of S:t Gertrud are two half-timbered houses. First the **Thott house** (1558), the oldest with half-timbering in the city, then the **Dieden house** (1620s), now the Savings Bank. Small shops were originally built under the high windows on either side of the entrance steps.

Östergatan comes out into **Drottningtorget** (Queen's Square). This was the hussars' parade ground and named after the consort of Gustav IV Adolf, who took a fancy to Malmö, stayed here six months in 1806–07 and thought of making it a second capital. He was deposed, but not before the city's largest square was named after him. The hussars' riding-school, the low cream-painted building, is now **Vagnmuseet** (the Carriage Museum) with a variety of coaches, bicycles and sledges. (Irregular opening hours—ask at tourist bureau.)

The light cavalry regiment known as the Crown Prince's Hussars was raised in 1758 and was held in special affection by local people until it was disbanded in 1929. A dedicated group still keep up the old traditions, however, and may sometimes be seen on special occasions. Many names in the city refer to the regiment—Regementsgatan, and the Kronprinsen shopping precinct, where the restaurant on the top floor is called Översten (The Colonel). The regiment fought against Napoleon at Bornhöved (now in Germany) in 1813.

Leave Drottningtorget by going out behind the Carriage Museum and turning left back along the canal, looking at the rear of S:t Gertrud on the way. This is Norra Vallgatan and was the medieval sea-line. Across the canal after about 600m is the **Central Station** with the tourist bureau. On the left is the **Forex Exchange Office** and then the Savoy Hotel. At this point in the canal the boat trip round the city starts. If you cross the bridge on your right, and walk past the station you come to the imposing main **post office** by Ferdinand Boberg. However, to return to Stortorget take Hamngatan on your left. The statue on the main road just beyond the entrance to Hamngatan is of Frans Suell, the Malmö harbour-builder, by Edvard Trulson (1912).

B.   The Castle Area

Gustav Adolfs torg to the south of the old town is on the site of former fortifications, which were razed in 1805 when the defensive canal was moved south to its present position. Here are the fast-food restaurants, bus-stops and starting points for bus tours. Cross the road to the west, heading for what looks like a park but is actually an old graveyard with the canal running across one corner. Pick your way more or less straight across, turn right up Slottsgatan and into the **Kungspark** as soon as you find an entrance. You could also reach this point by starting from Stortorget and taking the very narrow Isak Slaktaragatan on the west side of the square. This leads along Jakob Nilsgatan which has pretty cottages. The park is straight ahead.

Head north by any path and you will come to a main road with an obvious courthouse on the opposite side (Court of Appeals), turn left and follow the road round to the entrance to the castle—**Malmöhus**—on your left. Two massive outlying low cannon-towers flank the building and you cross a causeway over the canal which functions as a moat, to enter the courtyard under a tall gatehouse.

The castle began when Erik of Pomerania added a royal house to the sea-wall in 1434, and Kristofer of Bavaria installed a mint in 1444. The master of the mint was always a powerful local politician—Jörgen Kock, for example, took that office in 1518. Not much of this building was left when Christian III constructed his fortress in 1536 after he had finally subdued the rebellious inhabitants. This is the building to the left of the gatehouse. Christian defended his castle with a moat and cannon-towers. One of these, to the left of the entrance, remains, the one on the right is a reconstruction.

Frederik II lived here for five years before assuming the throne of Denmark in 1559. Another more reluctant inhabitant was the Earl of Bothwell, the third husband of Mary, Queen of Scots. He fled from Scotland in 1567 and was captured at Bergen where his ship was driven by a storm. He was imprisoned here for six years before being transferred to a prison in Denmark where he died in 1578. After the Treaty of Roskilde (1658) when Skåne became Swedish, Karl X Gustav extended and strengthened the fortifications but nothing remains of these now. During the years of Danish possession it had been a personal castle of the Danish kings, and now it became just another link in Swedish defences. From 1669 to 1674 the castle commandant was Erik Dahlberg who made Malmö into one of the chief towns of Sweden.

Erik Dahlberg was not an artist by profession but a distinguished military commander and governor who was also an engineer. (He it was who led the Swedish army over the frozen Great Belt in 1658.) Wherever his duties led him he put his considerable gifts into town-planning and designing churches and castles. Not only that, he was an extremely competent draughtsman, and was the publisher of the vast work *Suecia antiqua et hodierna* (1684) containing nearly 500 topographical engravings by the foremost artists of Swedish buildings and towns, an incomparable record for the historian.

Malmö Museum. Much of the castle was destroyed by fire in 1870 but additions and restorations have turned it into a museum (open daily pm, closed Mon except June–Aug). The ground floor has natural history with Swedish animals shown in their natural habitat, while the lower ground floor displays an aquarium and an unusual section with nocturnal animals. The walls of the staircase have Carl Larsson's enormous cartoons for his murals in the National Museum in Stockholm. On the first floor to the left at the top of the stairs there are furnished rooms of 17C–20C. At the end is the Skovgaard Hall named from Joakim Skovgaard's 'Christ in Majesty' cartoon for the apse mosaic in Lund cathedral (1924–25). Opposite this is S:t Petri's medieval organ, end 15C, restored several times. The textile gallery is also on this side of the stairs.

This is the most convenient point at which to visit the top floor with temporary exhibitions of mainly Scandinavian artists.

Right of the stairs on the first floor is a section on **Prehistoric Skåne**: finds and excavations, burials, food, building and a flint mine. In the first room on the left is a piece of prehistoric chewing-gum (*tuggummi*)—a chunk of resin dated to 6000 BC, with the teethmarks of an eleven-year-old. Beyond this section to the right is a series of old workshops from a smithy to a cobblers.

A left turn here brings you to the **medieval** exhibits, mostly from Malmö. There is a leaflet available in English and you can pick out the sections on monasteries, brick-building, hygiene, pottery and wood-carving. There are models of notable Malmö houses and a 5m-long relief of the city in the 1520s. At the end of this section, a left turn brings you out to the cannon-tower. Over the entrance is a copy of the oldest picture of Malmö, a print from a book of town illustrations (1582) where it is called 'Elbogen' (elbow—from the shape of the coast). The book itself is displayed nearby.

As you come out of the tower the entrance to the **castle** proper is straight ahead. Access is through the gatehouse tower: as you walk across the modern wooden landing the wall ahead is part of the original building. The **Knights' Hall**, the **King's Day Room** and the **King's Bedchamber** have large windows, with some shallow bays for extra light. These rooms contain furniture, unfortunately not labelled, and pictures of various centuries. The portraits are of royalty and nobility, one room for Danes and one for Swedes as well as Mary Stuart and James I of England. Magnus Stenbock the 'saviour of Sweden' at the battle of Helsingborg in 1710 is also portrayed. The treasury of S:t Knut's Guild is on display, and some of the furniture is very fine, such as the carved bed (1646) in the bedchamber.

The ground floor of the castle was divided into two apartments, the west one being for the castle commandant. The barrel-vaulted cellars incorporate some remains of the 15C structure. In the east part of the cellar Bothwell was imprisoned, but this cannot be visited. However, you can see the small windows of his rooms from the courtyard, on either side of steps leading to a door.

From the entrance to the castle you can see **Kommendanthuset** on the other side of the road, This is the late 18C arsenal now housing a military history museum, showing also a silver hoard of 1676, a toy museum and a marionette theatre (open summer). Continue along the road and in about 100m on the right-hand side there is a lane lined with picturesque fishermen's huts where fresh fish can be bought in the early mornings. The large brick building is the 17C Tannery. Here also the veteran tram can be boarded for short rides (tickets opposite the fishermen's huts).

Alongside the lane is **Teknikens och Sjöfartens Hus**, the Technical and Maritime Museums (open same times as the main museum, no information in English). The technical section has displays on planes, roads, power (steam, wind, water, etc.) and on a higher level local industries, sugar, cement, bricks and so on. You can enter a complete 1943 submarine (short stairs from power section). Up the main stairs is a science and technology section where you can set in motion experiments covering light, magnetism, gravitation and so on, but as yet the instructions and *warning notices* are only in Swedish. The centrepiece here is a model of Tycho Brahe's observatory on the island of Ven. On the other side of the building is the maritime museum with models of ships built in Malmö, Skåne harbours and lighthouses.

Retracing your steps back towards the castle, take the path which leads down the right side of it into the **Slottspark**. Ahead is a windmill on a knoll, which is actually a bastion of the castle. After crossing the bridge turn left and across the lake can be seen a replica of Carl Milles' **statue** 'Man and Pegasus' of 1950. For a closer view work your way around the lake. On this side also is the pretty Japanese-style garden 'Kärret' (swamp). The broad Kung Oscarsväg cuts through the park here and a left turn along it brings you back to the old graveyard via the gabled and turreted library of 1901, with its modern extension.

C. The theatre area and Pildammspark

From the library Fersensväg leads south to the **Stadsteater** (City Theatre), on the wide forecourt of which stands the spirited statue/fountain **Tragos** (1953) by Nils Sjögren. Figures on it include Hamlet and Charlie Chaplin. This theatre with a very large stage was opened in 1944 and it presents ballet, opera and musicals. (Tickets half-price an hour before the performance.) On the opposite side of the main road south is a tiny park beyond which lies the **Konsthall** (art gallery) which attracts some good exhibitions.

To reach the **Pildammspark**, the largest cultivated park in Sweden, go back to the theatre, cut through the car park behind it and along a short road to enter on the corner of Carl Gustafsväg and Roskildevägen. The park contains 200,000 trees, two lakes teeming with bird life, woods, statues, an open-air theatre (concerts in the summer) and a large clearing for open-air gymnastics, hot-air ballooning, midsummer maypole-dancing and the like. From the entrance skirt the small lake leaving it on your right. Continue along a high hedge. To the left is a 4m-high domestic iron of stone and metal, a sculpture by Hiroshi Koyama. Cross the road ahead and ascend a slope to the larger lake. Follow the shore anti-clockwise. On the other side of a small car park is a flower-walk leading to the pretty **Margareta Pavilion** which is of particular interest to British visitors.

Princess Margaret of Connaught (1882–1920), grand-daughter of Queen Victoria, known as Margareta in Sweden, married Gustav Adolf the Crown Prince of Sweden in 1905 but died before she could become queen. She was a talented amateur painter and garden-designer and some of her work is exhibited in this tiny building with photos and other mementoes.

The pavilion was built in 1914 as private quarters for the royal family during the Baltic Exhibition. The park is dotted with reminders of this great event. The architect Ferdinand Boberg designed his 50 ha 'White City' around the lake, with an exotic fantasy-castle as a restaurant on the island, then a peninsula. His daringly high 87m wooden entrance tower was modelled on the local Skåne church-towers with steeply pitched stepped gables. Extravagant national exhibitions were contributed by Germany, Denmark and Russia. (Poland and the Baltic States did not exist as such.) Lavishly designed displays showed the very latest in science, technology, industry, transport, architecture, art, furniture and fashion. Nearly a million people attended before the outbreak of war led to the withdrawal of Germany and Russia, and a gale had topped the grand tower.

Beyond the Margareta Pavilion steep flights of steps lead up to the open-air theatre. Back on the lakeside, behind the café, the three large fountains in the middle of the lake (coloured displays on summer evenings) can be viewed against the old water-tower (1903).

500m to the east of the Pildammspark exit on the corner of Carl Gustafs-vag and Pildammsvägen lies the old working-class district of Malmö centred on Möllevångstorget. Now the area is home to a thriving immigrant culture, with a large fruit and vegetable market at reasonable prices almost every day. The square is surrounded by small shops selling national foods. The large sculpture is 'Dignity of Labour' by Axel Ebbe (1930).

D. Outer suburbs

Limhamn used to be a separate village, but now is part of Malmö. The name means 'lime harbour', and limestone has been quarried here since the Middle Ages. The easiest way to get here is to take the coast road south (Limhamnsvägen). Here there is a dramatic limestone pit which can be viewed from Annetorpsvägen. A new science and amusement park is planned for the area. Ferries go to Dragør in Denmark and there is a large marina.

Hyllie Water Tower can be reached by driving south along Pildamms-vägen about 2.5km from the end of the Pildammspark. It is a 62m high white mushroom finished in 1973. The restaurant on top allows sightseers to go out on to the viewing balcony for a small fee to see the landmarks of Malmö and the flat fields of Skåne.

E. Excursions from Malmö

Dalby, Hällestad and Everlöv

From Malmö take the E22 towards Lund. 7km from the C-ring road and 1km past the windmill, at the Kronotorp junction turn on to road 11 towards Staffanstorp and Simrishamn. Just after getting on to road 11 a sign right points to **Burlövs By**. In the village is a group of attractive old buildings: the church, vicarage and school. The church (not always open) was built in the 12C and the nave and north chancel wall remain of this period. The tower was added in the 13C and later heightened. The south porch also has Gothic niches in the gable. The Renaissance altar was carved by Jakob Kremberg in Lund and there are two 18C pew-doors preserved. Opposite the entrance is the picturesque thatched vicarage of 1773 in its own garden, now a local museum (open summer Sunday afternoons). On the other side of the church is the 19C school, now used for local activities.

Continuing through Staffanstorp towards Dalby, the road passes the village of **Kyrkheddinge** where on the right-hand side of the road is a Romanesque **church** with later additions. The sandstone font is late 12C, the crucifix 15C and there is a brightly coloured Renaissance pulpit. The chunky tower of **Dalby church** now appears high on the skyline though still 5km away.

Dedicated to the Holy Cross, it is the oldest stone church still in use in Scandinavia, having been founded by King Sven Estridsen in 1060. It was a cathedral for six years before the see was transferred to Lund. The nave and south aisle are the oldest parts.

During major reconstruction a century later an entrance hall was added to the west which is now the crypt. (The spring here was used for baptisms before the font was acquired.) At the same time a small royal palace was built adjoining this entrance—this was the king's church, as opposed to the archbishop's church at Lund. An Augustinian monastery was founded in the 12C, one remaining wing of which is joined by a buttress to the north of the church. In the 13C the church was twice as long as it is today, extending to the east to a point marked by a tall wooden cross in the churchyard. In the 18C the tower over the entrance was removed and the present two-tiered structure was added.

Inside, the unplastered parts of the nave walls are from the 11C, and there is an unusual column set in one of the nave walls. The 12C crypt (originally the entrance-hall) has carved columns. By the entrance to the crypt is a wooden carving of St. Olof and a giraffe-necked dragon with a human crowned head. The vault paintings are from the 13C (restored) with heart-shaped palmette decoration on the rib-crossings and chevrons on the ribs. The 12C font is from the Byzantios workshop and shows the baptism of Christ. In a show-case are copies from the 'Book of Dalby', one of the oldest Scandinavian manuscripts, now kept in Copenhagen. There are two medieval choir-stalls, and the south door is also medieval. The carving of the face of Christ is from about 1500. The pulpit, the altar and the pews are from the 18C.

From Dalby a road goes west to **Torna Hällestad** (5km). In the village turn sharp right at the sign *kyrka*. The church has **vault-paintings** by the Master of Vittskövle, dated to the 1460s. The Entry into Jerusalem has Herod waiting at the city gate and Zaccheus in his sycamore tree, Christ washes the disciples' feet in a large basin, while Judas at the Last Supper is comically ugly. In the last two pictures Christ's accuser is shown in a jester's suit. Three runestones are built into the rear wall of the church, all carved as memorials using Danish rune language of around 1000.

To reach road 11, follow the signs to Veberöd. Turn left on to road 11, go through Veberöd and after 3km take the right turn towards Blentarp. After 2km follow signs to **Kulturens Östarp**, an open-air museum (open May–Aug, and Sept weekends, closed Mon).

Kulturen is the historical museum in Lund and they own the land which has a working farm, restaurant and open-air museum. The first group of buildings by the car park has a small museum (labels in Swedish only), a café and a restaurant which is a copy of an old inn near Malmö—it is worth taking a look inside. To the right a winding path leads across fields to two groups of buildings. On the right the working farm is private but visitors can enter the windmill, flax-preparing house and malt-house. On the left a path goes to the museum farm, passing a water-mill. The farm is built around a courtyard, and has some basic furniture and equipment, including painted chests and a loom.

Returning to the road, turn right still towards Blentarp. After 3km turn left to **Everlöv** church (open May–Sept). The church was built partly in the 12C and partly in the 13C. The great gate was formerly built into the wall surrounding the churchyard which was extended in the 19C. The simple vigorous **paintings** on the vaults were done at the end of the 15C by the so-called Master of Everlöv. The ribs of the vaults are unusually thick and the cells narrow which gives an odd effect of depth. Over the chancel are the symbols of the four Evangelists, the lion of Mark, the eagle of John, the ox of Luke, and Matthew as a man wearing glasses on the end of his nose. Over the nave each bay with its four cells represents four aspects of one event, the Creation, the Fall, Expulsion from Paradise and Lazarus and the

the other, devils push, pull and poke with sticks in a vain effort to force up the scale-pan. In the porch are a medieval door with decorative ironwork, a medieval poor-box, processional staves, wooden grave-spades and some gravestones.

If you return to Malmö by road 11, the St. Hans' Cross on the section missed by going to Hällestad leads in 2km to a 45m-long ship-setting of 39 stones in a muddy farmyard, while the other St. Hans' Cross nearby indicates a walking-trail to the top of the Romele ridge for a view over the plain.

Skanör and Falsterbo. These twin towns, once medieval strongholds and trading-centres, occupy the most south-westerly peninsula of Sweden. Take the E6/E22 to the south of Malmö, and branch off at Vellinge after 17km on to road 100. 7km after the turn the road crosses the Falsterbo canal which makes the peninsula technically an island. After the bridge the road runs through a thickly wooded nature-reserve which soon opens out to the left on to heathland, which is rare in Sweden. Here bell-heather and birds of prey thrive. At the roundabout turn right to **Skanör** church (signposted *kyrka*). At the T-junction turn left which brings you to the idyllic **town square** with the **church** on your right. It is white-washed and red-roofed, with crow-step gables, unfortunately rarely open. Dedicated to St. Olof, it was begun in the 13C. Behind it, signposted *borgruin*, is the site of the moated medieval castle, stones from which were used to build the town hall (18C) opposite the church.

Continue in the same direction out of the square, take the first turn on the left and in a few hundred metres there is a street-crossing for the town's flock of geese, with warning signs of a silhouetted goose and and white goose footmarks across the road. The charming centre has grass sidewalks and pastel-painted cottages with roses and hollyhocks by the doors.

To see **Falsterbo** which is very similar, continue south across the peninsula. Keep straight on through Falsterbo, turn left at the T-junction and continue until you are on a track under trees which leads you to the **church**. Built between the 13C and the 16C, and dedicated to St. Gertrude, if it is open you can see the medieval font, a 14C figure of St. Christopher, the 15C altar by a Lübeck artist, the 16C pulpit and several other works of art.

There is a small museum of local interest and picturesque streets. South-west of the church near the shore are the ruins of Falsterbo medieval castle. There has been a lighthouse here since the 13C, warning of a dangerous reef. The beaches are particularly good for swimming and amber is sometimes washed up. The island to the south is a bird sanctuary.

About half-way between here and Trelleborg to the east on the coast road there is an amber museum and shop (*bärnsten*).

Torup, Hyby and Svaneholm. Leave Malmö by the E65 towards Ystad. 4km after the junction of the E65 and the E20 turn off to Skabersjö and Torup. **Skabersjö** church (4km) at the road-junction is a typical Skåne church, with boxy tower, nave and chancel, trimmed with step-gables and a string of blind arcading under the eaves (though the step-gables were in fact added only in the 19C). It has a Renaissance pulpit.

Follow the signs for Torup (5km), through beech-woods with car parks and walking-trails, beautiful in late sping. **Torup castle** is set in extensive grounds in the woods (limited opening times, check with Malmö tourist bureau or try summer weekend afternoons. Swedish guided tours, but English notes are available).

Building was begun in the 16C, with streams being dammed to make a lake and the castle's stone cellar built on oak piles in the lake. In the 17C it was restored and partially rebuilt. A daughter of Christian IV of Denmark, Leonora Christina, was the wife of a 17C owner, Corfitz Ulfeldt. In that time of strife between the two countries the pair were implicated in treason against both Sweden and Denmark when the area passed from Danish to Swedish hands in 1658. Leonora Christina was imprisoned for many years and her husband died in exile.

In 1812 Torup was bought by the Coyet family, one of whom, Baroness Henriette Coyet, lived here for 57 years until she died in 1941 after putting much effort into its care, and the result is very much an evocation of her character and life. In 1899 Kaiser Wilhelm II visited for the hunting, and Crown Princess Margareta, grand-daughter of Queen Victoria, came on several occasions, as did Selma Lagerlöf, a friend of Henriette Coyet.

On the granite base there are three brick storeys surrounding a courtyard with two towers at diagonally opposite corners. The octagonal tower on the round base is probably a replacement for an earlier round one, and is later than its partner. The brick gable-ends are picked out in a pattern of white-painted blind lancets. There was an open arcade on one side of the courtyard, now filled by the library. Above the arcade are the coats of arms of the owners who repaired it in 1748.

The guided tour begins in the **octagonal tower** which contains paintings by Prince Eugen and Gustav Cederström. In the next room is a copy of a 1782 wall-hanging. The **hall** is hung with hunting trophies from the surrounding countryside, the ones with crowns having been bagged by royalty, and the statue at the end is Carl Milles' 'Solglitter'. On the staircase wall is a 17C Dutch **tapestry** of Adonis, and on the landing an Italian cupboard. There are pictures by Prince Eugen and a marble **head** of Amelie, Henriette's daughter, by Milles.

The **Green Drawing-Room** has **portraits** of Gustav III and Queen Sofia Magdalena by Per Krafft the Younger and the tapestry is from Beauvais. There is a tea-table from the Marieberg porcelain factory. In the upper tower room a screen of **silhouette portraits** of family, friends and guests includes Kaiser Wilhelm II. There are two landscapes by Carl Fredrik Hill, and the clock on the mantelpiece was a gift from Karl XIV Johan. The spiral staircase leads to a study and library. In a small side room there is a chair embroidered by Henriette Coyet and a portrait of her. The tile stove is from Rörstrand and the wrought-iron gate leads to an old privy. The long stick was used to measure visitors' height.

The **Red Drawing-Room** has 18C Aubusson **tapestries** showing Don Quixote. The Empire furniture is upholstered in red silk brocade, and the two inlaid **chests** are probably from the Georg Haupt workshop. Of the three family portraits the one of the girl, Henriette's daughter Amelie, is by Anders Zorn. The elaborate picnic-set was given by Napoleon to Princess Sofia Albertina. The beamed and panelled **Dining-Room** has rare Dutch gilded and painted pigskin **wall-coverings**, with biblical scenes (16C). There are royal portraits from the Ehrenstrahl workshop. The **library** downstairs, constructed on part of the courtyard, contains 6000 volumes. The principal treasure is a copy of Tycho Brahe's *Astronomiae Instauratae Mechanica*, printed in Germany in 1598 and hand-coloured. The enormous hand-written volume is a history of Torup by the Baroness, and there is a Gustav Vasa Bible of 1541. There is also a copy of a portrait of Leonora Christina, daughter of Christian IV of Denmark. A sculpted fireplace in Dutch Renaissance style is decorated with Ionic columns, lions' heads and coats of arms (1602), and near it is an escape-hole for emergencies.

The castle is set in extensive grounds and gardens, and across the road near the entrance is a pleasant outdoor café in the woods.

The old church at **Hyby**, 3km north-west, is a tiny white building beyond the 19C new church. This is the chancel of the 12C church which was used as a funerary chapel by the Trolle family until 1951. The 15C **wall-paintings** are well-preserved. The subjects include a Passion scene, the Last Judgment, apostles and St. Nicholas.

Road 108 goes south from Hyby to rejoin the E65 at Svedala (8km). It is 15km to the turn for **Svaneholm castle** (1km). Mourids Jepsen Sparre, a Danish nobleman (who is buried in Lund Cathedral), began the building of Svaneholm (Swan Island) in 1530 on an island in the Svaneholm lake. The south-west wing is the oldest part with a barrel-vaulted cellar and loopholes on the top floor. The other wings were added soon after. There is no defensive tower but projecting gables enabled the inhabitants to watch and repel intruders. In the 17C Axel Gyllenstierna (of the family of Hamlet's Guildenstern) rebuilt the south-east wing to look as if it had five storeys, but the top two are fake. Baron Rutger Macklean (or Maclean— Swedish with a Scottish ancestor) filled in the moat in the early 19C. The baron (1742–1816) was a well-known agricultural and social reformer and a member of the Academy of Science. Now the castle contains a restaurant, and a museum (open March–Sept, closed Mon). Textiles are displayed on the walls of the 17C staircase. On the ground floor there is a room devoted to Rutger Macklean, with his books and desk. Both this and the next room were decorated by a 17C Italian stucco-master, and there is a portrait medallion of the baron by Sergel. Collections include weapons and maps, with furniture, silver, pictures and china from the 18C and 19C, peasant costume, textiles and tools, with workshops and a school-room. The apartments of Countess Eva Ehrensvärd (d.1947) are preserved. In the gardens is a statue of Rutger Macklean by Axel Ebbe.

2

Malmo to Kristianstad

A. Direct

Total distance 94km. Malmö—E22 18km *Lund—22km turning for **Bosjökloster** (8km) and **Frostavallen** (10km further)—54km **Kristianstad**.

It is 18km from Malmö by the E22 to *Lund (pop. 63,000).

History. It used to be thought that Knut (Canute) the Great of Denmark and England founded Lund in 1020, but archaeological digs in the 1970s and 1980s produced evidence which could be dated to around 990. This was a wooden church, probably founded by Sven Forkbeard, with a graveyard, in the centre of the modern city. Lund was also important to Canute and he established a mint here. In 1060 it had a bishop, under the archdiocese of Hamburg-Bremen. In 1103 the Danish king persuaded the Pope to make Lund the seat of an independent archbishop over the entire area of Denmark, Sweden, Norway, Finland, Iceland and Greenland, making it the largest archdiocese in Europe.

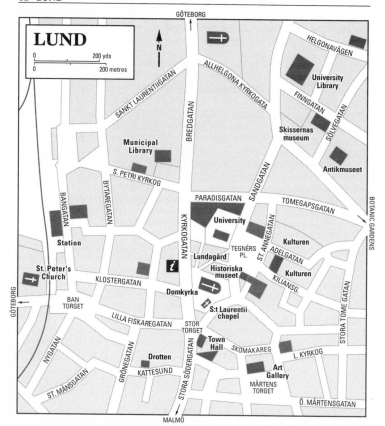

Lund became the cultural and commercial centre for much of Scandinavia, with the see itself owning land and playing a considerable part in politics. There were 27 churches as well as the cathedral. From the 13C to the 15C it was swept intermittently by war and fire, the worst incident being when it was fired by the Swedish army in 1452, after which it was never the same. In the 16C came the Reformation when it was reduced to a modest Danish bishopric, and in the next century it found itself under the Swedish flag. But this had its advantages. As part of a deliberate policy of 'Swedification' the university was founded by Karl XI in 1668 to make the ex-Danes into educated Swedish citizens. Soon the Danes tried to recapture Skåne, and the bloody battle of Lund in 1676 caused the death of thousands, and two years later the Danes fired the town. The unrest through the centuries has meant that there are not many old buildings remaining.

Today the university is the largest in Scandinavia with well over 20,000 students in 200 or so departments in Lund and Malmö. A newer institution is Ideon, a research park launched in 1983 to co-ordinate university research and industrial production. Large companies in Lund include Alfa-Laval, and Tetra Pak whose familiar cartons are exported in tens of billions every year all over the world.

Tourist bureau: Kyrkogatan 11 (opposite the cathedral), tel. (046) 35 50 40.

Post office: Knut den stores gata 1 (opposite the station).

Telephone, telegram: Klostergatan 6. Tel. (046) 14 87 00.

The motorway exit marked Lund C brings you in on **Stora Södergatan**. The main square with its modern town hall is a widening of the road just before the cathedral. To the left just before the square is Kattesund, a lane where an archaeological excavation is partly visible through large windows. These are the ruins of **Drotten's church** (Danish for 'Saviour' (open irregularly, leaflet in English available). This was where archaeologists found traces of a wooden church with graves which could be dated to the late 10C, as mentioned above.

Building history on this site is confused. In the 11C a church was built of stone to the south of the late 10C wooden church. Around the same time two wooden churches were built nearby but apparently soon razed—the outline of one of these can be seen marked in the pavement outside, by the department store. About 1150 a Premonstratensian monastery was founded and monastery buildings added, later becoming a parish church until the Reformation when it was destroyed. The excavations can be seen, together with an underground museum of finds and displays, with plans, tableaux and models.

Kyrkogatan leads north out of the main square and there is a golden swan on a shop-front to the left. This is the Swan Pharmacy, with much decorative woodwork inside featuring swans. There are flower-pictures on the front of the counter, and along the top of the wall-panelling the names and dates of past owners—there has been a pharmacy on this site since 1629. The **tourist bureau** is a little further on, opposite the cathedral. (There is a museum of telecommunications at Winstrupsgatan 6—left after the tourist bureau, then right.)

The *****cathedral** stands to one side of a small park (open daily). The astronomical clock plays at 12.00 and 15.00, Sun 13.00 and 15.00.

After Lund became an archdiocese, work began on the cathedral with the crypt and the western section, using local Skåne sandstone, and it was consecrated in 1145 by Archbishop Eskil. A fire destroyed the wooden roof in 1234 and it was then vaulted in stone, the weight of which became too much for the walls, and the fabric deteriorated.

In the 16C Adam van Düren restored it, adding buttresses and much decorative sculpture. Through the 18C, however, it crumbled progressively. A water-colour of 1836 and a lithograph of 1839 show a church almost unrecognisable today. Two plain squat towers are in the west, and the buttresses obscure the outlines. Even the apse, just recognisable, is crowned with zigzag crenellations. Inside, damage from the fire of 1234 was still visible.

The complete renovation of the 19C, first by C.G. Brunius and then by Helgo Zetterwall, carried a uniform Romanesque style throughout the church, with Northern Italian details.

The apse is the oldest and most authentic part. Finished in 1160, it sits on a heavy plinth, with three storeys of arcading, blind on the lowest, blind with alternating windows on the second and a delicate little open arcade at the top. The north door tympanum shows David, and that on the south has the Lamb of God with symbols of the Evangelists. Almost all of the western part with the towers was rebuilt in the 19C. The tympanum of the west doorway shows Christ, St. Laurence and St. Knut. The 19C bronze **doors** are by Carl Johan Dyfverman and show biblical history from Adam, the first three rows being Old Testament, the next four the Childhood of Christ and the last the symbols for earth, water, air and fire.

Just inside to the left is the **astronomical clock** with some parts going back to 1380; it was reconstructed in 1923. At the top are two knights who clash their swords to mark the hour. The top dial shows the paths of the sun and moon, and the signs of the zodiac as well as the time. Below this sits a

East end of Lund cathedral showing the apse (completed 1160) with its three storeys of arcading

Virgin and Child group. Twice a day the three kings and their servants march out one little side door and in the other to the strains of 'In dulci jubilo'. At the same time the heralds either side lift their trumpets. The lower dial is a calendar with details of days and dates from 1923 to 2023, and Chronos pointing at the present day. The figure at the centre is St. Laurence.

The canopied Renaissance **pulpit** (1592) is made of sandstone, limestone and black and white marble, with five alabaster reliefs of scenes from the life of Christ. It is by a German sculptor, Johannes Ganssog. The bronze **candle-holders** at the bottom of the chancel steps, with angels on columns with lions' feet are probably from the 13C. Between the choir-stalls is a bronze **column**, with St. Laurence and his gridiron, on a finely modelled base, of the 14C.

The 78 **choir-stalls** in the chancel date from the late 14C, roped off so that the visitor can see only the end ones in detail. The north row have Old Testament carvings, the south have allegories of the months, and prophets. The large end panel on the north has the Presentation in the Temple and the smaller has two prophets; on the south are the Annunciation, and the angel with Gideon.

The **altarpiece** was given by a wealthy local woman in 1398. It measures 7.5m by 2m, with Christ and the Virgin in the centre, and 40 saints under Gothic canopies. In the apse above is a **mosaic** of the Resurrection, with symbols of the Evangelists, by Joakim Skovgaard of Denmark (1927) mainly of Venetian glass. The stained-glass windows here and in the transepts are by the Norwegian artist Emanuel Vigeland (1930s).

In the north transept to the left there is a **door-canopy** with angels and lions in a somewhat Byzantine style, but with no apparent purpose. Opposite, the entrance to a chapel is framed by another, also Byzantine in feeling. An angel with three pairs of wings is in the centre, below him two people, with an animal each side. In the centre stands a 13C Gotland limestone font and against the end wall is the sarcophagus of Archbishop Andreas Sunnesson (1228). Nearby is a 14C **Virgin** carved in wood. In each transept sets of 18C carved doors back on to the choir-stalls. In the south transept is a **bench** for the clergy of the same period as the choir-stalls and a 5m-tall carved **tabernacle**. In the centre is a seven-branched bronze **candlestick**, 3.5m high, probably 15C, which has symbols of the four Evangelists, and in the end wall a **relief** of St. Laurence, the Virgin and St. Knut by Adam van Düren (c 1510).

Steps go down to the *crypt at both sides of the altar. The crypt is largely untouched since 1123 and some of its pillars are deeply incised with patterns, zigzags, barley-sugar twists, rope-designs and others. The most unusual feature is the pair of **columns** with figures clasping them. Interpretations abound, including Samson and Delilah, but the tale of the giant called Finn is much the most entertaining.

The English traveller Horace Marryat published a version of this in the mid 19C. There was once a giant called Finn—there is no suggestion that he is related to the Irish giant of the same name. He promised St. Laurence he would help to build the cathedral if, when he had finished, the saint could tell him what his, the giant's, name was. If not, the giant wanted to claim the sun and the moon as a forfeit. That was not possible, said the saint, so the giant asked for Laurence's eyes instead, and Laurence agreed. The giant built the church with the help of magic and was about to claim the saint's eyes, when Laurence overheard the giant's wife crooning to their child that his father Finn would bring him the monk's eyes to play with. When Laurence called the giant by name, Finn was so enraged that he, his wife and child rushed to tear down the church and were instantly turned to stone.

In front of the altar (1123) is the Renaissance **tomb** of Archbishop Birger Gunnarsson (1512) by Adam van Düren. He was the last Archbishop of Lund to die in office before the Reformation. On the extreme left is a **well-head** decorated by Adam van Düren, with heads of people, inscriptions, and what looks like a sea-creature attached to a locked chain devouring a sheep. Near this is the tomb of the last Danish bishop (1679) before the area became Swedish. There are many other tombs.

The small brick building south of the cathedral is variously called **S:t Laurentii chapel** and the old library. It is assumed to be the only remaining part of St. Laurence's monastery, and to have been used as a library, among other things. There is now a café in the vaulted crypt.

On the north-east side of the cathedral is **Historiska museet** which is linked by a walkway with **Domkyrkomuseet** (cathedral museum). The historical museum, a university department, was built as a bishop's residence in 1845. It will be closed for some time to come for complete renovation. (It will probably re-open to visitors at the same times: Tue–Fri, 11.00–13.00.) It will become more of a teaching resource for the interested university departments, with more space and the very latest multi-media aids. The following is a brief survey of some items previously on display. In the Stone Age section there is a skeleton from a dig at Skateholm (Skåne), dated to 5000 BC. In the Bronze Age section are figurines, neck-bands, swords and pottery, while the Iron Age division has gold clasps, pottery, jewellery, weapons and harness-fittings. The medieval section has a collection of *wood-carvings, and the large altar from St. Peter's friary in Ystad (c 1400). **Stone-carving** includes tympanums, fonts, columns and capitals. The reconstructed church with fittings from different periods will remain.

A new separate entrance will allow access to the **cathedral museum** even while the historical museum is being renovated. The items here have all come from the cathedral. The **textile section** has both pre- and post-Reformation vestments. Sculpture ranges from work by Adam van Düren to Baroque memorial tablets. 12C columns from the cathedral have been erected and behind them is the 1577 **altar**, in use until the 19C renovation. A separate section has models of the cathedral and a slide-show. The **Cabinet of Curiosities** (open by prior appointment, English-speaking guide) is based on a collection started in the 18C, and contains an eccentric and fascinating jumble of objects from the furthest corners of the earth.

The park by the cathedral is called **Lundagård** after the bishop's palace which used to stand here. Across from the cathedral the red brick building with the attached tower is the **King's house**, built for Fredrik II of Denmark in the 16C. It was given to the university at its foundation in 1668 by Karl XI, and used by it until 1882. Further on to the left is the white main **university building** (1882) which replaced the King's House. Behind this, on the crossroads beyond, are some attractive half-timbered buildings, c 1800, one in Bredgatan, and two or three in Sankt Petri Kyrkogatan, with old-fashioned shop-signs.

The path between the university building and the cathedral is known as the Philosophers' Walk. In front of the university is the traditional gathering-place for students. One of the big occasions is the proclaiming of spring, when on 30 April the students congregate wearing their white caps, the band plays, the choir sings, the church bells ring, a speech is made and the magnolias bloom. There is a similar concert the following day which is always televised live. In front of this is a mound ringed with **runestones** moved here from other sites, one of which bears the inscription 'God help their souls but they are buried in London'. The very large brick building labelled Akademiska Foreningen is the student union with a restaurant and a good bookshop, open to the public.

Across the road beyond is the entrance to *Kulturen, short for cultural-historical museum. In the front garden are several large, well-preserved **runestones**, with English translations of the inscriptions. The largest has a wolf, erected by two brothers to a third brother, and the one with a coiled inscription is also by a brother to a brother. One with no inscription has a witch riding on a wolf with snakes as reins and one has a cross. The broken one appears to have a picture of a warrior on it. Kulturen has both a conventional museum, the White House, and an open-air part (open May–Sept 11.00–17.00, otherwise 12.00–16.00). The buildings in the open-air section are always open when the museum is open, with one or two exceptions, and access is only through the main building. English leaflet with plan available. Some English labels and information cards.

In the **White House**, to the left on the ground floor are displays of weapons, armour and uniforms, with a panorama of the battle of Lützen in 1632 when Gustavus Adolphus was killed fighting in the Thirty Years War. Since the right-hand rooms lead eventually outside and there is a quicker exit from there, it makes sense to go upstairs at this point. On the first floor to the left are toys, games and dolls' houses of the 19C. To the right the first room is the only original one of the White House, built in 1854, with wall-panelling and a decorative wood ceiling. The next few rooms contain **Swedish folk art** and furniture. In the first room there are memorial pictures, ordered to commemorate important family events. Then come wooden and wrought-iron objects, painted chests, pottery and a good collection of Småland painted wall-hangings (*bonader*—see under Halmstad, Rte 7).

(This whole section may be occupied by temporary exhibitions hiding even the ceiling.) The top floor has pictures and temporary exhibitions. From the entrance hall the right hand door leads to displays on the archaeology and history of Lund with excavated finds and models. Displays continue through a linked building at the end of which there is the exit door for the open-air section before another linked building which has textiles and glass on three floors. In the basement are costumes and folk-dress, on the ground floor textiles and fans, and in the gallery are Swedish folk textiles, with a loom and spinning wheel. The glass collection is also on this floor. (English translation of Swedish information is on cards.)

As you go outside, to the right is first a smithy and beyond, a long low house. (The entrance is through the door to the right though it is not obvious. As advised in the Practical Information be sure to try all doors, stairs and corridors unless distinctly out of bounds.) In this building are displays of farming and fishing, and upstairs reconstructed farmhouses. An 18C **vicarage** is to the left of this.

A tunnel leads under Adelgatan. As you emerge and turn left there is an unfurnished medieval deacon's house. Behind it is a herb garden and an imposing 19C upper-class house whose basement has a **silver** collection (open 13.00–15.00) and the other two floors a large **ceramics** collection— Swedish, European and oriental. Beyond the herb garden the long house to the left has temporary exhibitions and there is a useful exit at this point. The two houses nearby were built as student residences, and there are some remains from a 12C church.

To the right at the rear of the upper-class house is a small garden and beyond, a huddle of buildings. First on the left, with wood-carving over door and window, is a 16C house from Ystad. This has displays on weights and measures and upstairs an old bank interior. At the back there is a way through to the next house with displays on various crafts and to the half-timbered house mentioned below.

The next house is a furnished **19C home** showing how a well-to-do academic lived (open 13.00–15.00), and the large **half-timbered house** contains an exhibition of **furnishing** and interiors, with panelling and painted furniture. Behind, the complex is mainly for administration.

Next comes a turf-roofed **farmhouse** (c 1700) with a low central section, furnished in the same period. By the pond is a modest 19C tenant farmer's house. Further on behind the larger farmhouse is a red-painted cottage containing a clog-maker's workshop. Behind this are offices housed in old buildings. The bell-tower was built in 1955. The house beside it is known as a loft-house as the main rooms are up the stairs. Passing a 19C summer-house, you come to the steep-roofed wooden **17C church** with 18C painting. The altar has a wood relief of the Last Supper and the pew doors are painted with flowers and the organ gallery with saints. There is also a votive ship. There is another loft-house just before the tunnel back to the White House, or you can use the quicker exit mentioned above.

On coming out of Kulturen have a look at picturesque **Adelgatan** under which Kulturen's tunnel goes, then go up Sankt Annegatan. At the corner with Tomegapsgatan, **Hökeriet**, Kulturen's shop selling old-fashioned sweets and other items, is open in the summer.

At the end of the road go left and then right up Sandgatan. To the left is a large area with university buildings, at the end on the right is a 19C student hostel, and ahead the large brick **Bishop's house** by Axel Nyström (1839). Bearing to the left round this you see the 1839 university library set on top of the hill (architects Nyström and Brunius). In the foyer is a very tall narrow runestone.

Finngatan is to the right. At No. 2 is *Skissernas Museet (Museum of Sketches, also called in tourist literature Konstmuseet or Arkiv för dekorativ konst; open Tues–Sat 12.00–16.00). This unusual collection displays preliminary sketches and models for finished art works. The first room is Swedish art, with much that is recognisable by the assiduous tourist who has done the sights of other cities. Engelbrekt's statue on the column in Stockholm City Hall gardens by Christian Eriksson is here, as is Ivar Johnsson's figure of a sailor's wife on a column at the Maritime Museum in Gothenburg, his Tycho Brahe on Ven Island and Carl Milles' Louis de Geer from Norrköping. In the passageway to the next room are stairs and a corridor. The stairs lead to photos and pictures showing the processes of applied art, including mosaic, enamel, frescoes, stained glass, stucco and icons. The corridor leads to an exhibit on the artwork for Stockholm underground stations. In the large international room are sketches by Chagall, Dubuffet, Matisse, Vuillard, Léger, Miró and many by Dufy. In the Scandinavian section the Danish exhibit includes Joakim Skovgaard's preliminary models for the apse mosaic in Lund cathedral. Upstairs from the Danish section are works by Mexican and African artists. The end room is the sculpture hall with a huge Henry Moore piece, and works by Oldenburg, Calder, Vasarely, a sketch by Le Corbusier and Picasso's sketch for his statue in Halmstad. There are also temporary exhibitions.

Continue along Finngatan and turn right into Sölvegatan. Near the end on the left is **Antikmuseet** (Museum of Classical Antiquities; open Mon–Fri 09.00–14.00, English notes to borrow or buy, ring the bell for admittance). The museum is basically a teaching display for the university, so most of the exhibits are copies. It contains items of Greek and Roman art with some Mesopotamian and Egyptian objects. The entrance-hall is dominated by a large kouros, and famous works include the discus-thrower, the calf-bearer from the Acropolis, Poseidon, and the Parthenon frieze from the British Museum. There is a selection of pottery, oil-lamps, figurines and other small items, and some papyri.

Continue to the end of Sölvegatan and turn right. At the end of the road is the entrance to the **Botanic Gardens** with thousands of labelled plants (open 06.00–20.00, tropical greenhouses 12.00–15.00). From here you can take Tomegatan, then go right and left and so work your way back to the cathedral through the narrow cobbled streets with a few attractive old houses.

Kiliansgatan runs from the rear of the cathedral, and at No. 10 is **Sveriges geologiska undersökning** (Swedish Geological Survey). There is a small exhibition of rocks found in Sweden with more detailed treatment of Skåne, and a large stone with a dinosaur's footprints. Continue until the road ends in Mårtenstorget. Here there is the **Konsthall** (art gallery) with changing exhibitions of contemporary art. In front of it is the little medieval brick **Krognos House**, also an art gallery.

Mårtensgatan leads out of the square to Stora Södergatan. Across the road is a medieval house called Stäket, now a restaurant. Turn left and two blocks down on the right is a gateway into the Cathedral School, whose predecessor was founded by St. Knut in the 11C. Also owned by it is the solid brick building next door where Karl XII lived from 1716 to 1718. The road to the right alongside this comes out opposite a park with a small planetarium, built as an observatory in the 1860s.

Grönegatan returns north and Stora Fiskaregatan to the left leads towards the station. Cross Bangatan (the station is to the right), turn left and then right, go under the overpass and take the steps to the right. Here is the red brick S:t Peters convent **church**, in Baltic Gothic style. The Benedictine convent was first mentioned in 1164 and the church was built in the 14C, while the convent has vanished. It is a simple buttressed building with a three-sided apse and no separate chancel or transepts. The tower on the north-west is later. The east and west gables are modestly ornamented with niches and circles, and a strip of brick decoration runs under the eaves. The only entrance is by the step-gabled south porch. Inside, the 15C German altarpiece has St. Catherine, St. Nicholas, the Virgin, a bishop and St. Barbara. The brass chandeliers and the pulpit with Evangelists are 17C. St. Peter in his niche on the north wall is modern. At the back under the organ gallery is a modern baptismal chapel.

South of the town-centre there is a medical museum in St. Lars' Hospital.

Leave Lund by the E22; another 22km brings the turn for road 23 to **Bosjökloster** (8km), situated on a peninsula which used to be an island in the Ringsjön (lake). Gardens open May–Oct 08.00–20.00, exhibitions and restaurant 10.00–18.00. Follow signs *slott* and *kyrka*.

A Benedictine convent was founded here in the 11C and became one of the most important and richest in Skåne. Many of the daughters of the upper classes were educated here. It was not destroyed at the Reformation—in Denmark there was not the same repression as in Sweden—and the nuns were allowed to continue living here but not to have new novices. The last archbishop of Lund was given the property when deprived of his archdiocese, on condition that he maintained the remaining nuns. In the late 19C Helgo Zetterwall restored and remodelled it, extending the theme of a typical Skåne church in chunky cubic shapes, white-washed and with red-tiled roofs and step-gables. The present ground plan is very similar to the original and some foundations and cellars remain. There was a west wing now replaced by the entrance and two gatehouses (17C). In the east wing the second storey was added in the 16C and the tower and gable in the 19C. Most of the lakeside façade of the south wing was redesigned by Zetterwall.

The **church** is built of the same sandstone as that used in Lund Cathedral, from a quarry near here. Most of the structure is 12C except for the 14C vaulting and the 19C tower, and the large windows, which were inserted in the 19C. The apse has unusual columns and a niche. Inside, the altarpiece (1515), probably Dutch or German, depicts the Descent from the Cross, with 16C Danish texts to either side. The backs of the doors have portraits of owners of the property. To the left on the chancel arch is a painting of St. Apollonia (14C), holding the pincers which took out her teeth—she is the patron saint of dentists. The large crucifix and the font are 14C. The 16C pulpit has been restored after many years' relegation to a storeroom. The oak pews are of the early 17C and are painted with coats of arms, dates, initials and other motifs. The tombstones are of owners of the 15C and 16C. The graveyard to the north of the church was for the nuns.

Most of the convent is now a private home, but one or two rooms are used for exhibitions in the summer—the beamed 17C Stone Hall and the vaulted medieval refectory. There is a small exhibition on convent life. Outside there are pleasant gardens, remains of a chapel, and a place for bathing and boating. An attractive walk in the park takes a figure of eight route, and at the crossing there is an oak reputed to be 1000 years old. Further on is a duck-pond.

At Frostavallen, 10km further on from Bosjökloster, via Höör, is **Skånes Djurpark**, a zoo specialising in Scandinavian animals which roam freely in large enclosures (open summer 09.00–17.00, winter 10.00–15.00). Elks, reindeer, red deer, lynxes, wolverines, bisons, bears, wolves and seals are among the animals to be seen, and there are sections for birds and reptiles. There is also a reconstruction of a Stone Age village and a 9C Viking grave. Children's zoo, amusements, playground, pool with waterslides, a barbecue site and refreshments are also provided.

You can rejoin the E22 8km from where you left it, by way of Höör and Hörby, then continue east towards Kristianstad. The landscape changes from flat and arable to wooded and rolling. The road crosses the boundary between Malmöhus and Kristianstad counties and goes over the Linderöd Ridge, to join road 19 in 32km.

Vä, after 4km and then 1km to the left, once had a town charter but had been devastated many times by Swedish troops, so that in 1614 Christian IV ordered the inhabitants to move to Kristianstad, his town which he had just founded. *Mariakyrkan (St. Mary's Church) was built in the 12C under royal patronage. Soon after, the Premonstratensian order established a monastery of which no trace remains. The wall and roof *paintings date from the end of the 12C, and are exceptional in that they form a complete set, linked by the text of the psalm Te Deum Laudamus. In the apse is Christ in Glory seated on a rainbow over the earth with a church, and surrounded by symbols of the Evangelists. Twenty-four roundels depict angels, apostles and saints in rich robes, while from one to the other goes a ribbon with the text. King Valdemar and Queen Sofia of Denmark, the donors of the church, are also depicted in the chancel.

After 2km you can take a right turn to Norra Åsum (3km) where the **church** has the broad defensive tower typical and necessary in the area, and a runestone in the porch which establishes the time of its foundation (late 12C) by referring to Archbishop Absalon who 'built the church'. There is a Romanesque font and a 17C carved pulpit.

The E22 joins the 21 in 4km and it is 4km to central Kristianstad.

Kristianstad (pop. 31,000) received its charter in 1614 when Christian IV of Denmark moved the inhabitants of Vä to this site and fortified it to be a secure base against the Swedes to the north. Unfortunately for Christian and Denmark the Treaty of Roskilde of 1658 meant that Kristianstad finally became Swedish. The grid plan of the centre is typical of the time. In 1852 the walls were razed and avenues laid out along their line, now called Östra and Västra Boulevarden, and Norra and Södra Kaserngatan.

Follow the signs to the centre. The road passes Tivoli Park laid out along the Helge river. The **tourist bureau** is set back from the main square (Stora torg) which has a large spiky fountain called 'Icarus', by Palle Pernevi. On the east side is the town hall of 1891, built in a Danish Renaissance style. It has a statue of Christian IV on the façade, a smaller copy of one by the Danish artist Thorwaldsen. The inscription 'Pax Vobis' is the king's message to the town 'Peace be with you'. To the south is the 19C Freemasons' hall and to the west a small square in front of the museum. To the north is the white Karl Johan (Empire) style courthouse (19C), also used by the army, hence the legend 'Legibus et armis'—to laws and weapons. To the right of this, across the road is the Mayor's house whose first two floors were built in the 17C.

The sandstone and brick **Trefaldighetskyrkan** (Holy Trinity church) is visible to the north-east, considered to be one of Christian IV's finest churches. In the flowerbed Christian's monogram may be picked out in pansies, depending on the time of year. Judging by the size and distinction of the church, Christian evidently had great plans for it, possibly as the seat of a bishop. It was financed by making all the churches of the dioceses of Roskilde (Denmark) and Lund donate a quarter of their income. The building was consecrated in 1658 on the feast of the Trinity to whom it is dedicated. It is 64.5m long by 44m wide. The stone plinth has many tombstones against it, which were previously in the floor of the church. Above this the brick façade is divided by tall round-headed windows under pediments, with sandstone volutes at the base. The seven elegant **gables** have volutes and other motifs in sandstone, and the three main ones are each finished with three statues. The north and south **doorways** are particularly fine, with reclining Evangelists, Matthew and John on the north and Mark and Luke on the south—this one is a copy of the original which is in the museum (see below). The tower to the west is crowned by a black tiered lantern added in 1865.

Inside, 12 slim granite pillars over 7m high support the Gothic rib vault. Many tombstones stand around the entrance, mainly from the 18C. The 17C oak **pew-ends** have cut-card foliage decoration. The all-different gable tops of the pews have human and animal heads, flowers and fruit. The chandeliers, including a very large one, are also 17C. The **pulpit** of the same date is of black marble with white marble statues and alabaster angels' heads. The high side galleries over the shallow transepts have carved oak panels. The font in the chancel is of sandstone and to either side of the chancel are picture frames intended for portraits of Christian and his queen, but now filled with biblical texts. A text also forms the centre of the **altarpiece** (17C)—the words of consecration from the Last Supper. Like the pulpit the altar is carved from black and white marble, and alabaster, and it has Ionic columns and statues of Christ and the four Evangelists. In each aisle hangs an opulent memorial tablet from the 17C. At the rear the ornate **organ façade** and gallery (1630) has the Danish coat of arms, King David playing his harp, the Muses and angels. Church silver is displayed in the baptismal chapel to the left.

On coming out of the church take Västra Storgatan to the north. No. 11 is a yellow two-storey inn of 1630; No. 7 is an ordinary home of 1641, and No. 6 opposite is the vicarage from 1770. Ahead is the **Norreport**, the North Gate, designed by Hårleman in 1766 (not the original site). To its right stands the 18C **barracks**. Go through the gate and across the car park to the 53m-high water-tower where you can enjoy the view from the café on top which is open from May to September. Return by Östra Storgatan parallel to Västra Storgatan to the east. No. 8 is an 18C house and Kippers restaurant next door has parts dating from 17C, both of which properties extend back to J H Dahlsgatan and can also be seen from there. Soon you are back on the main square in front of the museum. On the little square in front stand Folke Truedsson's tree-log statue 'Symphony', and Nils Möllerberg's 'Pomona'.

The **museum** (open Tue–Sun 12.00–16.00, Wed to 20.00) is in the stables, later armoury, of Christian IV's intended castle. On the ground floor to the right is a room for temporary exhibitions and to the left through the south door of the church you enter a military display, with uniforms and equipment, since this was a garrison town. Upstairs to the left are archaeology and local Skåne costumes. To the right is the **history of Kristianstad** (notes available in English for a nominal charge). There is a model of the town in 1620 as it replaced Vä as a defensive centre. The model of the white castle is of nearby Lillöhus, now a ruin. The brightly coloured painting of the town square has doors to open to show aspects of everyday life. An example of a 17C room is shown and, opposite, a wall of illuminated slides of Christian's other buildings. As can be seen, he was an enthusiastic builder, especially in Denmark, and especially in brick and sandstone. The pottery is mostly from Lillöhus. The model of a bastion has a window through which can be seen a model of Kristianstad as it was stormed by the Danes in 1676. (It had become Swedish in 1658.) Then comes an 18C shop, and 19C objects housed in typical attic storage compartments as found in Swedish blocks of flats. There is a selection of 19C shops and workshops. The third floor has temporary exhibitions.

If you leave by the rear of the museum you pass through the relocated **Södra Stadsporten**, the South Gate, designed by Jean Eric Rehn in 1780. Turn right and right again, then left down Östra Storgatan. At No. 53 the film museum (up four flights of stairs, open 13.00–16.00, closed Sat and Mon) is situated in Sweden's first film studio, active 1909–11. It has a reconstruction of an original set, some historic cameras and projectors, costumes and photos, with a small cinema for showing old films. The road comes out into Lilla Torg with its coloured fan-patterned cobbles. In Östra Vallgatan to the left there are two houses of 1637 (Nos 22–24). In Västra Storgatan to the right, No. 40 is the rusticated doorway of the house (1760) of General Cardell, a local commander, and opposite, the house where King Stanislaus of Poland lived in exile 1711–14.

Leaving Lilla torg by Östra Storgatan to the south and immediately turning left you find the large half-timbered **Garvaregården** of the 17C. Continue south one more block and turn right, left and right into Residensgatan. Near here was the site of the South Gate and appropriately the local school is called Söderportskolan. On the right at the end is the ochre Governor's **Residence** with rusticated ground floor (1860) by Scholander who worked on the royal palace in Stockholm. Ahead is the attractive **Tivoli Park** along the river, with a bird pond and rose garden. The green and white Art Nouveau building is the theatre and not far along is the Fornstuga, a dark wood Nordic style building which was the town's first museum (1886) with an open-air café in summer.

The wide road leading back north along Tivoli Park is Västra Boulevarden with some stately buildings including the old town hall (1872) with its façade on Tivoligatan, and on the corner with Nya Boulevarden the old savings bank (c 1900). Nya Boulevarden leads back to Stora Torg.

Just over 1km south of Stora Torg the **Järnvägsmuseum** (Railway Museum) is in a former station, at Hammarlundsvägen 2, reached by following Västra Storgatan to the south (open May–Sept pm, except Mon).

34km to the north-west of Kristianstad by road 21 is the 12C church of **Finja** with Romanesque wall-paintings by the so-called 'Master of Finja'.

B.   Coastal Route

Total distance 205km. Malmö—E6/E22, 31km Trelleborg—road 9, 46km **Ystad**—
10km junction with coast road via Ales Stenar—47km **Simrishamn**—road 9, 28km
Brösarp—road 19, 39km junction with road 21—4km Kristianstad.

Road E6/E22 to the south of Malmö leads through broad, fairly flat fields with few trees. At (17km) Vellinge, road 100 goes off to Skanör and Falsterbo (see Rte 1). After 7km the typical Skåne church of **Skegrie** is on the left of the road, Romanesque with a Gothic tower. On the other side of the road is a New Stone Age **tomb**, c 2700 BC, consisting of a central dolmen surrounded by standing stones.

After 2km at **Maglarp** the church, one of the oldest stone churches hereabouts, was begun in the late 12C, with a 17C broad tower, and gables more Dutch than Skåne. If it is open you can see the 14C and 15C vault-paintings, the 1568 pulpit, the 1759 reredos and, especially, the Romanesque font. There is also a 15C crucifix.

In 5km you reach **Trelleborg** (pop. 23,000). In the 1250s Trelleborg was given as a dowry to the Danish Princess Sophia when she married Valdemar of Sweden. It drew its riches from the sea in the form of herring, and nowadays much of its prosperity comes from the sea too, in the form of lively ferry traffic to North Germany. Do not be deceived about the climate here—the palm trees are taken in in the winter.

The **tourist bureau** is at Hamngatan 4 in a large 19C warehouse almost opposite the railway station as you come in on the coast road. Outside is a hefty statue by Bror Marklund. Walk along Hamngatan to the east and take the fourth turn on your right. Here is the attractive Gamla torg with the Mikaeli-Brunn, a fountain by Jonas Fröding with lively scenes. Go through the square and turn right to the newly reconstructed **Viking fort**. Take the next right past the 19C church to Stortorget, with an old water-tower. In the square is Axel Ebbe's spirited **fountain** 'Sea-serpent'. This artist came from southern Skåne, and more of his works are in a small red-brick **gallery** (open summer Tue–Sun pm, rest of year Sun pm) on the far side (west) of the pleasant park next to Stortorget.

From the Ebbe gallery turn south, cross Nygatan and take the next to the left. The **museum** is 800m away, at Östergatan 58 (open June–Aug, Tues–Sun 10.00–17.00, Sept–May, Tues–Sun 13.00–16.00). In front is a sculpture by Axel Wallenberg of a boy and two horses. The museum's archaeology section shows finds from Skateholm, a Stone Age (5000 BC) burial site, and the associated fishing settlement has been reconstructed. There is also some ethnography, a Viking section, local artists' displays, shop and café.

The coast road east out of Trelleborg leads along inviting beaches. The sea temperature here is usually slightly lower than on the west coast so the beaches are not over-populated by swimmers and sunbathers.

In 14km, Sweden's **most southerly point** (*Sveriges sydligaste udde* on the signpost) is at Smygehuk (shortly before the village of Smygehamn). Turn right down to the little harbour. On the way notice to the left the large figure of a goose, a reference to Selma Lagerlöf's much-loved children's geography of Sweden where little Nils Holgersson travels on the back of a goose all over the country, starting near here. At the harbour is a signpost with (sometimes surprising) distances to Moscow, London and so on. (*Treriksröset* is the point where Sweden meets Norway and Finland.) There is a café (open in summer) and a shop selling smoked fish. Many of these small harbours have their own smoke-houses which can be tracked down by the smell on the air. They have a wide selection of variously flavoured smoked fish and usually take-away snacks of bread and smoked fish. Across the grass beyond the café is a large round stone structure which was a lime-kiln.

Ystad is 32km further.

Ystad (pop. 16,000) grew up from the 13C around the Franciscan priory and rapidly became rich through its association with the Hanseatic League. It was attacked many times in the period of Danish rule. During the Napoleonic wars, English privateers who defied the blockade sold goods here. When the railways were constructed at the end of the 19C continental traffic went to Trelleborg, and Ystad declined in importance. Now ferries go to the Danish island of Bornholm and to Poland. It has a picturesque centre with many half-timbered houses and pastel-painted 18C and 19C cottages.

Continue along the coast road until you come to S:t Knuts torg on the left, opposite the station. The **tourist bureau** is in the square (open daily, except Sun am, mid-June–mid-Aug, otherwise Mon–Fri). Take Lingsgatan to the north out of the square. In Dammgatan, the first on the left, is **Charlotte Berlin's museum**, a furnished 19C house which can be visited.

Continue by way of Stickgatan to Stora Östergatan. To the right it leads past one or two historic houses, notably Pilgränds house on the corner of Pilgränd, and the charming courtyard of **Per Hälsas Gård** in Besökaregränd two blocks further. To the left on Stora Östergatan is the quaint little step-gabled **Birgitta house**, where Karl XII once stayed. On the square is the 1840 town hall, and behind it S:ta Maria church. The small brick house on the left is the **Latin School**, built in 1500. A quick detour to the left down Teatergatan and then right into Långgatan brings you past the picturesque 18C **malt factory**, and if you continue, then go right and right again you come back to Stora Västergatan with a photogenic **view** of the church tower and a half-timbered house on the left, partly from the 16C (complete with satellite dish and two TV aerials). Back at the church, there is a peaceful square of half-timbered houses opposite the west front.

The brick S:ta Maria **church**, originally from the beginning of the 12C has been restored many times. The chancel with the ambulatory is Late Gothic (15C), and the spire is from 1688. Following ancient tradition, a watchman still blows a horn from here at night to assure the citizenry that all is well. The baptismal chapel on the left of the church has a richly carved **altar** of 15C north German workmanship. Christ and the Virgin are in the centre with the apostles in groups of three; and below Augustine, Ambrose, Jerome and Gregory, the Fathers of the Church. The four paintings below are scenes from the life of Christ and the whole is surrounded by Gothic carving. The font is from Lübeck (1617) and the iron candelabra is a very early one of the 14C. The swords are Swedish and Danish, of the 17C and 18C. The 18C Baroque altar shows the Last Supper with the artist as the 14th person at the table. The 16C statues in the chancel are of the Virgin and John the Baptist. The latter was once used as a poor-box—he has a slot in his back. The crucifix is of the 16C. The front pews are constructed so the worshippers can turn to face the preacher during the sermon. The black and white limestone **pulpit** (1626) has Christian IV of Denmark's monogram. Memorial tablets include that of the mayor Johan Friis (d. 1630), who had 17 children. The organ gallery was painted in the 1720s with biblical scenes. The shield with Karl XII's monogram commemorates his stay in the town.

On leaving the church turn right and continue up Stora Norrgatan. At the crossroads are two fine houses. On the left is the **House of Angels** (1630) with carved faces, and on the diagonally opposite corner the **Brahe house**, built by Axel Pedersen Brahe who died in 1487 and is buried in the nearby **friary church**, which is reached by turning right down Sladdergatan. The ruins to the left of the church are from the friary. The church was begun in 1267 as part of the Franciscan friary of St. Peter. The nave is the oldest part, the chancel and south transept being added in the 14C. It contains a 14C font and many historic tombstones.

Reached by going round the church by way of a peaceful open space with a duck-pond is a wing of the Franciscan **friary**. It was built in the 13C and consisted of a square enclosing a courtyard. After the Reformation it was used variously as a hospital, brewery and granary, then became derelict. After restoration of the east wing, it is now a local museum, with displays on local living conditions through the centuries, costume and textiles, a model of the friary and some medieval work.

You can return to the main square through the narrow Bäckahästgränd with the 18C Garvare House, and then a right and a left turn round the 17C Apoteksgården.

Road 9 continues along the coast from Ystad in an attractive strip of woodland dotted with holiday cottages. 10km from Ystad road 9 turns north-east. The area to the south-east of the direct route to Simrishamn contains much of interest however so the following longer version is recommended. Take the coast road to the right and after 8km a right turn following signs for Kåseberga and the ship-setting site of Ales Stenar. From the car park it is a good ten-minute walk to the site, or for a shorter stiffer climb you can drive on down to the little harbour of Kåseberga and start from there. Nearby are smoke-houses (rökeri) with smoked fish and fish snacks for sale.

Steps and a sandy path wind up the steep hill until the grassy plateau on a cliff above the sea opens up. On this spectacular site lies Sweden's largest ship-setting, called ***Ales Stenar**, 'Stones of Ale' (a personal name). It is 67m long and consists of 58 stones (previously 60), not from the locality. The end ones are 3.3m and 2.5m high orientated north-west to south-east. No excavations have been carried out so there is no definite date, but it is thought to be from between 800 and 1050, late Viking/Iron Age. Theories have suggested its astrological use, or as a cult-site, or simply for burial. The more agile can scramble down the cliff and walk back along the stony beach.

On regaining the coast road, take the right turn. After 5km follow signs to **Backåkra**.

Dag Hammarskjöld (1905–61) became the second Secretary-General of the United Nations in 1953. Born in Jönköping, he worked first in the Swedish government service. As Secretary-General he aroused some controversy, but was a skilful diplomat. He was killed in an air-crash over Africa. In 1957 the area around Backåkra was threatened by developers, so he bought and restored the dilapidated farm. Sadly, he did not live to furnish and enjoy it, but he provided in his will for furniture, works of art and books to be moved here. He also wanted to build a chapel but lack of money forced an alternative—a 'meditation circle' on the heath nearby.

Dag Hammarskjöld's collections include works from Egypt, Greece, India and South-East Asia, and old maps and weapons were other interests. There are works of art by Picasso, Matisse, Braque and Barbara Hepworth. Furniture and paintings from Sweden and abroad, and many gifts from governments and individuals complete the collection.

Emerging again on to the coast road and turning left (the way you came), after 2km take a right turn to (4km) Löderup, where the originally 12C church has a sandstone ***font** (c 1160) by a sculptor known as the master of Tryde (a village 20km north-east of Ystad), or Magister Majestatis, who worked in Skåne and Gotland. It has two series of pictures, the Passion, with the main scene Christ in Glory, the motif from which this sculptor was given his Latin nickname, and the story of St. Olof. Round the base are four heads, animal and human. There is also a Renaissance pulpit by Jakob Kremberg and a Baroque baptismal altar.

Continuing north and then west towards Simrishamn by way of Borrby, the road reaches (10km) **Östra Hoby**. The church was begun in the 12C with the present apse. The broad west tower is a feature of churches in south-east and east Skåne where enemies and pirates could land from the sea. The earliest painting (13C) is in the apse, of God the Father, Christ and apostles below. Those on the chancel arch wall are somewhat later, and c 1500 the paintings in the west part of the nave and the apse vault were completed. The **font** is from the Tryde workshop, with a Christ in Majesty in a mandorla. The pulpit has the date 1654 but also the arms of Queen Anna who died in 1612. The altarpiece is from 1651.

From the crossroads at Östra Hoby it is 4km north to **Glimmingehus castle** which is well signposted (open April, May, Sept 09.00–17.00, June–Aug 10.00–18.00; café). It is thought the castle dates from the 13C or 14C. An uncompromising rectangular block surrounded by a moat, it concentrated more on defence than beauty, and although it is unfurnished it reveals something of the way of life of its inhabitants.

It belonged to the Ulfstand family and at the end of the 15C was owned by Jens Holgersen Ulfstand, a powerful Danish nobleman, governor of Gotland and Admiral of the Realm. He employed the architect and sculptor Adam van Düren who went on to work on Lund cathedral.

The quartzite walls are about 2m thick and the height is 26m. One of the Gothic step-gable-ends has a lion sculpture, the other had a 'wild man' which is now inside the castle. The brackets on the south show the position of privies. The holes above and below the top floor windows were for attaching an external archers' gallery of wood, but with the advent of heavy cannon the top floor itself had to be the firing position.

Over the main door is a panelled limestone **relief** showing Ulfstand flanked by his two wives, one a Trolle, the other a Brahe, two of the best-known families in Danish/Swedish history. Missiles could be dropped from the oriel projection above, which also served as a base for a hoist bringing goods through the door-opening below it.

In 1930 a semi-basement room was found under the entrance steps, but with no discernible purpose. Stairs lead down to the ground floor, where on the east was the kitchen, brewery and bakery. An ingenious central heating system led warmth from the kitchen to the upper storeys, and the well meant that an attacker could not cut off the water supply. On the west side was the beer and wine cellar.

On the stairs up to the first floor note the holes in the wall for shooting an enemy who got this far. The east part here was a guard room. Heavy cross-vaults rest on a central pillar with an octagonal ledge. There is a duct for the warm air from the kitchen under the vault. In an ante-room is the 'wild man' sculpture which used to be on the roof. At the other end was a living-room. The window embrasures have holes to support arquebuses, as do all the windows. There are seats in the embrasures, and a large fireplace. A storeroom is off the living-room.

On the second floor the large **Knight's Hall**, occupying two-thirds of the entire floor, was originally several smaller rooms. A carved fireplace shows the Ulfstand arms with a salamander and a herring (symbolising fire and water?). The coat of arms on the wall is that of Ulfstand's mother. Next is the most decorative room in the castle, for private devotion or possibly as a guest room. Over an opening which was formerly a cupboard is a relief of the Crucifixion by Adam van Düren (1505). The initials IH are probably those of Jens Holgersen Ulfstand, the kneeling man with the dog. The Madonna and Child is also by Adam van Düren. In a window embrasure is a carving of a knight with the Ulfstand and Brahe coats of arms and an inscription. The three-cusped arched doorway is likely to be of later date, possibly from Gotland.

The top floor is purely defensive, with cannon-ports all round, though Glimmingehus never actually had to defend itself. Even when the Swedish king directed it to be razed in 1676, the walls resisted and the attempt was broken off by the timely appearance of the Danish fleet in the distance.

The other buildings in the courtyard are much later. The wing to the east has the date 1640 and the initials HRK and LGS, Holger Rosenkrantz and Lene Gydenstierne—Rosenkrantz and Guildenstern were real Danish families whose names Shakespeare used in *Hamlet*. The same names crop up frequently all over Skåne in various spellings, and quite often in the rest of Sweden. The Rosenkrantz' owned Glimmingehus for many years. There is a museum showing among other things the finds from an excavation of the moat in the 1930s.

Continuing north from Glimmingehus brings you back to road 9 (Ystad to Simrishamn). (An **excursion** to the area to the north of the road brings you to three villages of interest. The moated **Tosterup** castle (15C, 16C and 17C) was the childhood home of Tycho Brahe. The local church has 15C paintings by the Vittskövle Master. North-west of Tosterup, **Övraby** church has a Romanesque apse-painting. At **Bollerup**, to the west of Tosterup, the castle is the result of several rebuildings. It has been restored more to its original style of Gothic with Renaissance windows. It has a vaulted cellar and ground floor, and the main hall has wall-paintings (c 16C). When the daughter of the house married a Brahe in 1502, the guests disposed of 20,000 litres of beer, mead and wine, ten oxen, 40 lambs and four cows.) From Bollerup it is 20km to Simrishamn and from Glimmingehus 10km.

Simrishamn (pop. 6000) has been a fishing town since the Middle Ages, the main centre of the area of east Skåne known as Österlen. Some of the streets are still narrow and winding, with low pastel-painted, red-roofed cottages.

S:t Nicolai church stands by the main square, of chunky sandstone blocks, with step-gables, and a brick porch. The present chancel was a fishermen's chapel in the 12C and the nave was added in the 13C, the vault in the 15C and later the porch and tower. The brightly-painted pulpit is from c 1626, though the figure of Moses underneath is later, carved by the same artist who made the altar-relief and the elaborate memorial to Peder Mörck opposite the entrance, as well as the crown and cover of the font. The pews and votive ships are from the 19C. Outside are two Carl Milles sculptures, 'The Sisters', and 'Angel with Trumpet'.

The building fronting on to the square next to the church is the town hall.

Storgatan runs east and west of the main square. A short distance up to the east is **Österlens museum**, in a 19C grain store (and the smell is still here). This contains some local archaeological finds, painted furniture, costumes and textiles, with farming and fishing (open pm, irregular hours).

Back in the main square, the next turning off to the right leads to an old courtyard with an enormous magnolia tree. Here and in the square are some original shop signs in metal, and some rosette-carvings on the doors, a local motif.

An attractive area of cottages lies on the other side of the church. Stora Rådmansgatan runs parallel to Storgatan, and half-way along is Lilla Torg, off which again runs Stora Norregatan, perhaps the prettiest street. The sea-front and fishing harbour are also a pleasant area for walking.

Leave Simrishamn by road 9 to the north. After 12km there is a turn for the village of **S:t Olof** (6km). According to local tradition St. Olof came to Skåne in 1026 on a military campaign, and some say he died here. Pilgrims flocked to honour the saint in the first 13C **church**, consisting of the present sacristy and chancel, so that the present nave had to be added in the early 15C. Once there were nine altars in the church, and even after the Reformation devotion to the saint continued—a scandalised bishop who visited in 1627 tore up the linen clothes which had been put on the statue.

The main **altar** is carved in wood, brightly painted with a blue background, and of 15C Lübeck workmanship. The central theme is the Crucifixion with a crowd of onlookers—notice the man on the left pulling a rude grimace. On the folding doors to each side are 16 saints with their attributes. When the doors are closed over the Crucifixion scene during Lent, one can see 16 Passion scenes in relief, no longer coloured. It is supposed there must have been a St. Olof altar since this was such an important place of pilgrimage, and the most likely place is where the Trinity altar now stands, against a pillar in the centre of the nave. However, in the chancel there is still a late medieval **St. Olof statue** with his traditional silver axe which was taken down by those seeking cures, who would stroke the affected part with it. This was done nine times, and the axe had to be put back for recharging after every third stroke. The custom was recorded even in the 1770s. The figure crushed under Olof's feet is traditional also, and may represent the old Viking religion or his heathen brother Harald. In the north-east corner of the nave the **Lady Altar** has the Virgin and Child surrounded by eight female saints, including St. Birgitta. The large central **Trinity altar** is again wooden and brightly painted, with the Father holding the Cross of the Son and a dove representing the Holy Ghost (15C North

The church of the village of S:t Olof (13C-15C) in typical Skåne style

German). On the pillar behind pilgrims scratched a prayer in runic script. Beside the south entrance with its original 15C door is the St. **Anne altar**, with Anne, the Virgin and Child. The **font** is the oldest object in the church, possibly 12C. The pulpit is from the 1620s and the pews from 1637 (restored). The walls and vaults retain some faded paintings of foliage and figures.

Back on road 9, after 3km there is a turn to **Stenshuvud**, a nature reserve and leisure area with car park, walks and views. After 3km **Kivik** is the centre for the extensive apple orchards in the region, with processing and storage plants and production of cider. It has a large fair and market in July.

The ***Kungagraven** (King's Grave, or 'Bredarör') is a cairn with a tomb from the Bronze Age c 1500 BC, south-east of the centre of Kivik (sign-posted; open summer). Originally the cairn was 75m in diameter and covered the grave completely. The entrance was made in the 1930s. The unusual feature is that it is the inside surfaces of the slabs of the tomb which are carved with pictures. On the first two stones to the left there is a sort of procession, with a two-wheeled cart drawn by two horses and two loose horses, and people, some making music, perhaps a funeral procession. On other stones there are figures and ornaments which are more like the motifs on rock carvings and bronze objects, including sun-wheels. The slab to the right of the entrance disappeared and had to be replaced using an 18C drawing as a model. This has a ship, as has the next slab which is the largest. The third one on this side has four horses.

After 3km a road goes to **Vitaby** (2km). The church is on a hill with a view over Hanö Bay. A massive flying buttress supports its 13C broad tower. The first 12C church had an apse, a lower chancel than now, and a short nave, and was enlarged over the centuries. The early 13C **crucifix** is in the early medieval 'triumphant' style. The crown is of gilded copper with three large mountain crystals. It is too big for the head, so was probably made for another figure. The font is also early medieval. In the chancel there is a 14C wall-painting remaining, with Passion scenes, other paintings having had to give way to the vaulting of 15C. The pulpit is 17C, and the 18C Rococo pews are painted with flowers. Pictures of the apostles are on the 19C gallery.

At (3km) **Ravlunda** the 13C church, remodelled in the 15C, has remnants of wall-paintings. In Romanesque times a large St. Christopher painting was on the north wall opposite the entrance but Gothic rebuilding destroyed most of it. On the 17C pulpit there is the monogram of Christian IV of Denmark. Some of the pews have delicate Rococo flower-paintings and there are opulent memorial tablets.

From Ravlunda you can take a road marked *Skepparpsgården* and *Haväng* (unsurfaced). After 3km near Skepparpsgården there is an Iron Age cemetery with standing stones and stone settings. The road ends in a car park and the Haväng **Stone Age tomb** is through the gate and to the left, on a cairn on the edge of a sandy beach. This is a cist of large stones surrounded by a frame 11m by 5.5m of other stones. Stone Age objects have been found under the grave.

At (4km) Brösarp, road 9 joins the 19, from where it is 14km to **Degeberga**. On the outskirts, a sign *Forsaker* leads to a car park (1km) from where there are woodland walks and two waterfalls, signposted *övre fallet* and *nedre fallet*. It is easier to go to the *övre fallet* first—about half-an-hour's walk.

From Degeberga it is 4km to **Vittskövle**. The grand **castle**, sadly not open to the public, stands within its moat beside the road. It is the largest in Skåne and was built in the 16C by the Brahe family. Two massive defensive towers and shot-holes angled down provided for security, and it has remained almost unaltered.

The **church** a little further on has important wall-paintings—indeed the artist is known as the Master of Vittskövle and worked in many local churches. The church was begun c 1200, and added to in the 15C by one of the Brahe family from the nearby castle. In the same century the roof was vaulted and painted—the outline of a Romanesque window can still be seen. In the chancel vault only the painting of St. Nicholas remains and it is likely that the rest of the vault was devoted to his life and works. The next two sections tell the story of the Creation, and to the west is the Fall and Expulsion from Paradise. The two bays of St. Anne's chapel on the north have female saints and Evangelists, and most of the rest of the surface is covered with foliage and writhing tendrils. On the south there is the Barnekov **funerary chapel** added in the 17C for the family who owned Vittskövle castle at the time, though two of the Brahes have coffins here. The font is medieval and the pulpit 17C, and there is an unusual wood-carving of Christ rising from the dead (18C). By the main door there is a 17C offertory box.

It is 13km to the junction with the E22 for Kristianstad (12km—see Rte 2A). About 16km east of the junction on the coast is **Åhus**, famous for its eels, with a delightful main square. The town hall with a small museum is on the north side and behind it is the Mariakyrka, in its present form from the 13C and 14C. Also in the town are the remains of a chapel of St. Anne and a house where Karl XI is said to have stayed (Kungsstugan).

3

Kristianstad to Kalmar

Total distance 178km. Kristianstad—road E22, 26km **Sölvesborg**—27km **Karls-hamn**—26km **Ronneby**—19km **Karlskrona**—89km *Kalmar.

Take the E22 out of Kristianstad towards Sölvesborg and Karlskrona. After 10km you can turn north for **Bäckaskog** (6km). Just after the turn a gigantic boulder, moved here by glacial action, stands by some farm buildings. This is the 'Troll's Stone', connected in legend to the castle of Trolle-Ljungby (see below). Follow the signs to Bäckaskog. There is a coin-operated turnstile so the grounds and exterior are accessible all year, but as most of the complex is now an hotel, facilities for visiting the interior can vary from year to year.

Bäckaskog was built as a monastery for Premonstratensian monks from France. The building was begun around 1250, in a position between the lakes Ivösjön and Oppmanasjön favoured with a mild climate, rich fishing and navigable waterways. The monastery was dissolved at the Reformation in 1537 and rebuilt as a fortified castle. In the 16C the south tower was added for defence. The Ulfstand and Ramel families owned it for 150 years, and in 1680 it came into state hands and was occupied by army officers. The last of these was Johan Christoffer Toll who carefully restored the castle and grounds. From 1845 to 1872 Karl XV used it as a summer home and played at being a farmer, and his daughter Queen Louise of Denmark used it until 1900.

From the entrance there is a good view across Ivösjön. The white building is the chapel, originally built in 1280 (tower 1640), and rebuilt after a fire in the 18C when the archway was made. The chapel crypt contains the grave of Henrik Ramel who died in 1653. In the courtyard can be seen the ships' cannons, here since 1863 when they were used to greet a visiting Danish king. A restaurant occupies the 16C cowshed and the barn and stables are also of this period. The channel is for the local stream which as in so many other monasteries around Europe was incorporated into the precinct, but here with the added refinement that the monks could fish through a window without even leaving the kitchen. The kitchen in the south-west corner was the first chapel. An old fireplace is still here with places for boiling, roasting and baking. The apartments on the first floor contain period furniture, some from when Karl XV used the castle in the 19C.

Beyond the courtyard there is a biblical garden with plants mentioned in the Bible and a herb garden which would have been essential to the monks for medicine and flavouring. Further afield is a rose garden. In the extensive park the largest trees are those planted by Field Marshal Johan Christoffer Toll—he said he planted a tree for each lady who turned down his proposal of marriage and there are twelve of them. The knoll on which they stand was then an island, before the level of the lake was lowered in the 19C. One special tree is the Betrothal Lime under which Karl XV's daughter Louise accepted the proposal of Crown Prince Fredrik of Denmark (Fredrik VIII). Karl XV used to sail the lake in an imitation Viking ship, singing with his courtiers. His horse Scheyk ('Sheik') is buried in the grounds, having been killed on the death of his owner, according to old tradition. Karl also built the conservatory near the entrance to the castle.

Back on the E22, after 1km a by-road goes to **Trolle-Ljungby** (2km),.a moated 17C castle. The imposing brick Dutch Renaissance building, owned by the Trolle-Wachtmeister family, is not open to the public but you can wander round the exterior and the grounds (Wed and Sat June–Aug). In a window is displayed the pipe and drinking-horn, probably medieval, said to have been stolen from the troll while he was enjoying his Yuletide feast at the Troll's Stone, mentioned above. Parts of the medieval castle remain, and the east wing was added in 1787.

Continuing on the E22, it is 15km to **Sölvesborg** (pop. 8000). The **tourist bureau** is at the roundabout called Blekingeporten on the E22, in the motorway service-station complex. From here to Kristianopel in the east is the 250km Blekinge Trail for walkers, and in the other direction the Skåne Trail (240km) leads to Torekov in north-west Skåne. Sölvesborg as its name implies had a fortress, built to preserve its thriving trade. The town was burnt many times in the constant Swedish–Danish wars, but through these and later vicissitudes the street pattern has been kept and the height of buildings limited so that it gives an impression of being older than it is and there are some charming little streets.

S:t Nicolai church is the oldest building, of brick with white-painted niches in the gables. The choir is of the 13C and the step-gabled towers 15C. In 1486 a Carmelite monastery was founded but was probably not finished before the Reformation put a stop to it. The **vault-paintings** date from the 15C, possibly from about the time of the building of the monastery because in the chancel they portray the life of the Virgin, especially honoured by Carmelites, while others show Christ, apostles and saints. There are more paintings in the south porch and there is also a runestone with a 6C inscription. The pulpit is from 1621, and besides the usual

Evangelists depicts Olaus Petri, who translated the Bible into Swedish, and Martin Luther. There is a 15C **crucifix**.

On the main square is Stig Blomberg's sculpture 'Ask och Embla' (1947). The signs *Museum* and *Konsthall* (art gallery) to the north-east of the square lead over a picturesque hump-backed railway bridge. Here by the shore near the harbour a 19C grain and spirit store displays archaeological and historical finds of the area and the gallery opposite has occasional exhibitions.

The stumpy remains of the castle (*Slottet*—marked by the St. Hans' Cross) can be reached by driving out of the square towards the north-east on the Östra Storgatan for a few minutes. The originally brick-clad keep was built in the 14C on a mound on the shore-line, and the walls and earth ramparts added over the centuries. In 1564 in the Nordic Seven Years War it was burnt by its own garrison. Until the Treaty of Roskilde (1658) it was used by the Danish administration for the area.

After 3km there is a signpost to **Nogersund** (10km). From here a boat goes to the island of **Hanö** (30 mins), where there is a cemetery for the many British sailors who died in the area during the Napoleonic blockade of Europe.

At 6km, **Ysane** has a 14C church dedicated to St. Gertrude, with 15C **vault-paintings** in the chancel. They were completed on the feast of the Assumption of the Virgin, 1459 as the inscription over the chancel arch says. Thanks to this inscription, uncovered in 1931, the name of the painter hitherto only known as the 'Vittskövle Master' was discovered to be 'Nicolai Haquini', interpreted in Swedish as Nils Håkansson. He was active in the north-east Skåne area, especially in Vittskövle. The best preserved painting shows Christ's entry into Jerusalem. Apart from the chancel the church is plain with a white wooden barrel-vaulted roof. It has a 17C pulpit. The name of the village is pre-Christian and Bronze Age mounds in the area are evidence of long settlement.

The E22 continues across the peninsula to rejoin the Baltic between Norje and (9km) Pukavik. Here the woods along the shore are the setting for holiday cottages and the inviting beaches are good for swimming and picnics, with kiosks and cafés.

In 9km **Karlshamn** (pop. 18,000) is reached. The **tourist bureau** is on the corner of Ågaten and Ronnebygatan.

The town's original name was Bodekull, but when Karl X Gustav favoured it with a town charter it changed its name in his honour (1666). It was then a thriving trading town but a serious fire in 1763 destroyed most of the wooden houses and the wealthy merchants set about constructing worthy homes for themselves, some of which survive today. When Denmark declared war in 1675, the castle was built on the island of Frisholmen, with 242 cannon and manned by a force of 400. Its most prosperous period was the late 19C, based on the manufacture of brandy and punch, and the processing of tobacco.

The signs to *Centrum* lead to the main square. Along the east side of this runs the long Drottninggatan, and many of the most interesting buildings are in a small area of Drottninggatan, north of the square. The Skottsberg-ska house at Drottninggatan 81 can be visited. It was built by a merchant called Olof Olsson the elder, and has a handsome doorway. The Smithska house is the oldest stone house in town and was built in 1765 by the richest man in town, Olof Berg. It now contains the **museum** of local history (open summer afternoons).

Vinkelgatan down by the side of the museum allows glimpses into the courtyard behind the museum with the picturesque **Holländar house**. On the other side is the art gallery (Konsthall), itself an old warehouse. Using the same entrance is a **punch museum** showing the manufacture of 'Karlshamns Flagg' the punch which meant so much to the town's economy in the 19C. (This is a sweet spirits-based drink flavoured with arrak.) Vinkelgatan comes out into Ågatan, where some old wooden houses and warehouses stand on the river-bank. On your left is the modern library, which has a model of the emigrant ship *Charlotta*. Turn to the left and follow the river. After six blocks the **tourist bureau** is on the corner of Ronnebygatan. From the quay here, in summer, a boat goes to the **castle** on Frisholmen island. This was begun in 1675, and the wall, powder magazine, casemates and gun-emplacements are well preserved. There is a dungeon and 'poisoned' well.

Following the shore round to the harbour will bring you to **Hamnparken** (harbour park). Here stands a **statue** which has great poignancy for those descended from the emigrants who went to America in the 19C. The statue was created by Axel Olsson (replicas exist elsewhere), and represents characters from Vilhelm Moberg's book *The Emigrants* and its sequels, a graphic account of the hardships and tribulations of those forced to leave their homeland by poverty (available in English translation). The farmer Karl-Oskar looks out to sea while his wife Kristina turns back to land. The relief is of the emigrant ship *Charlotta*. The 300-year-old turf-roofed cottage nearby was a fisherman's home and the larger wooden building was the pilot's house. In the attractive rose garden a little to the west there is a statue of a bare-footed girl called 'Maja', a character created by Alice Tegnér, a writer of children's songs, also the subject of a small exhibition in the museum.

The area to the north of the two parks contains idyllic streets of pastel-painted houses. The **Hotel Hoppet** (Hope) on the corner of Drottninggatan and Bergsgatan (to your left if you face into Bergsgatan) was used by emigrants. Note that Bergsgatan is in two parts separated by modern building.

Back in the main square the old **town hall** (1682), an attractive half-timbered and brick house, is used by a bank. On the south side of the square is the new town hall in Art Nouveau style, and on the north the **Carl-Gustav church**. Shortly after the town was granted its charter, it was decided that a new church should be built. Erik Dahlberg, who planned the town, also directed the building of the church, but for lack of money it was not completed until 1693. Much of the interior was decorated in the 19C. The elaborate brass font was made in 1717, but the bowl is 16C. The detached bell-tower, the building to the north-east with a cross on top, was built in 1793.

The E22 continues through rolling countryside with beech woods and some coniferous trees. The road here almost follows the boundary between the deciduous forest area to the south and the mixed forest area to the north. There are rocky outcrops where the road has had to be cut through pink-tinged granite. In 10km at Åryd you can leave the motorway and follow signs to **Eriksberg** (3km) a nature reserve with bisons, elks, deer and wildfowl. Visitors are driven in a bus on a 1½ hour tour.

After 16km you come to **Ronneby** (pop. 11,000). In the 13C this was the largest town in Blekinge and traded with the Hanseatic League. When the province became Swedish it lost its importance to Karlskrona, the new centre for the fleet. But in 1705 it was found that the waters of Ronneby were rich in iron, and by the 19C it was among the most famous spas in Sweden.

Signs to the *Centrum* lead to the Kulturcentrum beside the church. A **tourist bureau** is in part of the building, which is an old warehouse once used by Kockum's enamelling works, now containing craft workshops, studios and exhibitions. There is another tourist bureau by the Söderbro (southern bridge).

Heliga Kors kyrka (Holy Cross church) was begun in the 12C, the tower with its buttresses was added in the 15C, and the south porch in the 18C. The north transept contains the oldest wall-paintings, of St. George and the Dragon and St. Peter, of the 14C, while the 16C **chancel paintings** show man torn between good and evil, and a 'danse macabre' in poor condition on the wall. There are several 17C memorial tablets, a medieval crucifix and 17C pulpit. The 1652 altar contains a painting of the Last Supper in a richly carved surround. On the left of the nave is a battered **door** with an axe-slash and scorching from 1534 when Erik XIV's (Swedish) soldiers took the town in the so-called Ronneby Bloodbath during the Nordic Seven Years War and slaughtered those who had taken refuge in the church. The old part of the town around the church is called Bergslagen and there is a local museum here, originally the miller's house. (Follow the sign to *Mölle-backagården* and ignore the house with a similar name right by the church.) Just beyond the museum is the old water-mill.

The **spa-park** is a considerable distance away, on the edge of town. Follow signs to *Ronneby Brunn*. The very attractive park takes advantage of the natural situation where cliffs, a waterfall, lakes and woods are the background for elegant turn-of-the-century villas and a not-so-elegant modern conference centre and hotel, plus wide-ranging sporting facilities. A natural history centre occupies the pretty Villa Vera.

Rejoin the E22 and after 6km you can take the left turn and almost immediately on your right is a St. Hans' Cross sign for the **Björketorp prehistoric cemetery**. A 100m walk brings you to the Björketorp runestone inscribed about AD 700 with a curse on anyone who might desecrate it. The runestone is flanked by two standing stones and there is a circular stone-setting nearby. Altogether in this area there are 11 different grave monuments dating up to AD 500, and these are just some of those spread all along this ridge, called Johannishusåsen. You can continue to **Hjortsberga** (3km) where the bell-tower stands among 110 graves and 17 ship-settings dating between 700 and 1050. There are triangular and square stone-settings, barrows and upright stones. A brooch, knives and beads were among the grave-finds. The bell-tower is of oak and was first mentioned in 1665. The medieval church on the other side of the road has medieval wood-carvings, and 17C pulpit and pews.

Back on the E22 in 6km a signpost indicates *Hasslö* (10km), a town on an island linked to the mainland by a series of bridges. About 4km along this road is **Hjörtahammar** prehistoric cemetery with around 120 Viking (Swedish Iron Age) burials, including a 30m ship-setting.

8km further on, you can leave the E22 and it is 5km to the centre of **Karlskrona** (pop. 30,000), the capital of the old province of Blekinge which for once coincides with the modern county of the same name. Blekinge is the smallest province and like Skåne and Halland belonged to Denmark until 1658. The indented coastline is fringed with islands and inland the gentle scenery merging into northern forests has earned the name 'Garden of Sweden'. Blekinge embroidery in soft blues and pinks is on sale, in lotus and hibiscus patterns copied from porcelain. *Kroppskaka* is a local pork and potato dish similar to that found also in Småland and on Öland. The **tourist bureau** is in the library (Bibliotek) on the main square (Stortorget)—when the library is open you can collect maps and brochures even if the tourist desk is closed. (Library open daily and to 15.00 on Sat.)

In 1680 Karl XI decided on a naval base in his lately acquired southern provinces, and by the end of the century Karlskrona had become the second-largest city in Sweden.

Oak bell-tower at Hjortsberga (17C)

In July 1700 the biggest Swedish fleet ever organised sailed out of the harbour: 38 ships and eight frigates were commanded by Admiral Hans Wachtmeister from his ship *Kung Karl* which alone had nearly 1000 men and 108 guns. Their goal was the Öresund and the Danish fleet which they eventually defeated—though the war continued for 20 more years. Karlskrona was a Baroque town, but a disastrous fire in 1790, started by a laundry-maid in Amiralitetsgatan, meant rebuilding, and this was done mainly in neo-Classical style. The navy still dominates here, with its base including naval colleges, and the shipyard produces both naval and civilian vessels. In 1991 Karlskrona Shipbuilders launched a brand new 'stealth' ship, designed to evade detection and heavily armed, to travel at up to 50 knots.

Follow the signs from the E22 to the *Centrum*. The main square is on the highest point of the island, and contains two Baroque churches designed by Nicodemus Tessin the Younger, which escaped the fire. The circular **Trefaldighetskyrkan** or German church was completed in 1750 for the many Germans in Karlskrona. Tessin took the basic plan from the Pantheon in Rome, but his roof was destroyed in the great fire, and the present wooden roof is painted with trompe l'oeil coffering. The tomb of Admiral Hans Wachtmeister (1714) is in his family vault under the floor (inaccessible). The curved pews are painted in sober grey. Most of the furnishings are from the 19C, except for the red Öland limestone font of 1685.

Fredrikskyrkan (1744) in the middle of the square is called after the first Fredrik, 1720–51. There should have been spires on the squat towers according to the plans. The simple white interior with Ionic pilasters is a foil for the elaborately gilded organ. There are 35 bells in the south tower which are rung daily. Opposite this church is the neo-Classical Rådhus (town hall) of 1795, and also on the square is a statue of Karl XI by John Börjeson.

Continuing in the direction in which you entered the square, and leaving on your left the pseudo-medieval waterworks, you enter the broad Amiralitetstorg leading down the slope. The large wooden bell-tower in the middle belongs to the Admiralty church which is 500m away. Take Alameden (Spanish for poplar avenue), the second street on the left, which has some wooden houses from before the great fire. At the end is a statue of Admiral Hans Wachtmeister. Turn right and the Aurora bastion is ahead. *Kungsbro* is the old quay. Turn right again up Vallgatan. The pink and white building is the residence of the county governor. Here there is a bust of Erik Dahlberg who planned the city.

The first road on your left leads to the red-painted **Admiralty church** or Ulrica Pia. The wooden figure outside is called Rosenbom and is a poor-box (look under the hat). Legend says it is Constable Matts Rosenbom (c 1700) who fell ill and could not work so was granted permission to beg to keep his large family. The very spacious wooden church (1685) is named after queen Ulrica Eleonora, wife of Karl XI and it is supposed that Erik Dahlberg designed it. The altarpiece features a copy of Rubens' *Thrust of the Lance*. The cross on the altar in cedarwood, ivory, mother-of-pearl and ebony was given in 1744 by a sea-captain who obtained it from the Patriarch of Constantinople. The pulpit hourglass dates from 1693 and the votive ship is the corvette *Carlskrona* which foundered in 1846. There is a memorial tablet to Gilbert Sheldon of a family of English shipbuilders.

Turn left at the end of Vallgatan. Here is an area of restricted access as it belongs to the navy, but the **old shipyard** is open to visitors in the summer. It has a 300m-long wooden building of 1692 for making rope, a historic dock and Sweden's first submarine of 1905. Theoretically only Swedish nationals are allowed in.

The stately **Maritime Museum** (1880) is the first building as you start to ascend the hill on the other side. It contains four main sections—shipbuilding, figureheads by Johan Törnström, naval weapons and shipping technology. It also displays the work of the 18C shipbuilder Fredrik Henrik af Chapman. Behind the Maritime Museum the yellow wooden buildings are 18C officers' quarters.

To get to the oldest part of Karlskrona, return up the hill. On the corner of Borgmästaregatan is the soberly imposing **Nordenskjöldska Gården** (1795), built by rear-admiral Eneskiöld and used by the local council. In the courtyard behind all the buildings are of the same period, surrounding a walnut tree. The next street on the left is Hantverkaregatan. This leads to **Björkholmen**, another hilly island, where some 18C houses survive. This was the area where workers and seamen lived. The north–south streets are named after ship types and the east–west streets after Swedish admirals.

Returning along the north quay brings you to Fisktorget. Here is **Blekinge museum** in a series of old buildings. In the buildings along Fisktorget are exhibitions on stone-quarrying, fishing and shipping. The rest of the museum is reached through the Baroque garden and includes Admiral Hans Wachtmeister's imposing mansion of 1705, called Grevagården. This contains furniture and interiors of the 18C.

Keeping the sea on your left and continuing on to Borgmästarekajen, you will see the small three-masted fully rigged ship *Jarramas*, now a summertime café. *Jarramas* was built in 1900 and used until 1946 as a training-ship for cadets.

Excursions from Karlskrona include group tours to the 17C **Drottningskärs Fortress** a three-storey granite rectangle, an excellent example of Erik Dahlberg's fortifications—enquire at the tourist bureau. Enquire there also for **boat-trips** under the bridges of Karlskrona or out to the islands. Then there is **Vämoparken**, an open-air museum where 12 old buildings from Blekinge have been re-erected. To get there take the second motorway exit on your way out of the town and follow the signs. The ruins of the 16C castle of Lyckå are at Lyckeby, on the eastern edge of town.

The E22 leaves Karlskrona and turns east, then north up the coast to Kalmar. The church at (8km) **Ramdala** has a font, pews and pulpit of the 17C, the last presented by Christian IV, with illustrations from the Apocalypse and figures of the virtues. The east tower is the only remaining medieval part and contains the so-called 'monk's room' (no access).

After 4km you can make a detour to the **Bronze Age rock-carvings** at Möckleryd. Turn right at Jämjö, signposted Torhamn and after 7km there is a St. Hans' Cross on the right for Steneryd nature reserve. Follow signs *Möckleryd* and *Hällristning*. The carvings are mostly ships, with some footprints, animals and men.

On the E22, after 11km at Fågelmara a road goes east to **Kristianopel** (6km), founded by Christian III in 1600 to defend his Danish kingdom against the Swedes in Kalmar. Signs lead to the harbour (*hamn*) where remains of the fortifications line the sea-front. Gustav II Adolf captured the town in 1611 and destroyed the church. When the Swedes finally managed to oust the Danes for good in 1677 the walls were razed and the population removed to Ronneby, Växjö and Karlshamn. The **church** was rebuilt by the Danes in 1618. The east and west walls are considerably askew—this was to fit in with the old street pattern and still keep the east–west orientation. The wall behind the altar is painted with somewhat startling trees. On the left is the richly carved royal pew of 1635 and the pulpit and font are of the same century.

6km further north on the E22 at Brömsebro there is a sign *Fredssten* (peace stone) to the right. Here was the much fought-over border between Sweden and Denmark. Not only did the great Gustav Vasa meet Christian III here for negotiations, but here also was where the Peace of Brömsebro was signed in 1645 when Denmark relinquished three provinces to Sweden. A carved stone was erected in 1915 to commemorate the event. This is today still the border between Blekinge and Småland.

After 11km the area to the west of Bergkvara is a centre for handicrafts, and wood-carvings, textiles and pottery can be bought directly from the craftsmen in the villages around Torsås.

In 20km the road passes through **Hagby** with its delightful circular church, white-painted, with wood-shingled roof and separate bell-tower. The circular nave and apse were built in the second half of the 12C for defence—witness the loop-holes in the upper wall, formerly the defence storey. The porch was added in the 17C. There are a few remnants of wall-paintings, consecration crosses and a 14C crucifix. The modern crystal cross was made at the Orrefors glass factory. The 1770s pulpit has illustrations of Christ washing Peter's feet and a Road to Emmaus scene. The four figures on the wall to the left of the entrance are from an altar of 1760.

At 12km, **Hossmo** has another medieval fortified church with shingles on roof, tower and bell-tower. The carved door is dated 1653. After 8km there is the junction for Kalmar, with signs to the *Centrum*.

ˑKalmar (pop. 30,000) is the county town of Kalmar county, one of the three into which the old province of Småland is now divided. It is the gateway to the island of Öland, via the 6km bridge. The magnificent castle lies on an island of its own, and the old town is on the mainland nearby, though the later Baroque town on another island, Kvarnholmen, connected to the mainland by half-a-dozen bridges, is more rewarding to visit.

Tourist bureau: 6 Larmgatan (near the station). Tel. (0480) 153 50. Exchange.

Post office: Storgatan 1 (near Stortorget).

Travel information: Tel. (0491) 215 40.

Telephone, telegram: Storgatan 11. Tel. (0480) 893 60.

Kalmar was settled as early as the 8C. The Arabic geographer Idrisi put it on his world map of 1154, and it is mentioned in the *Gesta Danorum* of the late 12C. Snorri Sturluson the Icelandic historian mentions it in the early 13C as having been sacked by the Norwegians in 1123, but by the 13C it was an important trading town. Because Blekinge and Skåne to the south were Danish and it was the largest town near the border the castle was of immense strategic value—'The Key to the Kingdom'. A defensive tower was built c 1160 to protect the harbour and some remains of this lie under the present castle. The original settlement lay on the mainland just alongside. In 1397 the Union of Kalmar was formed through the energetic statesmanship of Margareta of Denmark, when Sweden, Norway and Denmark became briefly one kingdom. In the 16C under the Vasas it became one of the most significant centres in the country. Gustav Vasa and two of his sons each helped to rebuild the castle into a Renaissance palace. The town centre was removed, after a fire, to the island of Kvarnholmen and was built in the 1660s to designs of Nicodemus Tessin the Elder. After the Danes left southern Sweden in 1658 it lost its importance to Karlskrona. The original old town area was gradually rebuilt in the 17C and 18C.

To visit the **ˑcastle**, after following the signs *Centrum*, next follow the signs *slottet* (open May–Sept, closed Sun am, rest of year limited opening).

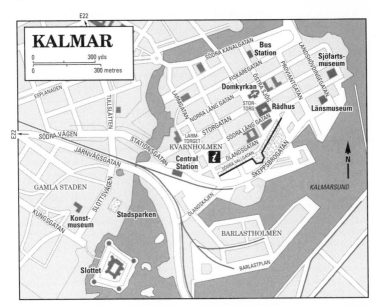

In the 12C, the Kalmar keep was part of an integrated defensive system which included a tower and fortified churches on Öland, and fortified churches on the mainland such as Hossmo and Hagby. New fortifications were erected in the reign of Magnus Ladulås (1274–90), who was married here in 1276. Erik of Pomerania, crowned king of the three realms by the Union of Kalmar but in reality only regent until Margareta's death in 1412, lived here 1407–09. In the early years of the 16C it was the scene of bitter conflict as Swedes and Danes conquered and reconquered it. Gustav Vasa captured it in 1525 and gave it to his queen as a wedding gift in 1532. Later he built ramparts and bastions, widened the moat, constructed a new drawbridge and strengthened or rebuilt the courtyard buildings. His sons concentrated on the interior, with lavish Renaissance decoration and furnishing. In 1611 it fell to the Danes for two years in the Kalmar War. Gustav II Adolf restored it but troubled times still lay ahead, as the Danes harried Småland. Finally peace came but it had lost its significance as guardian of the southern frontier and declined ignominiously into a storehouse, jail, granary and even a distillery. Restoration began in the mid 19C and continues, so certain rooms may be closed and exhibits moved.

The castle is approached by an 18C ravelin on the mainland, over a reconstructed drawbridge on to the castle island. Above the gateway is the Swedish coat of arms from 1568. The arch is set at an angle which made it impossible to shoot into the outer courtyard. The entrance to the inner courtyard is a Renaissance arch of 1554, and leads through a barrel-vaulted passage with restored decorations to match those in the chapel. The superb *well-cover inside is also Renaissance (1578), designed by Dominicus Pahr and made in Öland. The dolphin on the top replaced the original lion in 1851. The painted imitation stonework on the walls of the courtyard is a restoration of the 16C appearance.

The state apartments are entered on the north side by ascending the Queen's Staircase (1556) which is built with medieval tombstones from the 'reformed' churches and monasteries.

The **Queen's Apartment** (1555–56) is the first on the left. The change of pattern on the frieze shows where the room was divided in the 1580s, one side decorated at the end of the 16C, the other in 1620, where the window embrasures match the frieze. The fireplace is of grey limestone and it was painted in the 17C. On the wall is a 17C Brussels tapestry of the Sabine women, and there is a bust of Queen Margareta and a copy of the **Union of Kalmar document** of 1397. The next room is called the **Lozenge Hall** because of its intarsia work (1581) (the panels are in fact octagonal), both representational and purely decorative. This is divided by short Doric columns (1558–92, restored) with a Classical frieze half-way up the wall. The floor is a 19C version of the 16C original.

The **Grey Hall** was built in 1553 and was decorated by Johan III in the 1580s. The panelling has vanished but the 16C frescoes of the story of Samson by Arendt Lamprechts are still here, though pale and difficult to decipher. The coffered ceiling (restored) and the fireplace are of the 16C. The carved bed (1628) has the arms of the Danish families of Bille and Rosencrantz on the foot, and the head which is later has the arms of Gustav Adolf. The Rosencrantz arms are also on the **bridal chest** of 1579, beside those of the Hardenbergs. They were the forebears of Sophie Rosencrantz, the wife of Breide Rantzau who took the castle in 1611. The cupboard is from 1635.

The corner tower contains the **King's Chamber** (Kungsmak) of 1555–62. The exquisite *intarsia panelling (restored) is framed by Corinthian columns and shows landscapes and intricate patterns. One of these depicts the castle in 1560, and others are copies of well-known engravings. The panels are surmounted by painted stucco reliefs of hunting scenes (1585). The Baroque sandstone fireplace is dated 1657 with the monogram of Karl X Gustav. The floor is 19C.

The **Golden Hall** is named after the gilded ceiling (1576), which shows coats of arms with the three crowns—the Vasa arms—and the Göta arms (lion and three rivers in separate panels). The frieze was painted in the 16C and the fireplace is of the same period. Most of the paintings are copies and are of the Swedish royal family, including Gustav Vasa and Queen Kristina. The passage with the King's Staircase flanks the Watch Tower and leads into the **Green Hall**, so named because of its green and gold ceiling, with floral patterns in painted panels. Remains of 16C tempera paintings can be seen in the window embrasures.

Owing to the irregular shape of the castle, the **chapel** (1592) occupies most of the south wing. The barrel-vault and walls are 16C and the outer wall contains remnants of the 13C wall. The Queen's Chair and King's Chair and a few pews remain from the 17C and have the royal monograms. The limestone font is of the same period. The altar picture is a 17C copy. There is also direct access from the courtyard.

Passing the chapel staircase and the south antechamber with a clock mechanism of 1614, you enter the **Armoury**, originally a kitchen, as evidenced by the huge fireplace. The room contains military equipment and banners.

The **Burnt Hall** (1580s, burnt 1642, being restored) contains two fireplaces of 16C and 17C. It is the largest room in the castle. Next comes a small irregularly-shaped room which leads on to the landing again, but there is also a door leading to the Prison Tower and four small rooms running behind the Queen's Apartment and the Lozenge Hall. These were made when Queen Hedvig Eleanora came to visit in 1656, and are known as the Princesses' rooms. They contain a modest **maritime museum**.

Back on the **ground floor** (first landing) are the apartments of the governor of the castle. The rooms to the right form an exhibition illustrating furnishing styles. First an **antechamber** with a chequered ceiling contains a guide to different phases of Swedish art-history—Renaissance, Baroque, Rococo, Gustavian and so on, which are then each illustrated by the furnishings in the following rooms. On the floor the lines of brass tacks show the position of the walls of the medieval keep. (A booklet attached to the doorway of most rooms has an English summary at the back.)

To the left in the tower is the **round kitchen**, formerly a prison and then a powder store. The floor here was lowered to make the kitchen in c 1600. A baking oven is behind the fireplace. The holes in the wall mark the top of the dungeon which had no opening but a hole in its ceiling.

Back through the ante-room you can reach the Governor's Kitchen with old kitchen utensils. To the left a square tower room, once servants' quarters, has Empire style furnishings. The next room used to be part of the Governor's Kitchen, and has a Rococo fireplace and other Rococo furnishings. A tiny kitchen leads to the south room (Baroque), which has a ceiling painted with flowers and trophies. The furniture is also 17C and there are portraits of the Swedish royal family.

The square room to the left has some remains of red mural paintings, probably 17C. The stove is 16C and came from the cathedral. The furniture illustrates Renaissance style. The **Distillery Bookkeeper's Room** with the Great South Room once formed one large room. It has blue and white Rococo panels, and Rococo furniture.

In the **Governor's Hall**, decorated in 1692, there is furniture dating from the mid 17C to the mid 18C. The crystal chandelier once belonged to the Oxenstierna family. A tankard made of birchwood is among the objects on the table. The next room is called the **Nursery** and has clothes' chests of the 18C and 19C. On the other side of the landing are the deputy governor's apartments. The first is the memorial room of the Småland Hussars, the regiment created by Gustav Vasa in 1543. It was while commanding the regiment at the Battle of Lützen in 1632 that Gustav II Adolf met his death. The second room is called **Sven Månsson's Room** with murals of 1618, when he was governor. The model is of the medieval castle. Opposite the main entrance a narrow stair leads up to the two rooms used as a women's prison from the 17C on. As was the custom, the women were occupied with spinning.

Outside, it is a very pleasant walk around the ramparts by the sea. On the south and south-west are several 17C cannon.

On leaving the castle, the Kungsgatan straight ahead leads to the site of the first town where there are some 17C and 18C houses, among them the **Krusenstjernska** house, completely furnished and in its own garden. The entrance is on Stora Dammgatan, to the left off Kungsgatan about 500m from the castle (open June to mid-Sept pm only). If you continue through Stora Dammgatan, turn left and skirt the pond, you will find the Erik Bastion, part of the old defences. On the way back, the road parallel to Kungsgatan to the north (Gamla Kungsgatan) leads through narrow old streets, picturesquely decked with flowers. There is an old churchyard in the area, and the **Konstmuseum** (art gallery) is at Slottsvägen 1 (19C and 20C Swedish art, open daily) which brings you back to the castle.

The **park** on the other side of Slottsvägen, laid out along the waterfront, offers striking views of the castle. At the end nearest the castle is a neo-Gothic **monument** of 1851 commemorating Gustav Vasa's landing near here in 1520 after fleeing from Lübeck, three years before he won his throne.

To get on to the island of **Kvarnholmen** follow the *Centrum* signs. The island has an even grid of streets and the *****Domkyrka** (cathedral) looms large, so it is easy to find it in the middle of the main square, Stortorget. 'Domkyrka' is a misnomer, since the church is actually no longer a cathedral but the name continues though the see has been transferred to Växjö. Begun in 1660 and consecrated in 1682, both the Nicodemus Tessins, father and son, worked on it, though it was elder who planned it in 1660 immediately after returning from a visit to Italy, which is evident in its Roman Baroque appearance. The north and south façades could be regarded as a simplified version of Il Gesù in Rome.

The form is a cross with towers in the angles and apses at each end. It should have had a dome but this was never added. The heavy entablature running right round the building divides it into two storeys and it is supported on Tuscan pilasters of Öland limestone. Large rectangular windows topped by small square ones fill in the spaces below. Above this rise the four square towers which each have an octagonal crown. Between the towers each of the four façades has a triangular pediment and the north and south ones have a window flanked by two niches, while spiral volutes link them to the towers. Sandstone pinnacles crown all the high points of the roof.

The **interior** is high and light, the vaulting being 23m high, resting on a heavy cornice on massive Ionic pilasters. The side galleries are on slender Corinthian columns and the wood of the galleries is painted cool grey-green to match the pews. If the dome had been built the planned light from overhead would have balanced that from the choir windows. As it is, the **altapiece** is illuminated by electric light which leaves the top less well lit than it should be. It was designed by Nicodemus Tessin the Younger, the sculpture of the Creation is by Caspar Schröder and the Descent from the Cross probably painted by David von Krafft. The whole is surmounted by a sunburst and dove symbolising the Holy Spirit. The Latin text is from St. John's Gospel. The altar itself is decorated with laurels, palms and trophies and at each side the 18C statues represent Faith and Mercy.

The **pulpit** was made by Baltzar Hoppstedt in the 17C. The three-tier canopy has the Risen Christ, angels and allegorical figures of virtues. The figure supporting the pulpit is St. Christopher. The modern **font** of Öland limestone is in the shape of the Ark of Salvation. The floor of the chancel consists of carved 17C and 18C tombstones. A chapel off the chancel for private prayer is dedicated to St. Christopher. The organ in the west was constructed in the 19C. The bronze **chandelier** (1632) with 36 arms is from Lübeck and other chandeliers are of brass, from the 17C. The three bells of the cathedral were originally in the medieval church.

To the south of the cathedral is the 17C **Rådhus** (town hall), unusually with a rusticated central upper portion and pediment. The central carved roundel is the monogram of Karl XI (spelt with a C in those days), the one on the left with a flourishing tree tied firmly to a stake illustrates the motto 'obedience is best' and the one on the right exhorts those who judge to find out the facts first—note the measuring instruments. A central slim tower was originally planned.

Östra Sjögatan leads out of the square by the side of the town hall, to the south-east. At the first crossroads is the 17C house of the mayor Rosenlund, the oldest stone house on the island (on the right on the other side of Södra

Långgatan). It was once occupied by the architect Nicodemus Tessin the Younger, and at various other periods by a bishop and a school.

Turn left down Södra Långgatan and as the road ends in a square the **Sjöfartsmuseum** (Maritime Museum; open mid-June to mid-Aug. Mon closed) is on the left. This displays ship models, navigational instruments and the history of seafaring. Just beyond the Maritime Museum on the sea-front are considerable remains of **fortifications** with the Carolus Philippus bastion to the north and the Regeringen Bastion to the south. Cross the square from the Museum and turn right into Skeppsbrogatan. Immediately on the right is the **Länsmuseum** (open daily, except Sat and Sun am). Here in an old steam-mill are the finds from the warship *Kronan (Crown)*, sunk in 1679.

When *Kronan* was built in Stockholm between 1665 and 1672, she was one of the largest vessels in existence, nearly twice as large as the *Vasa* (see Rte 15). She measured 53m long at the waterline, with a 12.92m beam, a draught of 6.23m and 2140 tons displacement (*Vasa* 1300 tons). Her mast towered 50m above the waterline. She was the only ship of her time to have three complete decks. Her cost was astronomical for the time, 326,000 daler, twice the amount paid for a normal warship.

The Swedish king particularly chose an Englishman, Francis Sheldon, to design his ship because he wished to break the dominance of the Dutch in his shipyards. Sheldon was possibly influenced by his colleague Sir Anthony Deane, an eminent naval architect, author of *Doctrine of Naval Architecture* published in 1670. This lays down guidelines for calculating measurements based on the length of keel, and researchers have referred to the book in their work on *Kronan*. It is supposed that *Kronan* was taller and narrower than other Swedish ships of the time. To judge from a painting of 1680 and from carvings which have been saved, she was extravagantly ornamented with intricate woodwork, but as a warship she was also provided with 126 cannons and room for 840 men. She was commanded by Admiral Lorentz Creutz, originally from Finland, who was neither a soldier nor a seaman, simply a government administrator. In 1676 Admiral Creutz received an order to take the fleet of 60 ships to Gotland to recapture it from the Danes. The Danish and Dutch fleets pursued them in a strong wind and heavy seas. Level with Hulterstad on the island of Öland, as Creutz attempted to turn and engage the enemy, *Kronan* keeled over and exploded, probably because a falling lamp ignited the powder magazine. Forty-two men were saved out of the 840.

Kronan went down fully equipped and manned, unlike the *Vasa*, which means we will have a complete picture of life aboard, if and when all has been recovered. In the few years after the disaster 60 cannons were salvaged, using primitive diving bells. In 1980 the site was discovered 26m deep on the muddy bottom of the Baltic off Öland. Work is still continuing so the exhibition is constantly being expanded. In 1991, for example, an officer's uniform of red wollen material with metal trimmings and silk braid was discovered, an interesting discovery because uniforms were not generally worn until the 18C.

The exhibition is on the second floor, and a booklet in English can be borrowed explaining the displays. There are slide and video shows, some with English commentary (ask at the entrance desk for the latest information).

First comes a model of the wreck site on the sea-bed, showing the difficulties the divers faced. The show-cases and displays are fairly self-explanatory. Navigational instruments, utensils, furniture, pewter, china, jewellery and clothing are all here. The small everyday objects are perhaps the most intriguing—an officer's chest with contents, musical instruments, shoes and alcohol bottles, pocket-watches and snuff-boxes. The coin hoard is unique, with gold coins from Hungary, Spain, Venice and the Turkish Empire, as well as silver coins. There is a reconstruction of the seamen's quarters and an impression of the Admiral's cabin.

On coming out of the Länsmuseum you can continue along Skepps-brogatan. This leads to more of the old **fortifications** including the Cavalier Gate with Karl XI's monogram, and the Johannes Rex bastion. Go through the gate and turn left to **Lilla Torg** (small square). To your right is the **Dahmska house** with shaped gables and a fine doorway dated 1666, and a carved milestone at its corner dated 1737, originally painted and gilded. The engineer of the fortifications, Anders Berg, built the house for himself. Straight ahead is the old **Deanery** with its curving tiled roof, childhood home of the poet Stagnelius (1793–1823). In front of it is a modern fountain with a two-tailed mermaid. The large building on the corner between these two is the residence of the county Governor of the 17C and 18C, also with a good doorway, dated 1674.

Ölandsgatan continues west and comes out on to a strip of park extending to the right, laid on more fortifications, this time along the waterway between the mainland and the island of Kvarnholmen. On the mainland can be seen Prins Carl's ravelin and near the old water-tower on the island side is the West Gate for entrance by water. The park continues to the Malmbron bridge. On the other side of the canal to the right of the bridge the very large building is the Stagnelius School designed by the architect Ragnar Östberg (1866–1945) who created Stockholm City Hall. In front of the school is Carl Eldh's figure of a diver.

Suburbs and surroundings

About 2km north from the city centre along Stagneliusgatan and Kungs-gårdsvägen are the large grounds of the Renaissance manor of **Skälby**. Here are the municipal nurseries, with tropical and subtropical green-houses and tropical birds (open daily except Sat). Another kilometre or so beyond Skälby, the new water-tower can be climbed for the view.

Kläckeberga church is about 7km to the north-west of Kalmar centre. Leave the motorway at the exit after the one for Öland and the church is about 3km to the west. It is a fortified church, used as such in the 15C and 16C and even as late as the Kalmar War in 1611. The oldest parts are from the 12C with 17C chancel and 18C painted ceiling of sky, clouds and angels. The altar (1616) is by a German artist, Herman Hahn, with a painting of the Annunciation. It was looted from a Polish Jesuit church during the Polish–Swedish war, and was previously in the Storkyrka in Stockholm.

4

The Island of Öland

Total distance 290km. Träffpunkt Öland—road 136, 26km **Borgholm**—65km *Byxelkrok*—7km end of road 136—unnumbered road, 10km—road 136, 35km—unnumbered road 85km *Eketorp*—9km *Ottenby*—road 136, 53km *the bridge*.

*·**Öland** (pop. 24,000) is joined to the mainland at Kalmar by a 6km bridge. Road 137 to the bridge is well signposted in Kalmar—follow the signs to Öland.

The bridge, finished in 1972, is 6070m long and 13m wide with 155 piers. Low sections cross the land on either side and part of the sound, and over the shipping channel seven piers about 130m apart rise to give clearance of 36m. It took five years and 100,000 cubic metres of reinforced concrete to complete. There can be problems for high-sided vehicles when a strong wind is blowing. As the bridge crosses the island of Svinö, there is a turning for the look-out point (*utsiktsplats*) for an impressive view.

The island is 140km long and 17km broad at its widest point, Sweden's second-largest island after Gotland. It consists, unlike the granite mainland, mostly of limestone and sandstone. It has low rainfall and high sunshine figures so that its excellent beaches attract thousands of summer visitors. The flora includes 30 different orchids, and birdlife abounds, especially on Stora Alvaret, the bare heath in the south. Archaeological evidence goes back to 6000 BC, and Iron Age cemeteries and forts are thick on the ground, many unmarked and unexamined. Runestones are plentiful but more difficult to spot. The churches founded in the Middle Ages have mostly been altered through the centuries, though medieval furnishings and some wall-paintings remain. About 400 windmills picturesquely dot the countryside. Road 136 runs the length of the island on the western side and this is where the tourists and summer holiday visitors are. The most important cultural sites, with the exception of Eketorp, are concentrated in the middle third of the island.

Just over the bridge signs *Träffpunkt Öland* lead to the **tourist complex**. Tourist information, café and souvenir shops are complemented by the *Naturum*, a small exhibition on the natural history of the island (explanatory leaflets in English). The **Historium** (fee for entry, showings every 20 minutes) consists of a multi-slide presentation of the island's history, together with an exhibition, with English labels, including a mock megalithic tomb and medieval church. At the tourist bureau, look out for booklets of coupons, which are sometimes available, giving rebates on various attractions.

Follow the signs north to Borgholm and Byxelkrok. At (13km) Rälla you can turn off to see **Karums Alvar prehistoric remains** by taking the right turn to Högsrum, and after 3km the turn left marked *Gravfält*. Near the turn, on the right, are two standing stones called Oden's splinters, probably Iron Age. After 1km there is a small car park beside an area of heath with a prehistoric cemetery—opinions differ as to whether it is Iron Age or Bronze Age. Almost next to the car park are the remains of a 26m **ship-setting** called Noah's Ark. The outlines of the ship and the benches across can be seen in granite blocks level with the ground, while the stem and stern stones in limestone are upright. The large rock in the middle represents the mast. There are nearly 80 burial places here, mostly stone circles.

Back on the 136, after 2km, an art gallery at **Ekerum** shows the works of Per Ekström (1844–1935), a landscape painter. At 9km there is a sign *Solliden* and *Slottsruin*. **Solliden**, a modest white Italianate villa, was built in 1906 for the royal family. The gardens are open to the public (entry fee) for a few hours daily in the summer. There is an exhibition of royal pictures and other objects in a new pavilion. Nearby, dominating the landscape, lies the mighty shell of **Borgholm castle** (open May to Sept; museum; café).

Little remains of the medieval fortress except the outline of a tower in the courtyard, the present building having been constructed in the 17C and 18C. Johan III had employed the architect Dominicus Pahr for his grand new palace which was finished in 1589. It was damaged in the Kalmar War 1611–13, but even so a surviving drawing of 1634 shows a great medieval fortress crowned with Renaissance towers and turrets. Karl X Gustav lived here for some years before he came to the throne, having been given the castle by his cousin Queen Kristina. When he became king he employed Nicodemus Tessin the Elder as architect, but Karl's early death meant that these plans were never completed. Nevertheless, one elegant doorway in the courtyard plus the great staircases remain to give an inkling of former glory. There are extensive views from the upper storey.

In the small town of (2km) **Borgholm**, the 'capital' of Öland, is the local museum (Ölands Forngård, Köpmansgatan, May–Sept) with archaeological finds from the island on the ground floor, and furniture, costumes and silver on the other two floors. The museum itself is a typical Borgholm 19C villa with a ground floor of stone and the rest of wood. The entrance porch was added in the late 19C. Some old buildings have been reconstructed in the grounds.

After 28km there is a turning on the right to **Persnäs** (4km), where a 19C poorhouse, later used as a school, has been turned into a museum (Persnäs Skol-och Hembygdsmuseum; open summer afternoons, closed Mon). A turning on the left goes to **Sandvik** (2km), where an eight-storeyed windmill still has the original wooden working parts, and a restaurant.

Källa, 9km further north, has a 12C fortified church. It is signposted as *Ödekyrka*, meaning disused church. Turn right and then left from the village (2km). Churches were often built in the 11C or 12C and then fortified later against the attacks of 'heathens' from the other side of the Baltic. Here the outside looks like a large rectangular keep but inside some of the building history becomes clear. Original Romanesque arches have been built upon, up to high crenellations, and then these have been topped with a wooden ridge ceiling. The square plinth in the middle once supported a central pillar and there is a built-in pulpit.

At **Högby** in 7km there is a large stone-built Dutch windmill. The **church** has two medieval triptychs. The one of the Virgin is from the 14C, and the one with St. Peter, of North German workmanship, is from the 15C. There is also a crucifix of about 1500.

From (21km) Byxelkrok a boat-service goes to **Blå Jungfrun** (Blue Maiden), an 86m-high bare granite dome-shaped islet (usually out in the morning and back mid afternoon). The beach 2km north of the town has an odd stone formation called **Neptune's Fields**. This is a system of rolling wave-like raised beaches of shingle named by Carl von Linné (Linnaeus). There are also some Iron Age stone-settings.

At 3km there is a turning left which you can take for the northernmost point of the island (*norra udde*) where there is a lighthouse called Långe Erik. 2km further, road 136 ends and you join an unnumbered road. After another 3km you can turn left for '**Trollskogen**' ('magic wood') (2km), a nature reserve with trees twisted into weird contortions by the wind. A 4.5km marked walking trail takes you round, and there is an information centre.

Return west, rejoining the 136 in 7km by a left turn at a T-junction. 12km after (23km) Källa there is an unnumbered road down the east of the island, signposted *Föra*. After 1km **Föra church** (open mid-May to Aug) appears on the left, with a medieval defensive tower. There was originally also a tower over the chancel, like many of Öland's churches, giving rise to the name 'pack-saddle' churches. The pillar was the medieval church's central pillar. The figures of St. Nicholas (1390) and an apostle (c 1500) at the back of the church are from an old altar, and below them is an oak chest of 1671. The altar at the back is of Gotland limestone on a new base. The font is of 1250 and the crucifix from the 15C.

In 17km, **Egby church** (open daily) is the smallest on the island. It is Romanesque, with the original crudely hewn apse and a 12C font showing scenes from the birth of Christ. The medieval altar-table is of Öland limestone, and there is a wood-carved pietà of the 15C. The altarpiece on the side wall is of 1756, and there is a Rococo pulpit. In 4km there is a signpost for **Kapelludden** (2km). In 1374 a ship carrying St. Birgitta's remains from Rome stopped here on the way home to Vadstena. There are the ruins of a chapel and a tall cross. A lighthouse guards the point.

At (7km) **Gärdslösa**, the church is mainly Romanesque (1138). About 1200 the defensive storey was added, and the transepts and vaulted roof were built in the mid 14C. The faded wall-paintings are of different eras from the 13C to the 17C—the imitation stonework around the windows and arches is the earliest and the Old Testament scenes in the choir the latest. The font is 17C and the heavily restored votive ship is the *Nyckel*, sunk in 1679. Notice the capitals and brackets which are carved with faces. The crucifix is of about 1300 and the pulpit with its hourglass was made in 1666.

After 5km, the church at **Långlöt** has a medieval tower. Inside there are two fonts, one medieval and one of 1668, and a medieval oak figure of the Virgin. Here you can turn right to Himmelsberga and Ismanstorp. Just along the road is the excellent **Himmelsberga friluftsmuseum** (open-air museum). Three old farmhouses and 26 outbuildings have been meticulously furnished and equipped in traditional Öland style of the 18C and 19C (open May–Sept; very pleasant outdoor café).

Continue along the same side road for 5km to a left turn for **Ismanstorp**. The road ends after a kilometre, then there is a fair walk along a wooded track so do not lose confidence. Ismanstorp is the best preserved of the Iron Age forts on the island (c AD 400). Within the 125m-diameter ring-wall the bases of 88 dwellings have been found. Curiously, it had nine entrances, possibly an indication that it was a religious cult-site as well as for defence.

Return to Långlöt and continue south. At **Lerkaka** (2km) is a picturesque row of windmills and a runestone. Windmills came to Sweden via Germany in the 16C and the earliest on Öland is mentioned in a document of 1546. Their heyday was the 18C and 19C when nearly every farm had its own, and in 1820 there were 1713 of them on the island. Most were of the post-mill type where the whole body of the mill could be turned to catch the wind. In the north of the island many were built on a stone base. In the latter part of the 19C about 25 Dutch-type mills (where the top cap only could be turned) were constructed, some removed from the mainland.

Along this stretch of road one village succeeds another almost without a break. These are permanent homes, not holiday cottages like those clustered around road 136, and there are not so many tourist facilities.

At (8km) Norra Möckleby you can turn left for **Gråborg** (6km), the largest of Öland's Iron Age forts (6C AD) but not so well preserved as Ismanstorp. It has a 7m-high wall surrounding a rough oval 210m by 165m. It was occupied at intervals until the Middle Ages and there is a medieval archway built into the wall. Even in 1676 people are thought to have found refuge here from a Danish invasion.

From (7km) Sandby southwards, the interior of the island is occupied by **Stora Alvaret**, a treeless heath of unusual flora, including thousands of orchids. The bedrock is almost flat limestone with a very thin layer of soil. Mountain, tundra, steppe and Mediterranean plants are all to be found here in various pockets. Birds include Montagu's harrier, golden plover and skylark. The scrubby vegetation has varied through the ages with different levels of human exploitation, but is now being allowed to increase again.

The drive south can be somewhat tedious on this road. There are many unmarked fields of prehistoric cemeteries by the side of the road.

After 34km, **·Eketorp** is signposted as *fornborg* to the right and right again almost immediately (1km). (Open May to Sept; guided tours in English 13.00 mid-June to Aug). The crenellated wall surrounds half the circular fort. In the centre the comprehensive **museum** with hundreds of finds from the site occupies a huddle of thatched houses, and here there are models showing the three stages of settlement. (Labels in Swedish only, but you can buy an English translation.) **Eketorp I** which lasted from the 4C to the 5C consisted of a circular wall with stone dwellings fitted against it, apparently used only when danger threatened, since there are few household remains. **Eketorp II** (5C–7C) was twice as large, with dwellings in the middle as well as around the inside of the wall. The present reconstruction is meant to give a picture of this Migration Period settlement. **Eketorp III** was built in about 1000 and abandoned in the 13C, and it is planned to reconstruct this on the eastern half of the site. Meanwhile the reconstructed buildings include dwellings, storehouses, workshops and byres, with appropriate livestock—horses and geese, with hens scrambling on the thatched roofs, and a special breed of small black-spotted pigs which scamper appealingly about the visitor's feet.

On the road again, at Ottenby (9km) there is a sign left to the southern-most point (*södra udde*). On the point (4km) stands **Långe Jan**, a 42m-high lighthouse, built in 1785 by Russian prisoners-of-war, which may be climbed for the view. This area is a nature reserve and bird sanctuary where birds are studied and ringed. There is a **Fågelmuseum**, Bird Museum, open May to Sept.

Here at Ottenby there was a manor which was once a monastery and then a royal property. Join the 136 again for the drive back up the west coast. There are many prehistoric remains in the area. In 2km is the best view of **Karl X's wall** (1653) which runs for 5km right across the tip of the island and was built to contain the deer belonging to Ottenby royal manor.

At 16km you pass **Gettlinge Iron Age cemetery**, 1.5km long, with many different types of memorial, including a 30m-long ship-setting, mounds and stone circles. **Barby Borg** in 13km is an early **Iron Age fort** on a small escarpment, the old coast-line, giving a view over the surroundings.

3km further north is **Mysinge Bronze Age burial mound** by the side of the road, with other prehistoric remains. After 2km, **Resmo church** has fragments of Romanesque wall-paintings. It was originally a 'pack-saddle' church having two towers, the western one added in the 13C for defence. After 4km turn left at **Vickleby**. The church here too has a defensive tower and the village street is attractive. After 3km turn right to get on to the coast road. In 4km a sign *Karlevisten* points left into a field. This **runestone** is the oldest on Öland and tells of a Danish Viking who died in the 10C. Another 8km brings you back to the bridge.

5

Kalmar to Jönköping and Skara

Total distance 322km. Kalmar—road 25, 109km **Växjö**—road 30, 97km junction
with E4—20km **Jönköping**—coast road 7km junction with 47/48—39km roads
split—road 47, 25km **Falköping**—road 184, 25km **Skara**.

Road 25 from Kalmar to Växjö enters the forests of Småland, Swedish
glass-making country. Sixteen firms, ranging from Orrefors with nearly 400
workers down to Eneryda with a dozen, nestle in forest clearings.

In 1742 two retired generals, Koskull and Stael von Holstein, decided to start a
glass-factory and coined the name Kosta from the first letters of their names. So the
Swedish glass industry began.

In the glass-making process soda and potash are added to sand to lower the melting
point. These create bubbles, so saltpetre and antimony or arsenic are added. These
last two also help to decolorise the glass. Swedish sand with its high iron content does
not produce clear glass, so sand is imported from Britain, Holland and Belgium. The
red lead which gives glass its lustre, weight and that ringing sound, is a stabiliser. To
be called lead crystal, glass must have 24 per cent lead, and heavy lead crystal has 30
per cent. Health considerations now mean that the preparation of materials is done
centrally at Emmaboda for the whole Swedish glass industry.

In the workshops, craftsmen using blowing-pipes collect lumps of glass at 1200°C
from the furnaces, which are then smoothed by rolling on a metal plate. Air is blown
in, more glass is added, more shaping is done, coloured glass may be added, on the
inside or the outside or as a sandwich. The glass or vase must be kept turning or it will
distort, so trolleys with a surface of continually revolving wheels are used where a pipe
can be laid to revolve gently. The craftsmen work in teams. Some teams blow
free-hand, that is, without using a mould—free-hand blown glass is smoother and
shinier. It can be shaped by thick wooden scoops, scissors, flat metal or from time to
time a cool blast of air from an air-nozzle can be directed on to a specific spot. Stems
are coaxed out from the bottoms of glasses, feet are added, and a glass is created.

Engraving is done with grinding-discs or industrial diamonds in a hand-held drill on
a pattern which has been stencilled and painted on to the surface. A fixed copper
wheel can also be used. By boring a hole in the bottom the piece can be engraved from
inside using a water-chilled drill to reduce dust. Etching is done in an acid bath when
the negative of the pattern has first been traced in lacquer or wax. For cut glass,
carborundum or sandstone plates are used and the piece is finally polished with
pumice or by dipping in acid.

If the glass is painted with enamel this then has to be fired in a kiln. (At Strömbergshyttan you can try glass-painting for yourself.) Gold-painted detail has to be fired also,
and the shine revived by polishing with bloodstone.

Thirty or forty people will have worked on each piece before it is ready for sale. But
everyday pieces will probably have been either turned rather like pottery, cast for
decorative figures or blocks, pressed for the nearest thing to mass-production or spun
in a mould for bowls and vases with a pattern. Artworks in glass are now an important
area of production, but on a more mundane level the 'seconds' shop at each glassworks
is full of affordable delights. For example, 'snowball' candleholders are more or less
globular with a deep hole to take a nightlight-type candle and almost every glassworks
produces one or more variants. They say that the first one was in fact thrown into snow
and acquired a surface like rough ice.

Depending on the size of the enterprise there will be guided tours, a
museum, art gallery and a restaurant or café. (Usually visitors are welcome
(Mon to Fri until 15.00); most glassworks—*Glasbruk*—are well signposted.)
Road 25 passes by or near to the following glassworks: Pukeberg

(household and art glass), Nybro (ditto), Boda (bowls and vases), Åfors (art designs), Johansfors (Kosta Boda stemware), Skruf (hand-made), Bergdala (stemware and art), Strömbergshyttan (glass-painting). Further off the route, on road 28, are (12km) Sea (ornamental), and (2km) Kosta (large variety, museum and gallery). On road 31 16km from Nybro is **Orrefors**, second in the world for the production of crafted glass (after the Irish Waterford company), with every facility for tourists, and Målerås, Älghult, Rosdala and Lindshammer are on or near the same road.

The other thing the Småland forests are famous for is a large population of elks, which come out at dusk to browse at the edge of the woods.

Back on road 25 at **Lessebo** 71km from Kalmar there is a mill producing hand-made paper (open Mon–Fri 07.00–11.30, 12.30–16.00, guided tours in summer; museum).

Växjö (pop. 47,000) is another 38km. The town has a modern look, since after many fires little remains of its venerable past. St. Sigfrid, the English monk who baptised Olof Skötkonung, founded the church. It was a bishopric as early as the 1160s and by the 14C a market town. Its school, still standing, taught the botanist Carl von Linné (Linnaeus) and Per Henrik Ling, the father of Swedish gymnastics in the 18C. The 19C romantic poet Esaias Tegnér was bishop here and is buried in the graveyard.

Tourist bureau: Kronobergsgatan 8. Tel. (0470) 414 10.

Post office: Kronobergsgatan 18-20.

Travel information: Tel. 020 76 70 76. (Dial 020 even in town—cheap rate.)

Telephone, telegram: Kronobergsgatan 14. Tel. (0470) 464 90.

Follow the signs to the centre. The twin spires of the cathedral are to the south-east of the main square. The **tourist bureau** is in an old wooden house visible from the square (closed Sat pm and Sun, but leaflets can usually be taken from the letterbox). There are some solid 19C buildings about the centre such as the county governor's residence on the north of the square and the former town hall on the south.

The **cathedral** (open daily 08.00–20.00) was largely rebuilt in 1958–60 to restore the original medieval appearance, after an unsuccessful 19C attempt to recreate a Gothic church with an enthusiastic application of step-gables. In the porch a large plaque gives an eventful potted history: founded by St. Sigfrid in the 11C, burnt in 1276, ravaged by the Danes in 1570 and 1611, struck by lightning in 1740 and burnt, rebuilt 1746.

All this ensures that the artwork and fittings are modern. The **altar** has a striking bronze cross with behind it stained glass containing the words of a Swedish hymn, both designed by Jan Brazda, who also designed the font and pulpit. The **mosaic** in the south transept is by Bo Beskow and takes its themes from the Book of Revelations, with the 12 gates of the heavenly Jerusalem, and seven angels with trumpets. In the north transept is a painting of the Last Supper by Georg Engelhard Schröder (1751) which used to hang behind the altar.

In the nave floor a large brass S marks the spot where St. Sigfrid is said to have been buried.

Sigfrid, a missionary bishop sent by King Ethelred of England to evangelise the Norwegians and Swedes, baptised King Olof Skötkonung at Husaby in 1008. This is the real beginning of Christianity in Sweden after the failed attempts by Ansgar and others in earlier centuries. Sigfrid consecrated bishops to work in Sweden and founded his church in Växjö. He died here c 1045.

At the back of the church is a small chapel with faded remnants of 16C murals. The two stained-glass **windows** are by Bo Beskow, with the Tree of Life, and the Contest for Everyman, with a knight playing chess with Death. The organ is from 1940.

Up in the tower (keep climbing) is a small **museum** with vestments and coins, a 14C silver chalice, an 18C silver baptismal bowl, some memorial tablets and 18C tombstones.

To the north of the cathedral stands the handsome grammar school built between 1696 and 1715, and nearby is the statue of Esaias Tegnér the poet who was bishop here 1824–46, and an 11C runestone, whose inscription says it was erected by Tyke to Gunnar son of Grim. In the Linnépark beside the cathedral there is a bust of Carl von Linné the botanist.

Just across the bridge over the railway to the south is the building which makes Växjö a Mecca for Swedish-Americans, *Utvandrarnas Hus, the House of Emigrants (open Mon–Fri 09.00–16.00, Sat 11.00–15.00, Sun 13.00–17.00; archives open for private research Mon–Fri).

In Sweden in the 1860s a marked deterioration in the climate brought years of poor harvests, while from 1820 to 1860 the population had increased more than ever before. The system of strip-farming had previously led to problems, and in 1827 one of the most far-reaching of the land-reform acts was passed to amalgamate the strips into more viable areas, but this could not keep pace with the population, and also broke up the old social network. There were also many smallholders farming land previously not considered worth working, with a poor return. The Industrial Revolution attracted some to the towns, but life there was not much better in a restrictive stagnant society.

The idea of going to America was fostered by the increase in ease of communication, both in spreading the word about America, and in the feasibility of actually moving one's family and possessions. The welcome offered by America beckoned, with the possibility of owning land, and the need for workers on the American railroads and in other industries.

Between 1846 and 1930 c 1.3 million Swedes emigrated. The first great wave went in 1868–72, and others followed in the 1880s, 1890s and up to the First World War. Almost 20 per cent of the emigrants came from Småland and some parishes lost over 1000 people. America-fever took hold and the dream was self-perpetuating, though in fact one-fifth of the emigrants returned to Sweden eventually.

The journey was daunting—train to Gothenburg, ship to Hull, train to Liverpool and voyage to America. Eighty per cent of emigrants went through Gothenburg, and Sillgatan (Herring Street) there was devoted to hotels, restaurants and offices for them. By 1900 there were more Swedes in Chicago than in Gothenburg. In 1915 the Swedish-American Line started and emigrants could sail directly to the States.

In America many were pioneering farmers. One-tenth of all young men worked at some time on the railway. One entrepreneur said: 'Give me snuff, whiskey and Swedes and I will build a railroad to Hell'. Many of the women became sought-after domestics. Whole streets in some towns were Swedish, often called Snuff Street.

Växjö devotes the second weekend in August to celebrating the American connection.

On the ground floor of the House of Emigrants the permanent exhibition is called the **Dream of America**. There are photos, graphs and figures, mostly with English labels, showing living conditions in Sweden, conditions on the ships, work in America, Swedish churches, clubs and newspapers established by Swedes in America. Recordings with more information in Swedish and English are available.

Part of the exhibition deals with Vilhelm Moberg (1898–1973) the writer who is pre-eminently associated with the emigrant theme. He was born near Växjö, became an editor in Vadstena, but came to fame with his four *Emigrant* novels (1947–59; available in English translation). A room is devoted to him, and his study is recreated. His books have become so much a part of the Swedish perception of the emigrant years that his characters have almost taken on a life of their own. The most famous are Karl-Oskar and his wife Kristina, the subjects of the sculpture shown here (and in Karlshamn), and there is a display of dolls portraying Moberg's characters elsewhere in the museum. His vast quantity of research material was part of the basis for the archives of the Emigrant Institute, founded in 1965. Its collections of emigrant data are unique, and can be consulted. They contain church and club records, and many thousands of books, with much material also on computer disk.

Many works of art inspired by the emigrant saga are on display. Carl Milles' **fountain** in the courtyard shows a great fish with emigrants on its back. Other displays in the museum show such things as envelopes with postmarks from American towns with Swedish names, and how the very first emigrants tried to establish New Sweden in Delaware 1638–55.

Next to the House of Emigrants is the **Småland Museum** (same opening hours, English leaflet available). In the gardens are a few old local buildings, a windmill and a poor farmer's cottage. Entrance is through the newer section adjoining the old building on the hill.

The comprehensive *glass collection on the first floor has pride of place, as it documents the history of Swedish glass in chronological order. There is a considerable coin collection with bank-notes and medals from Sweden and around the world. Elsewhere are prehistoric and medieval finds from Småland, a corridor of 19C workshops, and local painting. The textiles collection shows costumes and techniques. Another section has exhibits from the life of Christina Nilsson, the opera singer, born near Växjö (1843–1921). A new conference centre, incorporating the 1912 bathhouse and overlooking Teaterparken, contains a concert-hall, art gallery, restaurant and café.

6km north of the centre are the imposing ruins of **Kronoberg Castle**, signposted *Kronobergs slottsruin*. It lies on an island in lake Helga, and is approached by a wooden footbridge (open summer 09.00–21.00, tickets at the café, itself an interesting old building). In medieval times the bishops of Växjö had their castle here. In the mid 1540s the rebel leader Nils Dacke captured it but Gustav Vasa won it back and remodelled it into a four-sided fortress, which however suffered in the next century at the hands of the Danes. Remains of the 15C are in the west and north wings. The various sections are provided with plans and explanations in English. From the jetty nearby the veteran wood-fired pleasure steamer *Thor* (1887) offers trips on the lake.

In the other direction in the southern suburb of Teleborg stands a more modern tourist attraction, **Ekotemplet**—the Echo Temple. In 1974 Växjö acquired a new water-tower, a drum standing on concrete legs. It was soon discovered that this produced a gratifying echo from the concave base of the water-drum, under the 4.5 million litres of water, and so many visitors came that a car park had to be laid out for them. *Teleborgs slott* nearby is a turn-of-the-century 'castle' (guided tours).

A narrow-gauge railway runs between Växjö and Västervik on the east coast (187km). It was abandoned by the State railways and is now run by a group of enthusiasts.

Excursions from Växjö

Bergkvara, Huseby and **Råshult**. Leave Växjö by road 23 going south-west. After 3km there is a sign to **Bergkvara** on the right where on the edge of a lake are the remains of a 15C keep once owned by the Trolle family. The later manor was built in 1780 and the grounds can be visited.

At (8km) Snugge there is the cottage where the singer Christina Nilsson was born, and after 6km you reach **Huseby Bruk** (open in summer, guided tours in Swedish of the manor at 13.00. Plan in English available from the tourist bureau on site). The ironworks was started in the 17C using bog ore from local lakes. In the 1840s the wealthy brothers Hugo and Malcolm Hamilton built the manor for themselves and furnished it appropriately, but they came upon hard times and had to sell the house and most of the furniture to Josef Stephens. To these were added the many-sided collections of Josef's father, an English professor, and Josef's daughter Florence in turn preserved and added to the collections until her death in 1979.

The first few buildings of the estate are used for selling antiques and pottery, and a bridge leads into the main area, where the water-mill has been set working again. To the right beyond the mill the large building is the **museum** where the history and examples of the products of the ironworks can be seen. The blast furnace was working until 1930.

The **manor house** is crammed with many and varied works of art and curios. Most of the iron items in the building, such as the balcony, stoves, light-fittings and mirror-frames, were made on the property. There are some original wallpapers and some older furniture. Among the heterogeneous collections may be mentioned a Meissen urn, a Brussels carpet, a small Rembrandt, jewellery belonging to Queen Kristina, a medieval figure of Christ, porcelain, silver and Sami handicrafts. Curiosities include a primitive shower-bath, some items which belonged to Queen Victoria, and a tiled stove with a recess used as an incubator for premature babies.

Also in the grounds is the **Statarmuseum**, an estate worker's cottage of the 19C, and a nature display in an old granary. Other buildings are those used for the farm which Josef Stephens started—dairy, carpenter's workshop, saw-works and so on.

After 34km a sign points to **Linnés Råshult** (5km), where Carl von Linné (1707–78) was born as Carl Linnaeus, son of the curate. He went to school in Växjö, then to Lund and Uppsala universities where he studied medicine. He travelled to Lappland in 1732 and spent some years in Holland, also visiting England and France. He became Admiralty physician in 1739 and professor of botany at Uppsala in 1741. His *Species Plantarum* and *Systema Naturae* revolutionised and systematised the classification of plants and animals. He was ennobled as Carl von Linné in 1762. The cottage has been rebuilt to give an impression of how it looked when Linné was born and contains some of his belongings (open mid-April to mid-Sept 09.00–18.00).

Dädesjö, **Granhult** and **Drev**. These three medieval churches can be reached by taking road 23 to the north-east towards Åseda. After 23km a sign points to **Dädesjö** on road 31. Follow the signs, and the new church is visible on the right, while the old church is set back on the left, a modest stone rectangle, in the churchyard. The Romanesque *painted wooden ceiling* was only preserved because an extra floor was put in for storage when the church was abandoned for the new one. The original chancel has gone, the arch being filled with stone slabs. The ceiling decoration (13C) consists of 28 roundels containing scenes from the Christmas gospel, together with legends from other sources. There are some notes in English but a full list only in Swedish, most of which can however be understood, but the three wise men are split up, Caspar being on his own and Balthazar and Melchior together (Nos 17 to 20, counting from the back, left to right).

Some themes are: No. 7 Gabriel foretelling the Virgin's death to her; No. 13 Herod ordering the slaughter of the innocents; No. 11 a legendary miracle associated with St. Stephen. No. 16 is another miracle legend and the last four are simply angels. It is assumed that these were painted by an artist named Sighmunder who signed his name in runes below the painting of St. Knut under the chancel arch. There are medieval wooden figures of the Virgin on the left and St. Olof on the right of the altar. The low stone benches at the sides are original. There are very faded wall-paintings, on the north wall the Passion of Christ and on the south the entrance into Jerusalem.

To get to Granhult from Dädesjö continue for 11km towards Lenhovda on road 31 and turn left (7km) still on the 31. (The short cut through Asby is unsurfaced.) Another kilometre or so brings you to the isolated wooden church of **Granhult**, built around 1220. It is known that it acquired its covering of wooden shingles some time later, since it was found that the walls under the shingles bore traces of weatherworn paint. The bell-tower is from the 17C.

Inside, the crucifix and background painting over the altar were done in 1699 by a Växjö artist. The chancel and nave **paintings** from the Book of Revelations are from the mid 18C, probably by an artist called Johan Zschotzscher. Some roundels can be seen underneath which may link the medieval decoration with Dädesjö. The chandeliers are 18C. In the vestry the paintings on the walls from the Old Testament are from the 17C and that of Christ on the ceiling from the early 18C. On the right wall of the chancel is a boarded-up leper squint. At the rear of the church a shrine with St. Olof, with the traditional human-faced dragon beneath his feet, and a Madonna and Child probably from Lübeck, are from the 15C.

Continue north on road 31 and after 5km rejoin the 23, and in 10km take a road right to Braås. Take a left at the (3km) crossroads and in another 3km follow the signs to *Drevs gamla kyrka* (2km). If the outsize key is not in the lock it can be requested at the yellow house.

The granite church of **Drev** consists of nave, chancel and apse, built about 1200. The **wall-paintings** executed in the 17C in the chancel represent the 12 apostles, in the apse the four Evangelists. Over the chancel arch are scenes from the Passion of Christ, while to left and right are wooden figures of the Madonna and Child, and St. Olof. In 1751 the scrolls in the apse, and the ceilings of the nave and chancel, were painted by Johan Zschotzscher, who also decorated the galleries and pews. Under the gallery are faded crowns and wreaths which were used to decorate coffins of children. The carved pulpit with Christ and the Evangelists dates from 1702.

Take road 30 out of Växjö to the north along the lake of Helgasjön. After 55km **Hjälmseryds Old Church** (*g:la k:a*, 7km past the new one) is a restored 12C building. In 10km you can turn off to **Nydala** (8km), the site of an important 12C Cistercian monastery. The mother-house being Clairvaux, 'bright valley', this one was named 'new valley' in Swedish, *Nydala*. Some parts of the medieval church are incorporated into the 17C one, which has a Baroque interior. There are remains of the monastery itself and also the parish church of the 15C.

In 32km road 30 joins the E4 which reaches Jönköping in 20km.

Jönköping (pop. 76,000) was given its town charter by Magnus Ladulås in 1284, but little remains of its long history. Gustav II Adolf had the town centre moved from the west to the east side of the lake of Munksjön, which is linked to Vättern by a short canal. Gustav also founded the beginnings of an arms factory, soon moved to Huskvarna. Some buildings remain from the 17C and 18C. Jönköping achieved fame in the 19C with the founding of the match factory, and the paper industry, started in 1862, was another source of prosperity. It is the administrative centre of the county of the same name, which is one of the three divisions once forming the very large Småland province, the other two being centred on Växjö and Kalmar.

The Match Industry. Experiments in various countries had developed a match in which phosphorus was used on the striking head, which proved both poisonous to the workers and dangerous in the box when the heads rubbed against each other. In 1855 Johan Edvard Lundström of Jönköping perfected the safety match using red amorphous phosphorus on the striking surface of the box itself. The Swedish match then went from strength to strength. In 1917 Ivar Kreuger formed Svenska Tändsticks AB and gradually obtained a complete monopoly of match production in a dozen countries, by extremely dubious methods. In the Depression his vast financial empire collapsed and he committed suicide in 1932. Today matches are no longer made here, but visitors can see the factory, now a museum.

Tourist bureau: Djurläkartorget 2. Tel. (036) 10 50 50.

Post office: Landmätargränd 5.

Bus station: Beside station. Travel information tel. (036) 19 95 50.

Telephone, telegram: Västra Storgatan 4. Tel. (036) 19 13 31.

The **tourist bureau** is in the comparatively new station complex on the lakeside—the station may have to be moved as it is already unsuitable for faster modern trains. Just along from the complex the area labelled *Tänd-sticksområdet* (Match Area) is the former industrial section of the town, now devoted to museums, theatre and crafts. The **Tändsticksmuseum** (Match Museum) is in a low grey wooden factory building of 1848 (open June–Aug Mon–Fri 10.00–17.00, Sat, Sun 10.00–15.00, rest of year closed Mon, shorter hours; copious English notes to borrow). Here the process of match-manu-facture can be followed with all the machinery on show, and models of the workers at their tasks, many of whom worked at home. Upstairs there is a large collection of match-box labels and a video is shown, in English on request.

In the surrounding buildings there are workshops, and a radio museum. Almost opposite the further end of the area is the wooden Johan III's Hospital (1570, restored), now a museum devoted to Victor Rydberg a local writer.

Going back east along Västra Storgaten you come to the Rådhus (town hall) in its gardens, and soon cross the short canal which joins the lakes of Vättern and Munksjön. The road now becomes Östra Storgatan and in another 500m there is the Kristine Church of 1673.

The area south from here has many old wooden houses. Turn right and right again to get to Östra Torget and, shortly after, Hovrättstorget, with a modern fountain showing symbols of Swedish laws and lawgivers such as Birger Jarl and Magnus Ladulås. This is appropriate, because on the south side is Göta Hovrätt, a 17C courthouse. On the west is the 17C town hall.

South again from Hovrättstorget is **Jönköpings Länsmuseum** in a modern building of interesting design (see the west end). Here is shown the history of the area over 10,000 years, with archaeology, some medieval items and progressing as far as the sewing-machine. Upstairs you can see into the workshop of a museum conservation expert, and there is a collection of Swedish art, concentrating on the work of John Bauer.

To get to the **Stadspark**, drive out along Västra Storgatan and follow the signs left at Dunkelhallavägen. From here there is a view over the town. On the left of the entrance beyond the restaurant is a commendable

Fågelmuseum (Bird Museum, open May–Aug; information in English). This has 1500 stuffed birds and 2500 eggs, representing species found in Sweden around the turn of the century when the collection was formed.

From the car park, signs point rather vaguely to various attractions. Straight ahead is the Friluftsmuseum (open-air museum). For the animal enclosures (Djurhagar) climb up to the right and take the left turn at the T-junction. The right turn leads to Bäckaby church and the bell-tower (Klockstapel). The oldest parts of the church are from the 14C (not always open).

On the left of the road towards Huskvarna not far beyond Saturnus Plan there is a rose garden, **Rosenlunds Rosarium**. **Rosenlund Nature Reserve** is a kilometre or so beyond, on the edge of the lake.

At the road junction to the east of the town there is a new shopping precinct which straddles the E4, Nya A6 Köpcenter or A6 Center for short, named after a regiment. Besides shops and restaurants, there is the absorbing **Tropikhuset** (the Tropical House) showing snakes, monkeys, crocodiles, fish, spiders, frogs and parrots—they are particularly proud of their home-bred dwarf marmosets. There is also the Forsvarsmuseum, dealing with the history of local defensive methods from the 14C on.

(For Huskvarna see Rte 13.)

North Småland has some attractions amid the forests. The principal road not covered by other routes is the E4 from Helsingborg (241km) which enters Jönköping from the south. Along the way **Ljungby** (111km from Jönköping) may be mentioned as including a delightful village of old buildings one of which has a collection of *bonader*, painted peasant wall-hangings. (Tourist bureau, information in English.) To the north-west of Värnamo (72km from Jönköping) near Kulltorp, is **High Chaparral**, a complete village like the set of a Western film with many events and activities for children and Western fans (June–Aug). **Smålandsstenar**, 40km to the west of Värnamo has the 'Småland Stones' which give the place its name—six prehistoric stone circles, 1.5km north-east of the town.

To the east of Jönköping, roads 31 and then 33 go towards **Västervik** (174km) on the E coast, a very attractive resort with a ruined castle, an old church and quaint boatmen's cottages. On the way, **Eksjö** (63km) has a picturesque and well-preserved Old Town area in three streets to the north of the main square. 62km further on, at **Vimmerby**, a children's story-book village has been arranged, based on the tales of Astrid Lindgren (creator of Pippi Longstocking). Fun, but expensive and can be crowded.

Leave Jönköping by the coast road to join (7km) the 47/48 following signposts to Skövde and Falköping. 7km after joining the 47/48 a sign points to *Habo church** (3km) (open in summer). This large wooden church built in 1723 has a nave and two lower aisles, which is unusual for a church made of wood, plus galleries built in on either side. There are pews for the gentry in cubicles beside the altar. Every surface of the interior is covered with *paintings** carried out by two artists 1741–43. The side walls illustrate the ten commandments with stories from the Old Testament, and on the ceilings under the galleries there is the Creed with pictures of the apostles, while above the galleries is the Lord's Prayer. The organ gallery is painted with ladies playing musical instruments. The two painters' work may be distinguished, since one has a more formal style in darker colours and the other paints more freely in lighter and softer colours. The sandstone altar is medieval, and the high altarpiece (1723) is crowned with a figure of

Christ. An unusual addition is the clock between the two main parts. High on the pulpit canopy but not so high as Christ on top of the altar stands a figure of Death. The sacristy is the only part of the church built in stone and contains somewhat damaged medieval carvings including a large 13C one of John the Baptist.

After 25km the 47 and 48 go their separate ways.

Before continuing on the 47 to Falköping you may like to take the 48 to see the churches of Suntak and Skörstorp. After 11km on the 48 follow signs to *Suntaks gamla k:a, hidden among trees, near a manor called Marieberg. With simple nave, chancel and apse, the exterior of the church looks very much as it did when it was built at the end of the 12C, except for the windows and roof, though the apse still has an old window opening. Inside the impression is of an 18C church painted all over in cheerful peasant-Baroque, though there are older faded paintings in the chancel by Master Amund (end 15C). The ceiling paintings are from 1769, the pulpit 1713 and the pews from the same period. The galleries are similarly painted. In the chancel is a copy of the 12C Suntak chair (original in the museum in Skara).

You can take road 193 just ahead to get back to the 47 and on the way you pass the little circular church of (9km) **Skörstorp**. (If locked ask for the key at the yellow house.) It was originally built for defence and the chancel, apse and chapel were added later. The extraordinary spire is from 1660. Inside it has been over-restored and re-restored, with now only the peasant Baroque altar and pulpit of the 18C as decorative elements. After 4km you can rejoin the 47, 15km from the 47/48 junction.

You will now see signposts including the word Ekomuseum. In the area between Falköping in the north and Ulricehamn to the south, historical sites have been grouped under this heading (cf. Bergslagen, Rte 14B), to give a picture of the district's history. All tourist bureaux in the area have leaflets in English.

To Karleby, Åsle Tå and Kungslena

Another 4km on the 47 brings a turn for **Karleby** (2km) where the modern road follows a very ancient communication route. Strung along the road for almost 3km are 13 Stone Age passage graves and nine stone cists, easily accessible. The largest passage grave, 17m, is called Ragvald's Grave. On the other side of the road is a very long row of farmhouses, an ancient dwelling site.

You can continue for 6km to Åsle and take the turn right in the village for **Åsle Tå**, almost immediately on your left. This is an open-air museum where all the cottages, some with turf roofs, are on their original sites and were inhabited by the very poorest people. Most were built in the 18C and 19C, and at least one was lived in until the 1960s. Some are furnished and can be visited in summer, and at other seasons one can wander around and look through the windows. The pig sties (*svinstian*) are nearly as big as the houses. A museum and an agricultural museum have been added. Right at the end of the straggling village is a little watermill.

From here you can continue north-east to **Kungslena** church (9km; open May–Sept) which is said to have been founded by King Erik Knutsson in memory of the battle of Lena near here in 1208 against Sverker Karlsson. The three spires are supposed to commemorate a meeting of three Scandinavian rulers in 1258, Birger Jarl of Sweden, Hakon of Norway and Valdemar of Denmark. The vault-paintings of swirling foliage are by Johan Risberg (1749). By a building in front of the church is a boulder which had to be lifted three times by any labourer who wanted employment, and seven times if he wished to marry the farmer's daughter.

Back on the 47, it is 6km to **Falköping**. The town (pop. 15,000) was first mentioned in the 12C, but since the area around contains about two-thirds of Sweden's 370 passage-graves, it is assumed that this was the first area to be settled in the New Stone Age, when the climate was warmer than now and favourable for first attempts at agriculture.

The **tourist bureau** is at Trädgårdsgatan 22.

You enter Falköping on Odengatan. Where this crosses St. Olofsgatan turn left to **S:t Olof church**. There is a legend that St. Sigfrid chose the site for this church in the 11C. The present church was built in the early 12C and was unusually large, possibly because the priest here often was also active at Skara cathedral. In the 13C the vaults were built and the nave lengthened. The tower came a couple of centuries later. Burnt by the Danes in 1566, it was later repaired. There are four wooden figures of the Evangelists from the 17C, two in the chancel and two under the organ. A leper-squint is to be seen on the right of the chancel.

South of the church is **Gamla stan**, with several streets of old buildings.

Return to Odengatan and cross straight over. A couple of hundred metres along on your left is the **Kyrkerör**, a New Stone Age passage-grave. Another couple of hundred metres along is the **museum** with a collection of local finds concentrating on the New Stone Age, and four models of S:t Olof's at various stages (open daily, pm).

Return again to Odengatan and turn right. At the roundabout turn right into Danska vägen. 350m along on the right, between Nos 201 and 203, is the enormous **King Björn's Grave**, 10.5m by 3m. It is New Stone Age but since Bronze Age finds were discovered there it was presumably re-used.

Another passage-grave can be seen at **Luttra** 6km south of Falköping on road 46, but there are so many of them in the region they cannot all be listed, and the same applies to medieval churches. For example, **Gökhem** (signposted from road 47, 8km west of Falköping), is mainly Romanesque with two 12C fonts, 15C paintings by Master Amund, the painter of Södra Råda, and a large wooden bell-tower.

Continue on the 184 (Danska vägen) north of Falköping. On the left at the edge of town is **Mösseberg**, a spa with a park and viewing tower. After 7km you could take the road right to **Gudhem** (1km), with the ruins of a Cistercian convent (1161) founded by King Karl Sverkersson. It was a stopping-place for pilgrims from the continent on their way to St. Olof's shrine at Trondheim. The finds from the excavations are in a small museum. Skara (see below) is now 18km by road 184 but going by way of Varnhem is highly recommended.

At Gudhem continue 3km on the same road, turn left at the T-junction and **Ekornavallen** is 3km further. On the left you see a couple of large fields on a slope, scattered with stones. There are four passage-graves, a cairn at the top of the hill, a stone cist, four round stone settings and assorted standing stones. The area was first used for burials in about 3000 BC, and continued to be used for 4000 years, through the New Stone Age, Bronze and Iron Ages. Ekornavallen is believed to have been the site of a 'ting' meeting in the 1220s at which the first provincial code of laws was formulated. The nearby lake, **Hornborgasjön**, attracts bird-watchers who come to watch the 'dance' of the cranes arriving in April from their winter quarters in Spain.

Continue on the same road to (12km) **Varnhem**. A Cistercian monastery was founded here in 1150 by monks from Alvastra using the mother-church at Clairvaux as their main model. The ruins are beside the church and clearly show the lay-out, with a small plan on a plinth to display the whole complex. A museum beyond the churchyard shows finds from the excavations. The oldest part now remaining of the church is the nave (1180–1234). After a fire in 1234 the semi-circular apse with chapels, and the vaulting, were built. In the mid 17C the church had fallen into disrepair, and Magnus Gabriel de la Gardie restored it to be his own burial place. It was he who added the buttresses and spires.

Magnus Gabriel de la Gardie (1622–86) belonged to one of the country's most influential and wealthy families, and became a favourite of Queen Kristina. He married Maria Euphrosyne, sister of King Karl X Gustav, and at one time owned over 1000 properties. During his lifetime he held several of the highest offices, including those of royal chancellor and treasurer, and head of the regency council for Karl XI. But he fell out of favour, lost his properties, and died in poverty.

As you enter the church there is the long lost (reconstructed) **tomb** of Birger Jarl (d 1266) the forerunner of the Folkung dynasty. Behind it is the reconstructed medieval lay brothers' altar. The pews are 17C, as is the **pulpit** by Georg Baselaque, de la Gardie's own sculptor, portraying seven virtues, and the de la Gardie arms. In the sacristy on the left can be seen a medieval piscina. The five **chapels** around the apse are memorial chapels for ancient kings, whose graves are under the floor near the high altar. The chapels have exuberant 17C vault decoration with a hanging crown in each. The first on the left is for King Erik Eriksson (1250) and the second Erik Knutsson (1216). The middle chapel is dedicated to three kings, the main one being Knut Eriksson (1196). The other two chapels are in memory of Inge Stenkilsson (1064) and, with an altar only, Birger Jarl.

Next come the two de la Gardie **burial chapels** with a **memorial chapel** in between. On the left are buried Gustav Adolf de la Gardie and his wife Elisabeth Oxenstierna in a tomb by Burchardt Precht, and on the right are Magnus himself and his wife Maria Euphrosyne of Pfalz-Zweibrücken. His sarcophagus was also designed by Burchardt Precht and the marble busts are presumed to be by Nicolaes Millich. In the chapel between are statues of Magnus (right) and his father Jakob, dressed as Romans, with banners and coats of arms.

From Varnhem take road 49 to (14km) Skara.

Skara (pop. 11,000) has a long history and was a cult-site in the Iron Age. By the early Middle Ages it had established itself as an important centre of communications, but its real significance derives from the establishment here in the early 11C of the first cathedral in Sweden and it was the heart of Swedish Christianity. (Lund cathedral is older but founded on what was then Danish soil.) Adam of Bremen mentions it and its founder King Olof Skötkonung in the 11C. In 1335 King Magnus Eriksson proclaimed the ending of serfdom here. Since the town's importance derived from the church, it was hard hit by the Reformation, but began to re-establish itself this time in the field of education, beginning as early as the 17C. Today Skara is known for its series of schools teaching the more unusual subjects—cycling, agriculture, stage arts, advertising and horse-management. The **tourist bureau** is at Skolgatan 1 behind the cathedral. Tel. (0511) 325 80.

The **cathedral** stands by the main square.

The first church on the site of the cathedral was consecrated in the mid 12C. It suffered attack and fire again and again and has been heavily restored, rebuilt and remodelled over the centuries. In the 13C and 14C it became successively early Gothic and Decorated, and in the following century Johan III had it richly embellished inside and out. After more Baroque refurbishing in the 18C, a 19C photograph shows a very different building from that of today with flat roofs on the towers known as 'the trousers of Skara'. It was in the late 19C under the direction of Helgo Zetterwall that an attempt was finally made to return to the 14C design, including plain rib vaulting in the nave, barrel-vaults in the aisles and the new triforium, a feature unique in Sweden. Some English influence may be discerned in the square east end instead of an apse.

The high altar (1663) by Hans Swant of Gothenburg depicts Christ's Birth, Resurrection and Ascension. Behind the high altar is a case showing ecclesiastical seals. The pulpit is from 1709 and the font from 1600. On the organ gallery are attractive figures of angels playing instruments.

Remains of the 12C crypt are accessible from the left of the chancel. In a grave here was found a tiny chalice belonging to Bishop Adalvard (d 1065) and a copy is displayed. Also from the first church are the expressive **sandstone reliefs** over the door to the vestry, just beyond the steps to the crypt. The chapel here is named after Brynolf Algotsson who was bishop of Skara 1278–1317. The altar of the Crown of Thorns alludes to the relic of a thorn which the bishop acquired for Skara.

On the right of the chancel is the extravagant Baroque **tomb** of Colonel Erik Soop (d. 1632) and his wife Anna Posse, which was made in Amsterdam in 1637 by Pieter de Keyser. The figures and reliefs are of alabaster against black marble. On the pewter coffin and the monument itself are scenes from the Thirty Years War. The almost life-size figures of Mars and Minerva belong to the composition.

The eight **stained-glass windows** are by Bo Beskow, made between 1945 and 1976. The colours are deep and rich, the effect medieval but the design distinctively modern. The windows from left to right are: Creation, with Noah and representations of good and evil; Patriarchs, with the stories of Abraham, Isaac, Jacob and Joseph; Prophets, with history from captivity in Egypt to captivity in Babylon; Skara window, with pre-Christian and Christian symbols; East window, with the Book of Revelations; Nativity showing the birth and childhood of Christ; Gospel window, with scenes from the life of Christ; Passion window with the Crucifixion and Resurrection. (Old Testament windows are to be read from top to bottom, New Testament ones from bottom to top.)

In the main square south-west of the cathedral is a **fountain** by Nils Sjögren with episodes from the town's history. Just down the road in front of the cathedral are the **ruins** of S:t Nicolai church (11C). To the east of the cathedral the **tourist bureau** is housed in a mid 19C wooden house, while the chapter house, looking like an 18C villa, is to the south-east. The neo-Gothic edifice to the south is a school designed by Helgo Zetterwall in 1871. On the north is the Diocesan Library which houses valuable archives, including the 12C Skara Missal.

The road down the side of the library leads to the museum and open-air museum. On the way you pass **Krak** manor house which consists of three separate buildings, and represents a typical Swedish manor of the 18C. They contain furniture and pictures of the 18C and 19C which can be viewed by asking for a guide at the museum. The vaulted cellar (not original) contains a restaurant.

Skaraborgs Länsmuseum (open daily) was at the time of writing undergoing renovation and much may be changed. There are some good medieval artefacts in the basement. A reliquary of wood sheathed in gilded copper with ecclesiastical figures and geometric designs, crowned with two animal heads is one of the most striking exhibits. The richly embroidered **vestments** show work by the nuns of Vadstena as well as from France and Italy. The very early **Suntak chair** with a wolf's head on one arm rest has a runic inscription on the back and a Romanesque door with intricate iron-work has an elaborate locking system and huge key. A later exhibit is the small 17C **Bjurum organ** made in Nurnberg and once owned by Per Brahe in his castle on Visingsö Island in Lake Vättern. This is part of a valuable collection of instruments owned by the museum. Upstairs there is a section on the geology of Kinnekulle—pull out the drawers to see rock specimens. In the section on embroidery and textiles drawers can also be opened to see more examples. Other exhibits include globes and timepieces, and a bronze shield of 600 BC.

Next to the museum is the open-air museum (*fornbyn*—open daily, except Sat and Sun am, buildings open May to Sept). Here among the usual cottages and cowsheds are more eccentric exhibits, a wind-powered saw-mill, a flax-kiln, an early transformer and a megalithic tomb.

There is also a veterinary museum to the west of Krak manor.

A narrow-gauge steam train runs 12km between Skara and Lundsbrunn, a former spa.

6

The Island of Gotland

*GOTLAND (pop. 57,000), the largest island in the Baltic, lies about 90km from the Swedish coast and 140km from Latvia. From north to south it is about 140km, and 50km at its greatest breadth. It tilts from cliffs of up to 40m in the west down to sloping beaches in the east and south-east. It consists, unlike the granite mainland, but like Öland and Skåne, predomi-nantly of limestone, with some sandstone in the south. The sea has carved terraces, cliffs and the distinctive *raukar*, single rock stacks occurring often in groups.

The climate is slightly milder than in the rest of Sweden, and the island is rich in flora, including orchids. There are many species of birds, but few of animals, of which the Gotland pony is a small hardy breed.

Ferries to Gotland go from Nynäshamn just south of Stockholm, and Oskarshamn on the south-east coast. Crossing times vary from four to six hours, and in the summer there are two ferries a day from each port.

History. There are some remains from the Stone Age, and many cairns and stone-set-tings from the Bronze Age, but it was the Iron Age which brought the first wave of prosperity to the island, with trade with the Roman Empire and further afield. In late Viking times (9C and 10C) Gotland became the northern centre of trade routes, and the shallow-draught Viking ships could land on the shelving beaches of the east coast. Half of the 200,000 silver Viking Age coins found in Scandinavia were discovered in Gotland.

About the mid 12C, German merchants started to expand their field of activities into this Scandinavian/Slav trading area, and settled in Visby, a natural harbour on the west coast, making it the most important town in the early Hanse, when the latter was a collection of merchants' associations. The Gotlanders in the countryside became alienated from the town, and this was emphasised with the beginning of the town wall in the middle of the 13C. In 1288 civil war broke out, but in spite of this, the 13C was the golden age of Visby, when spacious homes and warehouses were built for the merchants, and the religious orders and others built or expanded churches. German wine, Russian furs, Swedish swords, Norwich cloth, East Indian spices, Byzantine gold and Spanish rice all passed through the capacious warehouses of Visby.

But the 14C spelt the end. The plague raged in 1350, but just as disastrous was the invasion of the Danes under Valdemar Atterdag in 1361. The Gotlanders mustered some ineffectual forces, but the merchants slammed the town gates on them while Valdemar slaughtered the islanders. Visby then surrendered.

By this time Lübeck was taking over as the principal Hanseatic city, as the Hanse evolved into an association of trading towns. Land routes became preferable to sea routes, so the centre of action shifted and Visby was never the same again. Gotland was overrun by privateers, then the Teutonic Knights ruled it briefly, after which it was squabbled over by Sweden and Denmark until 1645 when it finally became Swedish. During these centuries the great stronghold of Visborg was built, and later blown up, and in 1525 Lübeck forces attacked and burnt much of the town.

Gotland picture-stones

These constitute a unique genre. There are three basic types. In the first period from the 5C and 6C, the stones are 3m or so high, with geometric and spiral decoration, or pairs of animals confronting each other (good and evil?), dragons or rowing-boats. The next type is from the 6C and 7C and the stones are smaller, with zigzags, birds, animals and boats.

It is, however, the third type which is most impressive, for in the 8C they become large again, rather the shape of a keyhole, with a broad curved top, and strip-cartoon pictures with strapwork ornament developing into writhing animals. At the top there is often a horseman, and if the horse has eight legs it is Sleipnir, Odin's horse, because he can run twice as fast as other horses. There is sometimes a woman offering a drinking-horn and it is thought that she is welcoming the dead into Valhalla. The scenes of fighting men may represent the pleasures of martial arts in Valhalla. But the most splendid pictures are those of the rigged sailing-ships often occupying the largest area. The sails are made of broad plaited strips of cloth giving a chequered effect, and the rigging is clearly shown plaited also, with rows of shields along the edge of the boat. This is interpreted as the ship ferrying the dead to Valhalla. A runic inscription was occasionally added.

The best are from the 8C though they continued to be produced off and on until the 11C. Before about 700 they were erected in cemeteries but then began to be placed alongside roads and in other public places.

Gotland churches

Christianity came to Gotland in the 11C and it was included in the diocese of Linköping. In 1572, after the Reformation and when the island was Danish, the Maria church was chosen to be the cathedral. The other churches of Visby were allowed to crumble, so that there are now ten church ruins within the town walls.

In the countryside there are over 90 remaining medieval churches which developed their own modest but distinctive style. To those accustomed to the medieval treasures of Europe this is an art of small-scale delights which have to be sought out. The churches usually have a square west tower with a short spire or cap, often octagonal. The towers in later years became more decorative with more windows, and the finest are by the architect known as 'Egypticus', named thus from the similarity of some of his sculpture to aspects of ancient Egyptian work. There are frequently two doorways on the south, one being into the chancel.

The typical doorway is deep, with slim clustered columns and a narrow carved frieze along the capitals. Above the door is a steep triangular pediment or hood, going up to the eaves, often cusped. Occasionally there are no windows on the north side. The early fonts are excellent, by such masters as Byzantios, Majestatis and Sigraf (see Art and Architecture). Wall-paintings or traces of them remain in a large number of churches. The earliest are 12C Byzantine style figures, as at Garde and the latest are the late 15C 'Passion friezes' by the 'Passion master'. In between, from about 1250 to 1350, are some delightful depictions of saints and devils, people and animals, and scenes from everyday life. Unfortunately many are very faded. The stained glass, though important in Swedish art history because of its rarity, looks quite insignificant to European visitors. Dalhem has the earliest and Lye has the most.

A. Visby

The medieval gem of *Visby lies within its almost complete town wall, with buildings from the Middle Ages onwards fringing its narrow streets, many framed in climbing roses, which have a long flowering period here. The brochures like to call it the town of ruins and roses. Beyond the wall lie modern suburbs (total pop. 21,000).

Tourist bureau: Donnersplats. Tel. (0498) 210 982.

Post office: Donnersplats.

Bus station: Between Österport and Söderport.

Telephone, telegram: Adelsgatan 16. Tel. (0498) 21 90 20.

Cars are banned from within the wall in summer, unless you are lodging inside. Good car parking is to be found at the Österport (East Gate) and Söderport (South Gate), and more along by the harbour. Bicycles are for hire at reasonable rates at the harbour and Österport among other places. A tourist 'train' runs from Österport and Inre Hamn (harbour). There is a Medieval Week in August. English tours available—ask at the tourist bureau.

The *town wall is c 3.5km long, and 27 towers remain out of 29. Building has been kept away from the outside of the wall, so you can appreciate it very much as it has always been. It is first mentioned in 1288 and must have been begun about the middle of the 13C. There are two sections, the sea wall and the land wall. The sea wall along the coast, built first, was about 5.3m high, crenellated and with a wooden gallery on the inside for archers. The wall incorporated original buildings of which the most significant is Kruttornet, the Powder Tower, of the 12C. The land wall was at first 6m high, with more crenellations than the sea wall, and an archers' gallery was supported on arches which can best be seen near Norderport. The Kaisar-tornet (Emperor Tower) on the east was built at the same time at the wall.

Early in the 14C the land wall was raised 3–4m, and its remaining towers were constructed. Saddle-towers, resting on the wall, were added, of which

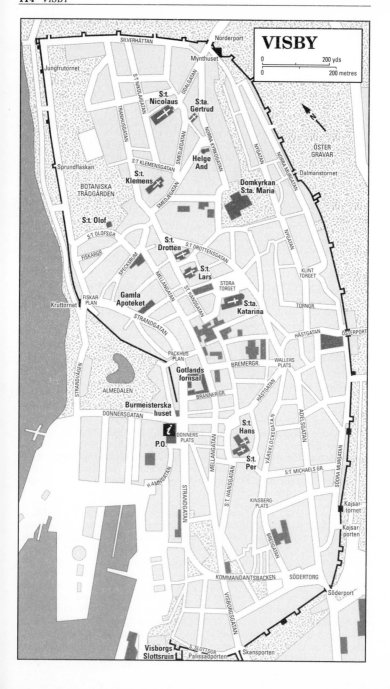

nine remain out of over 20. At the same time the sea wall was strengthened. Part of the wall is said to have been knocked down to allow Valdemar Atterdag's triumphal entry in 1361. The largest tower on the skyline is Dalmanstornet, once used as a guide mark for ships. At the beginning of the 15C Visborg castle was built against the wall to the south-west, and also in the 15C the sea wall towers Jungfrutornet (Maiden Tower), Sprund-flaskan and Kames were added. The defences were being strengthened even into the 18C.

Donnersplats is a square on the west side of Visby near the harbour, which is named after the substantial Donnerska house, now the post office and **tourist bureau**. Donnersplats is on Strandgatan, the Hanseatic high street, where wealthy merchants built lofty warehouses and dwellings, their gable-ends turned to the street. There are small plaques on some buildings with information in Swedish and English. The names of streets along here constitute a list of the towns with which Visby traded in the expansive Hanse days—Novgorod, Danzig, Lübeck (Lübska Gränd), Riga and Rostock, and elsewhere Bremen and Wismar are to be found.

Next to, but forward of the Donnerska house is the 17C wooden **Burmeisterska** house, built by a German merchant. Inside, the walls and ceilings are covered with lively decoration painted straight on to the planking, some with biblical scenes accompanied by German texts. There is a fireplace of 1662, a tiled stove and some furniture.

Opposite the Burmeisterska house is the **Naturmuseum**, with exhibits on Gotland's natural history (open summer 11.00–17.00). Continuing north, the tall narrow **Lange house** was a warehouse in the 13C and 14C. The brick-framed windows show the living-quarters.

The next building is ***Gotlands Fornsal**, the outstanding museum of Gotland history (open mid May to Aug 11.00–18.00, shorter hours in winter). The museum is mainly in an 18C brewery, but part of it is a medieval storehouse with restored interior on the lower floors. The ground floor has a good collection of ***picture-stones** (see above), large and small. In the next room are representative **burials** from the Stone Age, Bronze Age, Iron Age, Migration Period (c 500) and Viking. On the next floor, to the left, is a science and technology centre for children, and to the right objects from the Stone Age to the Viking period, with detailed English notes to borrow. The **treasury** has exhibits from some of the hundreds of treasure hoards found on Gotland, including a gilded weathervane. The Middle Ages shows trade, the civil war of 1288, and the building of the wall. There is a model of the fortress of Visborg. The Romanesque section has a model of a Gotland church with movable parts to illustrate the development of church architecture. The little ***Viklau Madonna** is among other wood-carved figures. The Gothic section has a collection of wood-carvings, with the retable from Ala and a triptych from Vall. From the textile section you can go down to the **medieval Visby** section in the restored storehouse, with a shop and merchant's office. Below this is the cellar with a model of Visby on a scale of 1:75, as viewed from a boat 100m off. Back on the first floor, this concludes with late and post medieval church art. The second floor has musical instruments, furnishing styles, an 18C farmhouse, a turn-of-the-century shop, and a costume display, and on the top floor is a section on seafaring.

The next buildings to the museum are the medieval **Liljehornska house**, and **Clematis house**, which functions as a 'medieval inn'. The small square here is Packhus Plan (Warehouse Square), with a fountain whose bronze figure represents the goddess of plenty. The gate in the wall here was a sea gate, and going out you find the site of the medieval harbour, now a park called *Almedalen*, with a duck-pond and one of the best views of the town. Here the wall itself, being the sea wall, is not so impressive, but because of that you can see the huddled buildings behind, towers, gables, tops of ruined churches, the cathedral and red roofs. Wharves were built all along the wall here for unloading.

Back on Strandgatan the next tall narrow medieval warehouse is called **Gamla Apoteket**, the Old Pharmacy, now used for craft displays. After Rostocksgränd is a pretty lane, Specksgränd, and to the left is **Kruttornet**, a tower which predated the wall. On its entrance level it has an exhibition explaining the history of the wall, and you can climb, with caution, the crumbling steps for the view from the top. Outside the wall is a strip of park between it and the sea, a particularly pleasant walk in the evening sun.

Continue on Strandgatan, where the second lane along, **Fiskargränd** is another picturesque one. Soon you are at the **Botanic Gardens**, with in one corner the ruins of **S:t Olof church**, the lower part of the west tower (13C). In the gardens, because of the mild winters, are specimens of almond trees, magnolias and acacias, besides vivid displays of flowers.

Skirt the gardens past S:t Olof towards the east, continuing into Vattu-gränd and Smedjegatan. Now you can go through a hotel car park on the left to the ruined **S:t Klemens church**, probably built in the mid 13C. It has a short broad nave with four round pillars which with the plainness of the decoration shows some Westphalian influence. The east end has three tall windows. This was probably a parish church since many graves have been found within its walls. Parts of the foundations of a previous church are marked.

Go round the east end of the church and take S:t Nikolaigatan almost opposite. **S:t Nikolai church** is a short distance along. If no other gateway is open go round the east end and try the wooden door in the wall beyond. The church still has most of its roof but the central tower has gone. There are remnants of Gothic tracery in the east windows and a damaged **rose window**, carved from one piece of stone, and originally in the chancel in the south-west. The **west gable** has rosettes and niches. The church was begun in the early 13C but underwent many renovations. It was taken over in the mid 13C by the Dominicans who altered and completed it finally in the late 14C. The first and most famous prior was Petrus de Dacia in the 1280s, who carried on a correspondence with a saintly Béguine (lay nun) and wrote her biography. A musical play based on this is performed every summer in the church.

Across the road from the east end of the church a low wooden gate in a wall allows you to peer through at the remains of S:ta Gertrud chapel (15C). Turn and go up Odalgaten to the **Norderport** (North Gate), to the right of which are the remains of Mynthuset (Mint House), built into the wall. To both sides of the gate you can appreciate the inside of the wall, with towers and arcades for the archers' gallery. Here is one end of the cliff that divides the town—Nygatan and Norra Murgatan run on the upper level, Norra Kyrkogatan below.

Return by way of Norra Kyrkogatan. Soon you see the round **Helgeand** (Holy Ghost) church. This was a hospital church, first mentioned in 1299, and apparently built before the mid 13C. It has two floors, but one chancel. The main doorway is on the south, with a smaller one on the north. The ground floor has cross-vaults, resting on four octagonal pillars. In the middle of the ceiling there is an octagonal opening to the upper floor, to which lead two staircases with arcading. Here it is somewhat lower than the floor below, with round pillars and missing roof. Another stairway goes up to roof level. Both floors are open to the chancel which has a semicircular apse.

The cathedral is straight ahead. On the way you catch glimpses of the cliff to the left. **Domkyrkan S:ta Maria** began as a church for German merchants and soon after its consecration in 1225 it was remodelled into a hall-church. The Romanesque south doorway of 1235 is called the **Bridal Door** and shows traces of Gothic feeling in the carving. In the mid 14C the Gothic **Great Chapel** was added in the south-west. The nave was given large Gothic windows and above it was built a huge storeroom so that from the outside it looks like a basilica again, with lower aisles. Inside, the Great Chapel to the right has slim clustered half-columns with carved capitals. At the end of the south aisle of the church is a sandstone altarpiece of the 17C and the main altar is 20C. In the north aisle is a low 17C confessional. The 17C pulpit has a fringe of very ugly angels' heads. The enormous font is of reddish limestone and above is a 13C wooden figure of the Risen Christ. Most of the memorial tablets are from the 16C and 17C.

Climbing the steps to the north-east of the church brings you to a plateau with a **view** of the upper part of the cathedral, the roofs of the town, the harbour and the sea. The large ruined church to the south-west is S:ta Karin (or Katarina).

Back on the lower level, Skolgatan leads west to two more ruins, S:t Drotten and S:t Lars. **S:t Drotten** ('the Lord', but in fact dedicated to the Trinity) is the one on the right, probably built in the early 13C, with a square tower. North of the chancel is a barrel-vaulted sacristy on two floors.

In the street to the north of this church the two-storey house with Gothic arcading on the upper floor is called the **Chapter House**, and was probably used by the Bishop of Linköping on his pastoral visits. On the other side, **S:t Lars**, also 13C, has a Greek cross plan, and is thought to show·influence from North-West Russia. The interior of the apse is horseshoe-shaped. Within the very thick walls you can climb up and round the gallery and down the other side. Other stairs lead to other levels.

Take Nunnegränd at the back of the churches to Stora Torget, the main square, where there is the ruin of **S:ta Karin church**. This was started by the Franciscans who came to Visby in 1233; it is mainly of the 14C and 15C. There is one wing left of the priory and in the summer there is an **exhibition** with models of all the Visby churches as they would have been. Underneath in the crypt there is an elaborate heating system among the gravestones. The church is the most romantic of the ruins of Visby, retaining as it does the great transverse arches of the vault, and some tracery of the windows in the apse.

Take the street behind the church on the south-west and turn left into S:t Hansgatan. At No. 21 is the **Konstmuseum**, showing changing modern art exhibitions. Beyond S:t Hans Plan are the ruins of **S:t Hans** and **S:t Per**, now with the tables and chairs of an outdoor café among the broken columns. S:t Per, on the right, is the older, then S:t Hans was built next door. Although they eventually had a common wall, they functioned separately.

Go up Hästgatan from S:t Hans Plan, turn right at Wallersplats and left up an alley opposite a café terrace which has a view over the town. Turn right and later left and you will arrive at the wall near the **Österport** (East Gate). Along here there are no buildings against the inside of the wall and you get a good impression of its construction. Outside the Österport also is one of the best views of the exterior. Turn right either inside or outside the wall and walk along to the next gate, the **Kajsarport** (Emperor Gate). The tower before this is the Kaisartornet (Emperor Tower) and was built at the same time as the wall. The wall between this gate and the Söderport is of different construction to the rest and is said to have been destroyed to allow Valdemar Atterdag's ceremonial entry into the town.

Walk round the outside and enter by the Söderport. Ahead is Adelsgatan, the main shopping street. To the left across the square is Artilleribacken and a left turn at the end of this brings you to the **Skansport**, flanked outside by the base of a barbican. The next gate is the Palissadport outside which is the site of the stronghold of Visborg, begun by Erik of Pomerania in 1411. When it returned to Swedish ownership it was blown up (1679). Take Slottsterrassen north again. After a small green area you come to the beginning of Strandgatan, and at No. 1 there is the 18C **residence** of the governor. Further along at No. 7 is the 17C residence, and soon you are back in Donnersplats.

B.   Southern Gotland

Total distance 204km. Visby—road 143, 44km junction with 144—road 144, 24km Hemse—road 142, 45km **Hoburgen**—return road 142, 23km Fidenäs—road 140, 68km Visby.

Note. As you tour the Gotland countryside you will see many signposts with names containing or ending with the word *äng* or *änge*. This means 'meadow', which will usually have wild flowers especially in late spring and early summer. Today these are cared for and encouraged. Fossils are plentiful on the island and are best sought on shores below cliffs.

Take the 143 to the south-east of Visby, signposted (15km) **Roma**. Here the church has the typical Gotland early Gothic steeple and deep doorway with steep triangular gable above going up to the eaves. It also has the typical foil and cusp decoration around the head of the door. The church was built in the 13C and the steeple is probably from the Egypticus workshop (14C). In the chancel the 13C tabernacle doors are of carved wood.

After 2km there is a sign for *Klosterruin* (monastery ruins—1km). Only the ruins of the **church** remain from the Cistercian monastery, founded in 1164 as the third Cistercian establishment in Sweden after Alvastra and Nydala. The unadorned Romanesque arches of the walls are still standing, and three of the five doorways.

Back on the road it is 4km to the turn-off for **Viklau** (4km). This church has given its name to the **Viklau Madonna**, a lime-wood figure of about 1160, from a North French school. The original is in Gotlands Fornsal in Visby, but the church has a copy, as well as a beechwood **crucifix**, also North French of the same period. The back of this was painted with acanthus in the 18C. The pews are 18C Rococo, and the 12C sandstone font is octagonal like those from the Byzantios workshop. The other font is 18C.

Again on the road, after 2km you pass a turning for Vänge and Buttle. **Vänge** church has a frieze of 12C reliefs possibly by Byzantios on the south façade and a font of the Hegwald school, while Buttle has remnants of 15C paintings by the Passion Master, a 13C font and a North German altarpiece of about 1400. Continue on the 143 passing (11km) the junction with the 146. After 1km you come to **Ala** church with Romanesque doorways with enigmatic carvings, a 13C font and some wall-paintings by the Passion Master. After 9km the 144 takes over 2km before Ljugarn, a holiday resort.

North-east of Ljugarn there is a dramatic stretch of *raukar, rock stacks up to 6m high, carved into weird configurations by the sea. (Follow the coast road from Ljugarn, about 3km.)

The 144 sets off west for Hemse. After 4km **Alskog** church has some stained glass and a 12C crucifix probably by the same artist as the Viklau Madonna. The chancel is higher than the nave, as often happened with rebuilding. In another 3km the church at **Garde** is important for its *Byzantine style figures painted under the tower arch (c 1200). The **chancel**, higher than the nave, and its **doorway** are the work of Egypticus and there is a **font** by Byzantios. Here there are still four lich-gates, one for each point of the compass, of typical Gotland design. From Garde you could make a detour south to **Lau** (5km) where the church has decorated doorways, 16C paintings, a defensive tower and the remains of a priest's house nearby.

4km from Garde the church at **Lye** has a sculpted **doorway** by Egypticus, with foil decoration all round and a deeper than usual capital frieze. The medieval stained glass is the largest area remaining in Sweden. There are paintings by the Passion Master. The same artist probably made both the 15C crucifix and the altarpiece, under which is a 15C painting of Christ's face on Veronica's cloth. Under the west tower are many runic inscriptions scratched in the plaster, with on the south a labyrinth and on the north a ship. North of Lye, **Etelhem** (3km) church has a font from the Hegwald school, a 14C crucifix, some wall-painting and some stained glass. The village also has a long-established pottery (*Krukmakeri*) with old and new workshops side by side.

At (4km) **Stånga** the nave and tower are the work of Egypticus. Alongside the main *doorway** several reliefs are set in the wall, presumably intended for elsewhere. The doorway itself is more richly decorated than most. The font is from the Hegwald group, while the 13C crucifix is, unusually for Sweden, installed on a rood-beam. Stånga is the scene of *Stångaspelet*, a recreation of traditional Gotland sports every July, which more than a little resembles the Highland Games of Scotland.

After 7km you could take the side-road to **Lojsta** church (wall-paintings) in 7km, where after another 1km, a right turn brings you to **Lojsta Slott** (2km), with foundations of a medieval fortress on a height surrounded by water, possibly belonging to the privateers who ruled Gotland briefly in the 14C, and by the car park a reconstruction of an **Iron Age house** (Lojstahallen).

The town of (2km) **Hemse**, the centre for the southern part of Gotland, has a church with a crucifix by the Viklau master and a Passion frieze. Here you join the 142 towards Burgsvik, and there is a short respite from medieval churches until you get to Grötlingbo (14km), unless you wish to look in at Alva (good crucifix) and Havdhem (retaining its Romanesque exterior).

At **Grötlingbo**, however, the church's interesting features include an Egypticus **doorway** and low reliefs from an older church set in the wall, possibly by Sigraf. The tower doorway is also decorated. The **crucifix** and **font** (by Sigraf) are from the older church. Notice the carved consoles, one with a face. There are paintings in the chancel, with dragons, by Egypticus and a carved wood tabernacle door.

After 2km a signpost points to **Kattlunds** (1km). This is an old farm where parts of the dwelling and great stone barn are medieval, though much has changed over the centuries (open in summer). Models show how the place would have looked in earlier times.

Öja church (after 10km it is 2km off the road) has one special treasure, the ***Öja crucifix**, where the circle around the cross, quite frequent in Gotland, has here been filled in with scenes and figures. The upper part shows angels and humans adoring Christ and the lower has two scenes with Adam and Eve. The Madonna on the rood-beam is a copy of the original in Gotlands Fornsal and St. John is a modern rendering. The church tower with carved **doorway** is by Egypticus and there are **wall-paintings** by an artist of the school of Albertus Pictor in the chancel, and some by the Passion Master in the nave. There are also the ruins of a defence tower.

After 5km a thatched building on the roadside heralds **Bottarve**, a 19C farm (open in summer), with outhouses thatched with the common Gotland *ag*, a variety of sedge (*Cladium mariscus*). This farm is typical of an earlier time, looking older than it is, and demonstrates the slowness of change on the island.

In 3km, **Vamlingbo church** lost its steeple in a storm. To the right of the entrance are 13C reliefs low in the wall. It has a mid 13C **painting** of the Archangel Michael weighing the soul of Emperor Heinrich II, who according to legend falsely accused his wife of adultery. Tendrils and leaves are painted in the chancel (13C) and there is an enormous painted figure of St. Christopher—he was painted extra large to emphasise his strength. The **font** is by Byzantios and there is a 15C altar.

In 2km there is a road for **Holmhällar** (6km), an area of rock stacks formed here of a type of limestone very rich in fossils, which can be better seen if water is poured on the rock.

The landscape here has become more bare, with stone walls and bushes taking the place of all the trees. **Sundre church** beside its defence tower in 5km has well-preserved wall-paintings, a Passion frieze and St. Laurence's martyrdom.

Follow the road for 4km. Where it forks, the right-hand road goes down to the shore, signposted *Hoburgsgubben*. Hoburgen is the name of the high point at the end of the road, not quite at the southernmost tip of Gotland. **Hoburgsgubben** means the Old Man of Hoburgen and if you follow the path to the left after the café you will find a signpost pointing at one of the highest misshapen rocks of the cliff. From a certain angle it is supposed to look like a button-nosed squat head, a *rauk* still attached to the cliff. Around are other rocks called his dining-room and bedroom. The left fork where you turned down leads to a point above the cliff, the road prosaically ended by a military installation.

Return by the same road 142 as far as (23km) Fidenäs and take the 140 towards Klintehamn and Visby. After 3km the sign *Vindkraftverk* points to a modern wind-energy plant, open to visitors in the summer. After 8km, **Hablingbo church** is a large 14C building by Egypticus. A **doorway** from the 12C church has survived with sculpture by Majestatis. The nave **doorway** has Egypticus' typical carving (with extra side-panels), as does the capital of the central pillar of the nave which here seems to justify his soubriquet. 1km along there is an unsurfaced road for **Petes** (4km), a 19C farmhouse, with older buildings around (open in summer). In 18km **Fröjel church** has a crucifix by the Öja workshop. There is a stone labyrinth pattern in the churchyard and the lower part of a tower nearby. About 2km later at Gannarve there is a reconstructed **Bronze Age ship-setting** by the side of the road on the left, 29m by 5m.

It is 4km to **Klintehamn**, a small town with a harbour from where you can reach the rocky island of **Stora Karlsö**. This is a nature reserve with hundreds of different birds, such as guillemots and razorbills, and plants, including orchids. There is a restaurant and natural history museum. Boats go out in the morning and back in the afternoon and a bus connects with Visby. The companion island **Lilla Karlsö**, also a nature reserve, can be visited only with a guide. This also has many birds and is grazed by Gotland sheep, a very old variety where both male and female have horns. It is accessible by fishing-boat from Djupvik fishing harbour. (No refreshments.) East of Klintehamn, **Klinte** church (2km) has some vault paintings, a sculpted chancel doorway and a 15C crucifix.

On the main route **Kovik** in 3km, an old fishing centre, has a **fishing museum** with fishermen's cabins, boats and equipment. At (10km) Tofta Strand, a holiday resort, **Vikingabyn** (Viking Village) aims to give the visitor a taste of Viking life, with opportunities to try on a helmet, wield a sword, grind flour and bake bread, work in the smithy or learn Viking handicrafts. (By the Toftagården Hotel, open Wed–Sun pm, July to mid-Aug.)

Gnisvärd (2km, then 3km by a left turn) was once one of the most profitable fishing villages on the island. About 40 fishermen's cabins line a 100m street, most of them from this century but some older. The arrangements of branches were for drying nets. Very shortly on the right is a turn to **Eskelhem** (3km), where the church has ceiling-paintings, a 13C crucifix and a font by Byzantios. Another 1km brings another turn for Gnisvärd, and 1km along this road is the largest Bronze Age **ship-setting** in Gotland, 47m by 7m. 50m south is another, and 100m south again, a third, and other grave-types are around.

Back on the 140 the church at (2km) **Tofta** has typical doorways and tower remnants of wall-paintings and a font by a follower of Byzantios. After 11km a road goes to *Högklint (4km), an overhanging cliff 48m above the sea. There is a wide **view** to the north-east towards Visby while to the south the cliffs continue. There are steps down to the shore where there are caves.

It is 3km to central Visby.

C. Northern Gotland

Total distance 172km. Visby—road 147, 2km junction for Dalhem—unnumbered roads 36km **Barlingbo, Dalhem** and junction with road 146—road 146, 1km Kräklingbo—return same road 146, 28km junction with road 148—road 147, 11km junction with road 148—road 148, 19km Fårösund—return same road 148, 31km **Tingstäde**—unnumbered road, 9km junction with road 149—road 149, 15km junction for Bro—unnumbered road 8km Bro—road 148, 12km Visby.

Leave Visby by the 147 and after 2km take the road signposted *Dalhem*. At (8km) **Endre**, where the church has a font with a remarkable **medieval cover**, take the unmade road marked (6km) **Barlingbo**. Here the church has a 13C steeple and typical deep doorway with gable, but its most treasured possession is its **font** (c 1150), with representations of the Archangel Gabriel, the Virgin, a man and a woman, possibly the Virgin's parents, and the Crucifixion. There is some 13C stained glass in the chancel, some wall-paintings from different periods and a crucifix from the 13C.

Turn to take the road a short distance back marked *Slite*, and follow the next signpost to **Dalhem**, 6km in all. The **church** has a 14C steeple, west rose window and west **doorway** with centaur, dragons, sphinx, a flute-player and a woman with twins, all by Egypticus or his school. Beside the north door a 12C tombstone of a priest has been inserted, possibly by Sigraf.

The church was unfortunately over-restored inside at the turn of the century, and covered with wall-paintings of this period. Of the **stained glass** in the chancel five panes are from the 13C—the Ascension, Pantocrater, Judas' kiss, the Flagellation, Carrying of the Cross and St. Margaret. There is a 12C **tabernacle door** by Byzantios and near it an oak processional cross of the 14C, the same period as the carved and painted choir stalls. The front panel of these is 17C, as is the bishop's chair. 14C wall-paintings remain in the south-east corner of the nave and on the south wall. To the east of Dalhem, you can visit **Hörsne church** (4km) which has an Egypticus doorway.

Continue on the same road from Dalhem for 16km towards **Kräklingbo**, joining the 146 1km before the village, where the church has restored Romanesque **wall-paintings**, interesting because they are not in Byzantine style like others of this date (compare Garde and Källunge), and a 13C crucifix.

To Torsburgen, Grogarnshuvud, Gammelgarn and Herrgårdsklint

From Kräklingbo you can take a worthwhile detour of 25km to the east, which includes Torsburgen prehistoric fort, a church, a lime-works, a cliff-view and two smaller prehistoric forts.

Take the unnumbered road towards Östergarn and 2km along there is a rough track through the woods to **Torsburgen** (3km). Torsburgen is a 1C Iron Age fort built on a natural limestone plateau 68m high and 1.5km across. On the west, north and east this is steep enough to afford protection, but on the south a rampart of limestone and shingle was built, 2km long on a 20m wide base and 7m high. It was probably for defence and refuge only, as no buildings have been found inside. It is the largest such fort in Sweden.

At a fork in the track, there is a signpost for **Ardre Lucka** 2km to the left where there is a car park and you can see the imposing man-made **rampart**, and at **Tjängvide Lucka** 0.8km to the right you can follow a steep rocky path from the car park, marked with red bands on the trees, to where an outlook tower gives you a **view** over the area. There was a serious forest fire in this district in 1993.

Continue, following signposts to (8km) **Katthammarsvik** on the coast where there are remains of lime-works. From here it is 2km to Grogarns-berget, from where you can walk out on to the head (**Grogarnshuvud**). On this cliff over the sea are the remains of an Iron Age fort. The shore is a favourite haunt of fossil-hunters. Go back to the turn-off for Katthammars-vik, turn right and shortly left on the Ljugarn road.

At (6km) **Gammelgarn** the **church** is accompanied by a typical 12C defensive tower. The church **doorway** has sculptures (14C) by the Egyp-ticus workshop, showing Adam and Eve, Cain and Abel, ending with Noah and his ark. Inside it has remains of paintings by the Passion Master, and a 14C altarpiece. Turn back towards Kräklingbo and 2km later there is a sign for **Herrgårdsklint** (3km), with remains of another Iron Age fort on a bluff, with a 2m high rampart. Inside are the foundations of five buildings. Kräklingbo is 5km.

From Kräklingbo take the 146 to the north. The church at (4km) **Anga** is mainly Romanesque with a frieze by the Passion Master. In 4km there is a road to Bringes (4km), via **Norrlanda church** which has an Egypticus doorway and a Passion frieze which has never been plastered over. At **Bringes** there are the remains of a **medieval house**, which originally had at least three storeys. The ground floor has a corridor and two vaulted rooms, and stairs lead to a similar floor above, with Gothic windows. There is no fireplace so it may have been a storehouse.

After 1km **Norrlanda Fornstuga** is 1km along a side-road. This is an open-air museum portraying everyday country life of the 18C, with a dwelling and outhouses. Opposite the turn for Norrlanda Fornstuga a road goes to **Trullhalsar** (6km), a cemetery from the Vendel period (late Iron Age 550–800) with stone-settings and cairns; all together there are about 340 graves deep in the woods.

After 7km, **Gothem** has a **church** with three medieval **lich-gates** and a ruined keep. The interior has **wall-paintings**, some fragmentary. On the north wall are scenes from the life of Christ, Birth, Magi, the Marriage in Cana (fragments) and the Flagellation, and below is a frieze showing the months. On the chancel arch are representations of the Passion, and above these the Annunciation and Descent from the Cross. On the south wall are the Resurrection and some fragments. The vault is scattered with foliage, eagles, monsters and knights. An inscription starting in the south-east corner and running around the nave gives the beginning of St. John's Gospel 'In principio erat verbum...'.

There are more paintings in the chancel, where there is also a 14C **choir-stall**, with painted rear panel, and carved borders and ends, including a panel with the Coronation of the Virgin. The front part was added in the 17C. The tabernacle door is from the 13C. The 17C **pews** are painted with grisaille biblical figures.

From Gothem you could visit Vallstena (7km) and Källunge (5km further). At **Vallstena** the church has some 14C paintings and a carved alms-box, while **Källunge** has fragments of **Byzantine-style paintings**, sculptured capitals and a 15C Lübeck altar. It has a very large Gothic chancel dwarfing the Romanesque nave and tower.

Back on the route, after 3km there is a turn for **Majsterrör** (2km), a 33m diameter cairn of the Bronze Age. **Tjelvars Grav** (Tjelvar's Grave; Bronze Age) is reached by a turning in 3km (with inconspicuous signpost). A rough track (2km) leads to an overgrown (restored) ship-setting, according to legend the grave of Tjelvar, the first man to set foot on Gotland. A prehistoric fort is visible just before it on the left.

In 5km the 146 joins the 147 which in 5km reaches Slite, Gotland's second largest town. In the 19C it depended on lime-works for its living, and in the 20C it has developed as Sweden's largest cement producer. In 6km the 147 joins the 148, and after 1km, you come to **Lärbro**. The **church** has an unusual octagonal **tower** and west **doorway** by Egypticus, with scenes from the childhood of Christ. Fragments of painting survive. In the chancel a winged **dragon** begins as a carved console, then becomes a relief, ending with a painted curly tail. In the vault is a painted Tree of Life and above the wooden doors of the tabernacle is the Crucifixion, and there are also figures of apostles. The **chair** is 13C. About 3km further on a road goes to **Kauparve** (1km) with a Bronze Age cairn. This has an outer ring and an inner chamber where a burial was found.

7km beyond, from Rute onwards the road is bordered either side by military areas forbidden to foreigners. Until 1991 this also included the entire island of Fårö, but now only the south part, about a quarter, is barred, with the exception of the road through. If you wish to visit these areas you can apply ten days in advance to the police in Visby. An exception is made in the case of tourists to (17km from Rute) **Bläse**, where there is a museum about the

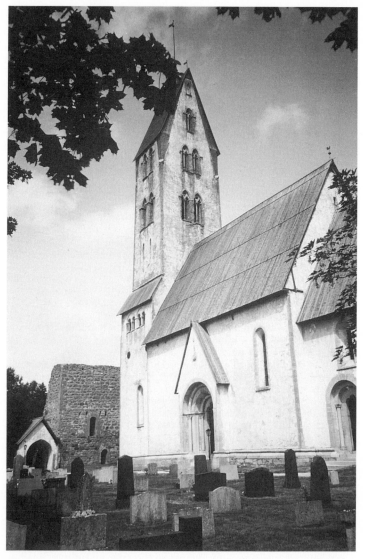

*Church of Gothem on the island of Gotland with typical tower by Egyp-
ticus and deep pediment over the doorway. To the left a medieval
lich-gate and remains of a defensive tower*

lime industry in the buildings. Bläse had its heyday as a lime-works in the
1920s and 1930s, and a great slagheap remains, with buildings from the
old works.

After 6km from Rute **Bunge church** has four medieval **lich-gates** and a deep **doorway**. The many **wall-paintings** include battle scenes, two Cruci-fixions, apostles and St. Olof. On the other side of the road is the little Skolmuseet (School Museum) in the old school of Bunge.

A couple of hundred metres further on is **Bunge kulturhistoriska museet**, an open-air museum (open mid-June to mid-Aug, 10.00–18.00, also from mid-May and to the end of August shorter hours. No English labels, English guide-book on sale). Inside the entrance gate, to the right, are reconstructed Bronze and Iron Age graves, including a 'wheel-grave' or 'sun-cross'—a cross in a circle. Ahead are four Gotland *picture-stones, with typical 'strip-cartoon' illustrations. One for example has a border of interlacing strapwork, scenes of fighting and a majestic Viking boat with chequered sail and criss-cross rigging. To the right are bun-shaped grave-stones which were laid on burials. Behind these is a stone-circle.

To the right beyond the prehistoric graves is the **18C farm**. The outhouses are gathered around the first courtyard, including a barn with a threshing-floor, a stable and cow-byre, and there is a wooden pump on the right. The dwelling-quarters lie within an enclosed yard, the *manbyggnad* being the main house, with painted beams, mottled walls, a box-bed, painted table and painted clock. The *undantagstuga* was for the retired parents, with a room for the visiting cobbler to stay and work in. Another small building was for brewing, and the farm-hands slept upstairs.

Beyond the farm is a very small windmill, which drove a mill, a lathe and a circular-saw. Turn left and the next building labelled *kalkugn* is a lime-kiln. On the other side of the path are first a stable and next a sheep-house, thatched with *ag*, a type of sedge growing in Gotland marshes. Ahead is a very large water-driven fulling-mill and two cottages used by a boatman. After a windmill on the left, beyond the main enclosure, is a **19C farm**, with a typically furnished dwelling.

Returning down the north side of the museum area, a cluster of buildings contain machinery which would have been driven by water, a fulling-mill, water-mill and water-powered saw-mill. Next is a tar-burning hearth and you can see how the tar would have trickled from the fire to the collecting-point. Then there is the sauna and charcoal-burner's hut, before you come to the **17C farm**—all these enterprises which needed fire were kept away from the farm-yard itself.

The main dwelling is on your right as you enter. It is furnished authenti-cally with fireplace, bed, cupboard, table, chairs, cradle and spinning-wheel. The adjoining cottage was used for guests or on occasions such as marriages or funerals. Next to this is the brewery and distillery, a privy, and a cold larder for meat and fish. Then come the carpenter's workshop, joined to the 'ox-house' and, opposite, a shed for carts. Behind, there is a modern store showing a collection of tools and equipment. Ahead are the byre and stable, joined by a diminutive two-storey house, geese on the ground floor and hens on the upper floor, accessible by a hen-sized ramp. The barn, completely of wood, labelled *ladu*, is from 1621, and finally there is the herb-garden near the house.

In 2km the road ends at Fårösund, from where ferries go every half an hour across the 1km sound to Fårö (Sheep Island—the same meaning as the Faroes). As mentioned above, the road through the south part, roughly a quarter of the island as far as the church, is bordered on each side by areas forbidden to foreigners. Beyond this, however, on the north-west coast are several areas of **raukar**—rock stacks—at Digerhuvud, Langhammar and

Gamlahamn. Fårö is comparatively unspoiled and buildings are mainly 18C and 19C.

Return by the 148 and continue to (31km) **Tingstäde**. In Tingstäde Lake there are the foundations of a pile construction known as Bulverket (Bulwark). The model in Gotlands Fornsal shows a platform in the shape of a hollow square measuring 175m in each direction, which had 7m wide sides. This seems to have been used for defence c 1000. It is visible only from a boat in still weather.

Tingstäde **church** retains the high stepped **gateway** to the priest's house—many similar ones still exist. The lower half of the church tower is Romanesque with galleries, the upper half Gothic. All three doorways are Romanesque. Inside, the capital of the central column and the tympanum of the sacristy door are similarly early medieval. The paintings under the tower are from the 14C and the 18C, and the acanthus and drapery paintings are 18C also; the crucifix is 14C.

From Tingstäde take the unnumbered road north-west to Stenkyrka. After 4km a road goes to **Martebo** (4km) where the **church** has three decorated **doorways** by the school of Egypticus, showing the Birth and Childhood of Christ on the north and chancel doorways, the story closing in the south doorways with the Passion and Christ in Limbo. The paintings inside show dragons and apostles.

Just before Stenkyrka at (3km) **Lilla Bjärs** there is a late Bronze and Iron Age cemetery on both sides of a wooded track, with round filled-in stone-settings and cairns. 1km further is the **church** of **Stenkyrka**, with a decorated chancel arch (13C) and other paintings of the 14C. There is a **font** by Majestatis and a 14C crucifix. About 500m on, in the grounds of the Hembygdmuseum (local museum), there is a reconstructed **wheel-grave** from the Lilla Bjärs site. This is by the roadside, past the entrance, and is 17m in diameter, with a central circle and a simple pattern of spokes.

Another 500m brings a T-junction with the 149 at Licknatte. To the right after 1km, is a turn for **Lickershamn** (1.5km) from where it is something under a kilometre's walk to the largest rock stack on Gotland, the **Jungfru** (Maiden), perched on the edge of a cliff. The stack is 11m high and 27m above sea-level, and the area is a nature reserve, with walks and views.

To the left after 11km there is a turn for the **caves** at Lummelunda (**Lummelunda grottorna**), with stalactite formations. The tour takes 25min and the temperature is 8°C. Also in the area is a gigantic mill-wheel and a restaurant in a 19C building. 2km further on is a winding lane for **Krusmyntaregården**, a comprehensive **herb-garden** with a view of the sea. (Shop and café.)

After another 2km take the unnumbered road marked *Väskinde 4*, but continue to (8km) **Bro church**, which has a capital frieze on the **doorway**. The **font** is by Sigraf, c 1200, painted in the 18C and the crucifix is of about the same date. The 18C foliage paintings partly hide medieval ones.

Turn south-west on the 148 to Visby. To visit **Stora Hästnäs**, substantial remains of a **medieval house**, follow the small signpost after 7km which says *St. Hästnäs 2* and *Golfbana*. The lane comes to a small parking area beside a farm wall. Hidden by trees, in the farmyard, is a 14C house with stepped gables. (When visited, the English notice was wrongly translated 12C.) This has a cellar and three floors. The ground floor has a vaulted ceiling and remnants of a fireplace, and a dark crumbling stairway leads to the wood-beamed first floor room with pillared Gothic windows. The third floor has a barrel vault. There would originally have been two lower flanking buildings, probably with stone basements and wooden upper floor.

It is 5km to Visby.

7

Malmö to Gothenburg

Total distance 280km. Malmö—E6/E20, 40km **Landskrona**—18km turning for **Helsingborg**—27km Ängelholm—53km **Halmstad**—40km Falkenberg—30km **Varberg**—46km Kungsbacka—26km Gothenburg.

Leave Malmö by the E6/E20 northwards towards Landskrona and Gothenburg. At 17km road 16 goes to Lund, and 1km along this road is **Fjelie** church (12C), which has wall-paintings from medieval times onwards, and a modern astronomical clock. After 5km there is a turning for **Borgeby** (1km), with 17C–19C manor buildings, and **Kävlinge** (6km), where the old church (*gamla kyrka*) has medieval wall-paintings and later pulpit, pews and a verger's chair.

Continuing on the E6/E20 at (4km) Barsebäck a road towards Barsebäckshamn leads to **Gillhög passage-grave** (3km) in a field off the road to the left 200m down a track. The passage-grave is from the New Stone Age (2300–1800 BC) and pottery from this period was found in the neighbourhood. Other later burials were found in the passage and in the mound. You need a torch to go down the cramped passage and into the chamber where the central stone of the roof is said to weigh 15 tonnes.

Barsebäck **nuclear power-station** (*kärnkraftsstation*) whose distinctive twin towers are visible from afar is 3km further on the same road. They have a small exhibition, with a guide and English information.

Sweden has 12 nuclear reactors of which two are here, producing about 1200MW, of a total for the country of nearly 10,000MW. A referendum was held in 1980 in which a majority agreed to the use of the 12 reactors for their lifetime of 25 years, with the aim of dismantling them as soon as possible, but not later than 2010.

After 14km there is a turn for Landskrona (3km).

Landskrona (pop. 27,000) received its charter from Erik of Pomerania in 1413, and in 1549 Christian III of Denmark started the citadel, whose fortifications were completed only under Swedish rule in the 17C and 18C. Much of the town was razed to make room for them.

The **citadel** (open June to mid-August) and its fortifications occupy a large area by the sea. There were three moats, with the inmost island a four-leaf clover shape. The main keep, joined to the west tower, is on the south-west side, with another tower at the east corner and corresponding low round buildings to the south and north. It was used as a prison, and the 19C house to the south-east was for the prison governor, while the north-east wing was a hospital. The keep has acquired decorative gables, and the buttresses on the courtyard are 18C. Inside, the vaults are 19C. To the right you can enter the west tower which was a dungeon, originally with access only from above. The next floor was for defence, with cannon-ports both in the main building and the tower. At the entrance to the tower the small room was used as a powder magazine. On the top floor of the west tower is a room now used for civil marriages, previously also a powder store. A gallery runs almost the whole length of the building from which arquebuses could be fired and other rooms used to be a chapel and armouries. Across the courtyard the east tower was a 19C and 20C **prison** which can be visited. In the round building on the south corner is a **museum** about the citadel. Near the shore to the south of the citadel is the new water-tower which is open in summer for the view from the top.

Landskrona Museum (open Mon–Fri 12.00–16.00, Thurs to 21.00, weekends 12.00–17.00) is in Slottsgatan which leads north from the citadel to the main square Rådhustorget. It is housed in an 18C barracks designed by the court architect Carl Hårleman. On the ground floor there is an art collection which belonged to Nell Walden, the wife of Herwarth Walden who was the founder and publisher of the German magazine *Der Sturm*, in the forefront of Expressionist art and literature. On the first floor are home interiors from the 18C to the 20C and on the second floor are a section on medical care and trade and craft interiors. Also here is an aeronautical section dealing with local aviators, and a prehistoric section. The top floor displays children's lives in the 19C and early 20C in the region, completed by a real play-school.

To the south is the **Sofia Albertina church** (1788) designed by Carl Hårleman. The writer Selma Lagerlöf lived in Landskrona between 1885 and 1897 in the 18C house at Kungsgatan 13 where she was a teacher. Here she wrote one of her most famous books *Gösta Berlings Saga* (1891).

North of the town at and beyond the holiday village of Borstahusen there are good beaches for swimming. There is a ferry-service from Landskrona to Denmark (90min), and to the island of **Ven** (30min)—there are also boats to Ven in the summer from Råå, just south of Helsingborg.

To the island of Ven

Ven's most illustrious period was undoubtedly when the astronomer Tycho Brahe lived here in the 16C. Latterly there were brickworks here—in 1930 there were six of them and nearly 1000 people. Now the brickworks have gone and 300 people are left. The island is c 4.5km by 2km.

The boat from Landskrona puts in at the little harbour of Backviken. At the top of the hill is a tourist bureau (open May–Sept) and a cycle-hire shop—highly recommended, even if it is a while since you rode a bike, and with more reasonable prices than Stockholm. Most of the sights have to do with Tycho Brahe.

Tycho Brahe (1546–1601) was born and brought up in Skåne, then Danish, the son of a Danish nobleman. He went to Copenhagen university then to Leipzig to study law, but found astronomy more to his liking. In 1572 he discovered a new star in the constellation Cassiopeia and proved it was more distant than the moon, which contradicted Aristotle's contention that the universe beyond the moon was unchangeable. Frederik II of Denmark gave him the island of Ven, the cost of his observatory and a salary. In the centre of the island at the highest point he built *Uraniborg*, of which nothing remains, but drawings show it to have been an extravagant building in Dutch Renaissance style. The wooden floors, however, did not hold the instruments steady so he had another observatory built to the south. He had his own printing-press and paper-mill. Brahe worked on Ven for 21 years. By all accounts he was very difficult to get along with, and quarrelled with the king. He went to Prague where Kepler was his assistant in an observatory provided by Emperor Rudolf II. His work however was systematic and accurate and the foundation for Kepler's laws of planetary motion was laid by Brahe's long years of daily observation, to some extent helping to disprove Aristotle and confirm Copernicus.

After 1.5km you will see a domed building on the left of the road. Above ground this is a reconstruction, but peering through the glass you can see down into the remains of Brahe's half-underground *Stjärneborg* (Star Castle) **observatory**, which he built when his palace proved inadequate for the job. A few metres on to the right is the site of the small and opulent palace, outlined by stones, and part of the **garden** has recently been restored. Ivar Johnsson's **statue** of the great man stands gazing heavenwards (erected in 1946—the 400th anniversary of his birth). The well which supplied Uraniborg with water in the kitchen is still here and there is also a cellar which would have been under the servants' living quarters. By the roadside a **museum** is devoted to Brahe, his work and his palace (open in summer).

The church here is known as the new church. To reach the 13C **church** of S:t Ibb (open June–August pm), situated on a height above the little harbour of Kyrkbacken, follow the road for 1km to Tuna By, and turn left for 1km. There are some picturesque half-timbered farms along the way.

8km after the Landskrona junction of the E6/E20 the road rises at Glumslöv and on top of the hill is the Skåne Rasta motorway service-station. From the car park and picnic area there is a wide view of the countryside. Behind the picnic area in a ploughed field is a group of seven Bronze Age barrows (1500–500 BC) and two New Stone Age passage-graves (c 2000 BC) which contained several successive burials by the local farming community. One of the barrows was used at one time as a gallows' hill. The barrows are visible from the car park, but approached only with some difficulty around the edge of the field.

7km further on you can turn off to take the old coast road to **Råå** (5km). This large fishing village is famous for its eels, has a harbour, a marina and a fishing and shipping museum (open weekends pm, May–Sept).

3km later take the E4 towards Helsingborg. To visit the old spa at **Ramlösa**, follow the signs *Ramlösa brunn* at the first junction. The spa park is on the left of the road, with yellow wooden buildings scattered about it, including the spa hotel, built in 1880 in Spanish–Moorish style, and former spa installations. The semi-circular building on the lower level is the 'new bathhouse' of 1919. Ramlösa mineral water has been promoted since 1707 when Johan Jakob Döbelius became convinced it cured every ill. Although the actual spa was closed in 1971, Ramlösa water is now a huge business and many Swedes use the name 'Ramlösa' to mean any mineral water. Döbelius' portrait is still on the bottle-labels.

The centre of **Helsingborg** (pop. 82,000) is 7km from the E20. At this point there is only 4km between Sweden and Denmark so it is not surprising that ferries cross here on average every 15 minutes in summer. The ultra-modern traffic-terminal (1991) unites the railway station and the port, the bus terminal and car parks, with the trains running underground in a 1200m tunnel. In the complex, known as **Knutpunkten** (Knot Point) are cafés, restaurants, shops, offices, post offices, banks and hotels. Millions of passengers and thousands of buses, lorries and cars cross every year to Helsingør (Elsinore).

Tourist bureau: Knutpunkten. Tel. (042) 12 03 10.

Post office: Storgatan 17.

Exchange: Knutpunkten.

Telephone, telegram: Bruksgatan 24. Tel. (042) 902 00.

Bus station: Knutpunkten. Travel information tel. (042) 10 72 00.

The **tourist bureau** is on the first floor of Knutpunkten and the useful *Helsingborg This Month* publication with maps, opening times and much other information is available here and elsewhere.

Helsingborg was known in the 11C when the Danes fortified it, and it suffered much in the wars between Sweden and Denmark. The castle of which the remaining keep is such a feature of the town was built in the 15C. One last heroic battle took place near Helsingborg in 1710, when the Swedes were led by Magnus Stenbock.

Just beyond Knutpunkten on the sea-front is Carl Milles' **seafaring monument** on a pillar, and beside it a **plaque** commemorating the landing here in 1810 of Marshal Bernadotte, come to take up the proffered position as Crown Prince of Sweden, later Karl XIV Johan. The ostentatious red brick town hall (1897) is on the right a little further on and by the side of it the elongated Stortorget leads up to Kärnan, the medieval keep. There is an equestrian **statue** of Helsingborg's hero Magnus Stenbock by John Börjeson (1901).

To the left Norra Storgatan has some half-timbered houses. No. 9, Gamlegård, is where Gustav III stayed, and opposite at No. 12 in a courtyard is the Henckel house (17C) with cream rendering instead of brick to show off the half-timbering. At the end on the left is the large Jacob Hansen's house (17C) and opposite, a fountain in the form of a celestial globe, a tribute to the astronomer Tycho Brahe.

Norra Storgatan continues into Fågelsångsgatan where at the end on the right is an early 19C wood-panelled house. The road ends in a T-junction with S:t Jörgen plats and Hälsovägen. In the square is a fountain 'Children Playing'. At the bottom of the hill Drottninggatan runs parallel to the coast and the concert hall (1932) and theatre (1976) can be seen across the road.

The road up the hill, Hälsovägen (Health Way), leads shortly to the Sofia spring on the right at the foot of Öresund park which is on a rocky plateau accessible here by steps. The water was formerly drunk for its health-giving properties. On the opposite side of the road more steps lead up to **Vikingsbergs Konstmuseum** built as a private home in 1875. This art museum has mainly earlier Swedish art and temporary exhibitions (open Tue–Sun 12.00–16.00, to 17.00 in summer).

Back on Stortorget, a monumental staircase leads up to **King Oskar's Terrace** (lift at nominal charge) with a view of the town and Denmark.

The entrance to the **Kärnan** (keep) is by a steep external stair to the 'ground' floor (open June–Aug 10.00–17.00, shorter hours in winter). The height of the tower is 34.5m, the area about 15m by 15m, with walls 4.5m thick at the bottom. The cellar could only be reached by a trap-door and the stairs are in the side turret.

On the **first floor** is the kitchen with an oven, a scullery with an outside drain, and a privy. In the kitchen, information boards give the history of the castle with notes in English. In the centre is a model of the area as it was in 1675, and pressing the button lights up the line of the medieval wall. The **second floor** is two storeys high combining the previous second and third floors. This was the home of the lord of the castle, and it has a fireplace and a privy above the one below. At one stage this room was a chapel, hence the vaulted ceiling, and the small adjoining 'chancel' cut into the thickness of the wall. The **third floor**, the original fourth, was also combined with the one above. The barrel vault was necessary in the 17C to support cannon. The previous battlements above this were demolished, but in 1894 the top was finished as it is now.

From the top there is a **view** of the town and across the sound to Elsinore and Hamlet's castle, in fact called Kronborg, squatting on the shore—an enjoyable excursion from Helsingborg, even if there is not much there to remind you of the play.

S:ta Maria church (turn left after descending from Kärnan) was built in the 15C in brick, on the site of an older church (open to 16.00, silver treasury Mon–Fri 13.00–14.00; ask the attendant for admission). In the entrance porch is a detailed time-chart, with dates and kings along the bottom and the developing plan of the church along the centre.

Turning to the left after entering the church itself you see on the left a copy of Lucas Cranach's portrait of Martin Luther and opposite is a painting of the parable of Lazarus and the rich man (1583). Under the picture is a 17C offertory chest. To the left again is the baptismal chapel at the back of which hangs a 15C tombstone of a local judge and his wife.

The Renaissance **pulpit** is from 1615 by Statius Otto, a German artist, with reliefs from the Old and New Testaments, divided by caryatids. The door and stair panel are carved and inlaid with intarsia, probably by a different artist. The medieval font in front of the chancel is of Gotland limestone with a brass bowl of the 17C. The chandeliers in the nave are also 17C, while the large crucifix is medieval.

The North German **altarpiece** is of c 1450, dated by the small coats of arms at the top, when Christian I was king of Denmark and Norway but not yet of Sweden. It is thought to come from Stralsund since the coins in the scene of the expulsion of the money-changers from the temple resemble those of Stralsund at that period. The altarpiece has two pairs of doors, painted on all eight sides, which are adjusted appropriately for Good Friday, Lent and Advent. Finally, fully opened it reveals reliefs and sculptures from the childhood of Christ. On the base are Christ and the Virgin with John the Baptist and eight apostles.

To the left of the chancel is a votive ship and on the wall behind is a small square tablet put up by Tycho Brahe in memory of his young daughter. Near here is the door to the vestry beneath which is the silver **treasury** containing church silver from the 16C onwards, and a Danish Bible of 1550 (notes in English available).

Round the apse are modern stained-glass windows by Erik Olsson, Einar Forseth and Martin Emond. On the wall behind the altar are the remains of medieval wall-paintings with St. Magnus of Scotland and St. Brendan of Ireland. In the south aisle is a memorial to Diderik (Dietrich) Buxtehude (1637–1707), the Danish organist and composer who was a native of Helsingborg. At the rear of the south aisle hangs a Renaissance clock-face and under it is the entrance to the tower with a chapel on the ground floor.

Södra Storgatan runs to the east of the church and following it to the south brings you shortly to **Stadsmuseet** at No. 31 (Town Museum; open Tue–Sun 12.00–16.00; information in three languages is on a revolving screen in each room). On the first floor the history of the town is shown from prehistoric times. Archaeological finds lead on to the medieval section where there is a model of Helsingborg in 1200. Another model shows the town in 1675, covering a larger area than the one in Kärnan. Local industry is represented by tin and stoneware manufactures and the Battle of Helsingborg is dealt with, including a preliminary model of the statue of Magnus Stenbock on Stortorget. A model also shows the old town hall demolished to make way for the present one at the end of the 19C, and there are many paintings showing Helsingborg over the centuries.

2km north-east of the centre is **Fredriksdal Friluftsmuseum** (open-air museum, open May–Sept 10.00–18.00)—take Hälsovägen or Stenbocksgatan. The main manor house is 18C with later farm buildings. A short distance away is the town quarter with shops and the old vicarage (prästgård), and the Grafiska museet (open 12.00–16.00), showing printing-presses, type and book-binding. In the gardens there is a recreation of an 18C French open-air theatre. The botanical garden shows native Skåne flora, and examples of garden styles.

Excursion to Kullaberg nature reserve

Take the coast road Drottninggatan north out of Helsingborg. On the outskirts is the suburb of Pålsjö, with a beech-wooded park on the hill to the right. Shortly afterwards the road passes **Sofiero**, the modest red brick palace built in 1865 for Queen Sofia, wife of Oskar II. In 1905 she gave it to her grandson Gustav VI Adolf as a wedding present. It is now a restaurant owned by the town of Helsingborg. The park which is open to the public (May to Sept) contains many varieties of roses and rhododendrons.

8km from Helsingborg the road joins the 111, and in 5km passes **Viken**, with an attractive centre clustered around the harbour.

After 7km, **Höganäs** (7km) is the hub of the pottery industry of north-west Skåne, exploiting the local layers of clay to make salt-glazed stoneware and other varieties, from creamy yellow to dark brown. There are about 50 factories and independent potters open for visitors and customers, often with cafés and shops. **Höganäs Museum** at Polhemsgatan 1, in a 19C sandstone house (open Mar to Dec afternoons, except Mon), concentrates on ceramics and pottery, with Höganäs history and local seafaring and mining.

At 5km there is a road to **Brunnby** (3km) where the medieval **church** has a 14C vault with contemporary **paintings**. This and other additions were paid for by the powerful and wealthy owner of Krapperup castle, Barbara Brahe, widow of one of the Krognos family. She had been on a pilgrimage to Rome with Queen Dorotea of Denmark. The vestry (previously the chancel) is painted with eight Old Testament figures, the present chancel with eight male saints, next come eight female saints, followed by apostles and church fathers, labelled with their names. A Gothic Madonna stands to the right of the altar. The pulpit is from 1623 and has Christian IV's monogram. The altarpiece is of 1731 and there are several votive ships. In the churchyard there is a rare **tithe-barn**. The main entrance to the church used to be through the barn archway, and seats against the side suggest it functioned as a sort of porch. To its left is a Gyllenstierna family tomb with their seven-pointed star.

From Brunnby a road goes north to **Arild** (1km) on the coast, another charming fishing village with a 12C chapel to St. Arild (the Lutheran one—the Catholic one looks old but isn't).

After 3km from the turn for Brunnby, **Krapperup** castle stands close to the road, but is not open to visitors. It has been owned by some of the foremost families in the land, the de la Gardies, the Brahes and now the Gyllenstiernas. The castle was rebuilt in the late 18C, and you can see in the rough finish of the surface how the ends of the side wings had been incorporated into a defensive wall. The seven-pointed star of the Gyllenstiernas can just be seen over the door in a carved sandstone wreath. The large building on the left by the roadside was the dairy, and the pig-house on the other side is half-timbered.

After 1km the road turns left for Mölle and Kullaberg. On the outskirts of (2km) **Mölle** the church on the right which looks medieval is in fact from 1935. Mölle is a holiday village clinging to the hillside as the land rises steeply. Just beyond is the entrance to **Kullaberg nature reserve and leisure area** (entrance fee per car). **Kullaberg** is a high rocky spur project-ing into the Öresund with steep cliffs down to the sea. On the north the broken edges give caves and crannies, jagged outcrops and strewn boulders. The highest point Håkull is 188m above sea-level and there are wide views. On the plateau itself there are woods and rich bird life, and some archaeological remains from the Stone Age have been found. The road ends in 2km in a car park. A few minutes' walk brings you to the point. There are good views along the north and south of the promontory. You can climb down to the **Silver Grotto**, a natural formation on the shore. The lighthouse nearby is open to visitors—there has been a lighthouse here since 1561 and the present light can be seen from 45km, the most powerful in Scandinavia.

Rejoin the E6/E20, at the junction 8km beyond the one from which you entered Helsingborg by taking Hälsovägen. To visit **Ängelholm**, after 19km you can leave the motorway at the junction marked Ängelholm Ö and follow signs to the centre. The **tourist bureau** is in the charming little 18C town hall beside the church. The bureau has an English leaflet giving a walk around the oldest buildings. The curious object on tourist literature looking vaguely like an antique lamp is an ocarina, a simple musical instrument made of pottery which has been manufactured in Ängelholm for 100 years.

The church has been renovated many times and is now 19C with 20C fittings. The enormous **statue of Christ** is a copy of one by the Danish sculptor Thorwaldsen. The 20C font is of Gotland sandstone and the painting above is ascribed to a pupil of Rubens. **Handverksmuseet** (Handi-craft Museum, open May to Sept) is in an 18C prison in a quiet square to the north of the church. This has displays of local crafts such as pottery, tanning and silversmithing. Walk east from the museum as far as the T-junction, turn left and **Skolmuseet** (School Museum) is in a handsome gabled building on the right. It has a school dentist's equipment from 1906 and a collection of 1100 educational posters, and many large and small items. Along Storgatan there are some 18C houses and by the river, crossed by a 19C bridge, there are pleasant leafy areas.

After 23km you come to the road junction of Östra Karup.

To Lugnarohögen and the Bjäre Peninsula

North of Ängelholm the Bjäre peninsula juts into the Kattegat—the end of the Halland Ridge which separates Skåne from Halland. The ridge is of gneiss, its highest point being 226m above sea-level. It has been a problem for rail traffic, but the planned 8.5km rail tunnel between Förslöv and Båstad should shorten journey times.

At Östra Karup you can leave the motorway to see the peninsula to the west and one or two sites to the east. Taking the 115 to the east, near Hasslöv, you can reach **Lugnarohögen**, a Bronze Age burial mound (open June–Aug Wed–Sun 14.00–16.00). You can enter the mound through the red cottage from which an underground passage leads into the chamber itself. This was excavated in 1926, and an 8m-long ship-setting from the late Bronze Age (c 700 BC) was discovered. There was a clay urn in a stone coffin containing burnt human bones, some woollen cloth, a miniature dagger, tweezers and a bronze awl. The remains of another person were also found. The whole is under a cairn covered with turf, the chamber now being provided with a ceiling.

1km to the north is **Hasslöv church** (19C) with older fittings and furnishings. 3km north-west of Hasslöv is the manor-house of **Skottorp** (open July, Tue and Thur 13.30). The present building was constructed in the 1820s, but its predecessor was designed by Nicodemus Tessin the Elder, and was the scene of the wedding of Karl XI and the Danish princess Ulrika Eleonora in 1680. The house has neo-Empire interiors, by the architect C.F. Sundwall, who also designed some of the furniture.

From the junction at Östra Karup it is 6km on road 115 to **Båstad** to the west, chiefly famous for its tennis championships, in some of which the late King Gustav V Adolf used to play. With its sandy beach close to the centre it is a favourite family resort.

Agardhsgatan is a long street of pretty houses, where at No. 9 there is a textile studio. The **church** is from the 15C, unusually with an ambulatory, and star-vaulting. There is a medieval Madonna and Child wood-carving, and below it the rough font is also medieval, with a runic inscription. There are remnants of vault-paintings in the north aisle and more complete ones with symbols of the Evangelists in the chapel to the right of the entrance.

To visit the gardens of **Norrvikens Trädgårdar** (2km), take road 115 past the church and turn right shortly after. Soon you arrive at the imposing gates (open May–Sept). On a terraced cliff above the sea various types of gardens can be seen—Japanese, Baroque, Renaissance, a water-garden and herb-garden. There are exhibitions, entertainment and refreshments.

Returning and continuing on the 115 you pass the local linen-weavers—*Vävaren*, besides enjoying the view. 7km from Båstad, at Hov, signposts point to **Hovs hallar**, a nature reserve with majestic sea-worn cliff scenery, standing stones, tumbled rocks and caves (fee per car). Maps of recommended walks are on display—go straight down from the car park to the cliff and turn right.

Torekov, an attractive holiday resort, is the village at the end of the 115. From the harbour a 20min boat trip brings you to **Hallands Väderö**, an island nature reserve, to which 'seal safaris' are sometimes organised.

The E6/E20 shortly leaves Skåne and enters Halland. At (9km from Östra Karup) Mellbystrand a turning goes to **Laholm** (6km; pop. 5000) an unpretentious town whose streets are embellished by no fewer than 25 **sculptures**. These were financed by performances of historical plays written by the local mayor from 1933–68, originally in order to be able to restore the ruined castle. The **tourist bureau** in the town hall (open in summer) on the main square has a leaflet in English showing where they all are, and runs guided tours (summer 12.00, start town hall), but most are easily met with by circling the main square and surrounding streets, within the area bounded by Lagavägen, Doktorstigen and Engelbrektsgata with the furthest away being Olof Palme's bust in the south part of the park. Around the church are attractive cobbled streets. The castle ruins to the north-east, for which the plays were written, are now crossed by road 117 and have a power-station on one side and a salmon-breeding centre on the other. (Exhibition open summer.)

Another 10km brings the road to Halmstad. Just before the town is 'Eurostop', a large service area (others at Örebro and Jönköping), with an hotel (reasonable), shopping centre, travel agency and information desk, exchange office, post office, picnic area and playground.

Halmstad (pop. 48,000) is the administrative capital of Halland, a county which has almost the same boundaries as the old province of the same name, and which belonged to Denmark until the Treaty of Roskilde in 1658. The town stands on the Nissan river, with a harbour and manufacturing industries. Christian IV of Denmark built fortifications in a crescent based on the river in the 1590s, with walls, bastions and a moat where the road Karl XI:s Väg is today. A fire devastated the town in 1619, sparing only the church, the castle, and some houses.

Tourist bureau: Lilla torg. Tel. (035) 10 93 45.

Post office: Kyrkogatan 3.

Doctor on call: Tel. (035) 13 10 00.

Telephone, telegram etc. Brogatan 19. Tel. (035) 15 90 70.

On the main square, **Stora Torg**, stands Carl Milles' **fountain** 'Europa and the Bull', and **Kungastenen** (King's Stone), a block-like sculpture by Edvin Ohrström (1952) commemorating the meeting of Gustavus Adolphus and Christian IV in Halmstad in 1619, swearing (a short-lived) peace.

S:t Nikolai church is to the south, orientated in reverse so that you enter by the east door under the tower. On either side of the entrance are raised Baroque funerary chapels each with a crypt underneath, so this was probably the original altar end. Some of the brick pillars are standing on bare rock. The vaulting is Gothic, and the clerestory windows are walled in. Eleven modern **stained-glass windows** were made between 1953 and 1978. The two round ones are by Erik Olson and the nine large ones by Einar Forseth, who designed the golden mosaics in Stockholm City Hall.

There are a few half-timbered houses, one on Stora Torg and some more in Kyrkogatan. On the other side of the broad Slottsgatan near the river is the castle, now the residence of the county governor, built at the beginning of the 17C by Christian IV. Cross the bridge near the castle to see on the left in the park by the river an enlarged version (15m) of a Picasso **sculpture** made with permission from the artist by Carl Nesjar in 1971. The sail-training ship *Najaden* (1897) moored near here can be visited. The library (Fredsgatan) and the theatre (Skansgatan) have examples of the art of the Halmstad Group (see below).

Back on the other side of the river in Vallgatan, two blocks west of Stora Torg, are some picturesque cottages. The one remaining town gate, **Norra Port**, with portions of old wall on either side is where Fredrikvallsgatan turns into Norra Vägen. 200m north is a sign right to the *museum (open Mon–Fri 10.00–16.00, Sat, Sun 12.00–16.00; notes in English available). In the basement are reconstructed craft workshops and on the ground floor is the history of Halmstad with a ceramic model of the town at the end of the 19C. In the medieval section you can try on medieval style clothes—mirror provided—and there is a prehistoric section.

On the first floor is the collection of *painted wall-hangings (*bonader*). These are blithely naive folk paintings common to Halland, Småland, Blekinge and North Skåne from the early 18C to the mid 19C. They were put up on cottage walls mainly for Christmas, hence the predominance of biblical scenes. Early ones were on cloth, later ones on paper and they were seldom signed. Some were produced by using a wooden stamp to give a black outline, then coloured by hand in bright primary colours. Favourite themes were the Three Wise Men, the Wedding in Cana (all guests and the bride outlined with the same stamp), and the parable of the ten wise and foolish virgins, all clad in 18C/19C dress, against 18C/19C backgrounds.

(Another large collection of wall-hangings has its own museum at **Unnaryd** about 55km north-east of Halmstad, within the local open-air museum by the river.)

On the top floor is an exhibition of ***paintings** by the Halmstad group of artists. The Halmstad Group, then post-Cubists who had studied with Léger, first gathered in 1929. They were the first in Sweden to paint in the Surrealist style in the early 1930s, since one of their number, Erik Olson, saw Dali's first exhibition in Paris in 1929. Others in the group were Axel Olson (Erik's brother), Waldemar Lorentzon, Sven Jonson, Esaias Thorén and Stellan Mörner. Besides works from these artists, often showing the influence of the Halland countryside, there is a selection from other modern painters.

The open-air museum, **Hallandsgården**, on Gallows' Hill is best approached from the south via Fogdegatan off Järnvägsleden. (Open mid-June to mid-Aug 13.00–18.00; viewing-tower; café.) Besides farm-houses, there is a flax-drying kiln, a water-powered sawmill and a horizon-tal watermill.

To visit **Mjällby** (5km) and another **exhibition** of the Halmstad artists, take the road towards Haverdal to the north-west. 2km past the airport there is a sign 'Mjällby 1'. (Check opening times before going.) Here Viveca Bosson, née Olson, daughter and niece of two of the Halmstad Group, shows paintings by the group, who settled and worked in nearby Sondrum from 1946–56, as well as other exhibitions. Further out on the coast is **Tylösand**, a holiday resort with an 18C S:t Olof chapel, and on the way, **Miniland** has Swedish buildings in miniature. The coast north of here is dotted with good bathing-places (often signposted *badplats*).

In 40km **Falkenberg** is a holiday resort (pop. 17,000) on the Ätran river. A new stretch of the E6 will soon bypass the town. In the centre is the stone Tullbron (toll bridge) of 1756, and the remains of a medieval castle. The bridge leads into Brogatan and the **tourist bureau** is on the corner of Holgersgatan. South of this is the old town, with the 18C S:t Laurentii church and cobbled streets. There are two **museums** here: Stadsmuseet deals with 18C and 19C Falkenberg, and another in an old granary treats its later history and industry, with emphasis on the 1950s. There is also a rock and fossil museum to the north of the old town (Stenmuseum).

North-east of Falkenberg **Svartrå church** (23km) has a painted wooden roof and organ gallery, as well as a medieval font and crucifix.

On the main route at (13km) Morup there is a sign *Varberg kustväg 18km*, the more scenic coastal route to Varberg. By the E6 it is 17km to the Varberg junction and a further 3km in to town.

Something of a geographical and cultural boundary cuts across Halland at the level of Varberg. Here the gently curving beaches and agricultural land of the south turn to rocky indented coasts and wooded ridges between the arable fields. To the south there is a Danish/Skåne influence in building styles, place-names and dialect, to the north a more Swedish/Norwegian orientation—many churches now have lantern towers under short turrets, more houses are built entirely of wood and there are no more place-names ending in *-arp* and *-rup*.

Varberg (pop. 22,000) became a fashionable bathing resort in the 19C and is still a popular summer holiday place. A ferry goes to Grenå in Denmark. The place is dominated by the huge **fortress** high on a rocky outcrop by the shore. The oldest parts date from the 13C, that is the north and south wings of the castle proper, the central rectangular complex built around the courtyard. In the 14C these were incorporated into a royal castle, and it was in this period that it became of great political importance. King Magnus Eriksson of Sweden and Norway lived here, and Valdemar Atterdag of Denmark visited him in 1343 to sign a peace treaty. In the 17C Christian IV of Denmark made the whole into a fortress with bastions and walls, but his possession was short-lived—he had to give it up to Sweden in 1645.

Follow the signs *Fästningen* (open daily); the entrance is by a steep path from the shore. On the left is the **White Monk Bastion**, and after passing through the well-protected entrance you see to the left the early 17C barracks, called the stables of Karl XI, with a small transport display. Other houses along here were officers' dwellings, now private homes. The last building down on your right before you enter **Middle Gate** (1612) was a prison, now a youth hostel.

The entrance to the castle is ahead (guided tours mid-June to mid-Aug every hour 10.00–17.00; also Sun, May and Sept 13.00–15.00, meet by Middle Gate). Highlights include a spiral ramp for moving cannon up the **Grey Monk Bastion**, **Eskil's Cellar** (16C) with above it the **Hall of State** (though with 20C floor and ceiling), and the **dungeons**.

The **museum** lies in the oldest part of the castle (open daily, closed Sat and Sun am except in summer; notes in English available). The most interesting exhibit is that of a 600-year-old **skeleton** and his complete clothing found in a bog at nearby Bocksten in 1936. His wardrobe included cloak and hood, stockings and shoes, and he carried with him belts, knives and one spare stocking. Three thick stakes through the body indicate that he had been murdered—they were to prevent his spirit seeking out his murderers.

A showcase is devoted to 'the bullet which killed Karl XII' in 1718 as he was besieging a fortress in Norway. It is in fact a brass button filled with lead, of a type found in Turkey. The belief was that the king could only be killed by magic power using something of his own property. The button, found in a gravel-pit in 1924, was supposed to have come from his clothing, and fits exactly the hole in the royal cranium—all clearly depicted here.

There are also works by the artists Karl Nordström, Richard Bergh and Nils Kreuger who worked here in 1893–96 and are referred to as the **Varberg School**. (The museum was being renovated at the time of visiting and will be much expanded and improved.)

Just below the fortress is the 19C cold bath-house with cupolas. The church in the town is 18C, and 19C buildings remain from the time when Varberg was a health resort for example, Societeshuset in the spa park, Societetspark.

It is 6km to rejoin the E20, and after 14km you can take a turning for **Ringhals** on the coast, a nuclear power-station with an information centre, and summer bus-tours of the area. In 16km there is a particularly attractive picnic site by a lake at Torpasjön Rastplats. In this area there are many granite outcrops.

To Tjolöholm, Hanhals and Fjärås

At the junction in 6km follow the signs to **Tjolöholm** (5km; open mid-June to mid-Aug 11.00–16.00; also weekends Apr, Sept, and Sun Oct). The manor is situated on the shore of a peninsula in the Kungsbacka fjord with a view of islands nearby, and beyond to the Kattegat. Take the path marked *slottet* from the car park. There are guided tours on the hour (in Swedish, but guides can help in English) or you can go around on your own with the aid of two leaflets in English.

James Fredrik Dickson was a prodigiously wealthy Gothenburg business-man whose grandfather had come from Scotland at the beginning of the 19C and whose father had built the luxurious Dickson house in Gothenburg. James Frederik was aiming at an English Tudor style and appointed Lars Israel Wahlman as architect. Unfortunately, he never lived to see it, and his widow supervised its completion (1904). It is built of rough-hewn reddish granite blocks with smooth ashlar quoins and other detailing. It is a concoction of Dutch gables, Tudor chimneys, towers, oriel windows, crenelations, Ionic columns and cupolas, with the servants' quarters added to one corner in half-timbering for good measure. It looks as if there are three 'storeys', but the floors do not run straight across the whole house—the rooms are at many different levels and there is a plethora of short stairways.

On the **ground floor** the **Great Hall** occupies the equivalent of two storeys. The 10m high fireplace is of Gotland sandstone, with the phrase *Coelum versus* carved on it ('towards heaven'). At one end two tall windows frame a painting of the Queen of Sheba by Julius Kronberg (1888). There is a mechanical organ and an English grandfather clock. Going through the hall and turning left you find a small **smoking-room** in luxuriant Moorish style with stalactite work in stucco, and walnut panelled ceiling and doors. The heating ducts and windows have turned wooden Moorish-style screens. Beyond is the top-lit **billiard-room** surrounded by built-in sofas. The lights over the billiard-table are of silver-plated bronze with the Dickson coat of arms. The study, panelled in dark oak, was fitted by Liberty's of London. The two concealed doors led to a safe and a wine-cellar. There is a portrait of James Dickson. On the other side of the hall is the high **dining-room** in Jacobean style with tall leaded windows looking out on the rear garden. The walls are panelled and the carved musicians' gallery is built in above the fireplace. The design of the stucco ceiling with heavy pendants is four-leaf-clover shape, with the coats of arms of the owners, which are also let into the windows. There are portraits of Queen Elizabeth I and Oliver Cromwell, and framed menus of banquets.

Upstairs from the carved baluster of the gallery with its fabulous beasts, you can see the hall better, and the painting on the upper part of the walls. At the bottom of the next staircase is a painting which is said to be the basis for the design of the mausoleum in the grounds. The **drawing-room** was used as a music-room and has a pianola, and Chippendale furniture. Watch for details throughout the house like the specially designed light-switches; here for example there is a mermaid holding a switch in each hand. The bay-window looks out over the gardens and the water. The **library** has oak shelves and many English books, and a decorated stucco ceiling. There are busts of the two Dicksons. Mrs Dickson's **boudoir** has a window overlooking the Great Hall, and has carved figures of characters from Shakespeare's *A Midsummer Night's Dream*. A frieze of imitation embossed leather runs around the room. The spiral staircase leads down to a small space arising from a miscalculation in the plans. An adjoining round alcove occupies the tower. The lady's **bedroom** is in dark oak panelling, and the dressing-room leads to the **bathroom**, very luxurious for the time. There was a bathroom on each floor, two with sunken baths, as here. The circular creation of metal tubes is a shower, with water coming from above, below and the sides. The lampshades are of shell.

On the next level are the rooms for babies and children, as well as cases with a display of clothes of the family, children and servants, and other household items including a paraffin-heated hair-drier. Right at the top is the **Royal Bedchamber**, prepared to receive a king who never came. The bed is a copy of Henry VIII's, and the porcelain is Limoges. Prince Philip, Duke of Edinburgh, once stayed here. Around the landing are 17C tapestries and there are several rooms with displays of plans and documents relating to the estate. You can descend by the servants' staircase.

The formal gardens stretch almost to the shore, and the mausoleum is to the right. Back near the car park the **Vagnmuseum** (Carriage Museum) has a varied collection, including the famous Tjolöholm **vacuum-cleaner** (*dammsugare*). It weighs 1 ton, and was drawn by two horses to the windows of the house, through which the 45m hose was led. Surprisingly modern-looking heads for the hose are hanging on the wall. The manège, for indoor riding, is now a café, and there is a bathing-beach (*badplats*)

A short distance from the car park towards the exit, a track leads to the village and church; the latter, in the same style as the manor, is too dilapidated to open. The village was started to accommodate estate workers' families, who were allocated one room and kitchen each, in semi-detached cottages, in typical Swedish red-and-white. There was a school, a village hall and reading-room and a cottage hospital, and later a shop.

Return towards the motorway and go under it, following signs **Fjärås**. The sign Äskhult 14km with a St. Hans' Cross refers to a settlement of 18C farms, showing how they were clustered in companiable groups before the 19C land reforms dispersed them in the name of efficiency. 3km from the motorway turn right and in 3km right again at a church. The **Fjärås ridge** of several kilometres on which you are driving was formed of gravel and clay in the ice-age, damming the valley. There are good **views**, especially over the lake of Lygnern. There are many prehistoric remains in the areas, one of which is about 1km south of the church, at **Li**, where there are over 100 standing stones, probably a Viking Age cemetery. Back past the church the other way is a natural history display (*Naturum*—restricted open times).

Return down the hill. At the T-junction you could turn right instead of left, to visit **Hanhals church** (2km; open in summer). It was originally Romanesque, then extended to the east in the 18C, but abandoned in 1890. The font is a copy of the original 13C one. The altar was completed in 1769 and the two votive ships are from the 1660s. (Fortunately the painted wooden **ceiling** had been preserved in Gothenburg museum so it could be restored. It was painted by Johan Durck in 1770, in rich colours, with three pairs of corresponding biblical scenes.)

Back on the motorway, at the next junction (8km) there is a turning for **Onsala church** (7km), which was founded in the 12C but remodelled in the 17C. In the 18C the tower, Gathenhielm crypt and small porch were added. The pulpit is Renaissance but most of the interior is from the late 17C and early 18C, so the overall impression is Baroque. The **ceiling-paintings** are in oval frames, with Old Testament scenes on one side and New Testament on the other, with clouds and angels in the centre. The organ gallery is also painted, with Christ, saints and prophets.

The altarpiece has a sculpted crucifixion against a painted background, with a relief of the Last Supper below and the Lamb seated on the book with seven seals above. The unprepossessing angel suspended in front of the altar is St. Michael. The chandeliers are of about the same period, and the votive shops are 19C.

On the north wall is a memorial to the brother of Lars Gathenhielm, the successful Gothenburg adventurer and privateer. Lars himself and his wife are buried in imposing white marble sarcophagi in the **crypt**, reached by the door to the left of the altar. Opposite the church there is a carriage museum (uncertain open times).

From (2km) the next junction you can reach **Kungsbacka** (2km). It has a cosy centre of low wooden buildings, mostly rebuilt after a fire in 1846. The church (1875) was restored in 1951.

The next town, Mölndal, now an industrial suburb of Gothenburg, used to exploit the waterfalls here to drive flour-mill and paper-mills. These gave way in the 19C to industries of more varied kinds. After 20km you can leave the road at the junction marked *Mölndal N* and *Gunnebo*. Follow the Gunnebo signs to see the manor, but on the way you may like to digress to the **Mill Village** following signs *Kvarnbyn*. This is a 19C industrial settlement on very hilly terrain alongside the falls which provided the vital power. It is not an open-air museum as such, since the houses and industries are owned privately or by the municipality, but tourists are welcome to wander and to visit the museums. Mölndal Museum has information and plans in English, as well as local finds and displays, and the local history society has two old houses with exhibitions including agriculture and industry in the area. The factories, mills and workers' dwellings clamber picturesquely over the hill.

Return and pick up the **Gunnebo** signs again. The *slott* or manor is situated on a height between the lakes Rådasjön and Stensjön. (Guided tours only, in Swedish but guide will speak English on request, Apr to Oct Mon–Sat 13.00–14,00, Sun 12.00, 13.00, 14.00, 15.00.)

The house, finished in 1796, was built as a summer retreat for the extremely prosperous Gothenburg businessman John Hall whose father had come to Sweden from Scotland. It has a formal terraced garden to front and rear and is surrounded by an 'English park'. It is a good example of Gustavian style, the Swedish version of neo-Classicism. The two main storeys are of wood painted to look like stone, resting on a basement of pink rendering, not visible from the front because of the slope of the land. The portico on the front has tall paired Ionic columns, and the windows have triangular pediments. At the rear is a grand stairway (reconstruction) over the basement to the terrace in front of the ground floor French windows. Above is a frieze of swags and above that a white-painted lead relief of harvest scenes.

One man, Carl Wilhelm Carlberg, was almost entirely responsible for the architecture and the interior design, plus the furnishings. Much of the sculpture, however, was carried out by an Italian artist, Gioacchino Frulli. The whole presents a picture of harmonious symmetry in tranquil colours.

An oval antechamber with Greek statues leads to the two-storey high **Grand Salon**, with large French windows, and mirrors between Ionic pilasters on the walls. The overdoors represent country pursuits—fishing, hunting, animal husbandry and gardening, and there are four statues of the seasons, with corresponding oval medallions above them. The ceiling is framed with elegant swags and a moulding of curving shapes, one of Carlberg's favourite motifs. The blue vases are East India Company porcelain (John Hall was a member of the Swedish East India Company). Two sham doors exist only for the sake of symmetry.

In the **dining-room**, a large relief of Amphitrite, the sea-goddess, should have been matched by one of the opposite wall. The overdoors have urns and vine-garlands. The tiled stove has urns, and a phoenix on top, of lead but made to look like bronze, and to one side is a warming-oven. In the alcove is an urn (copy) to which water could be pumped—an extraordinary refinement for the time.

On the other side of the Grand Salon is an **anteroom** with Wedgwood blue walls. The six armchairs are original, re-acquired from other owners, and the other chairs were made to match. There is a gilded table with a marble top. The watercolours show Gunnebo just when it was complete.

Mrs Hall's **bedroom** has green striped wallpaper. The chest is of continental design, while the chairs are Swedish. The overdoors have doves to symbolise love. Two further small rooms were for the lady's use, and on the other side of the hall were Mr Hall's rooms, very plain considering his wealth. The stove goes through to both rooms so it could be fed from the anteroom without disturbing him. There are portraits of Gustav III and Queen Sophia Magdalena.

Upstairs everything is much more modest, with trompe l'œil painting instead of sculpture. In one room is a series of portraits of owners and a model of the estate. In another is a portrait of Francesco de Miranda of Venezuela, who fell in love with Mrs Hall, and later became involved with the revolutionary struggle in South America. The story goes that he designed the revolutionary flag with yellow for her hair, blue for her eyes and red for her lips. Other rooms have displays of plans and sketches of architectural details for the house.

There is a café in the basement vaults. The rear garden has statues of the four seasons by Carlberg and ends in an oval pool with a fountain. The extensive grounds with attractive walks are open all year.

It is 6km to Gothenburg.

8

Gothenburg

***GOTHENBURG** (pop. 470,000, 'Göteborg' in Swedish), the second city of Sweden, has the most European feel of all Swedish cities. For 400 years it has been a gateway for the British and the Dutch who came to trade and settle. It is the country's greatest port, and its inhabitants have been used to lively commerce and to dealing with foreigners in the course of business. On the present site its charter dates only from 1621 so there are no winding medieval lanes. Instead, its history is that of a dynamic port and industrial city whose merchants built luxury mansions in spacious avenues and whose workers lived in quarters now regarded as picturesque. There are only two canals remaining, but the dominating influence is that of water all the same, from the great Göta river which enters the sea here, and where cargo vessels and jumbo ferries constantly manoeuvre.

The city has now of course spread out to modern suburbs but retains green spaces in the centre. Industry is concentrated on the north bank of the river. There is a university consisting of many colleges and institutes, and the city is the seat of a bishop. The respected Sahlgren hospital was founded in the 18C.

Tourist Information: Kungsportsplatsen 2, tel. (031) 10 07 40, hotel bookings, sightseeing tours, maps, timetables, leaflets (open Apr to Oct; shorter hours in Apr, Sept, Oct). There is also an office in Nordstan shopping precinct. There are two tourist publications which give opening times and other information, with English translations—'Vad händer i Göteborg' and 'Göteborg denna vecka'. Most museums are open only from 11.00 to 16.00, though there are exceptions. The **Gothenburg Card** saves money on museums, sights, parking, travel, boat trips and shopping.

Travel within the city. The easiest system to use is the tram, which to a great extent fulfils the function of an underground. The map is easy to grasp, each stop is clearly marked with its name, and each tram with its number and destination. The tramlines are usually in the middle of the road and cars take the sides. If you do not have a Gothenburg Card, tickets can be bought from the driver, or you can buy a plastic card from the driver or Pressbyrå which is then put in a machine on the tram for the appropriate amount to be deducted. The card is valid on all buses, trams and Älvsnabben, the boat from Lilla Bommen to Hisingen and Klippan. Tel. (031) 80 12 35 for travel information.

Emergencies. Police, Fire, Ambulance: tel. 90 000 (all over the country). **Medical information**: tel. (031) 41 55 00. **Clinic**: City-Akuten in NK building, tel. (031) 10 10 10, 08.00–20.00. **All-night chemist** (*apotek*) in Nordstan shopping precinct.

Telephone, Telegram and Telex: Hvitfeldsplatsen 9, near Kungsgatan, open Mon–Fri 09.00–18.00, Sat 10.00–14.00. Tel. (031) 770 78 15.

Exchange: Forex, Central Station, 08.00–21.00, tel. (031) 15 65 16.

Main post office: Drottningtorget. Exchange. Mon–Fri 09.00–18.00, Sat 09.00–12.00.

History. Present-day Gothenburg represents the fifth attempt to establish a port on the west coast of Sweden. In medieval times the town of Lödöse, 40km up the Göta river, was exporting iron and copper, hides and butter, and importing sugar, salt and textiles. It reached its heyday in the 13C and 14C. But Denmark and Norway controlled the area around Bohus fortress on the way out to the sea and collected drastic tolls, so in 1473 New Lödöse was founded in the area known as Gamlestaden considerably north of the present old centre. This was protected by the fortress of (Old) Älvsborg further down the river near the Älvsborg Bridge at Klippan.

Gustav Vasa then commanded the inhabitants to settle around the fortress, but Karl XI decided the north bank was a better position and founded the first town actually called Gothenburg on Hisingen. This was burnt by the Danes in 1611 during the Kalmar War. In the same war Älvsborg fortress fell and the Danes demanded the astronomical total of one million riksdaler for this and other properties.

It took Gustavus Adolphus six years to pay off the ransom and start planning his grand new city—where the centre is today. Building began in 1619, designed by Dutch engineers. The ground plan was based on a grid with four canals, Stora Hamnkanal, used as the harbour, and Vallgraven/Rosenlundskanal which are still there, and canals along what are now Västra Hamngatan and Östra Hamngatan.

Granite walls surrounded by moats were entered either by the canals or three land gates: the Kungsport Drottningport (King's Gate) at Kungsportsplatsen, the (Queen's Gate) on Drottningtorget by the Central Station, and Karls port (Karl's Gate) at the west end of Kungsgatan. The town rose within the walls and by the end of the century construction culminated in the two forts Skansen Kronan and Skansen Lejonet. English, Scottish, Dutch and German merchants were tempted to settle by such privileges as freedom from tax for 16 years and foreigners actually formed a majority on the city council.

In 1665 Gothenburg became the see of a bishop and in 1700 the seat of the local governor. By the 18C the town was solidly established and could turn its attention to trade and industry. Herring fishing was still a money-spinner, then came sugar-refining, and trade in iron and wood products.

In 1732 a ship of the Swedish East India Company sailed to Canton for the first time. The Swedish company in fact dealt mainly with China since the British monopolised India. Now the great merchant dynasties were founded, such as the Sahlgren family and many who came from Britain in this century and the next, such as the Chalmers and Dicksons. So began Gothenburg's period of prosperity and power, which could not be damped by fires or attacks from the Danes and Norwegians. The wealthy families gave generously of their riches and Niclas Sahlgren founded the hospital which bears his name, just as William Chalmers is still remembered in the name of Chalmers Tekniska Högskola, the technical college.

By 1800 the population was 18,000. A new boost to trade came with the opening of the Trollhätte Canal in 1800, and then the city profited mightily when Napoleon blockaded the rest of Europe, making Gothenburg a vital outlet for British trade. During the century canals were filled in, the railway was constructed (1856), and hotels opened hospitable doors. There were regular ships to England. Most emigrants passed through here, on their way to America via Hull and Liverpool, and bought their tickets in the building still labelled Amerikahus. (The road along the quay is called Emigrant-vägen.)

The population rose to 130,000 in 1900. The 20C brought shipbuilding, car manufacture and ball-bearings. Götaälvsbron (Göta Älv bridge) was built in 1939, and Älvborgsbron (Älvsborg bridge) in 1966. The Tingstad tunnel was finished two years later.

As Sweden was neutral in the Second World War, industry did not suffer. It was only in the 1970s with the decline of the shipping industry that Gothenburg started a modest decrease in population from 450,000 in 1975. Volvo is still here as a major industry, having been started in 1927 by two engineers from the ball-bearing factory SKF who decided to produce a tough car ('volvo' is Latin for 'I roll'). The shipyards now employ only a few thousand but the port is a major employer.

The port of Gothenburg is the largest port in Scandinavia, and the tenth largest in Europe; it is a company wholly owned by the City of Gothenburg. Part of the area, near Götaälvsbron, is designated a free port. In early years large ships could come up the Göta river to just beyond where Älvborgsbron is today. From this point rowing boats would take the goods to the harbour in the Stora Hamncanal. The river had to be dredged before ships could get any further. In 1845 the first stone quay, Stenpiren, was built, then came Skeppsbrokaj and Packhuskaj. The first 20 years of the 20C saw four more new quays plus one for the fishing port, and a harbour on the N side for coal imports.

The ships of the Wilson Line set off from Gothenburg to Hull taking emigrants on the first stage of the long journey to America. In 1915 the Swedish-American Line was started to take them directly to the States. In the 1960s new methods of transport of goods by sea demanded new harbours and almost 2km of land was reclaimed to make the ports of Skandia (1970), a container port, and Älvsborg, (1979) a roll-on-roll-off port. Cars and paper are important cargoes.

The value of the dry goods handled is greater than that of the oil, but oil is the biggest single product. There are three oil terminals, Ryahamn, Skarsvikshamn and Torshamn.

Today most of the port lies beyond the Älvborgsbron—on the city side are now mainly passenger ferries to Denmark and Germany.

The district called Hisingen on the north side of the river is actually an island, the fourth largest in Sweden (192km sq). In the 19C it became an important industrial area, with mechanical workshops. Some of these developed into shipyards: the Eriksberg, Lindholmen, Götaverket (now Cityvarvet) and Arendalsvarvet being active into the 1970s. Only one is now operating, which does maintenance work, and the future of that is uncertain since one of its main customers was the former USSR.

A.   Old Town North

Södra Vägen leads into the city from the E6—follow the signs *Göteborg C*. After crossing Engelbrektsgatan there is a large open space on the right, used for markets, football and car parking. Given the parking situation, and barred and one-way streets further in, this is a good option for the first-time visitor, Other useful car parks are at Gamla Ullevi, Nordstan shopping precinct and near Liseberg.

Södra Vägen then leads over a narrow park, and the Kungsportsbro (King's Gate Bridge) crosses the canal. Here is Kungsportsplatsen, with an equestrian statue of Karl IX by John Börjeson (1904), known to Gothenburgers as the Copper Mare, although it is a stallion. The **tourist bureau** is beside it on the right, and on the other side of the bridge is the pick-up point for **Paddan sightseeing boats** which tour the canals and harbour and go to Liseberg. Sightseeing buses also depart from here.

The centre of old Gothenburg is Gustav Adolfs torg, and this is most easily reached by continuing north along Östra Hamngatan. As the road passes over the next canal there is on the right a shady paved area, **Brunnsparken**. As the name suggests, there used to be a spa establishment here, and before that the iron-weighing house. Iron was brought by boat along the canal to be weighed for export: at the end of the 18C iron was the most important export from Sweden. In 1801 the weighing house was moved to Järntorget (see below). Now there on the square is a fountain with a statue by Per Hasselberg (1883) affectionately known as 'Johanna in Brunnsparken'.

The building behind has had a chequered history. Originally designed by Carl Hårleman in 1749, it included a sugar factory, to which cargo boats could tie up directly. It suffered in the great fire of 1792, and eventually was bought and remodelled into dwellings. A wealthy couple, Pontus and Göthilda Fürstenberg, moved in in 1880 and had the novel idea for the time of building a private art gallery on the top floor with lighting from above—as well as electric light, the first in Gothenburg. At the same time the interior was given a grand Baroque facelift. Now after standing empty for some time its future is uncertain. (See under Konstmuseet.)

The view from the other side of the bridge with Norra Hamngatan and Södra Hamngatan on either side of the canal gives an impression of the grandeur of the past, though many of the great houses have gone.

In the middle of **Gustav Adolfs torg**, to the left on the other side of the canal stands a **statue** of the founder of the city, Gustavus Adolphus. The original work of art was commissioned in Germany in the mid 19C, but on its journey to Sweden was lost overboard. The Heligolanders who rescued it demanded so much salvage money the thrifty citizens of Gothenburg decided to have another made instead.

To the east of the square next to the canal is the **Rådhus** (town hall) designed by Nicodemus Tessin the Elder in 1672. The third storey was added in the 19C. The rusticated ground floor supports a yellow-rendered façade with pilasters, topped with a pediment containing a clock and figures representing Law and Justice. In the courtyard is a fountain with a statue of a sitting girl by Gerhard Henning. The wing on the right, designed by Gunnar Asplund, creator of the Stockholm City Library, has **reliefs** by Eric Grate (1935–37).

The north side of the square begins with the Wenngren house, built for a city councillor in 1759, again with a 19C third storey. It has curiously shaped pediments over the windows. Next comes the 1746 Stadshus (city hall) designed by Bengt Wilhelm Carlberg. On the wall is a plaque commemorating Admiral Lord James de Saumarez (1757–1836), a British naval officer who commanded the British Baltic fleet sent to defend Sweden in 1809, when the Russians were trying to force Sweden to join the blockade of Britain. The Admiral brought his fleet to the coast at Vinga island and put paid to the threat.

Next to the city hall is the former Börsen (exchange) designed by Per Johan Ekman and finished in 1849. The ground floor portico is enclosed by five doors and the Classical columns support a balcony backed by five windows. The statues by Carl Gustav Quarnström represent hard work, good fortune, trade, seafaring, wealth and industry. It is a pity that it is not open to the public as it has a grand banqueting hall, works of art including Byström's Venus and Cupid and some mementoes of the composer Bedrich Smetana who lived and worked here in the mid 19C. It is the meeting-place of the city council.

Östra Hamngatan continues north towards the river. On the right is **Nordstan** Sweden's biggest shopping centre, built over several blocks cleared of slums so that the old streets continue through the glass doors and come out the other side, retaining their names. There is another **tourist bureau** and a 24-hour chemist in the precinct.

On the left at No. 11 is **Medicinhistoriska Museet** (open pm, except Mon) in the late 18C Oterdahl house, which served as a hospital from 1823 to 1854 (and later as police HQ). Here you may borrow a full English translation of the copious information. Room A: Health and Disease through the Ages, Room B: Folk medicine, Room C: Surgery and X-ray, Room D: Health

Care Professions, Room E: The Pharmacy, Room F: temporary displays, Room G: Gothenburg's health provision, Room H: a dentist's surgery. There are reconstructions of an operating theatre, a hospital ward, together with hundreds of instruments and samples of larger equipment.

Continue to the riverside. This area is called **Lilla Bommen** because it was a guarded entrance point when Östra Hamngatan was a canal—Bommen means 'the barrier'. You can either cross the perilous multi-stranded highway or use the glassed-in footbridge from Nordstan.

To the right rises **Utkiken** (Lookout) Gothenburg's skyscraper, in striking red and silver. It is 86m and 22 storeys high, the head offices of Skanska, a major building company, designed by Ralph Erskine and opened in 1989. The top offers spectacular **views**. The blue and white porcelain shards used decoratively here and there come from the East India Company ship *Götheborg* which sank in 1745 fully loaded with porcelain, tea, spices and silk from China; there are some modern paintings showing scenes from East India Company times. (Follow the signs *Göteborgs Utkiken* to the entrance and lift; open June–Aug 11.00–18.00; some refreshments at the top.)

Below Utkiken the graceful four-masted fully-rigged sailing ship is the *Viking*, built in 1907 as a training-vessel. Between the wars she plied between England and Australia making her last voyage in 1948. She is 91m long and her highest mast is 53m.

Across the little harbour is the impressive new **Opera House** (1994), with room for 1250 spectators in the main hall. In front stands Lenny Clarhäll's Venus (the two tall dark shapes), and the entrance wall reliefs each represent a composer. Other important new artworks are inside, notably the textile Scenrum by Britt-Marie Hansson. Along the quay behind are moored 12 vessels included in the **Maritima Centrum**. The ships and boats are open to visitors, and on the shore are a visitor centre, exhibitions and refreshments.

Return south by Torggatan or any parallel street, and at Kronhusgatan turn right to **Kronhuset**. This is Gothenburg's oldest secular building, erected 1642–55 in Dutch style as a granary and armoury. Here in 1660, the five-year-old Karl XI was proclaimed king after the death of his father in the Governor's Residence here in Gothenburg. From 1680 to 1898 it was used as a garrison church. The restored roof is in copper, replacing the original tiles. The ground floor is used for changing exhibitions and the upper floor portrays the first hundred years of **city history**, the 17C when Sweden was a European power. (Open 12.00–16.00, Sun 11.00–17.00, closed Mon, Sept–Apr. No labels in English.)

Aspects of Gothenburg history are grouped in sections, such as education, with a globe, wooden spanking implement and ABC book, and medicine with childbirth forceps and a bleeding-bowl with shaped rim. Other sections deal with the church, and punishment. There is a model of **Kronhuset** and one of the King's Gate of 1652 designed by Erik Dahlberg, now destroyed. The reconstructed one-room cottage is that of a local wise woman concocting herbal remedies, and there is an example of a prosperous home of the period. Many other items bear witness to the growing and confident wealth of the city in its first century. The courtyard outside is lined with small shops and workshops in the 18C wings. Pottery, glassware and silverware are made on the premises and there is a 19C grocer's with goods for sale. To one side is a small park with a herb garden.

Postgatan runs along the Kronhus area to the south. If you take this to the right and then Smedjegatan to the left you will be back on the canal on

Norra Hamngatan. On the right No. 4 has pretty stucco oriels while No. 6 (1732) was the most expensive house of its time.

No. 12 is the sober brick **Ostindiska huset** (East India House) built in 1750–62 by Bengt Wilhelm Carlberg, the city architect, and Carl Hårleman, the court architect, as offices, store and auction rooms for the powerful East India Company. Now it houses Gothenburg's principal museum, renamed Stadsmuseum, at the time of writing just beginning a far-reaching programme of rebuilding and reorganisation which should be complete by 1996. The historical and archaeological collections will remain here and will be joined by the collections of the former Industrimuseum and Skolmuseum. All are being totally rearranged in the new premises to provide a complete picture of the history of Gothenburg and western Sweden. Parts will reopen as they are completed.

Back on Norra Hamngatan, No. 14, the **Sahlgrenska** house built in 1753 and later renovated, is approached by imposing steps with wrought-iron railing and lampposts and with a broken pediment over the door. It was built by the widow of Jacob Sahlgren of the prominent Gothenburg family. Jacob was the brother of Niclas Sahlgren after whom the hospital here is still called—he financed the hospital in his will, and was said to be the richest man in the East India Company.

The **Kristine church**, named after Queen Kristina, or the German Church (open 12.00–15.00) was originally built in 1624 and the burial chapel to the east in 1682, but fires meant rebuilding in 1742–80. The tower is by Adelcrantz of 1783. Inside, the 19C stained glass with Evangelists, saints and prophets is set in Gothic-style tracery. The west half of the church has a gallery resting on slim Classical columns. Behind the altar is the eight-sided Baroque **Ascheberg burial chapel**. Rutger von Ascheberg (1621–93) was a Swedish field-marshal, member of the king's council and governor of Skåne, Halland and Bohuslän at the time these provinces were won from Denmark. His tomb is of worked metal over a fabric-covered base. The chapel contains also the tombs of six of his 25 offspring, some dying very young in the service of their country. On the walls are hung coats of arms and shields, and statues of saints stand in the niches.

Walking along the side of the town hall will bring you back to Gustav Adolfs torg.

B. Old Town South

Södra Hamngatan along the south bank of the Stora Hamncanal used to have the most elegant houses, two storeys in wood. After the fire of 1802 wooden buildings were forbidden, and No. 31, the **Frimurarhus** (Freemasons' Hall) (1806), is a good example of the rebuilding , with tall fluted Ionic pilasters rising through three storeys. The other façade still unchanged is No. 11, with rusticated ground floor and Ionic columns above. This is the Chalmerska house of 1805 by Carl Wilhelm Carlberg for William Chalmers, a Scottish businessman and director of the East India Company, who worked in Canton for many years. He was also a benefactor of the town and the Chalmers Technical College still bears his name.

Lilla Torg is a small open triangle by the bridge. The statue by John Börjeson of 1905 is of Jonas Alströmer, best known for introducing the potato to Sweden in the 18C. On the west side with the corner tower (of which the architect was especially proud) is the Wijkska house (1853) by A.W. Edelsvärd.

From here you can take Otterhällegatan which climbs steeply to the so-called **Drottning Kristinas jaktslott** (Queen Kristina's hunting lodge) (also accessible by a path from Kungsgatan). From here it is five or ten minutes' climb between flats and offices on one side, and hewn rock, perched on which is a circular block of flats, on the other. The diminutive villa which was originally elsewhere, is mainly 18C and therefore nothing to do with Queen Kristina. There is a café on the ground floor (open 11.00–16.00) and you can borrow a key to look at a room upstairs with a beamed ceiling and some later furniture.

From Lilla Torg continue to the end of Södra Hamngatan where No. 1 is the **Governor's Residence** with a carved doorway displaying the arms of Governor Lennart Torstensson and his wife Beate de la Gardie for whom the house was built in 1648. Karl X Gustav died here in 1660, precipitating the proclamation of his young son as king which took place in Kronhuset. The house was remodelled in 1855.

Across the road on the quayside is Stenpiren (the Stone Pier) where Carl Milles' **Delaware monument** commemorates the first Swedish settlement in the USA in 1638. This is a bronze cast (1938) of the original in Swedish granite which is in Wilmington, Delaware, USA. The ship on top of the 6m plinth is the *Calmare Nyckel*, one of two ships used by the emigrants. Among the reliefs on the sides, labelled in English, are Swedes buying land from the Indians and a runaway horse returned by Indians.

Many river and archipelago trips start near here, including those to Elfsborg and Vinga, and harbour tours.

Return past Lilla Torg and turn right down **Västra Hamngatan**. No. 6, originally a bank, is now **Antikhallarna**, the Antique Halls. Inside under the lavishly decorated ceiling are dozens of small antique shops on two levels, selling gold, silver, coins, books, porcelain, stamps and furniture among other things. (Closed at weekends; café on upper floor.)

Other houses in the street also reflect the wealth of the 19C, for example, No. 8 with grinning lions' heads and cartouches, and No. 10 with rusticated ground floor and stucco decoration over the windows. On the other side are No. 17, now the cathedral offices, and No. 15 which once housed the grammar school and then the telegraph offices.

The cathedral is on the even-numbered side. On the pavement in front of it is Jonas Hagberg's fountain of 1817, part of the city water system which brought water from Kalleback not far away. The present neo-Classical **Domkyrka** was designed by C.W. Carlberg, one of a family of Gothenburg architects, and consecrated in 1815, though the tower was not finished until ten years later. It stands on piles in the marshiest area of Gothenburg. Constructed in yellow brick, it has four massive Scottish sandstone columns supporting a pediment, while the windows are of almost domestic character. The tower is crowned by a black two-stage lantern with four clocks.

Inside, the dramatic gilded altarpiece immediately strikes you from the entrance. The shallow curved chancel wall is framed with Ionic pilasters and narrow galleries each side serve as transepts. Apart from the altar the impression is of restrained gilded decoration. To each side are enclosed wooden verandas, neatly net-curtained, one of which leads to the pulpit. Two stately hymn-number boards match the rest of the ornament. To the left of the entrance is a chapel with richly coloured modern stained glass and a textile hanging of Christian symbols in subdued blues and creams.

After visiting the cathedral take Kungsgatan almost opposite. 500m along is the 7m high bulk of the **Carolus Rex bastion**. At the top is an explanation in English, and a view of modern industrial Gothenburg, which with cranes and factory chimneys dwarfs the bastion. At the end of the 17C Erik Dahlberg modernised the defences of the city with ravelins, forts and bastions of which this is the only one left.

On descending from the bastion keep turning left to reach the canal bank. and a few hundred metres along you will find the **Feskekörka** (Fish church in Gothenburg dialect). This fish market was built in 1874 and its neo-Gothic style inspired its nickname. Inside, innumerable species of fish are on sale.

Along the canal bank you can still see the V-shape of a defensive ravelin jutting out. As you approach Kungsportsplatsen one of the main shopping areas is on the left, with pedestrianised streets. The barrel-roofed 1888 **Saluhall** looking as if it had been planned as a greenhouse is a food market, now a protected historic building. You are now back at Kungsportsplatsen.

The imposing **King's Gate** designed by Erik Dahlberg (model in Kron-huset) used to stand here and was demolished in 1839. The **Kungsport bridge** was opened in 1901 and the wrought-iron lamps were then lit by gas. Stora Nygatan continues north along the canal bank. At No. 11 some distance along, the composer Smetana lived (1857–58). He was conductor of the Gothenburg Philharmonic Orchestra 1856–59 and again in 1860.

C. Avenyn

At the south end of Kungsportsbro, Södra Vägen from the motorway meets **Kungsportsavenyn** which runs south-east to Götaplatsen. Called 'Avenyn' for short, it is the fashionable area of Gothenburg and still has some of its grand 19C buildings, once luxurious private homes, now with ground floors converted into shops and restaurants.

With your back to the end of the bridge, you see a little way to the left the entrance to **Trädgårdsföreningens Park** (literally Garden Association Park) with several attractions (open 09.00–21.00, entry fee May–Aug, free deckchairs, concerts in the summer). The park was started in 1842, and in 1878 the imposing **Palmhuset** was built by a Scottish firm which brought the parts from Scotland. Here there are succulents, flowering trees, tropical plants and water-lilies (open June–Aug 10.00–16.00).

Next to the Palm House is **Fjärilshuset**, the butterfly house, in a green-house (open all year, closed Mon, except June–Aug). This is in two sections, both tropical, the Old World (East Asia) on the left, and the New World (Central and South America) on the right. The temperature is 25°C and the humidity 80 per cent. There are 200–300 butterflies at any one time, each living for 2–3 weeks.

Further on is the **Rosarium**, an historical rose garden with 3000 species. The information boards are only in Swedish but you can follow the chrono-logy of rose history by noting the numbers at the top left of the boards. Wild Asian roses are grown beneath trees before you come to the formal rose garden. There is also a rock garden, a scented garden, a handicraft centre and a whole array of modern statuary. For example, near the Rosarium is the 'Vanished Bride' by Lars Stocks, showing such poignant remains as an umbrella and shoes. There is a bust of the poet Carl Michael Bellman and near the Södra Vägen entrance is 'The Climber' by Björn Therkelson (1986).

From the entrance to the park there are summertime tours of the city by miniature train.

In the small park between Södra Vägen and Avenyn, opposite the theatre, is a replica of the statue **Wrestlers** by Johan Peter Molin, a sculptor who came from Gothenburg. **Stora Teatern** (Grand Theatre) on the other side of the road was built in 1859, and functioned as an opera house until the new one on the riverside was built. Near it is a statue of John Ericsson (1803–89) who perfected the screw propeller and built several warships for the American navy.

The **Kungspark** behind the theatre along both sides of **Nya Allén** has limes, elms and chestnuts and is particularly attractive in early summer when the rhododendrons are in bloom, planted along the canal as they are also in Trädgårdsföreningen. There are a number of statues including that of a young deer behind the theatre and further along Tore Strindberg's 'Crocus Girl'. Nya Allén is a 2km-long avenue laid out in 1823; running parallel to it is Parkgatan. If you return from your walk in the Kungspark by **Parkgatan** the roads to the south afford glimpses of the prodigious wealth of 19C Gothenburg reflected in opulent mansions. **Parkgatan 25** (all the odd numbers are this side of Avenyn) possibly outdoes them all. It was built in 1885–89 by Adrian Peterson and the interior has been remodelled in Art Nouveau, but it is not open to the public. Parkgatan 2, on the other side of Avenyn where the even numbers are, is the **Dickson Villa** built for Oscar Dickson in 1859–62 by V. Boulnois, with Classical columns supporting the balcony, a closed veranda each side and pediments over the first floor windows. Restrained stucco borders edge the windows.

The eastern end of Parkgatan fringes **Heden**, the large open space which is used for fairs, sport and car parking. This used to be common grazing ground (Heden means 'heath'), then was a drilling ground for the local soldiery. Attempts are always being made to build on it, but the football players up to now have won the day.

Avenyn continues south-east and on the corner with Vasagatan to the right there is stone and brick building called **Valand** where the Gothenburg Art College (1886) had such distinguished teachers as Carl Larsson and Carl Wilhelmson. The college has moved but is still called Valand. In Vasagatan next to Valand there is ***Röhsska Konstslöjdsmuseet** (Museum of Arts and Crafts, open 11.00–16.00, closed Mon, Sept–April; plan in English). A pair of Chinese lions flank the entrance to this attractive brick building which looks older than it is (1914). The **basement** contains excellent **textiles**, and on the ground floor are displays from the **Mediterranean** and the **Near East**, including 600 BC reliefs from Babylon. The first floor is mainly for temporary exhibitions but also has European furniture and Swedish design. The second floor has good collections of **porcelain** including Sèvres and Meissen, **gold** and **silver**, both ecclesiastical and secular, and a comprehensive display of **book-bindings** from the 16C to the 20C. There is a Vasa Bible of the mid 16C translated by Laurentius and Olaus Petri—this translation was in fact superseded only in 1917—and an unusual display of **title pages**. The third floor has **Oriental art**, including silk paintings, carvings, statues, netsuke, pottery, bronzes and lacquer. **Japanese prints** 17C–19C are on pull-out screens. A new 20C design and craft section is soon to be added.

You could continue out along Vasagatan to Vasaparken where the university has its administrative building. Gothenburg University was formed in 1954 by the merging of the medical school with Gothenburg college.

Back on Avenyn, the block of buildings opposite Valand is another good example of the opulence of the 19C, with two sets of caryatids, and lush stucco work. Avenyn continues its stately way to *Götaplatsen, the cultural heart of the city. The vista culminates in the yellow brick Konstmuseum, rising high behind the gigantic **Poseidon statue** by Carl Milles (1930).

On the left the **library** has a display of 23 tiny reconstructions of workshops from the turn of the century, including wagon-maker's, upholsterer's and basketmaker's. Behind the library is the small **Teaterhistoriska Museum** housed at the back of the old Lorensberg Theatre, now restored after some years as a cinema. The museum has some sketches, costumes and photos showing Gothenburg theatre history from the 1920s onwards. Also on the left is the theatre.

On the right are the art gallery (**Konsthallen**) with changing exhibitions, and the **concert hall**, well known for its good acoustics.

The *Konstmuseum (Art Museum) is one of the best in the country (open Tue–Fri 11.00–16.00, also Wed to 21.00, Sat, Sun 10.00–17.00; open also Mon in summer. Café, bookshop). To the left as you approach are two Milles' statues, one of dancers, the other on a column called 'The Wings'. By October 1995 rebuilding work should be finished and the staircase replaced, from which such a splendid view of Avenyn can be enjoyed. Under the steps however a new entrance leads to the new Hasselblad photo-centre, and the Stena Hall (Hasselblad and Stena are financing the alterations) and the café and bookshop are also now on this level. A new interior staircase leads up to the former entrance hall which was also a Sculpture Hall, and may still be so. From the opposite side of the hall a staircase leads down to an imaginatively designed wing laid out in terraces displaying **post-war art**. (This again is liable to change.) Stairs at each end of the hall lead to the upper floors, the next one up being confusingly labelled 5 because the above-mentioned terraces are included in the numbering.

In a room at the right-hand end of the hall is (again, usually) a section devoted to lithographs and woodcuts by **Edvard Munch** the Norwegian artist (1863–1944). From this end you can reach Room 4 on Floor 5 where there are several paintings by David Klöcker Ehrenstrahl (1628–98), the Swedish court painter. Rooms 5–7 show paintings from Italy and Spain 1500–1750, and include works by Canaletto, Francesco Guardi, Giacomo Ceruti and Francesco de Zurbarán. In Room 8 is Rembrandt's _Knight with Falcon_, and in Room 9 Rubens' _Adoration of the Magi_. A long gallery displays the work of the Swedish neo-Classicist sculptor **Johan Tobias Sergel** (1740–1814). Rooms 12–15 have 19C Scandinavian art.

On Floor 6, Rooms 16–18 are a representation of the **Fürstenberg Gallery**. Pontus Fürstenberg (see Brunnsparken above) opened his innovative gallery in 1885 in his house on Brunnsparken. By the time he died in 1902 his art collection of 260 paintings and sculptures was the largest in Sweden, and included much by Carl Larsson who was one of his special protégés. After the Fürstenbergs died the collection went first to the museum in East India House, then when this art museum was built the interior of the original Fürstenberg gallery was reconstructed as a background for his collection.

In Room 16 can be seen a reproduction of a **water-colour** by Carl Larsson (1853–1919) showing Pontus sitting among the works of art in Room 18 (compare the picture in the background by Raphael Collin). Behind him his wife Göthilda is having her portrait painted by the artist Ernst Josephson (1857–1906). Pontus and Göthilda are also portrayed by **Anders Zorn** (1860–1920) in Room 18. There are other portraits by **Carl Larsson** which show the background of the gallery, and more of the best Swedish artists of the same period are in Room 20, with works by Anders Zorn, Ernst Josephson and Hugo Birger, whose **Scandinavian Artists' Breakfast** is in Room 18, with a key to who's who in the picture. These artists and others reflected the mood of national Romanticism and Symbolism c 1890, which was to be replaced by Expressionism, Modernism and Cubism. In Room 21 are the works of **Ivar Arosenius** (1878–1909). Born in Gothenburg, he led a short and dissipated life while producing caricatures of the Gothenburgers of his day.

Rooms 22–24 contain **Scandinavian art** 1890–1940 and there is a special section on Gothenburg artists 1920–60 in Room 24. About this time a group of artists who had all studied at Valand, the Gothenburg Art College, became known as the **Gothenburg Colourists**. The movement was triggered by a 1927 exhibit of Carl Kylberg, and as the name implies they used bright pure colour. The artists included Ivan Ivarson, Inge Schiöler, Åke Göransson and Ragnar Sandberg.

Room 25 has 18C artists such as **Alexander Roslin** and Elias Martin. Room 26 has medieval art and Rooms 27–29 French art 1800–1940. There are one or two works each by Monet, Renoir, Sisley, Gauguin, Degas, Henri Rousseau, Corot, Courbet, Delacroix, Pissarro, Rodin, Van Gogh, Dufy, Braque, Chagall, Derain and Picasso.

D. The Liseberg Area

Behind the art museum, **Renströmsparken** is reached by leaving Götaplatsen to the left of the museum and skirting **Artisten**, the new Music and Theatre College, part of the university, which has a programme of public concerts. In the park is a landscaped water-lily pond, and more rhododendrons, at their best in early summer. Beside the pond is a bust of Gustav III commemorating the fact that he was the first head of state to offer friendship to the United States after the War of Independence. Nearby is a sculpture of two young riders, presented by the town of Åbo in Finland. Behind stand the University Library (1954) and the Humanities Department.

The footpath to the left of the library leads down steps to the main road. Across the intersection is **Liseberg**, the amusement park which is Sweden's most-visited attraction with three million people a year. You can get there too by vintage tram from the central station, or by Paddan boat also from near the station.

It is open May to August, and April and September weekends. Times vary, usually opening at 12.00 but sometimes at 10.00 on weekday mornings without an entrance fee, for walking around only when the rides are not working. It is also open in the evenings for concerts, jazz, pop, rock, cabaret and folk dance, and the season finishes in September with fireworks. There are varying types of entrance ticket, to include different rides and refreshments—arrangements change from year to year.

With an area of 14 ha, Liseberg was opened in 1923 and aims to provide amusement for every age group. Care has been taken to retain trees and to lay out flower-beds. Attractions include the Flume Ride and roller-coaster, but there are rides for small children and plentiful opportunities for eating. Sverige plats (Sweden place) has an unusual fountain and the whole is perhaps at its best lit up after dark.

On leaving Liseberg on the same side as you entered you can continue east along Örgrytevägen, passing Svenska Mässan, the trade fair centre, and the jetty where the Liseberg Paddan boats from Slussplatsen moor. When you reach the E6 you can see **Örgryte Old Church** on the other side of the road among trees.

This is the oldest church in Gothenburg. There is a legend that St. Sigfrid founded a church on this spot, and the name of the road intersection is S:t Sigfrids Plan. The present church was begun c 1250 but the entrance-hall is 17C and the tower and chancel 18C as are the ceiling-paintings. These are the Trinity, Christ the Judge, and the fate of the blessed and the damned. There are memorial tablets to two Britons—Eliza Gordon (1811), the wife of the British Consul, and a businessman named David Low (1823). The pulpit is of 1780 and the font 1738.

On leaving the church it is a pleasant stroll along the side road parallel to the E6 towards the north as far as the footbridge over the E6. On the other side a road almost straight ahead comes out at the intersection of Åvägen and Valhallagatan. A left turn brings you to the **Etnografiska museet** (open Tue–Fri 11.00–16.00, Sat, Sun to 17.00. English leaflet, refreshments). The ethnographical collections moved here to the Industrimuseum premises in 1994, and at the time of writing the museum was building up its basic exhibitions. So far, there is a comprehensive section on the Indian races of both North and South America, with particular emphasis on textiles, and with artefacts dating back to 2500 BC. Displays will soon be expanded.

At Åvägen 15, two blocks to the north, an old transmission belt factory interior of about 1900 has been preserved. (Guided tours summer pm.)

Across the road from the ethnographical museum is the **Valhalla** indoor swimming pool behind which is the orange-painted **Scandinavium** indoor stadium with curving roof seating 12,500. At the end of Valhallagatan, Skånegatan to the right would bring you to the new **Ullevi** stadium holding 45,000, and Gamla Ullevi (old Ullevi) is not far away to the left. If you cross Skånegatan at the end of Valhallagatan and take Berzeliigatan, it will bring you back to Götaplatsen.

E. Haga

The area due south of the fortified town was the first working-class suburb. It was razed twice in the 17C to ease defence when the Danes attacked, but was rebuilt and retains some old houses on the original street pattern. After being neglected for many years an attempt is being made to clean and restore it.

Järntorget (Iron Square) to the west was so called because the iron-weighing house stood here after being moved from Brunnspark. The **fountain** is by Tore Strindberg (1927) and its statues represent the five continents to which the iron was exported. Around the bowl are the stamps of different iron companies. The north part of the square is now named Olof Palmes Plats.

In the streets to the south and east are many old wooden houses, often with a ground floor of stone. After so many fires wooden houses of more than two floors were forbidden, and stone houses of more than two floors were liable to sink into the clay on which the city rests. At the time of the industrial revolution so much new accommodation was required that a governor hit on the idea of a stone ground floor and wood above that—hence the name 'governor's houses', common in many parts of the city. Walking along Haga Nygatan and the adjoining streets gives an impression of the old quarter with occasional gems. At Haga Nygatan 7–9 a worker's house has been reconstructed which can be visited (ask at the tourist bureau).

On a steep tree-covered knoll to the south stands the fort **Skansen Kronan**, approached from Skanstorget or Lilla Risåsgatan. It is a stiff climb, and trees obscure the view from the top somewhat. The octagonal fort was planned by Erik Dahlberg as an integral part of the defences and was finished in 1697. It contains a small military museum (open Sat, Sun 12.00–15.00). On the first floor is a display of cannon; the wax models are wearing uniforms of 1794. On the second floor are uniforms through the ages, and on the top floor rifles, swords and some more modern uniforms and equipment, such as gas-masks.

(Skansen Kronan has a counterpart, **Skansen Lejonet**—Lion Fort—which has a lion on top. It was also designed by Erik Dahlberg, and is 1km north-east of the central station, along Kruthusgatan.)

F.   South-west Gothenburg

Masthugget and the Maritime Museum

Masthugget is so named because ships' masts were made here, and on Masthuggstorget is a modern wood sculpture based on masts. However, Stigbergstorget, the next stop on the tram-routes to Saltholmen and Frölunda, is nearer the church and museum. The church **Masthuggskyrkan** is reached by taking Bangatan to the south and then following the sign at the first turn left, climbing steeply. It is a good example of the national romantic style—it was finished in 1914. It is constructed of dark hand-made bricks and its tower is capped by a typical 'helm'. Inside, the romantic mood is furthered by the deep curved timbered roof reminiscent of a Viking ship. The ends of the timbers are visible and carved with patterns. The galleries are set on wooden columns and the organ gallery is carved with angels playing musical instruments. The striking carved and painted triptych on the altar is set off against the light-painted lower walls. From the terrace there is a **view** over the river, harbour and the Seaman's Tower.

On the other side of Bangatan towards Stigbergstorget is a substantial wooden house of c 1740, built for the widow of Lars Gathenhielm, an 18C privateer. The area south and west of the house was where seamen and shipyard workers lived and many 18C and 19C wooden houses are preserved especially around the idyllic **Pölgatan**.

Across Karl Johansgatan is the **Sjöfahrtsmuseum** (Maritime Museum, open Mon–Sat 12.00–16.00, Sun 11.00–17.00, closed Mon in winter). The museum is built on the site of the old shipyard once owned by Lars Gathenhielm, and it was also here that the last sailing-ship was built in 1887. The **aquarium** on the **ground floor** shows both local and tropical fish in large tanks depicting different environments such as stream, sea and harbour. In the tropical department there are snakes, turtles and alligators.

On the **first floor** is the history of ship-building from Viking times to the Middle Ages, including also the very early Nydam boat of the 4C which is shown in two possible reconstructions. There is a model of the **Gokstad ship**, now in Norway, of about 900, and of the **Calmare Nyckel** which carried the first settlers to Delaware in the 17C, shown on Milles' monument on Stenpiren. The exotic articles which were brought back from the east by the East India Company ships include carved ivory Chinese houseboats, carved boxes, porcelain and hundreds of other trinkets. There is a large collection of ships in bottles and a display of ropework. The many models in this section include the *G.D. Kennedy*, now the youth hostel ship, *af Chapman*, moored in Stockholm, and the *Viking*, moored in Gothenburg. Notice the array of **paintings of ships**—a captain would very often commission a painting of his ship for his home. The large central hall here has as its centre-piece a 1:12 model of the **Finland** which sailed to China in the late 18C. This room has many other models but its main function is to show off the collection of **figureheads**. On the other side of the central hall is a display on lighthouses and pilotage. Opening shortly on the rest of this floor will be an exhibition entitled Sail and Steam.

The **second floor** deals mainly with the 20C development of the port and shipyards, with maps, plans and large models. Unlike many maritime museums this one tries to present something of modern sea-faring and trade, for example there is a cut-away model of a large cargo ship. There is also a children's nautical playroom.

Behind the museum, the 62m-high **Sjömanstornet** (Seaman's Tower) (1934) is a war-memorial to Swedish seamen, with a figure of a woman looking out to sea, by Ivar Johnsson. The **view** from the top (lift) embraces the river, port and town to the east, and to the west the fishing harbour almost below, and down the river beyond.

The fishing harbour, reached by following the signposts *fiskhamn*, has fish auctions on weekday mornings at 07.00, a lively sight.

Klippan

The tram-stop Vagnhallen Majorna on the Kungssten or Högsbotorp route is a convenient approach to Klippan and there is also the Älvsnabben boat from Lilla Bommen (takes tram and bus cards, 30min).

Klippan Kulturreservat (Cultural Reserve) is on the waterfront beside Älvsborgsbron (bridge). The buildings are in general not open to the public but you can walk freely around them. Some of them were erected in the 18C for the East India Company whose ships docked here. The area later developed into an industrial estate with the sugar refinery, one of the most important industries in the 18C and early 19C, and the 19C Carnegie brewery. The sugar factory lasted until 1968 and the brewery a few years longer. Workers' houses, a school and chapel formed a complete community around the ruins of Älvsborg fortress. For the times this was something of a model industrial estate, with medical care, fixed wages and a savings' bank for the employees, to say nothing of the daily beer allowance.

On the left as you emerge from the underpass under Götaleden is a footpath running parallel to the main road. Just along here is a yellow manor house with older red-painted farm buildings around a farmyard. This was the site of Älvsborg royal manor from where the royal farms were managed. The animals were grazed on Slottsskogen (Castle Wood).

Return to the green behind the manor and cross it going towards the river. Across the small road you can enter a large **courtyard**. On the right, backing on to the road, is a terrace of houses for the employees of the sugar factory and brewery. Ahead to the right is the old stone **smithy** where anchors were made, originally a warehouse, and now an art gallery entered from the quayside, with a large anchor in front of the door.

On the edge of the river to the left the long low red wooden building was a **warehouse** for the East India Company, built in the 1770s. The light-coloured building further back off the road (1790s) also belonged to the company. At the other end of the lane to the side of this, the red wooden house on the corner was built in 1762, used variously as a dwelling, a bakehouse and customs-house.

On a knoll behind is **S:ta Birgitta's chapel**, built by the Scot David Carnegie in 1856 for his workers, in a style to remind him of the chapel in his home town of Balquidder. It has a wholly Swedish detached bell-tower. The brick house on the opposite side of the road was the school, and the pastel-painted wooden building was a gatekeeper's lodge.

Just along the shore is the Novotel Hotel, the exterior of which is a reconstructed version of **Carnegie's brewery**. The hotel has a leaflet on the history of the Carnegie industries and upstairs some photos of the reconstruction work. Behind the hotel is a silo and the new malthouse, while to the left is the old malthouse with characteristic kilns.

Beyond this group of buildings there are signs to **Gamla Älvsborg** which lead up to another rocky knoll with the ruins of Älvsborg fortress, roughly patched and covered with a roof. There was a wooden fort here in the 14C which became a stone castle in the 16C under the Vasas. It was supposed to defend New Lödöse (see History of Gothenburg) but was taken by the Danes and so expensively ransomed that it was decided to blow it up in 1660 and build Nya Elfsborg (see Excursions below). The fortress no longer has a good view of the river as it would have had in its heyday.

Beside the fortress is the loaf-sugar factory, and then come more 19C and early 20C industrial buildings also used in the sugar industry. The best view in the area is from the bridge, built in 1966, 45m high to give headroom to shipping.

Slottskogen

A tram labelled Marklandsgatan or Frölunda will stop at Linnéplatsen. (If driving, park inside the park at the end of Vegagatan; it is cheaper than the road outside.)

The very large park, **Slottskogen**, is where the royal animals were grazed. There are many attractions, signposted in Swedish with distances in metres. Some of the names are recognisable: the penguin pool and azalea valley, for example. There is an information board with English translations at the entrance. Some of the features are the aviary (*fågelhuset*), seal pool (*säldammen*), animal enclosures (*djurgårdarna*), children's zoo (*barnens zoo*). There are flamingoes from South America which have settled happily, though they tend to lose their pink colour after a time. Björngårdsvillan is a restaurant

On the edge of the park at the Vegagatan entrance is **Naturhistoriska Museet** (open Mon–Sat 09.00–16.00, Sun to 17.00; small leaflet in English, no English labels). The ground floor shows temporary exhibitions. The first floor has cases with fish, reptiles, sponges, insects and so on. There is a whale room reached off room 9 at one corner. The top floor has stuffed mammals in the centre and a very comprehensive collection of Scandinavian birds to one side and foreign birds on the other. The English leaflet points out some special items, for instance, the biggest animal, smallest bird and longest snake.

Not far below the museum is the small pond with a Henry Moore sculpture, 'Reclining Figure' (1961), near it. To the SE are some old farm-houses moved here from different parts of the country, some partly dating from the 18C (signboards in front of the first one, Gräfsnäsgården).

On the other side of the two parallel roads to the south-east of Slottskogen is the 175 ha **Botanic Garden**, entered at Carl Skottsbergs Gata 22 (open 09.00–18.00, greenhouse somewhat shorter hours). This is easily reached from town—tram-stop Botaniska Trädgården. Here plants flourish in Gothenburg's mild climate which otherwise grow only in Skåne. There are lilacs, Japanese cherries, azaleas, rhododendrons and berberis among many others, and a tropical greenhouse which has an orchid collection.

G.   Excursions from Gothenburg

Keillers Park—the name comes from another Scottish businessman—is on the north island of Hisingen and the highest point, **Ramberget**, offers a view of the city and the river.

Långedrag, with its marina, became a favourite resort in the 19C. It is the second to last stop on the Saltholmen tram, and **Saltholmen** itself offers bathing, and boats to the south part of the archipelago.

The archipelago. Vinga Island has a 19C lighthouse, which is on the logo used by the Port of Gothenburg, good swimming and fishing, and a museum with an Evert Taube exhibition, as the poet's father worked on the island. Despite the lighthouse and its predecessors the waters around the island are a ships' graveyard and the 19C pyramidal marker was made from wood from wrecks.

A boat goes to the island of **Marstrand** with its imposing castle, Carlsten Fortress, and streets of wooden houses (see Rte 10). Archipelago tours, ferries to the different islands, day or evening cruises, and trips on a vintage steamer are all on offer. Ask at the tourist bureau, or on the quaysides. The classic **Göta Canal trip** is quite expensive and takes 3–4 days (see Rte 9), but the canal boats offer day tours as well, and they also go out into the archipelago.

Nya Elfsborg. The nearest island with historical associations is Nya Elfsborg, a variant spelling of Älvsborg. Boats leave from Stenpiren where timetables are available. (Mid-May to beginning of Sept; guided tour of fortress in English included in price.) There is a commentary on the boat in English and Swedish pointing out areas of interest, such as the vast Scandia container terminal. Just before Älvsborgsbron is Klippan with the ruins of old Älvsborg. A red-painted stone after the bridge marks the old legal limit of the harbour area. A long white warehouse was a women's prison in the 19C.

The old Älvsborg fortress had to be ransomed from the Danes for 150,000 riksdaler in 1571, and when one million had to be paid again between 1614 and 1619 this was too much. So Nya (new) Elfsborg was sited on an island at the mouth of the Göta älv and stone from the old fortress was used for the new one. The fortress was planned by Johan Wärnschiöld but completed by the more famous Erik Dahlberg in 1660. It is an irregular pentagon with bastions, and casemates in the curtain walls. In the middle of the north curtain wall is a square tower. By the 1670s the Danes were back but were repulsed. However, in 1717 the threat was much more serious. The Norwegian Peder Tordenskiold with a Danish fleet made two attempts to take it and almost succeeded the second time, two years later, using a neighbouring island for cover. Later, until 1869, the building was used as a prison for serious offenders and persistent escapers.

After passing the little harbour and the defensive wall you arrive in the outer court. There was an inland harbour entered by an arch under the wall—it is hoped to restore this to its former state. The building to the right is the prison hospital built in 1773, now containing a museum usually visited at the end of the tour.

Perched on the centre wall, the tower contains a pretty little **chapel** designed by Jean de la Vallée, a good example of the 'Carolean' style—Swedish Baroque. The portrait over the altar is of Karl XII. The painted wooden gallery has portraits of Evangelists and prophets with decorative swags. The hole under the picture of Matthew was caused by a Danish cannon-ball. The story goes that it happened when soldiers were playing cards in the gallery during a service and the preacher was able to draw a salutary moral from the event. The cannon-ball over the door, however, was put there later. There is a trap-door in the floor through which ammunition was hauled up to the upper storey through a hole in the ceiling. In a cupboard in the gallery is a 1753 Bible and church silver. Outside stand two artillery shells adapted to serve as money-boxes.

The junior officers lived under the causeway to the church, and the senior officers and the commandant in the houses in the middle. The soldiers were accommodated in the east and south walls. The 18C and 19C prisoners' living-conditions in the cells in the walls are graphically described by the guide, and there are some illustrations, including the 'Elfsborg parade uniform', a set of iron shackles weighing 36.5kg, to prevent escapers swimming. The punishment cells, some completely dark, are also shown.

There is a picturesque café in a vaulted casemate.

The museum in the old hospital building has a model of the island in 1717, illustrations and much other information (Swedish) on the battles here and the people involved. There are also details about the subsequent prison, including prisoners' occupations—one was a student—and their daily menu, mostly porridge, pork and peas.

Borås, Hedared and Torpa

66km east from Gothenburg is the town of **Borås** (pop. 101,000), centre of the local textile industry. A new **textile museum** shows machines, fabrics and clothing (open Tue–Sun). The brick and granite town hall of 1910 was designed by Ivar Tengbom and Ernst Torulf, and the fountain on the square is by Nils Sjögren. There is an outdoor museum in Ramnaparken, and a zoo in Boråsparken, with African and Nordic animals—Borås lions have been exported to Longleat in England.

14km to the north-west on road 180 is **Hedared** with Sweden's only stave church, of the 16C, which is late for this type of construction. It is much plainer outside than its ornately carved Norwegian counterparts, and contains painting direct on the timber wall at the back of the altar from the 16C. This was discovered only in 1935, under the boards on which 18C paintings had been executed, which are now hinged to fold back. The other interior paintings are also 18C, with the Resurrection on a central roundel on the ceiling and seven apostles on the gallery. There is a medieval Madonna and two processional staves, with a stick for waking up sleepy members of the congregation.

24km east of Borås by way of Dannike (start by road 27, follow signs) **Torpa Stenhus** is a manor of which half is from the 15C and half from the 16C, built with defence in mind since it was near the border with Denmark. Some decoration and furnishing from the 16C is shown, and some weapons. There is a chapel, and you can explore the cellars and narrow servants' staircase.

9

The Göta Canal

Gustav Vasa in the 16C dreamed of cutting a waterway through Sweden from the Kattegat to the Baltic, and even that enterprising monarch was not the first to think of it. Between Gothenburg and Stockholm the rivers and lakes are so conveniently placed that, using the Baltic Sea as well, only about 100km needed to be excavated to achieve the entire through route of about 550km, which would avoid ships having to pass through the Öresund so close to the old enemy, Denmark.

Strictly speaking, the Göta Canal comprises the part between the two lakes of Vänern and Vättern in Västergötland and the section beyond Vättern to the Baltic, in Östergötland. The route between Gothenburg and Vänersborg is the Trollhätte Canal, and this is where efforts were first concentrated.

200 years after Gustav Vasa, in the reign of Karl XII, an attempt was made to bypass the Trollhättan Falls, the greatest obstacle, by the engineers Swedenborg and Polhem. It was not until 1800, however, that locks at last permitted passage through to Vänern. As for the rest of the route, it took the dynamic Baron Baltzar Bogislaus von Platen (1766–1829) to push through the ambitious plan to carve a navigable waterway to Stockholm.

He published his plan in 1806, and thought of it as not simply to further commerce but also for defence, to say nothing of the prestige which such a grand enterprise would give Sweden in the eyes of the world. In 1808 he brought Thomas Telford from Britain to survey and mark the route which he did, in just three weeks. (Telford helped to construct the Caledonian Canal in Scotland, and the two canals are now 'twinned'.)

In 1810 the Göta Canal Company received its charter and digging began. The statistics are staggering. It took 22 years, 58,000 soldiers (at various times), seven million man-days of 12 hours each. Eight million cubic metres of earth were removed with iron-clad wooden spades to a depth of 3m, and a width of 26m tapering down to 14m on the bottom. The west part was completed in 1822 and the whole finally inaugurated in 1832, sadly, three years after von Platen's death.

The **Trollhätte Canal** (see also Trollhättan) is 82km long, of which 10km is excavated channel, with six locks, and this part is still used today for serious commercial purposes. Through it, the ports on Vänern have an outlet to the sea, and millions of tonnes of oil, timber, paper, ore, coal and coke are transported every year. At the locks ships carrying up to 4000 tonnes are guided by illuminated screens which are also radar reflectors, and fluorescent leading lines guide them in. Transport times to Britain and Europe can be cut by up to a day by using the canal. The ports on Vänern are equipped with hot-water sprays and icebreakers, so business need not stop in winter.

The **Göta Canal** proper is now for leisure and holidays. Between one and two million people visit it a year and thousands of pleasure-boats pass through. For the classic trip from Gothenburg to Stockholm, and vice versa, three turn-of-the-century steamers, built to fit the locks and somewhat modernised, take about three and a half days, with stops and guided tours.

The Västergötland section starts at Sjötorp on Vänern and goes to Karlsborg on Vättern in 65km with 21 locks. The Östergötland section goes from Motala on Vättern to Mem on the Baltic in 92km with 37 locks. The highest point, 91.8m above sea level, is at (lake) Viken which serves as a reservoir for the locks.

There are several ways of enjoying the canal, which is generally open from mid May to the end of September.

1. The full trip Gothenburg to Stockholm or Stockholm to Gothenburg by historic steamer. The former direction is slightly preferable with more interesting stopping-places. Guided tours are arranged—there is a certain amount of spare time while the ship negotiates locks. For information, write to Rederiaktiebolaget Göta Kanal, Box 272, 401 24 Göteborg.

2. Shorter trips and day trips. Ask at any tourist bureau near the canal, or write to AB Göta Kanalbolag, Box 3, 591 21 Motala.

3. Your own boat or hired boat. Write to AB Göta Kanalbolag as above for details of fees, services and mooring-places.

4. Cycle along the towpath. Package available from Mariestads Turistbyrå, Hamnplan, 542 30 Mariestad, and bicycles for hire at many places—ask any tourist bureau.

The Göta Canal from Gothenburg to Stockholm

(Descriptions of places with names printed in **bold** will be found in the motoring routes.)

The first part of the route from Gothenburg is the Göta älv, and passes the massive fortress of **Bohus**, and the town of **Lödöse**. The first lock is at **Lilla Edet**, where Sweden's first lock was dug in 1647. Near **Trollhättan** is the beginning of the Trollhätte Canal and the first series of locks, and at **Vänersborg** boats enter Vänern. The height difference along this canal is 44m.

The route opens out into Vänern, Sweden's largest lake (5550 sq km), and passes on the right the white palace of **Läckö** and the distinctive **Kinnekulle plateau**. Vänern is almost divided into two by the Värmlandsnäs peninsula from the north, and the Kålland pensinsula with the island of Kållandsö (on which Läckö stands) from the south, with many small islands between them. The islands help to make Vänern calmer than Vättern. Because one-third of the country's drinking-water comes from the lake, massive purification plans were put into effect, with the unfortunate result that the water became too pure for the fish. Now it is hoped to achieve a balance between the needs of the human and aquatic population. Off the north-east of the lake runs the **Dalsland Canal**.

On the other side of Vänern the Västergötland section begins at Sjötorp where there are eight locks, a large harbour and a boatyard exhibition, as well as a preserved boatyard office. Von Platen had drawn up plans for a town here which were never implemented. The same fate befell his plans for the next town, Lyrestad. This has a medieval church and local museum. At Töreboda, Sweden's smallest ferry crosses the canal, as does the main Gothenburg–Stockholm railway.

At Lanthöjden there is an abandoned sharp corner of the canal, bypassed in 1933, forming a new island. Also at Lanthöjden an obelisk marks the highest point of the excavated section of the canal at 91.5m above sea-level, though (lake) Viken, into which the route soon passes at Tåtorp, is actually a fraction higher at 91.8m, and thus is the highest water-level.

The route winds on through Viken and thence into Botten by way of some narrow channels. The crag on the west shore is called Vaberget (140m). Botten is an inlet of Vättern, which it enters at **Karlsborg** with its fortress.

Vättern, the country's second biggest lake at 1912 sq km has far fewer islands than Vänern, the largest being **Visingsö**. There is a real danger of rough water with high waves due to south-east and north-west winds—the lake runs east-south-east to west-north-west.

At the other side of Vättern, the Östergötland section starts at **Motala**, where Baltzar von Platen's grave lies beside the canal. At Borenshult, the entrance to (lake) Boren, there are five locks and at the other end of the lake there is a manually operated lock at Borensberg. On the stretch just after this a new aqueduct has been completed, the second on the canal—joining the much older one at Ljungsbro not far ahead.

Between Ljungsbro and (lake) Roxen there is a total of 15 locks, culminating in a spectacular flight of seven together at Berg, at the outlet to the lake. **Vreta convent** is 1km away.

Off Roxen to the south runs the Kinda Canal to the lake of Åsunden, 80km long, designed for timber floating. With the Göta Canal and the Baltic Sea, and arrangements for transporting boats overland at one point, part of it makes a pleasure-boat route called the Blue Triangle for which tickets can be bought at the first lock or at Mem lock.

After Roxen the route consists partly of excavated canal and partly of natural waterway to **Söderköping**. Soon after Söderköping the lock at Mem means the end of the excavated canal and inland waterways, and boats take to the sea, first along a narrow inlet with the picturesque ruins of **Stegeborg castle**, then threading through the lovely S:ta Anna Archipelago and out into the Baltic.

Swinging north, the way to Stockholm leads eventually through Himmerfjärden and Hallsfjärden to reach **Södertälje**, now virtually a suburb of Stockholm. After 3km of the Södertälje Canal, boats have to pick their way through the intricate system of channels in the island-strewn lake of Mälaren, to tie up in **Stockholm**.

10

Gothenburg to the Norwegian border

Total distance 217km. Gothenburg—E6, 16km **Bohus**—4km and turn for road 168 to **Marstrand**—15km Jörlanda—road 160, 53km junction with road 161 and turning for Lysekil—road 161, 8km junction with E6—E6, 7km **Uddevalla**—62km **Tanumshede**—52km Norwegian border.

The E6 leaves Gothenburg northwards following the Oslo road, and runs along the left bank of the Göta älv, while the 45 goes up the right bank. The valley opens out and as the roads part company and the Nordre river splits from the Göta, there looms the bulk of **Bohus** fortress. Leave the motorway at (16km) the Rödbo junction following signs to *Bohus* and *Bohus Fästningen*. On the small square below the fortress there is a **tourist bureau**, and a large slab-like monument (1959) commemorating a meeting of the kings of Sweden, Denmark and Norway in 1101.

The present **fortress** (open May to mid-Aug, then pm to end Sept) is largely from the 17C. There was a wooden fort here in the 14C, built by the king of Norway (the border between Sweden and Norway/Denmark was here), and this was gradually replaced by a stone building. In the 16C it was rebuilt and furnished as a Renaissance palace, but was devastated by the continuing warfare. When the area became Swedish in 1658 it was thought necessary to fortify but not beautify the place. The fortification was achieved so thoroughly that in spite of 14 sieges it was never taken.

The spreading ravelins form an irregular polygon and the granite and brick castle is itself an irregular rectangle with towers or remains of them at the four corners. The walls are up to 9m thick in places, and at various points lower parts of medieval walls are visible. Much of the fabric is in a precarious state and the spiral staircases require extreme caution and preferably a torch.

The first gate is a modern reconstruction. From the first ravelin there is a view of the Nordre älv and the town of Kungälv. Directly below is the outline of a 17C church. In the courtyard is the 22m-deep well, gouged out with immense difficulty by Danish soldiers in the 17C.

The tower to the left (north) which gives the fortress its distinctive silhouette is called **Fars Hatt** (Father's Hat), and the one on the right (west) Mors Mössa (Mother's Cap). The east tower now ruined was the Red Tower, and the fourth was called Sven Hall's Tower. Between Father's Hat and Mother's Cap were the chapel and the commandant's quarters. Opposite is the **New Storehouse** (16C) with vaulted ceiling intact, which contained the brewery, bakery, granary and magazine. On the ruined south-west side was the Old Storehouse. A walkway with steps has been constructed so that visitors can see the view from the top.

In Father's Hat, designed by Erik Dahlberg, information panels (English) give the history of the fortress, and the models here represent servants of the 17C. In the walls you can see the ends of baulks of timber which once supported floors within the tower. Staircases, passages, casemates, the musket gallery (south-east) and the prison (north-east) can be explored, not forgetting outside the curtain walls where the pond and defensive cannon were located, and the view over the Göta älv from the east wall.

A few hundred metres away stands the 17C white wooden church of **Kungälv**, with Baroque furnishings and ceiling-paintings by Erik Grijs, a local artist (open June to mid-Aug). The square and the roads beyond the church, Östragatan and Västragatan, have pretty pastel-coloured houses of the 18C and 19C.

At the next junction on the E6 (4km) there is the turning on to road 168 for **Marstrand** with another fortress (27km). The road out over the deeply indented coastline is constructed over bridges and causeways and the **views** are very attractive, especially from the Instön bridge looking down over scattered rocky islets. Finally, within sight of the island and its castle, you must find a parking place (not always easy) and take the three-minute ferry-ride across the strait. You can also reach Marstrand from Gothenburg by boat, or a No. 312 bus.

Marstrand was a fishing community, then a fashionable 19C bathing resort. It is now popular with young Swedes as a summer day-trip, and along the harbour eating-places outnumber everything else. The streets lined with wooden houses climb steeply to **Carlsten fortress** (open June to Aug, pm) built on the highest point to command the archipelago with its round tower reminiscent of Bohus. As it is today, much of it is as designed by Erik Dahlberg in the 17C, but work continued until 1840 when it was finally considered finished.

The massive square central portion has alternating wide and narrow shot-holes, and overhanging privies, with the round tower to one side. The main entrance, Kungsporten, leads through a passage to a courtyard. Inside you can see the 18C commandant's house and 19C chapel. In the keep is the so-called King's Chamber—Gustav IV Adolf is supposed to have breakfasted here. A notorious 19C pirate, Lasse-Maja, held prisoner here for 25 years, is reported to have described life incarcerated here with breathtaking understatement as 'quite boring'. From the ramparts there is a view of the archipelago, the town and land beyond.

Down in the town the winding streets have many a decorative reminder of the modish days of the 19C and early 20C, with carved detailing on the façades. **Societetshuset** (Society House) of 1886 was one of the centres of activity, as was the warm bathhouse, now the Youth Hostel. In front of Societetshuset is a bust of Oskar II, the foremost patron of the bathing establishment.

From Jörlanda in 15km a more scenic alternative to the E6 to Uddevalla is to take the side road to Stenungsund (9km) and road 160 over the islands of Tjörn and Orust. The road (Tjörnaleden) passes over four bridges and is a rewarding drive. The islands are wooded and rocky with fishing villages like Skärhamn on the south coast of Tjörn, the main centre of population. Henån is the largest village on Orust which is Sweden's third largest island and was once famous for boat-building. Both islands have many prehistoric remains.

After 53km from Jörlanda the 160 meets the 161 on the mainland again. To the left the road goes to Lysekil (18km)—part of the way is the ferry across Gullmarn, Sweden's only true fjord, that is, with a bar across the mouth so the water is saltier than the Skagerrak and intrigues the marine biologists.

On the way (10km) you pass **Bokenäs** medieval church with later painted gallery, pews and ceiling. It has no windows on the north side, like many other churches, probably because evil was thought to come from the north. After 2km there is the ferry, a 2km crossing and 4km drive into **Lysekil**, a fashionable bathing-resort, now with restored buildings. In the Second

World War British torpedo boats fetched Swedish goods from the harbour, one of the few ways of obtaining foreign imports for the UK. The old town can be seen in Gamla Strandgatan and Banviksgatan, while Vikvarvets Museum in Turistgatan shows local fishing and quarrying, (open evenings). An imaginative new museum of the sea and aquarium, **Havets Hus**, with exhibitions and activities opened in 1993.

The 161 leads in the opposite direction to join the E6 and on to (15km) **Uddevalla** (pop. 30,000), which was once a ship-building town. Signs to the centre bring you in on Västerlånggatan. Just before this crosses the Bäveån, on the right you see the new salmon-pink and glass bus terminal (with air-terminal gadgetry) and the **tourist bureau** is in the same complex (closed weekends).

Across the road on the river-bank is the low modern **Bohuslän Museum** (open Tue–Fri 10.00–20.00, weekends to 16.00. Plan and some information in English). On the **ground floor** is the boat hall and displays by local artists. The history of the province of Bohuslän is shown on information boards on the mezzanine floor. The main displays on the history of Bohuslän are on the **top floor** where there are geological and natural history sections, occupations such as fishing, farming, quarrying, as well as preserving and women's work. A 19C farmer's cottage and workshops are reconstructed, while a series of models shows how the landscape has changed over the centuries. A gallery shows Bohuslän in paintings, and another contains a collection donated by a local inhabitant, which includes Flemish, German and Swedish painters. The colourful knitting of the area is illustrated and there is a room with earphones for listening to local folk music and dialect. In the café traditional local food is available such as *äggost* (egg cheese) made in decorative moulds.

On the main square **Kungstorget**, there is a statue of Karl X with Erik Dahlberg, the pair who made Bohuslän Swedish. On one side of the square is an old brick house which used to be the art gallery. Just off the square is the 19C church built after the great fire of 1806. The separate bell-tower (18C) high on a knoll at some distance escaped the fire.

Leaving Uddevalla by the E6 to the west, the route retraces the last part of the route from Tjörn and Orust. There are pleasant views of rolling wooded hills and granite outcrops. After 29km there is a turn for Lysekil by which you avoid the ferry. Taking this road, you can also reach **Nordens Ark** at **Åby** (12km). This is a zoo (open all year) for animals under threat of extinction, on the model of Gerald Durrell's zoo on Jersey which has the same aims. Here there are Scandinavian domestic and wild animals, as well as foreign animals suited to the climate, and the inmates include otters, arctic foxes and snow leopards. There are also training and research facilities.

It is 33km to **Tanumshede**, the central town of Tanum municipality, which has the greatest concentration of Bronze Age rock carvings in Scandinavia. Sweden has thousands of these carvings, and around Tanumshede are four large major sites, both interesting and easily accessible. They are best revealed by oblique light and Vitlycke museum organises tours after dark. The rocks are extremely slippery when wet.

The Bronze Age here lasted roughly from 1500 BC to 500 BC. On the ice-smoothed granite, Bronze Age man scratched and ground distinctive motifs, some now painted red for people to see more clearly. The simple cup-mark, a small circular depression, accounts for the vast majority, and the next greatest number is made up of boats. Then come humans and animals, then sun-wheels (crosses in circles), and such things as chariots. Predictably, interpretations are almost as numerous as the motifs themselves.

The boats are of many types. Sometimes they look like sledges, sometimes they have curly prows, and those with a criss-cross framework probably represent a basis of branches covered with skin. The crew are sometimes recognisable humans, sometimes mere matchsticks. Some have huge hands or carry axes, spears or bows, some are like witch-doctor figures with headdresses, others are leaping or running. The animals have been identified as deer, oxen, dogs, horses and many others. The footprints are among the most puzzling motifs, and there are handprints as well. The chariots have two or four wheels, and the draught-animal is shown in profile alongside. There are many baffling images, with labyrinths or nets, a few trees and in one place a maypole.

A book *Images of the Past* by John Coles is on sale in Bohuslän Museum (Uddevalla), and Vitlycke Museum, which gives a good introduction to the subject.

Just before reaching the church in Tanumshede, a signpost in three languages directs you to the carvings at *Fossum to the east (3km). The motifs here are mainly boats, all of the same style, and men brandishing different weapons, and deer. Two little men are jumping back to back. 1km further on an unobtrusive red sign indicates the museum of the Scandinavian Society for Prehistoric Art with exhibitions on the carvings (open in summer).

In Tanumshede, turn left at the church for the museum and three other sites. After 2km Vitlycke *Hällristningsmuseet is on one side of the road and a large area of carvings on the other. The museum (open May to mid-Sept 10.00–17.00) has an English translation of all the information, which can be borrowed, and there are books and leaflets on sale. Here interpretations are explored—did the carvings serve as fertility rites or were they a means of communication? Objects shown on the carvings are reconstructed and displayed next to reproductions of the motifs, boats, a cart, a splendid horn, bows and arrows. Animals are identified as horse, deer, hog, ox, duck, snake, lobster or whale.

Leave by the back door to visit the reconstruction of a **Bronze Age farm** where researchers are experimenting on the feasibility of various techniques in daily living. Among other things, they have found that it takes 30 minutes to grind out one cup-mark. Bronze Age farm buildings could be between 10m and 40m long. The one here is made of clay, willow-stems, oak and peat, roofed with thatch. The fire in the middle has an animal skin stretched over it to direct both sparks away from the thatch and smoke out through the vents in the roof. The bed also has a skin over it and consists of fur-covered boards. A loom has been reconstructed and pottery stands about. A breed of Gotland sheep, of which both sexes have curly horns, is being reared, which is thought to be as near as possible to animals of that era. In late spring you can see the lambs. In an outbuilding a bronze-casting furnace has been reconstructed, the furnace covered with clay, with an air-channel to a pit. There is a small enclosure for cultivation.

Opposite the museum across the road is a very large slab of granite with *rock carvings. Here there are different sorts of boat, one over 3m long, and many people and animals. There is a little cartoon-like scene of a man being chased by a snake, and the so-called 'love-couple'. There are other sites here in the woods and the museum has a booklet 'The Vitlycke Path' describing how to get to them.

There is a site 500m along the road at *Aspeberget, a little more difficult of access. Here the most important carvings have been covered by a roof so that it is not easy to see that here are some animals which look like yoked oxen, also some boats and humans. Other carvings are in the open a few metres beyond and still others in the vicinity.

Back on the road, after 500m an unmade road goes to the right to the *Litsleby site. After almost a kilometre the carvings are at the bottom of a hill in woodland to the left. The central figure is a 2m high man with a spear, surrounded by boats.

The E6 continues north from Tanumshede. After 20km you can take the 176 to **Strömstad** (12km). This was the first bathing resort on this coast at the end of the 19C, but fishing always remained important and today it has a well-known fish-auction. There is an open-air museum. 10km off the coast, Kosteröarna (the Koster Islands) are accessible by ferry and have interesting geology and flora.

On the E6, at 8km, **Skee** has a **church** a couple of kilometres off the road (probably open summer afternoons). The **'Skee Madonna'** is of black soapstone (13C), and the church also had a font of the same material and age, now in Historiska Museet in Stockholm. The 15C **altarpiece** from Lübeck has 17C Baroque doors, and portrays the crucifixion, surrounded by saints, some of whom are Scandinavian. The stone bell-tower is from the 17C. Nearby is an Iron Age cemetery with burial mounds.

In this area there are many other prehistoric remains. At Massleberg there is a passage grave, at Blomsholm two cemeteries one with a large stone circle, and at Grönehög there is a sizable tumulus.

The road reaches Norway in 24km. At the border there is a tourist bureau, called SveNo E6. The nearest Norwegian town is Halden and just to the south is the fortress of Fredriksten where the Swedish king Karl XII was fatally shot as he besieged it in 1718.

11

Gothenburg to Karlstad

Total distance 247km. Gothenburg—road 45, 73km **Trollhätten**—138 Segmon—E18, 36km **Karlstad**.

(For the first part of this route as far as Trollhättan see Gothenburg to Örebro, Rte 12.)

Vänersborg is 14km north of Trollhättan on road 45. It has a county museum, itself with some architectural pretensions, which contains among other things a collection of African birds. It has been newly refurbished to show the history of museum displays (open Tue–Fri, Sat am, Sun pm). The museum, the 18C church, the main square and the governor's residence are in a line in the grid-plan centre. The residence (1754) was designed by Carl Hårleman. In front of it and in the square are two statues by Carl Milles and an imaginative fountain by Carl Elmblad. The park is agreeably situated along the shores of Vänern and has a statue by Axel Wallenberg called 'Frida' at its east end. From here you can see at a distance the ships entering or leaving the canal where it joins the lake. Elk safaris to Halleberg can be booked here (see Rte 12).

Take the 45 north out of Vänersborg. This is now Dalsland, a small province, but with so many lakes that almost any drive is attractive, especially to the north. Canoeing and fishing are popular pastimes. The road leaves the shore of Vänern but begins to approach it again at (43km) **Mellerud**, which has a **museum** (open daily). This has reconstructed interiors of the homes of different social classes of the 19C and early 20C. Upstairs there are shops and a schoolroom, and a model of Dalaborg, a wooden castle of the 14C which was situated in this area. There is a genealogical section where visitors can research their ancestors of the area.

To the north-west the church at **Gunnarsnäs** (5km) has an unusual bell-tower sheathed with slate—Dalsland has supplied the slate roof of many a famous building. The church has a Renaissance pulpit and the ceiling was painted in the 18C by a local artist. The better-known Isak Schullström was responsible for the altar, and the apostles on the gallery. There is a 13C sandstone font, and a 17C pulpit. In the graveyard are some wrought-iron grave-crosses.

Back on the 45, after 4km you can take a turn for **Håverud** (12km) on the **Dalsland Canal**. The canal was built in the 1860s for transporting iron, and is 254km long, of which only 10km had actually to be dug to link the natural waterways. It has 29 locks. At Håverud the canal goes over rapids on an **aqueduct**, finished in 1868, a great feat of engineering of its time. It is 32m long, on granite pillars, and contains 33,000 rivets. A railway bridge goes 20m over the aqueduct while the road bridge affords one of the best views of this transport sandwich. You can also cross the road and climb to a viewing platform. Below the rapids is the **Dalsland Center** (open May to Sept) which is a trade exhibition area but has other interesting displays, a tourist information desk and a model of the aqueduct.

In the surrounding buildings are a salmon smoke-house, and craft work-shops, with the local **museum** across the path (open June–Aug). This deals with the canal, ironworking, saw-works and other industries of the area. There are boat-trips from Håverud to see rock carvings at Tisselskog.

On the way back to the 45 you can take a side-road after 4km to **Skållerud church** in a beautiful position above a lake. This looks like a modest red wooden church but inside it has exuberant **peasant-Baroque decoration**. The sculpture of the **altar** is by Isak Schullström (1760), with Moses and Aaron to either side and the Evangelists at the top. Erik Grijs painted the ceiling and the chancel arch with biblical scenes, and the gallery with apostles. Schullström carved the angels holding the hymn-number boards and the **pulpit** with apostles amid luxuriant brightly painted foliage with garlands underneath, and the Lamb of God, angels and coats of arms on the canopy. The medieval font is of soapstone—Dalsland has many Roman-esque fonts showing influence from Norway. In the porch are a previous door and some memorial tablets, and outside there are a few wrought-iron grave-crosses by the gate.

You can get back to the 45 on this road but the surface is very poor.

18km on the 45 from the junction for Håverud there is a turn for **Ånimskog** (2km) where the **church** has a colourful Baroque interior with 18C acanthus ceiling-paintings, pulpit and altarpiece, and a medieval sandstone font.

In 24km **Åmål** (pop. 10,000), the main town of Dalsland, has a harbour (**tourist bureau** nearby) on lake Vänern which was important for iron exports. The open centre with a little river running through the main square has kept some 18C and 19C wooden buildings around a green called Plantaget. On the north is the 18C **Vågmästare house**—the home of the 'weigh-master' who was responsible for weighing the iron for export, often also the mayor. On the east are two 18C houses and on the south one 18C and one 19C—the dates are on small metal plaques. The little bridge

(Mellanbron) is from the 17C. Down near the lake are the local **museum** (June to Aug, pm) and, opposite, the 17C church no longer in use.

Soon the road leaves Dalsland province and enters Värmland, which has some beautiful scenery with forests, hills and lakes. At (18km) Säffle a turn left goes to **Västra Smedbyn** (17km) where the 18C **Von Echstedt manor** has Rococo interior furnishings and paintings of biblical and hunting scenes. The entrance is guarded by painted grenadiers and the most reproduced painting is that of the elegantly attired owners sitting companionably on their privy. (Open mid-May to Aug 11.00–18.00.)

At (17km) Segmon the 45 joins forces with the E18 to just past Grums, where they split again, the 45 continuing north, and the E18 east round the top of lake Vänern into (36km) Karlstad.

Karlstad (pop. 53,000) was given its charter by Karl XI in 1584 before he came to the throne. It had already been a trading-centre with a natural harbour on the lake where the Klarälv river flows into it.

The Klarälv is one of Scandinavia's longest rivers, 500km, of which nearly half is in Norway under another name. This was the last river to be used for transporting timber—the last log floated past in 1991, the end of an almost 400-year tradition, which reached its peak in the 1950s and 1960s, when one million cubic metres of timber a year passed this way.

Floating of logs began in the 17C when individual forest owners used this economical means of transport, and as time went on saw-works and then pulp factories sprang up in the valley. The system of floating meant that timber had to be stored for long winter months, but now wood is transported fresh to the customer and storage costs are saved. Fresh timber also requires less use of chemicals than six-month-old wood, and the end of logging makes life easier for the hydro-electric power-stations on the river. Logs used to take 14 days to float down from north Värmland and from May to November the loggers toiled. In latter years much of the heavy labour was rationalised and mechanised. Loggers developed their own way of life and a special camaraderie, and have acquired a romantic aura in the popular mind.

In medieval times the Kläralv valley was a well-trodden pilgrim route to Trondheim, starting from the church in Hammarö.

Tourist bureau: Västra Torggatan 26. Tel. (054) 19 59 01.

Post office: Petersbergsgaten 1.

Telephone, telegram: Drottninggatan 30. Tel. (054) 19 23 45.

The present town of Karlstad, plagued by fires, was rebuilt in the second half of the 19C, with wide streets and squares. Follow signs to the centre. The main square (Stora Torget) has a 'peace monument' (1955) to the dissolution of the Sweden–Norway union in 1905, an aggressive female brandishing a broken sword and her foot planted firmly on a dismayed warrior's head. (The negotiations took place in Karlstad.) Behind her is the town hall of 1891 in neo-Classical style with two eagles on top.

Take Kungsgatan to the east where the cathedral is soon visible. Opposite the church is the orange 18C school designed by Hårleman and Cronstedt, with a school museum.

The **cathedral** was finished in 1730, basically a Greek-cross plan, with some additions. In the porch is a modern **tympanum** decoration by Heinz Decker with a golden Chi-Rho symbol surrounded by other symbols referring to various religions, the Bible, history, music, Värmland and other themes. Music for example is linked with Bach, there is Selma Lagerlöf's name with the name of her book *Jerusalem*, a Crown of Thorns, Alpha and Omega, an Egyptian scarab, St. Birgitta and Karl XI's monogram.

Inside, there is shallow rib-vaulting. The altarpiece was designed by Erik Palmstedt in 1790 with a cross swathed in a cloth, and to either side **angels** representing Religion and Devotion by Sergel. The pulpit is also by Palmstedt, neo-Classical, with angel-heads and laurel garlands. The modern altar is of Gotland limestone with an Orrefors crystal cross and the modern font is of crystal with a ceramic dove behind.

Take Norra Kyrkogatan to the north of the church and turn right to cross a bridge and left to come out on the riverbank. Along the river the tow-path leads to **Östra Bron** (East Bridge) of twelve granite arches, built in 1797 (no private cars).

Return along Norra Strandgatan. The red brick **Gamla Badhuset** (Old Bathhouse) on the right sometimes has exhibitions organised by the museum, and there are archives (*emigrantarchiv*) where people can research their forbears in the area. (Archives open weekdays, office hours; exhibitions shorter hours, but open weekends.)

Take Västra Torggatan to the right. The library is here with an art gallery and **tourist bureau** (closed Sun; also July Sat). Värmlands Museum is on its own further out to the left and runs temporary exhibitions of local interest.

Return down Västra Torggatan. The large two-storey yellow wooden building on the right with hipped mansard roof is the **Bishop's Palace** of 1780, said to have been saved from a fire by a doughty bishop's own fire-fighting efforts.

Turn right and left and you are on the river. Ahead is the characteristic **view** of Karlstad, with wide spaces and curving waterline. On the square at the end of the bridge is the 18C governor's **residence**, backing on to the town hall and across the river stands the white theatre. There are four statues around the bridge. On the north-west is the writhing 'Dwelling of' the Winds' (1967), a memorial to the many Finns who settled in Värmland at the end of the 16C. On the north-east sits Selma Lagerlöf the author (1968); on the south-west is Karl XI the founder of the town; and on the south-east a serving-girl of the late 18C/early 19C immortalised in verse.

Continuing along the riverbank you will see the boats which tour up the river and among the islands. In the next block to the left is **Almen**, an area of old wooden houses, spoiled by the intrusion of the modern town hall.

To the south of the town is **Mariebergsskogen**, an open-air leisure area, with fun-fair, children's zoo, a small open air museum, walks, views and a restaurant. (About 1km: take Klaraborgsgatan going south, then follow signs along Jungmansgatan and Långövägen.)

The 'island' of **Hammarö** further south is now a peninsula. The wooden church dates partly from the 14C and has 15C paintings. There is a 1748 carved **altarpiece** by Isak Schullström, and the previous altar is also preserved. The church was visited by pilgrims to Trondheim, hence the St. Olof figure in the sacristy. There is a 13C soapstone font. Prehistoric cemeteries are also to be found on the peninsula.

Excursion to Kristinehamn

Kristinehamn, a harbour town on lake Vänern, is 38km to the east of Karlstad by the E18. The modern centre is an attempt to recreate a nucleus of low-rise building amid greenery. The town hall is of 1798 and old houses still stand on Trädgårdsgatan. The church was designed in 1858 in neo-Gothic by C.G. Brunius, who worked on the restoration of Lund cathedral.

It has a medieval font and crucifix and 18C pulpit and altarpiece. Historic vestments are kept in a gallery with other ecclesiastical items.

The most famous artwork is undoubtedly the **Picasso sculpture** on the spit of land jutting into the lake (drive west to the lake, following signs). This is a 15m-high stylised head in cast concrete, made in 1965 by Carl Nesjar to Picasso's specifications.

Karlskoga, an industrial town 25km to the east of Kristinehamn, has a **museum** devoted to Alfred Nobel in the house he owned here. Nobel (1833–96) studied in Paris and the USA. He experimented with nitroglycerine until he could stabilise it to produce dynamite (1867). He laid the basis of his fortune with several factories in different countries, and had an experimental factory in Bofors. He left his fortune to establish prizes for those who benefited mankind in literature, physics, chemistry, medicine and peace.

12

Gothenburg to Örebro

Total distance 289km. Gothenburg—road 45, 73km **Trollhättan**—road 44, 57km **Lidköping**—23km Götene—E20, 136km **Örebro**.

Leave Gothenburg by road 45 through a heavily industrialised area. The 45 runs on the right of the Göta älv and the E6 on the left. After 9km the road is crossed by the 50m high Ångered bridge, which is nearly 1km long (40cm longer in summer!). After another 7km where the two roads part company at Kungälv, you can catch a glimpse of the imposing Bohus fortress behind refineries and factories (see Rte 10). Now the 45 swings into the country and follows the broad Göta valley.

After 5km a road right to Nödinge (2km) passes modern housing, then a right at the T-junction, a left and a right turn bring you to **Nödinge church** (open in summer). The wooden **ceiling** painted in 1741 has a flamboyant Judgment scene and Six Days of Creation. The pulpit, altar, organ gallery, pews, font and even the door to the vestry are all of the same period and style in luxuriant colour. During restoration work in the 1980s finds were unearthed which included walls of the 12C church, a medieval sword, coins and pieces of Limoges enamel, and below this, pre-Christian or early Christian ash and birchwood coffins.

In this area some of the prosperous-looking yellow wooden houses are very decorative, with their yellow or grey mansard roofs and a goodly provision of dormer windows, gables, balconies and bay windows.

After 18km the road passes through **Lödöse**, the original site of Gothenburg (see Rte 8). An expansive, purpose-built new **medieval museum** is being built, which will gather together all the finds from Lödöse and present a comprehensive picture of the first Gothenburg.

In 12km, **Lilla Edet** is an industrial town which has grown up where the valley narrows and the first lock was dug in 1607 for what was to become the Trollhätte Canal. The hydro-electric power-station takes care that the

400-year-old salmon-fishing fame of the place continues by providing a salmon-leap.

Trollhättan (pop. 40,000) is reached in 22km.

The town developed where the Göta älv fell 32m over spectacular falls. Using the power came naturally, even in the 17C when watermills and water-sawmills took advantage of it. In the mid 18C Christopher Polhem was engaged by Karl XII to build three locks, but the work was never finished. It was not until 1800 that a satisfactory system of eight locks was completed lower down the river. Other sets of locks were constructed in 1844 and 1916, these last being in use today (see Rte 9).

In the town there is a local museum at Kungsgatan 29, off the main square Drottningtorget (open Mon–Thurs, Sat am, Sun pm). The **tourist bureau** is at Karl Johans Torg (summer only). The main sights have to do with the canal and the hydro-electric power industry. Take Gärdhemsvägen to the north then Åkersbergsvägen to the left. (Straight ahead is Strömkarlsbron with a statue of a water-sprite by Carl Eldh.) After 1km **Kung Oskars Bro** (bridge) is on the right. From the middle of the bridge you can see where the falls would have tumbled down the ravine before the dam was built to provide hydro-electric power. On certain days in summer the waters are released as a spectacle for tourists—check times at the tourist bureau.

On the other side of the bridge is a stairway leading to a concave **rock** where 11 kings have scratched their names. This started when Adolf Fredrik and his queen Lovisa Ulrika came in 1754 to inaugurate one of Polhem's locks (Ekeblads lock a little further upriver). The last to sign in was Carl XVI Gustaf in 1975. Just here too is the large hole in the ground that was going to be Polhem's **middle lock**. The Hojum hydro-electric power-station near here was finished in 1942.

Continue over Kung Oskars Bro and up the steep hill. Near the top on the left is a parking place and a signpost to a footpath through the woods which says *Kopparklinten*, leading to a **viewpoint** high over the ravine and the town. All along the cliffs is an area for walking, continuing on the other side of the road leading up from the bridge, as far as Strömsbergs Turist-station. Here there is a small open-air museum (Forngård) and another view of the island-studded canal, power-canal and river.

Back on the lower road, after another half-kilometre or so there is the Olide power-station and the new 'energy centre' Insikten. The **power-station** can be visited (mid-May to mid-Aug, tours every hour, start from Insikten). **Insikten** (open mid-June to Aug 10.00–18.00) has models, computers and holograms illustrating electricity and energy, with a children's experimental section and displays on the natural history of the Göta älv. Outside there is a 15m model of the falls, and an outlook tower.

A kilometre or so further out there is **Kanalmuseet** showing the history of the canal, boats and construction work (open June to mid-Aug, plus some weekends). Further again is the **lock area**, where you can walk around the three sets of locks mentioned above (tours in summer).

Take road 44 to the east out of Trollhättan. After 20km a sign left points to **Hunneberg**. Hunneberg and Halleberg are two flat-topped hills like Kinnekulle (see below), mostly occupied by a nature reserve. Twilight elk safaris by bus to Halleberg may be booked in Vänersborg—money back if no elks are sighted. Failing twilit elks, take this side road for 2km and turn left to the lookout tower on Hunneberg (3km walk) for the view.

After 2km you can take road 47 to see the very fine **Sparlösa runestone**. After 12km turn left and follow the signs. The runestone is in a small glass house, usually open, but even if it isn't you can see the stone (guides in summer). Two of the sides have mainly runes. The one with the man holding up a beam is thought to say that Alrik set up the stone in memory of Ojuls son of Erik. The inscription along the top and right edge is believed to be 11C, and reads: 'Gisle erected this stone in memory of Gunnar his brother'. The side with the spirals includes the same names as the first inscription in a puzzling reference to Uppsala. A third side has a horseman, a deer, a lion, a ship and a large building, while the fourth has an involved picture with birds and snakes and an inscription again containing the same names.

Also in this area is the **runestone** at Levene. (Go on to the T-junction and turn right, then left after 4km.) Its only claim is that it is the tallest in Sweden (460cm). The inscription says it was erected by Harulv in memory of his sons Var and Targot. The church in whose graveyard the runestone stands has pretty wood-shingled steeples and there is a small open-air museum next-door. Nearby is an Iron Age cemetery (*gravfält*) and a nature reserve (*Levene Äng*).

The quickest way to Lidköping from here is to continue for 2km and turn left on to road 187, which after 20km rejoins the 44, 4km before Lidköping, 35km from where you left it. (North of Sparlösa, on the north-west side of the 44, at Tun, is a very large 'brimmed' Bronze Age cairn of 60m diameter, and a 1780 school.)

Lidköping (pop. 22,000) received its town charter in 1446 and was then sited on the east bank of the Lidan. In 1671 Chancellor Magnus de la Gardie decided to build a new town on the west bank and so there were two town halls and two mayors, with the two main squares facing each other across the river.

An area of wooden houses, **Limtorget**, signposted north-east of the old square, represents how the town used to look. In de la Gardie's new square (*Nya stadens torg*) is his wooden **hunting-lodge** (restored), transported from his estate to do duty as a town hall. It now contains the **tourist bureau** among other things. Also on the square is his statue by John Lundquist (1939). But Lidköping's fame in Sweden rests on the factory producing the historic **Rörstrand porcelain** (begun in Stockholm in 1746). They have a museum, exhibition, shop and café. (Open weekdays 09.30–18.00, Sat am and Sun pm. Follow the *Rörstrand* signs.)

There is a Handicraft and Maritime Museum on the corner of Esplanaden and Mellbygatan.

Excursion to the castle of Läckö

North of Lidköping the Kålland peninsula stretches into Lake Vänern, Sweden's largest lake with an area of 5550 sq km. On the west side of the peninsula at **Skalunda** 10km north-west of Lidköping is a very large **barrow**, probably Iron Age, 65m across and 7m high. 8km north of Lidköping is **Sunnersberg church** whose reredos is attributed to van Dyck. 17km further north is de la Gardie's white palace of Läckö on the large island of Kållandsö jutting into the lake.

***Läckö**, perched on a height and surrounded on three sides by water, with its white walls and capped towers and turrets, looks as if it came straight out of a fairy-tale. (Open May–Sept 10.00–18.00, guided tours, but you can wander at will. English notes to borrow.)

There was a castle on the site from the 1290s when it belonged to Bishop Brynolf Algotsson of Skara. It was added to over the years until it came into the possession of Magnus Gabriel de la Gardie in 1652. Not only was he powerful and wealthy (see note under Varnhem, Rte 5), he was also cultivated. It was he who donated historical treasures to Uppsala university library, like the Codex Argenteus, and sponsored Erik Dahlberg's monumental book of etchings *Suecia antiqua et hodierna*. He employed a German architect, Franz Stimer, to rebuild the castle though he contributed many ideas himself and kept a close eye on the progress of work. Some of the medieval fabric remains, as do some of the previous improvements of his father Jacob, for example, the pale fresco paintings here and there.

The main building is four storeys high, around an open courtyard, with a lower courtyard in front and the kitchen courtyard behind. It is surrounded on three sides by the waters of Vänern, but the moat on the land side is now dry.

In the first courtyard the **chapel** can be visited. This has remained more or less as completed by Magnus, with altarpiece, pulpit and organ façade of 1666. There are statues of the apostles in the window-recesses, and paintings of the articles of faith. You can also go down into the pretty little castle garden, on a terrace overlooking the lake.

The sandstone **gateway** into the main courtyard is from Jacob de la Gardie's time. One of the walls of this courtyard is opened up with a grand **arcade**, and let into the pillars are **statues** of Magnus and Jacob, replicas of those in Varnhem church. In the courtyard beyond, on the far side there is a kitchen, with a hearth, sinks and entrance to a dungeon. The well in the kitchen is 27m deep and half-way down a tunnel admits water from the lake.

The **apartments** are entered from the main courtyard. On the **first floor**, where some of the rooms have decorated ceilings, there are changing exhibitions. The **second floor** has the **state apartments**, the most splendid of which is **Riddarsalen**, the Knight's Hall. The ceiling is divided into panels painted with trophies of war. The nine large paintings (copies) tell the story of the Thirty Years War, and the sandstone fireplaces are carved with shields and inscriptions. In the next room, the **Fredssalen** (Hall of Peace), the painting on the ceiling shows the goddesses of peace and justice. There are portraits of the negotiators of the Peace of Westphalia which ended the Thirty Years War.

The **Österrikiska sal** (Austrian Hall) is devoted to the enemy in the war, with portraits of the Austrian royal family and of the generals, with the Austrian arms painted on the ceiling. Round the corner in the next wing are the **apartments** of Magnus' wife Princess Maria Euphrosyne, with her drawing-room, sumptuous bedroom, and little prayer-room off to one side. There are many portraits in the castle, well labelled. There hangs a portrait of the Princess herself, and in the dining-room is a copy of the wedding portrait of her and Magnus. The ceiling-painting represents the goddess of the harvest, Ceres. The last two rooms also have painted ceilings.

The **third floor** is annually devoted to a major **exhibition**, usually of impressive quality. However, do not miss the richly painted decoration on walls and ceilings while looking at the exhibition.

Continuing on the 44, 12km from Lidköping, Källby lies at a road junction. Turn left and immediately to the right you will see two very tall **runestones** on a little hill. One with a cross confronts the other with a pagan animal figure across an ancient highway.

You can continue on the same side road to Husaby and (2km) the start of **Kinnekulleleden**, a tourist route around the Kinnekulle, an oval plateau 307m high on the shores of Vänern. Kinnekulle is topped by a layer of diabase, a hard volcanic rock which has prevented its being weathered away. The strata beneath, mudstone shale, limestone, alum shale and sandstone, on a base of gneiss, have worn away on the sides to provide some nice object-lessons in geology and related botany.

You can follow the marked tourist route (do not be led astray by signs to Kinnekuller*ing*, which is the motor racing track). Most of the churches should be open in summer.

*Husaby is regarded as the cradle of Swedish Christianity, for it was here in 1008 that St. Sigfrid, an English missionary, is said to have baptised King Olof Skötkonung, the first Swedish king formally to abandon the Viking gods and embrace the new religion. The well where this is said to have taken place is to the east of the church. The **church** was the seat of a bishop until 1160 when the see was amalgamated with Skara.

The present building was begun in the mid 12C, and the vaulted roof was constructed in the 14C. Unfortunately the original vault-paintings in the nave were scraped off in 1901 but the chancel paintings were saved. The painted wooden **rood-screen** is extremely rare in Sweden. The hole in the wall beside it served as a pulpit. In the chancel are kept a medieval **bishop's throne** and **monks' bench**, both 13C. Just inside the rood-screen on the right is a medieval wooden **altarpiece** of the Virgin and Child carved from one piece of oak—the Child is carved from a branch. The **font** and **crucifix** are 13C, the **pulpit** and **altarpiece** 17C, donated by Magnus de la Gardie, owner of Läckö castle. Outside the entrance are two gravestones, one said to be that of King Olof and his wife Estrid, the other that of a bishop.

West of the church a couple of hundred metres are the substantial remains of a stately **bishop's palace** (1480s), with four-storeyed keep, forge, bakehouse and all conveniences. Unfortunately it was not long before the Reformation overtook it in 1527. A couple of hundred metres east of the church, an enclosed paved area with an 18C memorial to the coming of Christianity has steps going down to the well where St. Sigfrid is said to have baptised King Olof.

2km further (going round the route anti-clockwise) is a sign *Hällristningar* to the right. In a field is a 150m-long series of Bronze Age **rock carvings** picked out in red, mostly sun-wheels, ships and feet, but some distance along a dramatic man with an axe-like weapon appears.

At Kinne-Kleva the route turns left and passes Österplana Moor, a nature reserve with rare plants. The route soon runs near the town of Gössäter, beyond which to the north-east is **Forshem** (4km) where the 12C **church** has unusual sandstone carvings above the north and south doors and, inside, 17C roof-paintings, altarpiece and pulpit.

Continue from the Gössäter crossroads north towards Hällekis. Here you can take a road on the left up the **Högkullen**, the highest point of Kinnekulle (restaurant), for the wide views. Footpaths to the viewing-tower (*utsiktstorn*) are marked at various places.

Turn right to see the other side of the hill. Turn left at the junction at the bottom. (Or turn right to see Råbäck manor gardens.) Just past Medelplana church is an **Iron Age cemetery**, with three megaliths standing by the road. The large flat one has an inscription about the plague in Sweden in 1589. At 3km **Västerplana church** is medieval with 18C paintings, altarpiece and pulpit.

At Västerplana turn towards Husaby (4km). You can rejoin road 44 by driving south from Husaby to **Skälvum** 4km from where you left it. The **church** here is typically west Swedish Romanesque with some sculptural details by Othelric, a local artist, and a Baroque pulpit and altarpiece.

After 7km the industrial town of **Götene** has a medieval church best reached by ignoring the first two signposts to Götene and taking the road opposite that marked Kinne-Vedum. The **church** is unusually high with a simple nave and square chancel. Inside, the chancel is covered with **paintings** from the late 15C. The curious font is from the 12C and the altar triptych from the 15C.

The 44 almost immediately joins the E20 and after 10km there is a sign for **Årnäs** ruined medieval castle (12km), with excavated finds to be seen in a wing of the nearby 18C manor. In 7km the sign *Minnesfjäll* refers to an abandoned mine (3km) where once millstones were produced (guided tours in high summer only). In 8km leave the E20 to reach Mariestad in 3km.

Mariestad (pop. 16,000) received its charter in 1583 when it was named after Maria of Pfalz, the first wife of Duke Karl, later Karl IX. It is the administrative centre of Skaraborg county, about half the area covered by the old province of Västergötland.

The **tourist bureau** is beside the harbour. They produce a plan of a walk in the old town, with notes in English. They also have cycle-tours of the area, including along the towpath of the Göta Canal, and can book boat trips on the lake. Almost opposite the tourist bureau is the most picturesque **house** in town, now the youth hostel, with a café in the courtyard. It was a tannery, built after a great fire of 1693, when much was destroyed.

The **cathedral**, strictly speaking no longer a cathedral as it has no bishop, was constructed between 1593 and 1625. Duke Karl built it as a rival to that of his brother Johan III's cathedral in Skara, and his architect took as his model the church of S:ta Klara in Stockholm. The tower is a result of 19C renovation. Inside there is a recorded commentary in English. The tall three-stage Baroque **altar** is from c 1700 and has barley-sugar columns with symbols, both religious, and secular, referring to the town. The tombstones in the floor are of the 17C and 18C. The pulpit is of the same time as the altar, with figures of the apostles. At the back are portraits of Duke Karl and his wife Maria.

The walk suggested by the tourist bureau forms a figure of eight, crossing just by the churchyard. The most interesting roads are **Kyrkogatan** and **Västerlånggatan**. In Kyrkogatan, No. 21 was the first hospital (1761), and No. 20 was the first grammar school (1786). Västerlånggatan is prettier, with Nos 23, 21, 12, 10, 7 and 5 being noteworthy. On Gamla Torget there is an early 19C well-to-do merchant's house.

Halfway across Marieholmsbron (bridge) at the end of Kungsgatan, you can reach the 18C residence of the county governor, Marieholm, on an island. In one of the pavilions there is the **Vadsbo Museum** (open summer Tue, Sun 13.00–16.00), with local finds and the history of the town and the area. There are textile and coin displays, and carriages in another pavilion.

Excursions from Mariestad

*Södra Råda church is c 50km away to the north and has important wall-paintings. Take the E20 towards Stockholm and after 11km turn on the 64 towards Filipstad and Kristinehamn. On the way you pass near **Börstorps Slott**, from 17C/19C, with guided tours and varying exhibitions (open summer, closed Mon). The road also goes over the Göta Canal at Sjötorp where there is a small **canal museum**. Turn off at Gullspång, and follow signs to Södra Råda, then to *Södra Råda g:la kyrka*—7km of winding road.

The little wood-shingled church (open May to Sept; entrance fee) was built c 1310, with simple rectangular nave, chancel and porch. Inside, the wooden ceiling is trefoil-shaped, and every surface is covered with painting. In the *chancel these are dated 1323, with French high Gothic style figures, flowing draperies on swaying bodies, but the surrounding ornament seems to hark back to an earlier period. The subjects are the Trinity, the life of the Virgin, apostles and saints.

In the nave the **paintings** are from 1494, carried out by Master Amund. Here are the Last Judgment above the chancel arch, the life of the Virgin, the articles of faith and the Passion of Christ, as well as the story of the Prodigal Son and the legend of St. Eustace, with virtues and sins. The episodes are framed in roundels on the ceiling and rectangular sections on the walls. The 13C crucifix was given drops of blood by Master Amund, who also added the cut-out figures of the Virgin and John the Baptist.

The **fortress of Karlsborg**, although its buildings for all their size seem mundane, almost domestic, is in fact an astonishing example of a 19C defence installation. It is 64km away on the shore of Vättern by way of road 202. In Karlsborg village follow signs *Fästningen*. (The complex is open mid-May to Aug 09.30–19.00. Guided tours, with action and special effects, can be booked at the office outside the wall, in Swedish, but English can be arranged, given notice.)

It was begun in 1818 when Sweden had lost Finland and other territories and was surrounded by enemies. It was to serve as a last place of defence for the government, the royal family—and the country's supply of gold. At that time the strategy in mind was that enemies could be allowed to enter Sweden and then defeated on home ground. But by the time the 90- year construction project was finished, defence theory had changed—the foe was to be prevented from even setting foot on Swedish soil. By the same time too, of course, military weapons had overtaken Karlsborg, to the extent that its walls could no longer be expected to withstand determined attack.

The area of the complex is around 1 sq km, and the perimeter 5km. The south range is 678m long, said to be the longest building in Europe.

You can drive through the neo-Gothic archway to the car park in front of the central part of the long building. Here there is a **museum** (open June–Aug) and the **garrison chapel**. In the museum are objects relating to the history of the place, an air force section, and one on the life hussars, a regiment associated with Karlsborg, as well as local history. Upstairs is the large light garrison chapel.

Walking around the area, you can see the commandant's house, the arsenal and the clothing store among the ponderous buildings. Gathered around a square are some craft and souvenir shops and a café. You can climb the rampart for a view over Vättern.

Rejoin the E20 from 4km outside Mariestad and, after 18km, cross the Göta Canal and in another 12km you could turn at Hova, for **Älgarås** (7km), where the 15C church, beyond the far end of the village, has a 13C Madonna shrine, Crucifixion group, font and bell. The faded 18C paintings are of the Resurrection, Ascension and Last Judgment. Back on the E20, from Finnerödja after 14km you could reach the town of Tived, and Tiveden, the legendary haunt of trolls.

Tiveden is a plateau of ice-hewn granite c 30km square, covered with forests, lakes and bogs. In the wildest part of the interior, between the lakes of Unden and Vättern, the Tiveden National Park has been established, where no one has ever lived, and the aim is to keep this as an example of primeval forest, with no human intervention. The forest was ravaged by fire in 1835, and though some trees survived, most now standing are the result of self-seeding. Animals, birds and plants thrive largely undisturbed, though walking trails cross the area—note that there is some difficult terrain to negotiate. Other walking trails thread through the larger area around. The main information centre is at **Stenkälla**, where there is parking and refreshments, but you can get information from any local tourist bureau about routes, accommodation and sights.

In 9km the road leaves the province of Västergötland for that of Närke. In 29km the E20 is joined at Hallsberg by the 50 from the east coast of Vättern. Here a road goes north to **Hardemo** (5km) which has an 18C **church** dedicated to St. Olof, and 10km further north-west is the ruined monastery of **Riseberga**, once an important Cistercian foundation.

5km on is the junction with the 51, from which after 9km you could visit the prehistoric remains of **Hjortsberga** (9km) with standing stones and burial mounds. 12km later a side-road leads to **Mosjö** (2km) with a medieval **church** (signposted *Mosås*). From here it is 12km to the centre of Örebro.

Örebro (pop. 86,000) has a history dating back to the mid 13C when a fort was founded, probably by Birger Jarl. The river Svartån was important for the growing prosperity of the town since German merchants became interested in trading in the products of the Bergslagen region—copper, iron and furs. In 1434, Engelbrekt the rebel leader besieged and occupied the castle. In the 17C the Hjälmare Canal was excavated to link the town with Stockholm. (The canal was resited to the east in the 19C.) Several meetings of the Riksdag (parliament) were held here, notably the one which approved Marshal Jean Baptiste Bernadotte as Crown Prince of Sweden in 1810. It is the administrative centre of Örebro county, which includes the old province of Närke and parts of other provinces.

Tourist bureau: Castle courtyard. Tel. (019) 21 21 21.

Post office: Storgatan 3.

Travel information: Tel. (019) 128 000.

Telephone, telegram: Våghustorget 1. Tel. (019) 19 16 44.

At one end of the long narrow **Stortorget** is **S:t Nicolai church**, originally from the 13C but very much restored in the 19C. Engelbrekt is said to be buried in the church (1436). Beside it is a modern statue by Nils Sjögren of the brothers Olaus and Laurentius Petri, natives of Örebro. Olaus (see under Stockholm Storkyrka) was the leading churchman of the Reformation, and Laurentius was the first Protestant archbishop.

The **tourist bureau** is in the courtyard of the castle, to the north of Stortorget. The **castle**, situated on an island in the Svartån, dominates the centre of town. The original keep is the part with a step-gable, next to the south-west tower. Much of the present appearance of the building comes from the late 16C and early 17C, but the whole has been restored and re-restored so that it has a grand romantic exterior, but not much remains inside, where a conference centre has now been established. (Castle open 12.00–16.00, longer at weekends and in summer. Closed Mon. except June to Aug. Guided tours, also English, daily mid-June to mid-Aug.)

The Baroque-style **gateway** is a late copy of that on the Arvfurstens Palats in Stockholm, but inside the courtyard are two original Renaissance double **doorways**, in the south-west and north-east corners. They have heavy rusticated bands on columns supporting pediments.

The **apartments** shown are on the fourth and fifth floors. On the fourth, the anteroom has a 1928 floor inlaid with symbols and coats of arms, and there is a statue of Engelbrekt. To one side in the south-west tower is a circular waiting-room, constructed c 1900, rather in the style of a medieval chapter-house. The beamed Rikssalen (Parliament Hall), remodelled 1927–30, has portraits, the principal one being that of Karl XI and his family by Ehrenstrahl. Further rooms are the tower room, popular for weddings, and Gustavus Adolphus' Room. On the next floor is the **Bernadotte Salon**, and a long room with portraits of provincial governors', since the castle was their residence. Also in the castle the newly-organised **Slottsmuseet** takes over the function of a country museum and displays the history of Örebro county from the Stone Age onwards. Their special treasure is the **Eketorp** hoard of coins and ornaments from c AD 1000, and there are displays on the Vikings and the Finnish settlers.

On the west of the castle is the elegant **theatre** of 1853, and west of that, the rambling brick building looking like a pastiche on the Holsten Gate at Lübeck, is the office of the local newspaper. Beyond are pretty walks along the river and on to **Frimurare holmen** (Freemasons' Island).

On the north side of the castle is the **Biologiska Museum** (open summer, around midday), a large room in a building of the Karolinska Skolan, an historic school. The museum began in 1864 as a teaching aid, and the animals include an appealing elk and other Scandinavian natives, with fish and birds in the gallery.

To the east of the castle by Hamnbron (Harbour Bridge) is **Tekniska Museet** (open June to Aug 12.00–18.00) in an old warehouse. This shows industry of the area with old printing presses, and domestic and office electrical equipment. Other local industries included mining, shoe-manufacturing and photography. (No English information.)

Back across the main road on the corner with Engelbrektsgatan is the new **Konstmuseet** (Art Museum) in the old Länsmuseum building, with varying art exhibitions. From near the technical museum there are summer boat-trips, and also from there you can walk along the river to Stadsparken, the town park. About 700m from the museum you reach **Wadköping**, the open-air museum with houses from the 16C onwards (open 11.00–17.00). It is also accessible by road. The square is the most picturesque part, and the most interesting house is **Kungstugan**, the King's House. This is of medieval type, built in the 16C. You can ask the guide to take you in to see the rare **wall-paintings**. Other houses belonged to a shoe-maker, glove-maker, smith and weaver. Some are private, and some have art and craft shops.

There is another open-air museum at **Karlslund**, 3.5km to the west. (Take Karlslundsgatan from Vasatorget.) Spread over a large area is a collection of old buildings including a manor and an agricultural museum in the mill.

About 2.5km north of the town centre is the water-tower known as **Svampen**, 'the mushroom', (1957), from which there is a wide view from 58m up. Take Östra Bangatan to the north and there is no way you can miss seeing it.

To the south, about 2km from centre, is a leisure area called **Gustavsvik**, with adventure pool, outdoor pool, camp-site and car museum.

13

Jönköping to Stockholm

Total distance 332km. Jönköping—E4, 39km **Gränna**—27km Ödeshög and road 50 to *Vadstena—62km **Linköping**—43km **Norrköping**—59km **Nyköping**—102km Stockholm.

The centre of Huskvarna is 6km from the centre of Jönköping, but the two virtually coalesce.

Huskvarna (the older spelling 'Husquarna' is retained in the name of the firm; see below) is named after a 'house mill' on the waterfall. (Compare English 'quern', a stone handmill.) Where the road to the centre leads to a pedestrians-only street, take the right turn up the hill (Jönköpingsvägen) until you cross a bridge and immediately on the right is a car park. Beyond this is **Smedbyn**, 'Smiths' village', a street of picturesque cottages where the armament workers lived.

A small-arms factory was founded in 1689, and was the beginning of today's Husqvarna company which makes household equipment. Almost opposite on the other side of the bridge is **Husqvarna Fabriksmuseum**, in the buildings once used for arms manufacture (open 13.00–17.00). The high brick building which houses the museum stands by the side of a narrow ravine in the river from where water-power was obtained. There are examples of all the objects made here, from outboard motors and chain saws to bicycles and sewing-machines. Machines for manufacturing guns and household equipment are also shown, and there is a collection of hunting weapons in the *Vapenmuseum*.

Returning down the hill and continuing on the same road, Jönköpingsvägen, then bearing north along the lake, you find **Dr Skoras Vaxkabinett** (open summer 10.00–19.00) with wax models of Swedish royalty, pop and film stars. Almost opposite in a 1771 powder store is the **Stadsmuseum**, with displays on the history of the town (open Sat pm May to Aug). This has archaeological finds, objects retrieved from the lake, photos, paintings, weapons and medals, and one of the first sewing-machines of 1875. The building beside this, Kroatorpet, is a café in a 19C environment. The next road on the right leads into Ådalsvägen which climbs the hill affording good views over the surroundings.

The E4 continues along the shore of Vättern and is one of the most beautifully situated motorways in the country.

It is 33km to Gränna but you may choose the first approach road a couple of kilometres earlier, which takes you past **Gyllene Uttern**, 'the Golden Otter', a pseudo-castle which is a hotel, and near the old industrial village of **Röttle** with a 17C mill. (Village accessible to tourists in summer.)

Gränna is a pretty little town of cobbled streets and painted wooden houses, interspersed with large red and white advertisements for *polkagrisar* ('polka pigs'), sticks of striped peppermint rock which you can see being made. The **tourist bureau** is on the main street in the same building as the Andrée museum, devoted to the efforts of a local balloonist to reach the North Pole in 1897. There is an open-air museum on Grännaberget above the town.

To the island of Visingsö

Amiralsvägen leads down to the harbour where smoked fish is often on sale, and there are ferries to **Visingsö** (25min). The island is the largest in Vättern and is 14km by 3km. Most of the sights are near the harbour but for visiting further afield you can hire a bicycle or use a horse-drawn *remmalag*, where the passengers sit back to back.

There was a fort on the island in the 12C, **Näs castle**, which was on the south end (ruins), where Magnus Ladulås died in 1290. More substantial ruins remain of **Visingsborg castle** near the harbour. Per Brahe the elder received the island from the crown in 1562 and using stone from Alvastra convent built the castle, which burnt down in 1718. Per Brahe the younger extended his power by building also Brahehus and Västanå castles on the mainland. The **Brahe church** not far away was begun by Magnus Brahe in the 17C. It is decorated with energetic wall-paintings by local artists. Several Brahe family members are buried in the funerary chapel. The pulpit has intarsia work. Ebba Brahe's wedding crown is displayed, and there is a 13C reliquary from Limoges, as well as a 15C carving of St. Birgitta similar to one in Vadstena. The sacristy door with decorative ironwork is from the medieval church—such ironwork on doors is a feature of the district.

Also near the harbour is the herb garden (*örtagård*) with old-fashioned herbs and roses and, a little futher, half-timbered 18C barns said to have been built by Russian prisoners-of-war who were kept on the island. Further away to the north, **Kumlaby church** was begun in the 12C, then Per Brahe had an observation platform built on top of the tower. Inside it has some 15C vault-paintings.

From Gränna there is an old coast road to Ödeshög. If you rejoin the E4, however, you will see after 6km the ruins of **Brahehus castle** on the cliff. There is a motorway service area from which the castle can be reached by a footpath under the E4. Using stone from Alvastra monastery, Per Brahe built the castle in the mid 17C, commanding wide views. It had two floors, cellar and attic, in the form of a keep with surrounding courtyard.

After 21km the E4 turns north-east at Ödeshög.

To Alvastra and Vadstena

At this point road 50 continues up the lake shore towards Vadstena and Motala. 7km along road 50 there is a sign to *Alvastra klosterruin* (2km). The sign *Pålbyggnad* points to the site of a Late Stone Age pile dwelling. The dig has been filled in, but there is an information-board. Simple huts were erected on a platform on piles in the marshy ground, and evidence of foods such as fruit, cereal, fish and meat has been found. The sign *Strand* leads to the home of a writer called Ellen Key.

Alvastra monastery was founded in 1143 by Cistercian monks invited from Clairvaux by Queen Ulfhild and King Sverker. There are considerable remains of the church, which had a barrel-vaulted nave with transverse barrel-vaults in the aisles, a straight-ended chancel and short transepts. Sweden's first archbishop, Stefan, was buried in the chancel, and St. Birgitta's husband Ulf Gudmarsson was buried in the north chapel. You can also see lesser remains of the cloister, chapter-house, kitchen and other buildings. A model of what it looked like is shown near the entrance. The monastery became very powerful and by 1500 owned over 400 properties. It was dissolved in the 1530s, and much of the stone carted away for building material.

Remains of Alvastra monastery church, founded 1143 by Cistercian monks

You can continue in the same direction to rejoin the 50, but you can also cross straight over the 50 to reach **Heda church** (2km), 12C but heavily restored, which contains **wood-carvings**, mainly gathered in the baptismal chapel. The **Madonna** on the left, known as 'Queen of Heaven in Heda' is from the 12C. The top part of the font is 13C and in the wall is an unusual carved **piscina**. The figure of Christ is presumed to have come from a crucifix and the other Madonna is also medieval. The **altar** too contains medieval figures in a plain frame.

Road 50 now skirts the **Omberg**, a granite horst 10km by 3km, whose highest point, Hjässan, is 175m over the water-level of Vättern. Several roads lead on to it, well signposted. The lakeside edge has dramatic cliffs, and there are viewing-points, some prehistoric remains, a nature display, a youth hostel and picnic areas.

8km from the Alvastra turn-off, **Väversunda church**, a short distance off the road, has retained its medieval exterior and has a **door** with decorative ironwork illustrating the Crucifixion and the Fall of Man. From here too you can reach the lake of **Tåkern** (10km), a nature reserve and bird sanctuary. There are three areas for visitors, with viewing-towers, on the north, south and east, the one on the east being accessible to the handicapped. There are of course certain regulations to protect wild-life. Ninety species of birds nest near the lake and a large number of spring and autumn migrants stop here. The flora and insects are also interesting.

After 4km you can turn to Rogslösa (1km) with probably the best ironwork-clad **door**, possibly depicting St. Hubert (a hunting scene), and St. Michael and the dragon. In 10km a road goes to **Nässja domarring** (stone circle) (6km). It is 3km to Vadstena.

•**Vadstena** (pop. 5500) is known to have had a church in the 12C, where the Red Tower, remnant of a later church, still stands. The village which grew up belonged to the Bjälbo family, ancestors of the Folkung dynasty of rulers. It was one of the Folkungs, Magnus Eriksson, who married

Blanche of Namur and at whose court St. Birgitta was lady-in-waiting. Blanche and Magnus gave Birgitta the Bjälbo palace to start her convent. After the saint's death in Rome in 1373 her body was brought back to Vadstena and a great cult sprang up, drawing crowds of pilgrims of all classes and nationalities, who brought income to the town. Even councils of state were held here, and trade naturally prospered.

The Reformation put an end to the streams of pilgrims, but the man who instigated the Reformation also put new life into Vadstena by founding one of the country's great castles. Gustav Vasa planned this as part of a chain of defence for the heartland around Stockholm. The medieval town plan can still be seen in the centre, and many houses with parts from the Middle Ages remain. Today Vadstena is delightful, but do not count on finding accommodation easily.

St. Birgitta (1303–73) was the daughter of the well-to-do and well-connected governor of Uppland, Birger Persson. She married Ulf Gudmarsson of Ulvåsa, later also a provincial governor, when she was 13 and had eight children, one of them St. Katarina. She was lady-in-waiting at court, in the the Bjälbo Palace in Vadstena, and while there began to have visions which inspired her throughout her life. In 1339 the couple made a pilgrimage to Nidaros (Trondheim), the shrine of St. Olof. Subsequently they travelled to Compostella, and Ulf died shortly after, being buried in Alvastra convent. In 1346 Birgitta was given the Bjälbo Palace by the royal couple to found a monastery for both monks and nuns, according to her revelations the central theme of which was to be simplicity and poverty. In order to obtain papal approval for her new order, Birgitta went to Rome, but the Pope was in Avignon. In fact it was not until 1370 that she was given the required permission, and in the interval she campaigned for the Pope's return to Rome, and worked for the destitute and ill. She then went on a pilgrimage to Jerusalem, and shortly after her return to Rome she died without seeing Vadstena again. She was canonised in 1391. Her daughter Katarina carried on her work, saw to the building of the church, and in turn was canonised in 1484.

The way into the town leads between the castle and the station, and parking is available nearby. Storgatan is the main street and a little way along in Rådhustorget the **tourist bureau** is housed in a a building with a history from the 16C. All historic houses in the town have a small plaque with information in Swedish and English.

Rådhustorget is the setting for the pretty little **town hall** which was begun in the 15C, but renovated many times. You can see the ground floor which is a restaurant, and entering through the tower the upper chamber which is used for exhibitions. In the same block there is a shop specialising in Vadstena bobbin-lace, where someone may demonstrate how it is made, and there is a small lace museum. Also in the square is the pharmacy (*apotek*, 19C) and Vadstena Museum (open an hour or two daily in summer) with parts dating from the 16C.

Storgatan has the greatest number of old houses, for example Helgeands-gården at No. 18, but the side streets to the west are more picturesque. Storgatan progresses through the main square, Stora Torget, and later comes to Rödtornet (the Red Tower) on the left. This is all that remains of S:t Pers church (15C) which was the church of the townspeople. It has step-gables and blind lancet decoration. The building now attached to it was originally for a school. On the other side of the road set back on private property you can see the 15C and 16C **Bishop's house**.

North of the Red Tower, signposted *Klosterområde* is the monastery area. However if instead of Klockaregatan you take the street parallel on the east, Lastköpingsgatan, and then the first on the right you will find the quaint **Mården Skinnare's house**. Mården was a wealthy furrier (*skinnare*) who started a hostel and hospital on this site for pilgrims, the poor and the ill. This was probably a residence belonging to the hospital (open July 13.00–16.00, also tours 12.00 June and Aug). The ground floor was for storage and the upper had living quarters, and there was originally a third floor also. Next door is the 1757 purpose-built mental hospital, now a museum of treatment of the mentally ill (open as above).

From these two houses you can go back a little way and approach the *monastery church through a gate in the medieval wall, crossing the churchyard to arrive at the very plain gabled façade. The church (Lutheran, open 10.00–17.00, later in summer), consecrated in 1430, was built of Omberg limestone and according to Birgitta's instructions without ornamentation. It is orientated in reverse, and this is the east end, with two insignificant doorways. The lancet windows have no stained glass, and there are no sculptural details. It is a hall-church, with aisles the same height as the nave. A model in the church shows how it had altar-rails, steps and galleries built in to accommodate the nuns. The ribs of the star-vaults are painted with foliage and chevrons in red and green. Though so unostentatious in architecture, it now houses a veritable treasury of *medieval wood-carving.

At the back are two enclosed pews used by the Dowager Queen Hedvig Eleanora. The **tomb** a little further in is that of Duke Magnus, son of Gustav Vasa (1595). The pillar beside it has a small statue of St. Jerome attached to it, probably by Bernt Notke of Lübeck. Round the pillar on the right are three **carvings**—a 15C St. Anne, a figure of Christ and one of St. Andrew.

The next pair of pillars each have a famous carving of St. Birgitta. On the left is the **'portrait' Birgitta** (c 1440), on the right **St. Birgitta in ecstasy** (1435) receiving one of her revelations. Her usual attribute (symbol) is a book.

Against the right-hand wall is a series of **carvings**. Above is a 14C crucifix, and under it an altarpiece, known as the Rosary Altar—the original roses have gone. To either side are figures of angels and saints. Above to the left is a Madonna in a niche which was a door by which the nuns entered the wooden gallery. The door further along was the one by which a nun entered the convent and never returned, except in her coffin for burial.

At the west end of the south aisle are several tombstones, of minor royalty and aristocracy, and against the pillar is a statue of St. Anne. The 16C font stands in front of the 1521 Brussels *altarpiece, showing the Assumption and Coronation of the Virgin. Above is a large **crucifix** made in Lübeck, contemporary with the church.

Steps lead down to the Monk's Choir where there is the altarpiece known as the *Birgitta Triptych (Lübeck 1459). The saint is dictating her visions to small cardinals. Also depicted are monks, nuns, apostles and saints. On the doors are scenes from the childhood of Christ and life of the Virgin. St. Birgitta's **reliquary** made at the time of her canonisation (1391) is in a glass case. It is covered in red velvet and has silver gilt medallions with the arms of those who made gifts to the monastery. Fewer than half of these now remain. The relics within include some from Birgitta.

At the end of the north aisle is another well-known carved figure, the 'beautiful Madonna', a Dutch work of 1450. Nearby is a statue of John the Baptist.

To the north of the church is the **palace of the Bjälbos**, given to Birgitta for her convent. This was where she had lived as lady-in-waiting to the court. (Open July 13.00–16.00, shorter hours June and Aug.) The Gothic doorways

Statue of St. Birgitta in ecstacy (North German c 1435)

on the left are from the palace, the row of small windows were put in for the nuns' cells, one window between two. The stately doorway was sculpted with martial emblems in 1677 when the building was used as a home for soldiers. Inside, much restored, you can see the King's Hall with pillars and arches, and upstairs the corridor with nuns' cells. A small side tower contains a vaulted chapel with 16C paintings of the Evangelists, and the catafalque and coffin in which Birgitta's body was brought home from Rome. The vaulted chapter-house was built c 1400.

The wing on the west, now the main entrance of a hotel, originally had the convent kitchen and refectory, and the one on the east had a sickroom and access for the nuns to the church. To the west of the church are excavations from a brewery and sickroom, and beyond, the large building, now partly a restaurant, contains some remains from the time when it was a simple monastery for Birgitta's monks. It then had just one storey, and the vaulted chapter-house remains in the right wing. Behind the car park is the herb-garden, part of the monks' garden.

Across the green is the new Catholic St. Birgitta's convent, church and guest-house. Religious orders were banished from Sweden after the Reformation, but Brigittine convents continued abroad and in 1935 some sisters returned to run a guest-house. In 1962 they were able to establish a new branch of the order here. In 1992 four novices were professed in the old church, the first for 400 years. The new church (1980) is entered from the far side of the complex (open for services and guided tours in summer).

The *castle is a few minutes' walk away (open mid-May to mid-Aug 12.00–16.00, longer in July). It is a good example of Swedish Renaissance, and one of the few castles anywhere with a marina in the moat. It consists of a block with three square towers forming one wing of a square with massive round towers at the corners, now linked by puny 19C walls. It was begun by Gustav Vasa in 1545, and finished in 1620 with the decorative west gable, the east gable being completed some years earlier. Emphasis is on the symmetrical and horizontal, and there are rows of plain windows, broken only by the Gothic windows of the chapel in the third floor added by Johan III. Gustav married his third wife here, his mentally handicapped son Duke Magnus was a resident, and the Dowager Queen Hedvig Eleanora spent much time here in the 17C.

A bridge leads to the main gate. Between two bulging half-columns a fine Renaissance doorway (1563) is carved with Duke Magnus' coat of arms and initials. The inner side is simpler but of similar quality. Both are French in style.

Inside, up on the **first floor** there are temporary exhibitions. On the **second floor** (turn right where the stairs divide) there is the Bridal Hall with some wall-painting and painted beams, which is used for opera performances by the Vadstena Academy. On the **third floor** (go back to where the stairs divide and go up the other side) four rooms have been provided with furniture and paintings. The dining-room has Baroque chairs, an intarsia chest and two German cabinets. There are two paintings by the Fleming Frans Snyders, and royal portraits. Between the windows is a Baroque **mirror** of c 1700. The Cabinet has paintings by Ehrenstrahl and his school, and by David von Krafft. In the bedroom the richly carved bed is from North Germany. An intricately-worked 17C Antwerp **cabinet** of wood, tortoise-shell and brass stands in the Anteroom and there are two Flemish paintings. The Small Hall of State has a Brussels tapestry showing Dido and Aeneas, and there are more royal portraits. The **chapel**, though built in the 17C, has a star-vault, lancet and rose windows. The altar painting is by Sir Anthony van Dyck. The room is stone-floored, with an exceptional echo. The two adjoining small rooms were once part of the chapel and one later served as library and sacristy.

Tours of the town by tourist 'train' leave from beside the castle. Behind it are two old harbour warehouses, one of which has facilities for visiting yachtsmen. From the station across the road a veteran train (steam or diesel) goes to Fågelstad (10km) twice a day in summer.

The north-east shore of Vättern

Further north up road 50 is (16km) **Motala**, a town planned by Baltzar von Platen, creator of the Göta Canal. The fan-shaped street pattern is his, and Motala Verkstad, on the island between the canal and Motala river, was the engineering works founded to service the canal. Von Platen's **statue** is on the main square, and his **grave** is on the canal bank—follow the tow-path on the north side about 700m.

At the mouth of the river there is a bridge of 1787, and on the north bank of the canal there is the **Kanal-och Sjöfartsmuseum** (Canal and Maritime Museum) in the old building of the canal company (open mid-May to Aug). This shows the construction of the canal, tools and techniques. Upstairs there are models of canal boats and a video is shown, with English soundtrack on request. You can also ask here for the key to look over the lock-keeper's cottage just over the bridge. Nearby, the crankshaft set up as a monument is a tribute to Motala Verkstad. There is also a Radio Museum, and Motala Museum in Charlottenborg 17C manor (about 1.5km along the south bank), with local history and art.

To the north-east of Motala the ruins of St. Birgitta's home are on a point of land, **Birgittas Udde**, in lake Boren—confusing, because the manor, called Ulvåsa, was later rebuilt on the next point east in the lake, where there is now a 19C manor of Ulvåsa.

After 11km north on road 50 there is a turning for **Övralid** (2km), the beautifully situated home of the poet Verner von Heidenstam (1859–1940), open to the public. **Medevi Brunn** (spa) in 5km has preserved spa buildings, and you can drink the water. In another 27km there is a turn for **Kinaparken** (Chinese Park) in an old quarry, with Chinese bridges, pavilions, waterlily-ponds, trees and plants.

The road crosses the north arm of the lake at Hammar with pleasant views and, a little further on, **Stjernsund** 'castle' with luxurious 19C interior is open in summer.

The E4 from Ödeshög turns north-east and after 10km a road is signposted *Rökstenen*, where you will find the **Rök runestone (1km), the most famous if not the most attractive runestone in the country (accessible all the year round). Now situated by the church gate, it was discovered in the 1840s having been used as a building stone in a small building belonging to the church. It is 2.5m high with another 1.5m underground, weighs four tonnes, but what makes it so unusual is that it is almost completely covered with 800 runic letters. It was erected in the first half of the 9C by Varin in memory of his son Vaemod, and is a baffling collection of myth, legend and history in poetic and grandiose verse or prose or even code, which has not yet been fully interpreted. The adjoining exhibition is in Swedish only, but English information is available at the **tourist bureau** at the entrance in summer.

Back on the E4 there are signs to the lake of Tåkern (see above) after 4km and again after another 4km. From here it is 12km on the E4 to Mjölby, but from here you can also go to **Skänninge** passing on the way near **Bjälbo**, the home-village of the Bjälbo/Folkung family (connected with Birger Jarl and St. Birgitta), where the church has a defensive tower from the 12C.

Skänninge (16km from Rök), a pretty village with old wooden houses and a medieval church was early inhabited by Hanse merchants, hence the brick **church**, finished c 1300, is in Baltic Gothic style. The step-gable is ornamented with blind lancets, cross and large rosette. The altar-painting is a 17C copy of that in Linköping, and the pulpit is of the same date. The wood relief of St. Ingrid, a local saint, is a modern version of a 17C fresco in Florence. There are many 17C memorial tablets.

North of the church is the main square with the 18C town hall, and on the other side under the arch the **old town**, covering several streets of old cottages. Beyond, reached by crossing the river, turning left and going over the crossroads for about 100m, are the scanty remains of St. Ingrid's convent for Dominican nuns (1270).

On the way back to the E4 which you can rejoin at Mjölby in 8km, you could digress a couple of kilometres to see the **Högby Runestone**. (Somewhat vaguely signposted after the first sign—at the junction of several tracks take the second on the right, then after some distance on a rough track, at the T-junction it is just to the left on a wooded mound.) The carver was named Torkel and it commemorates, at the behest of their niece, five brothers slain in different lands (early 11C). From Mjölby it is 32km to Linköping.

*Linköping (pop. 82,000), now the administrative centre of the county of Östergötland, was an important ecclesiastical centre in the Middle Ages, being the seat of a bishop in the early 12C. In 1152, a meeting here proclaimed that Sweden was a province of the Roman Catholic Church, whilst in the 13C King Valdemar was crowned in the cathedral. In 1598, Sigismund of Poland (grandson of Gustav Vasa) was defeated by his uncle Duke Karl, later Karl IX, just outside the town and in 1600 some of Sigismund's supporters were executed in the 'Linköping Bloodbath'. The town was destroyed by fire in 1700, but the cathedral escaped.

Linköping has closed its tourist bureau. Some hotels marked by the green and white 'i' sign usually on genuine tourist bureaux have a few tourist leaflets, and hotel staff may spare time to answer basic questions. It is to be hoped that at the very least town plans and lists of accommodation will soon be made available.

Post office: Kungsgatan 20.

Telephone, telegram: Ågatan 29. Tel. (013) 20 22 25.

Follow signs to *Domkyrkan*, the *cathedral, whose spire is also a good guide. The building material is limestone. The transepts, which do not now project, form the oldest part dating from 1232, and were joined to an older narrower nave and a chancel built at the same time. In the 14C a longer nave was built, as wide as the transepts, and in the 15C the present chancel. A west tower was built in the 18C, which now has a spire. On the exterior there is sparse ornament in the form of blind arcading, but the lancet windows have very varied tracery patterns. It is a hall-church, with an ambulatory and three chapels at the east end.

The south door **tympanum** (restored 19C) has a central figure of Christ and scenes from the Passion. The west door now has a modern mosaic. The interior columns are round, octagonal or clustered and the nave and aisles are roofed with cross-vaulting, the east end by star-vaulting or a variant.

The church, though striking the European visitor as sober, is richer in sculpted decoration than most others in the country. Inside on the side walls can be seen blind **arcading**, in both Romanesque and Gothic style. The point where they join shows two building phases, late 13C and early 14C. The Gothic arcades, by English artists, are decorated with sculpture, heads and foliage being the main motifs, with little animals and birds. The round arches have ornament only on the capitals. Otherwise the main columns of the nave have modest capital sculpture, mostly foliage. **Corbels** have heads or small figures; vault **bosses** are also carved, with faces, flowers and coats of arms.

The three altar paintings are by the Norwegian artist Henrik Sörensen (1936). The large crucifix is from the 14C, a local work, while the **pulpit** is Baroque. The three ambulatory **chapels** were constructed by masons from

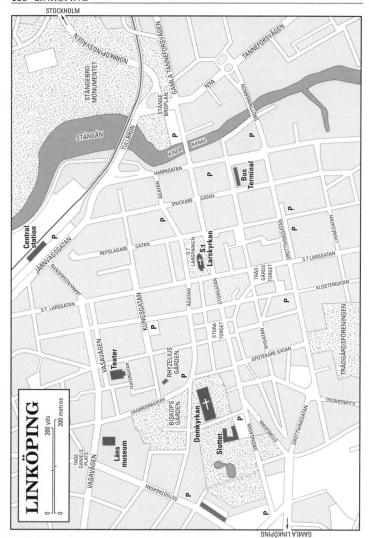

Cologne. The first chapel on the left is dedicated to a medieval bishop, Nicolaus Hermanni, and the tombs are of one of Gustav Vasa's three mothers-in-law (1549) and a 17C provincial governor. The central chapel, the Lady Chapel, has unique new **windows** (1993) of etched glass, with the Virgin's head and hands among plants and flowers. The 15C North German bronze **font** stands behind the main altar, and modern tapestries (1938) hang there. The third chapel is dedicated to St. Thomas à Becket of Canterbury. Beside it is a 1542 altar painting, a **triptych** formerly on the main altar, by Marten van Heemskerk from Holland, with crowded scenes from the Passion of Christ.

The **castle** (*slottet*) is almost opposite the west front of the cathedral (no admittance). In the 13C the Bishop of Linköping built a castle here which has been many times rebuilt. Some decoration from the 14C defence tower remains on the north façade. Gustav Vasa strengthened it, and his son Johan made it into a Renaissance palace. Here Sigismund of Poland and Duke Karl signed their treaty, and here in 1600 Duke Karl was proclaimed king. Several monarchs stayed in the castle. It had its last major face-lift in the 18C and it is now the residence of the county governor.

The main square is three blocks to the west, the scene of the Linköping Bloodbath. There is an entertaining **fountain** by Carl Milles portraying Folke Filbyter, a legendary figure searching for his grandson, while on the base are lively scenes from the history of the province of Östergötland, with Kings Valdemar and Magnus Ladulås, and St. Birgitta on her way to Rome.

A few blocks to the south is the pleasant **Trädgårdsföreningen park**, with a belvedere some distance in.

To the north of the cathedral, if you go up Gråbrödragatan (Greyfriars Street) you pass on the right the site of the monastery and an old building called **Rhyzeliusgården**, once the post-Reformation bishop's palace. This houses some stonework details from the cathedral and you can ask at the museum for the key.

In the park on the left you can see the present Bishop's Palace, with a projecting circular section (18C) and, opposite, the modern concert hall, where you also come upon **Östergötlands Länsmuseum** (open Tue–Thurs 11.00–21.00, Fri–Sun 11.00–16.00). Archaeological finds include an important Boat Axe (Stone Age) burial, found in the town, consisting of a whole family. Gold coins from Arabia show the far-flung trade of later centuries. There are some medieval finds, but paintings form the greater number of the exhibits. The main areas are German Renaissance, of which the centrepiece is **Lucas Cranach**'s *Fall of Man*, 17C Dutch and 18C Swedish and French. 20C Swedish art includes the Gothenburg Colourists. A special darkened room shows the **Königsmark embroideries** of 1689, probably made for the wedding of Amalia Königsmark.

Out to the west, about 2km along Malmslättsvägen, is *Gamla Linköping, a particularly imaginative example of a local open-air museum. (Accessible all the year round, with many events and activities in summer, especially pm.) Over 80 predominantly 19C buildings have been transplanted from the centre of town to form a village centred on Kryddbotorget, the market square. Shops and workshops show how trade was carried on and wares manufactured, from ropes to chocolate, and houses show how life was lived. The bank and school are museums. You can travel the streets in a horse-drawn carriage or little 'train'. The inhabitants wear period costumes and engage in everyday pursuits, like small befrilled girls trundling iron hoops. Do not get in the way of the villainous-looking thief pelting round a corner, still less of the portly constable in ponderous pursuit. Altercations and other vignettes are staged on the square.

Another 4km out in the same direction is the **Flygvapenmuseum**, the national air-force museum with a large collection of veteran planes (open pm). Leave the motorway at the second junction and follow the signs.

On the north-east edge of town across the river Stångeån, is the **Stångebro Monument** commemorating the battle between Sigismund and Duke Karl on the site.

Excursions from Linköping

8km north of the centre (take Bergsvägen), is **Vreta Klosters Kyrka** (Vreta Convent church), of great significance in the Middle Ages. About half-way there, off the road, is **Kaga** church decorated with medieval paintings by different artists, including the Risinge Master and Master Amund.

Vreta was founded in about 1120 and later taken over by the Cistercians, but lost its considerable influence when Vadstena flourished. The nave was constructed in the 14C, and much of the church has been restored to resemble as far as possible its appearance when it was rebuilt in 1289 after a fire. The 17C funerary chapel was added for Field-Marshal Count Robert Douglas (d 1663) and his family. There is a 12C Madonna and other wood-carvings in a raised sacristy on the north, and a 16C royal pew. The 17C pulpit is South German/Italian, of oak and birch. Of the convent itself only ruins remain, which are incorporated into a garden. Tombstones and other fragments found in the ruins are kept in the granary about 100m to the south.

To Ekenäs castle

From Linköping you can visit **Ekenäs slott** (23km), by taking road 35 to the south-east (well signposted), or reach it also from the E4 to Norrköping. (Guided tours July Tue–Sun pm; also weekends May, June, Aug. Swedish, but guide will explain in English.)

The present castle was built in 1617–50. It is romantically perched on a wooded rocky outcrop, with three square towers whose caps and the roof are covered with wooden shingles. The approach is over the moat and under one of the towers. The separate pavilions are from 1700, and one houses a tea-room. In the castle there is 18C and 19C décor and furniture, most in Karl Johan (Empire) style, but a 17C bed and an 18C Dutch intarsia cabinet may be singled out, and in the dining-room a long series of portraits of Swedish monarchs. There are stately tiled stoves, carved and panelled walls and doors, and remnants of a ceiling-painting, as well as a curious stone carving of the goddess of justice from the previous house (16C). Down in the basement are vaulted 16C cellars, a good ghost story and a 19C kitchen.

Leave Linköping by the E4, north of the town. After 2km the road crosses the Kinda Canal, and after 20km there is a turn for Ekenäs slott (see above). After 4km the road passes over the Göta Canal and in another 8km a sign points to **Löfstad slott** (1km) (guided tours, Swedish, June–Aug pm), rebuilt in 1753 by the wealthy and influential Major-General Axel von Fersen and his wife Hedvig Catarina of the de la Gardie family. Their daughter married into the Piper family who owned the place until 1940.

The castle consists of three separate wings, with the main entrance set in a projecting pedimented centre portion, the three doorways framed with carving. The roof is of the double-sloped 'säteri' type, and a sandstone frieze of heads and coats of arms runs between the first and second floors. Inside there is a large collection of good furniture, some by Georg Haupt, and portraits, some by Ehrenstrahl. The dining-room has a silver collection, glass, porcelain, including the 'Löfstad service', 19C tapestries, and portraits. The study has a 1590 South German intarsia cabinet illustrating the months. The library, with 5000 books in leather bindings, was fitted out in the 19C; two large mirrors were saved from the previous building. The salon has a rich mixture of furniture styles—Baroque, Rococo, Gustavian and Karl Johan—with a portrait by Ehrenstrahl among many others, and a cabinet of miniatures. The bedroom has a Georg Haupt writing-table.

In the grounds is a memorial erected by Sophie Piper to her brother Axel von Fersen the younger, who was a distinguished soldier and diplomat, fought in the American War of Independence, was rumoured to be Marie Antoinette's lover, engineered the French royal couple's abortive escape attempt and was murdered by a rabble in Stockholm, suspected of having poisoned the heir to the throne.

It is 9km on the E4 to Norrköping. Alternatively, you may detour via Kimstad and Skärblacka to *S:ta **Maria** church (26km) near Risinge, following signposts to *Risinge* and *'S:ta Maria K:a'*, the old church being 4km south of the present village. (Check opening times at a tourist bureau before going, or possibly try a summer weekday before 15.00.) It has a wood-shingled roof and the double churchyard wall is roofed in the same way. The church was begun in the 12C and had a new vault in the early 15C. This was then painted by the so-called Risinge Master, whose artistic production was small but of high quality. The *scenes, on five vault-bays, are composed within medallions in frames, some of which are lettered with texts. The small spaces between are crowded with animals, foliage and patterns. The faces are always in three-quarter profile. The subjects range right through the Bible, starting with the Creation, and include, for example, the stories of Isaac, and Joseph, and the Assumption of the Virgin. There is also a 15C Lübeck altarpiece.

You can then get to Norrköping by joining road 51 at the village of Risinge 4km further on. (From here, in the other direction **Finspång** (5km west) is an industrial town with some workers' houses remaining of the old iron-works, and a works' museum. The 17C manor is private.) Completing the circuit of the lake of Glan to Norrköping to the south-east, you pass a sign *Glasbruk*, indicating Rejmyre glassworks.

Norrköping (pop. 83,000) received its town charter in 1384. Thanks to the rushing waters of the Motala river which powered its machinery, it became 'Sweden's Manchester', with great textile mills, now silent. Along the river the 19C industrial environment has taken on a evocative quality. Today, the port is one of the most important on the east coast. There are various tourist cards on sale, giving discounts on activities in the town and the zoo at Kolmården. The yellow trams will take you across town but most sights are near the centre. There are boat trips in summer.

Tourist bureau: Drottninggatan 11. Tel. (011) 15 15 00.

Post office: Drottninggatan 20.

Telephone, telegram: Drottninggatan 28. Tel. (011) 19 50 74.

Bus station: Opposite the station.

Just north of the tourist bureau the **town hall tower** provides a panorama from 50m up (mid-June to mid Aug 11.00; meet at the tourist bureau). There are 48 bells in the tower which play at certain times. North of this again is the river and on the north bank lies Karl Johans Park, which has luxuriant and creative **cactus displays** in summer.

The industrial landscape is back to the south-west along the river. Take Drottninggatan south to Gamla Torget (Old Square) where stands Carl Milles' **statue** of Louis de Geer, the 17C Dutchman who did so much for Sweden's industry. Turn up Järnbrogatan and cross the Gamlebro (Old Bridge) after which the whole area is turn-of-the century industrial in red brick. Continue along Västgötegatan to No. 19 where there is the **Stads-museum** (town museum, open Tue–Fri 10.00–16.00, Thurs to 20.00, Sat, Sun 11.00–17.00; textile machines shown working Tue, Wed 14.00, Thurs 18.00).

The museum consists of several linked old industrial buildings, which makes the lay-out extremely confusing, but fortunately there is a plan and short guide in English. On four floors there are exhibits reflecting Norrköp-ing history with particular emphasis on the textile industry. On the ground floor are shown preparation and dyeing, on the first spinning and weaving. A street of craftmen's shops is also on the first floor, and on the second there is the workshop area, and the social conditions of workers. The top floor has handicrafts.

Down by the side of the Stadsmuseum you can walk through to the **Arbetsmuseum** (Museum of Work, open daily 11.00–17.00). This is in 'The Iron', a striking seven-storey cotton-mill of 1917, oddly shaped in order to fit the shore-line it stands on—the basement is in fact below the water-line. It contains long-term but temporary exhibitions on the theme of work. The only permanent exhibition is that around the stair-well, illustrating the life of Alva Carlsson, a typical worker at The Iron from 1927 to 1966.

From here you can explore both sides of the river in the historic **industrial townscape**, with solid and sometimes handsome red-brick factories. If you happen to start from the north side of the river you can take Bredgatan and reach the riverside after some minutes. Then it is an enjoyable walk to the footbridge over the weir, and along the south bank, eventually reaching **Färgaregården**, a dyer's household, now an open-air museum. You can also reach it by car along S:t Persgatan. It consists of a dyer's home and workshops from the early 19C. (Accessible all year, buildings open May to Aug 12.00–16.00; café.) The dyer and his assistants lived and worked in the scattered buildings, the pressing-house, dyeing shop with vats, and mill-ing-house with water-wheel. The herb-garden grows plants for dyeing.

The **Konstmuseum** (Art Museum, 12.00–16.00, also summer evenings, closed Mon Sept–May) is just to the south of where Drottinggatan meets Södra Promenaden. It is set in a **Sculpture Park** (English leaflet available), of which perhaps the most striking exhibit is the slowly moving 'Spiral Gesture' by Arne Jones. The museum has a representative **collection of Swedish art** from the 17C to the present (English leaflet). It starts in the **basement** with such as Roslin and von Krafft. The **ground floor** has the most recent works with post-modernism and other isms, while the **first floor** has the 19C, cubism, and the Gothenburg Colourists, among others.

The district called **Himmelstalund** is to the north-west of the centre, reached from the E4. There is a large leisure area on both sides of the river with swimming-pool, camp-site and bathing. Half a kilometre from the car park, on rocks forming a rise, there are Bronze Age **rock carvings**, some of which have been picked out in red. There are boats, footprints, sun-wheels, swords, horses and bear paw-marks.

Excursion from Norrköping

From Norrköping taking the E22 to the south, you can visit **Söderköping** (17km; pop. 7000), a charming little town once one of the most important in the country. In the Middle Ages, Hanse merchants brought it prosperity, because the river was then navigable up to the town hall, and later Gustav Vasa spent considerable time at Stegeborg castle nearby, which brought the centre of power close to hand. But what with the river silting up, the decline of the Hanse and the Danes burning it in 1567, Söderköping lost its significance, and not much is left of its medieval past, when even Riksdag sessions were held in the town. In the 18C the spa was developed, and in the 19C the Göta Canal brought business back, but not enough.

The **tourist bureau** is in the 1777 town hall on Rådhustorget. To the west, in an 18C district, is the small white **Drothems church** with its decorated step-gable and square tower, founded in the 13C. It was the church for the country-dwellers, whereas S:t Laurentii was the town church. Inside it has deep-ribbed star-vaults. The late 15C **altarpiece** was carved in Lübeck, and the centre figure represents the Trinity, with saints to either side under carved canopies. The 18C pulpit has foliage decoration.

S:t Laurentii church is just across the river and makes a quite different impression—large and imposing in red-brick Baltic Gothic with a great sweeping double-sloped roof and broad gables with blind decoration. It was originally from the late 13C, the vaults 15C and the gables 16C. The medieval chapels along the north aisle were converted after the Reformation into another parallel aisle. The **triptych** (1500) on the altar shows the Descent from the Cross and on the wings are 24 Old Testament figures. The pulpit was made in Vadstena (1671). There are chandeliers from the 16C and 17C, many memorial tablets, and medieval carvings of St. Catherine of Alexandria, Martin of Tours and St. Christopher. There is an unusual wooden bell-tower nearby (16C).

Walk along Prästgatan to the east and in the street on the left there is the old school-house, with the **Stadsmuseum** (town museum, open Mon–Thurs am, Sun pm, mid-June to mid-Aug 11.00–17.00). Trade, churches, the spa and the Göta Canal are among subjects covered, and there is a model of the late medieval town.

The district round this bend in the river is 19C in character, with enjoyable walks especially along the river, Storgatan and Ågatan. To the north, short streets lead to the canal, with the lock, and attractive paths to follow. The cliff on the other side is called Ramunderberget, and paths lead up to a good view.

Further to the east is the **spa area**. There is a legend that the spring gushed up to save the life of St. Ragnhild, about to be burnt at the stake (unjustly, of course). The spa received a royal charter in 1774, and in the 19C was a flourishing resort. Now the hotel is a conference centre as well, though you can still drink the water, which is available in the foyer. Across the river among the trees in the park is the little spa chapel and the spa hospital, used until 1974, is nearby. Boats moored in the river complete the scene.

Further out to the south-east is an open-air museum, **Korskullen**, with a group of old buildings.

East of Söderköping the excavated part of the Göta Canal comes to an end at Mem, which has a fine manor-house, now used for conferences. The canal route goes through Slätbaken, an inlet of the Baltic, and on an islet are the ruins of the once imposing **Stegeborg castle**, built to defend Söderköping. Now you can see the 25m-tall round tower and the remains of the courtyard buildings from the 15C. Gustav Vasa used to stay, and his son Johan III was born here. Later, as he did with so many of his father's castles, Johan made it into a Renaissance palace.

Beyond lies the panorama of the **S:ta Anna Archipelago**. There is an ecumenical chapel (Capella Ecumenica), a co-operative venture of twelve different churches, on one of the islands, reached by boat from Kungshäll-sudden on Sundays.

The E22 continues south from Söderköping to Kalmar (226km), passing through Västervik and Oskarshamn, from both of which ferries ply to Gotland.

The main route the E4 heads north out of Norrköping to turn east round the head of the long Bråviken inlet. After 17km you may follow the signs to **Kolmården Djurpark-Zoo**. In 5km the village of Kolmården is reached and after 1km there is a sign to the disused marble quarry *Marmorbruket*. The cool green Kolmården marble was quarried here from 1722 to 1970, and has been used in the most distinguished buildings, notably Stockholm City Hall. You can walk past the workshops to see the quarry.

The zoo is another 3km (open May to Sept 10.00–15.00, 16.00 or 17.00; feeding times tend to be in the afternoon). This is an expensive outing and it is worth examining all the various ways of buying tickets. The zoo can be included on a card with Norrköping sightseeing, or its three main attractions can be included on one ticket.

The safari park comes first, and cars are led through the enclosures in convoy. There are Scandinavian animals as well as the usual lions and giraffes. Further on, between the car park and the entrance to the zoo, is the **Tropicarium**, an excellent collection of such fauna as snakes, crocodiles, parrots, tropical fish and butterflies, with perhaps the stars of the show being the sharks in their 1-million-litre plexi-glass tank. The prettiest exhibit must be the coral grotto. Names are given in Swedish and Latin, with maps showing where they are found. The zoo itself has all the usual animals, including areas especially geared for children. There are special displays with birds of prey, elephants and dolphins. A cable-car circles the whole area (summer only).

Back on the E4, in 4km you leave Östergötland and enter Södermanland, often shortened to Sörmland. In 22km you can take a parallel road to Nyköping which will bring you past the **church** at **Tuna**, begun c 1300. This has paintings in the chancel vault of Christ and the saints from the 17C, and over the chancel arch of SS. Peter and Paul of the early 14C. The Madonna is North German from the end of the 15C. The columns have unusual pierced-brick capitals.

Nyköping is 16km from where you left the E4. The town (pop. 26,000) is the administrative capital of Södermanland. In medieval times it was a thriving harbour and market. Here in 1317 took place the infamous 'banquet of Nyköping' (see below). The town was burnt by the Russians in 1719, so the oldest parts now date from the 18C.

There is a **tourist bureau** in the 17C town hall in Stora Torget. Opposite is the 18C governor's residence and S:t Nicolai church, and in the square a fountain designed by Ragnar Östberg, architect of Stockholm City Hall. The **church** has a complicated building history, dating from the 13C. The carved sandstone south doors are from the 17C. The most striking object inside is the 1748 **pulpit** modelled on that of the Storkyrka in Stockholm. On the other side is a late Gothic carved altarpiece with the Virgin and two bishops. The main altar **picture** of the Last Supper was painted by Georg Engelhard Schröder (1739).

Since the church tower was damaged by fire in 1665, it was decided to build a separate **bell-tower**, a high red wooden tower perched on a rock to the west of the church, the oldest wooden building in the town.

You can walk along the river bank from Storgatan southwards to the **castle** of Nyköpingshus, now the museum. Opposite is the art gallery, also part of the museum, which has temporary exhibitions on themes of history or art (open Tue–Sun 12.00–16.00; also July Mon).

A defensive tower was built to protect the town in the 13C, and Magnus Ladulås soon converted it to a fortress. The most notorious event was when Magnus' son Birger invited his brothers Erik and Valdemar to a banquet, and then shut them in a dungeon to starve, the 'banquet of Nyköping'. Gustav Vasa strengthened the castle, and his son Karl IX turned it into a Renaissance palace. Karl X Gustav was born here in 1622. In 1633 Gustavus Adolphus' (Gustav II Adolf) embalmed body remained here for 11 months after his death in the Battle of Lützen, while his mortuary chapel was being built in Riddarholm church in Stockholm. An engraving of the mid 17C shows a flurry of decorated spires, towers and gables on solid defensive walls. The castle was severely damaged by fire in 1665 and never recovered its importance.

The **Gatehouse** has the coat of arms of Karl IX. The main historical exhibitions are in the Kungstornet, King's Tower. Around the stairs are stone carvings from the Renaissance palace. In the **first floor** guardroom there are models of the castle at various stages, and by pressing buttons you can see lights come on in different sections which illustrate, for example, the events leading up to the banquet of Nyköping. On the **second floor** the craft of medieval wood-carving is illustrated, with some good medieval figures, while the **top floor** has later history with portraits of royalty and a section on the stay here of Gustavus Adolphus' body, his widow and the six-year-old Queen Kristina. There is also a model of the Renaissance castle.

In the old **governor's residence** (*Gamla residenset*) there are displays of archaeology and social history, with furniture, craft and costumes. Events are staged in the courtyard in the summer, including an historical pageant.

The grounds along the river are attractive, and a little further on there is a small open-air museum, in one of whose buildings, **Tovastugan**, there are wall-paintings of 1641 (summer café).

You can continue your walk along the river to the pleasant harbour area with old buildings. A plan is afoot to convert this district into an arts, crafts, leisure and eating complex.

To Runtuna, Lid and Uppsa Kulle

As the E4 approaches Stockholm the area on either side has many historic castles and churches. To the north of Nyköping, by taking road 223 you can visit Runtuna and Lid churches, and the prehistoric mound of Uppsa Kulle. **Runtuna**, 3km off the 223, has a late Gothic North German altarpiece, a Baroque pulpit and wall-paintings by the artist known as the Union Master. The church of **Lid**, 5km further, on an unmade road, has painted vaults (15C) and a 13C crucifix. You can return to rejoin the 223 at Aspa (very rough road) where a runestone stands by the roadside. Turning south again on the 223, in 5km you can digress to **Uppsa Kulle** (2km), a burial mound probably contemporary with those at Uppsala (c 6C). This is the third largest in Sweden, 55m across and 9.5m high. From the top there is a gentle spreading view of all the elements of a typical Swedish landscape, scattered red wooden houses among lakes, fields and woods.

To Nynäs and Stendörren

As for the other side of the E4, after 17km from Nyköping, you can turn for Nynäs castle (14km), and after another 12km Stendörren nature reserve.

Nynäs Slott (open mid-June to mid-Aug 11.00–16.00; also weekends a month before and after) has a history going back to the 14C. As it is now, parts date from the 17C and 18C, with the entrance portico and balcony from the 19C. The entrance hall has a vaulted ceiling and there is a turn-of the-century kitchen, but the most arresting feature of the building is the extravagant 17C **stucco-work** on the first floor. In the main salon the ceiling has a central medallion with the four elements and four putti around a star. (Nynäs was owned by the Gyllenstierna family whose name means 'golden star'.) There are coats of arms in the corner roundels, the spaces between being filled with a profusion of shells and foliage. The bedroom has an alcove partially screened by free-standing stucco urns and garlands, with a ceiling to match. There are portraits and some furniture which it is hoped to complete in appropriate style. The stately 1909 orangery designed by Isak Gustaf Clason has a café. The castle stables now ingeniously provide for picnickers, with a table and chairs in each stall.

Stendörren nature reserve about 12km away is on the next spit of land to the W; follow signposts to *Stendörrens naturreservat*. At the first car park on the left of the road, cut through the trees on the right, from where you can walk out over the islands—linked by three **footbridges**—seeing some of the archipelago without a boat. The road ahead leads to a larger car park from where you can walk 1km to another point with a view. (Maps at the car parks.)

To Trosa and Tullgarn

39km from Nyköping on the E4, at Vagnhärad, you can turn to visit **Trosa**, an idyllic little town on the coast (9km). On the way you pass *Trosa lands kyrka*, the church for the country-dwellers of the parish of Trosa. Once the medieval town stood here, but the rising of the land forced a move to the new coast-line. The church was begun in the 13C, and most of the walls are of this time, with vaults and tower of the 15C. Fragments of wall-painting remain. The crucifix is 14C and the **pulpit** is by a pupil of Burchardt Precht whose work is in Stockholm Storkyrka.

The tiny town hall with onion tower on top stands in the market square. From here you can take **Östra Långgatan** to the south, with an example of a fisherman's cottage, beside the café called Tre Små Rum. Turn right to reach the river, on either side of which are picturesque **walks**, either back into the centre or down towards the harbour where eventually a bridge leads on to a large island with woods, a camp-site and swimming.

If you can tear yourself away from the river you may return to the centre by **Västra Långgatan**, parallel to Östra Långgatan on the west of the river. On the left is the diminutive ex-police and fire-station with a similar turret to the town hall, only red instead of black. Further up is **Kåkstaden**, the so-called 'shanty-town', with 18C red-painted wooden cottages. Among them, **Garvaregården** is the tanner's establishment with a café in the courtyard, and the **Stadsmuseum** (town museum, open in summer) in one wing. This has old photos, displays on fishing and trade, and a map of the Russian invasion of Stockholm archipelago in 1719 when so much was burnt.

The **church** is on the other side of the road, approached by a lane between the houses. It was built in the 17C after the town had to be moved from its medieval setting. The bell-tower is from about 1700. The **altar** was made in 1711, but the painting is 19C, while the oldest object is a little wood-carved altarpiece of the late 15C. The **pulpit**, also 1711, may be by the same artist as that in the older Trosa church, a pupil of Burchardt Precht. Some distance to the north, the town mill is now a craft centre.

From near the older Trosa church a road goes to **Tullgarns Slott** (6km), situated on a rise by the water. (Open early May to mid-Sept 11.00–16.00. Guided tours in Swedish, but there are comprehensive English notes to borrow, with a free copy if you buy the glossy Swedish guide.) The estate was founded c 1600 by Count Carl Sture. The castle was rebuilt in 1727 by Magnus Julius de la Gardie and bought as a holiday palace for Prince Fredrik Adolf in 1772, since when it has been owned by various members of the royal family. It has 18C and 19C interiors, furniture, paintings and tiled stoves.

The castle forms three sides of a square, the open side facing south to the water. The main north **façade** has three doors in a pedimented centre section and a short clock tower. The ground floor is rusticated, with two storeys above. Because of the slope of the ground, in the courtyard there are only two storeys, and below, a graceful arrangement of stairways with wrought-iron balustrades.

The **entrance hall** is clad with blue Dutch tiles and there is a copy of the well-known mosaic dog from Pompeii *Cave canem*. Up a flight of stairs you are at the original rear main entrance, on the level of the courtyard. The **stairwell** was painted by Anders Hultgren, Prince Fredrik Adolf's painter, with—since money was short—trompe l'oeil statuary and decorative carving. The **Great Dining-Room** is the largest room, and has Greek-inspired décor, with pilasters and an imitation Wedgwood frieze. The Tullgarn china service is on display, and there is a large painting of the Battle of Fredriksten. After the billiard-room with several objects from Egypt, the **Blue Drawing-Room** is decorated in neo-Rococo (1890), light duck-egg blue, with flower and bird scenes over the doors. The **Music-Room** has musical symbols in the décor, and a guest-book with the signatures of very distinguished and famous visitors. The **Red Room** was decorated in the late 18C with a frieze, and medallions over the gold-panelled doors, and the **Great Bedchamber** was designed by the Masreliez brothers also at the end of the 18C, in Pompeian style. It has an elegant tiled stove, and in fact some of the stoves here are works of art in their own right. The **Writing-Room** in Rococo has writing **cabinets**, one of which is certainly and the other probably by Georg Haupt. The Duke's Wardrobe has Stockholm scenes by Elias Martin over the doors. On the ground floor, the **Breakfast-Room** was fitted out at the end of the 19C as a German Bierstube, with 17C and 18C South German furniture.

From Vagnhärad it is 27km to **Södertälje**, an industrial town now virtually a suburb of Stockholm, with a commuter train service to the city. There is not much evidence left of its long history dating back to Viking times, which includes also being burnt down three times by the Russians. The Södertälje Canal which forms part of the Göta Canal route was dug in 1819 to let ships through into lake Mälaren and so to Stockholm. S:ta Ragnhild church on Stortorget has some parts dating from the 11C. The old town hall has been moved to beside the canal. Torekällberget is the local museum area, with town history and old buildings.

From here it is 36km to central Stockholm; see Rte 15.

14

Örebro to Stockholm

A. Southern Route

Total distance 187km. Örebro—E18/E20, 39km **Arboga**—E20, 15km Kungsör—23km **Eskilstuna**—30km *Strängnäs**—17km turn for Gripsholm—27km Södertälje—36km Stockholm.

Leave Örebro by the E18/E20 towards Stockholm. After 14km there is a turn for **Glanshammar church** (open Mon—Fri; English recorded guide) with interior paintings of the 1580s and several medieval carvings. The Reuter burial chapel is from 1679.

In 25km **Arboga** (pop. 11,600) is an appealing little town on the banks of the Arboga river, in a narrow pocket of the province of Västmanland between the provinces of Närke and Södermanland. It was a commercial centre in the Middle Ages, dealing in the iron from Bergslagen. Here in 1435 Engelbrekt was elected ruler of Sweden in opposition to Erik of Pomerania, in a meeting in which all four estates were represented, thus considered the first real parliament. When plague broke out in Stockholm in 1710, Arboga became the provisional capital. In 1856 the electrical workshop was founded which eventually became the electro-technical giant Asea·Brown Boveri.

The main square has an 18C town hall, and a wooden building with a café has carved decoration. South of the square is a bridge from which there are good **views** of the old houses along the water, and just on the other side is the **tourist bureau**. On either side of the river are picturesque streets. **Storgatan** along the south side is lined with wooden houses including the 18C Crugska Gården at No. 20. Near the next bridge, there is an interesting attempt to build updated versions in red-painted wood to harmonise with the older houses. Pretty lanes run down to the river, as they do from **Västerlånggatan** on the north side.

You can walk back along the other side of the river on Strandgatan. Here there is **Heliga Trefaldighetskyrka** (Holy Trinity church), originally part of a Franciscan friary. It has considerable remains of medieval **wall-paintings** including scenes from the life of St. Francis, other saints and biblical scenes as well as a depiction of the church itself. The **pulpit** is from the workshop of Burchardt Precht, and the very large chandeliers are from the 17C and 18C. The modern central cross is from 1980. In front of the church is a statue of Engelbrekt by Carl Eldh (1935).

The good local **museum** is in one of the houses of an old courtyard in Smedjegatan to the north-west of the main square (open mid-June to mid-Aug pm, English notes). The building itself has medieval parts to which you can walk through from the entrance. In the Stone Hall are church vestments, coins, and the catafalque on which Karl XII's coffin lay. Elsewhere are archaeological finds, furniture, costume, silver, pewter, toys and musical instruments.

Nikolaikyrka, the church for the country dwellers of the area, is just beyond the centre to the north-east, on the other side of the ring road,

Centrumleden. The North German **triptych** is from the beginning of the 16C, and there is a model showing how it closes, and the paintings on the double doors. In the chapel to the right is a 15C figure of God with Christ, and at the rear is a 17C painted altar enclosure.

There is a brewery museum (open summer pm) in Skandiagatan, off Centrumleden to the north-west, in a brick granary once belonging to the local brewery.

2km from the centre of Arboga, the E18 turns north, while the E20 continues west, crosses the Hjälmare Canal which connects lake Hjälmaren with the Arboga river and Mälaren, and arrives at **Kungsör** (pop. 6000) in 13km. The church, **Kung Karls Kyrka**, was designed by Nicodemus Tessin the Younger, and finished in 1700. Centrally planned in Greek cross form, it has a large dome. The **altar** was carved by Burchardt Precht with a painting by Ehrenstrahl. The pulpit is from the same time, and was meant for the chapel of the palace in Stockholm. There is a collection of church silver, and a case with old bibles. The open-air museum at Kungsudden includes remains of a house built by Gustav Vasa.

To Julita

From Kungsör you could visit **Julita Gård** (manor), which is 36km south. Follow signs after 32km at Äs. This large estate (open June–Aug 11.00–17.00) began when Cistercian monks founded a monastery in 1180, and it became a place of pilgrimage. At the Reformation most of the buildings were torn down and the material used for building Vasa castles. The **manor** built in 1675 was largely rebuilt after a fire in 1744. In 1902 the estate was inherited by Arthur Backström, an avid collector and preserver of the past, who laid the foundations of the various small **museums** here today—the dairy museum, the carriage museum, the fire brigade museum, and others. There are guided tours (Swedish) of the manor with its furnishings of the 18C and 19C, and the work of one gifted craftsman, Gustaf Henning Forsman (d 1956), who was employed on the estate for 40 years.

In the romantically designed **museum**, built in 1930, there is furniture, costume, agricultural and craft equipment, local displays and temporary exhibitions. The **church**, built just after the museum, is reached through the museum by way of a little courtyard hung with climbing plants. Houses from the locality have been gathered to form a small **open-air museum**, and other buildings are open to the public including the stables with real horses, and a reconstruction of Forsman's workshop. The **abbot's house** from the monastery, somewhat remodelled, can also be seen.

Further south **Katrineholm**, a modern industrial centre, has a leisure area around the manor of Stora Djulö. To the north-east of the town is the **church** of **Floda**, with some vaults painted by Albertus Pictor, and a Baroque burial chapel with extravagant stucco-work made for a field-marshal in the Thirty Years War.

On the way from Kungsör to Eskilstuna there are two churches of note. **Torpa** is 1km off the E20 where, according to legend, the **church** was founded by St. David, the English monk described as the 'apostle of Västmanland', said to have been the 11C first bishop of Västerås (not to be confused with St. David of Wales). The present chancel was the nave of the Romanesque church and the vault and chancel arch paintings are from the 15C. The triptych is of about the same time, North German or Swedish. The paintings in the porch are 17C and fragments of Romanesque painting have been found. The horn-blowing Archangel Michael is 13C, as is the sitting Madonna and an apostle, while the Madonna shrine and crucifix are 15C.

Tumbo church is 6km off the road. There is a wrought-iron-decorated door now in the porch, where there is also a carved **bridal seat** with reversible back, of the 16C. The curious round stone is a pre-Christian grave-marker. Inside, the modest main altarpiece is from the 14C and the more elaborate one at the rear of the church from the 15C, as is the Madonna on the left of the chancel.

17km from Kungsör you can take a turn for **Torshälla** (3km; pop. 8000). In the main square in the old part of the town with many wooden cottages are the wooden 19C town hall and the church with its step-gabled tower, much rebuilt in the 19C. This has the tomb of Reinhold Rademacher (1668) who founded the Rademachersmedjorna in Eskilstuna. There are vault paintings of the 15C. From the 16C there are carved figures of SS. Katarina, Gertrude, Birgitta and George. On the square is the sculpture 'Ying-yang' by Arne Jones (1967). Following the sign *Bergströmska gården* brings you to the local **museum** in an old wooden house, which contains 19C interiors and local exhibits (open July pm, also some Thurs). In the middle of the river is the powerful statue **Thor's Goats**, by Allan Ebeling (1960), an artist from the area. (The name Torshälla comes from 'Thor'.) Ebeling has another work on Östra Torget, the 'Water-carrier' of 1967.

The centre of **Eskilstuna** (pop. 60,000) is 6km further. The town was named after St. Eskil, an English missionary, who became bishop of Strängnäs. He was stoned to death in a pagan reaction c 1080. Eskilstuna early became an industrial town, largely owing to Reinhold Rademacher (1608–68) who founded the workshops or smithies bearing his name, Rademachersmedjorna. For a time it was a Free Town. Present-day products continue the old tradition with stainless steel, surgical instruments and cutlery.

Tourist bureau: Hamngatan 19. Tel. (016) 11 45 00.

Post office: Rademachergatan 6.

Telephone, telegram: OBS Interiör, Sveaplan. Tel. (021) 19 28 27.

Follow the signs to **Rademachersmedjorna**, where the **tourist bureau** is housed in the 1772 town hall. They have a good map with notes in English. Upstairs is a room for exhibitions, typically the modern products of Eskilstuna industries.

Most of the **workshops** (open daily, except winter Sun and Mon) were designed by the royal architect Jean de la Vallée in 1658, each to include living and working quarters for several smiths, journeymen and apprentices. At the end of the 17C there were 72 workers here, 20 of them German. In 1771 the Free Town was established to encourage the venture, hence the town hall of 1772. The **Berglundska smedja** is the best preserved, with earth floor and 18C furniture and fittings. In another there is an exhibition of tools, and in another later building you can see where the workers slept. Some of the workshops house craftsmen carrying on similar trades, working with gold, silver, steel and copper.

Across the road on an island in the river are two museums in the buildings of the old arms factory, **Faktorimuseet** and Vapentekniska Museet. The first, the Factory Museum (open daily 11.00–16.00 not Mon, no English information), includes much more than its name suggests. Local **archaeological finds** up to the Middle Ages are shown on the **ground floor**. In the **technical section**, there is a workshop of 1860 which made the Remington rifle, and steam engines, with the first steam locomotive and the first fire engine. There is a mechanical workshop of the 1910s. **Upstairs** is a well-arranged **display of interiors** to illustrate historical furnishing styles from the Renaissance onwards. A section on Eskilstuna history is in preparation. In the nearby **Vapentekniska Museet** (open summer not Mon) there are weapons ranging from crossbows and swords to rifles for hunting and fighting, as well as modern weapons up to the 1980s from many countries. On the other side of the river the former Bolinder Munktell factory has been renovated to become a hotel.

The next bridge to the east is Nybron and near it is **Klosters church** built in 1929. The town park is attractively situated on the river-bank, with Carl Milles' sculpture the 'Hand of God'. On the other side of the bridge is another Milles group, the comical 'Jonah and the Whale'.

Following the river which now turns to the south, there is **Fors church** on the west bank, which was begun in the 11C, and is now mainly 14C and 17C. It contains several late medieval **carvings**, two 15C Madonnas, and a group of five saints, as well as a crucifix and St. Martin of the same period.

A little further along is **Konstmuseet** (Art Museum, open daily, not Mon 12.00–16.00) with Swedish art from the 17C to the present day, as well as a few 17C Dutch and Flemish paintings. There are pictures by Ehrenstrahl, Roslin, Liljefors, Wilhelmson and Carl Larsson. but most works are from the 20C, with Isaac Grünewald, Sven Erixon and Bror Hjorth, as well as the Art Concret painter Otto G. Carlsund. Södermanland artists are represented, and temporary exhibitions are arranged.

Across the river from Fors church the **old town** occupies two streets along the river, with 18C and 19C houses, including the old theatre where 18C drama is revived. Tingsgården near the bridge, late 18C, has art and craft workshops.

Continuing out east along the main road brings you to the entrance to a park where there is a mound on the left with a prehistoric fort. Further in is **Sörmlandsgården**, a typical central Swedish farm, recreated by assembling buildings from the province, which are furnished and equipped. The cylindrical construction is for smoking meat. In the summer various events are staged, with a week in July devoted to folk music and crafts.

Parken Zoo on the west side of town is signposted from most main roads. The zoo is most famous for its white tigers, but there are amusements and entertainments, swimming pools and floral sculptures as well. (Open May–Sept 10.00–15.30, 16.30 or 17.30 depending on month. Expensive; ask at tourist bureau about cheap days or deals.)

Excursion from Eskilstuna

9km to the north-east of Eskilstuna there is the leisure area and marina of **Sundbyholm**, surrounding a manor house now part of a conference centre. A few kilometres before arriving there, a sign points to **Sigurdsristningen**, the Sigurd carving, an 11C inscription with runes and illustrations on an outcrop of rock. The runes say that a bridge was built here by a wife in memory of her husband. The pictures show scenes from the Sigurd (Siegfried) story—the Nibelung legend. Sigurd kills the dragon, and roasts him, burns his finger and sucks it, which enables him to understand the language of the birds. His horse carries the Nibelung treasure.

On the way back you may like to take the side-road you passed before you turned off for the carving, which will bring you to **Jäder church** (4km), the burial place of the powerful Oxenstierna family. Originally 12C, it was rebuilt in French/Dutch Renaissance style, with typical gables and doorways, by Jean de la Vallée and Nicodemus Tessin the Elder on the commission of the great chancellor Axel Oxenstierna. Tessin designed the chancel with the vault where the chancellor himself is buried. Jean de la Vallée designed the vestry on the north and the Brahe chapel on the south which has a delicate wrought-iron grille (1659). No fewer than 53 carved funeral standards adorn the walls, and there is a 16C Flemish altarpiece.

A new stretch of the E20 will run south of the present alignment cutting the slight curve between the outskirts of Eskilstuna and Härad. On the present E20 to Strängnäs, after 9km a sign points to *gravfält*, an Iron Age cemetery, somewhat damaged, with mounds and a runestone. At **Härad** after 14km, the **church**, begun in the 12C, possesses a rare **reliquary chest** in carved stone, probably the work of the Skåne artist Majestatis, who produced so many superb fonts in the 12C. The altarpiece is a Swedish work of the late 15C. On the left there is a Madonna shrine, and on the right an unusual one with Mary Magdalene of the same date, with paintings of her life.

It is 7km to the centre of •**Strängnäs** (pop. 11,500). If you leave the E20 by the exit marked Strängnäs V, this brings you in on Eskilstunavägen, to a useful car park by the bus station. The **tourist bureau** is diagonally across the road at the junction of Storgatan and Järnvägsgatan. (Note that accommodation can be difficult in Strängnäs.)

You can cut through the small park behind the tourist bureau and walk up the narrow **Klockarbacken**, turning right and then left to approach the cathedral by way of Gyllenhielmsgatan, through an area of low wooden cottages. The Lion Gate is the entrance to the precinct, flanked by the museum and the chapter house. The chapter house on the right dates from the 15C, and was the seminary where Olaus Petri the reformer taught for a time. On the left is the **museum** in an 18C printing-works (open 12.00–15.00 or 16.00, closed Mon off-season. Detailed English information in booklets hanging in each room). Among other things are local archaeological finds, a model of the cathedral in 1330 before all the chapels were built, a model of the Dominican priory once here, and an enlarged photograph of the aftermath of the devastating fire of 1871.

The •**Domkyrka** was consecrated in 1291, and of this the present nave remains. During the 14C and 15C, the tower up to the white strip, the chapels all around, the nave vault and a large new chancel with five-sided apse were added. The top of the tower was finished off in 1745 by Carl Hårleman. There is modest exterior decoration, with a narrow frieze on the vertical part between the nave and aisle roofs. In the walls are embedded several runestones, and more stand about the grounds. Most are damaged. One near the apse was, unusually, made to lie and not to stand.

Inside, the brick pillars have varied contours. The **nave vaults** were painted in the early 1500s. The first chapel on the right is the **Lady Chapel** with remains of 15C paintings of the life of the Virgin. Next to it the double chapel with star vaulting has Kolmården marble sarcophagi for the mistress of Fredrik I and her daughter. On a nearby pillar is a faded painting of the *Man of Sorrows*, and attached to the other side parts of a medieval altarpiece. Next is the south porch and on the other side of the inner wall you can see remnants of the early medieval doorway. Here there are also figures (1952) of Olaus Petri and Laurentius Andreae, leading figures of the Reformation. Olaus Petri was a deacon in Strängnäs and taught at the seminary.

The most ornate chapel is the next, the **Gyllenhielm burial chapel**. Admiral Carl Carlsson Gyllenhielm (d 1651) was the illegitimate son of Karl IX, and half-brother of Gustavus Adolphus. Henrik Damer of Lübeck sculpted the **statues** and the **baldaquin**, and the **stucco decoration** was done by Daniel Anckerman, with large detailed depictions of two of the Admiral's battles occupying the walls. On the coat of arms is half a vase (half a Vasa!). The shackles which he wore as a prisoner in Poland are hanging on the wall. The chapel is closed by an elegant wrought-iron grille.

The Scholars' Chapel was for students at the seminary. The **Stenbock chapel** was the first to be built (14C), and contains a memorial to Admiral Gustaf Otto Stenbock (d 1685) in carved wood imitating marble. The **vaults** here and across the nave at this end have well-preserved **paintings**. While looking up you can observe the **arches** through which a narrow gallery would have run each side of the nave at the top of the pillars, and a remaining part of the iron balustrade can be seen on the opposite side.

The paintings on the chancel vaults are from 1462. The magnificent main *****altarpiece** was made in Brussels in 1490, the gift of Archbishop Kort Rogge. A model shows how the altar closes and the paintings on the doors. On the right is another no less superb *****altarpiece** of about the same date and also from Brussels, and in front of it the **tomb** of Sten Sture the Elder, regent of Sweden who died in 1497, but whose monument was designed only in the 18C by Jean Eric Rehn. On the left the huge *****monument** to King Karl IX has a horse and rider in gilded copper armour, surrounded by a graceful iron grille. The various parts of this were made between 1589 and 1611.

One of the most touching memorials anywhere is the cherubic little figure of two-year-old Princess Isabella, daughter of Johan III, who died while her parents were imprisoned in Gripsholm Castle. Her *****tomb** was carved by Willem Boy in 1580. The medieval bronze **font** has letters spelling the Ave Maria.

Back in the nave, returning down the north side, you can see a medieval choir-stall, and there is a sculpture of **St. Erik** by Bernt Notke. The **pulpit** is from 1789, by the royal sculptor Peter Ljung. The north porch has some reconstructed parts of the early doorway. Next come two burial chapels, near which on a pillar is a 15C Madonna. The Baptismal Chapel has another outstanding *****altarpiece** from Brussels, of 1515, and the room beside the tower contains the cathedral library with rare books.

Outside, behind the apse stands **Roggeborgen**, built as his palace by Bishop Kort Rogge at the end of the 15C. There is a tradition that Gustav Vasa was elected king of Sweden in the hall of state on the first floor, remodelled in the 19C (open summer lunchtimes). It was a school from 1626 until the 1930s, and now houses part of the Royal Library. (The large building to the north looking like a 19C factory is used as a sports hall.)

Roggeborgen is only one of four bishops' residences around the cathedral. To the south the building with elegant curly gables is the present **bishop's palace** of the late 17C. The more modest **Paulinska house** on the other side of Biskopsgränd was built by a bishop in the early 17C. Another is the small red wooden house called Luktan, of the 16C.

Biskopsgränd runs down to one of the harbours, with walks along the shore. From here there are boat-trips to Stockholm, Birka and Västerås. On summer Saturdays a boat takes tourists round the island of Selaön, with views of the castles of Tynnelsö and Mälsåker.

Walking north brings you to Tosteröbron (bridge), carrying a road to the north part of Strängnäs and on to Enköping. From the bridge there is a view of the cathedral and Roggeborgen across the water. Continuing west along Norra Strandvägen, you see a sign *Klosterruin*, but the ruin is marked only by hedges on a steep terrace. This was the site of the Dominican priory from

1268 until the Reformation. More rewarding is the **old town** on the point, surrounding the windmill. Västerviksgatan and Kvarngatan are both picturesque, and the courtyard house called Grassagården, with a café, has parts from the 17C. Beyond and below the windmill is the marina, and the bus station car park.

To Fogdön, Aspön and Selaön

The convoluted shores of Mälaren can be further explored by penetrating the peninsula and two islands to the north of Strängnäs. On **Fogdön**, the peninsula to the west, **Vansö church** has a 15C Lübeck altar and two other shrines, and paintings by Peter Målare. **Fogdö church** was begun in the 12C, with the sacristy and Berghammar burial chapel added in the 17C. There are paintings by the Union Master (15C). Taking a right turn at Fogdö church brings you to the ruins of **Vårfruberga convent**, from where the skyline of Strängnäs can be seen across the water. This was a Cistercian foundation and the walls have been restored enough to make the ground plan visible. There is an entry into the brick vaulted refectory at the rear of the area. There are prehistoric remains marked *fornminne* in various parts of the peninsula, but they are difficult to find.

The main road to Enköping crosses the island of Tosterön, then goes on to **Aspön** where the church of Aspö has a medieval altarpiece and other carvings, and a chair of the 13C. From the 17C come the pulpit, many memorial tablets and especially carved funerary standards.

The island of **Selaön** has a Late Iron Age cemetery at Östra Sjöhage, and further on, on the side road marked **Åsa Gravfält** one of the same era lies in a flower meadow, with stone settings and mounds (500–1050). Continuing north, you can visit the **church** at **Överselö** with mid 15C vault-paintings belonging to the Mälaren group of churches, decorated earlier than those of Peter Målare and Albertus Pictor. The subjects are mainly saints, amid spirals, flowers and foliage. The **Överselö Madonna**, early 14C, is in the chancel, and there is a late medieval altarpiece and other figures, including St. Erik and St. Olof. A side road goes to the coast where across a narrow channel you can see the castle of Tynnelsö, not open to the public.

Back near the bridge to the mainland, a road goes to **Ytterselö**, where the church has a small **altarpiece** from Antwerp with the Södermanland saints Botvid and Eskil. The present chancel was added in 1728 to provide a **burial vault** for Anna Maria Soop of Mälsåker and her family. The south funerary chapel with its original iron grille is also for a member of the same family, as are the carved funerary standards. There is a Madonna of c 1500 and a 12C font. From outside you can look into the vault under the chancel through a small low door. The large **tomb** under its own roof in the graveyard is for Hans Åkesson Soop. The road continues to the 17C manor of **Mälsåker**, the home of the Soops, designed by Tessin the Elder. (Being restored, may eventually be open to the public.)

From Strängnäs, the E20 turns south-east and after 12km reaches Åker. Gustav Vasa established a gunpowder factory (Åkers Krutbruk) in 1552, and about the same time started the canon factory (Åkers Styckebruk) which continued until 1866. Some buildings remain, and there is a museum (open summer weekends). About 11km to the south, **Skottvångs historic iron mine** which supplied Åker also has preserved buildings and a museum (open in summer).

After 5km there is a turn for Mariefred and Gripsholm (see Rte 15). In 17km you can leave the road to get to **Turinge church**, where military commander and architect Erik Dahlberg designed his own lavish **funerary chapel** with stucco ceiling, and two sculptures by Nicolaes Millich (1690s). A very large funeral standard, and a portrait of Dahlberg by Ehrenstrahl are also preserved.

It is 10km to Södertälje (see Rte 13) and 36km to Stockholm (see Rte 15).

B. Northern Route

Total distance 203km. Örebro—E18/20, 39km **Arboga**—E18 17km **Köping**—18km Hallstahammar—20km **Västerås**—33km Enköping—4km junction with road 263—road 263, 21km Övergran and turn for Skokloster (16km)—5km Bålsta— E18, 46km Stockholm.

The E18 and the E20 are combined to just past Arboga (see Rte 14A), and there the E18 turns north to reach Köping in 17km.

Köping (pop. 19,000) received its town charter in 1474 and became an important port for iron from Bergslagen. The name of the town comes from *köpa*, Swedish for 'to buy', so this and the nine or so compounds like Jönköping and Linköping mean 'marketplace'.

The chemist Carl Wilhelm Scheele (1742–82) worked in Köping for a time, and discovered oxygen independently of Priestley, and a dozen acids. He separated chlorine, glycerine and hydrogen sulphide as well as making other important discoveries. There is a section in the local museum devoted to him and a reconstruction of his working environment. There is a.**statue** of him by Carl Milles (1912) beside the main square, in summer a green and flowery space refreshingly unlike the usual main square car park.

The **tourist bureau** is opposite the right side of the town hall—maps available even when closed. The **church** on the other side of the town hall is from the 15C, renovated in the 18C to designs by Nicodemus Tessin the Younger. It has a 16C North German **altarpiece**.

Down **Österlånggatan** opposite the town hall you can walk through an area of old houses to reach the **museum** (open weekdays pm) where Järnvägsgatan crosses the river—something under a kilometre.

The small but attractive **open-air museum** is called Gammelgården, on the other side of the river at the end of Otto Hallströms Väg, off Glasgatan.

Leave Köping by the E18 which after 2km turns right. If instead you take the 250 ahead you will see immediately on your left a Late Iron Age burial mound called **Ströbohög** (500–1050), 35m in diameter. The spot was on the route of the Eriksgata, which newly crowned kings followed to receive homage, and legends of giants and dragons surround it.

Excursions from Hallstahammar

To **Strömsholm**, **Dingtuna** and **Tidö**. After 16km near Hallstahammar you can turn south to visit **Strömsholm castle** (9km), and also the church of Dingtuna and the castle of Tidö on the same double peninsula between Köping and Västerås. Strömsholm is situated in formal grounds on an island in the river, near the beginning of the Strömsholm Canal. The castle (open May–Aug 12.00–16.00; also weekends before and after) was designed by Nicodemus Tessin the Elder for Karl X's widow Hedwig Eleanora (1672). It is most famous for its works by David Klöcker Ehrenstrahl the court artist, especially his horse paintings. The estate has been associated with horses since Vasa times, when a stud farm was started to breed horses for the army. Now it is a venue for racing, and there is a riding school for instructors.

It has sparse interiors from the 18C, notably the Chinese Room, which you can visit at will, though there are also guided tours. The **art collection** however, with Ehrenstrahl's work, repays study, and the chapel at the top, by Tessin and Hårleman, has a well-known organ, of which you can choose to hear recordings. There is a café in the old kitchen with a huge fireplace in a detached pavilion.

Vagnmuseet, the Carriage Museum, is on the other side of the main road, up the steep track to the left. This is part of Stockholm's Livrustkammaren (armoury) carriage museum and is particularly interesting because it preserves less exotic examples of the royal carriage-maker's art. Here is a red-velvet upholstered hunting carriage, a State sleigh, a mail coach and many others, with old prams and saddles for good measure (labels in English).

You can continue past Strömsholm, after joining the 56 following signs to **Dingtuna** c 10km north-east. The church is mainly from about 1300, with 15C vaulting, tower and porch. The *paintings belong to Albertus Pictor's early work, c 1470, and are lively and expressive scenes from the Old Testament with single saints and Evangelists, such as the determined St. Olof who sails through devil-infested seas. There is a medieval St. Birgitta carving and the altar and pulpit are from the 18C. In the sacristy are some figures in a medieval altarpiece.

Tidö castle is 12km to the south, by an involved route of minor roads—keep following the signs *Tidö slott*. (Remember the way because returning is worse!) The castle (open June–Aug not Mon 12.00–17.00, State Apartments shown 14.00) was built by Axel Oxenstierna, royal chancellor and regent for Queen Kristina, and finished in 1652.

The long low frontage is broken only by the carved archway leading into the courtyard. The fourth side of the square is the castle proper which is higher than the three wings. It has a 'säteri' roof, and little decoration except for the stately entrance with steps leading to a carved **doorway**. Above the door at roof level is a handsome pediment. Inside many rooms are open for visitors to wander freely and art exhibitions are held here. The most outstanding feature of the castle is the beautiful *intarsia work on the doors and surrounds, no fewer than 43 of them in the whole building (mid 1630s). The guided tour takes in the **Hall of State** which has four of these doors, an imposing painted ceiling, portraits of Axel Oxenstierna and his family, and many objects which were booty from the Thirty Years War. The **Yellow Salon** on the other hand is elegantly 18C, and the view from it encompasses the grounds and lake. There is a toy museum, café and shop.

If you walk half a kilometre down past the right-hand side of the castle you come to the shore of Asköviken, an inlet of Mälaren around which lies a **nature reserve**, particularly rich in bird life. Here you can walk out on a footway to an observation point, and on the way back from Tidö car park to the road there is another car park from where you can get to another observation point, Rudöklippan. On the way to Dingtuna the sign Asköviken leads to yet another car park for the walk to the bird-watching tower on the north shore.

To the ironworks of Bergslagen

The road junction at Hallstahammar can also be the starting-point for another longer diversion (46km, 91km or 226km; see below), this time into the old iron-working region of **Bergslagen**. Bergslagen is an area of about 150km by 100km north of Örebro, with an adjoining strip stretching out eastwards to the coast between Uppsala and Gävle. (Most of the sights in this strip are dealt with elsewhere.) Tourist authorities have combined the sights in different groupings and publish much information and suggested routes, including a tourist map with notes in English, and separate leaflets on each site. One of these groupings is called **Ekomuseum Bergslagen**, concentrating on the central area around the Strömsholm Canal. Many places have limited opening hours, but will be pleased to show interested visitors around—ask at a tourist bureau. Often too you can wander around the estate even if the buildings are not open. There are many activities— gold-panning, canoeing, beaver safaris and mineral-hunting.

Iron-working has been going on in this area for 2000 years, beginning with bog ore. The Middle Ages developed blast furnaces, and when explosives came into use in the 18C the industry became the most important in Sweden, needed to finance the wars of that period. Then came the ability to harness water for power and the refinement of charcoal to produce high quality iron, eventually leading to the modern steel industry.

The Strömsholm Canal came into being for the transport of iron, and was built between 1777 and 1795. It is 107km long, passing through 14 lakes, with 26 locks covering a total drop of 100m. It runs from Mälaren near Strömsholm castle to Smedjebacken in the north. It is now used only by pleasure craft, including canoes, for which there are ramps at the locks.

The route below is 226km, not counting detours, from Hallstahammar back to Örebro. Going to Ängelsberg (46km) and back will give you a flavour of the area, and to Smedjebacken (91km) will show you the length of the Strömsholm Canal.

Hallstahammar (pop. 12,000) has a canal museum which also includes a display on Strömsholm castle. Opposite is an island which is a leisure area, with the Sörkvarn rapids, swimming-pool camp site and marina. Follow signs to *Kanalmuseet* or *Skantzen*. The canal museum deals with the Strömsholm Canal.

Take the 252 north from Hallstahammar. At (14km) Sura you can cross the canal to **Surahammar** where the tourist bureau is in the Stone House (1847), where exhibitions are also held. The ironworks museum is nearby (open certain hours in summer) and on the green is a 1 ton hammer from 1895.

Back in Sura, the 252 continues north and crosses road 65 so that the waterway is now on the left. Other industrial sites are at **Ramnäs**, an iron-working settlement surrounding the old manor, now an hotel, and **Dunshammar**, where there are remains of primitive furnaces.

From (32km) Ängelsberg you can reach **Oljeön**, an island where an oil refinery was established in 1875. Crude oil was imported from the USA and other raw materials from Russia and Spain, making use of the Strömsholm Canal for transport, and production grew to 200 tons a year. Workers and their families lived on the island and you can see their homes and other preserved buildings including the interior of the refinery and some machinery. (Ferries in summer.)

The **ironworks** at **Ängelsberg** is a little out of town, signposted with the spelling *Engelsbergs bruk* (open in summer, guided tours, but visitors can also wander around on their own). Here you can explore the timber buildings containing the blast furnace, water-wheel and other machinery. An avenue leads to the 1746 manor-house, with the smithy, brewery and bakery, as well as farm buildings and the works office.

At 12km, Fagersta is a steel-working town on the Kolbäcksån. The Bruksmuseum shows ironworking history. From the town take the 68 across the river and almost immediately turn right (2km). Here at **Västanfors** is an area with a local **open-air museum**, including a manor-house, school museum, theatre museum, pottery and various exhibitions. Crossing the river by the locks you can get to the old power-station (*Gamla Kraftverk*), also a museum, and nearby stands an 1866 Bessemer converter. (Most of these open May–Aug 11.00–18.00.) 13km to the north-east of Fagersta is the town of **Norberg** with a mining museum 3km to the north.

Take the 68 to the south-west and turn right after 3km towards Ludvika on the 65, a pretty wooded road by the water. At 27km a sign points to **Flatenbergs hytta**, a kilometre or so off the road. Here the 19C foundry buildings are to a great extent intact, with the 11m-high blast furnace. At one stage 3000 tons of pig-iron were produced here. (Guided tours summer pm, but grounds are open.) After 3km the road passes Smedjebacken the end of the Strömsholm Canal, where by the harbour there is a narrow gauge railway, a steam locomotive and in an old warehouse a display on transport. 6km later a rutted track leads to the **iron-mine** at **Flogberget** (*Flogbergets Besöksgruva*—guided tours only, summer pm).

The road, with lake views, leads in 8km to **Ludvika** where there is an unusual outdoor **mining museum** with large exhibits, showing for example how ore was transported. To reach this, go through the open-air museum, here called Gammelgård. (Both open in summer 11.00–16.00.)

You can return south to Örebro by way of road ·60 from Ludvika to **Grängesberg** with a locomotive museum, to **Kopparberg** with a mining museum, to **Lindesberg** with a wealthy mine-owner's home and the Löa mine workshop, and **Nora** with a railway museum and the Pershyttan ironworks.

On the main route, it is 20km from Hallstahammar to *Västerås (pop. 98,000), the capital of the county of Västmanland, now smaller than the old province of the same name. The name of the town comes from 'Västra Aros', hence the Aros Conference Center in the 25-storey skyscraper. The logo of the town, the initials AM entwined in medieval characters, probably comes from 'Ave Maria', since the cathedral was dedicated to the Virgin. The town was first mentioned in 1120 and soon became the head of a diocese. The Riksdag was held here on several occasions—in 1527 the Reformation was decided upon (in the Dominican priory), and in 1544 the crown was established as hereditary in the Vasa family (in the castle). A great fire in 1714 halted the town's progress somewhat. Nowadays it is an industrial town, best known as the home of ABB, Asea Brown Boveri, the electro-technical conglomerate, and one of their three main research centres is here. The church-like brick tower with onion-domed top on Södra Ringvägen belongs to them.

Tourist bureau: Stora Gatan 40. Tel. (021) 10 37 00.

Post office: Sture Gatan 18.

Bus station: At Centralstation, Travel information: tel. (021) 11 72 00.

Telephone, telegram: Gallerian 7. Tel. (021) 19 12 57.

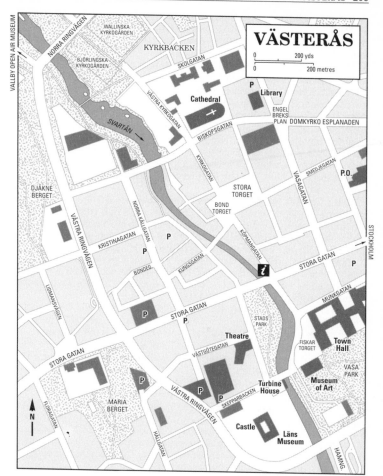

VÄSTERÅS

0 _____ 200 yds
0 _____ 200 metres

Ringvägen is the ring road (prefixed by south or west, etc. as required) encircling the town centre, which is crossed by Kopparbergsvägen and Stora Gatan. There is a large multi-storey car park where these two meet which makes a useful base (entrance in Munkgatan). This is part of the 'Multi-center', four blocks of shops and restaurants linked by glassed-in streets. You will emerge on the pedestrianised part of Stora Gatan which will lead you (left) to the **tourist bureau** at the corner with Köpmangatan. The bridge there affords a picture-postcard **view** of crooked wooden and half-timbered houses and warehouses reflected in the river Svartån.

The cathedral and the old town are to the north by way of Köpmangatan which leads to **Stora Torget**, the main square. A lane to the left leads to another picturesque view from a bridge. In the square is a series of figures of cyclists, the 'Asea stream' (1989), representing the workers of Asea as they used to pedal to work. Continue on the same street to reach the cathedral. In front of it is a **statue** of Johannes Rudbeckius by Carl Milles (1923). Rudbeckius (1581–1646) was an influential bishop who founded a secondary school here in 1623, repaired churches and made organisational reforms.

The *cathedral is in brick with double-sloped roof, and blind decoration in zigzags and lancets. It was begun in the 13C, and during the 14C and 15C it was lengthened and widened so that it now has five aisles, the outer two incorporating original chapels. The spire was built in 1693 by Nicodemus Tessin the Younger.

On each side of the west door is a **stone relief** (1500), one of the Virgin and one of John the Baptist with St. David the apostle of Västmanland. Inside, once past the entrance tower, you are in the 13C church, where remnants of low arches can be seen on the brick pillars, and the lighting is deliberately subdued. The large 14C **crucifix** hangs on a rood-beam where the chancel arch was.

On the right is a remarkable free-standing *baptismal chapel, a ten-sided enclosure made in Lübeck in 1622. It is carved in oak with very secular caryatids on the slim columns above and figures in niches on panels below. Inside is the **font** and the extraordinary **font-cover**, even more luxuriantly decorated. Beyond on the right is the baptism chapel proper, with a 16C *altarpiece from Antwerp showing the Virgin as Queen of Heaven. The font here is a cast of an original of 1391. Over the south door a modern round window links images of St. Peter's in Rome, with Västerås cathedral tower, the ABB tower and the town hall.

Beyond the brick-pillared 13C core the white section is from a 19C neo-Gothic rebuilding, and further on the red columns are 15C. There are many ornate 17C and 18C memorial tablets throughout the cathedral.

The main *altarpiece carved in gilded oak was made in Antwerp, and depicts the Passion and Resurrection. It was donated by Sten Sture the Younger, regent of Sweden, in 1516. There is a model to demonstrate how the doors can be opened to show further paintings on leaves which can again be folded back to reveal yet more paintings.

On the right is the **tomb** of Erik XIV (d 1577, tomb 1797) in Carrara marble, with copies of royal regalia on top. At the very back there is the brightly painted Veronica altar, the only one of stone in the church (1514). On the other side of the main altar the imposing tall **memorial** is that of Magnus Brahe, Marshal of the Realm, and his two wives. The monument is of black and white marble, with alabaster figures (1641).

Another valuable *altarpiece is in the Chapel of the Apostles, west of the north door. This one is from Brussels, c 1500. Nearby against a pillar are two medieval carved **pew-ends**.

There is a museum with vestments, silver, books and assorted exhibits associated with the cathedral.

To the east of the cathedral there are the botanical gardens, and to the north beyond the Rudbeckius school lies the **old town** district of Kyrkbackan with steep cobbled lanes lined with 18C and 19C houses and cottages. The ones nearest the cathedral were for such as church officials and teachers, further away were the craftsmen, and beyond lived the poorest citizens. In the middle is a minute park called the hop garden.

The other sights are to the south of Stora Gatan, reached by returning to the tourist bureau and following the river-bank to **Fiskartorget**, where there used to be a fish market. The modern **town hall** (English leaflet from the tourist bureau) was built between 1953 and 1988 on the site of a Dominican priory, and over 2000 skeletons were found during excavation. They were those of monks, soldiers and ordinary citizens, probably victims of Gustav Vasa's attack on the Danish-occupied priory in 1521. Works of art surround the building. 'The Bull' by Allan Runefeldt stands menacingly on a column in the square and in front of the main door there is the 'Cave of the Winds' by Eric Grate, referred to by the irreverent populace as 'the municipal deaf ear'. Walking round anti-clockwise, you have the peaceful open space of **Vasaparken** on the south side, and near the building there are the outlines of the priory, and a plan of it on a small plinth. On,the way round you pass a chunky sculpture of a centaur.

Across Fiskartorget is the old town hall (1857) now the **Konstmuseum** (Art Museum, open 11.00–16.00, Sun 12.00–16.00, closed Mon). This shows Swedish and other Scandinavian contemporary art in temporary exhibitions.

On the bridge over the falls the old **Turbinhus** (turbine house) is part of the museum. It was built in 1891 to harness the power from the falls, and was the reason ABB moved from Arboga. It had three turbines with a combined horse-power of 150. It is open an hour a day in summer—ask at the museum.

The **museum** is on the west bank, in the uncompromising square block of Västerås castle. The medieval rectangular keep is incorporated in one wing. After a fire in 1736 it was renovated to designs of Carl Hårleman, but you can still see traces of round-headed openings and other clues to its earlier origins. Johan III married his second wife Gunilla Bielke here, and the important Riksdag of 1544 was held in the castle (see above). The museum (open Tue–Sun 12.00–16.00) has Iron Age exhibits on the first floor and coins, medals and textiles on the second. On the third is the beamed Rikssalen, the Hall of State (19C reconstruction), and displays on medieval Västerås and industrial development. (The county governor lives on the top floor.)

Vallby open-air museum, Västerås, with a pigsty and, beyond, a turf-roofed galleried farmhouse

It is a pleasant walk back to the centre through **Stadsparken** on the west bank of the river.

Beyond the west ring road, Västra Ringvägen, is **Djäkneberget**, Deacon Hill, a hilly park best entered from Kristinagatan. There is a view of the town and the usual activities, but the oddest feature is the 500 **inscriptions** carved on rocks, with sayings, prayers and memorials to famous Swedes in ten languages. These were completed between 1862 and 1897 at the instigation of one Sam Lidman.

Vallby Friluftsmuseum (open-air museum) is beside the E18 at the Vallby junction on the north-west of the town, or you can take Vallbyleden from the centre. (Area accessible almost all the time; information in English at the shop and the café.) A goodly collection of buildings from Västmanland are well grouped on an inviting site. Details include the decorative pagoda-type **telephone booth**, designed in 1900 and manufactured again in 1950, in the town square.

You enter near the village shop. To the right there is a large **farm complex**, whose **dwelling-house** has murals in the best parlour. Beyond is a complete town square, and further, a manor-house. Many of the buildings are used by craft workers, a silversmith, brush-maker and potter among others. On the left of the entrance are more scattered buildings including a school, and at the end a reconstruction of a **Viking long-house**, which it is planned to equip and furnish. Small Viking field enclosures illustrate farming methods.

Excursions from Västerås

Boat trips from Västerås go to Birka, Strängnäs and Gripsholm (Mariefred).

Skultuna. This is 14km to the north-west and is the site of a brassworks (*Messingsbruk*) founded by Karl IX in 1607, though the present buildings except for the *brännhytta* (melting shop), are much later. Here they had the necessary water supply and charcoal, while copper was obtained from Falun, and zinc from Poland. The skilled workers were imported from Germany and Holland. You can see some of the finishing processes on a guided tour, and there is a gift shop for their own production, mainly candlesticks, as well as a large general kitchen-ware shop in an old factory building. The brassworks is picturesquely set in the Svartån valley with walks either side, and there is a rhododendron plantation, rare so far north.

The Badelunda Ridge (Badelundaåsen). Along this boulder ridge to the north-east Västerås there are many Iron Age sites. From the E18 4km from the ring road follow the sign *Anundshög* (Anund's Mound). The ridge stretches from here to Badelunda church (3km). Along the way at the village of Tibble you can see where the houses are today still in a row along the road, a medieval pattern. Just off the road here a prehistoric maze (*labyrint*) is on top of a small hill. Continue towards *****Anundshög**, taking a right turn. This is the largest mound in Sweden, 60m in diameter and 14m high, of the period AD 400–700. It has not been excavated but it is thought to contain a cremation burial within a stone cist. The 20 or so other graves around have yielded rich finds. Beside it are two very large end-to-end **ship-settings**, 53m and 50m, and many other standing stones are in the clearing. The **runestone** is from c 1000, and says that stones were raised to the memory of Heden, Anund's brother, but any link with the mound is dubious.

While on this side of town you may like to continue to (7km) **Tortuna church**, built about 1300, with 15C vault and **wall-paintings**. In the vaults these picture an array of saints, from apostles and Evangelists to church fathers and Swedish saints, in small medallions and larger standing figures. On the north wall the seven sacraments are depicted. The style and choice of motif are unlike those of other Mälar valley painters and the artist is known simply as the Tortuna Master. They are also difficult to date, and are probably from c 1500, therefore at the time when Albertus Pictor was active (see below).

Two large end-to-end ship-settings beside the Anundshög burial mound (late Iron Age)

The castle of Ängsö. Ängsö, or Engsö, (24km) is signposted from the same junction of the E18 as Anundshög, and also more directly from the E18 on the way to Enköping (open mid-June to mid-Aug Tue–Sun 13.00–17.00, plus weekends before and after). It lies on a large island of the same name, which is a nature reserve. The Sparre family built the first castle in 1480, and owned it almost continuously until 1710, when the Pipers bought it. It was theirs until 1971 and they still run it.

The cellars are 15C and the next two floors 17C. In the first half of the 18C Carl Hårleman renovated it and added the top floor and the free-standing pavilions. You may look at the building without a guide, starting in the dungeon and proceeding to the other floors where the interior decorations were mainly completed after the rebuilding in the 18C for Carl Fredrik Piper and his wife. On the **first floor** there is a large dining-room and the Countess' suite, on the second the Rococo ball-room and guest-rooms. The **top floor** has the Count's suite, with study, armoury and library. Throughout there are portraits, and good tiled stoves. The gold chain in a niche on the staircase is said to have been won by Johan Sparre, an early owner, from a ghost in a dice game.

The **church** was begun in the 14C and has faded medieval paintings. The Piper funerary chapel was added at the east end in the 1730s for Count Carl Piper who died a prisoner in Russia. His son Carl Fredrik had the west tower designed by Hårleman, and provided new fittings. There is a medieval St. Anne shrine.

In an 18C wooden storehouse there is a display about the island's nature reserve. You can for example press a button to hear the song of a particular bird. Maps with walking trails are provided.

Continuing from Västerås on the E18 towards Enköping, after 19km there is another road to Ängsö, and 1km later the road crosses the border between Västmanland and Uppland. It is 13km to **Enköping** (pop. 18,600), a town with a long history but with not much of it visible today. Vårfrukyrkan, Our Lady's Church, stands on a height overlooking the town and dates from the 12C and 15C. Below it lie the ruins of a 14C church. The local museum is in an 18C house in Rådhusgatan. In the main square there is a fountain called the 'Four Elements', by Nils Sjögren. 18C warehouses line the harbour from where there are summer trips in an 1888 steamer, while on the other side of the river are the ruins of a 13C Franciscan priory.

The region on both sides of the lake of Mälaren with its innumerable inlets was settled early because of the ease of water transport. Once Stockholm was established as the capital there was even more incentive for the heartland to expand and prosper, so the area is packed with medieval churches and Renaissance and Baroque castles. (However, most of the latter are not open for visitors.)

Excursions from Enköping

To **Boglösa** and **Veckholm**. One or two churches can be seen on the large peninsula to the south of Enköping. In addition, the region all around Enköping has many Bronze Age rock carvings, especially to the north towards Örsundsbro, but on this southern peninsula near Boglösa (10km), more of an effort has been made to make them accessible. The subjects include foot-soles, ships, men, animals and sun-wheels. Near the church of **Boglösa** there is a small museum (*Hällristningsgård*—open summer weekends plus daily July pm). This has leaflets with maps and notes in English. The most famous carving is the 4m-long **Brandskog ship**, showing rowers paddling, 1km north of Boglösa church. Some carvings can be seen at the far end of a cattle-field, and/or along obscure tracks, and many have not been painted, making them difficult for the non-specialist to spot, but for the enthusiast blessed with good weather and sturdy footwear it is a happy hunting-ground.

Boglösa church was founded in medieval times and has a door and some carving along the edge of the porch roof which is also from this period. The altarpiece is from the 15C and the pulpit from the 18C.

You can continue to (12km) **Veckholm church**, originally medieval. Magnus Gabriel de la Gardie employed Nicodemus Tessin the Elder to design a family **funerary chapel**, but it was never finished since at that point the previously immensely wealthy Magnus lost his fortune. The chapel was heavily restored in the 19C. The grandiose **memorial** to Johan de la Gardie (d 1640) was intended to be in the south transept and the centre should have been kept free. Also buried here is General Fredrik Pontus de la Gardie (d 1791) in a sarcophagus of Kolmården marble, and there is a funerary standard for Magnus' one-year-old son. (Magnus himself is buried in Varnhem church.) The 16C **altarpiece** is from Brussels. On each side is a medieval figure, and the ornate **organ façade** and **pulpit** are 17C. There is a late medieval **pew** with delicate carving. Outside, small doors allow you to peer into the de la Gardie crypt. The 17C bell-tower has 19C sundials.

South-east of Veckholm the nature reserve of **Härjarö** stretches into the lake on a smaller peninsula, and to the west there is **Kungs Husby** where the church (open summer weekends) has medieval paintings, crucifix and Madonna, with an 18C pulpit. To the south of this you can cross a bridge to the island of Grönsö (unmade road) with an 18C manor whose grounds are open to the public. The neighbouring island also has a manor, Utöhus, not generally open to the public.

To Härnevi, Härkeberga and Kvekgården

Take the 70 towards Sala out of Enköping and soon turn right at the sign Härkeberga 8. Now ignore signs to Härkeberga for the moment and concentrate on **Härnevi**, to which there is an unmade road after 7km. The **·church** rivals the more famous Härkeberga in the splendour of its paintings by Albertus Pictor—here his colours are at their best.

Albertus Pictor (d c 1510) was the most accomplished church painter of the late Middle Ages. He is sometimes called also by the Swedish version 'Albert Målare'—Albert the Painter—or Albert the Embroiderer, since he occupied himself in the winter months by producing some of the finest textile work of the period (now in the Historical Museum in Stockholm). He probably came of German stock and was first heard of in the Stockholm region in the 1470s. He decorated the interiors of c 30 churches, mainly in Uppland but also in Västmanland and Södermanland. The late Gothic period was a time of prosperity and artistic blossoming, when wooden church roofs were exchanged for new brick vaults. These were then plastered and painted *al secco* on dry plaster, thus the paintings are not frescoes in the strict sense. Albertus must have had a workshop of talented artists to help with the volume of production.

In the early years his figures were slim and stylish, but his later work became more realistic and down-to-earth, with a shrewd eye for telling detail, amusing caricature and the dress of everyday life. Animals and musical instruments play an important role—sometimes together, with comic results. When portraying biblical scenes he made use of the woodcuts of *Biblia Pauperum Predicatorum* (the 'Bible of the Poor') as basic designs, at the same time being concerned to point a moral. Scenes and figures are framed in three-dimensional-looking tendrils and foliage, though pre-prepared patterns were used to fill empty spaces. With time his reds have darkened to browns, but still the colours can be enjoyed, especially in the six churches where the paintings have never been white-washed over—Härnevi, Härkeberga, Floda, Kumla, Odensala and Täby.

At Härnevi the walls were once over-painted so the paintings are not in such good condition as on the vaults. Here the artist used expensive paints like purple and blue, which have lasted well. The *paintings can be dated to c 1480, at the height of Albertus' powers, and it is thought that he painted in person here and in Härkeberga. (English booklet on sale with detailed interpretation.) Even in the porch the vault and walls are painted—Christ with worldly and holy men, St. Martin, St. George and St. Veronica. In the chancel on the intricate star vault are the Nativity, the Trinity, Moses, Samson and scenes from the childhood of Christ. In the nave vault can be seen Cain and Abel, Moses, the Archangel Michael, the Coronation of the Virgin and Pentecost. Entertaining details are in the spandrels and other irregular spaces, such as the organ-playing pig and the bagpipe-playing goat, and the odd devil lurks here and there. St. Apollonia, patron of dentists (with pincers) is on one pillar while behind the organ Judas is hanging, with his money-bag round his neck.

Return to the main road, turn right and follow signs to (7km) *Härkeberga. As in Härnevi, the walls were once white-washed and the paintings are faded. Albertus completed his work at Härkeberga in the mid 1480s. (Recorded description and leaflet in English.)

In the chancel vault are the Evangelists, Samson, Christ, and the life of the Virgin, in the nave the Coronation of the Virgin and Old Testament figures such as David and Goliath, Daniel and Isaac. The next vault tells the story of Joseph as well as showing Moses, Cain, Esau, the Assumption of the Virgin, with the Last Judgment. Everywhere there are devils, animals, musicians and dancers tucked into unexpected corners. In the porch are St. George, St. Gregory, Adam and Eve, the Wheel of Life, and St. Martin. The furnishings of the church are 18C, the **pulpit** being a work of Jean Baptiste Masreliez.

In 7km you can join the 55 to Uppsala, going north to Örsundsbro from where **Kvekgården** is a kilometre or so off the road. Kvekgården is an 18C farm but built in medieval style. The horizontal timbers interlock at the corners, log-cabin fashion, and the wood has never been treated with the later ubiquitous Falun red. The buildings have weathered to a silvery grey, roofed with thatch, instead of tiles or turf. The furnishings are mid 19C. (Open in summer, but you can see the exterior any time.)

From here you could continue north and then east to the castle of **Vik**, following signs *Viks slott* (guided tours twice a day in summer). Originally medieval this was renovated in the 17C, with upper floors, carved doorway, centre staircase and bigger windows being added. The Hall of Knights has a stucco ceiling and pillared fireplace, and there are portraits and furniture. Return south by the 55 and in 5km it meets the 263 at Litslena.

The main route, road 263, leaves Enköping to the east and after 11km you can see the **church** of **Litslena** which has a 1480 Lübeck **altarpiece**, with Scandinavian saints, Eskil, Botvid, Olof, Erik and Birgitta among the 24 figures. The doors close twice to reveal first paintings for Christmas and Lent, and then the Crucifixion and St. Gregory. The **wall-paintings** are the work of an unknown artist c 1470. On the south wall the Creed is illustrated with apostles and prophets, while the west end has the Last Judgment. The north wall has a Passion series, and in the vaults are single saints.

Continue east on the 263. The **church** of **Husby-Sjutolft** is 5km off the road. Here only the walls have paintings but they bear Albertus Pictor's signature. They have been restored but are still enjoyable. The altarpiece is from Lübeck (15C). At **Övergran** (14km from Litslena), Albertus was again the painter, but the pictures are faded and damaged.

To Skokloster

Beyond Övergran church there is a turn for Skokloster (16km), and just past the turn by a bridge a runestone stands on a height. This is the **Varpsund stone** which commemorates a victim of an expedition to Russia (1040s).

*Skokloster is considered the supreme example of Swedish Baroque taste in the country, combining as it does interior decoration with contemporary fittings and furnishings. (Open May–Sept. Guided tours every hour 11.00–16.00—avoid 13.00 and 14.00 which are usually very crowded. English-speaking guides.)

A Cistercian convent was established here in the 13C. In the 17C the estate was given to Herman Wrangel, an Estonian in the service of Karl IX. His son Carl Gustav Wrangel became a Count, as well as Admiral and Councillor of the Realm, Governor General of Pomerania and adviser to the Regency of Karl XI. He had castles built in Swedish possessions on the continent, and rebuilt the Wrangel Palace in Stockholm. At Skokloster he employed Casper Vogel as architect but Nicodemus Tessin the Elder made some suggestions, such as having the façades rusticated, and Jean de la Vallée drew designs for the grounds (not carried out). After 14 years' construction the exterior was completed in 1668, and much of the interior also dates from about this time. However, when Carl Gustav died in 1676 work was broken off and some parts are still unfinished. What remains is a flamboyant compote of stucco ceilings, carved firesurrounds, gilt leather wall-coverings, expensive tapestries, elegant furniture and well-known paintings.

Skokloster (1668), Carl Gustav Wrangel's luxurious Baroque palace

The white four-storey castle stands on a height, built around a courtyard with octagonal towers at each corner. The material is mainly brick, with Swedish stone, Dutch roofing tiles and Italian marble. In the *entrance hall paired marble Ionic columns support a shallow vaulted ceiling. The reception area occupies what was the main kitchen, and other rooms on the ground floor were workshops and storerooms.

The stairs are of Öland limestone. The **first floor** (labelled 'second' in the English leaflet) contains the most sumptuous *apartments. Around the walls of the Classically decorated corridors are inscribed proverbs in several languages, and between the windows the portraits are of Herman Wrangel's fellow-officers. The ceiling has grisaille paintings.

The **Count's Drawing-Room**, which functioned as a waiting-room, is dominated by Ehrenstrahl's large equestrian **painting** of the Count. The deeply carved wooden **fire-surround** incorporates a painting of Apollo and Daphne. The gilt leather **wall-covering** (probably 18C) is almost invisible behind close-ranged portraits, including those of the Count's wife and some of his children. Winged putti decorate the **stucco ceiling**, and furniture includes a fine walnut **chest** and a **cabinet** displaying china.

The **Count's Bedroom** is even more luxurious since he received visitors from his bed (he slept elsewhere). The stucco **ceiling** here has warlike trophies and weapons, and the carved **fire-surround** in black and gold has the Wrangel arms. Here as in other rooms the fireplace is supplemented with a tiled stove alongside. The **tapestries** are 17C Dutch, and there is a **cabinet** inlaid with tortoiseshell. The **bed** is draped with red silk damask dotted with spangles, mentioned in a document of 1672. The walls are hung with portraits.

The tower room is a tribute to Karl XIV Johan. The **Hall of Kings**, so called because of the royal portraits from Gustav Vasa to Gustav IV Adolf, has the most distinctive **ceiling** in the castle, if not the most artistic. Figures representing the four continents surround a dragon fight, and the four elements are represented. The ebony and ivory **cabinet** came from Augsburg and there is a 16C gilt bronze **clock**.

The **Countess' Drawing-Room** has a stucco **ceiling**, with the four seasons, putti, flowers and birds. **Porcelain** is displayed in a Dutch cabinet, and here the **chairs** as well as the **walls** are clad in leather. The **Countess' Bedroom** has her and her husband's arms on the ceiling, and the **tapestries** are from the same series as those in the Count's Bedroom. Yet another florid **fire-surround** here has two carved Amazons.

The **silver collection** with many other expensive trinkets is in the next tower room. The **Yellow Drawing-Room** has a stucco ceiling with a curious wavy profile. The chairs are French Rococo and the rest of the furniture is in mixed styles including Empire. After the Queen's Bedchamber with chinoiserie furniture and portraits of the count and countess, the Dining-room has a table laid as it would have been in the mid 17C.

On the **second floor** (named 'third' in the leaflet) is the great two-storey-high **banqueting-hall** which remains incomplete, almost as it was when the count died. You can see through to the bare roof, and tools and carpenters' benches as they would have been at the time. Nine guest rooms on this floor are named after European cities (not usually shown). They contain furniture in mixed styles, portraits, tapestries and ceilings painted to imitate stucco. On the **top floor** are collections garnered by owners from the 17C to the 19C, of armour and weapons, a Greenland kayak, stuffed animals, models of castles, American Indian artefacts and a Turkish tent. There is also a valuable library occupying seven rooms.

The brick **church** was originally built for the Cistercian convent. The funerary chapel was added for Herman Wrangel, and the altar, pulpit and font were brought from Poland in 1660. Further away there is a motor museum with 40 or so cars and motorbikes. (Information in English; open all year.)

Back on the 263, it is 3km from Övergran to **Yttergran**, where the church has **paintings** (1480s) by Albertus Pictor which have been restored. In the chancel are prophets and scenes from the life of the Virgin, in the nave vault Evangelists and church fathers, and on the walls the Passion of Christ. Hidden by the organ is the Last Judgment. In the porch are St. George and the Dragon and symbolic scenes. The altarpiece is late medieval and there is a 17C bridal seat of medieval type.

From Yttergran it is 2km to the E18 at Bålsta, and after crossing the Sigtuna fjord the outer suburbs of Stockholm soon begin. It is 46km from Bålsta to the centre of Stockholm.

15

Stockholm

*STOCKHOLM is the capital and largest city of Sweden (population of built-up area 1,040,000, of Greater Stockholm 1,500,000).

A city built on 14 islands linked by over 50 bridges cannot fail to have charm. The presence of so much water means wide horizons and picturesque views, and climbing a hill or a tower turns the views from picturesque to spectacular. The usual comparison with Venice is misleading, since the waterways do not penetrate the old town, and although ferries bustle about the archipelago, the network of bridges means the emphasis is on road and rail rather than water-borne traffic.

The economy of the city is based on the service sector not on industry, which spares it much dreary industrial suburbia. More than half of the largest Swedish companies have their headquarters here, and nearly half of all computer personnel, a third of civil engineers and over a third of those in financial services work here. It has a university, and university institutes of medicine, economics and technology.

The major national museums are located here, and there is lively music, theatre and art. In the summer street-life provides entertainment with open-air cafés, music in the parks, outdoor exhibitions and pleasure boats on the waterways. The principal tourist attractions are the old town, the Royal Palace, the Vasa museum, Skansen open-air museum and Drottningholm Palace.

Tourist Information: The main tourist bureau is at Sverigehuset (Sweden House), Kungsträdgården. (Open mid-June to August 08.30–18.00, Sat, Sun 08.00–17.00, Sept to mid-June 09.00–17.00, Sat, Sun 09.00–14.00. Tel (08) 789 20 00, Sat, Sun (08) 789 24 90. Toilet available on request.) They book excursions and can tell you about places outside the city like Sigtuna and Skokloster (highly recommended) There are other offices at the Kaknäs Tower (open all year) and in the City Hall (summer). Some tourist information is also available at Hotellcentralen in the Central Station.

The essential publication is *Stockholm This Week* (free) which gives maps and details of shopping, museums, restaurants, entertainment, transport, taxis, emergency medical treatment and more. You can buy the **Stockholm card** which gives free admission to all the museums, free transport and (valuable) parking. Linked to the Stockholm Water Festival in August the **Water Pass** can be bought which gives reductions on food, transport, accommodation and entertainment; most also available in June and July. The bookshop on the first floor sells every sort of publication about Sweden.

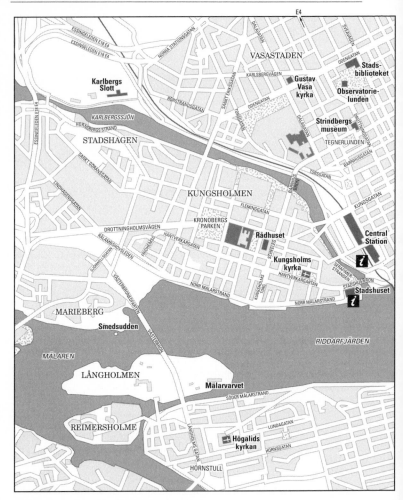

Accommodation: This costs even more in the capital than in the rest of the country, so it is even more vital to seek out weekend and summer rates (still high), or settle for somewhere on the fringes of the underground or local train system. If you prefer to book before you leave home ask your travel agent or the Swedish Tourist Office for information on the various deals on offer by the hotel chains, which can amount to good discounts if booked in your home country. Otherwise Hotellcentralen in the Central Station (tel. (08) 24 08 80) will do free advance bookings in hotels or hostels but charges a fee for immediate bookings. Private rooms (no breakfast) are few and far between, but you can always ask the tourist bureau to put you in touch with a firm such as Allrum, Wallingatan 34, 111 24 Stockholm (tel. (08) 21 37 89/21 37 90) which deals with them. There are six youth hostels in the inner city (book ahead, especially for the hugely popular af Chapman boat), plus two open in the summer only, and about a dozen in the Greater Stockholm area.

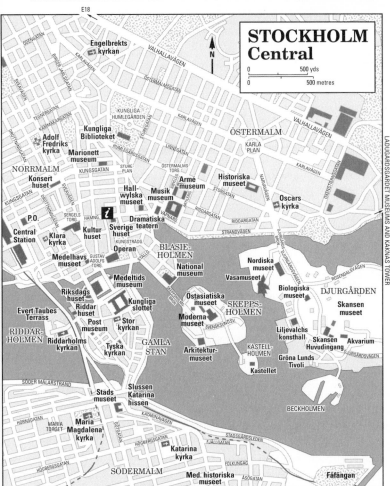

Travel within the city. A new ring road, or rather tunnel, is planned for the late 1990s, and a toll will be payable to travel on it or to cross it into the centre of the city, according to present plans. Parking is as difficult and expensive as in any other capital city, but the **Stockholm Card** helps with the cost. It makes sense to leave the car on the edge of the underground system. There are various **tourist travel cards**, covering all means of transport, including some boats and some tourist attractions. If you are going to be in the city only a day or two you can buy tickets at the entrance to underground stations or from the bus-driver. Pensioners are entitled to a reduction. For longer stays you can buy a strip of *Rabattkuponger* at Pressbyrå kiosks which give a reduction of about a third. The city is divided into zones and the number of coupons for a journey varies according to how many zones you travel through. At the SL office on the lower level of Sergels Torg you can find maps, timetables and information on all transport in the city and the county (tel. (08) 23 60 00). There are information kiosks at Slussen and Norrmalmstorg.

The easiest transport for the visitor to use is the **underground**. All lines meet at T-Centralen, the central underground station (note the railway station is called Centralstation or simply Centralen for short while Cityterminalen is the ultra-modern bus station). Blue-and-white signs with a T for Tunnelbana mark the entrances. (See note below on the artistic side of the underground.) The **Tourist Line bus** (mid-June to mid-August daily, Sundays in spring and autumn) is good value. The fare covers all travel for one day on a figure-of-eight route, with 14 stops so you can get off and on as often as you wish. You see the bus stops at major tourist points like the Royal Palace, Skansen and the central station.

Do not forget **water transport**—there are dozens of ferries, local sightseeing ones, commuter travel ones, long trips in the archipelago. The main tourist boats operate from Nybroplan (by the theatre), Strömkajen (near the Grand Hotel and the National Museum) and the City Hall. A stroll along these quays will collect you handfuls of brochures. **Bicycles** can be hired but are much more expensive than in the rest of the country. There is a cycle-hire place at Djurgårds bridge below the Nordic Museum.

Sightseeing. The boat-trips are a satisfying experience, but there are also coach tours, or combined coach and boat trips, or walking tours: details from Sweden House. A short walking tour of some intimate corners of the old town may start in the summer from the obelisk by the Royal Palace. (Check at the tourist bureau, or try the obelisk at 18.30.)

Toilets. Public toilets in very popular places are extremely expensive, for example, in the west wing of the Royal Palace, Kungsträdgården, Gallerian shopping centre and the central station. Even cafés and restaurants may have a coin-operated toilet, or you may have to ask for the key (*nyckel*), and in the capital the churches, otherwise a good source, either do not have them or open them only during services. Most big squares have one if you hunt around, but they may be open only in summer. On the maps in *Stockholm This Week* they are marked WC (T stands for underground!). The following is the list published by Stockholm Information Service (omitting the ones just mentioned): Hötorget and Östermalmstorg underground stations, Rotunda, Norra Bantorget, Skeppsbron, Slussen, Götgatan, Ringen, Fridhemsplan, Fridhemsgatan, Odenplan, Strandvägen, Djurgårds bridge, Vasa park (summer only). Others are at City Hall Quay, Kulturhuset, corner Hamngatan/Nybroplan, Strömparterren, Riddarholmen car park and Mariatorget.

The tourist season. Although major attractions stay open longer than in the rest of Sweden (see Practical Information) it is still possible to be caught out by restricted opening times and tourist services before mid June and after mid August. The moral is, check on the spot before making a long trip. Bear in mind that printed programmes are no guarantee, so ring up the company or organisers, or the tourist bureau. If you can read a little Swedish (German will help) get the newspaper *Dagens Nyheter* on a Friday for their section *På Stan*, a full breakdown of what is available for the week. *Stockholm This Week* is fairly reliable but is printed some time in advance. **Opening hours in this book can be only a guide.**

Shopping areas. Hamngatan: department stores, NK, the Duty Free Showroom and Gallerian shopping precinct. Biblioteksgatan, Stureplan, Grev Turegatan, Nybrogatan: more exclusive. Drottninggatan: PUB and Åhlens department stores. Västerlånggatan: main shopping area in the old town; also Österlånggatan. Köpmangatan (old town): antiques. Hornsgatan, east end (Södermalm): art, handicraft, antiques. Most museums have souvenir shops.

Emergencies. Police, Fire, Ambulance: as in the rest of the country, tel. 90 000. **Medical Information:** tel. (08) 44 92 00. **Doctor on call:** tel. (08) 44 90 00. **Dental treatment:** S:t Erik's Hospital, Fleminggatan 22. After 21.00 tel. (08) 44 92 00. **All-night chemist:** Klarabergsgatan 64, tel. (08) 24 82 80. **Lost Property:** Central Station. **Police:** Tjärhovsgatan 21, and SL (Stockholm Transport): Rådmansgatan underground.

Exchange: Forex, Central Station.

Telephone, telegram, etc: Kungsgatan 36

Main Post Office: Vasagatan 28–34.

Art in the underground. About half of the underground stations have been decorated by some of the best artists in Sweden. Many look like grottoes, and there are sculptures, paintings, mosaics, engravings, reliefs, even ponds. SL produce a leaflet in English 'Welcome to the World's Longest Art Exhibition' (available in their Sergels Torg office) which details and illustrates the most innovative. The most entertaining line is perhaps the latest, No. 10/11 from Kungsträdgården to Hjulsta/Akalla. T-Centralen has the most art, there are cuddly penguins at Tensta and classical sculptures at Kungsträdgården. Other goodies are at Solna, Farsta Centrum, Gärdet, Stadion and Västra Skogen. Breaking your journey to have a look costs no extra.

History. Excavations have shown that there was earlier settlement on Helgeandsholmen, where the Parliament building stands, than on Stadsholmen, City Island, where the old town—*Gamla stan*—lies (also known as *Staden mellan broarna*, the town between the bridges). Over the centuries the land had risen, creating a sill between the Baltic and lake Mälaren, and by the 13C the island of Stadsholmen, though still smaller then than now, seemed the obvious place both for defending the entrance to lake Mälaren from the Baltic, and for developing trade.

Birger Jarl built a fort on the site of the present royal palace, and in 1252 he granted Stockholm its city charter, its first mention in history. By the end of the century the city wall had been built, and the Franciscan friary founded. Soon Stockholm was the most important town in the country, and then an international trading market. Taking its place in the great Baltic network it came to be heavily influenced by the mighty Hanseatic League as German merchants settled and assumed more and more power in business, culture and even government. Its wealth was built mainly on the export of the products of the Bergslagen mining area.

From the 14C to the 16C the city played a key role in the perpetual struggles for power, both within Scandinavia and on the continent. In 1471 the Swedes, led by Sten Sture the Elder, defeated the Danes at the battle of Brunkeberg (in the present-day Norrmalm district) and the city became Swedish. In 1520, the Danes took Stockholm and Christian II of Denmark was crowned king. After joyful feasting, however, Christian had bishops, noblement and some passers-by slaughtered on the main square in the Bloodbath of Stockholm. (See below, Rte 15A.)

The young Gustav Vasa landed in the south of the country from Germany in 1520 and after three years' struggle won back the city, the last stronghold of the Danes in Sweden except for the southern provinces. Gustav was crowned king in 1523. He restored the castle—known as *Tre Kronor* (Three Crowns)—and his son Johan turned it into a Renaissance palace. Together the Vasas improved the city, mainly with money from the 'reformed' churches and monasteries.

Now the royal chancellery and the central administration of the country were established here. The Parhelion painting (Vädersolstavlan—see under Cathedral) shows what the city looked like at this time, with the cathedral and the defensive tower of the castle surrounded by houses crammed on to the island, and empty hills behind.

During the Thirty Years War (1618–48) Sweden acquired lands ringing the Baltic and was a major world power, and now in 1634 was the moment for Stockholm to be declared the national capital.

Gustav II Adolf, better known to Europeans as Gustavus Adolphus, expanded the harbour to improve trade, instituted tolls and subsidised trading companies. Wooden buildings were prohibited, and the fortifications were dismantled when Vaxholm fortress was built and customs posts established. So there was space, opportunity and money available for the grand houses on Riddarholmen and Stadsholmen. The styles ranged from German and Dutch Renaissance at the beginning of the century, through Dutch Classical to Roman Baroque at the end of the century. In 1697 the Three Crowns castle was burnt down and opened the way for Tessin's masterpiece. The city began to spread beyond the islands on to the mainland.

The royal palace was the greatest building achievement of the 18C. The waning of Sweden's international power brought some slowing of the capital's vitality, which was not helped by the plague in 1710 and periodic fires. But trade and shipping were given impetus later in the century by the formation of the East India Company, while Gustav III encouraged new building and expansive parks and gardens.

In the late 19C the city experienced a new surge of building in the Östermalm and Vasastaden area, and Djurgården became a public park. Skansen was opened in 1891.

In 1905 the Parliament building and the national bank alongside it on Helgeandsholmen were completed. The Olympic Stadium was built for the 1912 games. Modern engineering meant that the Brunkeberg ridge and the heights of Södermalm could at last be tamed into terrain suitable for motor traffic. Stockholm's symbol, the City Hall, was opened in 1923. The first underground line was completed in 1930.

Between 1930 and the 1960s the population of the inner city increased from 300,000 to over 800,000, since when numbers have dropped somewhat. After the Second World War Sweden could start to build rapidly with new prosperity hardly touched by the war. A great spurt of building took place, and the tidying up and gentrification of the old town began, which in some instances meant destroying historic houses. Banks, offices, stores and administration swept into old residential areas. Now conservation has become as important here as in the rest of Europe, and the destruction of old houses in Gamla Stan and elsewhere has been halted.

Today Stockholm is a cleaner, safer capital city than most, civilised attributes now coming to be appreciated more and more by the visitor.

A.   The Central Islands

The Old Town

The island of Stadsholmen, better known as Gamla Stan—the Old Town—is linked by bridges for every form of transport to the mainland north and south. It is joined on the north to Helgeandsholmen (Holy Ghost Island) which is occupied by the House of Parliament, and on the west to Riddarholmen (Knights' Island). An islet called Strömsborg containing one building is accessible only from the Vasa bridge.

Much of this old town area is a warren of narrow lanes with houses dating from medieval times onwards. The lanes open unexpectedly into tiny tranquil squares or wide streets lined with mansions. It encompasses the cathedral, the royal palace, the German church, the House of Nobility, the palaces of the rich and the cramped quarters of the poor through the ages.

It is easy to be seduced into following other lanes than those described here. The thing to remember is that the wealth of architectural ornament is often above eye-level, above modern shop-fronts and cafés. You will find overdoors of luxuriant swags, cartouches and consoles, goods' hoists and shop-signs, coats of arms, and fire insurance plaques with a phoenix rising from the flames (so the fire brigade could concentrate on the right house). At eye-level there are carved door-posts, door-knockers and wrought-iron gates. There are inscriptions here and there, often in German, testimony to the influence of German merchants in Hanseatic times.

The iron ties holding interior beams in place are a study in themselves. There are many varieties, but among them curly X-shaped ones are medieval, then 16C fork-shapes developed horned and curly ends in the 17C, a thick band around a bar is 18C and a plain keyhole is 19C.

Besides looking up, try going down—many cafés and restaurants are in medieval cellars and vaults. At pavement level the boulders against corners of houses were to protect them from passing carriages.

The island used to be smaller and the old sea-line can be experienced wherever there is a steep change in level as in Mårten Trotzigs Gränd and Köpmantorget. The 13C fortifications may have run just inside this line, more or less along Prästgatan, Baggensgatan and Bollhusgränd. By the 15C the land had risen so much that another wall had to be built further out, almost along Lilla Nygatan and Myntgatan, and nearly as far out as Skeppsbron.

Every street block in the old town is provided with a Classical name. All blocks in Sweden have names for the convenience of planners and

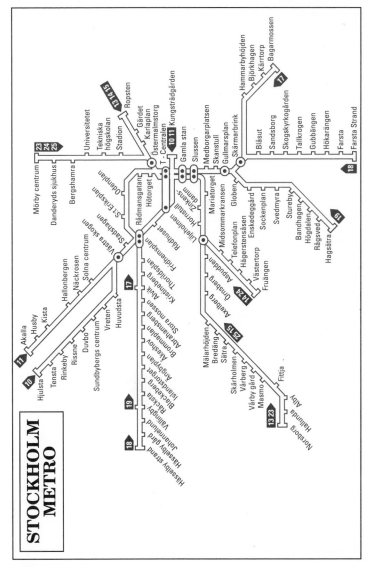

architects, but this is one of the few areas where they are on the street name-plates, eg. *kv. Venus*. The names here were given about the year 1700.

The easiest approach is by underground. Come out of Gamla Stan underground station by the exit marked 'Gamla Stan'. At the top of the steps turn left and then right up **Kåkbrinken** which climbs straight up towards the main square, Stortorget, crossing several wider roads. As it crosses Prästgatan, on the upper right corner which is protected by the barrel of a cannon, there is a **runestone** built into the wall of No. 17. The runic inscription from about the 11C says: 'Torsten and Frögunn had the stone erected to their son'.

Stortorget is on top of the island plateau, almost in the exact centre. It has been the hub of Stockholm's history from the 13C. Here on the market-place were the first council meetings and later political meetings, here too the stocks and the place of execution.

On 4 November 1520 Christian II of Denmark was crowned in the cathedral as king of Sweden and Denmark. There were three days of peace and festivity with Danes and Swedes seemingly at last united—but on 7 November Christian had over 80 of the leading churchmen and lords tried and executed on the square, the bodies left in a heap there as a salutary warning. The Bloodbath of Stockholm was to help to galvanise the young Gustav Vasa into action and propel him towards his own coronation in the same church three years later as king of an independent Sweden.

On the east side of the square the 17C red gabled house is said to have as many white stones in its façade as there were victims of the Bloodbath. There is sandstone carving on the gable and the ornate doorway has a German text. On either side are other graceful gables.

The white building with Classical and Rococo details is the **Stock Exchange** designed by Erik Palmstedt (1767–76). It is on the site of the old town hall which was used as a meeting-place for the Estate of Burgers. The building also houses the Nobel Library and the Swedish Academy. On the west side, No. 3 has two curved 17C gables and No. 5 on the corner of Svartmangatan has a painted wooden ceiling of the 17C, with flowers, fruit and animals, visible through the display-windows. The fountain in the centre of the square is from the 18C.

Leave the square by Trångsund down the left of the Stock Exchange. Ahead on the right is the façade of the Storkyrka (cathedral) and just before it is where the graveyard used to be, now paved over. Alongside the iron gates are statues representing Reason and Divine Love (17C) at this end, and Prudence and Hope (early 18C) at the other.

The *Storkyrka (Great Church) is dedicated to St. Nicholas of Myra and was consecrated in 1306. (Open daily; sometimes there are English guided tours in summer. The tower containing a small museum and the old cathedral smithy is open in summer Tue–Fri 14.00.)

The cathedral is first mentioned in a document of 1279 when it was a simple three-aisled church. About 1340 side-chapels began to be added, the first being the Lady Chapel, as high as the nave and with a four-bay vault still preserved. Gradually chapels along north and south made the church broader than it was long. About 1400 it was lengthened by adding a new chancel with a five-sided apse and in 1420 a defensive tower was built to the west, together with Själakor (All Souls' Chapel) between the tower and the south aisle.

The next step was to remove the walls between the side-chapels, creating a five-aisled church. The roof and the tower were heightened and new vaulting provided except in the Lady Chapel and All Souls' Chapel, which still has its 1470s' paintings. Gustav Vasa thought the church was too close to the south-west bastion of his castle and wanted to raze it, but he was persuaded simply to remove the end of the chancel.

When Nicodemus Tessin the Younger built the new palace at the beginning of the 18C the church was regarded as hopelessly outmoded and the exterior was completely remodelled, finished c 1740 to the Baroque designs of Johan Eberhard Carlberg, and a new Rococo top was added to the tower. Finally in the early years of the 20C a thorough restoration removed the plaster from the vault-ribs and pillars revealing large areas of red brick which purists complain is not historically accurate.

The cathedral is Sweden's national church where royal marriages are celebrated, but there has been no coronation ceremony since the 19C. A painting by Carl Gustav Pilo in the National Museum shows the coronation here of Gustav III and Sofia in 1772.

In the porch are gilded reliefs, most from Riga in the 16C. Inside, the late Gothic vaults and pillars belie the exterior but many of the furnishings and art-works are Baroque.

To the left of the entrance is a modern globular **candle-stand** with 49 candles. The designer Torolf Engström wanted to have 490 to represent the 'seventy times seven' times St. Matthew's Gospel says we should forgive our brother but space allowed only one for every ten. In the north aisle are tombs from the 16C and 17C with sculpted or relief figures on top.

At the east end of the north aisle is the cathedral's treasure and masterpiece, ***St. George and the Dragon** by Bernt Notke of Lübeck. Carved in oak (the dragon's fins are of elkhorn), 3.6m high, it was dedicated in 1489, a gift from Sten Sture the Elder to the cathedral in thanks for the victory over the Danes at Brunkeberg. Its vigour, imagination and technical mastery of the medium make it one of the most outstanding works of its age north of the Alps. The pyramidal form of the group holds together the flailing shapes of the dragon which lead up through the solid strength of the horse to the saint's tensely upraised sword. Bernt Notke, like many of his countrymen, worked for some years in Sweden. It is likely, of course, that much of the less important work was completed by his assistants in his workshop. The plinth is from the 20C but the reliefs are original. Given the circumstances, we assume that the dragon is Denmark and the princess, kneeling on a representation of a castle, is Sweden.

On the north wall by St. George is David Klöcker Ehrenstrahl's monumental 17C painting of the **Last Judgment** originally destined for the chapel of

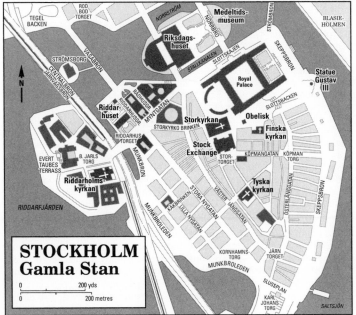

STOCKHOLM
Gamla Stan

0   200 yds

0   200 metres

the old castle. When the castle was burnt the picture and the same artist's Crucifixion (in the south aisle) was saved, but the architect thought they were too old-fashioned for his new chapel. The tomb framed by Corinthian pillars behind St. George is of a 17C royal chancellor. Beside it stands a large bell of 1493.

The Baroque ***high altar** is of ebony and silver. In the centre are scenes from Christ's Death and Resurrection, which were made in Hamburg in 1652, while the wings were made in Sweden. In front of the altar is a bronze seven-branch candlestick nearly 4m high, made in 1470.

The ***royal pews**, with their surging gilded draperies and crown canopies held by angels, were designed by Nicodemus Tessin the Younger and sculpted by the German Burchardt Precht in 1684. The gilded ***pulpit** with angels holding the canopy and a sunburst behind is also by Precht (1702), after he had been to Rome and been influenced by artistic works there.

Under the pulpit lies the modest **grave** of Olaus Petri, rediscovered near this position in 1907, and opposite is a memorial to him.

Olaus Petri (1493–1552) the driving force in the Church behind the Swedish Reformation was born in Örebro and studied in Uppsala, Leipzig and Wittenberg, where he was one of Luther's pupils. In 1525 he was the first Swedish priest to marry. On his return from Germany he rose rapidly to become Chancellor (1531–33). He was popularly known as 'Olof in the basket', the basket being the pulpit in which people mostly saw him. He preached against both Catholicism, which suited Gustav Vasa for economic reasons, and the royal power, which did not. In 1540 the king condemned him to death for treason but reprieved him, and by 1543 he was vicar of Stockholm. He translated the New Testament (1526) and most of the Old Testament (1541) into Swedish, as well as writing hymns, sermons, history and a play.

The **font** is of 1514 and the silver and gold **chandelier** was bequeathed in 1652 by Ebba Brahe, the first love of Gustavus Adolphus. In the right-hand aisle is the Olaus Petri chapel with Ehrenstrahl's **Crucifixion**. A tablet on the east wall commemorates Crown Princess Margareta, grand-daughter of Queen Victoria, who died in 1920. On the base of one of the pillars is a **carving** by Adam van Düren of two lions snapping at an eel—interpreted as Sweden being harried by the Danes. Also in the right aisle is Carl Milles' marble **monument** to the three generations of architects in the Tessin family (1933).

To the west are the four 14C ***bays of the Lady Chapel** with original painted vaults. At the rear of the right aisle is a treasure which could be overlooked. Known in English as the ***Parhelion painting**, it is the first picture of Stockholm (1535), and shows the church, the old Three Crowns castle, walls, towers and houses, under a sky with parhelic circles, halos caused by ice crystals. It is said that Olaus Petri ordered the painting to record the omens caused by the king's overbearing actions, or alternatively to defuse Catholic propaganda on the subject by setting it up in church. There is an illuminated enlargement of this in the Medieval Museum which is much easier to see and study in detail.

Here too is a display-case of historic Bibles.

Come out of the cathedral and turn right. Ahead is the late Renaissance **mansion** designed by Jean de la Vallée for Axel Oxenstierna, Queen Kristina's Chancellor. Sadly he did not live to occupy it and died in 1654. Because the house is at an angle to Trångsund, the door and window-frames are slanted to make then appear straight ahead.

Turn right and you see one of the curved wings of the royal palace. (For the palace and its museums see below.) Continue round the cathedral. In the cobbles is a line of stones showing the outline of the medieval apse, and not far away more stones show where the bastion has been, so one can judge of Gustav Vasa's prudence in having the apse removed. At the centre of the east end of the cathedral stands a statue of Olaus Petri by Thomas Lundberg (1898).

The **obelisk** at the top of the slope (known to Stockholmers as 'the toothpick') was one of five planned by Gustav III as thanks to the city for its staunchness during the war with Russia. In the event it was built by his son Gustav IV in 1799.

On the left of the cathedral is the rear of the Stock Exchange. Further down the slope the low yellow building is the **Finska kyrkan** (Finnish church). It was built in the 17C as a games hall, and was acquired by the Finns in 1725. Inside on the gallery are painted Finnish coats of arms. The chandeliers are late 17C and the altar painting of the Resurrection is a copy made in 1734. The pulpit is from 1767. Behind the church is a small garden with a fountain, one of many quiet green retreats in the old town.

Next down the hill at No. 4 is the restrained and elegant façade of the **palace** which Nicodemus Tessin the Younger built for himself opposite the royal palace which was his creation. The more decorative interior, rear and garden are not open to the public.

Before leaving Slottsbacken, have a look down the slope to the waterside where stands one of Sergel's best works, his *statue of Gustav III (1808).

Take Bollhusgränd (named from the 'ball-house'—the games hall) to the right after Tessin's palace. No. 3A has a Baroque doorway with lions and coats of arms. The lane comes out on to Köpmangatan and to the left you see Köpmantorg with a copy of St. George and the Dragon from the cathedral. Here stood one of the city gates torn down in 1685. From the statue's vantage-point on the height of the medieval shoreline you can look up and down Österlånggatan.

Österlånggatan is a quiet street which has lost its former character as a centre for shipping and trade when it was on the waterline. Of all the taverns only Den Gylden Freden (Golden Peace), No. 51, has survived from 1722 the year after peace was concluded with Russia. It was made famous in song by the poet Bellman, owned once by the painter Anders Zorn, and frequented by another poet Evert Taube. The street is fringed with narrow lanes leading down to the present waterline at Skeppsbron.

Go back up Köpmangatan. The second on the left is **Själagårdsgatan** where No. 2 has a doorway with angels and warriors and No. 3 has a coat of arms and the date 1643. Here the road opens into a cool triangular space, with a chestnut tree and benches, called Brända Tomten—the Burnt Property.

Back on Köpmangatan the gate at No. 11 has a cartouche with flowers and cherubs dated 1730. Through the gate is an unexpected open area obtained by clearing away old houses in the 1930s. No. 15 has a carved overdoor with fruit and initials.

Now you are in the main square again. Turn left and left again down Svartmangatan. Svartman is 'Black Man', that is, a Black Friar. In 1336 King Magnus Eriksson gave the Dominicans land to build a friary, which can be seen on the Parhelion painting in the cathedral. Interesting houses here include No. 6 with coats of arms, and No. 17 in Rococo style of 1768. Here is also **Tyska kyrkan**, the German church, for this was the area where German merchants tended to gather in the Middle Ages. Two lanes are still called 'German'—Tyska Brinken and Tyska Skolgränd, and there is Tyska Brunnsplan and Tyska Stallplan as well.

The site of the church was where the German merchants had their guild hall in the 14C, though they soon admitted Swedes, and here Knut Knutsson was elected king in 1448. In the 16C, after the Reformation, the building was expanded to a church. The 96m copper-covered spire was rebuilt after a fire in 1878. The bells play German hymn-tunes (familiar through English translation) at 08.00, 12.00, 16.00 and 20.00.

The main entrance is by the imposing **south door**, which has figures of Moses and Christ, with Faith, Hope and Charity above. Inside, the vaulted ceiling (17C) is sprinkled with angels' heads and two pillars stand in the centre. Under the gallery over the entrance are paintings from the Old and New Testaments. The most striking object is the two-storey **royal pew**, designed by Tessin the Elder in lush Baroque. The gilded 9m **high altar** of German workmanship has three central paintings and to the sides are figures of the Evangelists and apostles. The most interesting artistically is the ebony and alabaster **pulpit** (c 1660) with its figures of Christ and the apostles. To the right of the altar is the baptismal chapel with a gilded silver font of the 17C, and the two armchairs are a gift from German-born Queen Victoria of Sweden.

Svartmangatan soon opens out into the small Tyska Brunnsplan, with a **fountain** of 1787 by the architect Erik Palmstedt. There is a school on the right which was the site of the Dominican friary (the cellars still exist), and it was here that in the 1660s the court painter David Klöcker Ehrenstrahl built himself a mansion, now very much altered.

Take Tyska Stallplan to the right which will bring you to Prästgatan. Across the road almost opposite is the narrowest lane in Stockholm, **Mårten Trotzigs Gränd** with steps down to Västerlånggatan. In places it is less than a metre wide. Turn left at the end and you are in Järntorget, where iron used to be traded ('järn' is iron). Directly opposite on the other side of the square is a building designed as a **bank** in 1680 by Nicodemus Tessin the Elder, in Roman Baroque style. It was extended down to Skeppsbron in the rear by Carl Hårleman in the 1730s.

Take Triewaldsgränd to the south. At the end a left turn leads to Slussen. Slussen means 'the lock' and there has been one here since the 17C. The present lock is called the Karl Johan, and there is an equestrian statue of Karl XIV Johan in Karl Johans torg. (For more on Slussen, see Södermalm route.)

Skeppsbron runs up the east side of the island and at this end ferries leave for Djurgården. Here is also Carl Milles' leering **Sea-god** (1913).

Turning right at the end of Triewaldsgränd brings you to Kornhamnstorg, 'corn harbour square' whose name speaks for its history. The statue of the archer is by Christian Eriksson and represents the rebel leader Engelbrekt. House No. 51 is the Scharenbergska house and has an ornamental oriel window of the 17C.

Take one of the lanes to the north back to Västerlånggatan. This is the main shopping street of the old town, but some of the old buildings remain, or parts of them, especially the upper floors. No. 68 is the **Von der Lindeska house** of the 1630s with a Baroque doorway carved in sandstone. No. 67 has cornucopias of fruit and No. 54 has a doorway dated 1662. Many more such details can be found along here.

At Tyska Brinken you can turn right, cross Prästgatan and turn left into Skomakaregatan where there are also many old houses, Nos 5, 7 and 9 being particularly worth examining, and there is a goods' hoist on No. 3. When you reach the main square, turn down Kåkbrinken to get back on to Västerlånggatan. At No. 29 the façade above the modern shop is a row of **Gothic windows** discovered under plaster in 1946 (reconstructed). Olof Palme lived next door at No. 31.

Gåsgränd to the left near here leads into another open courtyard with many details such as figures carved on the corners of one building, the shoemaker's shop-sign and an amusing sculpture of small heavyweight boxers watched by a row of eager spectators' heads (Sven Lundquist, 1967).

Västerlånggatan continues and Storkyrkbrinken is the next big crossroads. (Ahead, No. 7 Västerlånggatan is 18C with 19C painted decoration.) A left turn here leads down to Riddarhustorget. On the right is the government administration building on land created by clearing the interior of an old block in the late 1940s. Some original houses are still incorporated in the complex. The round courtyard with a fountain, 'Morning of Life' by Ivar Johnsson, can be seen by entering for example through Klockgjutaregränd off Västerlånggatan.

At the end of Storkyrkbrinken, the white building opposite with two wings in front is the **Supreme Court**, once the Bonde Palace, designed by Jean de la Vallée in French Classical style, with pilasters and festoons on the façade (1662–73). It served as town hall between 1732 and 1915.

Next door is ***Riddarhuset**, the House of Nobility, generally considered to be the most beautiful building in Stockholm (open Mon–Fri 11.30–12.30). In front there is a statue of Gustav Vasa by L'Archevêque (1774).

Riddarhuset (the House of Nobility) finished in 1674

Several architects had a hand in the planning, Simon de la Vallée, Heinrich Wilhelm, Joost Vingboons and Jean de la Vallée (son of Simon). The façade is by Vingboons and true to his native country he used Dutch Classical style, but in a restrained version influenced by Palladianism which reached Sweden c 1640—hence the colossal Corinthian pilasters—and with emphasis on the horizontal rather than the vertical. It is of muted red brick and sandstone, the sandstone pilasters being crowned by a frieze, cornice and pediment. The upper storey has triangular pediments and the lower segmental. Festoons and garlands in sandstone articulate the façade.

The handsome 'säteri' roof is by Jean de la Vallée. 'Säteri' means manor-house, and such roofs have two planes, separated by a low vertical step. The figures on the roof represent various virtues mentioned in the Latin inscriptions on the façade.

The building was used by the Estate of Nobles as a meeting-place and has had its share of historic events, one of the most dramatic being Gustav III's unorthodox arrival in 1789 to assert his supremacy over the recalcitrant nobles. Previously the power of the nobles had been such that the country was virtually run from the Riddarhus.

You enter by the front door on Riddarhustorg, although the fact is not advertised except in small print to the side of the doorway. The broad stairway, by Jean de la Vallée, with a painting by Gustav Cederström of Karl X Gustav crossing the ice of the Great Belt, leads to a landing off which to the right is the **Great Hall**. The walls are covered with over 2000 **coats of arms** on copper of noble families. The **ceiling-painting** by David Klöcker Ehrenstrahl (1669–75) represents Mother Svea (Sweden) with the three graces, and Fame and Eternity. There are detailed notes in English on the painting available in the hall.

The **chair** of the Land-Marshal (chairman of the House of Nobility) is of carved ivory and ebony borders with inlaid ivory representations of the Old Testament (North German, early 17C).

Two staircases in front of the dais lead down to other rooms. The anteroom at the bottom has 17C portraits and porcelain with coats of arms. The Land-Marshal's hall has portraits of 17C and 18C Land-Marshals while the small reception-room on the other side has portraits of 19C Land-Marshals. Back up through the Great Hall and across the landing in the Chancery may be seen more porcelain and the seals of the noble families.

In the garden behind stands a **statue** of Axel Oxenstierna by John Börjeson of 1890. (The land for the Riddarhus was bought from him.) The two pavilions were built only in 1870.

From the front of the Riddarhus is a good view of the Riddarholm Church across the bridge on the island of Riddarholm.

With your back to the Riddarhus cross straight over to an open triangular space called Munkbron. This means Monk Bridge and the next road to the left is Stora Gråmunkegränd—'Big Greymonk Lane'. The grey friars were the Franciscans on Riddarholm. The façade on the short side of Munkbron is that of the **Petersenska house**, built by Christian Julius Döteber from Leipzig in 1645–49. The double doors are framed in rich sandstone sculpture, the windows have carving above and the gables are edged with scrolls and finials.

Passing the less impressive front of the Petersenska house in Lilla Nygatan and continuing, you will find in the next block the **Post museum** in a Classical building from the 1630s (open Tue–Sat 11.00–15.00, Wed to 20.00, Sun to 16.00. Small café and shop). On the ground floor is displayed the history of the Swedish mails, including old post-vehicles. On the first floor there is a comprehensive collection of stamps on pull-out screens, and a reconstruction of a stamp-printing works with old stamp-presses. On the top floor are hundreds of the small objects used by the post office, pen-stands, punches, posthorns, blotters and lamps, among other things.

Take the next right into Kåkbrinken and this will bring you back to Gamla Stan underground station along Munkbrogatan. If you continue a few steps into Mälartorget you will be rewarded by the heart-warming **sculpture** 'Family' by Pye Engström.

The Royal Palace

There are seven sections of the *ROYAL PALACE (Kungliga slott) open to the public, all with different opening times and seasons. Some are very restricted, and some may be closed for a variety of reasons, including state visits and ceremonies. It would call for a very high degree of ingenuity to see them all in one day, so if you are short of time it is essential to check opening hours in *Stockholm This Week*, and/or the tourist bureau, and again on the noticeboards on the spot. As a **rough guide** so that you may see what you are up against, opening hours at the time of writing are given below.

The Royal Apartments are entered on the west, between the curved wings (open May–Aug Tue–Sat 10.00–15.00, Sun 12.00–15.00, Sept–Apr 12.00–15.00, closed Mon).

The **Hall of State** (*Rikssalen*) and the **Chapel** (*Slottskyrkan*) are entered from the south (both open May–Sept 12.00–15.00). The **Treasury** (*Skattkammaren*) has the same entrance (Mon–Sat May–Aug 11.00–16.00, Sept–Apr 11.00–15.00, Sun all year 12.00–16.00).

The **Armoury** (*Livrustkammaren*) is on the south side also but further down the slope (open Tue–Fri 10.00–16.00, Sat–Sun 11.00–16.00, also Mon in summer).

On the north, there is **Gustav III's Museum of Antiquities** (open June–Aug 12.00–15.00), and further along under the arches of Lejonbacken is the **Palace Museum** (*Slottsmuseum*), (May–Sept 12.00–15.00).

Slottsbodarna is the gift shop in the right-hand curved wing on the south.

Changing of the guard: Weekdays 12.15, Sundays 13.15.

Concerts are held in the palace in summer.

By 1692 Karl XI already had Nicodemus Tessin the Younger working on a renovation plan for the old Three Crowns Castle. The north wing had been finished when in 1697 Karl died. A month later, before the King's funeral, fire swept through the castle and destroyed everything except the new wing. What with war, Tessin's death and other vicissitudes the palace was not ready for occupation until 1754, and not complete until 1770. Tessin's son Carl Gustav took over the direction of the work together with Carl Hårleman, using the original plans.

The east façade of Stockholm royal palace (late 17C–mid 18C) with the cathedral (13C–16C) on the left

The problem of the hilly terrain was solved on the north by creating a grand entrance one floor up and having Lejonbacken lead up at each side. A bronze lion guards each end—the name means Lion Slope. The severe north façade is patterned on early Roman Baroque palaces although with more emphasis on the horizontal. The mezzanine above the ground floor was to accommodate the height of the original chapel here, hence the row of small square windows. The massive doorway has a balcony above, with the central French window of the Bernadotte gallery surmounted by the Swedish coat of arms.

On the east two long low wings enclose a garden (closed to the public), which again is one floor up, with a stairway leading up to the railing so that from the road it is difficult to get a near view. It has a nine-window-broad central portion with rusticated ground floor and colossal pilasters uniting the top two floors. It seems that Tessin was thinking of Bernini's Palazzo Odescalchi in Rome when he designed this façade.

The south façade has the function of a ceremonial entrance to the Great Hall and the Chapel and so has a monumental central portion resembling a triumphal arch. Six great Corinthian columns frame niches with sculptures.

On the west Tessin had another problem. The cathedral was too close for him to build two long wings as on the east. Therefore he made one long and one very short, but he completed the design with two curved free-standing wings enclosing the outer court. The west façade is the most decorative. A nine-window-wide central section has banded Doric columns on the ground floor, caryatids with Ionic capitals on the first floor, and Corinthian pilasters on the second, between which are medallion portraits of Swedish rulers.

The inner courtyard is 89m by 77m. The façades are comparatively plain, especially the north and south entrances which have rustic portals as their only ornament. The west and east façades have a rusticated arcade on the ground floor, with colossal Corinthian pilasters above and pediments over the windows on the first floor.

Looking at the disposition and function of the rooms it is apparent that Tessin divided the palace into a masculine and a feminine side. On the west are the apartments for the king and princes, the Hall of State and council-chamber, and also on the west was the outer courtyard with sentries and cannons. On the east were the apartments for the queen and princesses, the chapel, library, (planned) theatre, and outside, the garden. The most resplendent hall of the palace, Karl XI's gallery, which links the two sides, reflects the idea in its decoration.

The **Royal Apartments**, consisting of the Bernadotte, Guest and State Apartments, are entered on the west side. On the **ground floor** are rooms used for temporary exhibitions, and the magnificent *staircase is the ceremonial entrance to the Apartments. Tessin was particularly pleased with the staircases, especially the fact that four flights of stairs lead to the first floor, and three, turning in the other direction, to the second floor. They occupy the full breadth of the wing. Much of the decoration, however, came later. In the mid 18C, reliefs, architectural paintings and the lights on the newel posts supported by Jacques Philippe Bouchardon's bronze putti were added. Under Oskar II in the 19C most of the other decorative details including the ceiling with paintings by Julius Kronberg were completed.

On the **first floor** are the *Bernadotte apartments** with decoration and fixtures from the 1730s and 1740s which were first carried out for King Adolf

Fredrik and Queen Lovisa Ulrika in 1754 and were last lived in by King Oskar II (d 1907) and Queen Sofia.

The **Anteroom** was originally a guard-room—notice the overdoors with symbols of war. The coronation of the first Bernadotte king, Karl XIV Johan, in the cathedral is the subject of the painting by Per Krafft the Younger. The 18C busts are of Fredrik I and Adolf Fredrik, and the relief portraits are of Gustav VI Adolf and Carl XVI Gustaf (both 20C).

The **Pillared Hall** occupies the corner between the west and north wings. The round **ceiling painting** of Svea (Sweden) and the four seasons was done by Alessandro Feretti in 1736–37 and the 12 Ionic columns and 16 pilasters (later 20) are of the same time. The delicate Rococo painting round the windows came in the 1750s. The overdoors and mirror-frames were completed by Jean-Baptiste Masreliez in 1780. The **statues** of Apollo and Venus are by Johan Tobias Sergel.

The **Viktoria Drawing-Room** was originally two rooms. It was almost completely remodelled in the 1860s in neo-Rococo style by the architect Scholander and the furniture is all of this period except the two German stucco-topped tables which are earlier. The pink velvet wall-coverings were previously in Lovisa Ulrika's audience room.

The next room is an octagonal anteroom which, with its twin at the other end of the Bernadotte gallery, has a ceiling by Guillaume Thomas Taraval (one depicts Peace under Arms, the other Freedom).

From this first anteroom the visitor can look into Oskar II's study, kept as it was when he died in 1907. Personal objects, photographs and portraits crowd the room, and there are writing implements, folk-art textiles and a cabinet with presents from the Tsar of Russia.

The *Bernadotte gallery** contains **paintings** and articles relating to the Bernadotte dynasty. It was decorated in the 1730s to plans by Carl Hårleman. Much of the wall decoration was taken away by Gustav III who wanted space for his pictures. The painted overdoors are probably by Taraval and the doors and wall-panels on the window wall by Jean Bourguignon, French artists brought here by Hårleman. Taraval also did the ceiling-paintings which show the Praise of Virtue, framed by birds, cherubs, flowers and foliage.

As you enter there is a display of some of Karl XIV Johan's belongings, including his marshal's baton bestowed by Napoleon in 1804. On the inner wall are two large portraits of Karl XIV Johan himself and his queen, Desirée, known in Sweden as Desideria, both by Gérard. In the centre of the wall is Queen Josefina, wife of Oskar I, who is portrayed to the right on a large canvas. The many other portraits are of members of the Bernadotte dynasty.

From this gallery you can look into Oskar II and Sofia's breakfast-room.

Lovisa Ulrika's Audience-Chamber has been restored to its original pink decoration. The **tapestries** are from Beauvais in 1745 and show scenes from the story of Cupid and Psyche, after cartoons by François Boucher. The throne and canopy were designed by Jean Eric Rehn and the bust of Lovisa Ulrika is by Sergel. The decoration of the ceiling is from the 1730s.

Similarly, the next room, **Lovisa Ulrika's Salon**, has been restored to its first colour, this time blue, but the original Rococo decoration has gone except for the gilt stucco ceiling and two overdoors. Notable, however, are the **paintings** belonging to Queen Josefina, (granddaughter of Empress Josephine) to whom Napoleon gave an Italian castle with its art collection. Here you can see Piero di Cosimo's Madonna and Botticini's *Portrait of a Boy*.

The **Dining-Room** at the corner of the north and east wings has also been restored. The hunting scene by Jean-Baptiste Oudry has been put back into the original frame carved by Bourguignon. The carved wooden pilasters are original and also the overdoors by Oudry. The silk damask wall-covering is a reproduction.

In the last accessible room of this suite there are royal portraits of recent times. These include Crown Princess Margareta (from England), the painter Prince Eugen, and Queen Ingrid of Denmark. The last two on the right are Queen Louise (a Mountbatten—d 1965) and Gustav V (d 1950). The two young princes on the other wall are Gustav VI Adolf (d 1973) and Wilhelm.

The *Guest Apartments are on the next floor. They were planned as living quarters for Crown Prince Fredrik Adolf in 1781. Jean Eric Rehn supervised the renovation to the plans of Carl Fredrik Adelcrantz.

The **Guard Room** contains many portraits, the two large ones being Karl XI on the left and Karl X Gustav on the right, and Karl XII between the windows. The malachite vases are from Russia.

The **Salon**, which reflects Gustavian Classicism in its sober ornament, has Brussels tapestries from c 1700 of scenes from Ovid's *Metamorphoses*. The furniture is mainly from Karl XIV Johan's time (French Empire—'Karl Johan style') and there are several French Empire bronzes. The large portrait is of Louis XV and the vases are from the St. Petersburg factory.

The **Audience Chamber** is also hung with Brussels tapestries, here representing the legend of Meleager. There are two Rococo bureaux flanking Gustav IV's writing desk which was designed by Louis Masreliez.

The **Bedchamber** is Rococo in decoration and there are medallions by Boucher over two of the doors. The bed was designed by Jean-Baptiste Masreliez and the two bureaux on the outside wall were made by Lorents Nordin, a Swedish cabinet-maker.

The **Small Bedchamber** is in restrained late Gustavian style. The door-mouldings are by Per Ljung from 1783. Another small bedchamber containing a Jan Brueghel painting leads to the Inner Salon whose decoration was carried out about 1790 in a style derived from Pompeii, but the furniture is mostly Swedish Empire. Two bookcases by Georg Haupt have sliding fronts (18C). Finally, a small room is devoted to the paintings of Crown Princess Margareta. A travelling-case by Georg Haupt s exhibited here.

The *State Apartments on the same floor are the most sumptuous in the palace and they contain among others the oldest interiors designed by Tessin himself. First come two guard-rooms designed by Carl Hårleman. The second has statues by Johan Niklas Byström of Gustav II Adolf, Karl X, and Karl XI. On the corner of the west and north wings the **Council Chamber** hung with Gobelins and Karlsberg tapestries. The two Gobelins ones (1771) represent Jason and Medea, and the three from Karlsberg Meleager and Atalanta. (Queen Ulrika Eleanora set up a tapestry-weaving centre for orphans at Karlsberg.) The overdoors also show Jason and Medea. Most of the fixtures here are by Scholander of the 19C except the doors which date from Tessin's time. There are busts of the Bernadotte kings from Karl XIV Johan to Gustav V, and Fredrik Westin's equestrian portrait is also of Karl Johan.

The **Audience Chamber** is one of the earliest interiors. Bernard Foucquet carried out the Venus and Mars on the ceiling and other French artists worked on the rest of the decoration. Foucquet portrayed scenes from the life of Alexander the Great in the half-circle paintings and René Chauveau made the stucco statues in the corners which depict Venus. The **tapestries** with woodland scenes were woven in Delft on the orders of Queen Kristina for her coronation in 1650. The canopy is 16C Italian but the initials C.R. on the backcloth were probably added for Queen Kristina. There are two portraits by Frans Hals (1638). The set of folding stools are mid 18C.

Gustav III's Bedchamber retains its Baroque ceiling with paintings by Jacques Foucquet and Jacques de Meaux of the young Karl XII with Fame, Minerva, Hercules and other allegorical figures, with sculptural details by Chauveau. The corner paintings are of the Muses. The walls are white and gold with Gustavian pilasters (1770s). The Gobelins **tapestry** represents a scene from Lully's opera *Roland*. This is set in an alcove which was newly added in the 1770s. Three French ebony **cabinets** (late 18C) stand in the alcove. The centre one has a flower inlay of agate, lapis lazuli and mother-of-pearl which is older than the cabinet itself. On the right is a bust of Gustav III by Sergel (1777) and on the left one of Karl XII by Bouchardon. The Louis XVI style *writing-table is by Georg Haupt (1770) and belonged to Gustav III. This is probably Haupt's best work.

The great *Gallery of Karl XI represents the summit of Tessin's work as an interior designer. It is in the top centre of the north wing and looks out over Lejonbacken to Norrmalm. It is 47m long and 6m wide. The walls are comparatively plain. One of Tessin's principles was that a rich ceiling should be balanced by sober walls and vice versa. Mirrors on the inside wall (inspired by those at Versailles?) correspond to windows on the outer wall. Corinthian pilasters lead up to a carved corniche. The **ceiling-paintings** by Jacques Foucquet are allegories of Karl XI's Danish War. The gallery was first planned to be three rooms, a large one in the centre with at the west end a War Cabinet and on the east a Peace Cabinet, and these themes can be seen in the decoration of the ceiling. The sections are divided by heavy consoles, and the Cabinets have paintings of Janus in a warlike and peaceful guise respectively, corresponding also to the king's/masculine side and the the queen's/feminine side of the palace. In the main section Vulcan is preparing weapons, then comes Karl XI as a Roman emperor, and finally Peace between Sweden and Denmark. The Virtues in high relief line each side above the cornice. The overdoors are by Claude Henrion. Through a door you can look into the **White Chamber** which has a Rococo ceiling and neo-Classical walls with garlands and festoons of leaves and flowers. The **cabinet** facing the door is by Georg Haupt and pulls out to form a servant's or guard's bed.

Against the mirrors stands a row of *display-cabinets with some of the objects from the royal collections, in porcelain, amber, silver, ivory and jewellery. Since these are among the choicest objects of the collections, all are worth examining, but it is naturally the most lavish which catch the eye. Some of these are: the **enamelled bowl** studded with cameos (No. 22), the rock-crystal **tankard** with diamonds, rubies and a sapphire (220), the ivory and silver-gilt **salt-cellar** (143) and the travelling **medicine chest** with 12 amber bottles (324). Queen Kristina's gold and enamel **watch-case** (224) is attributed to Pierre Signac, and has allegorical scenes relating to the Queen.

Sofia Magdalena's State Bedchamber was, like her husband Gustav III's, designed in the 1770s by Rehn. It has a ceiling-painting by Taraval of the four continents. The gold and white pilasters are carved with a rose pattern by Jean-Baptiste Masreliez who also made the mirror-frames. The plaster medallions above the mirrors are ascribed to L'Archevêque. The portraits of Eugène de Beauharnais and Augusta Amelia (parents of Queen Josefina) are by François Gérard.

In the **Don Quixote Room** the light has to be excluded to preserve the **Gobelins tapestries** (18C) and in fact they cannot all be exhibited all the time for their own protection. They portray scenes from Cervantes' novel, hence the name of the room. The ceiling is by Taraval, of Juno and the winds, and the overdoors by Boucher in frames by Rehn.

The **White Sea** is the name of the large hall in the corner of the north and east wings. It used to be two rooms, made into one in the mid 19C. In the north part the ceiling-painting represents the Triumph of Sweden by Dominico Francia. In the south, Francia collaborated with Taraval and Johan Pasch on the Triumph of Fredrik I. The walls of the north part were remodelled in 1845 by Axel Nyström who also built the gallery in the south. The perspective architectural features can be viewed from a certain spot to be correct to the eye. Some of Gustav V's collection of silver is on display and some Sèvres porcelain which was a gift from Louis XV to Gustav III in 1771.

The ***royal chapel** was conceived by Tessin as part of a grand design for the south wing. Together with the hall of state, the vestibule between and the exterior façade, it formed a complete entity and for once he was able to do as he wished since there were no constraints as in other parts of the palace.

From the vestibule double curved staircases lead up either side, with the plinth of the columns occupying the height of the ground floor. The chapel is on the right. Trophies decorate the curving walls and the entrance door is surmounted by a triangular pediment. The interior was modified after Tessin's death by Carl Hårleman to conform to the Rococo style which was by then in fashion. The **ceiling-paintings**, centred on the Ascension, are by Taraval and Pasch, framed by Bouchardon's sculptured surrounds. Bouchardon, with help from Adrien Masreliez, made the gilded **pulpit** with its sweeping draperies and four Evangelists. The **altar**, with its representation of Christ in Gethsemane, was started by Bouchardon, continued by L'Archevêque and finished by Sergel. The pews were made for Tessin's first chapel in the north wing.

On the left of the vestibule is the ***hall of state**. The lower part corresponds to Tessin's plans but again Carl Hårleman introduced Rococo decoration in accordance with the mode. Colossal columns frame the throne and canopy. The two large **statues** are by Byström, of Gustav II Adolf and Karl XIV Johan. The heavy cornice supports a row of windows between which are alternating female and child allegorical groups by Charles-Guillaume Cousin, Bouchardon, L'Archevêque, and others. Cousin was also responsible for the sculpture above the window over the throne.

The silver ***throne** made in Augsburg was given to Queen Kristina by Magnus de la Gardie. On the back is a crowned wreath of laurel between the figures of Justice and Prudence. The blue velvet canopy ornamented with silver and gold was designed by Rehn.

Under the hall of state the ***royal treasury** houses the Swedish crown jewels and other priceless objects. The regalia of Sweden were last used for a coronation in 1873 at the crowning of Oskar II. Until 1973 they were put on display at the state opening of Parliament, and are still brought out on the occasion of royal marriages and funerals. The items most closely linked with the monarchy are the crown, orb, sceptre and, unusually, a large gold key.

The **crown** and **orb** were made by Cornelis ver Weiden for Erik XIV's coronation in 1561. The orb represents a globe with a world map. The **sceptre** and **key** were also made for Erik in the same year. The oldest items (c 1540) are two ceremonial **swords** of Gustav Vasa, one etched with Biblical scenes and one with scenes from Roman history.

Karl XI had a gold and jewelled **anointing-horn** made for his coronation in 1607. Another unusual object is an orb specifically for a queen (1585). Karl X Gustav's crown as heir apparent and Maria Eleanora's crown of 1620, totally covered with gold and jewels, are also noteworthy. The **silver font** was made for the baptism of Karl XI in the early 18C and is still used for royal baptisms.

Crowns of 18C and 19C non-reigning members of the royal family are grouped in one case and are comparatively modest, in gold over blue material. Also on display is Oskar II's coronation cloak.

At the rear of the rooms hangs the **King Sveno Tapestry** of the late 1560s showing the legend of Sveno the son of Magog, one of the earliest tapestries made in Sweden.

The **Armoury** has an inconspicuous entrance on the lower level of the south façade. This has not only armour, but royal clothing and a collection of royal carriages. Among the armour is **Gustav Vasa's helmet** of 1540. Some superb suits of armour are shown, in particular the **ceremonial armour** for Sigismund II of Poland, grandson of Gustav Vasa. This is a complete suit for horse and rider (1550), the horse being given a pair of curly horns. A 17C set of tournament armour is in black velvet and gold and opposite is the ceremonial funeral armour of Karl X Gustav.

Examples of court dress of the 18C and early 19C occupy a large section and many **costumes** of Karl X are preserved. Clothing of the three kings who met a violent death is shown—Gustavus Adolphus who fell at Lützen in 1632, Karl XII who was killed on campaign in Norway in 1718, and Gustav III who was shot in the old Stockholm opera-house in 1792. Gustavus Adolphus' blood has been subjected to DNA analysis to establish inherited factors and illnesses, and the results are displayed here. Other items include saddles, pistols and other weapons. A multi-slide show on iron and its working is shown with English commentary at 12.00 and 14.00. The upstairs gallery has temporary exhibitions.

In the basement is the collection of **royal carriages**. This includes the 18C **Crown Prince's coach** made for Gustav III, a **royal sledge** in gilded Rococo of 1777 and the **coronation coach** drawn by eight horses, for the coronation of Adolf Fredrik and Lovisa Ulrika in 1751.

Gustav III:s Antikmuseum was started after his death as a memorial to the king. During his Italian journey he had collected nearly 200 pieces of sculpture, ranging from fine examples to restorations, reconstructions and downright forgeries. Over the years the collections became the basis for the National Museum, but the sculptures for some time have been kept in the palace. In 1992, 200 years after Gustav's death, the galleries were restored to as near their original state as possible. Three large pictures (1794), exhibited here, by the court painter Pehr Hilleström the Elder were an important basis for the restoration.

The large gallery was first meant as an orangery, the neo-Classical decoration being the work of Carl Fredrik Sundvall. Here the reclining figure of **Endymion** is probably from the Hellenistic period, while opposite is a **priestess**, probably a Roman copy, between two richly decorated candelabras from the workshop of Giovanni Battista Piranesi, made up of components from different periods. Apollo, Minerva and the nine Muses

(Roman copies) occupy the north wall. In the smaller gallery there are copies of four columns whose originals are in the National Museum. The figures on top, like most of the pieces in this gallery, come from the Piranesi workshop. In the middle is a large square Roman cinerary urn, once used as a fountain, and other exhibits include fauns, hermaphrodite figures, and a large collection of portrait busts, many of which are 18C imitations. Temporary exhibitions are also arranged.

The **Palace Museum** is approached under the central arches on Lejonbacken on the north. The vault of the cellar is from Gustav Vasa's time and has been excavated to show a wall from the 13C, a medieval well and a kitchen from Johan III's reign (16C). There are prints and plans of the castle at various epochs, as well as a diagram showing the composition of the personnel at the castle in 1585—in that year the court was composed of 1245 people, of whom just six were the royal family. On display is a collection of objects found on the castle premises, keys, pieces of carved stone, brick and tile, workmen's tools, pottery, cannon-balls and so on, as well as fragments of a boat.

Riddarholmen

From Riddarhustorget the Riddarholm bridge crosses on to Riddarholmen—the Island of Knights. The first inhabitants were the Franciscan friars who built a church and priory under the protection of King Magnus Ladulås at the end of the 13C.

The triangular open space is **Birger Jarls Torg**, and **Birger Jarl's statue** by Bengt Fogelberg (1854) stands on top of a pillar here even though Birger Jarl had nothing to do with the island which was uninhabited in his time (mid 13C).

The palace with two wings facing the bridge is the **Wrangel palace** by Nicodemus Tessin the Elder and Jean de la Vallée (finished in 1660). Field-Marshal Carl Gustav Wrangel was a powerful and wealthy statesman and soldier, governor of Pomerania, who also built Skokloster castle. When Three Crowns Castle burnt down, the court moved here from 1697 to 1754 and it was known as the King's House. After this it was occupied by various official bodies and it is now a Court of Appeal. The original decoration has been destroyed by fires, and it has undergone major renovations. The other buildings on this square—besides the church—were built in the 17C and are now government departments.

***Riddarholm church** is red brick Gothic with the addition of later brick chapels and one in Gotland sandstone (open May–Aug Mon–Sat 10.00–15.00, Sun 12.00–15.00).

This is the Swedish pantheon—almost all Swedish monarchs and their families are buried here. It was started c 1300 as the friary church and had two aisles. In the mid 15C the south aisle was added, and in the late 16C the tower.

Gustavus Adolphus added the Gustavian chapel on the south-east in 1629–34. Then his military leaders followed suit and before the century was out five of them had built chapels of their own, four on the north and one on the south, where the Vasaborg chapel was also situated. On the north-east Karl XI built the Baroque Karolinska chapel beginning in 1671. Nicodemus Tessin the Elder designed it but it was left to Carl Hårleman to complete.

The Bernadotte chapel on the south was added in 1858–60 by Fredrik Wilhelm Scholander for the Bernadotte dynasty. The 16C tower was destroyed by fire in the 19C and the cast-iron one erected to replace it lasted just over a century when it was replaced in 1970 by a non-rust replica.

As you enter there is to the left a display board giving the history of the friary, in Swedish but there is a drawing of the probable appearance of the church and friary in the 14C.

The church has no pews as no services are held and the eye goes immediately to the two great *tombs in front of the altar. These are of King Magnus Ladulås (left), who died in 1290, the founder of the friary, and King Karl Knutsson (d 1470). They are actually buried under the floor and it was not until Johan III's time that they acquired their Renaissance tombs (16C) with sculpted figures on top, by Lucas van der Werdt.

The Baroque altar was designed by Nicodemus Tessin the Elder in 1678.

Beside each chapel, plans show the names of those buried in each coffin. To the left of the tombs of Magnus Ladulås and Knut Knutsson is the **Karolinska** (Carolean) **chapel** on two levels. In the upper part is the black marble sarcophagus of Karl XII (1718) and two green marble ones, and below are the golden coffins of Karl X Gustav and Karl XI with their families, including the small ones of young children.

Opposite is the **Gustavian chapel** with Gustavus Adolphus' sarcophagus in Italian marble. Other monarchs are buried in the non-accessible crypt. Next is the **Bernadotte chapel** with Karl XIV Johan's **sarcophagus** in Swedish granite (1844). This is not Älvdalen porphyry as popularly supposed, though made at Älvdalen porphyry works. (See under Älvdalen.) His wife Desideria is buried in a sarcophagus of green Kolmården marble. Others of the dynasty are buried in brown limestone sarcophagi.

The other chapels on the south are the Vasaborg chapel with the tomb of Gustavus Adolphus' illegitimate son, and the Banér chapel for the commander-in-chief of the army. On the north side are the two Lewenhaupt chapels with Marshals of the family, and the Wachtmeister chapel with the tomb of a general. Near the entrance is the Torstensson chapel for another army leader.

The north porch is part of the original building, and the gravestones on the floor were laid later. The **coats of arms** covering the walls are those of the Knights of the Order of Seraphim. The shields are in certain groups, foreign rulers in the apse, Swedish nobility on the north wall, foreign royalty and nobility together and so on. The dates are when the order was conferred and the date of death.

The Order of Seraphim is Sweden's highest order of chivalry. The badge of the Order has gold seraphs' heads round a white eight-pointed star with I.H.S. (Jesus Hominum Salvator) and the three golden crowns of Sweden. A cross and the nails of the Crucifixion are included. When a knight dies, the church bells are tolled and his shield is hung here. Swedish nationals are no longer eligible for the order.

On coming out of the church take Wrangelska Backen down by the side of the Wrangel palace. This leads down on to **Evert Taubes Terrass**, a broad walk with a **view** down the Riddarfjärd to Västerbron (bridge) beyond which is lake Mälaren. Slightly to the right is the classic **view** of the city hall across the water on the island of Kungsholmen. To its right is the Stadshuskaj (City Hall Quay) from which many sightseeing boats depart. To the left (south) is the island of Södermalm, and on it some distance away can be seen the twin towers of Högalid church. The very large red building on the waterfront is a former brewery. Nearer, old houses climb the heights of Södermalm from the quay, and the tower of Maria Magdalena church rises among them. Moored here is the *Mälardrottning*, a large yacht previously owned by Barbara Hutton, now a hotel. On the terrace is Christian Berg's sculpture called 'Sun-boat', and further on is a figure of

Evert Taube playing and singing. At the end of the terrace in the corner between two buildings is **'Birger Jarl's Tower'**, which has nothing to do with Birger Jarl, having been constructed in the 16C as part of Gustav Vasa's fortifications.

Helgeandsholmen

The surface of the island is occupied almost entirely by the **Riksdag** (Parliament) building, while the **Museum of Medieval Stockholm** is underground. The name means Holy Ghost Island, and it is the site of the first settlement in the city.

Two buildings were planned in the late 19C, the parliament to the west and the national bank to the east. They were constructed between 1894 and 1905 by the architect Aron Johansson in neo-Baroque style. The parliament building was designed to accommodate two chambers, so when the single-chamber system was inaugurated in 1971 the total number of members was too great for either of the rooms previously used. Parliament moved to Kulturhuset on Sergels torg until 1983 when the remodelled building was ready.

The solution was to take over the almost hemispherical bank and raise it by adding two storeys with a mainly glass façade, making this the new chamber. The old Parliament building is used for committees, ministers, library and other services. Corridors connecting the two have been constructed under cover of the monumental archways.

The Swedish Parliament has 349 members in 28 constituencies, and members sit in the Chamber grouped by constituencies, not by parties. All proposals to Parliament are discussed and prepared beforehand by 16 committees of 17 members each, reflecting the comparative strength of the parties in Parliament. The Speaker is elected by the members and has wide powers—it is even possible for him to act as regent in certain circumstances. There are elections every three years and voting age is 18. The electoral system used is proportional representation.

From 1932 to 1991 with few breaks the Social Democrats were in power, supported traditionally by the Party of the Left (formerly the Communist Party). In 1991 the conservative elements, led by the Moderates, took over. But their programme of cuts in the welfare services and greater encouragement to private enterprise did not flourish in the economic climate of the 90's, and in 1994 the Social Democrats under Ingvar Carlsson again took the lead.

The east façade facing Strömparterren is ornamented with sculpture, 'Mother Svea' (Sweden) and the four estates. The entrance for tourists is on the north, to the right of the archway. (Free guided tours in English late June to early Sept 12.30 and 15.00.)

From the curved glass-fronted members' lobby outside the chamber in the eastern section there is a view of Riddarfjärden and the City Hall, the Central bridge, the Vasa bridge and the tiny island of Strömsborg.

The **chamber** itself is designed to emphasise national characteristics. Pale Swedish birchwood is used for the panelling and semi-circular rows of seats, and the large woven wall-hanging behind the platform is a stylised Swedish landscape in pale blue-grey tones. Each desk is equipped with push-button voting in case a stand-up vote leaves an issue in doubt. There is an upper gallery for spectators who may enter to listen to the debates.

Downstairs the old bank hall has kept much of its character since the bank counters have been replaced by a post office, travel agency and other services for members. Paintings attached to the ceiling represent Northern Sweden (mining) and Southern Sweden (agriculture).

In the western section the two former chambers are now used by the two largest parties. The old second chamber has wall-paintings by Axel Törneman. They are linked by a vaulted corridor now used as a reception area. In its centre is a lantern ringed by coats of arms of the Swedish counties.

The **entrance hall** is in pale green and white, top-lit. Two graceful staircases lead up to the surrounding gallery, consisting of Carrara marble Ionic columns and Corinthian pilasters on stucco walls. The complex is connected by a glass corridor under the bridge (Stallbron) to the south with the members' building in Gamla stan. This, which used to be the Chancellery (1936), has a narrow portico at right angles to the canal and contains offices and sleeping accommodation for members, as well as a chapel and swimming-pool.

With the renovation of the parliament building it was planned to make an underground car park for members. However, the excavations turned up such valuable archaeological evidence that **Medeltidsmuseet**, the Museum of Medieval Stockholm, was constructed underground to incorporate as much as possible of the findings. The entrance to the museum (open June–Aug Tue–Thurs 11.00–19.00, Fri–Sun 11.00–17.00, Sept–May Tue–Sun 11.00–17.00, Wed to 19.00) is through a vault under the road in front of the parliament. Steps lead down to Strömparterren, a small semi-circular park occupying the opposite end of the island from the similarly-shaped west part. There is one of Carl Milles' most celebrated statues, the **'Sun-singer'**, in the park.

On coming through the vault of the museum entrance you are met by an illuminated enlargement of the **Parhelion picture** from the cathedral, showing Stockholm in 1525 in considerable detail. The first section is on medieval religious life and leads into the museum proper. Ahead is a **boat**, found on this island. Behind it runs a length of the **town wall** of c 1530. To the left is a section on **building methods** and in the next corner is an excavated passage from the 18C. A series of reconstructed wooden buildings shows the **medieval harbour**, complete with sound-effects, and in the centre is the **'Big House'**. It is made of medieval bricks from the island and shows crafts on the ground floor and a town-council chamber above. To the right of this is a wall of the 14C which used to surround the churchyard, beside which is a display on the scientists' work on the period, with geology, dendrochronology, and osteological work. Behind this exhibit is a 22m long clinker-built **warship** of c 1520 which was salvaged in 1930, with three cannons. Along the rear wall are sections on shipbuilding, defence and crime and punishment. Turning back towards the entrance you will see a representation of the runestone in the old town and on the walls a pictorial history from Birger Jarl to Gustav Vasa. Films and slide-shows are given, but not in English at the time of writing.

Blasieholmen and Skeppsholmen

Blasieholmen and Skeppsholmen are noteworthy for their museums. **Blasieholmen** is no longer an island in spite of the name 'holmen', simply a peninsula dividing Strömkajen from Nybroplan. It was the original Skeppsholmen (Ship Island) because the shipyards were here—the *Vasa* was built here. When the shipyards moved on to the next island to the south, the name went too. The neck of the peninsula is crossed by Stallgatan, off which is Blasieholmstorg, a quiet square with a large bronze horse at each end. Facing on to Nybrokajen is the Musical Academy designed by Johan Fredrik Åbom in 1878.

The prestigious ***National Museum** stands on the waterfront facing the royal palace (open Tue–Sun 10.00–17.00, Sept–June also Tue to 21.00.

Slide-show introduction in English mid-June to end Aug 14.30, 15.30. Lecture-tours in English on different themes in summer—varying times).

The National Museum contains much that was collected by Carl Gustav Tessin, the third of that illustrious family, who was Swedish ambassador in Paris. From 1739 to 1742 he shrewdly garnered paintings, sculpture and drawings, including unique architectural designs of the 17C and 18C, and graphic works, as well as French contemporary art. When he came upon hard times, he sold them to the king and queen. To these were added Adolf Fredrik and Lovisa Ulrika's private collections, and later their son Gustav III's Greek and Roman statuary which he brought back from his Italian journey. After his death the whole was made available to the public in the Royal Museum which opened in the palace in 1794. In 1885 Karl XV's collection was added. The present building was opened in 1866 and now displays European fine and applied arts from late medieval times to the end of the 19C. (20C art is in the Museum of Modern Art, Gustav III's antiquities and Far Eastern art have their own museums and there is a separate Museum of Mediterranean and Near Eastern Antiquities.)

The architect of the Neues Museum in Berlin, Friedrich August Stüler, designed the limestone façade and its reliefs with allegories of art in neo-Renaissance style, and Fredrik Wilhelm Scholander, designer of several rooms in the royal palace, planned the interior.

In the small garden to the left of the museum are some **sculptures**—Johan Peter Molin's 'Wrestlers', John Börjeson's 'Boy with a Tortoise' and Theodor Lundberg's 'Fosterbrothers'.

The entrance-hall is decorated with **wall-paintings** by Carl Larsson, depicting moments in Swedish art history. The subjects are: Ehrenstrahl painting Karl XI, Nicodemus Tessin and Carl Hårleman, the architects of the royal palace, Taraval and the Drawing Academy, Boucher's Triumph of Venus presented to Lovisa Ulrika, Gustav III receiving antiques and Sergel working on Cupid and Psyche. The painting on the upper east wall of Gustav Vasa entering Stockholm is also by Carl Larsson.

Two rooms on the ground floor are devoted to temporary exhibitions and there is a shop, restaurant and auditorium.

The **Department of Drawings and Graphic Art** does not have works on show but anyone can ask to see any work in the collections. (Go through Room 101 on the left of the entrance-hall and ring at the glass door at the end.) The range of drawings include works by Raphael, Rubens, Dürer, Van Dyck, Watteau and Boucher, and the Swedish artists Sergel, Hill and Josephson. Architectural drawing and interior designs include some by Le Brun, Jean de la Vallée, the Tessins, Hårleman and Rehn. The graphic art collection specialises in European 17C and 18C works and Swedish art to the present day, and includes Rembrandt and Anders Zorn.

The first floor contains the **Department of Applied Arts**. Here there are items from the 16C to the present day. Collections of pottery and porcelain include the **'Kristina' majolica service** and the 14C **Alhambra vase**, with Meissen, Delft, Rörstrand and Marieberg exhibits. There are good 16C **tapestries**, and the **Bielke bed** is a striking creation in silk and velvet. Swedish **glass** and **silver** are well represented, as well as furniture and some 20C design.

The * **Fine Art Department** is on the top floor. (On the way up the numbers on the risers of the stairs are seat numbers for the popular summer Tuesday evening concerts by the museum's own chamber orchestra.) On the landing are four large paintings, two by Goya, *Poetry and Poets*, and *Spain, Time and History*, and Gustaf Cederström's *Bringing Home the Body of Karl XII* and Nils Forsberg's *Death of a Hero*.

At the top of the stairs to the right in **Room 306** are paintings by artists of **15C and 16C Europe** including **El Greco** and **Lucas Cranach**. In the small rooms bordering Room 306 is an excellent collection of **icons** and other religious art. Artists from Flanders and southern Europe are in **Room 307**, including Rubens. In **Room 308** is 17C Dutch art where pride of place is given to Rembrandt's very large **Oath of the Batavians**. Here there are also bronzes by Adriaen de Vries. Off Room 308 there is Spanish and Italian religious art of the 15C and 16C, including Murillo's *Return of the Holy Family from Egypt*. In **Room 317** are early **18C French** paintings with Watteau, Chardin and Boucher. In the small rooms in the corner off **Room 318** is an important collection of French and English **miniatures**. Room 318 itself has **Swedish 18C** art and here Roslin's *Lady in a Veil* (1763) is perhaps the most attractive piece, certainly one of the best-known paintings in Sweden and now a symbol for the museum. Per Krafft is represented, and Carl Gustav Pilo's painting of the *Coronation of Gustav III* in the cathedral is also here.

In the small parallel rooms are works by Elias Martin and David Klöcker Ehrenstrahl. In the large **Room 327** are gathered works from *18C Europe including Canaletto, Gainsborough, Reynolds, and Sergel's *Cupid and Psyche* sculpture. *19C French art is in **Room 333** with Cézanne, Gauguin, Sisley, Courbet, Corot, Millet and Delacroix. Renoir's *La Grenouillère* is particularly notable. **Room 334** contains **19C Swedish art**, with Anders Zorn, Prince Eugen, Carl Larsson, Bruno Liljefors and Carl Wilhelmson. **Room 335** shows Swedish art at the turn of the century and includes Ernst Josephson and Carl Fredrik Hill.

Skeppsholm bridge just after the museum leads on to Skeppsholmen. The gabled building high on a bluff ahead is **Admiralty House**, remodelled by Fredrik Blom in the 1840s, an example of the medievalism prevalent at the time. To the right is moored the *af Chapman*, the best-known and most popular youth hostel in Sweden.

The *af Chapman* began life in the Whitehaven (Cumbria, England) shipyards. A fully-rigged three-masted sailing-ship, she was bought by a Dublin company and christened *Dunboyne*. The letters of this name are still visible under the paint at the bow. Her first voyage was in 1887, and she subsequently travelled the world. After a period under the name G.D. Kennedy, in 1923 she was renamed *af Chapman* after a Swedish admiral and after the Second World War took up her place at Skeppsholmen as a youth hostel.

On the left, immediately after the bridge from Blasieholmen, a path climbs through the trees up to the long low *Östasiatiska Museet (Museum of Far Eastern Antiquities), open Tue 11.00–21.00, Wed–Sun 11.00–17.00). The building was designed by Nicodemus Tessin the Younger in 1700 for military use. Most of the material is Chinese as Swedish archaeologists have been particularly active in China. The museum also contains Gustav VI Adolf's collection of jade, bronze, porcelain, ivory and rhino horn.

Chinese Stone Age pottery starts on the ground floor. On the first floor is a comprehensive collection of **Chinese ceramics** from the 7C to 1644, the end of the Ming period. Chronologically the exhibits start from the back of the room with Tang tomb figures. There is a booklet in English available for consultation. Across the landing are **Chinese applied art**, and **Korean** and **Japanese art**, including a magnificent set of 17C-style Samurai armour, a gift from the Crown Prince of Japan in the 1920s.

On the second floor **Chinese Bronze Age** art is shown and across the landing are **Chinese** and **Indian sculpture**, and **Chinese paintings** on paper and silk from the 11C. On the third floor there is **Chinese ceramics** from 1644 to 1912 (Ch'ing period), including porcelain ordered in Sweden and brought back by the East India Company in the 18C.

On leaving the museum you will see Karl Johan's church to your left, an octagonal building with a cupola, of 1824–42, by Fredrik Blom. The circular interior is surrounded by Ionic columns and the altar painting is by Johan Gustav Sandberg (1840).

Skirt the church and continue in the same direction along the hill above the road and in a minute or two you come to the entrance of *Moderna **Museet** (Modern Art, open Tue–Fri 11.00–21.00, Sat, Sun 11.00–17.00. Shop, restaurant.) The old entrance-hall used to be a naval drill hall, designed by Fredrik Blom, finished in 1834, but the whole is now being rebuilt to an architecturally interesting modern design, and until it is finished the works can be seen at Birger Jarlsgatan 57, near Eriksbergsplan. The museum possesses works by almost every 20C artist of note—Picasso, Braque, Utrillo, Kandinsky, Max Ernst, de Chirico, Giacometti, Dali, Mondrian, Duchamp-Villon, Pollock, Matisse, Chagall, Magritte, Miró, Brancusi, Léger, Warhol, Rauschenberg and others. There will also of course be temporary exhibitions. At the time of writing it is not clear whether the museum of photography will continue in a gallery of this building with several important exhibitions every year, drawing on its comprehensive archives.

On coming out of the museum of modern art, descend to Svensksundsvägen and almost opposite you will find the **Arkitektur-museum** in an 1870s house designed by Victor Ringheim (open Wed–Sun 11.00–17.00, Tue 11.00–21.00. Drawing and Picture Archives Tue–Fri 09.00–12.00). The museum concentrates on architecture of the last 100 years. The **Drawing Archives** contain work by Swedish architects, including Ragnar Östberg, Gunnar Asplund and Ivar Tengbom. The **Picture Archives** have photos and slides of 20C architecture. Between six and ten exhibitions are arranged every year, with models, plans and photographs, often on suitable anniversaries, or on specific themes, areas or periods.

Continue on Svensksundsvägen which now bears left. The buildings here, as all over the island, bear a military stamp—most of them were constructed for the navy, a natural development from the old shipyards. At the crossroads turn right to the shore. Ahead, across the Kastellholm bridge, is the rocky island of Kastellholmen, crowned with a 19C pseudo-fortress. From its base there is a good view in nearly all directions. This building also belongs to the navy and the Swedish flag is hoisted on top every morning at 08.00, to show Sweden is at peace. Considerable heat was generated when economies stopped the practice. A group of seamen landed and raised the flag themselves in protest, since when the ceremony has been resumed.

B. Inner Stockholm

Djurgården

The name means Deer Park, and **Djurgården** was once part of a much larger royal hunting enclosure. Now it is devoted to amusement and culture, with Skansen, the *Vasa*, Nordic and Biology museums, Waldemar-sudde, Liljevalchs and Thiel galleries, and Rosendal palace.

The classic way of arriving on Djurgården is by boat, and in the summer there are almost non-stop ferries from the south end of Skeppsbron, and Nybrokajen (May to mid-August). You can drive there but the island is closed to cars at the weekends. Alternatively, there are buses, plus the tourist trams Nos 7 and 7E called Djurgårdslinie. The nearest underground station is Karlaplan, about a kilometre walk to the Nordic Museum and the Vasa Museum, a few minutes longer to the Hazelius entrance to Skansen.

From the ferry, the way up to the main road passes on the right Gröna Lund, an amusement park. The area to the south (right) was inhabited in the 18C by shipyard workers and a few buildings from the 18C and 19C remain. To the left a short distance along is **Aquaria**, a museum dealing with water. This has a rain-forest hall with light and sound effects, an ocean aquarium and living coral reef, both glass-sided for close study, and a section on Swedish wetlands.

As you reach the main road, a right turn leads to the principal entrance to Skansen, and further on Waldemarsudde, while to the left are the *Vasa*, the Nordic and the Biology museums. Taking the left turn first, the road passes **Liljevalchs Art Gallery** on the left. This arranges various temporary exhibitions and an influential spring show. The building, by Carl Bergsten 1913–16, is an interesting example of architecture of the time.

After a few minutes you come to a roundabout where there are bus-stops, the Hazelius entrance to Skansen and **Biologiska Museet**. The museum (open summer 10.00–16.00, winter 10.00–15.00) was built in 1913 to recall a medieval stave church or Viking hall, completely clad in wood shingles. The carved door is particularly striking. Inside, the walls of the circular hall were painted by the artist **Bruno Liljefors** to portray the Swedish landscape, merging from cliff to sea, then to marsh and forest. Against this are many hundreds of stuffed birds and animals shown in their natural habitat, viewed from an ingenious double curved staircase.

The main road continues north and on the left is a churchyard where are buried many seafarers, including the remains found in the *Vasa*. In a few more minutes the grandiose pile of *Nordiska Museet appears on the left. The Nordic Museum (open Mon–Fri 10.00–16.00, Sat, Sun 11.00–16.00, closed Mon Sept–May) was opened in 1907. It was designed by Isak Clason to house the collection begun by Artur Hazelius. The architecture reflects the still prevailing love of a plethora of turrets and gables, combined with the new rejection of manufactured materials such as stucco and rendering, and a preference for genuine brick or stone. The entrance doorway was sculpted by Carl Eldh.

The museum takes as its brief the depiction of life in Sweden from the Reformation to modern times. In the central hall a vast **oak figure** by Carl Milles represents Gustav Vasa, the Reformation and Renaissance king. The exhibitions surround the central open hall in three galleries, and continue in the basement. There are stairs each side of the entrance and in each corner of the building, and two lifts in the central part—this description starts at the top.

On the **top floor** there is a section on **Swedish homes** through the ages (leaflet in English available). A reconstruction of a 19C wooden cottage illustrates the farmer's home. Other displays show a manor house and a wealthy brewer's house. Continuing clockwise round the galleries, you come to temporary exhibits, and in the curved section at the rear there are some cases with small household items, and then a survey of periods of **Swedish furniture**, including carved and painted pieces.

On the next floor down (**first floor**) are household **textiles** for floor, wall, bed and table, arranged in cases labelled with dates in Swedish. (Note that '1800-talet' means 19C etc.) Parallel to this exhibit is a narrow gallery with toys and dolls' houses. Still continuing clockwise, the display called the **Rise of Modern Sweden** 1870–1980 occupies the short side of the museum, leading into **Food and Drink**, with table-settings and china. (The dim lighting can be augmented by finding the light switches on the fronts of the cabinets.)

The next section has temporary shows and on the next short side is **Scandinavian Folk Art**, which includes work from other Nordic countries as well as Swedish painted wall-hangings. Then comes the **Costume Gallery**, where there are also old pattern books and fashion magazines.

Down in the **entrance hall** the right-hand side has temporary exhibitions, a book shop which doubles as an information desk, and the restaurant.

The left-hand side seems at first sight to be completely occupied by a colossal drum set on its edge. This is the 'videograph' and inside old films are shown. Surrounding this, starting on the left is a panoramic history of Sweden from 1870 to 1980. Called *Modell Sverige, it traces the country's development into an industrialised and technological society. Scenes and displays are set up in the alcoves while a mass of further information is provided on pull-out trays in different languages in the chests in front. The themes range from emigration and consumerism, to working conditions and packaging, in a chronological sequence.

In the **basement** there is a substantial section on *Sami or Lapp culture. There are reconstructions of a furnished tent, and storage hut on legs, with displays on reindeer, clothing and equipment. There is a series of small scenes showing living quarters in different seasons and in different types of terrain. These are (left to right): 1. Coastal Sami—turf hut, part for animals, 2, 3 and 6. Fell Sami—summer, spring and autumn, and winter, 4. Inland Sami—cottages, 5. Forest Sami—summer huts, 7. Finland—winter cottages. Also in the basement are **folk costumes**. The curved showcase shows the variation in folk costume throughout Sweden, from south to north (right to left). Here also are costumes for various occasions and activities. Generally such costumes were not worn for work after the mid 19C and they became the subject of study by historians and artists. Towards the end of the 19C the upper and middle classes 'discovered' folk costume and it became fashionable to own a set.

The *Vasa Museum is behind the Nordic Museum to the right (open June to Aug 09.30–19.00, Sept–May 10.00–17.00. All information in English. Guided tours in English. Film every hour. Shop, restaurant). The name is spelt either Wasa or Vasa. The ship was christened *Wasa* but nowadays all old words with 'w' are spelt with 'v', and the museum has officially chosen 'v'.

In 1625 Gustavus Adolphus, embroiled in the Thirty Years War, ordered a new warship for Sweden. The shipyard was on Blasieholmen, the shipwright in charge was Henrik Hybertsson from Holland. She was 68m long including the bowsprit, 11.3m broad and 52m from keel to masthead, lavishly carved and with gilded ornamentation. Her fire power consisted of 64 cannons, her sail area was $1200m^2$. She was designed to carry 100 seamen, 20 gunners and 300 soldiers. Her maiden voyage on 10 August 1628 was also her last. Less than 2km from her yard she keeled over and sank near Beckholmen (off Djurgården), because of lack of stability. Attempts were made to salvage her contents with primitive diving-bells in the 17C and some cannons were recovered.

In 1956 Anders Franzén traced the wreck in 33m of water. An immense rescue operation began. The bolts holding her together had all rusted away and had to be replaced. All organic material had to be stored in water until treatment against shrinkage and rotting could begin. Six of her ten sails were retrieved and treated. The remains of a man with well-preserved clothing were also found. There were about 24,000 separate finds, all of which had to be sorted and classified, then fitted together. All but 10 per cent of the wood was oak, the rest pine and lime. The oak and pine resisted the rotting process better than the soft lime which is one reason why so much of the fabric remained. The other important factor was that the termite *Teredo navalis*, which normally thrives on wood in other seas, does not like the lack of salt in the Baltic.

More than 700 pieces of carved wood were dredged up, of different sizes, importance and degree of deterioration, according to their depth in the mud, and whether they were of the more resistant oak and pine or the softer lime. After exhaustive research, experimentation and lengthy preservative procedures, the sculpture was gradually reconstructed. The stern decoration is awe-inspiring. Stylistically, its ancestors are north German and Dutch late Renaissance sculpture, of the late 16C and early 17C, which arrived in Stockholm in the second quarter of the 17C. Some of the works can be ascribed to named artists working in Stockholm at the time.

The main subjects of the carvings are Roman history, Greek mythology, the Bible, flora, fauna and grotesque figures. Traces of paint and gilt prove that this would all have been a riot of colour, its purpose to emphasise to friend and foe alike the might, the wealth and the glory of the Swedish nation.

A temporary museum was provided until in 1990 a specially-designed home for the reconstructed *Vasa* was opened here on Djurgården, close to where she foundered.

On the roof of the museum are three masts showing the height the *Vasa's* masts would have been. The mechanism of the fountain outside is part of the equipment used in salvage. The museum goes down three floors below ground level, so you enter on **Level 4**. The ship, set on the lowest level, towers through seven floors and the viewing and exhibition galleries encircle her. The displays are constantly updated, and there are also temporary exhibitions, so what follows may vary somewhat. There will soon also be displays on naval warfare, the Stockholm shipyard, and the symbolism of the ship's carvings.

On the entrance level the information desk is just inside the door to the right. Further along is a rigged model of the *Vasa*, to one-tenth scale. Displays on this floor concentrate on the **techniques** and **equipment** of the salvage operation.

The next floor up up (**Level 5**) shows **life on board**, food, coins, clothing, punishment, tools, chests, personal articles, dishes and pots, bronze and pewter objects.

At the time of writing the top two levels are viewing galleries only, and it is from here that the superbly decorated 20m high stern can be closely examined (see below).

Down on **Level 3** are sections on life in Sweden in 1628, such as the all-important mining industry, and the influence of the church.

On **Level 2** are computers where you can use the screen to visit various parts of the ship, or you can try to see what difference it would have made to her fate to vary the ballast or sails for example. Outside are moored an icebreaker, **S:t Erik**, of 1915, and the lightship *Finngrundet* (1903) which can also be visited.

The core of the museum, however, literally and figuratively, is the ***ship** itself, and thanks to the design of the building the visitor can view it from all angles and all levels. It is naturally the ***carving** on the stern which draws all eyes. At the top are two griffons holding a crown over a figure representing Gustavus Adolphus. Below that are two lions holding the Vasa dynasty coat of arms, the Vasa sheaf of corn, the three crowns and lions. Next come two cherubs holding the Vasa sheaf. The galleries are supported by Roman warriors. As the galleries continue round the sides they are decorated with warriors, mermaids, tritons and carved cupolas. Although the stern is the most richly embellished, the rest of the ship deserves close examination also. Inside, too, many details were found, lintels, balustrades and panelling profusely carved.

•**Skansen** has three entrances, the Hazelius gate, the main entrance and Sollidsporten. From the museums the Hazelius gate is the nearest (beside the Biology Museum) and you can take the funicular to the top of the hill (extra fee payable). From the ferry the main entrance is the nearest, and there is a free escalator. Sollidsporten is further along to the east. There are also two gates which are exits only. (Open summer 09.00–22.00, buildings open 11.00–17.00, winter 09.00–17.00, (not all) buildings 11.00–15.00. Guided tours in English from 12.00. Many concerts and festivals. Cafés, restaurants, shops.)

Skansen, opened in 1891 as one of the world's first open-air museums was founded by Artur Hazelius who also started the Nordic Museum. He began the process of moving homes, farms, windmills, a school and a church to an area of hilly parkland which now covers 33ha. Today there are about 150 buildings, a zoo and an aquarium.

Over the years the entertainment side has increased. Stockholmers tend to gather here for the numerous festivals of the Swedish year from the Christmas market, New Year and the welcoming of spring to midsummer's day and Sweden's national day. Many concerts, of all types of music, folk dancing and fireworks are organised, and it is a popular place to eat in the evenings. (Book ahead.) In the houses and farmsteads in the summer people in authentic costume demonstrate crafts such as baking traditional food, glass-blowing or pottery.

The territory is arranged with some reference to geography, with the Skåne farm in the south, the elks, bears and the Sami encampment in the north and the Mora farmhouse north of centre.

Inside the main entrance, on the left before the escalator to the upper level, is the **Tobacco Museum**. This is housed in a local inn of c 1820, with a café on the ground floor. The museum (summer 11.00–17.00, winter 11.00–15.00) has displays on all floors of the building showing the history of tobacco, an old tobacco shop, pipes, cigars, cigarettes and snuff, a reproduction of a cigar-maker's home and a display of lighters and oddities.

At the top of the escalator from the main entrance the visitor arrives in the **Town Quarter**, with a grocer, bookbinder, combmaker, bakery, pottery, glassworks, pharmacy and savings bank. The 'industrial area' next to it includes a joinery and engineering works.

To the right of this complex is a plateau with a restaurant commanding a wide view over the surroundings. Near the two Öland windmills to the east is a reproduction of the maze from Gotland, 'Trojeborg'. Take the path between the windmills and the maze and then turn right and you will find **Skogaholm manor**, a typical 17C house with 18C furnishings. Costumed chamber music concerts are given in the courtyard.

To the north (rear) of the manor is the market-place, lined with stalls. To the left is the post office and to its right the **Älvros peasant farm** of 17C north Swedish log-cabin construction, with log roof lined with birch-bark as waterproofing.

Take the road north to the right of the farm, passing the Bagarstuga, a cabin specially for baking flat crispbread. The road curves left to the **bell-tower** from Håsjö (1779), near the top of the funicular from the Hazelius gate. Nearby is **Skogens hus** (Forest House) with an exhibition on forestry.

North of here are two particularly handsome farms—from **Delsbo** (early 19C) and from **Mora**. The Mora farmstead is the oldest in Skansen, dating from the 16C, in north Swedish log-cabin style, with birch-bark waterproofing.

North again is the **Fäbod**, a cluster of huts used during summer pasturage where cheese and butter were made. Then comes the **Sami** (Lapp) **encampment**, dwelling and storage huts, with the zoo of Nordic and other animals ranged along the north perimeter. These include reindeer (reached by a wooden footway to the left before the Sami encampment), elks, wolves, bisons, wild boars, otters, seals, deer, lynxes and bears. The spring litter of baby bears annually causes an influx of captivated visitors.

Returning by the east side, you pass **Bredablick**, a 19C outlook tower from which the layout of Skansen and the view of Stockholm can be appreciated

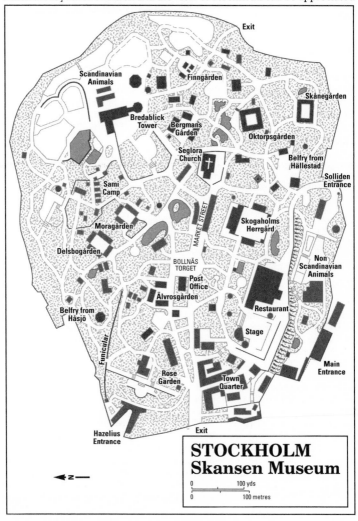

STOCKHOLM
Skansen Museum

(entrance fee). South of Bredablick are the **Kyrkhultstuga** from south Sweden, a low dwelling sandwiched between two taller storehouses, and **Bergmansgården**, a 17C mine-owner's home with a turf roof. Almost in line with these is **Finngården**, a settlement of Finns in Värmland, very similar to the Sami encampment. Near Finngården is an **exit** called Bellmansroporten.

Near the centre of Skansen is **Seglora church**, very popular for weddings. It is a typical Västergötland church built in 1730 of pine, and the tower and sacristy were added in 1780. The Baroque pulpit is from 1700, the altar from 1780. The painted ceiling is 18C.

On the way back to the entrance the main buildings are **Oktorpsgården**, an 18C peasant farm, and **Skånegården**, brought to replace a burnt-out farm in 1972, with half-timbering and thatching. It was last inhabited in 1920 and the interior, outhouses, tools and equipment, portray this period.

The great **bell-tower** from Hällestad, Sweden's tallest at 42m, stands near the Sollidsporten entrance.

Working your way back to the main entrance along the lower level you pass the monkey house and the aquarium, with Cuban crocodiles, bushbabies, loris, tarsiers, pygmy kangaroos, fish, snakes and insects.

It is c 1.5km from the main entrance of Skansen to **Waldemarsudde**. The 47 bus, however, covers c 1km of that. Follow the shore to Waldemarsudde (open June–Aug Tue–Sun 11.00–17.00, Tue and Thurs also 19.00–21.00, Sept–May (not Dec) Tue–Sun 11.00–16.00).

Prince Eugen (1865–47) was the youngest son of Oskar II and a well-regarded painter as well as a collector. In 1903–05 the architect Fredrik Boberg built a home for him here on the low cliff on the south-west point of Djurgården. In 1913 the prince had a gallery added for his large collection of mainly Swedish contemporary artists, and the building was extended in 1945. The contents of the house and gallery constitute an all-embracing survey of Swedish art from 1870 to 1940.

In the house the art works are set in the environment of the Prince's own home where he lived for over 40 years and gathered the best of living Swedish artists around him. His period furniture and the superb flower-arrangements, still continued as in his time, are the background for art packed closely on walls and all horizontal surfaces. The garden too is set with sculpture.

There was already a house here—to the right of the main building—known as Gamla huset, the Old House, built in c 1785 by a businessman who also built the windmill for producing linseed oil. Prince Eugen lived there before his own home was ready.

Entrance is directly into the gallery. This has four rooms of paintings, and one with statues by Per Hasselberg. The end room contains paintings by the Prince himself and the rest have works by his contemporaries including Ernst Josephson, Carl Fredrik Hill and Richard Bergh.

The house is reached by a long underground passage from the gallery. As you emerge you can visit the Prince's kitchen, now a café.

The rooms are grouped round the hall. All are crowded with works of art and almost every object is worth at least a glance. Artists to look out for are Bruno Liljefors, Nils Kreuger, Karl Nordström, Eugene Jansson, Ernst Josephson, Carl Fredrik Hill, Karl Isakson, Carl Milles, Carl Eldh, Anders Zorn, Richard Bergh, Sven Erixson, Otte Sköld and Bror Hjorth.

The **Dining Room** was decorated by the architect in late-Gustavian style (neo-Classical) in blue, white and gold, with rounded corners. The antique furniture includes Empire chairs and two English sideboards. The firescreen was painted by Elias Martin in a frame by Jean-Baptiste Masreliez. Two well-known paintings by the Prince hang here, *The Cloud* and *A Last Ray of Sun*.

Turf-roofed South Swedish farmhouse in Skansen open-air museum

To continue clockwise, the **Salon**, in white and pale-yellow, contains 18C furniture and is the setting for Ernst Josephson's *Strömkarlen* painting, and Anders Zorn's portrait of Queen Sofia, the Prince's mother. The overdoors are in grisaille by Georg Pauli.

The **Flower Room** is as its name implies full of (real) flowers. It has a view over Stockholm across the water and contains 18C furniture, and Milles' bronze Europa and the Bull. The library has leather furniture, and many small sculptures and etchings by Anders Zorn. The Prince's **study** has a collection of French paintings, including Poussin, Corot and Delacroix. The top two floors are used for temporary exhibitions.

Outside, the **gardens** laid out on a terrace above the water display sculpture, including a copy of Rodin's *Thinker* and works by Per Hasselberg, Carl Milles and Carl Eldh. To the right of the house and gallery, Gamla huset (The Old House) shows items from the prince's childhood and early life, and early paintings, with furniture belonging to the house and a collection of flintware. On the west side is the Prince's tomb.

On the other side of the main house, beyond the terrace, is the large linseed oil mill of 1784, said to be the only one in Sweden (open in summer).

Rosendal Palace is on the north side of Djurgården (guided tours only, on the hour June–Aug Tue–Sun 12.00–15.00, Sept weekends 13.00–15.00. Swedish only, but guides can usually speak English and give assistance). There is no public transport and it is c 2km from Djurgårds bridge. (Remember the island is closed to cars at the weekend.) Take Rosendalsvägen from the roundabout at the Hazelius entrance to Skansen. (Keep on Rosendalsvägen in spite of turnings and forks. The palace is partly screened by trees opposite the end of the road called Rosendalsterrassen.) Alternatively if you were in Skansen you could leave by the Bellmansro exit (but no re-entry here), turn left and then right past the car park, taking the winding Rosendalsterrassen to come out opposite the palace—c 0.5km, thus leaving only the return walk to the bridge to do.

In 1810, a year after the accession of Karl XIII, Jean Baptiste Bernadotte, Marshal of France, was chosen to be Heir Apparent and Crown Prince of Sweden. He eventually succeeded to the throne as Karl XIV Johan in 1818. He naturally brought with him his French tastes, and Rosendal is the essence of French Empire style translated to Sweden.

The architect Fredrik Blom had perfected a type of 'movable' house of wooden sections which could be prefabricated, and Rosendal is built in this manner with the walls faced with brick and rendered. Karl XIV Johan in his new country wanted to surround himself with the current style he had left behind. So Empire with all its Classical allusions, mahogany furnishings, and gilded bronze, its strong colours, pomp and grandeur took root in Sweden and became 'Karl Johan style', later spreading even to the middle classes in a modified form.

The plan is a shallow E, with the roofs of the two end sections at right angles to the façade to give triangular pediments which contain laurel wreaths. In the centre a wrought-iron balcony rests on columns of Kolmården marble.

Most of the furniture is typical Karl Johan style in mahogany, the tiled stoves are also Empire with gold decoration, and porphyry objects abound, as the King owned the porphyry works in Älvdalen. Another recurrent theme is that of bronze, either French or Swedish, in the shape of clocks and light-fittings of various kinds with Classical themes or forms. Embroidered firescreens are another feature, and there are many portraits, of the King and members of his family. Notice also the opulent chandeliers and the French carpets.

The large room in the left-hand wing is the **Blue Salon** and contains good examples of the style, with 1830s chandeliers, and stoves. Fredric Westin's painting of Hebe and the eagle hangs on one wall. The **Dining Room**, built on to the side of the building, is decorated to resemble a Roman commander's tent, with draped ceiling. The table is laid to represent authentic dining splendour.

The large **Yellow Salon** is central in the palace, behind the entrance hall, with décor by Per Emanuel Limnell. It has overdoors in grisaille and the doors themselves are delicately ornamented.

The two following rooms contain furniture from the King's combined bedroom and study in the Stockholm royal palace, with his desk, small personal belongings, pictures and bookcases.

The mahogany staircase leads up to a narrow landing crowded with the King's collection of landscape paintings. To the left is the **Red Salon** (over the Blue Salon). Pleated red silk covers the walls and these are surmounted by a painted frieze in grisaille. This represents the early history of Sweden according to myth with Odin's arrival in Sweden, the founding of Sigtuna and so on, painted by Hjalmar Mörner c 1829. Where the handclasp of peace between two former enemies is shown, directly below is Olof Södermark's portrait of the king, regarded as having brought peace between Sweden and Russia. The furniture is of mahogany, with red upholstery and gold carved beading.

The **Orange Room**, with a portrait of Crown Princess Josefina by Fredric Westin, is between the Red Salon and the Lantern. The ***Lantern** is central, above the Yellow Salon and is one of the foremost examples in Sweden of French Empire style, in gold, deep rose and white. The walls are divided by Corinthian pilasters, with mirrors and paintings between them. The wall paintings are from the tale of Cupid and Psyche, and in the cupola Limnell painted the four seasons. The round porcelain and bronze table was a gift from Louis-Philippe of France. There is a French ***chandelier** with swans.

On the other side of the lantern are the **Blue Anteroom** with a portrait of

Queen Desideria by Olof Södermark, the Blue and Yellow Room and the Library.

The 2.5m high **Rosendal Vase** in the gardens is popularly supposed to be of porphyry. Though made at the Älvdalen porphyry works, it is of granite—it would not be possible to carve a porphyry object of this size and shape.

Also on Djurgården almost on the furthest east point several kilometres from Skansen is the Thiel art gallery, but if you do not have a car it is very much more easily reached by bus from the Kaknäs Tower (see Ladugårdsgärdet route).

Norrmalm

This route has the sights of more general interest towards the beginning and the end, so that at any point you can abbreviate the walk by crossing from west to east and continuing.

Norrmalm was originally an island, divided from north to south by the Brunkeberg ridge, scene of an important Danish defeat in 1471. It began as a suburb of the centre of trade and government in Gamla Stan. Now the ridge has been almost entirely flattened, and commerce and government have moved onto Norrmalm. Much mid 20C building has taken the place of the old districts.

Gustav Adolfs Torg is the large square looking across the Norrbro (North Bridge, 1807) to the royal palace. In the centre is an **equestrian statue** of Gustavus Adolphus by Pierre Hubert L'Archevêque (1796). To the east is the **opera house** (1890s), with a well-known restaurant *Operakällaran* (Opera Cellar). It was in the previous opera house on the same site that Gustav III was shot at a masked ball in 1792, the subject of Verdi's *Un Ballo in Maschera*.

On the opposite side of the square is **Arvfurstens Palats** (Crown Prince's Palace), with rusticated ground floor and colossal Corinthian pilasters, built in 1782 by Erik Palmstedt, now the foreign office. On the north-west corner of the square at Fredsgatan 2 is **Medelhavsmuseet** (the Museum of Mediterranean and Near Eastern Antiquities, open Wed–Sun 11.00–16.00, Tue 11.00–21.00. Information in English on pull-out trays). The building was designed by Rudolf Arbolius as a bank, the central hall being modelled on the Palazzo Bevilacqua in Bologna. This central part holds the Greek and Roman collection. The Greek displays shows objects from the Bronze Age to the hellenistic period, with vases and small sculptures. The Roman collection has everyday objects from all periods of Roman history. Most of the Egyptian collection is down in the former bank vaults. Mummy cases from Deir el Bahari, pottery, mummy portraits and masks are among the exhibits. Smaller displays are in the surrounding rooms but the most important is the **Cyprus collection**. From 1927 to 1931 Einar Gjerstad led a Swedish archaeological excavation in Cyprus. The terracotta warriors, large and small, of about 650–500 BC, are from Ajia Irini, in north Cyprus.

Take **Strömgatan** westwards along the waterline, and in the next block is **Rosenbad**, an Art Nouveau building with delicate detailing, built by Ferdinand Boberg in 1902–04 as a bank and office-block. It is now the seat of the Prime Minister and central government.

Drottninggatan runs north between Rosenbad and Arvfurstens Palats. This street had its heyday in the 19C and some imposing buildings remain from the late 19C and early 20C, for example, Nos 5 and 17 among others.

About 350m along, **Brunkebergsgatan** on the left leads to **Klara church** (open weekdays 09.00–18.00, Sun 11.00–18.00. English leaflets available).

St. Klara's (Clare's) Franciscan convent was founded by Magnus Ladulås in the 13C as the female counterpart to the friary on Riddarholmen, but disappeared at the Reformation in 1527. In the late 16C two Dutch architects designed a brick church on the old site. After a fire in the 18C it was restored by Carl Hårleman and Carl Adelcrantz.

The tower and spire were restored in the 19C when the main doorway was also carved. The ceiling-paintings are from the early 20C and show Old and New Testament scenes. The altar is made of Öland marble, designed by Adelcrantz, and the *Descent from the Cross* is by Jonas Hoffman (1766). On either side are two **angels** copied from plaster casts by Johan Tobias Sergel. The gilded wood pulpit is from the mid 18C, probably designed by Hårleman. Most of the **memorial tablets** were designed by Jean Eric Rehn, including his own. The fine organ was built in the early 20C. In the churchyard is the grave of the poet Carl Michael Bellman.

Continuing along Drottninggatan you see **Sergels Torg** opening up almost immediately. It is dominated by Edvin Öhrström's columnar glass sculpture (1974), 37.5m high, illuminated at night. The square has two levels—the lower is a lively shopping precinct round an open space. The useful SL (Stockholm transport) centre, covering transport in the city and county, is here. Another useful institution is **Kulturhuset** (Culture House) on the south side. This has an exhibition and information centre, and a theatre. It opened in 1974, but Parliament occupied the theatre and part of the exhibition centre until 1983, when it was able to move to its new premises. Now the main building has on its five floors cafés, a reading-room and library with newspapers and magazines, varied exhibitions and a bookshop, while the theatre has taken up its original purpose.

It is c 250m to **Hötorget** north by way of the pedestrian street Sergelsgatan. The square is dominated by the **concert house**, built by Ivar Tengbom (1923–26) with a row of colossal Corinthian columns striding across the façade. The Nobel prize-giving ceremony is usually held here, with the exception of the Peace prize which is presented in Oslo.

In front is Carl Milles' **Orpheus** fountain with Orpheus surrounded by spellbound listeners. Hötorget means Hay Square, where hay and livestock markets were held, and is still today a centre of trade with markets on the square, an underground food hall, a shopping precinct (Hötorgscity) as well as the department store PUB.

Kungsgatan runs across the north side of Hötorget, and is one of the main commercial arteries of Norrmalm. It had to be cut through the Brunkeberg ridge and viaducts constructed for the crossing streets Malmskillnadsgatan and Regeringsgatan. In the section to your right the two 17-storey towers at the first viaduct were Stockholm's first skyscrapers, built in the 1920s.

Return to Drottninggatan and continue north. About 250m further north is Barnhusgatan on the left. In No. 12–14 Folkets Hus, a lecture centre owned by the trade unions, houses **Dansmuseet** (Dance Museum, open Tue–Sun 12.00–16.00, closed July). The Dance Museum shows dance as an art form and religious rite, European and Asiatic folk dance, stage models and design sketches, with costumes and masks. It also has valuable archives. The large yellow building opposite is a former school, designed by Helgo Zetterwall in 1876.

The **Hologram Museum** is at Drottninggatan 100 on your right after another 200m or so. It is an exhibition and shop combined, so displays change. Artists from various countries exhibit and there are reproductions of world-famous art objects, portraits of well-known people and experimental artwork.

The **Strindberg Museum**, the celebrated Blue Tower, and Strindberg's last home, is on the left a little further on, at No. 85 (open Tue–Fri 10.00–16.00, also Tue to 21.00, Sat, Sun 12.00–16.00). An old-fashioned lift will take you to the third floor (called fourth in Sweden).

August Strindberg (1849–1912) was born in Stockholm and lived in 24 different homes in the city. He had an unhappy childhood and three unhappy marriages. After an interrupted university career and initial failure of his dramas he lived abroad for some years. His first major work was *Mäster Olof* (1872) about Olaus Petri. *The Red Room* is a satire on artistic society in Stockholm. (See below, Berns Salon in Berzelii Park.) When his collection of stories *Married* was published he was tried for blasphemy and acquitted. In *The Father* (1887), *Miss Julie* and *The Creditors* (both 1888), he displays crime and abnormality, castigating the corruption around him. These works were in a naturalistic style but he then developed a realistic mode, notably in historical plays, and *Crime and Crimes, Easter* and *Dance of Death*. Later he experimented with symbolic dramas, containing early indications of expressionism, surrealism and the theatre of the absurd. He was also an accomplished painter, still exhibited in Sweden, including in the National Museum.

He moved into this flat in 1908 when it was new, with the latest electric light, central heating, telephone and lift, and stayed here until his death four years later, writing his last significant play *The Great Highway*, as well as many books and innumerable newspaper articles.

Here you can see his apartment reconstructed, and also the adjoining apartment containing more mementoes. His furnishings and works of art (the sculptures are cheap casts), and his study with his books are more or less as he left them. From his balcony he viewed the processions which marked his 60th and 63rd birthdays. Displays extend into the adjoining apartment and here there is an interesting set of photos taken by Strindberg himself using remote shutter-release, of himself and his family in Switzerland in 1886. Posters for productions of his plays are also here. A film with English commentary is shown. In 1909 he rented the attic for his library, which is still there and available to researchers.

Return down Drottninggatan to Tegnérgatan. To the right it leads to **Tegnérlunden**, a little park with a statue of Strindberg by Carl Eldh. To the left it leads to Sveavägen, another of the city's main arteries.

Turn right and ahead on the right is the neo-Classical **Adolf Fredrik's church**. This was designed by Carl Fredrik Adelcrantz and finished in 1783. The **altar**, **pulpit** and **organ gallery** were designed by the architect. Sergel sculpted the **Resurrection** for the altar, as well as the **memorial** on the right of the chancel to the philosopher René Descartes who died in Stockholm in 1650. There is an unusual modern font and baptismal lamp by Liss Eriksson. The ceiling-paintings are by Julius Kronberg. In the churchyard is the grave (south of the church) of the assassinated prime minister Olof Palme (1986), as well as those of the sculptor Sergel, the painter Elias Martin and another prime minister Hjalmar Branting (1925).

Return down **Sveavägen**. On the corner of Tunnelgatan is the spot where Olof Palme was killed which for many years afterwards was marked with fresh flowers. The next to the left is Brunnsgatan, and at No. 6 is the **Marionette Museum and Theatre**, with puppets from around the world (open 13.00–16.00, closed in summer). Brunnsgatan comes out in **Birger Jarlsgatan**, the border between Norrmalm and Östermalm. (While the Modern Museum is undergoing lengthy renovation, the works of art can be seen at Birger Jarlsgatan 57.) Turn right and this leads to **Nybroplan**, a busy traffic junction for buses and ferries.

Just as Birger Jarlsgatan reaches Nybroplan, **Hamngatan** joins it on the right. At Hamngatan 4 is the sandstone and granite façade of the **Hallwyl Museum** (open June–Aug 11.00–16.00, Sept–May Tue–Fri 12.00–15.00, Sat, Sun 12.00–16.00. English guided tour mid-June to mid-Aug daily 13.00, rest of year Sun 13.00).

In the 1890s Count and Countess Walther von Hallwyl had this mansion built by Isak Clason. He was influenced by Venetian and Spanish Gothic/Renaissance transitional styles, seen in the impressive courtyard which almost completely shuts out the surrounding buildings. The left-hand door with the horseshoe was the stable entrance. Inside, the fittings and furnishings span styles from turn of the century historical romanticism to Art Nouveau and national romanticism. The countess spent most of her life, starting at the age of 17, collecting for what amounted to her private museum. She was extremely wealthy in her own right, and filled her home with the choicest antiques she could find from all over the world.

The first landing is surrounded by family portraits, copies made by Julius Kronberg, and has a ceiling with stucco foliage. To the left is the **Dining Room**, beamed and panelled in Baroque style, with 18C French tapestries and a 17C chandelier. Portraits of the children of the family are in the next room. The **armour collection** includes a 15C Turkish suit of armour. The purpose-designed billiard-room has a coffered ceiling and leather wall-covering, with built-in cupboards for cues. The large painting is *Pomona* by F. Floris. Next, the **china collection** has porcelain from the major European manufacturers such as Meissen, Wedgwood, Copenhagen and Capo di Monte.

Also on the first floor, but may be shown later, the smoking-room in sombre colours has portraits by Julius Kronberg, and this leads to the **Great Salon** in Baroque style, with lavish use of gilt. The ceiling painting is the *Concert of Peace* by Kronberg, the **tapestries** are 16C Brussels and the carved reliefs over the doors depict the arts. The glass-fronted gilt cabinet is Italian. Next is the small **Red Salon** with a ceiling-painting from the school of Ehrenstrahl and furnished in Rococo style.

Halfway up the stairs a locked room with silver and family jewellery can be shown to smaller groups. On the next landing are two good marquetry chests. On this floor visitors see the bedroom with lighter Rococo décor, the shaving-room with all a gentleman's necessities including those for moustache-grooming, and the bathroom, a new-fangled idea for the time—the shower was cold for use after the bath. Next come various guest rooms and sitting-rooms.

The **art gallery** is on the top floor where Flemish and Dutch artists predominate, and these include van Dyck and Frans Hals. Parallel to this runs the library, with books behind green panelled doors and another display of china. The house also possesses an important collection of Chinese ceramics.

The Hallwyl Museum overlooks **Berzelii Park**, with Milles' 'Playing Bears' sculptures at the north-east entrance, and in the pavement is the joke sculpture of a workman appearing from a manhole, 'Humour' by Karl Göte Bejemark. Also in the park is Veikko Keränen's sculpture 'We Two' (1993) like a pair of black seals.

The building to the west of the park is **Berns Salon**, built in 1863 as a restaurant which rose to fame (or notoriety) through August Strindberg's *Red Room* in which he describes it as a sort of smart young bachelor's club, part of the contemporary salon culture. Now it has been refurbished as a hotel, restaurant and conference centre. The Red Room has been preserved, and is used as a breakfast room for the hotel.

Across the park and the square stands the **Drama Theatre** (Dramaten) built 1901–08, with reliefs by Christian Eriksson. Take Hamngatan to the west and after passing Norrmalmstorg you come to **Kungsträdgården** (King's Garden), the centre of outdoor life in Stockholm, known to Stockholmers as Kungsan.

This was the royal kitchen garden until the middle of the 17C when the royal vegetables were removed to Humlegården (Östermalm) and Kungsträdgården became an elegant Baroque park. A palace called Makalös was built on the south part for Jacob de la Gardie, which burnt down in the 19C. The sculptures in the nearest underground station entrance in Arsenalsgatan represent those from Makalös. In 1971 the park was the scene of bitter controversy when planners wanted to fell a group of elms to dig for an underground station. Conservationists demonstrated night and day and sat in the trees. Workmen protected by police were to begin felling but the confrontation grew too violent and the trees were saved.

At the north-west end of Kungsträdgården is Sverigehuset (Sweden House), which houses the main tourist bureau. Opposite Sweden House on the other side of Hamngatan is NK, one of the leading Swedish department stores. The park is lined with fast-food stalls in the summer, and there is very often some kind of open-air entertainment going on, as well as outdoor chess with giant pieces.

There are several sculptures in the park including Karl XIII by E.G.C. Göthe (1821), Molin's large **fountain** (1873) with allegorical figures, and further south Molin's **statue** of Karl XII, the king who died in 1718 on campaign in Norway. Round the base are four mortars captured in battle in 1701. Not far away are Romeo and Juliet (1982).

This area of the park is called Karl XII:s Torg and is flanked to the west by the opera house, on the other side of which is Gustav Adolfs torg where the route began. To the north of the opera house is the **Jakob church** (open 11.00–17.00). Johan III founded the church on the site of an older chapel of St. James (Jakob). But his death in 1592 interrupted the work and it was not completed until 1644. From the latest building period come the three **doorways** by Henrik Blume from Holland, of which the most impressive is on the **south** side. The statues on either side are of Moses and St. James. The Corinthian columns support putti and inscribed tablets, and above these is an orb with a cross surrounded by clouds with figures representing the Trinity.

Inside, there are signs of the long building time, overlapping both Gothic and Renaissance. The fittings and furnishings are mostly of a later period except for the 17C font. Carl Hårleman designed the organ gallery in the 18C and the altar is a 20C work in 17C style. There is a modern flame-shaped candle-stand by Lennart Vintermyrs. The habit of lighting candles used to be abhorred as too Roman for the Swedish church, but in the last decade or so the provision of candle-stands has become almost universal.

Kungsholmen

The name means King's Island. Queen Kristina gave it to the city, and later it became a centre for craftsmen of all kinds. In the 19C heavy industry moved in, and with it workers' dwellings, many of which have survived. Along Norr Mälarstrand old workshops were cleared and substantial houses for the gentry constructed.

In 1923 it acquired its and Stockholm's most outstanding modern building, the ***City Hall** (Stadshus), on the south-east corner of the island. The unmistakable silhouette rises on the edge of Riddarfjärden, and is visible from a distance from all directions except north. It is the building of which the city and country are perhaps most proud.

The City Hall took 12 years to complete. Ragnar Östberg (1866–1945) created his masterpiece in a national romantic style with Venetian overtones in his use of arcades and columns. Some of the dark-red bricks were hand-made to give authentic texture to the the surfaces. The tapering tower rises to 106m with a lantern top from which rise the three gold crowns of the Swedish coat of arms. On the tower are figures of four saints connected with Stockholm, Mary Magdalene, Clare, Nicholas and Erik.

Stockholm City Hall (1923) by Ragnar Östberg

On the south side of the roof are **statues** representing painting, music, sculpture and architecture. On the short Maiden Tower to the north is the large gilded group St. George and the Dragon by Christian Eriksson.

At either side of the north entrance are granite **reliefs**, one of Stockholm in the 16C and one in the 20C. This entrance leads under an arch into the Citizens' Courtyard. Over the arcade to the right are bronze figures of Olof Skötkonung, Johannes Rudbeckius, Olaus Petri and Sten Sture the Elder, representing Mälaren towns. There is a tourist bureau and souvenir shop. (Tours in English mid June–Aug 10.00, 11.00, 12.00, 14.00, Sept–mid June 10.00, 12.00, but may be cancelled for civic functions.)

The tour gathers in the **ʻBlue Hall**. There is no blue anywhere as the intended painting of the walls was never carried out. There are Classically-inspired columns under round arches, and Islamic-inspired star-patterns under the top gallery and in the narrow interior windows. The hall is lit by small windows near the ceiling. The floor is of marble from Kolmården. Up in the south-east corner under the clock is a niche with a figure of Ragnar Östberg holding the city hall in his hands. It is in this hall that the banquet is given after the presentation of the Nobel prizes in the Concert Hall.

The wide stairs lead to the Council Corridor, with carvings of heads of workers who were employed in building. The Aldermen's Room contains a 12C wooden figure of St. Erik. The **Council Chamber** in its décor harks back to Viking times, with its dark wood and rich but subdued colours. It has a wooden ceiling through whose beams you can see the central blue portion to represent sky, surrounded by red, with views of Stockholm. There are seats for the 101 council members and room for the press and spectators.

The **Vault of the Hundred** is situated under the tower. It has 100 sections in its 31m high vault, and is said to take its name from the fact that the council members enter through it. On the wall a device makes figures of St. George and the dragon, with a princess and her page, move round to the strains of a medieval carillon, a Swedish war song. (Visible inside and out May–Sept 12.00 and 18.00.)

The **Oval** is an ante-room hung with 17C Beauvais tapestries, and is used for civil marriages. The 47m long **Prince's Gallery** is so called because the artist Prince Eugen painted the mural of the shores of Stockholm along the inner wall. Opposite through the windows over the south terrace is the real view of the same surroundings.

After passing through the Three Crowns Room with a view of Stockholm by Elias Martin (18C, clothes overpainted in 1800) the tour ends with the pièce de résistance, the ***Golden Hall**. The effect is stunning. Almost 20 million tesserae, most of them gilt, were organised by Einar Forseth (whose mosaic work is also in Coventry Cathedral) into what for the time was a highly controversial design. The 44m long hall is dominated by the Queen of Mälaren mosaic on the north wall. A gigantic woman with snake-like hair and the city hall, cathedral and palace on her knee symbolises the City of Stockholm receiving homage from the world. On the left are the countries of the west and also southern Sweden (note the twin towers of Lund Cathedral), and on the right the countries of the east with northern Sweden, represented by the mining industry. The rear wall shows the medieval royal palace and the building of the city hall. On the left side of the hall are scenes from the history of Sweden, and on the right notable Swedish people, including Birger Jarl, St. Birgitta, Olaus Petri and Strindberg. The floor is of Kolmården marble.

The **tower** (open May–Sept 10.00–15.00, (separate entrance and fee) has a lift which takes you to the level of the main roof. You come out into a circular area decorated with statuary. From here there are first stairs, then a seemingly never-ending gentle ramp round the four sides of the tower. The first stopping-point is the top of the Maiden Tower with the golden St. George and the dragon. After this there are few opportunities to look out except through the very small windows. However, the *view from the top is breath-taking looking down on Riddarholm with Gamla Stan behind. From here you can appreciate how much water there is in the centre of the city and the relationship of one island to another.

Outside, the **garden** is laid out on the terrace to the south, accessible through an open colonnade. In the colonnade at the west end are several works of art, including a relief of Carl Larsson the painter on a column, and on the end wall memorials to noted Swedes, including Nobel, Hazelius (founder of Skansen), the poet Bellman and three Polar explorers. On the terrace there are **sculptures** by Carl Eldh. To the right are his statues of Ernst Josephson, the painter, Gustav Fröding, the poet, and August Strindberg, the dramatist. On the balustrade on the shore are his figures representing Dance and Song.

Towards the east end is what looks like a piece of tree-trunk. The story goes that from Sigtuna, Stockholm's predecessor as capital, the city fathers floated a tree-trunk down the lake, determined that where it came ashore would be their new capital. Folk etymology says that this is the origin of the the name Stockholm—'tree-trunk-island'. The figure on the **column** at the east end is Engelbrekt, the rebel hero, by Christian Eriksson. The grotto is called Loke's punishment, an episode from Norse mythology. Round the corner is a tomb-like cenotaph commemorating Birger Jarl.

From the City Hall it is an agreeable walk along the Serafimer Strand to the north. On the tree-lined grassy strip is a sculpture by Tyra Lundgren called Bluebird (Blå fågel).

Along the south shore, **Norr Mälarstrand**, 19C houses, several with fanciful curly or stepped gables, make a backdrop for the boats moored at the long quay. No. 76 was designed by Ragnar Östberg, architect of the city hall. In between these two fringes lies the old working-class district centred on **Hantverkargatan** (literally 'hand-worker-street'). At No. 2 is the former hospital of the Order of the Seraphim, with a gate from 1792. No. 5 on the other side of the road was the Royal Mint (Kungliga Myntet).

Kungsholm church on the right is a Baroque building on a Greek cross plan, with additions in the 18C (ceiling) and the 19C (tower). This area has now become home to many administrative bodies. In **Scheelegatan** to the right further on, is the Rådhus, here used as law courts, in national romantic style (1914). The sprawling ornate building behind in the next street is police headquarters, and beyond is a park called Kronobergspark.

Back on Hantverkargatan, at No. 45 is the Landstingshus, the county headquarters with Classical façade, and behind it a pleasant area of scattered old wooden houses now used for administration. The island broadens here, and to the north is the district of **Stadshagen**, with open spaces, and Stockholm's oldest allotments from the 1920s towards the edge of the Karlbergsjön.

This 'lake' gets its name from the palace of **Karlberg**, the long white three-storey building on the opposite bank. In 1669 Magnus de la Gardie bought the central part and remodelled it while later owners expanded it. In the 18C it was a royal residence, and since 1792 it has been a military academy. The Karlberg canal was dug in 1719 probably by Russian prisoners of war. Here Essingeleden, the E3/E4, divides the island from north to south, crossing bridges on to the islands of Lilla Essingen and Stora Essingen on its way south. Lilla Essingen is the most thickly populated island in Stockholm, while Stora Essingen has prosperous villas.

In the north-west part of the island there is the residential area of Kristineberg. On the south-west corner is a beach for swimming, as there is also on the south coast in the suburb of **Marieberg** at Smedsudden, between Lilla Essingen and Västerbron (bridge). From here there is another good view of the city. Marieberg is the newspaper quarter and the two skyscrapers are occupied by the newspapers *Expressen* (largest circulation) and *Dagens Nyheter* in one and *Svenska Dagbladet* in the other—the latter two are the most authoritative in the country.

Västerbron (the West Bridge) was built in 1935 to join the two biggest islands of Kungsholmen and Södermalm, passing over Långholmen on the way. As might be expected it has an excellent view up and down the lake. On the east side of the bridge is the large Rålambshov park running down to the shore with several sculptures and an open-air theatre.

Östermalm

Östermalm was undeveloped until the late 19C when the broad avenues and star-shaped junctions were laid out on the model of Paris. The wealthy middle-classes moved here to live in spacious new mansions reflecting the current fashions of neo-Renaissance, neo-Gothic or Art Nouveau. Of the several museums and other sights, the most significant is *Historiska Museet** on Narvavägen, which runs north from Djurgårds bridge—third block up on the left (open Tue–Sun 12.00–17.00).

On the **ground floor** the pre-history section has full information in English, explaining such things as dendrochronology and pollen analysis. The Stone Age section has important burial finds, and Stone Age art, then comes the Stone Age in the north of the country, and the Bronze Age in South Sweden and Denmark. In the Iron Age section there is an interesting comparison of Sami (Lapp) artefacts with those from Germanic races. Heavy gold neck ornaments from the Roman Empire are shown, with gold brachteates and horns, and a finely-worked weathervane of gilded bronze. Some Gotland picture-stones and runestones stand next to large decorated boulders, which are assumed to have had magical purposes.

In the Viking section a wall of Nordic designs forms a background for boats, jewellery, weapons and pottery. *Finds from Birka**, the Viking town on an island in lake Mälaren, where new excavations began in 1990, are displayed, together with a model reconstruction of the town with log houses along the narrow streets. Themes include religion, textiles and children. As digging continues, displays will be expanded. For more details, see under Birka.

The medieval section occupies the **first floor**. The large **Romanesque hall** shows fonts, including one with runes, doors with intricate wrought-iron decoration (see the one from Högby), and a series of painted wooden panels hanging on the walls. The 11C Hemse **stave church** from Gotland has modest carved decoration.

Small items like keys and horseshoes are gathered in one room and the Romanesque area continues with chests, pews and other items. In the Romanesque gallery note especially the embossed gilt copper *altar frontal** from the 12C, with matching reredos and cross. The **stained glass**, mainly from Gotland, is effectively shown lit from behind. The **jewellery** section has information on pull-out trays beneath the cases, and near-by are drinking-horns and a small case with bone, horn and ivory carvings.

At the beginning of the **Gothic hall** a chapel devoted to St. Birgitta, Sweden's greatest saint, contains altars depicting scenes from her life and revelations. The statue by the window is the oldest known of her and the gravestone is that of her husband. The hall has a notable collection of *altarpieces**, mainly of North German workmanship, including the original altar for the Storkyrka of 1468. Also here is a large seated figure of St. Thomas à Becket of Canterbury, said to be modelled on the likeness of a Swedish bishop. After the armour section there is a display of **textiles**. Look especially for those attributed to **Albertus Pictor**, of the second half of the 15C.

Post-medieval church art is gathered in a church-like interior with pulpits, altars and pews, even a painted wooden ceiling. Ecclesiastical vessels, candlesticks and baptismal bowls are in display-cases.

A new *treasury** (*Skattkammare*) in an underground vault will by now have replaced the former Goldsmiths' Gallery. Three magnificent *gold collars** of the 5C will take pride of place, with a 20cm jewel-encrusted gold **buckle**, as well as the Timboholm treasure of undecorated gold rings and spirals, and sacrificial offerings of snake-headed rings from Öland. Priceless *reliquaries** include those from Linköping cathedral buried by the shrewd Bishop Brask when Gustav Vasa was going to confiscate them. The silver section has bracelets and collars, and coins from Arabia. Audio-visual presentations will explain techniques and interpret the makers' intentions.

The **Coin Museum** is on the **top floor** (leaflet in English). The comprehensive collection is labelled with dates, from about the year 1000. (Remember *1700-talet* means 18C.) Medals and banknotes are also included.

Almost opposite the museum, the Oskarskyrka has stained glass windows by the Norwegian artist Emanuel Vigeland, brother of the sculptor.

Return west by Storgatan and after about 700m you pass the octagonal **Hedwig Eleanora church**. This was finished in 1737, though the dome was added in the 19C. Inside it has slim Corinthian columns under the galleries and large half-columns supporting the dome. The carved wooden 'Golden Altar' of 1747 has a painting of the crucifixion (1738) and a modern round stained glass window in the centre of the broken pediment above. The neo-Classical pulpit with swinging golden drapery was designed by Jean Eric Rehn in 1784.

Just beyond the church is **Östermalmstorg**, where the Saluhall (food market) of 1889 has arcades, turrets and Chinese dragons on the roof.

Take Sibyllegatan down by the side of the church which comes out in **Riddargatan**. You will have no difficulty identifying on your left **Armé-museet** (Army Museum), with crossed axe-heads on the railings and a courtyard bristling with cannon (open 11.00–16.00, closed Mon except in summer). The main building is an artillery store built in the 18C. Chronologically the displays begin on the **second floor**, where military history is traced from Vasa times onwards. A model of the Battle of Lützen (1632) where Gustavus Adolphus was killed accompanies material on the Thirty Years War, and there are models of the fortresses built by Erik Dahlberg later in the 17C. Much of the 18C history is taken up with the wars leading to the loss of Finland, and this floor concludes in the 19C. The **first floor** is mainly occupied by Sweden in the Second World War, while on the **ground floor** can be seen the development of artillery.

Almost opposite the museum you can cut through a yard to **Musikmuseet** in the refurbished 17C army bakery (open Tue–Sun 11.00–16.00). Here a section on the nature of sound and of music where you can listen and experiment, leads into a display of pianos. A door leads to the stairs down to the basement where the history of music in Sweden is displayed. Other areas have temporary exhibitions and there are substantial archives, a reference library and recorded music collections.

South of this building runs **Väpnargatan** where at No. 1 there is the entrance to the Royal Mews (guided tours at 14.00, check days at tourist bureau). Visitors are shown the stables, saddle-room and carriage collection.

Facing Nybroplan is **Dramaten**, the theatre completed in 1908, with reliefs of a Dionysis procession and a commedia dell'arte group by Christian Eriksson, and playing children by Carl Milles at the entrance. The foyer is in white marble, bronze and stucco, and in the cream and gold auditorium, Julius Kronberg's paintings decorate the ceiling amid more stucco work.

Somewhat to the north of this area of Östermalm lies Kungliga Humlegården (King's Hop Garden) a large park where there is the neo-Renaissance Royal Library (1877). This is a national library, entitled to receive a copy of every book published in Sweden.

North again on a hill in Östermalmsgatan is the **Engelbrekt church** (1914), a prime example of national romantic style. Built in granite and brick, it has a slim tower on the south-west. Inside it has an elliptical vault, and amid the low-relief ornament you can find references to several historical styles, including Greek and Byzantine, with some runes for good measure.

Ladugårdsgärdet and the Thiel Gallery

Ladugårdsgärdet, known as Gärdet for short, was a military area until 1949, and even now has much undeveloped land. It has, however, four museums, somewhat indigestibly grouped side by side—you might split them up with a visit to the Kaknäs Tower nearby. You can go by car, or 68 or 69 bus from Sergels torg. The bus-route goes along Strandvägen with its imposing turn-of-the-century mansions, round Nobel Park, then passes the embassy district and the English church, before reaching an open area.

The first museum is the **Sjöhistoriska** (Maritime), a curved building with central rotunda, designed by Ragnar Östberg, architect of the City Hall (open 10.00–17.00. Some English information). You enter on the **first floor**. To the right is naval ship-building of the 20C with submarines and other warships, and parallel to this 19C ships, with large models, a master's cabin and so on. In the central section is a large exhibit on the Battle of Svensksund of 1790 (detailed English information) when Sweden defeated Russia. The decorative stern of the royal schooner *Amphion* looms behind. In the left wing this subject continues, and a series of interiors follows the fate of a young oarsman.

On the **second floor** there is a section called Sea and Man, with navigation, lighthouses, and the seaman's life. At the end small models trace the history of the ship from 800 to 1890. In the **central rotunda** is an exhibit on Columbus and in the other wing a display on the Swedish East India Company's ship *Götheborg*.

Down on the **ground floor**, below the entrance floor, merchant shipbuilding of the 18C is illustrated with Stockholm Shipbuilding and East India Company ships. The 19C then leads into a section on the Johnson Line through its long history of over a century.

Next door is **Tekniska Museet** through which one can reach Telemuseet—Telecommunications Museum (both open Mon–Fri 10.00–16.00, Sat, Sun 12.00–16.00, some information in English). The entrance is on floor 2. The **central hall** has an exhibition called Technology and Man, and to the right down a corridor is the history of electricity with transport, turbines, installation and distribution, and modern entertainment.

From the central hall steps go down to the **machinery hall** with as centrepiece Sweden's oldest steam engine, surrounded by cars, water-wheels and turbines. To the right is the entrance to the reconstructed mine (ask at reception for this). Ahead is an activity centre.

On the next floor there is an exhibit on the Swedish building industry through the centuries, a section on technology in the home, and mechanical engineering. There is a large number of wooden models of machinery from the Royal Model Collection, some dating back to the 18C.

A considerable area of the **top floor** deals with the history of printing from Gutenberg to today. The history of chemistry starts with alchemy, and includes a reconstructed laboratory of the early 20C. Then comes the theory of chemistry and the Swedish chemical industry. There is also a section on the forestry industry.

Telemuseet is accessible from the central hall of Tekniska Museet. Here there is not much information in English, though you can buy a guide-book—on the other hand, much is self-evident. On the **ground floor** there is the development of telegraphy from other signalling systems. Serried ranks of telephones illustrate their history, and early switchboards are shown. Upstairs is the history of the Swedish phone company, and radio, with a studio, and the use of radio in coast-guard work, and satellites. This leads into the development of TV and finally computers.

In the centre of the building is the **L.M. Ericsson Room**. (Detailed notes in English.) Lars Magnus Ericsson founded his successful telecommunications company in 1876. This room, decorated and furnished in 1903, was intended for board meetings, and the telephone has been incorporated as a motif into every possible item, even the ceiling.

The library and archives can be visited (Mon–Fri 13.00–15.00) and the complete set of telephone directories from 1890 could be useful to those engaged in genealogical research.

Finally, there is the **Folkens Museum** (Ethnographical: open Tue–Fri 11.00–16.00, Sat, Sun 12.00–17.00, good restaurant). The permanent exhibition is on the **first floor**, and deals with Central and North Africa, Mongolia, and North American Indians. There are reconstructions of dwellings with some displays on religion and social life. One corner has sketches by the explorer Sven Hedin (1865–1952). On the balustrade of the stairs are the labels for the collection of boats displayed below and opposite.

It is less than 10 minutes' walk to the **Kaknäs Tower**, at 155m the tallest construction in Scandinavia, built in 1967 for the telephone company (observation galleries open mid April–mid Sept 09.00–22.30, rest of year 09.00–18.00). At the bottom is a tourist bureau and souvenir shop. The lift goes up at 5m a second so you are soon at the restaurant on floor 28, or the first observation gallery on floor 30 (refreshments). This floor is walled with insulating glass, and there are numbered photos to help you identify landmarks and areas like Skansen and Gamla stan. The floor above is protected only by a thick wire grille and there are coin-in-the-slot binoculars for the spectacular **view**.

Back on the road, you can take a 69 bus to the **Thiel Gallery** which is on the island of Djurgården, not quite at the furthermost point, Blockhusudden. The gallery (open Mon–Sat 12.00–16.00, Sun 13.00–16.00) is set above the road on the left, a white mansion built by architect Ferdinand Boberg for the banker Ernest Thiel in 1905. Thiel was friend and patron to many in Konstnärsförbundet, a group influenced by the French Barbizon school, and most of the artists exhibited here were members of it.

The gallery begins on the **first floor** where there are temporary exhibitions. On the stairway to the **second floor** there are pictures by Bruno Liljefors, and to the right more by this artist and Anders Zorn. A side room is devoted to Carl Larsson. To the left a large top-lit room shows Carl Wilhelmson, Richard Bergh, Ernst Josephson and Gustav Fjaestad. The large room at the end, also top-lit, has some Vuillard, Toulouse-Lautrec, Gauguin and Strindberg on the upper level and below are many pictures by Edvard Munch, and a set of furniture designed by Fjaestad.

Upstairs are one or two small rooms, one again devoted to Munch. In the garden are several sculptures by Emanuel Vigeland (brother of Gustav).

Södermalm

Södermalm did not become an island until the construction of the Hammarby canal with the lock which can accommodate much larger ships than the old lock at Slussen. Now Södermalm counts as the largest island of the 14 which make up inner Stockholm.

The name means south height, and it is indeed rocky as can be seen from the way the old houses climb the ridge from Riddarfjärden opposite the City Hall. For a long time it was inhabited mainly by the poorer sections of the populace, but as modern machinery makes it possible to conquer the terrain, it is gradually changing character, though 18C pockets remain and many 19C houses. By the nature of things there are fine views. Because of the steepness in places, it can be difficult to navigate in a car since what looks like a possible through road may in fact be cut off by a cliff. However, road works are continuous, and the situation should improve.

Slussen (The Lock) has become the name for the whole area of the traffic complex which joins Södermalm to Gamla Stan. The first lock was built in 1637, because of difficulties caused by the rising of the land. Christopher Polhem (see also under Trollhättan) renovated this in 1744, and it was renovated again in 1850 and 1935. This last rebuilding was done when the nearby traffic-junction was constructed, providing what was at the time an epoch-making solution to congestion—a clover-leaf shape. The main road south, Söderleden, divides the island into two.

Södermalm east

The square just south of the traffic complex has market stalls and fast-food kiosks. On the west side is the **Stockholm City Museum** (Stadsmuseum), housed in what used to be the town hall, designed by the two Nicodemus Tessins in the 1640s. It is a Baroque mansion, with a 'säteri' roof (raised centre section, like that of Riddarhuset). (Open Fri–Mon 11.00–17.00, Tue–Thur 11.00–19.00. Shop, 19C café, which expands to the handsome courtyard in the summer.) On the **ground floor** are the archaeological finds from the city. On the first floor are displays of Stockholm as the capital of a great power in the 17C. There is a **model** of the Three Crowns Castle, and other models, a 17C building site, painted panels and other building elements. A selection of prints shows the city in different ages. The **treasury** contains silver from the 17C to the 19C. On the **second floor** the growth of the city is shown on maps, and there are temporary exhibitions. The **third floor** concentrates on **Stockholm in 1897**, the growth of industry, workers' conditions, and their homes, with sound effects.

Opposite the City Museum the tall tower is the **Katerina Lift** (Katerinahissen, small fee) and its top is joined to a walkway which leads directly on to the cliff and the higher level of the island (**views** all the way). You can progress from here to **Mosebacke Torg** with its theatre and another view from the terrace to the left of the theatre.

Alternatively at the bottom of the lift you can take the steep road to the left going up the hill, **Katerinavägen**. Where the road turns right, take the small street to the left (**Fjällgatan**). Not only is the street itself lined with 18C houses, but it affords also one of those classic views of Stockholm—hence all the tourist buses.

Below there may be moored two large brightly-painted ships. These are icebreakers called *Ymer* and *Frej* after Norse gods (Ymer was born from ice). Their winter work is in the Baltic where they crunch through a metre of solid ice or 15–25m of ice-floe. Beyond are the islands, Gamla stan to the left, then Skeppsholmen and little Kastellholmen with the tower flying the Swedish flag, then Djurgården, and on a point of Djurgården to the right, Waldemarsudde.

Yet another viewpoint is **Fåfängen**, a small park with a little summerhouse a kilometre or so away on the eastern point of Södermalm. Below is the

Viking Line Terminal whose outsize passenger ships ply to Finland carrying several million passengers a year. Inland are quiet areas of 18C and 19C houses around Nytorget and Åsoberget.

The **Medical History Museum** is at Åsogatan 146 (open Wed, Thurs pm and occasional Sun). If you climb the hill from which you turned into Fjällgatan, Åsogatan is the fourth on the left.

In **Hobergsgatan** about half a kilometre north of Åsogatan is the **Katarina church**, being rebuilt after being devastated by fire in 1990. The intention is to make a replica so that visitors can appreciate Jean de la Vallée's 17C design of a Greek cross with cupola. The Baroque altar, pulpit and 18C Rococo organ façade are not being reconstructed, and the interior will be redesigned to fit modern needs.

Along the south-east shore of Södermalm is the Hammarby Canal on the other side of which is what used to be the old port and industrial area. Industries remaining in Stockholm have now moved to the north of the city.

A large mound made of refuse, called Hammarby Hill, is used for skiing in the winter, and sometimes it is possible to skate on the lake.

The main roads cross Hammarby lock from Södermalm by a combination of bridges. Nynäsvägen in 1km leads to **Stockholm Globe Arena**, opened in 1989. This glaringly visible white sphere is 85m high and accommodates 16,000 spectators for sports and other events. Beside it is **Sveriges Riksidrottsmuseum** (Swedish National Sports Museum).

Södermalm west

Take **Hornsgatan** down by the right of the City Museum. Cross Götgatan. (No. 16A a little way along on the right is the mid 17C palace of Ebbe Brahe.)

On the other side of Södergatan is the **Maria Magdalena kyrka** (open 11.00–16.00). It is mainly of the 17C, reconstructed in the 18C after a fire to the same design which had been partly by the two Tessins. The pulpit and organ façade are from the 18C while the font is 17C, and the altarpicture was painted c 1800. The poet Erik Johan Stagnelius is buried in the churchyard.

Along the first part of Hornsgatan and in the blocks behind, going down to the waterfront are 18C houses, those which make such a picturesque impression from the other islands. Where Hornsgatan has to surmount a small steep hill, half of the road has been levelled for cars, so that older houses remain on the hill, and steps are provided for pedestrians to cross the road. In this area old houses have been renovated and art galleries and craft shops have moved in.

Further along is **Mariatorget**, a small green dominated by a fountain with a muscular **statue** of Thor and his fish by Anders Henrik Wissler. At Mariatorget 1C there is a toy museum with dolls, lead soldiers, vehicles of all kinds and a large section for pianolas, musical boxes and other music-producing machines.

About 1.5km further on is the red-brick **Högalid church** (1923), its twin towers visible from a distance. The architect Ivar Tengbom designed it in national romantic style with medieval nuances, the towers for example are supposed to be inspired by those of Visby Cathedral on Gotland. Wall-paintings are by Gunnar Torhamn, and there is a mosaic by Einar Forseth, who designed the mosaics in the City Hall.

Just beyond Högalid church Västerbron (bridge) crosses the tip of Söder-malm after passing over Långholmen, a green and rocky island occupied in summer by holiday-makers busily boating and bathing. The long yellow building with the black roof, now a hotel and youth hostel, was a prison until 1971. On the east tip of Långholmen is the last working shipyard in Stockholm, Mälarvarvet, which now does repairs only.

On the north shore of Södermalm is **Skinnarvikspark** with another view. The very large dark red building is a former brewery. The south-western shore is rocky and green with a large hospital standing on the cliff (1943).

The smaller island off the east end of Södermalm is Reimersholme, once an industrial area.

C. Suburbs

Millesgården

Lidingö is an attractive residential island on the eastern edge of the city, linked to the mainland since 1924 by a 1km long bridge. It is the site of Carl Milles' home and garden full of sculpture set on terraces on the water's edge (open May–Sept 10.00–17.00, Oct–Apr Tue–Sun 11.00–16.00. Shop, café). To get there, take the underground to Ropsten (east terminus of lines 13/14/15). Do not leave the platform but walk forward to get the small local train (Lidingöbanan) to the first stop across the bridge at Torsvik. (You can also take a bus—check the number from the notice on the platform.) *Millesgården is on the hill to the right as you face inland and there is a footpath up to it from the train-stop. Alternatively, from June to mid-August there are boats from Nybrokajen and Strömkajen.

Carl Milles (1875–1955) was born near Uppsala and educated in Stockholm. He studied woodwork, carving and modelling in the evenings while working as an apprentice cabinet-maker. From 1897 to 1904 he lived in Paris on a scholarship supporting himself precariously while studying, and had the opportunity of working with Rodin. He was also influenced by Puvis de Chavannes, Maurice Denis and Antoine Louis Barye.

In 1905 he married Olga, an Austrian painter, and in 1906 returned to Sweden where he had gained enough of a reputation to be sought after. At this time he began the massive wooden figure of Gustav Vasa for the National Museum.

The Baltic Exhibition in Malmö in 1914 brought him greater recognition. In 1920 he became Professor of Modelling at the Royal Academy of Art in Stockholm. In 1931 he moved to the United States, becoming Head of the Department of Sculpture at the Cranbrook Academy of Art. For the next 20 years he lived in America and was laden with honours and awards. In 1945 he and his wife became American citizens. In 1951 he moved to the American Academy in Rome but spent the summers in Sweden. He died at Millesgården.

His early works were realistic but soon became simplified and more decorative. He was inspired by many different styles, including archaic Greek, Romanesque, Chinese and Italian Mannerist works. His work tends to be exuberant, even humorous, but also lyrical or mystical on occasion, especially in later life when some figures seem to be floating, and angels are a constant theme.

The range of size is remarkable, from the monumental Poseidon to the intricacies of very small figures, as is the contrast between the almost tangible movement of the Aganippe fountain figures and the stillness of À la Belle Étoile. He liked to set his figures on columns and indeed collected columns of all kinds. Here you can find a sandstone column from Gustav III's opera house in Stockholm with a Corinthian capital said to be by Sergel, columns of white Italian marble and columns of Älvdalen porphyry. Fountains were another fascination, where he could experiment with the combination of the stillness of bronze and the movement of running water.

Since so much of his work is in bronze, Millesgården can show replicas of works now all over the world. The sculptures are displayed on three main terraces and several smaller ones, among landscaped gardens, trees, flowers and fountains. In the house and studio is the art collection which Milles built up, as well as smaller works of his own and studies for larger works.

In the house much of the art collection is in the **Music Room** with a Beauvais tapestry, and works by Claude Lorrain, Canaletto, Utrillo and Pissarro as well as German and Austrian wood carvings. In the **Red Room** are Milles' early smaller works, including 'Sunglitter'. A small room known as the **Monk's Cell** contains Chinese carvings. Other Milles works are in the **Main Studio** (plaster casts) and the **Gallery**. The breakfast room has cupboards with designs painted by Olga, and old Delft tiles on the wall. The **Antique Gallery** has the artist's collection of Greek and Roman státues and fragments.

On the **upper terrace** alongside the house the main group is **The Dancing Girls**, and further on the **Susanna Fountain**. There are details and studies from other larger works including the 'Emigrants on a Fish', which is in the House of Emigrants, Växjö.

The narrow **middle terrace** is edged with plain granite columns and the central sculpture is a study for a monument to Sven Hedin, the explorer. On each side of a narrow flight of steps is a wild boar. At the top of the broad steps is the **Sunsinger**.

To the left is the tiny terrace called **Little Austria**, a present to Olga from her husband, now with the couple's graves. This leads to **Olga's Terrace** with the **Aganippe fountain**. The three figures on dolphins symbolise the Musician, the Painter and the Sculptor. Beyond is the rose terrace with a café.

The lowest terrace is a large irregular L-shaped area on the water-front with dozens of works of art. On the furthest point stands the massive **Poseidon** (from Götaplatsen in Gothenburg). Nearby is **Man and Pegasus**, original in Des Moines, Iowa, replicas in Malmö, Antwerp and Tokyo.

Behind in the pool are **Sunglitter, Europa and the Bull** as well as tritons, and the fish from the Poseidon statue. At the end of the pool is **Anne's House**, planned for Milles' secretary but lived in by the artist and his wife during their summers in Sweden.

On the other side of Poseidon are the columns with sculptures perched on high, adding to the sense of lightness and showing their silhouettes against the sky. Perhaps the best-known is the **Hand of God**, especially as it is used in all publicity material for Millesgården (original in Eskilstuna). There are six angel musicians.

At the other end of the terrace is the amusing chubby **Folke Filbyter** (a character in a legend) from the fountain in Linköping, while behind in the greenery are the Buddha-like **Jonah** and his whale.

Haga

To get to **Haga Park** with its Pavilion and other attractions you can take a 515 bus from Odenplan underground station, and get off at Haga Norra or drive out the E4 to the north. Inside the park there are signposts to the various places of interest.

First on the north is **Fjärilshuset** (Butterfly House, open Tue–Fri 10.00–16.00, Sat, Sun 11.00–17.00, shorter hours in winter) in one of the green-houses. You can buy a coloured leaflet in English to help with identification. There are about 300 butterflies of 30 species, each individual of which lives an average of 2½ weeks. The temperature is kept at 25°C and the humidity 75 per cent. The little birds on the ground are Chinese dwarf quail which eat insects and snails. At the end of the greenhouse is a case with larvae. Flitting amid the tropical foliage are species which range from the large Owl Butterfly down to the diminutive Red Pierrot, by way of the Giant Purple Emperor and the Painted Jezebel. The butterflies are more active on sunny days.

South of the greenhouses are the so-called **Copper Tents**, a copy of barracks originally from 1787, supposed to resemble Roman campaign tents, now with a restaurant, and a display of Gustav III's plans for the park, never completed. Beyond, the **Great Lawn** sweeps grandly down to Brunnsviken, an inlet of the sea. After taking the path to the left, near the bottom of the slope you can follow a path signposted *Slottsruinen* up to the mighty foundations of what was to have been Gustav III's answer to the palace of Versailles but was cut short by his assassination in 1792. Southeast of the ruin is a house called **Haga slott**, built in 1802–04 and lived in by 19C monarchs. Renovated in the 1930s, it was the childhood home of Carl XVI Gustaf and his sisters, the 'Haga princesses'. It is now used for foreign state visitors—Nikita Kruschow once stayed here.

Next on the right is *****Gustav III's Pavilion** (open June–Aug 12.00–16.00 and some weekends) originally a manor, and remodelled in the late 18C inspired by the Petit Trianon at Versailles. The architect was Olof Tempelman, and the chief interior designer was Louis Masreliez. After his Italian journey Gustav was enthusiastic about antique art, and the discoveries at Pompeii were another impetus to what became known as Gustavian style, of which this Pavilion is probably the best example.

In the **dining-room**, which has undergone considerable restoration, the décor is mainly in grisaille painting on friezes, niches and overdoors. The chairs are original, with Chippendale-style backs and the remainder Gustavian. Masreliez designed the console tables. The chandeliers are original.

The **large salon** is the hub of the building, and here Masreliez' decoration has not been altered. This is decorated in Pompeian style with brightly painted panels featuring Jupiter, Juno, Apollo and Minerva. The furniture is also original, based on antique designs, The mahogany tables are by Adam Weissweiler, and the china is Sèvres and Meissen. In the blue antechamber, narrow gilt carved strips outline the panelling.

The end wall of the **Mirror Room** consists almost entirely of glass panels divided by marble columns, to frame a view of Brunnsviken and the woods beyond. The gold and white panels between the mirrors are decorated in an Adam-inspired style. The grisaille friezes represent Apollo, Minerva, Homer and Virgil—Gustav liked to think of himself as Apollo. The chairs were inspired by Roman models, and there are two alabaster urns and a bust of Gustav by Sergel.

Back in the large salon a door leads off to the King's bedroom with blue-grey hangings and upholstery. The painting of Henry IV of France and Sully is by Alexander Roslin. The furniture is Gustavian rather than antique.

The **library** is lined with gold-tooled books, and above the marble fireplace is a relief portrait medallion by Sergel, with two gilt light-brackets. The table is by Georg Haupt and the library steps with intarsia are original.

Upstairs the **King's 'Divan'** has a long wall-sofa (reconstructed). This was the first room decorated by Masreliez and has remained unchanged. The central wall-painting is of Apollo and there are alabaster figures in niches at the sides. The chairs are upholstered in hand-painted Chinese silk, and there are ingenious little storage spaces under the windows. The antechamber to this room has Pompeian painting with Mars and Minerva and there is a small Laocoön group on a porphyry base. Other small rooms are shown, two for servants, one for the Crown Prince and one for his tutor, sparsely furnished and decorated.

Near the Pavilion, **Ekotemplet** (the Echo Temple) stands on a mound. This is a roofed oval colonnade used as an outdoor dining-room, built in 1790, with some remnants of ceiling painting.

It is a very pleasant walk around the head of the inlet, and thence south along its shore, bearing left past the café. When the path reaches the shore again there is a gate to the **Royal Cemetery** (open Sun and holidays 13.00–15.00) where are buried Gustav VI Adolf and non-reigning members of the royal family, including Gustav's two wives Crown Princess Margareta, granddaughter of Queen Victoria, and Queen Louise (Mountbatten).

From here the path continues round the bay and soon you can cut across to another exit from the park, passing the early 20C courthouse painted in 'Stockholm yellow', and beyond the car park to the left you can see Stallmästaregården, a restaurant partly dating from the 17C.

Ulriksdal

A 540 bus from the underground station of Bergshamra takes you quickly to Ulriksdal if you wish to save a 20-minute walk, or you can drive out the E4 beyond Haga. The bus turns at Confidencen, an 18C theatre now used again for performances. The next building on the left is **Stallgården**, where there is a wing containing a reconstruction of Queen Kristina's coronation coach with original textiles—her coronation procession started from Ulriksdal. Opposite is the 19C palace church, and ahead through the gates is the **Ulriksdal palace** (open mid May–mid Sept 12.00–16.00, closed Mon).

The original 17C palace was rebuilt in the 18C by Fredrik I and Ulrika Eleanora, and it was renovated in the 19C by Karl XV, and again in the 1920s for Gustav VI Adolf, then Crown Prince. It is these last two periods which are represented in the interior, and there is much interesting furniture, of which only a selection can be mentioned here. There is an English leaflet available at moderate cost.

Off the entrance hall, originally three rooms, is an audience room, and then room No. 3, the **General's Room**, has an 18C Dutch cabinet of intarsia work with oriental plates set into it. The **Drinking Hall** has 18C gilt leather hangings, and inlay round the door, furnished with early 18C Scandinavian chairs and sofa. The bedroom on the right has an ebony cabinet with marble inlay and two walnut corner cupboards. The bedroom on the left has a 17C oak bed. Princess Sofia Albertina and her ladies are said to have embroidered the wall-hangings in the next room.

Upstairs, the antechamber (No. 8) has gilt leather wall-coverings, and the two chests are 18C Dutch, while the cabinet with ivory figures is German. The bedchamber also has gilt leather, and a large cabinet has 16C carved reliefs on a 19C base. **Karl XV's bedchamber** has a 17C walnut bed and a portrait of the king by David von Krafft. There follow two rooms with paintings by Karl XV and his artistic friends. The king did the one of Djurgården in the snow. In Room 12 there is an intarsia secretaire. In Room 14 the two portraits are by Ehrenstrahl, of Karl XI and Ulrika Eleanora, and the next two rooms serve as a library. The dining-room provides a complete contrast, being from the 1920s.

Out on the landing is a model of Ulriksdal as designed in 1745 by Carl Hårleman, and portraits of Karl XV and Queen Lovisa. The 1920s living-room was presented to Gustav VI Adolf, then Crown Prince, and Princess Louise by the people of Stockholm. The wedding goblet is from Orrefors and there is a picture by Prince Eugen on the left by the window, with paintings by other well-known Swedish artists. Other rooms have displays of stoneware and silver, and finally there is the **Balcony Room** with 18C wall-panels.

As you leave the palace the **Orangery** is ahead to the right. This was designed by Nicodemus Tessin the Younger (somewhat altered since) and contains an exhibition of Swedish sculpture from the 18C onwards, with models, reduced-scale versions and plaster casts. Artists represented include Sergel, Fogelberg, Byström, Börjeson, Hasselberg and Qvarnström. In the centre portion are three large statues of Norse gods.

Other places of interest within the city

1. **Vasastan** is the district to the north of Norrmalm. The best known building here is the **City Library** designed by Gunnar Asplund (1928), at the corner of Sveavägen and Odengatan. The square base with rotunda above has a plain surface with only a narrow low relief frieze resembling Egyptian hieroglyphs, symbolising the areas of knowledge to be found within. The rotunda contains the lending area as well as shelves, and fanning off are rooms for specialised subjects. This was the first library in Sweden where the borrowers could help themselves to books.

The little park alongside is called **Observatorielunden**, and on top of the mound hidden in the trees is the old observatory designed by Carl Hårleman (1753, renovated c 1870). There is now a small museum here, with astronomical instruments. In 1931 the work of the observatory was moved out to Saltsjöbaden.

Considerably further to the north is the Wine and Spirits Museum, at Dalagatan 100, and at Lögebodavägen 10 there is the studio of the sculptor Carl Eldh with many of his works of art.

2. The university area is appropriately served by the underground station *Universitetet*, close to which is **Naturhistoriska Riksmuseet** (Natural History Museum), at Frescativägen 40. This is a sprawling grandiose 1915 building most of which is occupied by researchers and administration. However, the exhibition areas at the time of writing were in the throes of far-reaching expansion and reorganisation, with plans for new displays. The ultra-modern theatre/planetarium Cosmonova has an all-embracing screen for a total experience of space exploration, rainforests and such.

Not far away (signposted) is the Bergianska Botaniska Trädgården, the Botanical Gardens. Here too changes are in the air, with ambitious plans for a large covered winter garden on the shores of Brunnsviken, with Mediterranean and sub-tropical plants.

3. **Spårvägsmuseet** (Tramway Museum) at Tegelviksgatan 22 (on the west edge of Södermalm, buses 46, 53, 66) shows public transport from the 19C onwards.

D. Excursions from Stockholm

Drottningholm

You can reach *Drottningholm palace by car, public transport (underground to Brommaplan, then bus) or by boat from Stadshusbron (City Hall). (Open May–Aug 11.00–16.30, and Sept shorter hours. Beautifully situated outdoor restaurant not recommended to those short of time or money. Café near Chinese Pavilion in high season.) The palace was begun in 1662 by the Dowager Queen Hedvig Eleanora, employing successively the Nicodemus Tessins, father and son, as architects. The main section has a square plan, with a rusticated ground floor and two main floors. The 'säteri' roof (with raised centre portion) has a vertical section deep enough to put windows in, and there are also round dormer windows. In 1744 Lovisa Ulrika (later Queen) acquired the palace on her marriage to the Crown Prince. She had another storey added to the lower side wings, designed by Carl Hårleman, and redecorated so that much of it was transformed from Baroque to Rococo. There are French style Baroque gardens and extensive grounds beyond, where there is a Chinese pavilion (*Kina slott*).

The visitor enters by the lakeside façade. The *staircase is predominantly pink/purple simulated marble with stone detailing. The lowest section is painted in trompe l'oeil, to lengthen the perspective as you enter. The stairwell is surrounded by Classical statues on the balustrade and in niches, and busts of kings of the Goths by Nicolaes Millich. Lavish stucco alternates with allegorical roundels and paintings of palace interiors with strange visitors. The ceiling-painting is by Ehrenstrahl the court painter, with Apollo and Minerva holding Queen Hedvig Eleanora's monogram in the lantern and trompe l'oeil allegories around.

On the **first floor** the vestibule has a ceiling painting by Johan Sylvius of the triumph of a Roman commander surrounded by stucco work designed by Tessin the Elder. The hall of the bodyguard retains original gilt leather wall-coverings made in Venice in the 17C, depicting the siege of Vienna by the Turks in 1683. There is a large wardrobe with perspective carving on the doors. The picture with the dromedary is by Ehrenstrahl.

The **Green Drawing Room** has a ceiling painting of Hercules and Minerva and overdoors with Hedvig Eleanora's monogram. On the left are portraits of Queen Lovisa Ulrika's parents and between them Louis XV of France. To the right are portraits of Louis XVI and Catherine II of Russia. There are busts of Lovisa Ulrika by Sergel and of Hedvig Eleanora and two of her grandchildren by Millich.

Next to the right comes the **Gallery of Karl X**, intended by Hedvig Eleanora to be a memorial to her husband. The German artist Johan Philip Lemke painted the battle scenes to designs of Erik Dahlberg who took part in some of the exploits.

Back in the Green Drawing Room, to the left is the **Ehrenstrahl Drawing Room** with six wall-paintings and ceiling painting by this artist. These depict symbolic themes from the lives of Hedvig Eleanora and Karl XI. The furniture is French Rococo and the bureau is from 1782.

Hedvig Eleanora's dazzling *State Bedchamber in green and gold was designed by Tessin the Elder and finished in 1683. The floor is composed of six different sorts of wood. The alcove is supported on Ionic columns and the ceiling by Corinthian pilasters. Ehrenstrahl painted the pictures, and every other surface is covered in gilt crowns, roundels, monograms, angels, fruit and foliage. A candle-stand with cut-glass drops is at each side of the bed and two Baroque tables in front of the alcove with a Savonnerie fire-screen, the only later addition to the room. Two large Delft urns also stand here. In the **Green Cabinet** with wall-covering of silk damask are portraits of the royal family with, among others, Gustav III as a baby and young child, and Karl XIII as a baby. It is assumed Lovisa Ulrika and her ladies embroidered the upholstery for the furniture here. Above the mirror is a small still life by Jean-Baptiste Oudry.

You now pass through an antechamber with more family portraits into the **Blue Cabinet** which Lovisa Ulrika used as a writing-room. The urns on the mantelpiece are from Berlin and the child's portrait is that of the daughter of the artist Carle van Loo. From here you can look down the long **library**. This was fitted by Jean Eric Rehn for Lovisa Ulrika in 1760. The escritoire and library steps are by Georg Haupt. In the small passage room are pictures of Drottningholm and Vadstena and you return to the Green Cabinet to reach Lovisa Ulrika's **dressing-room** in pale turquoise panels painted with flower-garlands (1740s). From here you are back at the stairs and go up to the **second floor**.

From the landing there is a long view of the gardens. The ceiling paintings are by Sylvius, of Greek gods. In the guardroom next door the ceiling is also by Sylvius, of the seasons. In the ante-room with its Gustavian blue/grey paint and flowers there is an 18C bureau and chest.

In the **Blue Drawing Room**, or Corner Salon, with damask-covered walls, the overdoors are by Elias Martin. The intarsia cabinet made to contain silk samples shows various stages in silk manufacturing on its doors. The **Chinese Drawing Room** is so called from the Chinese-style stove probably made in St. Petersburg. In three stages, it is a confection of green, pink and blue, with statues and roundels of landscapes. The Gobelins tapestry of Theseus was given to Gustav III by Louis XVI in 1784. The piece of furniture which looks like a bureau opens out to become a guard's bed, by Georg Haupt, who also made the one in Stockholm palace. In **King Oskar's Hall** is a set of Mortlake tapestries of the story of Hero and Leander—unfortunately one was cut in half to fit the space. Some statue or vase stands and two little desk-like pieces are covered in Boulle marquetry. There is a portrait of Oskar II. The **Generals' Hall** in dark blue and gold has battle-scenes and portraits of generals of the wars of Karl XII, together with a portrait of the king, all by David von Krafft.

The **Karl XI Gallery** looks out over the water at one side and there is a good view of the staircase on the other. The hall is dedicated to the warlike deeds of this king in the Skåne wars with twelve somewhat faded battle pictures by Lemke (1670s). Sylvius painted the Greek allegory on the ceiling, and there is a bust of Karl XI. The **Yellow Drawing Room** is hung with 17C Brussels tapestries showing the seasons, months and elements, and from here you can look into the Queen's Hall with a writing-desk by Georg Haupt of 1770.

The **Hall of State** has an original ceiling with trompe l'œil painting of columns and balustrade surrounding a scene of Greek gods. The rest was redecorated in white and gold in the 19C by Scholander. All around are portraits of European monarchs of the 19C. Finally, the decorative so-called **guard-room** with heavy stucco-work and ceiling by Sylvius of the fall of Phaeton functioned as an ante-room to the Hall of State.

The **chapel** in the north pavilion was finished in the 1730s, with white walls and marbled pillars. The altar has a picture painted by Georg Engelhart Schröder the court painter.

The ***Drottningholm Court Theatre** is to the right of the palace (open May–Aug 12.00–16.30, Sept 13.00–15.00. Guided tours in English). Queen Lovisa Ulrika came from Prussia and was accustomed to European culture and amusements, so she had the theatre built in 1766 by Carl Fredrik Adelcrantz, who actually finished by paying for most of it himself. The materials were simple—stucco, wood, plaster and papier maché were combined and worked to produce a true Rococo décor. That cultivated monarch Gustav III made the place into a lively meeting-point for the arts. Unfortunately, Gustav met his death by the assassin's bullet in another opera house, in Stockholm, and after such a patron and such an end, interest in theatre in general and this one in particular languished for many years. The building mouldered in dust and cobwebs until 1921 when a researcher suddenly realised he had found an 18C theatre in which time had stood still. The original scenery was there and has been faithfully copied for use. The stage machinery, however, owing much to shipboard techniques with capstans, needed only new ropes to function again. There are machines for waves, clouds and storms and of course trapdoors.

The tour begins in a small room to the right of the entrance foyer, which was once given to the architect to live in, and after another small room the visitor goes up to the ***auditorium**. This seats 450 people and few changes have been made to the décor apart from installing electric light. The line of chandeliers goes down the sides of the auditorium and across the front of the stage, linking them together, which is also achieved by the way in which the cornice continues on to the stage. There are six boxes borne on consoles, the middle ones at each side being for the king and the queen.

The acoustics, with all the wood and plaster, are very good. The stage is exceptionally deep, almost 20m, with 4 per cent tilt. The ceiling is stretched canvas, painted to resemble stucco and the rest of the theatre similarly conveys a complete Rococo image. Since virtually no maintenance has been done for 200 years the illusion needs the dim lighting. Now between 30 and 40 performances are given annually and authenticity of period is the main preoccupation, from the works performed to musical instruments and costumes. (Behind the scenes were living-quarters for the actors, not on view because of their fragility.)

Next shown is the **veranda**, a large light neo-Classical room added by Gustav III for socialising. The French architect had planned an open loggia but Swedish weather inspired the sky-like covering which gains its effect because of the galleries just below. In the Carousel Room there are two large paintings by Pehr Hilleström (1779) illustrating the pageants which were held here with all the court taking part. The original flowered wall-paper is still here, nailed and not stuck, for easy removal and use elsewhere.

Behind the palace are the Baroque gardens with fountains and formal parterres originally laid out by Nicodemus Tessin the Elder. The bronzes are by Adriaen de Vries, war-booty from Prague and Denmark.

North of this is the English garden. There is a lake with an island containing 250 lime trees planted in radiating lines. The octagonal 'Gothic tower' was built in 1790. Signs _Kina slott_ pointing down the garden and then left lead to the Chinese Pavilion. On the way you pass a wooden tent-like structure, a guard post designed by Adelcrantz.

The **Chinese Pavilion**, newly restored in shining red lacquer, was finished in 1769 to designs by Adelcrantz and interiors by Rehn. With its wavy eaves-line, golden roof decorations, and curving wings linking its main rooms, it is an 18C European concoction of chinoiserie liberally dosed with Swedish Rococo.

The octagonal marble entrance hall leads on the left to the **Red Room** with gold and red panelling containing 18C Chinese lacquer screens of landscapes in gold, silver and a little colour. This is the only really Chinese room in the building. Next comes the curved Yellow Gallery with two cases of oriental pieces, and the wing ends in the Green Drawing Room in green, gold and white with lattice-work and foliage.

The oval **Mirrored Drawing Room**, straight ahead from the entrance hall, is in cream and gold. The headings of the mirrors have dragons while the overdoors incorporate 'Chinese' scenes. The sewing-table is in lacquer, with gold and silver ornament, and the fittings are carved ivory. On the left is the bedchamber with walls covered with pink watered silk. The three pictures are made of feathers, cloth and bone, and there is a genuine Chinese bamboo table. On the right of the drawing-room is the deep rose-pink **Sewn Room**, named after the embroidered wall-hangings of foliage, trees and birds made by the Queen and her attendants.

To the right of the entrance hall the **Yellow Room** has lacquer panels, and Japanese geisha figures on the mantelpiece. The Green Galley leads to the **Blue Drawing Room** with paintings inspired by Boucher and Watteau. The large urns are Chinese famille rose of 1740 and there is an 18C lacquer screen.

Upstairs, the **Octagon** has original taffeta wall-coverings of flowers, foliage and birds. To the left the library contains books mainly in French and in matching bindings. There is a collection of Chinese trinkets, figurines, dogs and birds. There is also an ante-room with Chinese wall-paper, from which one looks into the **Yellow Cabinet** hung with Chinese silks, containing lacquer boxes and Chinese figures. Gustav III's oval study contains 12 Chinese paintings on glass of women musicians (18C).

Outside there are four detached pavilions. The one further away on the left is the Confidence, which was used as a dining-room. To the right the corresponding pavilion was used by King Adolf Fredrik as a carpentry workshop, and the nearer pavilion was a billiard-room.

Gripsholm

The dramatic castle of •**Gripsholm** on an islet beside the little town of Mariefred is the national portrait gallery of Sweden. It has 4000 portraits in its possession (1200 of them on display), original interiors and other valuable works of art (open May–Aug 10.00–16.00). If you are not driving, you can reach it by boat (fast or slow), or train to Läggesta, then bus or at certain times a veteran narrow-gauge steam railway. There is an all-in excursion ticket available at the tourist bureau.

There has been a castle here since the 14C, but it was Gustav Vasa who began the present building, and his successors over the centuries added to, remodelled and redecorated the place.

The Queen Dowager Hedvig Eleonora was one of those who made considerable changes (beginning of the 18C) as was Gustav III (end of the 18C), and there was a thorough renovation in the 1890s. Today there is a small irregular courtyard framed by the Grip or Griffin Tower, then (clockwise) the Vasa Tower, the Theatre Tower and the Prison Tower. Attached to this core is a larger courtyard with lower wings.

As you go over the drawbridge and into the first courtyard the massive **Griffin Tower** is ahead. This is named after the coat of arms of the first builder of a fortress here. On the right of the arch you have just come through are the royal housekeeper's apartments and on the wall by the arch are two casts of medieval reliefs. The wing to the right was built in the 1690s. Directly to the left is the Commander's Wing and beyond, the Cavalier Wing (18C) and Karl IX's wing (16C). Two ornamented Russian cannon are in the courtyard.

The way leads into the small inner courtyard, with a carved timber oriel room over the entrance steps. The door to the left leads out on to a jetty.

There are no labels in English and the only information in English is in the guide-book on sale. On the other hand the pictures themselves are all labelled and in more or less chronological sequence as you follow the room numbers. **Rooms 1–7** were remodelled in the 1890s to look like 16C interiors. **Room 1** is called the Astrak room after the tiles on the floor and the portraits are of Gustav Vasa and his sons and their contemporaries, such as the Sture family who opposed them. An important portrait here is the relief of **Gustav Vasa** by Willem Boy. The next room with an original ceiling has 17C portraits. You can look into **Room 3**, *Duke Karl's Chamber** which has original panelling, painted ceiling and built-in furniture from the 1570s, a rare example of Renaissance interior decoration. **Room 4** has a **coffered 16C ceiling** (not originally here) and a North German bridal chest, while **Room 5** has a painting of the architect Nicodemus Tessin the Younger and **Room 6** of the court painter Ehrenstrahl. **Room 7** with portraits from the reign of Karl XII has the sculptor Precht and the engineer Polhem, and **Room 8** is the round Lower Armoury in the Griffin Tower, with an inscription in red, opposite the door, by two prisoners of 1600.

On the second floor most of the décor is 18C. No. 9, the **Throne Room**, is the largest in the castle. Behind the throne as part of the canopy is a very fine Spanish 16C *hanging** showing Zeus, Callisto and Eros. The portraits are 17C copies, and the ceiling was raised in the 19C to make room for them.

Rooms 10–13 were fitted in the 1780s for Gustav III's sister Princess Sofia Albertina. They start with the **Audience Chamber** with **corner cupboards** by Georg Haupt, and an 18C gilt-framed **mirror**. The portraits are from 1720–72. The **Bedchamber** has original décor from 1782 and there is a portrait of the princess. The bureau is 18C and the clock is French of c 1800. There follow the princess' study and the maids' room. From the narrow **Room 14** you can look into rooms used by the Mistress of the Household and Gustav III's doctor. There are portraits of King Adolf Fredrik and Queen Lovisa Ulrika.

Rooms 17–26 are the **King's Apartments**. After the Wardrobe and the Tower Room comes **Room 19**, the **King's Bedchamber**, with painted beamed ceiling of the 17C and panelling from the 18C by Jean Eric Rehn. The Japanese lacquer **chest** (c 1600) is patterned in gold, mother of pearl and gilt brass. The **mirror** (mid 17C German) is framed in silver. The **bed** is French Baroque with silk and silver embroidery.

After the Lesser Cabinet, with two pictures of the castle, comes the **Council Chamber** with a 16C coffered ceiling and imitation gilt leather wall-covering of 1890. The 17C **table** has a top of ivory, mother of pearl and tortoiseshell, and the silver brocade chairs are 19C. The **amber chest** in the glass case is early 18C probably from Germany and the ebony and tortoiseshell **cabinet** is 17C. The large **family portrait** is by Ehrenstrahl (Karl XI and family) and opposite is an **equestrian portrait** of Karl XI again by Ehrenstrahl, while the other **equestrian portrait** is of Karl XII.

After a 19C Audience Chamber, the **Guard Room** has an excellent 16C **ceiling** and you can go into the Oriel (19C) above the courtyard, with pictures of Gripsholm. The **Upper Ante-chamber** has late 18C pictures, with personalities from the reign of Gustav III.

The **White Drawing Room** in the Theatre Tower, in lavish gilt and white, was designed by Rehn, with portraits of contemporary rulers, including George III of England. Gustav's own **portrait** is by Alexander Roslin.

The **Queen's Apartments** are **Rooms 27–33**. The **Green Drawing Room** was decorated in 1780 and the Gustavian furniture is original, though with 19C covers, and the bureaux are 18C French. There are portraits of Adolf Fredrik and Lovisa Ulrika. A long narrow audience chamber leads into the **Queen's Bedchamber** (1780), with panelling, mirrors and silk hangings in Gustavian style. Here the **corner cabinets** have paintings after Boucher. From the dressing room you can reach the long Westphalian Gallery with portraits of the delegates discussing the Peace of Westphalia in 1648.

After the Dressing Room, Wardrobe and Tower Room with the Gripsholm china service, stairs to the next floor lead to the theatre vestibule. To the left is the *theatre (1781) a masterpiece of Gustavian design fitted with great ingenuity into the confines of the tower. It was designed by Erik Palmstedt for Gustav III, with great fluted columns and mirrors, boxes for eminent guests and two statues by Sergel. The portraits on this floor are 19C and 20C. After some guest rooms and the sentry corridor you can look into 'Erik XIV's Prison', so-called, but not in fact where he was kept.

The large gallery, **Room 44**, has group portraits from the late 17C to today. The Upper Armoury, **Room 45**, has a stuffed lion, given (live) to Fredrik I. There are guest apartments and then the Tower Room with self-portraits. After **Room 53** with modern portraits, you can see Duke Fredrik Adolf's apartments. Back on the ground floor there are a few more rooms including the **Lower Roundel** with foreign portraits.

The pretty little town of **Mariefred** has an 18C town hall (with tourist bureau), a 17C church and a restored old inn on the lake shore. The church and the inn are on the foundations of the 15C Carthusian priory which gave the town its name (Pax Mariae).

Birka

The first Viking town worthy of the name was on an island called Björkö (Birch Island) in lake Mälaren, 30km west of Stockholm. It lies on a junction of waterways from Uppsala to Södertälje (north to south) and from Stockholm and the Baltic to the western reaches of the lake, also passable in winter by sledge. Local farmers on Björkö were always turning up curious objects while ploughing and even in the 17C some attempts were made at excavation. In the 19C a local scientist began to dig, and collected thousands of finds, which somehow dropped into obscurity until the 1930s. The latest investigation started in 1990, in the area known as the 'Black Earth'—black because of the occupation deposits.

You can drive to Rastaholm (Ekerö) and take a ferry, or take a two-hour boat-trip from the City Hall. (Tours run mid May–mid Aug. Guided tours are included in the price of the boat-trip, though you can wander on your own. Some English guided tours—extra fee.)

The remains of **Birka** are on the north-west part of the island. In Viking times there were two islands as the sea was 5m higher then, and remains of jetties have been found on the old shoreline. There was a rampart along most of the landward side of the settlement enclosing an area of c 7ha, and near the sea a protective fort for emergencies. Burials naturally took place outside the rampart, and there are about 2500 mounds, ship-settings, triangles and single standing stones.

Inside the rampart the inhabitants lived in single dwellings with 6–10 people in each. The fort was built round a natural outcrop, surrounded by an earth rampart with a palisade on top. 700–1000 people lived here between the end of the 8C and c 980, and to judge by the finds, led a varied, even cosmopolitan existence. Mirrors, bone combs, swords, scissors, brooches, beads, amber, keys, clasps, pottery, bronze dishes, iron rings, arrowheads, games boards, needle-cases and wooden buckets reflect their interests, occupations and habits. The finds are in the Historical Museum in Stockholm.

It is assumed that this town was ruled from the king's seat on the nearby island of Adelsö. The town had its own council (*ting*) and was a thriving craft and trade centre—Arab coins and Chinese silk have even been found. Furs of fox, squirrel and marten were traded and bronze-casting was also carried on.

In 829 the monk, Ansgar, from Corvey in Germany, arrived to try to convert the Swedes. Despite being attacked and robbed by pirates, he persevered and received permission from King Björn to preach. He stayed for 18 months but by all accounts was only moderately successful. A later second visit had not much more lasting effect. Birka is mentioned in Vita Ansgarii (870) and Adam of Bremen (1070s) mentions it as a 'town of the Goths'.

On arriving on the island you can join the guide who leads the group to the most important areas. The route goes straight ahead from the landing-stage then bears left through a gate. At the first fork in the path a map shows where everything is. (There is also an English map with notes for sale at the kiosk by the landing-stage, as well as an English booklet with considerable archaeological detail.) Taking the right fork brings you to an area of about 400 graves, mostly mounds, but some stone-settings also. Leaving the path and cutting across to the left, you find a single standing-stone among the mounds, probably originally coloured in black, white and red. (There are only fragments of runes on Birka, because their heyday was later than that of Birka.) Some mounds have a hollow in the top where hopeful looters dug, only to be disappointed, since in this cemetery the grave-goods were cremated with the bodies.

North of this area with graves is the **fort** on the highest point of the island, with several entrances through the earth rampart, the largest of which is called the King's Gate. There were no buildings in the fort as it was simply for emergency protection. On the highest part of the rock a Celtic cross was erected in 1934, commemorating the year 1829, a thousand years after Ansgar arrived. North of the fort an area of 200 chambered tombs was found. These were lined with wood, with inhumed, not cremated, bodies and very rich grave-goods. To the north-west there may have been some sort of guardhouse since weapons have been found.

From the fort you can see for a considerable distance. To the north-west on the next island Adelsö, you can see a white church near which the site of a king's palace has been found, probably the place from which Birka was ruled. Below the fort in a field to the north is the modern excavation. Further to the north-east, beyond the town rampart, is a very large area of grave-mounds, about 1600 of them. To the east is the village of **Björkby** and beyond you can make out the dark shape of St. Ansgar's Chapel (1930).

This has works by Carl Milles and Carl Eldh. Another area of mounds is to the south-east at Kärrbäcka, and there are isolated mounds here and there.

A favourite walk is to take the road past the excavations round to the chapel, but do not miss your boat as it is quite a way. Near the landing-stage a temporary exhibition gives further information which will be extended and improved as work continues.

The Archipelago and the Lake

Stockholm Archipelago is dear to the hearts of all Stockholmers, who take to the water and the islands in their thousands in the summer, retreating to the remotest and quietest areas where they have their summer cottages and boats. Estimates of the number of islands are generally between 24,000 and 30,000, depending on what you mean by an island.

Ways of seeing some of them are many, ranging from a half-hour ferry-trip to a luxury day-cruise or an island-hopping card offering unlimited travel for a couple of weeks. There are various forms of accommodation on the islands—youth hostels should be booked ahead. Some islands have no water-supply.

For a short sample trip you might try Fjäderholmarna (25min) where there is an aquarium of Baltic fish, a smoke-house and restaurants. Other islands are Själbottna, Svartlöga, Rödlöga and Arholma to the north, Grinda, Sandhamn, Möja and Finnhamn to the east, and Dalarö, Fjärdlång and Utö to the south.

A trip with some historical interest is that to **Vaxholm**, where there is a 19C fortress. You can get there by boat (1hr) or by buses 670–673 from Tekniska Högskolan underground station. In the town there are some 18C and 19C wooden houses—the tourist bureau has an English leaflet describing them. Waxholm Hotel is from the turn of the century, and the oldest streets are in the east part of the town. There is a local museum on the north coast, and an 18C church, and 19C town hall.

The fortress is on an islet just off the coast (open mid May–Aug, half-hourly ferry). There was a fort here from Gustav Vasa's time, but as it is now, it was completed in 1863. It contains a museum with displays on the defence of the archipelago, and fortification, as well as on the local mine at Ytterby which gave its name to the element Yttrium.

To the west lies lake Mälaren on the shores of which are some of the most impressive sights of the Stockholm region, accessible by boat. Besides Drottningholm, Gripsholm and Birka, mentioned above, you can also reach Sigtuna, Uppsala, Skokloster, Strängnäs and Västerås by water.

16

Stockholm to Gävle

A. Direct

Total distance 173km. Stockholm—E4 70km *Uppsala—103km **Gävle**.

The E4 runs north through Stockholm suburbs passing Haga Park, then through Sollentuna and Upplands Väsby. The next junction (36km) Arlandastad is the nearest to Norrsunda Church and Rosersberg castle. The church has 15C paintings and a 17C Dutch Renaissance funerary chapel built for Johan Sparre.

Rosersbergs slott is c 5km south-east of the junction (guided tours mid May–mid Sept on the hour 12.00–15.00, Swedish only but guides can usually give some help in English). The castle was begun in the 17C but remodelled as a Baroque palace in the 18C by Nicodemus Tessin the Younger, and remodelled again in 1797–1815. This renovation was for Duke Karl (later Karl XIII), and the other members of the royal family particularly associated with it were Karl XIV Johan and his widow Desideria. It contains interiors from the period 1795–1825, and has extensive grounds.

Some ground-floor rooms have isolated displays. On the first floor, the **Dining Room** retains some of its décor by Jean Eric Rehn. Part of the Rosersberg china service by Rörstrand is shown. The very large picture is by Louis Bélanger, and other pictures are of Swedish castles. The next room is in Empire style, while the **Red Salon** has damask wall-coverings and late 18C furniture. The next room which was used as a bedchamber is decorated with laurel wreaths and has four overdoors painted with the times of day. There is an inlaid mahogany sewing-table. After two smaller rooms, the 'conversation room' has a curved sofa fitted into an apse-like niche. Desideria's **bedchamber** at the end of the building has an elaborate turquoise and gold draped bed-canopy. The roundels depict the seasons. To the other side of the central axis the emphasis is more masculine with royal portraits, and a council room with a large portrait of Karl XIII holding the document of adoption of Karl XIV Johan. The sculpture of the woman with the lion is Mother Svea (Sweden).

Upstairs there are war pictures, with a giant sea battle piece (1788) by Louis Jean Desprez, in a room whose décor is devoted to battle honours. Other rooms are the audience room with mirrors and pilasters, the picture gallery, museum room and library. The last room shown is one designed in 1823 by Fredrik Blom with green draperies over the bed and on the walls, inspired by Roman campaign tents, and incorporating a triumphal arch and Ionic columns. There is also an inlaid desk, and typical stoves in the form of truncated columns.

To reach Sigtuna you can either continue on the side-roads or return to the E4 and leave at (2km) the next junction. (Sigtuna can also be conveniently reached by public transport from Stockholm. Take the commuter train (*pendeltåg*) to Märsta, and then bus 570 or 575—check the number. There are boat-trips in summer from the city hall quay.)

*Sigtuna (pop. 5000) boasts the oldest street in Sweden, in the same position as when the town was founded. It used to be thought that Olof Skötkonung founded it in the 11C, but recent finds suggest it was already in existence c 970. It replaced Birka as the foremost trading centre in the country and was the first to mint coins. It has three ruined churches of the 11C which is an indication of its stature at that time. In 1164 the diocese which had been established here was moved to Uppsala, and in the 13C Stockholm took over its place as the premier trading centre. The Dominican friary founded in 1247 was razed at the Reformation. Today it is a picturesque little town of painted wooden 18C and 19C houses and shops. It has a famous boarding-school.

From the car park take **Stora gatan** towards the west—this is the street still on its historic line. Soon on the right is a small square with the diminutive 18C **town hall** (open summer 12.00–16.00, like everything else here). Inside on the left is a room which was used as a prison, on the right the council chamber with decorative frieze, eight royal portraits and 18C furniture (detailed leaflet in English).

Back on the main street the **tourist bureau** is in Drakegården, an 18C inn, with a small café. Two blocks along is Lundströmska Gården, a middle-class home of c 1900, open to the public. As Stora gatan swings to the right there is the museum, with exhibitions on the history of the town (leaflet in English), soon to expand.

The next main road to the right leads shortly to the ruins of **S:t Per church** on the left, built in the first half of the 12C. Much of the central tower is intact and under it is one of the oldest cross-vaults in the country. The church has a chancel, apse and transepts with apses. The nave is double-aisled, and there are the remains of the west tower. It has been suggested that this may have been the cathedral.

Return towards the centre by Prästgatan opposite the church. The next lane to the left has two runestones. Further along Prästgatan are the remains of the tower of S:t Lars church and more runestones. Just after this is the brick Gothic Maria church, and standing in the churchyard the ruined **S:t Olof church**. This has 1m thick walls and heavy square pillars in a cruciform plan, with central tower. The nave is so short that it could be supposed that it was never fully completed. The large grave beside the church with the name Olof Palme is that of the uncle of the assassinated Prime Minister of the same name.

The 13C **Maria church** (open 10.00–18.00) was one of the first brick churches in Sweden (as the country's boundaries were then). The outlines of the cloisters of the friary can be seen on the south wall. It has one small tower on the north-west corner, decorated step-gables and a straight east end.

Inside, it has a nave and two aisles. By the entrance above the organ is a 15C painting of the Trinity. In the north aisle there are more **paintings** of the same century and a Swedish altarpiece again of the 15C with a modern stained-glass window above.

The main **altarpiece** is from North Germany with figures of the 14C and 15C. To the left is a 14C wall-painting and the statues on either side are St. Dominic and Christ. The carved wood pulpit is from the 17C and the large crucifix 15C or 16C. There are medieval figures in a case at the end of the south aisle.

From here it takes a minute or two back to Stora gatan, but if you have time the shores of the Sigtuna fjord beyond offer an agreeable walk.

From Sigtuna you could also visit Skokloster castle, about 23km (see Örebro to Stockholm route).

It is 32km to the old university town of ***UPPSALA**, the fourth largest conurbation (pop. 100,500).

Gamla Uppsala (Old Uppsala), 4km to the north of the present town centre, was the main place of worship of the pagan Svea tribe. Attempts were made to eradicate the old religion in the first years of Christianity by building a church on the site of the temple. The church became the cathedral (the archdiocese was established in 1164) but in c 1273 the bishop took up his see in the small settlement of Uppsala itself, then known as Östra Aros. The Pope stipulated that the name should be transferred with the see, and the precious relics of St. Erik (see below).

At that time the lower land level meant that Uppsala was easily in touch with the open Baltic, with a thriving market and port, and also the seat of the king. When Stockholm took over as main government centre Uppsala retained the spiritual supremacy and coronations continued to take place here.

The university was founded in 1477 and was the chief function of the town for centuries. Gustav Vasa began the building of the castle in 1549 and his sons completed it and turned it into a Renaissance palace. It has been the scene of many stirring events of Swedish history (see below), including the Uppsala Assembly when the Lutheran faith was formally adopted as the state religion, and the abdication of Queen Kristina.

In 1702 a great fire destroyed much of the town, including large parts of the cathedral and castle. When the railways came in the 19C industry came too, so that Uppsala is now as industrial as it is academic. But the sights and sites, architectural, religious and historic, to interest the tourist are gathered harmoniously on one side of the Fyrisån which winds an attractive course through the centre, and the modern shopping area is just over on the other side. Fyrishov is a leisure complex with large adventure pool, campsite, chalets and many amenities.

Tourist bureau: Fyris torg and the castle. Tel. (018) 11 75 00.

Post office: Kungsgatan 11.

Bus station: By Centralstation.

Telephone, telegram: Bangårdsgatan 7. Tel. (018) 19 14 75.

For the first-time visitor parking at the castle has the advantages that it is easy to find (*slottet*), easy to park and cheaper than the very centre of town.

The ***castle** was begun by Gustav Vasa in the mid 16C and, as so often happened with Gustav's castles, was fashioned by his sons into a Renaissance palace. Here one of them, Erik XIV, in a fit of madness instigated the murder of Svante and Nils Sture and other prominent men on suspicion of treason. The Uppsala Assembly of 1593, which established the supremacy of the Lutheran Church in Sweden, took place in the Hall of State, where also Parliament resolved to enter the Thirty Years War (1630). Gustavus Adolphus and Axel Oxenstierna deliberated over the war in the Council Chamber. In 1653 plague broke out in Stockholm, and Queen Kristina moved here for the last year of her reign before her abdication of 1654 at a ceremony in the Hall of State.

After the fire of 1702 the castle was never rebuilt in its original rectangular form. Instead it was restored by the court architect Carl Hårleman to an L-shape, and so it has remained with few changes. The fourth corner is marked by the Styrbiskop bastion, on which the Gunilla Bell stands. The original bell (recast in the 18C) was presented by Gunilla Bielke the second wife of Johan III. Here Uppsala students celebrate the coming of spring (*Valborgsmässoafton* or Walpurgis Night, 30 April) by a torchlight procession. The castle is now mainly occupied by the county governor, county offices and such, but there are three sections open to the public (open daily mid April–Sept).

The way in to the **Hall of State** (Rikssalen) is through the tourist bureau and café. On the ground floor there are royal portraits and some miniature

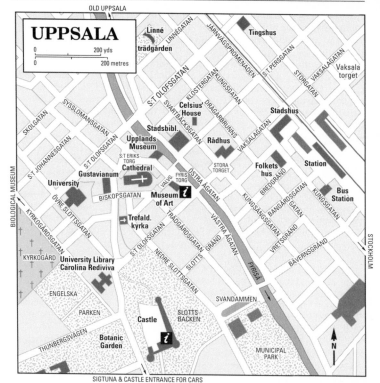

OLD UPPSALA

UPPSALA

0   200 yds

0   200 metres

Linné
trädgården

LINNÉGATAN

JÄRNVÄGSPROMENADEN

Tingshus

S:T PERSGATAN

STORGATAN

VAKSALAGATAN

Vaksala
torget

S:T OLOFSGATAN

KLOSTERGATAN

KUNGSGATAN

SVARTBÄCKSGATAN

DRAGARBRUNNS

Celsius'
House

Stadshus

VAKSALAGATAN

SYSSLOMANSGATAN

SKOLGATAN

Stadsbibl.

Upplands
Museum

Rådhus

S:T JOHANNESGATAN

S:T OLOFSGATAN

S:T ERIKS
TORG

Cathedral

STORA
TORGET

Folkets
hus

Station

BREDGRAND

BANGÅRDSGATAN

KUNGSGATAN

BIOLOGICAL MUSEUM

Gustavianum

University

ÖVRE SLOTTSGATAN

KYRKOGÅRDSGATAN

BISKOPSGATAN

VÅNG

FYRIS
TORG

Museum
of Art

ÖSTRA ÅGATAN

KUNGSÄNGSGATAN

Bus
Station

Trefald.
kyrka

TRÄDGÅRDSGATAN

VÅNG

VÄSTRA ÅGATAN

GRÄND

VRETGRÄND

STOCKHOLM

KYRKOGÅRD

University Library
Carolina Rediviva

S:T OLOFSGATAN

NEDRE SLOTTSGATAN

SLOTTS
GRÄND

FYRISÅ

BÄVERNSGRÄND

ENGELSKA

PARKEN

Castle

SLOTTS
BACKEN

SVANDAMMEN

THUNBERGSVÄGEN

Botanic
Garden

MUNICIPAL
PARK

N

SIGTUNA & CASTLE ENTRANCE FOR CARS

historic costumes in cases. On the stairway is a large portrait of Archbishop Nathan Söderblom (d 1931) who worked for ecumenism and received the Nobel Peace Prize. At the top is a copy of the well-known equestrian portrait of Queen Kristina (original by Sébastien Bourdon in the Prado), and more royal portraits. The Hall of State was made higher by Carl Hårleman (the former height can be seen), and is now hung with 17C **Flemish tapestries**. The hall can also be viewed from the upper floor, where there are copies of Classical sculptures in Athens.

The other two sections of the castle are approached under the arch called King Johan's Gate. To the left in the cellar is the castle **museum** which traces the building history with models and plans. There is an informative video shown in Swedish and English. The display starts with Gustav Vasa's castle with keep and courtyard, begun in 1549. Model 3 represents Johan III's plans, never completed. There is a picture of the great fire of 1702 and a model of the restored castle by Carl Hårleman. The original plans and a model of the Hall of State are shown, and how the chapel communicated with it. Illustrations of the stucco-work in the chapel are shown—at the moment inaccessible but may soon be open to the public.

To the right of the arch the ruins of the **Gräsgården bastion**, the oldest part of the castle remaining, have been made safe and walkways constructed under cover of the building around. Here and there scenes from the life of Vasa times 'Vasa vignettes' have been arranged with models and sound effects, such as the royal kitchen, the nursery and bedchamber. One room is called the Sture prison though it may well have been a guardroom. There is some information in English as you go round.

Standing by the Gunilla Bell on the Styrbiskop bastion you have a view over the cathedral and from the long side of the courtyard you can see the 18C-style garden below, part of the **Botanical Gardens**. This was the castle garden, and was given to the university by Gustav III in 1787 when Linné's garden (see below) became too small. Behind is the Classical-style Botanicum (Department of Botany), designed late 18C, finished early 19C, part of which is the **Orangery**, open to the public, as is the tropical greenhouse.

Walking down from the castle you see on the left the imposing *university library on its height facing Drottninggatan. The previous library was called Carolina after Karl IX and the new one built in the 19C was named Carolina Rediviva in honour of Karl XIV Johan. Its exhibition hall to the right of the entrance has a replica of the *Codex Argenteus (Silver Bible), written in silver on purple vellum, a very rare translation into the now extinct Gothic language of the gospels by Bishop Wulfila. This dates from the reign of Theoderich the Great (d 526), and was probably written in North Italy. It was in Germany for centuries, was captured by the Swedes when they looted Prague in 1648, and passed through many hands before coming to rest here. Other treasures are the **Carta Marina**, printed in Venice in 1539, drawn by Olaus Magnus, the last Catholic archbishop in Sweden, a 16C **map of Mexico**, books annotated by Copernicus, and examples of Ethiopian, Persian, Greek and Arabic MSS. There are several illuminated books, and facsimiles of the oldest book printed in Sweden and Snorre Sturlasson's *Edda*. Handwritten pieces by famous people include those by St. Birgitta and by Gustav III as a boy of eight.

Behind the library is the 'English park'—i.e. consisting of trees and grass, with a statue of Karl XIV Johan.

Almost opposite the library is the strip of park leading to the cathedral and a short distance along on the right is **Trefaldighetskyrkan** (Holy Trinity church). This was begun in stone and the brick parts are 14C—it survived the fire of 1702 relatively unscathed and was the only church in Uppsala where services could be held in the summer of 1702. It has a sturdy square tower over the entrance, with modest decoration of crosses and blind niches here and there. Inside, the clustered columns and vault-ribs are of brick, and some painting remains, with work by Albertus Pictor in the transepts.

This is the second church dedicated to the Trinity in Uppsala. The first was on the site of the cathedral, and it was there that King Erik in 1160 attended Mass after which he went out to fight the Danes on S:t Eriks torg where he met his death. Miracles were related about the healing qualities of his blood and a holy spring on the spot where he died, and he was shortly canonised.

The *cathedral just ahead was probably begun in the 1270s. The cathedral at Gamla Uppsala had been damaged by fire and the question of relocating the archdiocese had been debated for decades. French builders were engaged and brought the latest French ideas, but carried them out in native brick. The cathedral was finally consecrated in 1435. In the fire of 1702 it was almost destroyed, and was restored by Carl Hårleman. In 1885–93 Helgo Zetterwall rigorously restored the Gothic plan and added the steeples to the same height as the length of the church. The 19C surface of machine-made bricks was restored again in the 1930s, and the use of burnt bricks at regular intervals gives a spotty effect. Chapels surround the apse and sides, and there are transepts about half-way along the total length.

The **west doorway** was completed in 1431 but the figure of St. Erik is 19C. The **north doorway** remains from the 13C, as do parts of the south doorway. Inside, clustered columns are linked to the vaults by slim shafts up through the almost closed gallery with small round windows and the clerestory.

In the floor at the end of the left aisle is the gravestone of Carl von Linné (Linnaeus), and on the right a candle-stand, the 'Tree of Reconciled Peoples'. In the first chapel to the left is a modern textile hanging showing the building of the cathedral, and the next chapel is the burial place of Carl Banér and has a memorial to Linnaeus. It is also the temporary home of a medieval statue of St. Olof which is known to have come to Uppsala at the end of the 13C. In the next chapel, the scene with modern figures is changed according to the church's year.

The **pulpit** (1710) was carved by Burchardt Precht, with gilt scrolls and swags and a heavy elaborate canopy. The central vault-bay at the crossing is the Coronation Vault where Swedish kings were crowned until the 17C. The large chapel on the left is the Jagellonica Chapel, named after Katarina Jagellonica the first wife of Johan III. The couple's **Renaissance tombs** (Johan is actually buried with his father) have paintings above them, one of Stockholm, one of Cracow, the native cities of Johan and Katarina respectively.

The **Sture Chapel** is a memorial to the family murdered by Erik XIV, and also contains the grave of Ebba Brahe whom Gustavus Adolphus loved but never married. The **triptych** is from Brussels (16C), with the story of St. Anne. The Finsta Chapel contains the greatest treasure of the cathedral, the gilded silver **·shrine** of St. Erik. St. Birgitta's father, Birger Persson of Finsta, and her mother, are buried in this chapel. The slab has a representation of their seven children, including St. Birgitta.

In the centre chapel, which should be the Lady Chapel, is the great **Renaissance tomb** of Gustav Vasa, surrounded by obelisks. He has a wife to either side, and he, all three of his queens, and his son Johan III with his second wife Gunilla Bielke lie in the crypt below. The tomb, in alabaster with details of gilded bronze, was completed in 1571 by Willem Boy who made several funeral monuments for the Vasa family, including those of Princess Isabella in Strängnäs, and Katarina Jagellonica (above).

The main altar has a 3m high cross of silver and crystal. Around the ambulatory are capital and corbel **carvings** which survived the fire. The largest chapel on the right of the altar has two **sarcophagi** designed by Nicodemus Tessin the Younger, one for Bengt Oxenstierna (d 1702), chancellor to Karl XI, the other for Magnus Stenbock (d 1717) the final victor over the Danes. Past the transept are the Chapel of Peace and the Chapel of Prayer, then the Baroque tomb of Gustaf Banér (beheaded 1600). The tomb of Emanuel Swedenborg (1688–1772), the theologian and philosopher, is in the second chapel from the end.

The cathedral **museum** is in the north tower. Tickets are available at the book-stall, and the lift takes you to the fourth floor from where you walk down through exhibits on three floors. The museum contains medieval embroidered copes and jewel-encrusted chalices, a 12C reliquary and chasubles from the Albertus Pictor workshops. On the second floor are later chasubles and copes, collecting-bags of the 18C and 19C, as well as bishops' mitres. One case contains regalia, with crowns, orbs and sceptres, and in another are costumes belonging to the Stures murdered in 1567.

Opposite the cathedral is the **Gustavium**, rebuilt from a medieval building in the 17C for the university, under the auspices of Gustavus Adolphus who wanted educated men for his government. The building, restored in the 18C, sufficed for its purpose until the mid 19C, and now houses three small museums attached to the university, and the remarkable anatomical theatre in the cupola (open June–Aug 11.00–15.00). The **Egyptian collection** has mummy cases, vases, inscriptions, figurines and jewellery, and the **Nordic Department** has displays of clothing, tools, weapons and harness illustrating pre-Christian life in Scandinavia, including finds from the *boat-graves in Valsgärde. The Classical display has vases, heads and figurines, many from the Swedish expeditions to Cyprus.

On the **third floor** there is access to the tall cylindrical *Anatomical Theatre (1662—reconstructed), extending into the cupola from which it is top-lit. In the centre is the slab for dissection, and around climb steep narrow galleries with standing-room for students—no seats. The galleries are supported by Classical pilasters, Tuscan, Doric, Ionic, Corinthian and Composite, and there is the monogram of Karl XII in a cartouche in the cupola.

You can leave the Gustavium by the rear door and climb the hill to **Universitetshuset**, the imposing university building (open for guided tours in Swedish and English July–Aug 11.00, 13.00 and 14.00, but you can also go in as far as the foyer and its galleries without joining a tour).

The university was founded, the first in Scandinavia, by Archbishop Jakob Ulfsson in 1477 to educate priests, and has always been looked on as the foremost academic institution of the country. Carl von Linné and Anders Celsius were two of its leading luminaries. The present building was erected to the designs of Herman Holmgren, influenced by the Florentine Renaissance and was finished in 1887.

On the exterior the names of famous people are inscribed in roundels, and over the entrance stand four statues symbolising different faculties. The spacious foyer, reminiscent of the Baths of Caracalla in Rome, has three coffered domes. The green columns and the balustrades are of Kolmården marble, and there are replicas of Classical statues on the galleries.

The black-walled **Senate Room** where the board of the university meets is hung with portraits of royalty. (The university has the next largest collection of portraits after Gripsholm castle.) The painted panelled ceiling includes symbols of the faculties.

The entrance to the grand **Aula**, the main hall of the building, has the motto 'To think freely is great, to think rightly is greater' above the entrance. The hall is spectacularly decorated in gold, blue, red and green, with most attention riveted on the apse over the stage, with its pediment above and flanked by statues of Demosthenes and Sophocles. On the ceiling are oak-leaves for strength and on the gallery columns laurels for victory. The hall was built so that all 1500 students could gather in one place, but now there are 35,000 of them, so it is used for graduation and other ceremonies, and for concerts.

Upstairs the visitor is shown a series of faculty rooms and a lecture room. In the **Chancellor's Room** is the **Augsburg Cabinet**, a gift from that city to Gustavus Adolphus in 1632. It is an extraordinary creation which defies classification. It is made of oak, ebony and mother of pearl, and on top are heaped natural objects to symbolise the natural world. One part of it plays music, another is a dressing-table with toilet articles. Scenes from the Bible are painted on small alabaster panels. In the next room are exhibited more objects from its interior and it is evidently intended to unite all knowledge with the arts and more mundane needs.

After visiting Universitetshuset you can descend the grassy slope bearing left and join S:t Olofsgatan towards the river. In the block on the right just before the river **Walmstedtska Gården** (open weekends p.m.) shows a professor's home of the 19C.

Cross the river and take the second on the left, Svartbäcksgatan. **Linné's garden** is in the second block on the right. The garden was redesigned by Linné in 1745 and has now been recreated to the same plan which illustrates Linné's classification of plants. The building beyond is the **Orangery** with art exhibitions and the two pavilions are elegant tool sheds. Linné's house is on the right of the entrance to the garden and is where he lived, worked and gave lectures from 1743 until his death in 1778. On the ground floor are the dining-room, kitchen and his wife's room, and on the first floor his study, library and lecture-room, and there is a display of his works.

Return along Svartbäcksgatan, crossing S:t Olofsgatan into the shopping area. A short distance along, askew to the street, is the house where Anders Celsius (1701–44), originator of the Celsius temperature scale, worked from 1741 until his early death. He was Professor of Astronomy and had an observatory here, designed by Carl Hårleman, which continued in use until 1853.

Take the next to the right. (Straight ahead leads to Stora torget, the main square.) The white building on a tongue of land jutting into the river which you can see from the bridge is **Upplandsmuseet**, the county museum, and to get to it you pass the end of Fyris torg with the **tourist bureau**, and the **Art Gallery** (Konstmuseum) in a former hotel.

Turn right to reach the museum, in an old mill (open summer 11.00–16.00, rest of year 12.00–16.00). Here there are temporary displays on the **ground floor** and on the **first floor** the geological development of Uppland. **Folk art** includes 18C and 19C painted furniture and textiles, while folk music of the area shows the 'key-harp' (nyckelharpa), a complicated stringed instrument also found in other areas. You can ask at reception to listen to tapes.

On the **second floor** there is the history of Uppsala, with detailed English notes to borrow. The highlights of the town's history are chronicled, like St. Erik's death, the building of the cathedral and the founding of the university. There is a model of the cathedral hill in the late Middle Ages, and a reconstructed 15C dwelling, as well as a good carving of St. Anne of the 15C. A small section pictures Linné's Uppsala with the various crafts which would have been practised. There is another floor with a miscellany of objects, and a small display of rya rugs and how they developed from bedspreads to floorcoverings.

Beyond the museum is **S:t Eriks torg**, the traditional place of the saint's death.

On the way back towards Fyris Torg there is an attractive café in a medieval vault where you can also sit out on the river bank.

Turn right up Valvgatan which leads under an arch through a house called **Skyttaneum**, rebuilt in the 17C for use by the university, named after the owner. Now you are back at the cathedral.

Two museums lie just beyond the centre. The house of the artist **Bror Hjorth** is at Norbyvägen 26 (open July–Aug Tue–Sun p.m., fewer days rest of year). Norbyvägen starts opposite the south end of the castle, and the house is about 800m along, on a corner on the left. This is crammed with

Hjorth's works and gives a good idea of his range. He lived 1894–1968, and evolved a primitive style in wood, bronze and glaring colour in paint, of which his altarpiece in Jukkasjärvi (Lappland) is perhaps the example best known to tourists and through reproductions.

The **Biology Museum** is in a park at Vasagatan 4 and contains dioramas against which are shown Swedish animals (check at tourist bureau for opening times).

***Gamla Uppsala** (Old Uppsala) is well signposted to the north of the town (4km) on road 290. The ancient Svea tribe had made (Gamla) Uppsala into an important trading and communications centre, and in time it became a centre of administration also, where the *ting* council met. The first mound you come to, as yet not fenced in, is the Tingshögen or Ting Mound, the site of the council meetings, which continued to the 16C.

Beyond are the three tumuli surrounded by a fence, the ***Mounds of the Kings** (c 6C). The first and third were excavated in the mid 19C and contained cairns with cremation burials. The middle one has not been fully explored, but it is assumed its cairn is the largest. Remains of burnt grave goods indicate that food, weapons and horses accompanied the king. The kings have been identified as Egil, in the east mound, his father Aun in the centre, and his grandson Adil. It is hoped to have a special museum here for the finds which are at present scattered in Stockholm and Uppsala.

From here you can look across the plain to Uppsala and see the steeples of the cathedral against the sky. Beyond the mounds is a large area with many other burials from the late Iron Age. Boat-graves have also been found in the vicarage garden west of the church (9C or 10C) and at Valsgärde (500–1100) 2km away—these were different in that they were not cremations and there were rich finds.

The ***church** is beside the 'ting' mound.

The cult of the Aesir (the collective name for the Norse gods) known principally from Snorre Sturlasson's *Edda*, had three main gods, Odin, Thor and Frey, and the three mounds have sometimes been linked with them. Adam of Bremen (11C) gives an account of the temple of Uppsala, decked with gold, a gold chain on the roof and the scene of bloody sacrifices before statues of the three gods. The temple proved a stumbling-block to Christian missionaries, who having converted the people of Sigtuna, turned their attention to Uppsala.

Evidence of post-holes under the present church support the assumption that this was the site of the great temple, and it seems reasonable to suppose that the church was deliberately placed on this spot. A small stave church was first built, then some time in the 12C a large cathedral replaced it. The present church represents the chancel and crossing of this. The transepts and nave, which extended to the present churchyard wall, had been demolished following a fire some time in the first half of the 13C. The apse was enlarged later. Stout foundations point to a heavy western gallery and a taller tower than today. The ground plan is related to that of the churches of S:t Per and S:t Olof in Sigtuna, to Vår Fru Kyrka in Enköping and to St. Petri in Bremen, showing traits of Anglo-Norman and Anglo-Saxon traditions, with its apses on the transepts and central tower. The brick buttresses mark the position of the transepts and the supporting pillars of the central tower can be seen, as well as damage by the 13C fire.

The church soon became the centre for the cult of St. Erik and then it became a cathedral, the seat of the first Archbishop of Sweden, Stefan of Alvastra, appointed in 1164. Until then, Sweden had been part of the archdiocese of all Scandinavia whose archbishop's seat was in Lund, then under Danish rule.

In the porch are two collecting chests. One is made from an oak log fitted with iron bands and locks, dating from the earliest days of the church. The other is 17C and has no fewer than seven locks, so that seven people have to agree on opening it—today it is used to collect money for post-cards. Entering the nave, the former crossing, you can see on the left a case of church silver which includes a 14C chalice and a 13C censer. The plain font is from the 13C, rescued from the churchyard where it did duty as a tombstone. On the left wall of the nave there is a memorial to Anders Celsius (the upper one). The ceiling paintings are from the 15C when the vault was built. They contain the arms of the Oxenstierna family, the horns of an ox. The Virgin and Child sculpture is of the 15C, probably Swedish. The **altarpiece** is also Swedish 15C and features several Scandinavian saints. SS Olof and Eskil are at the top left, St. Erik and Bishop Henrik top right, and St. Birgitta is bottom centre, with a book. The altar consists of the tomb-stone of St. Erik once in the floor of the church, now set on a modern plinth. The crucifix on the rood beam has a figure of Christ of the 15C and on the south side is a 13C crucifix. The bishop's throne is from the 12C. The detached bell-tower was built in 1514.

The local open-air museum **Disagården** is half a kilometre away (open all day in summer, guided tours pm. English leaflet). The three farms have been gathered to give an idea of an Uppland village. The largest dwelling is from the early 19C and is furnished. Most of the other buildings are 18C and 19C, with one or two earlier examples. The cottage from Bärby is decorated with 19C wall-paintings, and there are all the usual farm out-houses, with vegetable and herb gardens.

From Gamla Uppsala you could cut across on a side-road to road 288, to the **church** at **Vaksala**, also about 4km from the centre, or of course start from Uppsala itself.

The church was begun in the 12C but remodelled in the 14C with rib vaults. In the 15C two side chapels were added. The ***triptych** was made in Antwerp c 1510. Being specially commissioned for the church, it has the parable of the wise and foolish virgins—this is a pun on the place-name, for 'vak' comes from 'to watch' or 'be wakeful'. The two saints to whom the church is dedicated, St. Andrew and St. John the Baptist are on the doors. Scandinavian saints are in evidence—St. Birgitta, St. Erik, St. Olof, St. Botvid with a fish and St. Sigfrid holding a pail with children's heads.

The oversized font is a copy of the 14C one. The bishop's chair or bridal chair is from the 13C. In the chapel to the left can be seen the wise virgins again, this time painted. The paintings date from the 14C and 15C (ceiling) and include strange half-human, half-animal figures. In front of the church are a 15C tithe barn and church hostel.

Excursions from Uppsala

The main excursions are to Sigtuna and Skokloster, treated elsewhere. These can also be reached by boat from Uppsala on summer weekends. *MS Enköping*, built in 1868, has been refurbished as she was at the turn of the century and offers cruises. A narrow-gauge railway run by enthusiasts puffs between Uppsala and Länna on summer weekends, which can be combined with *MS Enköping*.

Linnés Hammarby and **Mora Stenar**. Carl von Linné had a two-storey wooden cottage built at Hammarby in 1762 as a summer home which remains much as it was in Linné's time and contains possessions and mementoes. Linné made part of the grounds into a botanical garden and built a stone house as museum and lecture room (open summer pm. Tue–Sun). It can be reached by taking road 282 east from its junction with the E4 and following the signposts '*Linnés Hammarby*', past (10km) the church at Danmark which has 15C paintings.

Not far south of Hammarby are the **Mora Stenar** (Mora Stones) in a small white building. The central stone is missing but the surrounding ones remain. It was here that kings of Sweden were elected from 1275 to 1457, after which they would set out on the Eriksgata, a tour through the kingdom to receive homage from their subjects. The Eriksgata went through Uppland, Södermanland, Östergötland, North Småland and Västmanland, back to here. The Eriksgata continued to be a custom, and the last was by Karl XI in 1609.

East Uppland. A day-trip east of the E4 of somewhat over 100km can produce an interesting mix of late medieval church painting and industrial history in the shape of old ironworks, with a minor castle and prehistoric cemetery or two thrown in.

Take the 290 out past Gamla Uppsala. In 7km the sign **Valsgärde Gravfält** indicates the late Iron Age cemetery where rich finds were discovered in boat-graves. The cemetery is on a moraine divided by a depression which may have been a road. There is one mound, 29 stone circles and signs of the 15 boat-graves where the weapons, harness, sacrificial animals and household articles were found (Vendel and Viking periods 550–1050).

From (13km) Vattholma follow the signs to (5km) '*Tensta k:a*'. Just before the church is a sign to Gödåker prehistoric cemetery which has mounds and stone-settings, damaged by cultivation. **Tensta church** is high and brick-faced, with no tower, like many in Uppland. It was begun in the 13C with later additions and alterations, and has unusual tall blind arches on the exterior, and a round west window with oak tracery. The wall and vault **paintings** are mainly from 1437, by the German Johannes Rosenrod, with strong expressive figures—this is the only work known of this artist. On the north wall of the chancel is a painting of the donor Bengt Jonsson Oxenstierna, while the west bay of the nave has a series of scenes from the life of St. Birgitta. There is a late 15C altarpiece.

Follow the signs to (5km) Viksta. Two medieval lich-gates lead into the churchyard. The **church** was begun at the end of the 13C and the brick vault was added in the 15C when the gable ornament of symbols and patterns in the brick surface was made.

The **paintings** inside date from 1503, by two different painters. The two westernmost bays are from Albertus Pictor's workshop while the rest are of the Tierp type—note the 'chain' design. Saints, evangelists and apostles in variety are depicted. The font and large crucifix are 13C and the altar crucifix is 14C, of gilded copper. The statue on the right of the altar is St. Birgitta, but the other cannot be identified—both are 15C.

Continue to Husby where there is a prehistoric **mound** called Ottarshögen, according to legend the burial-place of Ottar, the son of Egil and father of Adil buried at Gamla Uppsala, and the area has other burials.

Continue towards Örbyhus to (12km) **Vendel**, which has given its name to a whole section of Swedish cultural history—the Vendel Period (550–800). In the 14 boat-graves excavated here were found opulently decorated grave-goods. Each chieftain was buried in his clinker-built boat 5–10m long, with his horse, weapons and armour. Many objects had superb gilt-bronze mounts, often with writhing animals and interlacing. A helmet and shield of early Vendel style, imports from Sweden, were found at Sutton Hoo in England. A small exhibition about the finds is in the medieval gate-house on the south of the church.

The **church** was consecrated in 1310 and the vault and wall **paintings** were executed in 1451–52 by Johannes Iwan, the main painter of the Tierp school, whose painted ornament owes something to Johannes Rosenrod at Tensta, but whose figures are less powerful and more harmonious.

Continue towards Örbyhus. After 9km **Örbyhus slott** (castle) is just off the road on the right (open summer p.m., grounds open all day). There was a fortress here in the 15C, later rebuilt into a small Baroque palace in the 17C and renovated in the 19C. This was where Erik XIV was held prisoner by his brother Johan III and died in 1577, according to legend after eating poisoned pea-soup. Tests on his body this century appear to show he had consumed arsenic. His prison is shown.

At the town of Örbyhus turn right towards Dannemora and Österbybruk. It is about 10km to the turn-off for **Dannemora**, the site of one of the great mines which financed Sweden's foreign adventures in the 18C. First it was a silver mine, then in Vasa times iron began to be exploited. Nowadays mining is underground, but the vast open mine can be seen, 200m long, and there are guided tours in the summer.

4km away, at **Österbybruk**, was where the Dannemora iron was worked. This was a *Vallonbruk*—Walloon works—since French-speaking Walloons from South Belgium contributed their expertise to the great expansion of the Swedish iron industry in the 17C. In 1643, a Dutchman, Louis de Geer, bought the works at Österbybruk, Gimo and Lövstabruk. Österbybruk had had ironworks since the 15C but de Geer and his Walloons meant a new era of productivity and prosperity. In Österbybruk you can see the forge originally built by Walloon workers and reconstructed in 1794 (open June–Aug). The forge building is part of a complex consisting of the 18C manor-house which has a modest church in a free-standing wing—de Geer's coat of arms is on the pulpit. There are also storehouses, workshops and other buildings belonging to the ironworks, a self-sufficient community.

Return by the 290. After 19km near Salsta a sign *fornborg* points to a prehistoric fort. At Salsta there is also a Baroque palace, not open to the public, designed by Nicodemus Tessin the Elder.

It is 22km back to central Uppsala.

The E4 continues north from Uppsala. At 19km **Björklinge** has a church begun in the 14C and remodelled in the 17C. It has 15C paintings by the artists of Tierp and Arentuna.

After 34km, **Tierp** has a **church** whose **paintings** have given its name to the Tierp school of church painters, probably taught or led by one Johannes Iwan (15C)—see also Vendel above. This school's characteristic chain motif is in evidence as a sort of backbone to the vault design.

In 6km a turning goes to Söderfors (13km), where there was a settlement centred on an anchor foundry. The Rococo manor, neo-Classical church and workers' homes remain (grounds open to tourists).

At 22km the E4 crosses from Uppland province into Gästrikland, and thereby leaves Svealand, the middle section of Sweden, and enters Norrland the vast empty northern part of the country with 54 per cent of the area, 14 per cent of the population and under five inhabitants per km^2. (Norrland should not be confused with Norrbotten, which was the name of an old province and now is the northernmost modern county. For Norrbotten see under Luleå.) In 22km comes the turning for Gävle (4km).

Gävle (pop. 67,000) is the largest and oldest town in Norrland, its charter dating from 1446. Its first castle was built by Johan III in the 16C and it developed into a port and industrial town. One of its best-known products is Gevalia coffee, named from a Latinised version of Gävle. The town centre is comparatively modern, as a result of a disastrous fire in 1869. The broad esplanade was laid out partly as a fire barrier, but also provides a relaxed spaciousness beside the business and shopping areas.

Tourist bureau: Kyrkogatan 14. Tel. (026) 10 16 00.

Post office: Drottninggatan 16.

Telephone, telegram: Drottninggatan 29-31. Tel. (026) 90 100.

Follow the signs to the **tourist bureau** which is in a 19C courtyard called Berggrenska Gården, best approached by Norra Strandgatan by the river-side. Other parts of the courtyard are occupied by art and craft shops. A block to the north of the tourist bureau is Stortorget, the lively main square adorned with pink 'pylons', which have reliefs of aspects of the history of the town, community, work, religion and the arts. A block to the east is the esplanade, with at the north end the **theatre** (1878) designed by Axel Nyström.

The **esplanade** has **fountains** by Karl Johan Dyfverman (1880), flowerbeds and a café. Near the town hall at the southern end is Eric Grate's **sculpture** 'Goddess by the Hyperborean Sea', symbolising Gävle by the Bothnian Sea. The town hall was designed by Carl Fredrik Adelcrantz in the late 18C and was restored after the fire of 1869.

Take Norra Strandgatan to the east. After crossing the railway line there is an area of **old warehouses** in three streets parallel to the river. Cross the river by the nearby bridge. Just along this shore to the left is the starting-point for boat-trips to the archipelago. Turn right from the bridge and soon on the left is the **Länsmuseum**, the county museum (open Tue–Fri 10.00–16.00, Sat, Sun 13.00–17.00).

The **first floor** has the history of Gävle, including pictures of the fire of 1869. There is a **censer** from Baghdad with an Arabic inscription, probably brought back by a Viking, and remains of a boat of c 400 AD. The **peasant culture displays** are of particular interest, with carved boxes, furniture, tools and harness, and a peasant house interior. Also on this floor are textiles and costume, silver and porcelain, and shipping and fishing. The **second** and **third floors** are devoted mainly to art from the 17C to the 20C, but may give way to temporary exhibitions. Artists represented include Elias Martin, Alexander Roslin, Tobias Sergel and Carl Larsson, and local artists are also shown.

Down the next turn after the museum is **Gamla Gefle**, a picturesque cobbled area of 18C and 19C houses which escaped the fire. Back on the riverside you come to an open space facing the town hall over the river, and on the grassy mound is Henry Moore's three-part reclining **figure** of 1976. On the other side of Södra Kungsgatan is **Slottstorget**, the place where on the first Sunday of Advent every year a gigantic *julbock* is set up—a straw goat which is a Swedish Christmas symbol, normally seen in more manageable sizes, down to 3cm high. Bets are taken as to whether it will be burnt down before Christmas

Beyond is the 18C castle, on the site of one built by the Vasas in the 16C, now the seat of the county governor. Cut through the castle grounds, take Slottsträdgårdensgatan and then cross the river by the footbridge. Up-stream from here along the river with its little rapids is an extensive **park** area, first Stadsträdgården, and then Boulognerskogen. Carl Milles' figures of five angels playing musical instruments are here.

On the edge of the park, about 1km from the centre along Kungsbäcks-vägen is **Silvanum**, the forestry museum (open Tue–Sun 10.00–16.00). The exhibit goes anticlockwise around the building. (The museum intends to produce a guide in English.) The displays are history of forestry, growth of trees, seeds and plants, cultivation and management, economic factors, enemies of the forest from storms to elks, processing, wood technology and the natural environment with animals, birds and plants. Video films, pictures, maps and graphs, as well as tapes of birdsong, illustrate the themes, and there are also temporary exhibitions. The museum also has a 10ha **arboretum**, Valls Hage, to the north-west on the other side of Västra Vägen.

Back at the footbridge it is a few steps to Trefaldighetskyrkan, the **church** dedicated to the Trinity and consecrated in 1654, on the site of a medieval church. It has had to be considerably renovated through the centuries because of problems with subsidence. The best items are the 17C **pulpit** and **altarpiece** by Ewerdt Friis of Schleswig-Holstein. Both remained unpainted until the 19C. The altar shows the Last Supper, Crucifixion, Resurrection, Ascension and Christ in Judgement, with saints to either side, and the pulpit with its stair are similarly carved, with scenes from the life of Christ. The font is from the 12C. Historic vestments are in a glass case covered by a curtain (pull the cord at the side).

Following the river will bring you back to the tourist bureau.

Järnvägsmuseet (the Swedish Railway Museum, open 10.00–16.00, Mon closed, check times at tourist bureau) is south of the centre. Take Södra Kungsgatan for about 2km and at Hemsta follow the signs *Järnvägs-museum* for three left turns. The building used to be Gävle's engine shed, built in 1907. The museum has a collection of about 50 steam locomotives and nearly 30 specialised carriages. Sixteen of the engines are over 100 years old and five are in working order. You can see a model of Sweden's first locomotive of 1853, Förstlingen, and the preserved second one, Fryckstad of 1855. Early carriages include that of Karl XV from 1859. There are narrow-gauges in the next room and the exhibition continues chrono-logically. Oskar II's audience carriage of 1874 is perhaps the most luxurious, while at the other extreme is the carriage for transporting convicts. Lastly there are modern locomotives and future projections. There is a café in a 1950s carriage.

On the other side of the entrance are the small exhibits which portray Swedish railway history, from the first horse-drawn line in 1798. One section shows how a railway is built, and you can hear a tape of the songs of navvies. There is a model of the railway through Stockholm and a map where the red lines were government railways and the green ones privately constructed. Train ferries have a section to themselves as do modern trains. At summer weekends a **veteran steam train** travels three times a day from the museum to Furuvik.

B.   Coastal Route

Total distance 224km. Stockholm—E18 65km Norrtälje—road 76 159km Gävle.

The E18 leaves Stockholm to the north-east and reaches Norrtälje in 65km. This is the capital of the district of Roslagen which is characterised by its broken coastline of inlets and islands. The Vikings from Roslagen were called Rus, and gave their name to Russia.

Norrtälje was a medieval market-place. In 1719 the Russians burnt the town, and the town hall and church date from the rebuilding. It eventually became a popular bathing resort for Stockholmers. There is a museum in an old arms factory as well as a museum of humour.

Take the 76 to the north. From (17km) Söderby-Karl you could take a road on to the elongated island of Väddö, then north to the town of Grisslehamn and further over bridges to two other islands, or explore south, crossing on to still other islands.

At 19km, **Edebo** church has 16C ceiling paintings. From there you could go to Häverö (8km), where the **church** has an altarpiece from Antwerp and a 16C wooden bell-tower. At 23km, in Harg there are buildings remaining from the 18C ironworks, with the manor-house in its grounds, and a summertime modern art exhibition. After 9km, **Östhammar** is a pleasant harbour town with a 17C church and 18C town hall. From Östhammar you can reach Gimo (16km south) with another old ironworks complex. Nearby Skäfthammar church has 16C paintings.

After 6km you can reach Öregrund (11km) out on the peninsula, a fishing and holiday village. Another 11km brings **Forsmark**, where there was yet another large ironworks, from which many buildings have been preserved (*Forsmarks bruk*). The complex is centred round the **manor** designed by Jean Eric Rehn (1774), a three-storey house with two gables facing front, with colossal columns on the façades (not open to the public). The streets of low workers' homes lead from the manor to the **church** (1800, by Olof Tempelman), and the museum is open daily in summer. On the coast (3km) is the nuclear power-station (tours daily during summer, weekdays the rest of the year, summer bus tours round the area); follow signs *Kraftstation*.

In 17km at **Lövstabruk** there is another well-preserved **ironworks** settlement, complete except for the actual ironworks which finished working in the 1920s. Louis de Geer from Holland bought Lövstabruk in 1643 and the family continued there for 300 years. By the 18C the works formed a self-contained community round the imposing manor, set beyond gardens and the river. The **house**, designed by Jean Eric Rehn, is shown on guided tours in the summer (Tue–Sun 13.00 and 14.00), and contains **interiors** by Rehn and by Isak Gustaf Clason. There is a small natural history collection and a library in the detached wings. There is also a display of carriages of the 18C and 19C, in the stables to the right behind the house, and in the malthouse in the other direction an exhibition on brewing (collect an English plan from the **tourist bureau** on the main street). The church (1727) with its 'säteri' roof has a well-known organ by Johan Niclas Cahman. The de Geer coat of arms can be seen on the pulpit canopy and the altar. Workers' homes line the main street and behind lie old storehouses, the school and barn, now a silversmith's.

South of Lövstabruk (15km on a poor road) is Florarna, a nature reserve, with interesting bog plants. This ancient name is connected to the English 'floor', referring to the flat surface.

At (19km) **Karlholmsbruk** is another of de Geer's ironworks, with 18C manor, church and bell-tower. The workers' homes are now inhabited by pensioners, and the Lancashire smithy has been restored for viewing.

It is 11km to **Älvkarleby**, where the once impressive waterfall now dammed to produce electricity is released once a year for the tourists. The Dalälv splits in three above the falls and unites again lower down. In the middle is the island of Laxön, an attractive leisure area. The power station and the salmon-breeding centre can be visited in summer as can Vatten-fall's laboratory with exhibitions on modern energy techniques. The **church** is from the 15C, with vaults painted by Eghil, the artist of Ytterlännas. Karl XIII's bridge dates from 1816.

At (14km) **Furuvik** there is an amusement park (Furuviksparken) with zoo, circus and bathing beach (threatened with closure). A steam train runs to Gävle.

It is 13km to Gävle.

17

Stockholm to Mora

Total distance 312km. Stockholm E18 73km Enköping—road 70 44km **Sala**—37km Avesta—59km Borlänge—43km **Leksand**—20km **Rättvik**—36km **Mora**.

Take the E18 out of Stockholm to the north-west. For the route as far as Enköping see Örebro to Stockholm, which includes the churches of *Härkeberga and *Härnevi.

At Enköping take road 70 towards Sala and Avesta. After 35km you can take a turn for **Kumla** church, built about 1300, which has *vault-paintings by Albertus Pictor (1482), never whitewashed over. The paintings on the walls are fragmentary. The main colours are ochre, green and reddish-brown, and the motifs are fitted into the cross-vaults and star-vaults. The subjects are Evangelists, Scandinavian saints, the life of the Virgin, fathers of the church and prophets, surrounded by waving foliage and coats of arms. Under the chancel arch is the Tree of Jesse, and in the porch legends are depicted. The work represents the beginning of the artist's most brilliant period (see note under Härnevi).

In 9km road 70 reaches **Sala** (pop. 12,000), best known for its historic silver mine. Follow the signs for the **tourist bureau** in the centre. To the north of the centre is a **museum** devoted to the art of Ivan Aguéli (1869–1917). Take Rådmansgatan from the main square north, and it is just over the river at Norra Esplanaden 7. Aguéli was born in Sala, and worked mainly in France, but also in Egypt and Spain, painting landscapes and portraits.

1km to the west of the Aguéli museum is **Väsby Kungsgård** (open p.m. in summer, also weekends the rest of the year). This royal manor is chiefly famous as the setting for the romance of Gustavus Adolphus and Ebba Brahe in the 17C, but the present building is 18C, on the 16C cellar, and contains a collection of weapons, paintings and furniture. In the grounds are exhibitions dealing with linen, carriages and agriculture.

The **church** 1km north of the Aguéli museum is from the 14C and contains paintings by Albertus Pictor and a 16C Brussels altarpiece (may not be open).

The *silver mine is well signposted *silvergruva*—take the main road Ringgatan to the west and turn left where signposted. The mine is about 2km further. (Open in summer.)

The legend is that once upon a time a bull was butting the ground when his owner notices his horns were covered in silver. Be that as it may, there were silver-workings here from the late 15C, and by Gustav Vasa's time one-third of the country's silver came from this mine. Convicts and prisoners of war were compelled to work in the depths—prisoners of war were allowed up only on Sundays. The only source of power was water, so watercourses were altered and a reservoir was formed from which a system of canals and tunnels led the water to the mine.

On the way in to the reception centre, you pass the surface building (1858) of **Queen Kristina's Shaft**. This shaft, now 257m deep, was begun in 1650 and for many years was the principal one, being used also for the transport of the workers and equipment. The deepest shaft is **Karl XI's**, begun in 1670 (318.4m), and its round surface building is from 1834. The brick machine-house is also from the 19C. The other important shaft is that named after **Gustav III** (267m) from the early 18C.

In the reception building, the original stables for the mine's horses, there is a model of the mine and you can book to descend to 40m or 60m. The tunnels and galleries have a total length of 20km. In Queen Kristina's Shaft one can stand 26m below the ground, look down to a water surface 155m below and be told that the shaft goes 100m below that. In places, sooty walls are a legacy of the early methods of mining by building fires against the rock.

There is a café in the house of the manager of the mine's waterworks. The **museum** is in the 18C home of the mine engineer. (The moon over the door is the ancient symbol for silver.) In the museum is a large collection of objects found in and around the mine and its buildings, personal effects, coins, glass, pottery, tools and weapons. Processes of mining and associated techniques are shown such as smelting, the water-system and fire-precautions, as well as the processing of lead, which began in 1879.

To the south can be seen the gaping hole of **Stens Botten**, the earliest mine, the roof of which collapsed in 1581. South of this again is **Torg-schaktet**, a shaft which in the 19C was used in manufacturing lead shot. Warm lead drops fell 90m into water and became neatly spherical. Art exhibitions are held in the **Director's House** of 1828, and other shafts and buildings repay a leisurely visit.

There are good walking-trails in the area (ask the tourist bureau for a map), often following the watercourses dug for the silver mine, and amid woods, meadows and bogs.

The **Traktormusuem** is 4km south-east of Sala, with 60 or so tractors (open in summer). Take road 72 towards Uppsala for 1km for the junction with the Stockholm, road and follow the signs.

Road 70 continues 37km to **Avesta** (pop. 17,000), the southernmost town in the province of Dalarna.

Dalarna is sometimes translated into English as 'Dalecardia'. The name means 'the valleys', referring to the valleys of the Österdalälv and the Västerdalälv rivers, uniting at Djurås to become the Dalälv proper. Almost all of the province is now the county of Kopparberg, but that is only for bureaucrats. This is the 'folklore centre of Sweden' and much of foreigners' romantic vision of Sweden comes from the arts and crafts of this province. The old crafts are carefully preserved, and here you can see folk paintings and costumes and hear folk music.

The paintings are known as *dalmåleri*. In the 18C it became the custom to decorate furniture and utensils with scrolls of swirling foliage, representing the tree of Jonah in the Old Testament. In the 1790s figures began to be introduced, mainly in biblical scenes, but also showing contemporary events, both political and more homely. The composition of the biblical scenes was often taken from the *Biblia Pauperum Predicatorum* (Bible of the Poor), a picture Bible first published in Germany in the 13C and in many later versions. Although the composition was stereotyped, the figures and buildings were as the artists saw them in their daily life, a delightful anachronism giving a picture of contemporary clothing and the Dalarna milieu. The figures were set in frames of floral extravaganza as on the furniture. The two main centres were Leksand, using a colour-scheme of mainly blue, ochre and red, and Rättvik, using red and green. The art lasted c 100 years, to the late 19C.

The folk music is based on the fiddle, but the key-harp (*nyckelharpa*—in several museums), bagpipes, clarinet and accordion are also played. Some museums provide tapes for listening to recordings, and there are folk music festivals in several areas, the largest in Bingsjö, north-east of Rättvik.

The local costumes are very varied and can be seen in museums. Crafts of the region include leather, brass, woven braid, baskets woven from wood-shavings, and furniture. The principal museum of Dalarna is in Falun, but there are gems in unexpected places.

At the main junction for Avesta the eye is assailed by a 13m high concrete Dala horse in traditional orange, with blue, white and yellow swirling patterned bands. Dala horses are native to Dalarna, but have become a tourist souvenir for all of Sweden (see under Nusnäs for their manufacture). Also at the junction are the **tourist bureau**, shops and eating-places.

Avesta had smithies in the 14C, which used the power from the river. In the 17C the copper-works of Säter moved here and copper from Falun was processed. Swedish copper coins were minted in Avesta from 1644 to 1831. Now the town produces stainless steel instead of copper.

The road to the centre crosses the Dalälv. On the other shore on the right are the **Dead Falls**, left dry when the river changed its course, a centuries-long process ending around 4000 BC. Along a footpath you can see Stora Helvetet, Lilla Helvetet and Södra Helvetet (Big, Little and South Hell), once waterfalls.

Turn right at the next junction. Just past the turning to the next bridge is the entrance to **Gamla Byn**, the Old Village, with buildings from the 17C onwards, though most are 19C, following a fire. This was where the first copper-works and mint were situated.

The **church** was consecrated in 1655, built by the master of the mint, Markus Kock, who was influenced by the design of the German church in Stockholm with its two-aisled plan. It has an elegant Rococo pulpit and a 17C altarpiece. The tower is 19C.

Take Badhusgatan to the river bank, turn right and almost under the bridge is the **Myntmuseum** (Mint Museum—check opening hours at the tourist bureau) in the cellar of an old stone grain store. It shows the history of Swedish money, especially, of course, copper, but also banknotes and medals. It possesses what is claimed to be the largest coin in the world, from 1644, which weighs nearly 20kg.

There is a **Bison Park** (*Visentpark*) reached by continuing on Bergslagsvägen to the T-junction, turning left and following the signs.

The 70 continues 19km north-west from the Dala horse to **Hedemora** (pop. 7500), with the oldest town charter in Dalarna (1446). The **tourist bureau** is in a restored 18C apothecary's shop. Near the bureau is the main square with 18C town hall and 19C hotel. The unusual **Theatre Barn** a block or so to the north was built in the 19C with a theatre above the ground-floor grain store. The church is from the 14C with 12C crucifix and font, and a Baroque pulpit. There is an open-air museum (Gammelgård) on Åsgatan.

From Hedemora by the 270 to the north you can reach **Husbyringen** (12km), a 60km tourist route which aims to show the effect of man on the landscape (leaflets in English are available at the tourist bureau). On the route are a manor, a church, a forest trail, several ironworks, a ruined monastery, a geology trail and Christopher Polhem's works at Stjärnsund, where there are exhibitions on the great engineer and his inventions.

Branching off the 270 before you reach Husbyringen, you could visit **Garpenberg** site of an iron mine, with a 17C wooden mine chapel, an 18C church and an open-air museum.

Continuing on the 70 from Hedemora, after 10km a side-road goes to **Vikmanshyttan** (7km) where there is an ironworks museum, an old smithy and a modern church.

Soon to the north of the road is **Bispbergs Klack**, a granite outcrop 175m over the surroundings, with its south precipice host to flora which by rights should not thrive so far north.

On the outskirts of (6km) **Säter** is the **Bil & MC Museum**, in a low brick building with a round corner on the road, which has a large collection of cars and motorcycles, from a 1904 Ford onwards. In another part of the same building is **Biografmuseet** (cinema museum) tracing the history of moving pictures.

500m on, the **tourist bureau** is on the left and on the right the approach to **Säterdalen**, the Säter Valley, a 5km long system of 35 ravines carved by ice, with the winding river Ljusterån below. Walking trails explore the area, with its views and interesting geology, flora and fauna.

The centre of the town has wooden buildings from the 19C and before. In 19km, Stora Tuna **church** was consecrated in 1469. In the porch can be seen the original brick façade before the tower was added in front of it. Inside, it is a three-aisled hall church in late Gothic style with star vaults. The large crucifix (the figure of Christ is 2m tall) is from c 1500. The outsize pulpit (1757) was carved by Johan Ljung who also worked at Stockholm castle. The altar picture is a copy of one by the court painter Ehrenstrahl in the Storkyrka in Stockholm. There are several memorial tablets on the walls, the oldest to Gustavus Adolphus of 1643, and there are two royal portraits, of Karl XI and Karl XII. There is a small exhibition in the sacristy. The opera-singer Jussi Björling (1911–60) is buried in the churchyard.

In 4km you can turn right to Ornäs (5km), to see **Ornässtugan**, somewhat off the road but well signposted. This is a very attractive timber house in a lovely situation on Runn lake (guided tours on the hour June–Aug 10.00–17.00, English leaflet available). The owner of the estate was a farmer and part-owner of Falun copper-mine, and built it in the late 15C to accommodate guests. The 18C owner added the exterior staircase and put in windows. Its claim to fame in Swedish history is that in 1520 Gustav Vasa, in flight from the Danes, hid in the privy, and was lowered from there by the wife of the owner on to a waiting sled below by which he made his escape.

The long balcony has sections at each end where the women would sit and work. In the **King's Room** there are items relating to Gustav Vasa and his epic escape, with a map of his route, family paintings and a genealogical tree. A clothes closet has tools and other items and the famous privy is shown. The banqueting hall has later furniture and royal portraits.

From the roundabout it is 1km to the centre of **Borlänge**, (pop. 40,000) where the main roundabout has a striking modern fountain. The domed building beyond is a shopping centre. The parking areas along Ovanbro-

Ornässtugan (late 15C) from which Gustav Vasa made one of his many dramatic escapes from the Danes

gatan to the left are useful for visiting the **tourist bureau**, the Geological Museum and hantverksbyn (Craftsmen's Village).

Geologiska Museet (open June–Aug 11.00–17.00, otherwise Sun p.m.) is excellent considering the size of the town. There is, however, little information in English, though most labels are understandable. The collection comprises 5000 items, including 300 different porphyries—porphyry comes principally from Älvdalen, further to the north-west in Dalarna. Minerals from Dalarna form one of the main displays, and other highlights are radio-active and fluorescent minerals (wait for the effect). Fossils are in another display and there are 250 rocks in a special Russian section. Some large crystalline samples are astonishing, like the great amethyst. The houses in the 'village' surrounding the museum are from the late 19C and are mainly arts and crafts shops.

Not far past the tourist bureau on the other side of two roads and the railway is Folkets Hus with Framtidsmuseet (Museum of the Future) with some history and technology displays.

To reach the **open-air museum** take Ovanbrogatan to the T-junction and follow the sings *Gammelgården* (guided tours in summer). There are some 30 buildings and a guide will show you four or five in great detail, usually a representative one from each century. The most internationally interesting is the small **Jussi Björling museum**. The singer was born and brought up in Borlänge, and here are gathered some costumes, photos, programmes and other memorabilia. The guide will play tapes of his singing. Other buildings usually shown are Kullesgården (17C), Anders Matsgården (18C) and Gubbstugan (19C), crammed with contemporary furnishings and authentic detail. There are also storehouses, stables, barns, a school, a smithy and a mill.

Also in the town, a museum called Pylonen deals with the history of road-building.

After 20km the road comes to Djurås where the Österdalälv and Västerdalälv meet, and the 70 pursues the valley of the Österdalälv to where it leaves lake Siljan at (23km) **Leksand**. The depression of Siljan was formed 370 million years ago by the impact of a meteorite. The area is rich in fossils, and attempts have been made to drill for oil and methane in the lake, but so far without significant success.

The **tourist bureau** in Leksand (pop. 5500) is just down the road to left after you cross the river. Here and elsewhere you can buy the Siljanspass, giving many reductions. On the right a little further on is the **Kulturhus** with exhibitions of **Dalarna painting** on paper, chests and boxes, and a collection of local **costumes** (open summer, weekdays 11.00–17.00, Sat to 16.00, Sun 13.00–16.00, and other seasons shorter hours).

Down the same road you come first after half a kilometre or so to the **open-air museum** (*Hembygdsgårdar*), and later after swinging to the left to the **church** out on a peninsula. The nave is the original 13C church, now with many accretions. The onion-domed top of the spire is 18C. The many galleries are unusual. The best work of art is the large crucifix of c 1400, probably of Swedish workmanship. There are memorial tablets of the 17C and 18C, and the altarpiece is 18C. The shingle-clad bell-tower is from 1628.

In **Släktforskarnas hus** they have parish archives from 1920 on micro-film which can be consulted. There is a summer music festival every year, centred on Leksand and Rättvik. There are also 'church boat' races on the lake.

It is a pleasant drive of about 30km to explore a little of the west coast of the lake before taking the main road on the east side of the lake to Mora. The road leads between red painted wooden houses and then along the shore with glimpses of the lake. Over the causeway between the lake and the inlet Byrviken, the road soon runs below the hill on which is the village of **Siljansnäs**. Having climbed the hill to the village square, you can pursue one of the signposts: *Gammelgården 1km* (open-air museum), *Naturum 2km* (natural history), or *Björkberget 1km* (view). You can return round the other side of Byrviken via Alvik.

The 70 turns north to (20km) Rättvik, but the longer coast road passes through (8km) Hjörtnäs which has a tin model museum (Tennfigurmuseum) with set-pieces illustrating historical events, and in 4km **Tällberg** has an open-air museum, Holens Gammelgård, on the top of a hill. On the way up you pass clusters of buildings which look as if they might be an open-air museum—one of the hazards of being a tourist in Dalarna. At the top, the buildings are from the 17C and 18C with interlocking corner timbers and birch-bark waterproofing. The artist Gustaf Anckarcrona gathered the buildings and had his home and studio here. There is a typical house with a gallery, on a courtyard, and some buildings are furnished.

After 13km you are in **Rättvik**. The **tourist bureau** is in the centre. There is a long pier, first built 1895, which is a stopping-point for boat-trips and it makes a pleasant stroll to the island at the end. For the church and museum take Storgatan to the north-west, and the church is off the road near the shore. It was founded in the 12C, but is now mostly from the late 18C. The large crucifix is 14C, the pulpit 17C and altarpiece 18C. There is a medieval cope. On the shore is the landing-place for 'church boats' which used to be rowed here for Sunday service. Close to the church on the south is the **Vasa monument**, one of many in Dalarna. This one commemorates Gustav Vasa's speech to the people on this spot in 1520. To the other side of the church is a line of 16C/17C **church stables**, for the horses to wait in during the service.

From here you can reach the open-air museum (**Gammelgård**) by crossing the railway and turning left (open in summer). One building has **wall-paintings**, one has **painted furniture** and there are **costumes** in another.

The road turns west towards Mora. After 26km there is a turning for **Nusnäs** (4km). This is the main place where Sweden's prime souvenir, the Dala horse, is manufactured, and you can watch the process in the workshops. Traditionally they were made of pine and spruce, and in the 19C they began to be decorated with floral-based patterns. They come in a variety of sizes. The first block shape is cut by machine, then they are hand-carved. After dipping in red, black or blue paint, they are ready for hand-painting in traditional fashion, with deft and swift brush-strokes. Cockerels are now also made, and the tall painted Mora clocks. The souvenir shops are tempting but crowded.

It is 10km to Mora by the coast road.

***Mora** (pop. 11,000) is the tourist heart of Dalarna. It was the home of Anders Zorn, the best known Swedish painter abroad, and has a museum devoted to his work. For most Swedes, however, Mora conjures up a vision of skiing, and in particular of the Vasa ski race (Vasaloppet). The course is 90km long, from Sälen to Mora, held every year since 1922 when there were 199 competitors—now the numbers run into thousands. The race commemorates Gustav Vasa's return to Mora in 1520, after the best skiers in Dalarna caught him up on his flight to Norway, promising their support against the Danes.

The crowded centre of Mora comes as a rude surprise after the quiet towns just passed. The **tourist bureau** is on the main road by the harbour. The **church** on Vasagatan, originally medieval, was remodelled in the 17C and renovated many times since. Vaulting and the west gable, visible under the tower, remain from medieval times. The paintings of royalty were a gift from Zorn. There are cases with examples of building workers' marks. Anders Zorn is buried in the churchyard.

Opposite the church is a statue of Zorn and along the road to the east is a **statue** of Gustav Vasa by the artist, near the finishing line of the Vasa ski race. A statue of a Vasa skier is also on Vasagatan.

A few steps away is a set of buildings devoted to Zorn.

Anders Zorn (1860–1920) was born in Mora and studied in Stockholm, Paris and London. He began as watercolourist, and leaned towards Impressionism. He started to paint in oils in 1888 when he moved to Paris and in 1896 came to live in Mora. He took up portrait painting and also etching, in both of which he became extremely successful, even portraying American presidents Cleveland, Theodore Rooseveldt and Taft. It is considered, however, that his best work dates from before 1900.

The elaborately rustic **house** (open all year), was designed by Zorn and contains furnishings, textiles and works of art by Zorn and others, and his considerable collections. His workroom is open to the church-like roof and is hung with tapestries. The small house to the right (possibly 12C) was his studio.

The ***museum** is in a modern stone building (open all year). In the basement are Dalarna folk-paintings and costumes, and a collection of etchings, paintings and sketches. The ground floor has temporary exhibitions and on the top floor are works by such Swedish artists as Liljefors, Nordström, Ekström and Kreuger, as well as Italian paintings. Anders

Zorn's best known works here are *Sunday Morning, Margit, Mora Market* (the church), *Julottan* and the self-portrait.

Zorn also started the local open-air museum **Zorns Gammelgård**, reached by Yvradsvägen, with buildings from the surrounding countryside, including examples of cottages with central fireplaces. The oldest building is from the 14C, and a new one has been constructed to house Zorn's collection of local **textiles**.

From here take the next fork left and follow signs to **Vasamonumentet**, the Vasa monument (open summer 12.00–18.00). This is a sort of temple built in 1860, the 300th anniversary of Gustav Vasa's death, over the cellar of a house which was the scene of one of Gustav's many escapes. As all the provinces contributed, their coats of arms go round the outside. Inside, there is a trapdoor with a rough stair descending to the historic cellar where Gustav is said to have hidden. The three pictures on the walls tell of his adventures. First there is Ornässtugan, the house near Borlänge (see above) where Gustav was helped to escape by a woman, and here in Mora, too, a woman was instrumental in saving him from the Danes by sending him into the cellar and installing her beer barrel on the trapdoor (second picture). The third painting is of the farm in Sälen, where the Dalarna skiers are said to have caught up with him and brought him back to win his kingdom.

There is a 16C log cabin nearby.

Excursions from Mora

A drive to Sollerön, an island in Siljan, takes you down the west side of the lake. Take the 45 for 10km and turn left for (6km) **Gesunda**. From here you can drive a couple of kilometres up Gesunda hill, marked *Gesundaberget* and *Tomteland* (Santa World). Here in his big wooden chalet Santa welcomes children all the year round (quite expensive) with various activities. From the top of the hill (cable railway) there is a wide view.

Take the road to Sollerön, which is joined to the mainland by two bridges. It is 5km to the 18C church (should now be open, after restoration). The signs *Bengtsarvet* and *Hembygdsgård* lead in 1km to the open-air museum, and through its grounds to the Iron Age cemetery with barrows, stretching for 1km, where rich grave goods have been found. Return to the church for the road back to Mora (12km).

•**Älvdalen** (37km) lies on road 70 to the north-west of Mora and was the centre of porphyry production and working. The way lies among hills, lakes and thick woods. At 22km a sign points to Zorns Gopsmorstuga, the artist's wilderness studio.

Porphyry was much prized by the ancient Egyptians. The name comes from the Greek for 'purple' and is thus associated with royalty—Louis XIV appreciated it. It is a volcanic rock containing quartz, feldspar and mica and is comparatively hard, 7 on the Mohs scale. It is in fact not only red but comes in innumerable different shades. The best known Swedish variety, Bredvad porphyry, is a deep red.

The porphyry works were founded here in 1788, at Porfyrgården, north-west of the town. In 1818 they were bought by King Karl XIV Johan. The two objects most associated with the king are the 2.5m high Rosendal Vase, weighing 9.5 tons, and his 16 ton sarcophagus, both in Stockholm. Because these were made in Älvdalen they are popularly believed to be porphyry, but in fact that would be impossible, given their size. They are made of granite from Garberg. After the king's death the works gradually ran down, but in 1897 were restarted in another village Västermyckeläng (often shortened to Västäng) which continued production until 1986. Now porphyry is used only for jewellery and small items.

The **tourist bureau** is near the centre of town. (Check the times of guided tours at Västäng and Porfyrgården before planning your day.)

The **church** is on the other side of the road. Started in the 16C, it has been renovated several times. The pillars under the organ gallery are of Garberg granite. There is a 17C wedding seat and in the vestry a 15C crucifix. Near the church are two wooden **cabins**. The first is claimed to be the oldest wooden building in the country, a **tithe barn** of 1285 with some remains of medieval decoration. Next to it is a gallery house of 1585 used by guests to the vicarage.

To get to the new porphyry works at Västäng go back a little from the tourist bureau and follow signs to the right, to **Nya Porfyrverket**, about 1km, in a battered wooden building on the left of the road. Here you can see the water-driven machinery which was still in use when the works closed in 1986. Machinery was brought here from the old porphyry works in 1897, added to and adapted, but not much was renewed. There were up to eight workers, employed solely on work to order, since it was so expensive—it took an hour to cut 1cm. Samples of porphyry can be seen in various stages of shaping and grinding.

The *museum is in the centre of town, on the left past the church (open summer Mon–Fri 12.00–17.00, weekends 13.00–17.00, rest of year closed Mon. English leaflet to borrow). Near the entrance are stately Blyberg **porphyry urns** with bronze handles, and a round **table** containing a colour sample of every type of porphyry. The show-cases are filled with exquisite objects, bowls, vases, butter-dishes, candlesticks, salt-cellars, knife-handles and paper-weights. Displays deal with the two great objects made here but not of porphyry, the **Rosendal Vase** and Karl XIV Johan's **sarcophagus**. The sarcophagus took eight years to make, and since it was so heavy it could only be moved on sledges, it was another four years before the weather was suitable. 180 men pulled the sledges, one for the sarcophagus and one for the lid, to Gävle, where the two pieces were shipped to Stockholm and taken to the Riddarholm church where Swedish royalty are buried.

On the other side of the road is the courthouse in whose grounds stands the last large porphyry piece made in Älvdalen, in 1936.

Porfyrgården is c 2km to the northwest on the main road and then a kilometre or so following signs to the right. Porfyrgården is the name of the manor house which is now a restaurant, and other buildings are now arts and crafts workshops. The lake was used as a reservoir for water-power to drive the machinery. The grindery (*Västra Sliphuset*) and its machinery is a reconstruction, with its large water-wheel outside. Inside the intricate wooden drive-wheels and beams are set in motion so you can see how it works.

Back on the main road you could turn right for less than 1km in order to see **Rots Skans**, an attractive open-air museum on the site of a military outpost on the former border with Norway. The log houses have overlapping ridge timbers, interlocking corners and birch-bark waterproofing. Notice the diminutive mill-house and at the north end a reconstructed bog-iron blast-furnace.

This north part of Dalarna offers many adventure holiday pursuits. Besides the usual canoeing and fishing, there are wild-life safaris to see bears and elks, canoe-safaris to see beavers, plane-trips and visits to summer pasture settlements (*fäbodar*).

Due west of Älvdalen but accessible only by a roundabout route is **Sälen** just south of which the Vasa ski race starts, on the frozen surface of the river Västerdalälven. There is a **monument** to the race on the main road, and **Olnispagården**, an old farm building, is supposed to have sheltered Gustav Vasa on his flight. It was owned by the same family from Vasa times to 1945. There is a painting of it in the Vasa monument in Mora.

Beyond Älvdalen road 70 goes towards Norway through wilder country. From Särna you could reach (drive and then walk) the highest waterfall in Sweden, **Njupeskär**, with a total drop of 125m, on the edge of Fulufjäll. From Idre (31km) you can get to Idre Fjäll where there is skiing from October to May, with every sort of winter sports facility from paraskiing to sledging with huskies, and in the summer beaver-safaris, canoeing and geology tours. You can visit Aernie South-Sami centre, based on the most southerly Sami 'village'.

18

Karlstad to Mora

Total distance 292km. Karlstad—E18 6km—road 61 25km Fagerås—road 45 74km Torsby—road 239 36km **Ekshärad**—road 62 34km junction with the 45—road 45 117km Mora.

Leave Karlstad by the E18 to the west, and pick up the 61 after 6km, turning north to (25km) Fagerås, where you take the 45 towards Sunne and Torsby. There are three long narrow lakes in this valley, the Lower, Middle and Upper Fryken, (Nedre, Mellan and Övre Fryken), and the road gradually approaches their waterline.

At 34km you can follow the signs to **Rottneros** (1km), a 40ha park of gardens and sculpture (open mid May–mid Sept 09.00–18.00. Adapted for the disabled and those with impaired sight and hearing). The estate, which was originally an ironworks, is celebrated in Swedish literature as the site of Ekeby Manor in Selma Lagerlöf's *Gösta Berlings Saga*, but the present manor dates only from 1932. The grounds are scattered with 100 pieces of **sculpture**, mainly by Scandinavian artists of the first half of the 20C, but there are also copies of Classical statues, such as the Nike from Samothrace.

The main path goes south from the entrance, and on the left are enclosures with sculptures, notably the Carl Milles **fountain**. At the main 'crossroads' stands the manor, with formal pool in front. Behind are the oak park and arboretum, beyond which the grounds extend to the lake, while on the extreme left is Selma Lagerlöf's garden. Also to the left of the main path are the rose-garden and the **Carl Eldh parterre** with his sculptures, as well as the sculpture garden and the king's garden. Returning along the west side you find sculpture by **Vigeland**, and a large area stocked with birds and animals, before coming to the east–west path along which you can look to the manor. The two buildings near the main path are the **Cavaliers' Wings**, mentioned in *Gösta Berlings Saga*. Next come the flower garden and the lake, then back at the entrance are the herb garden and the refreshment places.

At (4km) Sunne you can cross between the lakes on road 241 and then follow the signs to **Mårbacka** (11km), Selma Lagerlöf's home.

Selma Lagerlöf (1858–1940) was born and died at Mårbacka. She trained as a teacher and taught for ten years. The estate had to be sold on her father's death, but through her literary success she was able to buy back first the house, and then after she received the Nobel prize for literature in 1909 the estate itself. She had the house completely rebuilt, designed by Isak Gustaf Clason, with 'säteri' roof and portico supporting a long balcony.

Her first novel was *Gösta Berlings Saga* (1891), a collection of episodes linked by the central character. She was the first woman to receive the Nobel prize for literature and the first woman member of the Swedish Academy. Her other most famous work is probably *Nils Holgerssons underbara resa genom Sverige (Nils Holgersson's wonderful journey through Sweden;* 1906–07), a child's geography of Sweden interwoven with fantasy and adventure. *Jerusalem* (1901–02) is a tale of Swedish peasants in the Holy Land.

Parts of the author's childhood home have been reconstructed in the house (open mid May–mid Sept 10.00–18.00, guided tours). Selma managed to buy back much of the dispersed furniture from her father's time and you can see the sitting-room with portraits and furniture, and the 1920s kitchen. Upstairs is her study preserved as she left it, and the panelled library with an almost complete collection, including translations, of her prolific work.

Back in Sunne, you could detour to the other side of the main road to look at the **church** in Gräsmark (20km north-west). This has a late Baroque interior with painted wooden ceiling. The local open-air museum has some buildings recalling the wave of Finnish immigrants to this province. (See under Torsby.)

After 18km you can drive up a winding road to the top of **Tossebergsklätten**, where an outlook tower gives added height from which to enjoy the *view of lakes, forests and hills (picnic site, refreshments).

At (18km) Torsby a new centre called **Niittaho** (check open times at the tourist bureau) aims to research and gather information, and organise exhibitions about the life of the Finnish settlers who began to come to Värmland in the mid 16C. Some found employment in the mines, others worked land despised by Swedish farmers, cutting and burning the woods to make fields for growing rye. They brought their language and customs, their building and farming methods. Finnish continued to be spoken into the 20C, while Finnish cooking can still be found. In the forests to the west and north of Torsby are several old Finnish settlements which can be visited, Kvarntorp, Ritamaki, Purala, Mattila, Juhola, Abborrtjärnsberg, Rikenberg and others. (Guided tours from the tourist bureau in Torsby.)

From Torsby take the 239 for 36km to **Ekshärad** which is the best place to see wrought-iron **grave-crosses**. (You could of course continue straight up the 45, shortening the route.)

'Cross' is a misnomer, for these extraordinary creations represent the Tree of Life. They are to be found in Värmland, Dalsland and West Småland, and it is thought the idea was brought here by Walloon settlers. In the early 17C they were simple rings, then developed a bell shape, and remained relatively plain until the middle of the 19C, when with new technology they blossomed into a profusion of intricate ornament. Some have one arm, some have many, some are topped with bridal crowns, some have an iron flag or streamer, some a dragon's head or cock, but the most common decoration is single leaves swinging freely, and spiralling tendrils. Smiths and peasants received iron as part of their wages, and used it to honour the resting-place of their dead. There are c 320 crosses at Ekshärad, 200 of them from before 1900.

As for the church itself, it is the third on this site, the first probably founded by Cistercians to cater to the needs of pilgrims making their way up the well-trodden pilgrims' way to Trondheim, by way of the broad Klarälv valley. The pilgrimages to St. Olof's shrine there continued for 500 years until Gustav Vasa forbade them in 1544. St. Olof attracted pilgrims from Greenland and Germany, England and the Faroes who every year converged on Trondheim, then called Nidaros, by 28 July for the feast of the saint on 29th. (St. Olof, the warrior king Olaf of Norway, imposed Christianity on his people and was killed in battle in 1030.)

The present shingle-clad **church** was built in 1686. The altarpiece (1697) has Evangelists surrounding the central painting of the Crucifixion. The pulpit is Renaissance and the medieval font is of Norwegian soapstone. On the wall is a late medieval altar from the old church, with St. Anne, the Virgin and Child. On the organ gallery is an unusual row of **portraits** of monarchs (1764) and the ceiling is painted with angels and clouds. Two rooms display items belonging to the church, including vestments, a Gustav Vasa Bible, a 17C ciborium, a 17C bridal chest and bridal crowns, which were lent to brides on their wedding-day.

Near the church are the **church stables**, now selling handicrafts, and across the road an open-air local history museum. In the Nils Ols-rummet **wall-paintings** by a travelling Dalarna painter are preserved (open summer pm.).

Take road 62 following the pilgrims' route up the Klarälv valley. At 32km the shingle-covered **church** (1764) of **Norra Ny** is on the left of the road. The local school has had the excellent idea of having the children prepare and translate an illustrated booklet in English which may still be available. The altarpiece represents the Crucifixion and Resurrection with figures of John the Baptist and Moses. There are also two triptychs, one with a Madonna and Child of the 13C and another of the 15C with the Descent from the Cross. The font is medieval, of soapstone, the wooden figure of St. Olof is from the 13C, and there is a processional cross of the same century.

At the crossroads in 2km join the 45 again with a right turn. In 16km you leave the province of Värmland and enter Dalarna. On either side are forests, sometimes clearing to allow views over marsh as the road climbs and descends. At (30km) **Malung** the road crosses the Västerdalälv. Malung is a leather-working town, and has a church founded in the Middle Ages and an open-air museum.

The road continues over marshy country with linked and meandering streams, ponds and lakes. At (52km) **Siljansfors** there is a Skogsmuseum (Forestry Museum, open June–Aug) and the remains of an old ironworks. A 5km nature trail leads to the top of Harkenberget (366m above sea-level).

In 7km there is a turn to Gesunda and Sollerön, and further to Mora, while the main road continues and reaches Mora in 12km. These two roads are described in the form of a circular excursion from Mora (see Stockholm to Mora Rte 17).

19

Gävle to Mora

Total distance 173km. Gävle—road 80 84km turn for **Sundborn**—6km *Falun—83km Mora.

Road 80 leaves Gävle to the west and reaches **Sandviken** on Storsjön lake in 24km. There are modern homes designed by Ralph Erskine in the Nya Bruket quarter, and Smedsgården is a house showing how ironworkers lived at the turn of the century and in the 1940s (limited open times).

From here the 272 goes north to **Högbo** (5km), where a large area once belonging to an ironworks has been turned into a tourist complex. There is a tourist bureau, and near it the **Vagnsmuseum** (carriage museum). To the north of these is the **Textilmuseum**, based on the collections of Hedwig Ulfsparre (d 1963) who gathered specimens of different textile techniques such as weaving, embroidery and lace from many districts of Sweden.

To the east is a watercourse which powered the works, and on either side of it the Old Manor (1737) and the New Manor. On the water's edge is the **Öfra Hammaren** (Upper Hammer) of 1666, now with exhibitions on the iron industry. There are pleasant walks, canoeing, fishing, refreshments and a hotel, including rooms fitted in the former workers' homes. The church is from 1777. (Most of these are open June–Aug from 12.00 onwards, tourist bureau and refreshments from 10.00.)

Also accessible from Sandviken is the 4.5km veteran railway from Jädraås to Tallås, run by enthusiasts. (30km northwest. Runs June–Aug, Sun and some Sat.) At **Jädraås** there is also an old ironworks with 19C manor, Lancashire forge, workers' homes and other buildings.

The 272 to the south of Sandviken leads across the middle of Storsjön (lake) to Årsunda (15km) where the church has a 16C Antwerp **altarpiece** and 16C ceiling-paintings by Eghil. This road continues to (34km) **Gysinge**, with the remains of a large ironworks and other displays and attractions.

Back on the 80, after 17km a road runs south to **Torsåker** (7km) where the local museum is the early 19C home of a mine manager, with other buildings.

At **Hofors** in 12km, the local museum (the second building from the car park) contains worker's homes from three different periods, the late 19C, the 1920s and the 1950s. The building, from the 1870s, originally held eight one-room flats.

In 9km there is a turning for Långshyttan (14km). Any name with *bruk* or *hytt* is a relic from the ironworking era. This one is on the *Husbyringen* tourist route (see Stockholm to Mora, Rte 17), and there are remains of the ironworks and a museum.

In 22km, follow the somewhat winding route to **Sundborn** (10km), very well signposted because this is a top-favourite outing for Swedes. It was the home of the artist Carl Larsson, and even if you do not care for his art, Sundborn provides an insight into the Swedish mind.

Carl Larsson (1853–1919) was born in Stockholm and was a member of the Scandinavian artists' colony in Grez, France, in the 1880s. Here in the open air he painted in water-colour, producing delicate airy effects. He was for a time teacher at the Gothenburg art college and was a protégé of Pontus Fürstenberg (see Gothenburg). Carl and his wife Karin, also a budding painter whom he met in Grez, then settled in Sundborn where they rebuilt and extended the previous house on this site. At Sundborn he began to paint meticulously detailed portrayals of his home and family. His wife abandoned her painting, and took to textiles of all kinds, using new bright warm colours. Carl's paintings of the Sundborn interiors have deeply influenced the Swedish enthusiasm for home decoration and the way Swedes regard their homes. His best loved work is the series *Ett hem* ('a home'). But at the same time the artist had a third side to his work—he was also a monumental painter, and decorated the entrance hall of the National Museum in Stockholm with huge wall-paintings, as well as the Opera House and Dramaten (theatre).

The house, **Carl Larsson-gården**, (open May–Sept, guided tours, long waiting time possible) has over the main door a welcome message from the artist and his wife. Inside, the interiors are recognisable from the paintings, with Karin's cheerful textiles and Carl's pictures everywhere. His studio is also shown. A short distance away is Stora Hyttnäs, a complete preserved turn-of-the-century home.

The 18C wooden **church** with some wall-paintings by Larsson is reached by going back to the main road, crossing it and continuing for some distance, a pleasant walk along the waterside. Nearby is a building with a collection of Larsson's portraits.

From where you left road 80 it is 6km to Falun but you can also follow the signposts more directly to the town. On the way at Sveden the sign *Bröllopsstugan* points to Linnaeus' wedding cottage which has wall-paintings.

****Falun** (pop. 35,000) is the administrative centre of the county of Kopparberg, whose borders more or less correspond with those of the old province of Dalarna. For more on Dalarna see under Avesta, Rte 17.

Copper was being mined in Falun as early as the 11C and continued until 1992. In 1288 Bishop Peter of Västerås is recorded as owning one-eighth of the mine, regarded as the first share transaction in Sweden. Prosperity reached its zenith in the 17C, as the town became the second largest in the country with 6000 inhabitants. With at times up to 1200 employees, it became the world's largest copper producer and helped to finance Sweden's overseas adventures and wars of that period.

On midsummer day 1687, when by great good fortune no-one was working underground, there was a catastrophic collapse of the carelessly planned honeycomb of tunnels, to form *Stora Stöten*—the Great Pit—which has been a tourist attraction for centuries.

Falun has given its name to two products still popular today. One is *Falukorv*, the fat Falun sausage, which was originally made from the meat of the oxen slaughtered for their hides to make rope for the copper works. Today it is made of various different meats.

The other product is *Falu rödfärg*, Falun red paint, which, applied to almost every country cottage, is a part of the Swedish vision of the perfect retreat in the woods, beside a lake or on an island. It is not paint in the strict sense of the word. Mine-waste with little copper but containing some iron is weathered over many years, washed, dehydrated, roasted and ground. The recipe also includes oil, starch and water. Today it is produced in other colours, with the same penetrating and preservative qualities.

The **tourist bureau** is on the main square Stora Torget. Opposite is the brick **Kristine church** which was built in the 17C and restored in the 20C. The German artist Evert (or Ewerdt) Friis carved the pulpit and the altarpiece in 1669. In the sacristy are historic vestments, and the church also has silver ecclesiastical vessels.

Leave the square by Falugatan to the south which leads over the Faluån. Immediately on the right is ****Dalarnas Museum** (open Mon–Thur 10.00–17.00, Fri–Sun 12.00–17.00).

On the ground floor there are art exhibitions, with local graphic artists. There is also the interior of Selma Lagerlöf's study and library from her house in Falun. The authoress came here because her mother and sister were here, and lived in flats before she bought the house which she kept until 1933, though she had by then bought back the family home in Mårbacka. The house has been demolished, but its interior was transferred to the museum and a few additions made.

Dala panting in Dalarnas Museum of the Queen of Sheba coming to visit Solomon (1808)

On the **first floor** are the *****peasant culture** displays. It is perhaps the collection of Dalarna **folk-paintings** that most catch the eye, but the **painted furniture** is almost equally captivating. There are two rooms with wall and ceiling-paintings. The folk-music section shows that unusual instrument the key-harp (*nyckelharpa*). You can ask at reception for ear-phones to listen to the music, which is based mainly on fiddles, and you can buy cassettes. The costume section has a useful map of where the costumes come from and the textile display has extra exhibits on pull-out trays. (See under Avesta for more on Dalarna folk-art.)

On the **second floor** there are interiors of a copper-mine manager's room and a worker's room. There is a display of finished copper articles as well as other local applied art, furniture, books and photos.

To the south of the museum, across Falugatan and Gruvgatan, there is **Elsborg**, a pleasant area of wooden houses, formerly inhabited by mine-workers. To the north of centre are two other areas of wooden houses, **Gamla Herrgården**, where those who worked on the copper from the mine lived, and **Östanfors** which was used by farmers who came to do business in the town. These areas have buildings from the 16C to the 19C.

Further out, straight along Gruvgatan, about 1km from the river, is what most tourists have come to see, the *****Great Pit**, inside the grounds belonging to the company Stora Kopparberget. This is part of the very large Stora group, whose logo is the ancient symbol for copper (and Venus), a circle with a cross below it, as seen on a tower at the edge of the crater.

The first thing everyone does is to go to the edge of the chasm to look down into it—there is a small viewing tower. The pit is 100m deep and 300–400m wide. The next thing is to book a **tour** of the underground mine which starts at the small building in front of the manor-house (guided tours May–Aug 10.00–16.30, also spring and autumn weekends pm.).

Visitors wear hard hats and waterproof capes (your shoes are likely to pick up red smudges). There are 30km of tunnels in the mine, and 4000 named locations such as the General Peace Chamber which is 20m high and 60m long. A lift takes you down to 55m, where the temperature is 5°–8°C. Here you are told the story of Kåre the white billy-goat whose goatherd noticed red stains on his horns after butting the ground. In the Creutz shaft 208m deep, there is a bucket on a rope which supported seven men as well as the ore going up to and down from the surface. A constantly tolling bell at the surface meant all was well—sudden silence was an alarm signal. Down here the acid in the water preserves organic matter. There is a tale of a man lost for 42 years whose body was so perfectly preserved that his former fiancée could recognise him. Methods of working are explained, first with making fires, then with explosives. Tools and equipment are shown, such as one of the 6000-a-day torches. Horses were kept in stables down in the mine. The 'Royal guest-book' is a section of wall with carved signatures of royal visitors.

The **museum** is in the yellow manor-house (open daily). Here there are tools, clothing, copper coins and machinery, including large models of hoisting gear. There are displays on copper manufacture and products, and a reconstructed board-room of the company. Relevant art-works are exhibited, and there is the history of the company and a section on Falun red paint, which can also be seen in the shed which now serves refreshments, alongside the enormous figure of the billy-goat who started it all.

The oldest building in Falun is Stora Kopparberg **church**, north of the centre, on the other side of the railway line. This was begun in the 14C, the chancel and sacristy being built in 1690 and the tower in the 18C. It has a pietà probably from Lübeck and a Madonna and Child both of the late 15C and an oak carved pulpit of c 1620. Church silver is kept in a side- chapel.

Leave Falun to the north-west, continuing on the 80. After 14km **Grycksbo** has a paper-mill founded in 1740. Tours twice a week in summer show paper-making by hand, and you can also have a tour of the modern paper-mill.

In 6km **Bjursås** has a local open-air museum, Stadigsgården, on a hill (Dössberget) with a view. From here there is a walking-trail of 35km taking in summer pasture settlements.

Road 80 joins the 70 in 24km, 3km from Rättvik. See Rte 17 Stockholm to Mora for the remainder of the way to Mora.

20

Mora to Östersund

Total distance 320km. Mora—road 45 124km Sveg—road 84 60km turn for **Flatruet** (100km) and road 315 30km—road 316 23km Åsarna—road 45 83km *Östersund.

Leave Mora by the 45 going first east then north to skirt Orsa lake (Orsasjön) with good views. Just before (14km) **Orsa** (pop. 5100) at Trunna parking place with an information board, is the local open-air museum with examples of buildings from the district. The tourist bureau in Orsa is in Centralgatan which runs from the station to the church. In the next block north from the tourist bureau is Kulturhuset with a display of local folk costumes and art. The church, largely rebuilt in the 14C and 15C possesses a North German crucifix of the 14C, and a font of the same period which has strange mouth-to-mouth dragons' heads on its base. A possible explanation is that the dragons could thus wreak no evil on the infant. There are some 14C wall-paintings. Orsa library has picture archives from the area.

From here there is an unusual excursion to the **bear park** at Grönklitt, claimed to be Europe's largest. It is 15km from Orsa, signposted *Björnpark* (open May–Sept/Oct. Binoculars can be useful). The bears are in enclosures in a natural environment and walkways have been constructed for visitors. In the winter, TV cameras in the hibernation lairs relay continuous pictures to the holiday chalets nearby—the place is a winter sports' centre.

Continue on the 45.

To Helvetesfallet, Mässbäcken and Skattungbyn

After 4km road 296 goes east towards Voxna. From this road you could after 5km turn towards Storstupet (7km), a waterfall on the Ämån, and from there continue to **Helvetesfallet** (Hell's Falls) where water roars down a 30m deep canyon. You can return by Tallhed.

After another 1km on the 296, the village of **Mässbäcken** is the centre for the local grindstone industry, for everything from the traditional knife-grinding to cosmetic use. From here the sign *fäbodar* brings you to (12km) an old summer pasture settlement, still functioning and selling traditional refreshments.

The village of **Skattungbyn** (5km) has a wide view of the surrounding forest. The 19C church has two medieval altarpieces.

Back on the 45, the road reaches Emådalen in 20km. From here Helvetesfallet, mentioned above, is to the south-east, and to the north-west a long stretch of the Ämån tumbles down three other falls, Pilstupet, Bössfallet and Lusbostupet.

From here northwards Finnish place-names such as Noppikoski start to appear. Settlers came here from Finland in the 16C and 17C and the area is called Orsa Finnmark. After 29km a way leads to the top of the hill of **Pilkalampinoppi**, with a tower built for fire-watching from which you can admire the view.

Soon the small **Hamra National Park** is on the right, after which Tandsjön (lake) is on the right and later Fågelsjön on the left. After 67km the 45 swings west into Sveg and doubles out again eastward. (The 45 is a recent confection, the Via Lappia, pieced together out of many former road numbers, designed to link the towns of inland Sweden from Gothenburg to Karesuando, as far north as you can get in Sweden.)

Sveg, situated where the Ljusnan flows out of Svegssjön (lake), is the administrative centre of Härjedalen. Härjedalen, an ancient province now part of the county of Jämtland, forms just one municipality because of its sparse population, with less than one person per square kilometre. It is very mountainous with over 40 peaks more than 1000m high. Sveg is the only community with more than 1000 inhabitants. It has a local open-air musuem.

The village of Älvros 16km along road 45 has houses from the 17C onwards. The church is mainly 18C, with a wooden vault by Jonas Granberg of Klövsjö who also made the altarpiece. The bell-tower is by Pål Persson.

However, instead of the 45, the following route is recommended as a slower but more interesting alternative as far as Åsarna, using the 84 and the 315, with a possible detour to Flatruet.

Road 84 follows the Ljusnan valley and its associated lakes to the north-west of Sveg, first skirting Svegssjön. In 15km, **Gammelremsgård** is an 18C farmhouse of log-cabin construction and log roof, with well-preserved ceiling and wall-paintings from 1774.

The road turns north at (15km) Linsell and the river broadens. To the left is **Sånfjället** a fell massif 1277m high which is a national park. The name means Sun Mountain. When the park was established in 1910 one bear was found, now there are more than 20, out of a total Swedish bear population of 800. The five peaks are bare of trees, and moss and lichens abound because reindeer (all of which are domesticated and belong to someone) do not graze here. Lower down are birch and spruce, some of the latter being 250 years old. Access roads are sign-posted from Linsell and Hedeviken, and you can drive as far as Nyvallen. There are car-parks, the occasional shelter and cabin, toilet and campfire facilities. The tourist bureaux (main bureau in Hede) have details of tours, bear-safaris and other activities, with maps and leaflets on the flora (in English).

At 30km is the turning right on to the 315 to Vemdalen, Svenstavik and Östersund.

To the Flatruet plateau

A rewarding detour is to take the 84 to Hede and the **Flatruet plateau** (100km). At (11km) **Hede** the **church** is on a road parallel to the 84 to the south. The typical large **bell-tower** was built in 1751. The church has also the typical deep double-sloped roof and has been restored to a great extent to its 18C appearance, with among other things a **pulpit canopy** of that time. The pulpit itself was made earlier, but has been remodelled. The tall carved angel is also 18C and there is a Rococo **rood-arch** linked to carved tops to the front pews. The carvings in square frames on the fronts of these pews are from the 17C.

Just after Hede is an attractive picnic site on the river, on the right c 100m off the road. At 13km the village of Långå has the remains of a 17C **fort** (Långå skans) built to protect the newly Swedish region from the Danes and Norwegians. It had star-shaped fortifications, and barracks, brewery, bakery and stables.

After 33km **Tännäs** is a mountain village popular with holiday-makers, 1km down the 311 towards Särna. (This is not a good route to Särna as the surface is extremely poor.) The church here is 17C, renovated in 1855.

Continue to (15km) Funäsdalen and turn right towards Mittådalen, Flatruet and Ljungdalen. The track is rough and climbs all the way to the bare Flatruet plateau, with only electricity poles striding over the empty land. The highest point (975m above sea-level, the country's highest public road) is marked by a concrete pillar and a heap of stones with names of visitors. The *view is vast and desolate in all directions.

This road continues to Ljungdalen from where one could drive back to Åsarna, but the road is not good.

Turn right on to the 315 from the 84. All over this area are Sami (Lapp) shops selling smoked (*rökt*) or dried (*torkat*) reindeer meat (*ren*) and soft reindeer leather products. There are also cafés specialising in hot waffles (*våffel*) with cream and jam (check price before you order).

In 8km **Vemdalen church** was completed in 1763. It is eight-sided with a deep two-stage roof and a central onion-turret. The bell-tower was built in 1755. Inside, the 18C altar was carved by Jonas Granberg from Klövsjö, and the pulpit with its bulging panels of inlaid cherrywood and deal was made by another local artist from Ljungdalen. The Rococo style and colour-scheme is carried through to the chancel arch and the hymn-number board. In the sacristy there are recently discovered 17C paintings. The iron-ore chandeliers are of 17C and the wrought-iron candleholders, one for each pew, are modern.

Continue east. After 22km take road 316 to Klövsjö, Åsarna and Östersund. **Klövsjö** in 5km, is set on the slope of a hill with a view across a lake to the mountains in the west. On the outskirts of the village a sign to the left points to **Tomtangården**, an old farm of 14 clustered buildings open to the public. Some of the outbuildings are from the 17C and the rest from the 18C or early 19C.

You can work your way to the centre of the village by continuing for 0.5km and turning right up the hill, or else the main road will bring you to the **tourist bureau** where you turn left. Take the first left for the **church** which is very close.

The medieval pilgrims to Trondheim stopped here so there was a chapel before the present wooden church was built in 1795–97 by Pål Persson the bell-tower builder. Jonas Granberg who also worked at Vemdalen and for Trondheim cathedral here made the altar and font. The obelisk-shaped wooden pillars each side of the chancel entrance are a north Swedish feature. The pews are a modern reconstruction to complete the 18C image.

Continue north, descending through forests. The road joins the 45 at (18km) Åsarna, an important skiing centre, and in fact the entire district is geared to winter holidays.

On the Ljungan there are small rapids, Åsanforsen. At (17km) Svenstavik the road passes the south point of Storsjön (the Great Lake).

To the west of Storsjön

Road 321 goes left up the other side of the lake and after 7km you can drive on to Hoverberget, a steep tree-clad hill (548m) on a pensinsula, with an outlook tower on top, and a cave which can be visited (Hoverbergsgrottan). At Persåsen, 12km further on, a road leads west which passes several summer pasture settlements (*fäbodar*). You can continue south to Börtnan or north-west to Glen on the edge of the mountain Oviksfjällen.

After 25km on road 45 **·Hackås** has a church in an idyllic situation on the shore of the lake. Follow the sign *Hackås k:a* (1km). The hill above was once the site of ancient councils, trials and executions. There are numerous Iron Age burials in the district, covered by two archaeological trails.

This too was a resting-place for pilgrims to Trondheim. As they had to get to Trondheim on 28 July for the feast of St, Olof the next day, they were accustomed to be here on 20 July and celebrate the feast of St. Margaret. That is perhaps why the **apse paintings** (13C) relate her martyrdom in the time of Diocletian. The present **apse** and **sacristy** were the original church built in about 1130, though tradition says a church was founded here by the nephew or grandson of St. Olof in the 11C. In the 15C a nave was added with **wall-paintings** done in 1601, and the paintings show clearly how long this nave was. The rest was added in 1770.

The **pulpit** and **retable** (1780–81) are by Johan Edler. In the apse is a 15C censer, in the sacristy a crown with the Skånke crest (a boot) and 17C votive ship, and in the chancel a 15C candlestick and a 17C font carved out of a tree-trunk. The crest of the Skånkes, who are said to be descended from the founder of the 11C church and the rebuilder of the 15C, is also in the nave. The stately **bell-tower** was built in the 18C to replace a defensive tower like the one at Brunflo (see below) which had been struck by lightning. (From Hackås a local road continues up the lake and passes a 1.3km bridge across to Oviken where there is a medieval church and an open-air museum. If you do not cross the bridge you can continue to (17km) Sunne where there are the ruins of a medieval church and a defensive tower.)

The 45 continues 25km to Brunflo where it joins the E75. Brunflo **church** was built on the site of a medieval one in the 18C. Here the roof is more like a mansard roof than the Swedish *säteri* version with a vertical section between the two planes as at Hede and Vemdalen. The local craftsman Johan Edler made the **altar** and the **pulpit** with a Gethsemane scene. There is a font of Gotland sandstone of c 1200 by Sigraf, a tall painted wooden clock of 1834 and a good organ. The 30m **tower** beside the church was built in the late 12C for defence, and its 19C top houses the church bells.

From Brunflo it is 16km to Östersund.

Östersund (pop. 43,000) has an enviable situation on Storsjön (lake), in the centre of the Jämtland lake district and with the spectacular mountain region further off along the Norwegian border to the west. Consequently it is fairly full all the year round, with Swedish holiday-makers, foreign tourists, and conference participants. More facilities remain open in winter where they tend to close in southern Sweden, and there are many extras for the winter tourist—floodlit ski-slopes, competitions and festivals, not forgetting car-heaters and warm garages at some hotels. The electronics and engineering industries are the biggest employers. There is a significant military presence, with regiments based here, and military training schools so that many conscripts on military service pass through each year. The **Inlandsbanan** (Inland Railway) from Östersund to Gällivare is (or was) a great tourist attraction, with a guide on board and stops for photography and berry-picking. Its future however hangs by a thread, and each year is threatened to be its last.

Tourist bureau: Rådhusgatan 44. Tel. (063) 14 40 01.

Post office: Storgatan 38.

Telephone, telegram: Kyrkgatan 62. Tel. (063) 90 100.

The island of Frösön close to the shore, named after Frö the fertility god, was the first site of settlement. In about the 7C a fort was built on the island. Soon Frösön became a market-place and a centre of local government with a *ting* council-meeting and a local governor. In 1645 Jämtland province became Swedish at the Peace of Brömsebro, and to educate the newly Swedish citizens a school was established. The church was built on a pagan place of sacrifice. A find under the altar in 1984 consisted of models of animals significant to the old Viking religion, surrounding a tree-stump, which it is thought represents Yggdrasil, the Tree of the World in Norse myth.

Östersund itself was founded in 1786 by Gustav III and retains its central grid plan and some original houses. It became important only when the railway from Sundsvall was constructed in 1879. It is the capital of Jämtland county which includes the two ancient provinces of Jämtland and Härjedalen, with small parts of Ångermanland and Hälsingland. The scenery in the county is superb, ranging from placid lake-country to mountains rising above the tree-line, which are the main centre for down-hill skiing in Sweden. There are bears and even muskoxen, though the muskoxen are few (20–30 altogether in Sweden) and live along the Norwegian border. The lake is said to be inhabited by a monster which figures largely in the tourist literature—notice the logo, and all the little monsters for sale.

Follow the signs to the **tourist bureau** in the centre of town where there is parking space in front of the school building (1849) in which the tourist bureau has its offices (open Mon–Sat 09.00–22.00, Sun hols 11.00–20.00, winter Mon–Fri 09.00–17.00).

If you intend to stay more than a day it will be worth buying the **Storsjö card** which gives free or reduced tickets for coach and walking tours, museums, lake-trips in the old coal-fired steamer Thomée, entertainment, parking, the adventure pool Storsjöbadet and the open-air heated pool on Frösön, Lövstabadet.

Behind (to the east of) the tourist bureau is the large brick town hall of 1912 with a central tower modelled on the bell-tower of Håsjö (replica in Skansen).

North of the bureau is the **Town Museum** (*Stadsmuseum*. Open 13.00–15.00. Displays on the history of Östersund). To the north again is the **Gamla kyrka** (Old Church) begun in 1834 (open 11.00–17.00).

A turn left will bring you to the main square with a view across the lake. The theatre is to the right and there is a sculpture called 'The Choir' by Thomas Qvarnsebo. Ahead is the pleasant Badhuspark extending into the lake and leading to the pedestrian bridge across to Frösön.

The **streets** south of the main square, Prästgatan and Storgatan, have 18C houses, wood-panelled, pastel-painted, some with fretted wood balconies. Just south of where road 45 joins Rådhusgatan is the **Stora kyrka** (Great church) with a view of the fells and lake. It was built in 1940 with somewhat Gothic and Byzantine nuances, and a green and gold turret. The fresco above the altar is by Hilding Linnqvist.

On the northern edge of town are the two museums Jamtli (open-air museum) and the Länsmuseum (county museum).

Jamtli calls itself History Land (buildings open summer 11.00–17.00, but you can walk in the grounds at other times and in winter. Leaflets and plans in English. Stalls, café, restaurant). It is indeed more history-based than other open-air museums, with archways proclaiming which period you are entering as you approach a group of buildings. There is emphasis here too on audience-participation and you can learn the old crafts. Children can feed animals, milk cows and play old games. In many buildings costumed and often bare-foot inhabitants are working with real animals or real products and you are greeted with an historically-accurate equivalent of 'good-day'.

From the entrance you are in the year 1900 with the market stalls from Frösön on the right selling old-fashioned goodies, and town buildings to the left. Turn left and then right before the children's section and after passing the courthouse with a trial going on you reach the large enclosed farmyard of **Lillhärdalsgården**. Everything is done as in the year 1785 and the extended family is busy on the farm chores. Nearby is the smithy. Return across to the main north–south path where several large buildings extend almost in a line. After the Hov restaurant the 19C is represented by **Näsgården farmhouse** with a bakery where flat crispbread is made, and Hammerdalsgården where old crafts are demonstrated, a school-room and a gunsmith's workshop. At the end there is a **fäbod** (summer pasture settlement where butter and cheese are made), a forest-worker's hut and a Sami (Lapp) dwelling.

On coming out of Jamtli, **Jämtlands Länsmuseum** (County Museum) is straight ahead on the left (open Mon–Fri 09.00–16.00, Tue to 21.00, Sat, Sun 12.00–16.00).

Immediately to the left of the entrance is a small section on the **Great Lake Monster**. Sightings report him to be very similar to the Loch Ness monster, 6m to 12m long, snake-like body and small dog-like head with ears or fins. In the 19C concerted efforts were made to catch him, and in 1894 a company was formed for the purpose with King Oskar II as patron. A gigantic pair of tweezers, a harpoon and two crooks were manufactured, and the bait was pigs or calves. To withstand the expected sudden strain the equipment was anchored to a special jetty on the shore. The equipment is displayed here with other exhibits. A law has now been passed declaring the monster a protected species.

The main exhibitions are on the two upper floors. On the **first floor** to the right are **pre-historic finds** from the county, from the Stone and Iron Ages to Viking times. Important exhibits are the Rödö Urn, the 6C Brunflo and Häste clasps and the Offerdal spearhead.

To the left are temporary exhibitions and *Fäbodliv*—life in the mountain pasture huts used from June to September. There were 3000–4000 of these in 1900 and in 1967 there were still 206. One farmer might have several of these settlements, each consisting of cottage, barn and milk-shed. One woman could look after several, making butter and cheese there. Also on this floor are local music and folksong, coins and medals, and religious art, including a 14C Madonna and three 17C altarpieces, together with assorted local wood-carvings.

Upstairs on the **second floor** to the right is the museum's treasure, the *tapestries from Överhögdal. (English booklet available to consult and also to buy in the bookstall downstairs.)

The tapestries, from the 9C or 10C, were found in a dusty heap in an old storehouse in 1910. Other pieces were then searched for and found, one being used as a doll's blanket (the child was pacified with 2kr) and another having a narrow escape from being used as a cleaning-rag. The technique is the one used in oriental soumak weaving, where the pattern thread is looped round two or three warp threads. This was probably worked on an upright loom. The base was flax and the pattern threads wool from local sheep, coloured with plant dyes, mainly deep reds and blues. There are few other tapestries using this technique in Scandinavia. One is in the National History Museum in Stockholm and another was found in the Oseberg ship in Norway.

The tapestries are crowded with pictures of animals—horses, elks, reindeer, birds, dogs and unknown creatures. There are also houses, boats, trees and various symbols. One piece which has been carbon-dated to the 11C can be called Christian. It has been interpreted as the story of the Christianisation of Jämtland by St. Staffan of Bremen. The subject matter of the other pieces is debatable—scenes from a saga, or perhaps fertility symbols for a wedding or the victory of Christianity over the old heathen gods.

The rest of the textile sections show techniques, materials and costumes from Jämtland. Clothes for different occasions are displayed, for winter, for best, for working. The remainder of the floor is occupied by picture archives, the children's section and temporary exhibitions.

The island of **Frösön** is joined to the mainland by a pedestrian bridge and a vehicle bridge. At the end of the vehicle bridge, drive straight ahead for the runestone, the outlook tower and the zoo, though the latter two can be approached also from the other road to the left.

Follow the signs *runsten* in a short but winding route to the courtyard of a municipal building. The stone originally stood near the bridge and is the most northerly in Sweden, from the mid 11C. It says 'Östman Gudfast's son had this stone raised, and this bridge made and christianised Jämtland. Äsbjörn made the bridge, Tryn carved and Sten made the runes'. It is the only Swedish runestone which mentions Christianisation.

Return to Frösövägen and turn south. Turn right into Nybovägen then left into Byvägen which shortly turns right. Follow the signs *utsiktstornet*. This is the Frösö tower on top of Östberg hill from which there is a **view** of the lake and much of Jämtland. The zoo is another kilometre or so on the same road and includes a tropical house, nature museum and children's playground.

Work your way south to join the main road Vallaleden, or from the bridge, follow the signs *Frösö k:a* (Frösö church) which is 5km away to the west. After 2km from the bridge the road turns right past Öneberget, a hill on which is an Iron Age fort on the edge of a bluff.

Frösö church stands on a rise with a view of the lake and fells. It has an imposing Baroque onion-domed wooden **bell-tower**. Built in 1754, it is clad in wood shingles in typical south Norrland style. The large bell is the 14C Birgitta bell—St. Birgitta is said to have stopped here on pilgrimage to Trondheim. The other bell is from the 18C. Against the south wall is the grave of the composer Wilhelm Peterson-Berger (1867–1942) whose home Sommarhagen is near here (open to the public).

The church was founded c 1200 but two 19C fires destroyed much of the fabric. The ceiling is a wooden barrel-vault with cloud paintings. The 18C altar depicts the Nativity below and Christ above flanked by angels. A medieval reliquary stands in a niche. The Rococo pulpit by Johan Edler shows the four Evangelists seated round a table with angels and scrolls. On the organ gallery are paintings of the prophets in 16C costumes, previously on galleries at the sides.

About 1km further on is Frösön **open-air museum** (open summer 09.00–21.00, museum 12.00–16.00). Here too there is an outlook tower. To the left of the entrance is a cabin used for storing riding equipment for a cavalry officer in Jämtlands corps. There is a café in the large wooden building to the left and inside across the ceiling are beams from which food stores were slung. To the right the white house is the museum with exhibits on school, home and farming. This was part of the school founded in 1674 after Jämtland became Swedish. Before this pupils went to Copenhagen or Trondheim. There were between 50 and 130 pupils and they lived in scattered cabins, bringing with them food enough for the whole term. In 1847 the school moved to Östersund (the tourist bureau building). It was called a *Trivialskola* from the Roman *trivium*, the first three subjects studied. Ahead is a small wooden teacher's house of 1735 and other old wooden buildings lie beyond.

21

Gävle to Sundsvall

Total distance 210km. Gävle—E4 74km Söderhamn—54km **Hudiksvall**—82km **Sundsvall**.

Going north on the E4 from Gävle, this is still the old ironworking region and there are preserved ironworks to be seen, such as at Oslättfors. After passing (28km) Hagsta, in 4km there is a cluster of communities to the right of the road, Hamrånge, Bergby and Vifors. At Hamrånge the 19C church has medieval carvings, and there is a local museum at Bergby. The old ironworks at Vifors has a Rococo manor and several other buildings. From here you can reach Norrsundet (8km) on the coast, where there is a workers' museum, and an industrial museum in the fort-like machine-room of the steam-powered saw-works. The disused station has been turned into a church.

After 3km you can turn to **Axmar bruk** (13km), an ironworks estate where you can see the foundry, blast furnace with 20C, tar factory, mill, storehouses, workers' homes and associated buildings from the 19C. In the grounds there is a 19C neo-Gothic summer-house.

In 11km at Tönnebro, just after the road leaves Gästrikland province and enters Hälsingland, there is an attractive motorway stop overlooking the Noran lakes. In 28km you reach **Söderhamn** (pop. 13,000), dominated by the 19C mock-castle viewing tower of Oscarsborg on Östra Berget, a hill above the town.

The **tourist bureau** is on the right as you enter. To reach the museum you have to continue along Brädgårdsgatan and double back from the square to the right. The **museum** is in part of the arms factory designed by Christopher Polhem in 1748 (open summer p.m. except Mon), and deals with the history of Söderhamn. The gabled brick town hall is from the late 19C. Further along and off to the left is the Ulrika Eleonora **church** named after Karl XI's queen, and designed by Nicodemus Tessin the Younger, finished in 1693. It has a Greek-cross plan, with a 17C pulpit and many ornate memorial tablets.

Fjärilshuset (the Butterfly House, open all year) is a kilometre or so out on road 301 towards Bollnäs. This claims to be the world's most northerly butterfly house, with specimens from the Philippines and Malaysia. The species to be seen vary throughout the year, and are kept at 75 per cent humidity and a temperature of 25°C.

2km out on the same road is **Söderala**, where there is a stone **church** begun in the 12C with a Greek-cross plan, thought to be influenced by the

Sigtuna churches. The medieval **vault-paintings** are here in a different style to the others in Hälsingland. There is a Gotland sandstone font of c 1200.

Continuing on the E4, in 10km you can turn for **Trönö old church** (4km), signposted *Trönö g:la kyrka*, which is some kilometres from the village of that name. It was begun c 1200 and extended in the 16C. With its 17C bell-tower of stave-church construction, and the churchyard wall with lichgates, it makes a picturesque scene. Inside it has **wood-carvings**, some by Haaken Gulleson, including the altarpiece and a Madonna. The statues of Faith and Hope to either side of the altar are from 1737, and the pews are also 18C. Across the railway, Söderblomsgården is a local museum, in the house where Archbishop Nathan Söderblom was born. He was awarded the Nobel Peace Prize in 1930.

·Enånger in 22km has two churches. The medieval one is off the main road, signposted *gammal kyrka*. This was built in the 15C and is little changed except for the windows. The **walls** and **vaults** are painted by an artist of the Tierp school known as 'Eghil' with events from the Bible and ecclesiastical history, framed in luxuriant painted foliage. The same artist did the paintings at Ytterlännas and Torsåker.

The talented wood-carver **Haaken Gulleson** had his workshop near Enånger in the early 16C, and he and his associates were active in Hälsingland and all the surrounding provinces, as well as Ångermanland to the north. His work is recognisable by solid forms, doll-like round faces with pink cheeks and corkscrew curls, and broken folds of the garments. Here he carved the main **altar** and **St. Anne with Madonna and Child**. There is a 16C German altar on the north wall and in the sacristy another **triptych**, **St. Roch** by Gulleson and the Archangel Michael with a dragon. The carving on the rear galleries was done in the 18C by the same artists who carved the pulpit.

In another 10km Gulleson's work is also to be seen, in the **church** at **Njutånger**. The **altarpiece** shows a Calvary scene with saints on the doors including Scandinavian saints, St. Olof, St. Erik and St. Katarina (daughter of St. Birgitta). A **Virgin and Child** and an unknown **saint** are on the south wall, the work of Haaken Gulleson or his school. The **vault-paintings** are probably 16C, because the Vasa emblem, a wheatsheaf, is incorporated into the painting. (An English leaflet identifies the saints on the vaults.) The Gotland limestone font is 13C, and outside, the bell-tower with its onion-domed cupola is probably from the 1720s.

4km later at **Iggesund** you can follow the signs to '*Bruksmuseum*', the **ironworks museum** (free guided tours in English. English booklet. Open mid June–mid Aug).

The ironworks was founded at Iggesund in 1685. There was no iron nearby, but an abundance of wood which was consumed in very large quantities by the industry, and it was easier to bring the iron from Dannemora and Utö than transport the wood there. In 1721 the Russians razed the place, but it was rebuilt and improved, and enjoyed considerable prosperity in the 18C and 19C. The forestry side of the company was gradually expanded also, so that when the iron industry faded in the 20C and the ironworks finally closed in 1953, the company continued with wood products. Today it concentrates on sawn timber, paperboard and cellulose.

At the entrance end of the machine-hall the huge brick furnace is sur-rounded by all the associated installations. Wooden stairs and walkways wind between, above and below in a maze of different sections and levels. At the very top you can see how the ore, charcoal and limestone are manoeuvred into the blast furnace. Charcoal was used because it gave better quality than coal when used with this particular technology, and limestone made the slag more liquid. The smelting works and the tool-maker's forge are nearby.

Further on are the bulbous Bessemer converters for making steel and at the end are hammers and rollers. In the side rooms there is an exhibition about the industry, the foundry and its workers, with a worker's home of the 1930s. The estate functioned as an independent community organised by the company, with its own shop, school and post office. There is also an exhibition on the development of the office milieu. **Grillska gården**, the elegant manor house, was built in 1724. (No admittance.)

It is 8km to **Hudiksvall** (pop. 15,000). The **tourist bureau** is down near the harbour on the Hudiksvall fjord. Nearby are **19C warehouses** on either side of the inlet Strömmingssundet which forms the end of the canal. Cross the bridge at the end of this and take Lilla Kyrkogatan towards the church. On the right, the middle house is the vicarage, which escaped a destructive fire in 1792.

S:t Jakob church had to be rebuilt in the early 18C and the interior is mainly from the 19C and 20C. Return down Norra Kyrkesplanaden—you can see the other side of the old vicarage—to the narrower part of the canal, cross it and take Sundsesplanaden, the next road on the left. Storgatan, which soon crosses at right-angles, is the main shopping street, and on the opposite corner is **Hälsinglands Museum**, in a former bank (open all year, except off-season weekends a.m.). In the central room on the ground floor are local **archaeological finds**, including an Iron Age burial and the Malsta runestone which is inscribed without the usual upright strokes, in so-called 'staveless runes'. The local medieval ***wood-carving** on show is mostly by Haaken Gulleson who had his workshop near Enånger. The fishing and seafaring exhibition has some boats, models and equipment.

On the next floor is the history of Hudiksvall, and the textile display with local linen, lace, knitting and embroidery. The museum possesses good ***peasant art** collections, with chests, clocks, cupboards, sledges, textiles, costumes, and harness, carved and painted, but these may give way to temporary displays. There are painted peasant interiors and middle-class interiors from the late 18C and early 19C. On the second floor there is (usually) Swedish art.

Continue north, turn left, right and left to Lillfjärden (Little Fjord), today a lake joined to the sea by a canal, but 400 years ago it was the harbour, eventually cut off by the rising of the land. There is a nature trail all round it, with plentiful bird life, especially Canada geese.

Continue along the lake and take Marknadsgatan as far as Town Hall Park—with no town hall. The sculptures here symbolise the town's relation-ship with the sea. **Långgatan** on the left leads into the old fishermen's quarter with low wooden houses. Drop down to Hamngatan and turn right. On the corner of Brunnsgatan is the early 19C property of Julius Brun the apothecary who built Stenegård in Järvsö. Return along the harbour to the tourist bureau.

A view of the town and the fjord can be had from the hill of Köpmanberget, reached by going out along Hamngatan about 1km and following signs.

Excursion to the Dellen lakes and Järvsö

Leave Hudiksvall to the west on road 84. **Forsa church** in 10km was completely rebuilt in the 19C but contains much late medieval art. The **altarpiece** on the north wall of the chancel is the work of Haaken Gulleson and the carved centre section represents the Intercession of Christ on behalf of mankind. The wings of the triptych are painted. The almost 3m high **Madonna and Child** on the side-altar is signed by Gulleson himself. The large crucifix is from c 1500. Over the sacristy door is a 14C figure of an apostle and on the south wall there is a Madonna of the early 16C and St. Michael from the same century. On the rear wall are St. Barbara (16C), St. Olof (1300), St. Erik (16C) and Christ (15C). (These dates are not agreed by all.) St. Michael on the south wall is also from the Gulleson workshop, and there is a 14C apostle in the chancel. Ecclesiastical textiles mainly from the 18C are displayed in a cabinet. In the 'Birgitta room' at the back is a copy of the **Forsa ring**, a large iron door-ring, c 1100, with a runic inscription about ecclesiastical duties, and another **altarpiece** probably from the Gulleson workshop, with carving on all three sections, and paintings on the backs of the doors. The somewhat worn figure of **St. Birgitta** is from c 1500.

Outside there are some remaining 19C **church stables**, which were large enough to drive the vehicle in as well. To the south near the lake is *Gillestugan* a medieval two-storey stone building with an outside staircase, whose purpose is not clear.

Delsbo in 24km is on the Dellen lakes, formed by the impact of a meteorite about 200 million years ago. (From here there is a pleasant drive going north on road 305. On the way you could visit Delsbo forngård—open-air museum—with peasant art and the church with an onion-domed bell-tower, and Bjuråker forngård with more wall-paintings and a summer pasture settlement. From Friggesund you could drive up the hill of Avholmsberget for the view, and proceed to Moviken with a well-preserved blast furnace. A road also goes from Bjuråker along the north shore to the south lake.)

The Dellen folk music festival takes place in July with venues all over the area.

It is 27km to **Ljusdal** where there is a stately 18C **bell-tower**. The **church** has an **altar** made in Antwerp c 1500. The pulpit (1773) was carved by the same artist as the large angel statues. There is an open-air museum by the river and a conventional museum in the centre of town.

Turn south on to road 83 towards Bollnäs, to **Järvsö** (18km). This has a free-range zoo, called **Järvzoo** (open all year), where a 3km long wooden walkway has been constructed between and sometimes above the animal enclosures. Here Scandinavian animals roam in terrain which varies according to species—muskoxen, foxes, wolverines, deer, elks, wolves, beavers and bears. There is a plan to complement this by establishing Scandinavian birds. You can hire binoculars, and there are suitable rest places.

Another attraction in Järvsö is **Stenegård**, a 19C estate with original buildings, arts and crafts workers' shops and gardens. This is on the other side of the river from the centre of town and on the way you see the 19C church on its island—it has a small museum in the tower. Stenegård was started by an apothecary called Johan Julius Brun in 1857, and was a working farm. There are two parallel manor-houses, a large gatehouse with tourist bureau and other buildings now housing such enterprises as a silversmith's, baker's, linen and glass shops. The lower garden is used for public events and the upper garden has a herb section. The gazebo is a modern copy. To the north of Stenegård are the church stables, which you can reach on the way back to the centre by turning right where you would otherwise turn left for the bridge.

2km south of Järvsö is **Karlsgården**, a large farmstead with buildings from the 17C and 18C complete with good **furnishings** and **equipment**. Note the three-seater privy with a view.

From Hudiksvall the E4 continues north and reaches (5km) Hälsingtuna. The **church** was begun in the 12C and the tower which served for defence has remained from that time. There are several **medieval wood-carvings**, including a Calvary group of 13C, and St. Michael and St. Nicholas of the 16C. The altar and pulpit are 17C and the majestic **bell-tower** was constructed in 1777.

Just after Hälsingtuna a minor road goes to Hög (2km) with another 18C bell-tower by the church (not always open). The lich-gate is medieval and there are two runestones in front of it. The place-name means 'mound' and there are pre-historic tumuli in the neighbourhood, one of which is near the vicarage.

From here too you can reach the large Hornslandet peninsula in 20km or so, with interesting flora and fauna. The main village Arnön has a museum about the peninsula, and there are two other fishing-villages.

After 29km at Jättendal you could take a road to Mellanfjärden (7km) on the coast, a fishing-village with a museum of the coast, a summer art-gallery and rope-works which can be visited.

In 6km the road comes to Gnarp. There are many summer pasture settlements (*fäbodar*) in the region such as Vallenbodarna, north of Gnarp. 11km from Gnarp you can turn off to **Galtström** (9km) where the ironworks was founded in 1672. Much has been preserved, including the 17C church, the blast furnace, roasting furnace, and a little steam locomotive used for transport within the grounds and to the harbour.

This is now the small province of Medelpad. At (14km) Njurunda there is a local open-air museum. Soon the road crosses the Ljungan. About 2km north of Njurunda there is an area of scattered prehistoric remains to the west of the road, with mounds and stone circles. It is 15km to Sundsvall.

The E4 comes in to **Sundsvall** as Landsvägsallén and turns left to skirt the Sundsvall fjord.

Sundsvall (pop. 50,000) is situated between two great rivers, the Indalälv and Ljungan, and surrounded by hills. It received its charter from Gustavus Adolphus in 1624. In 1721 it was burned by the Russians. Relative obscurity continued until the 19C when saw-milling brought prosperity from the timber floated down the two rivers, and it is still the centre of the Swedish forestry industry. After a great fire in 1888 only stone houses were allowed to be built, and many remain from this period. A hundred mansions were built within ten years from the wealth flowing here from the timber business, so that it is known as the town of stone. It was the capital of the small Medelpad province, which is graced by scenery of rivers, forests and indented coastline. Now it is included in the county of Västernorrland, of which is it the largest municipality.

Tourist bureau: Main square. Tel. (060) 11 42 35.

Post office: Köpmangatan 19.

Bus station: South side of Norrmalmsbro (bridge). Tel. information: (060) 15 31 00.

Telephone, telegram: Kyrkogatan 11. Tel. (060) 90 100.

Storgatan runs across the north end of Stora Torget, the main square. The **tourist bureau** is in a low building on the north-east and has much information in English (open 09.00–17.00, June–Aug to 21.00).

In the centre of the square is a **statue** of Gustavus Adolphus (1621) the founder of the city. To the south is the cream-coloured town hall (1865–68).

The two sculpture groups (1891) are symbols of local government activities, such as government, justice and police, and music and social life. On the west is the scroll-gabled **Hirschska house** of brick and stucco, with rusticated ground floor. On the north are the brick **Gran's house** with stepped gables and turrets, and Edvall's the jeweller's shop with interior from the 1890s.

Leave the square by the south-west corner and take Kyrkogatan. In the second block on the right is the **house** built by one of the many 19C timber barons, Johan August Hedberg. The park opposite is called after him and contains a bust of him.

Ahead is the brick neo-Gothic church built after the 1888 fire. In 1952 much was simplified and the sculptures round the main door 'Praise to the Lord' were added. Inside there are white walls and vaults with brick pillars and vault-ribs. In the baptismal chapel the old font and part of an old altar-piece are retained. The pulpit is from 1952 with intarsia renderings of parables. Above the south gallery with its figures of Luke and John is the Luther window (1920), and opposite are Matthew and Mark, with Gustavus Adolphus in the window (1920). The votive ship in the seafarers' chapel is a model of the *Västernorrland*, the last ship built in Sundsvall. The chancel windows (1895) represent the Creation, Birth of Christ, Resurrection, Ascension and the Holy Ghost. Below are carved wooden figures on the wall in a modern version of a reredos, with Christ, Madonna and child, and three missionaries.

Return to the main square and take Storgatan to the east, lined by imposing buildings. The broad road at right angles is Esplanaden. Next to this are small public gardens called Vängåvan with a fountain (1886) by Sofia Gisberg. The top figure is Art, the others Industry, Manual Work, Trade, Shipping, Science and Wisdom.

On the right is a bank of 1906 and on the next corner is the renowned **Hotel Knaust** (1890), which has an even more renowned neo-Baroque staircase. It may soon be restored to its real function, after a period as Patent Office. Across the road are more grand mansions—small plaques give dates, and some information in Swedish.

Take the next road to the left. You can already see the striking **Kultur-magasinet** (Culture Warehouse), ingeniously constructed by linking four old warehouse blocks. The intervening streets have been glassed in and roofed with glass, from which some solar energy is derived. The warehouses were built in the 1890s by leading architects and were given the names of ships. The ground floors were offices and the upper floors used for storage. They had to be capacious as the frozen sea meant nothing could be moved by ship from December to April. To the left is the library, to the right the museum. The complex houses also the County Archives, a café and a nursery school which you can visit.

The **museum** (open Mon–Fri 10.00-17.00, often later Sat 11.00–16.00) is on four floors and two buildings, linked by footbridges at each level. The buildings are called Barkassen (longboat) and Skonerten (schooner).

In **Barkassen** on the first floor is a **history of Sundsvall** from the 17C to the 19C. The dynamic period of the late 19C is shown separately. This was when Sundsvall was the centre of the world's largest timber-working area. The rebuilding of the city after the fire is shown with models, drawings and photos (detailed notes in English available). On the second floor the art gallery shows 20C Swedish artists, and on the third is a section on local artist Carl Frisendahl.

Over in **Skonerten** on the second floor is Sun, Rock, Water (notes in English), an exhibition on the geology and landscape of Medelpad province, and on the third floor is shown the heyday of the **sawmills**, with models, photos and trade union banners. The other floors are used for temporary exhibitions. Displays are planned on the Iron Age in Medelpad, and a sawmill worker's home. In the summer there are regular concerts under the glass roof and in the museum, and city walks can be be booked here.

A hill to the north (Norra Berget) has a view, small museum and restaurant. Follow the signs N Stadsberget. The museum (open daily, short hours in winter) is on the right. It has one famous exhibit the **'Skvader'**, a stuffed animal, half hare and half wood-grouse, supposed to have been shot in 1874. This originated as a tall story by a local hunter. The rest of the museum shows the history of shipbuilding in the area, and there are sections on copper-working, shoe-making, clock-making, bookbinding and printing. In the basement are reconstructions of an old bakery, smithy and dairy.

In the large wooden house nearby, which once produced wine, there is a pottery, and behind the buildings is a small zoo of farmyard animals and deer. A *fäbod*, summer pasture cottage, serves old-fashioned snacks at summer weekends. At the end of the road there is a **view** over Sundsvall and the island of Alnön, and a restaurant.

22

Sundsvall to Östersund and Åre

Total distance 285km. Sundsvall—E14 82km **Borgsjö**—88km Brunflo—16km Östersund (or Sundsvall—road 86 86km Bispfors—road 87 117km Östersund)—50km Mattmar—49km **Åre**.

Take the E14 out of Sundsvall to the west towards Östersund. On the outskirts of Sundsvall at Högom there is an Iron Age cemetery with four large mounds, seven smaller ones and a runestone.

16km from Sundsvall at Vattjom there is an extensive area of Iron Age remains, among them **Starkotter's Grave**, a large rectangular stone-setting between the river and the road. About 6km south, through Matfors, is **Attmar church** of the 18C with a **crucifix** and a **Madonna** by Haaken Gulleson, and a bell-tower of the 16C. By the lake there is a 1920s tar-factory.

The road now follows the Ljungan. The Ljungan is 350km long, and was in early times a considerable trade route, and later a medieval pilgrim route to Trondheim in Norway. Today it is important for hydro-electric power, and several power-stations exploit its great falls. Soon the river broadens into Stödesjön. Wooded hills with birches and pines alternate with some cultivation and occasional crags and cliffs. The woodworking industry is very much in evidence.

Just before (35km) Torpshammar a road goes south to **Flataklocken hill** (465m), on the south-west side of which is the geographical mid-point of

Sweden. On the top is a viewing tower easily accessible from the car-park, and you can buy a certificate to prove you have been there.

Back on the E14, in 14km in Fränsta is the 18C Torp church, and 2km further there is a road to the wooden Vik bridge, 133m long, built in 1888, which you can drive to, but not over. After 15km the church and bell-tower of Borgsjö are visible from the road but you have to pass and return on a minor road.

Borgsjö church (open summer 08.00–16.00) was built by Daniel Hagman in 1766, and is one of the most complete remaining Rococo churches in Sweden. The local woodcarver Johan Edler made the Rococo **pulpit** and the altar in 1771 and 1783. The woodwork is decorated with paintings of flowers, landscapes, apostles and Evangelists. A bridal bench stands in the chancel. The **figure of St. Olof** by Haaken Gulleson is from the early 16C and the font from the 17C. The **sacristy door** is from the previous church and has a carved 13C Christ with later apostles and a deacon. A 15C censer is in the sacristy.

Outside, the gateway was added in the 19C by the son of the original builder, and the *bell-tower is by Pål Persson of Stugun (1782). Of all his bell-towers, this is reckoned to be his finest. The smallest bell is from the 17C, the other two from the 18C.

After Borgsjö the forest closes in. The road passes from Medelpad into Jämtland, now turning north-west. This is the beginning of the lake district with many attractive views.

In 88km the road reaches Brunflo and in 16km Östersund. (For Brunflo and Östersund see Mora to Östersund Rte 20.)

Alternative route from Sundsvall to Östersund

An alternative way from Sundsvall to Östersund (203km instead of 186km) is to take road 86 along the Indalälv to Bispfors and then the 87 to Östersund. The 86 joins the river at Indal (24km). The Indalälv is 430km long and is one of the most important in producing water-power. The valley offers many **viewpoints** from which to appreciate the landscape.

Near Liden in 22km there are several viewing places, Vättaberg being one, over the river and the valley. Liden 15C church has a Madonna and other carvings, some from the 13C.

At Bispfors in 40km take the 87 to Östersund. **Döda Fallet** (Dead Fall) at 8km is the result of an 18C mistake. To try to bypass the 20m falls so that timber could be floated down, a canal was dug, but the river took advantage of the canal and changed course, emptying the former Ragunda lake and leaving the empty falls. A new waterfall was formed further back where the power-station is today.

In 12km, the granite **Ragunda church** with wood-shingle roof is medieval, with Renaissance and Baroque decorations and furnishings. The Danish coat of arms is on one wall, from the early 17C when Jämtland was controlled by Denmark/Norway. There is a rood-screen, unusual in Sweden.

Stugun in 47km was the home of the great bell-tower builder Pål Persson, and he built the older **church** here in 1786. At 38km there is a turning for Kyrkås church (see Östersund to Storuman Rte 27), and after 12km Östersund (see Rte 20).

The E14 leaves Östersund to the north and gradually turns west for Åre at (22km) Krokom, where the road crosses the Indal river and begins to climb giving views of the Storsjön lake to the left.

After 8km there is a turning for Glösa (16km) where there are **rock carvings** (*hällristningar*) with small stylised figures, mostly animals, probably elk and reindeer (2000 BC). These are about 400m walk from the car park. There are also prehistoric trapping-pits about 1km to the east.

In 5km a sign points to Mus-Olles museum, an eccentric collection of boxes and packaging from the 19C to 1950, as well as coins, photographs, stamps. china and textiles all gathered by a hoarder called P.O. Nilsson (1874–1955).

Mattmar church in 15km is by the side of the road, with a **tourist bureau**, picnic area and old buildings of the local museum. The **church** is medieval with the chancel and vestry added in the 18C. On the left wall are six carved **medieval figures**, probably from an altarpiece, a saint, St. Birgitta, Christ, St. Olof crushing the old Viking faith under his feet, St. Sigfrid and a Madonna and Child. On the opposite wall are another St. Birgitta and Madonna and child. The **St. Anne group** over the baptismal altar is by Haaken Gulleson. There is a crystal cross on the baptismal altar, and a 17C wooden font. The pulpit was made in 1662. The **bell-tower** is of the Jämtland type with onion-domed top.

The road runs along a lake and at (24km) Järpen crosses the broad Järpe river. A road from here leads north to Kall (19km), from which you can reach a **rock-painting** site in a walk of about 1km. (*Hästskotjärns Hällmålningar.*) These Stone Age paintings are done with ochre mixed with animal fat, and they occur mostly in north Jämtland. The pictures are mainly of elks, though other animals occur and sometimes people.

After 5km there is a sign to Ristafallet on the left. This is a series of waterfalls, the highest 14m above a wooded island and others below.

The town of **Åre** (20km) is dominated by the mountain of Åreskutan (1420m) which rises directly from the main square. The E14 bypasses the town so you come in on Årevägen. Where the road forks take either road—the **church** lies between them.

There is a recording in various languages which tells you about the church. It was built in the 13C and extended in 1736. The wooden star-vault was added in the 18C. The **altarpiece** is from 1736–41 and the **organ-gallery** is also 18C. A **statue** of St. Olof of about 1300 is wearing an 18C hat. The Renaissance **pulpit** was made in 1673 and the galleries are painted with flowers and landscapes. The elaborately carved and richly coloured **font** has a pelican on top and is supported by human figures. (The stone-pine-cone is a symbol of fertility.) The bell-tower was built in 1755–60.

Åre is pre-eminently a winter sports centre—there are five months of snow a year. Throngs of visitors are catered for by a cable railway and chair-lifts, hotels, flats and chalets.

The **tourist bureau** is in the main square. The cable railway starts from the centre and the mountain gives an unusually wide **view** from 1274m because it is so isolated. In the summer there are climbing and riding courses, canoeing and shooting rapids, fishing, gold-panning, boat-tours and cave-tours. In the winter every type of skiing is available, ferrying by helicopter, paraskiing, snowboards, snow-scooter safaris, hang-gliding, dog-team driving and climbing.

There is a local museum on the old shore road to Duved, and Njarka Sami encampment can also be visited. To the east is Fröå gruva (10km), an old copper-mining area.

The E14 continues towards Norway. After 13km a road goes to Tännforsen (8km). This waterfall is 60m broad and falls 37m into the Norn lake.

From (30km) Enafors, Handöl is 5km along a side-road. Soapstone has been quarried here since the 16C. The Handöl falls, the second highest in Sweden with a total drop of 120m, are easy to approach, 200m from the road. There is a Sami chapel of 1804 with a late medieval altar-piece.

The last town in Sweden is (17km) Storlien, a tourist resort. The Bridal Veil (*Brudslöjan*) is a 24m waterfall 4km to the west. 3km after Storlien the E14 enters Norway.

23

Sundsvall to Umeå

Total distance 248km. Sundsvall—E4 19km Bergeforsen—30km **Härnösand**— 40km Lunde and turning for road 90 to **Sollefteå** and *Nämforsen—78km **Örnskjöldvik**—111km **Umeå**.

Take the E4 out of Sundsvall to the north. You can follow the signs to **Alnön**, a 15km-long island joined to the mainland by a 1km bridge, with interesting geology and flora. Alnön was inhabited by 2000 BC, and the many prehistoric sites are marked by the usual St. Hans' Cross sign. In the heyday of the timber industry its coast was lined with sawmills. The medieval **church** dates from the 12C with vaults and paintings of the 16C (open mid June–mid Aug 09.00–19.00). The **crucifix** is by Haaken Gulleson (c 1500). The local museum has exhibitions on sawmilling. Nearby are the remains of a defence tower. The neo-Gothic 'new' church was built by Ferdinand Boberg in 1899 and contains a remarkable 12C **font** carved from pine, with interlaced foliage and animals.

At (19km) **Bergeforsen** the power station with attendant salmon-breeding station and aquarium can be visited (all three are open at varying times, but mainly June–Aug 12.00–15.30, aquarium longer). The tours are organised from **Älvens Hus** (House of the River) situated on a height above the river (open May–Sept 10.00–17.00, late June–mid Aug to 20.00. Salmon specialities in the café) The salmon-breeding centre in Bergeforsen releases nearly 400,000 smolt (young salmon) every year to find their way to the Baltic. In the aquarium the grown salmon can be seen, some up to 20kg.

Älvens Hus is a co-operative enterprise by the water-power companies. The displays concentrate on the river, power and fish. Information is provided by a variety of media at a variety of levels. You can be linked to a computer in Stockholm which regulates the water, or obtain facts and figures from a video. A multi-slide show takes viewers on a journey from the Indal's source to its mouth in the Baltic. A section on life beside the river goes back to the rock-carvings of 3000 BC. The legend of the water-sprite whose music was heard in the great waterfalls is also illustrated.

The E4 bends round the inlet of Klingerfjärden but a planned new bridge will cut the bend. At 3km there is a sign for Lögdö bruk where there are wooden buildings belonging to an old ironworks (not open to the public). There is a café in the manor-house. The works chapel has a St. George by Haaken Gulleson.

Just after the turning for Lögdö, road 331 goes north to **Västanå** (20km) where there is a high waterfall. At the foot of the fall are some of the buildings remaining from the ironworks which flourished from the mid 18C to the mid 19C. The works bought iron from Bergslagen which was ferried by boat to Härnösand and by wagons from there. It manufactured iron fittings for use in shipbuilding, and up to 100 people lived in the area.

The E4 continues through granite outcrops and coniferous woods and reaches **Härnösand** (pop. 19,000) in 27km.

The oldest part of Härnösand is on the island of Härnön, 7km by 10km, which grew up as a medieval trading centre. It received its charter in 1585. A grammar school was founded in 1647. After it was burnt by the Russians in the same year as Sundsvall (1721) it took a long time to recover. The 19C brought prosperity, and the streets were lit by electricity as early as 1885. The neo-Classical architecture of the turn of the century inspired the name 'Athens of Norrland'. It was the capital of the old province of Ångerman-land, and is now the capital of the county of Västernorrland, comprising most of old Ångermanland plus Medelpad. Inland this is an area of vast forests and plunging rivers. Just north of the town is the beginning of the beautiful High Coast (Höga kusten), a deeply indented coastline best appreciated from the sea. There are boat-trips from here, and from several other places further north.

The E4 enters as Södra Vägen. You can drive on to Härnön by Storgatan, which crosses two bridges and the small island of Mellanholmen, and bears left. The **tourist bureau** is at Storgatan 15 (open mid June–Aug).

The main square, Stora Torget, is just left and then right from the tourist bureau. On the west is the governor's **residence** (1785–91), designed by the court architect Olof Tempelman in neo-Classical style using local brick. On the south is the neo-Renaissance provincial government building, now an art gallery (1863) (open Tue–Fri 11.00–15.00, Sat, Sun 12.00–15.00).

The massive blocks of Labrador granite in the centre of the square form one of three parts of the **sculpture** Evolution (1991) by the Norwegian Hagbart Solløs. Two smaller parts are on the little island of Mellanholmen. A 'water staircase' forms a symbolic link between the parts.

Continue north to the broad Nybrogatan which on the left crosses another bridge from the mainland. On the stretch of road to the right are some of the ostentatious **houses** built at the turn of the century. On the corner with Köpmangatan is the yellow neo-Baroque Freemasons' House (1904) with festoons and a double-sloped ('säteri') roof.

No. 5 is an Art Nouveau house of 1905 with a corner turret and dragons under the windows. Opposite is the former post and telegraph building, with heavy tower, turrets and a balcony. No. 7 in neo-Renaissance has pilasters and balconies. Opposite is the neo-Classical **town hall** with a graceful semi-circular portico, originally built as a school by the same architect as the governor's residence, Olof Tempelman (1791). On the left is a neo-Renaissance bank (1895) with gilded Swedish coat of arms, and No. 10 on the right is in the same style.

Across Brunnshusgatan are government buildings. On the left corner is the county administration (1905–10), neo-Baroque and Art Nouveau. Ahead is a grey and white wooden building of the 1870s, now a college.

Return to Brunnshusgatan and turn left, then right into Trädgårdsgatan where the elegant wooden building was finished in 1871. Opposite is the cathedral in a small park where there is a **monument** (1910) by Carl Milles to the local bishop and poet Frans Michael Franzén (1772–1847). The two figures Selma and Fanny were his inspiration.

The neo-Classical **cathedral** was built in 1846 by Johan Adolf Hawerman. It has a Greek temple façade but with two turrets above, and there is a cupola above the chancel. Inside it has a barrel vault and side galleries on columns. The 18C altar is from an earlier church as is the organ gallery. The chandeliers are from the 17C. Up in the galleries are kept some vestments, including bishop's robes, and the cathedral museum is there.

Between the cathedral and the canal is the district of **Östanbäcken**, which means east of the stream. The stream was formerly the source for an 18C spa, but the spa building was torn down to make room for Nybrogatan's mansions. Östanbäcken has the same street plan as in the 1630s, and the oldest buildings date from just after the fire of 1721. Cobblestones still remain, and the street called **Östanbäcksgatan** with its side lanes is particularly picturesque.

To the north facing the bridge is the **Bodenska house** of the 1840s, in wood. Across the bridge on Mellanholmen is the **Wikmanska house**, another large wooden building partly dating from the mid 1700s. The library and theatre are on the island. The other two parts of the sculpture Evolution are here, and there is a symbolic sculpture by the library in memory of local writer Ludvig Nordström by Bengt Helleberg (1963). In front of the theatre is a sculpture by Eric Grate.

About 2km south of the centre is Vårdkasberget (Beacon Hill—175m) with a view over the surroundings. This is one end of the High Coast walking trail. On the east shore is Smitingen where there is seabathing, and caves.

Follow the signs to **Murberget** open-air museum on the north edge of town about 1.5km from the bridge (buildings open late June–early Aug 11.00–17.00, when crafts such as spinning and weaving are demonstrated and there are many activities). Over 80 buildings have been moved here or reconstructed.

The car park is just after a manor-house. On the left is the town square with reception and information in the old Härnösand **town hall**. Opposite is the village shop with early 20C wares for sale, and around are other houses of wealthy citizens.

Beyond this to the left after some small buildings is the church, modelled after Hackås church near Östersund, with genuine fittings, however. The **bell-tower** is also genuine, moved from another district. To the north of the church is the vicarage and further north the Sami dwellings.

The **Spjute Inn** of 1801 is still a restaurant. The long narrow building is a **skittle alley** (1910s) where you can play—skittles came to Sweden in the Middle Ages from Germany. In the north-west corner is a summer pasture settlement (*fäbod*) and south of this a sawmilling section with a sawmill and workers' huts.

Turning back towards the entrance, you can see the furnished and decorated **Ångermanland farmhouse**, which is inhabited and worked in the summer, and you can join in the chores. At the **school** you can sit and learn as in the old days or ask the costumed schoolmistress about the history of Swedish education—her English is excellent. The new **Länsmuseum** is also on this site with exhibitions on the history of the county of Västernorr-land.

The E4/90 leaves Härnösand winding north to (40km) Lunde where it meets the Ångermanälv. The river is 450km long and is another of Sweden's great sources of water power, with eight power-stations, of which three can be visited. (See also below: Vattenfall and Water Power.)

Lunde was the scene of a stormy encounter in 1931 when five demon-strating workers were killed by police. An expressive **monument** by Lenny Clarhäll (1981) has been erected near the river commemorating the event.

To Sollefteå and Nämforsen

For **Sollefteå** (50km) and the rock-carvings at *Nämforsen (40km further) take road 90 to the north-west following the river. The road passes through Kramfors, an industrial town. On the far side of (18km) Bollstabruk a road goes right to Nyland which you can take to get to Ytterlännas. The first church is the new one—continue for 1.5km to the *old church of Ytterlännas. The **vault** with *paintings by a member of the Tierp workshop known as 'Eghil' dates from the end of the 15C. Flowers, foliage, geo-metrical designs and figures crowd the surface, in mainly blues and browns. The early 16C Madonna is by Haaken Gulleson. The **inner door**, previously the outer door, is thought to be from an earlier church and the lion **door-knocker** possibly came from the Middle East. The **lower gallery** and the **pews** were constructed in 1718. The brightly painted **pulpit** was made in 1761, and the altar-piece is of 1739.

On the outskirts of (32km) **Sollefteå** (pop. 9000) road 90 passes the entrance of a large establishment called Statens Hundskola. This is the national **dog-training centre** where dogs are trained for the police, customs, the blind, the army and rescue services. Every year 100 trained dogs graduate from the school, which shows its work to the public (Mon–Fri 13.30 in summer, with special demonstrations on certain days).

About 1km further the 90 turns right. The **church** is in Kyrkvägen, the first turn on the left. The first church was medieval, but was completely remodelled in 1770 by Daniel Hagman in Rococo. The wooden bell-tower was built in the early 19C. Johan Edler carved the **altar-piece** and Rococo **pulpit** with four Evangelists round a table (18C).

Continue towards the town. As the 90 turns left into Storgatan a road goes right towards Ådalsbyn, the local open-air museum with nine old buildings and a café. After another 1km Kungsgatan (still road 90) on the right leads to the bridge over the Ångermanälv. In the middle is a **monument** to the loggers who used to work on the river.

The 90 now turns left and goes up the other bank of the river. Näsåker in 40km is the village where the falls of Nämforsen are situated. Signs lead off the 90 a couple of kilometres before the dam. Cross the river and pass the power-station to the **tourist bureau** in the disused railway station. On the tracks outside stands a steam-engine of 1915, used until 1972.

There is a small nature exhibit with items on beavers and bears. Another display explains the *rock-carvings (detailed notes in English available). Further information and a video are in the railway carriage.

The carvings are New Stone Age, influenced by the beginnings of the Bronze Age, done over a period of several thousand years. The area around the rapids became a meeting-place around 3000 BC, where hunters would gather in the summer. 1750 carvings have been catalogued, and most are on two islands difficult of access. Enthusiasts can borrow a rowing-boat to get to one of them.

The most common motif is an elk, including some with a head at each end. There are also bears, reindeer, birds and salmon, with some human figures, sun-wheels and human footprints. There are almost 400 stylised boats with people. The average size of the carvings is 25–30cm. It seems clear these were ritualistic carvings in connection with catching elks, by hunting them to the rapids where they would fall in and be washed ashore further down. The 'boomerang' wielded by some figures may be for killing birds, or according to another theory may be ritualistic.

Among the items found on the dwelling-site on the south bank were arrowheads, axes, scrapers and knives of quartz, quartzite and schist, contemporary with the carvings, as well as iron tools and medieval coins. Thus it seems the place was inhabited over a period of 4000 years. The largest number of finds was from the Bronze Age.

On the south side of the river close to the tourist bureau is the **power-station** (guided tours mid June–mid Aug 10.00–15.00). When it was being planned in the 1940s the rock-carvings were investigated by archaeologists and found to be so valuable that the power-station site was moved. The machine-room is, unusually, above ground and one wall is living rock. Here is Tyra Lundgren's large **stone-ware relief** (1950) depicting the history of the river, including loggers at work. In summer the falls are partially released for the tourists. Other power-stations do not do this, but have a *Fallens dag*, (Falls' Day) in July where the waters are released totally. These days have now become an institution, and real folk-festivals—see under Stornorrfors. Here there is also a *'Fallens dag'*, besides the partial release.

On the other bank of the river a path goes down to the wooden footways constructed for comfortable viewing of a small section of the **carvings** which have here been painted red to make them easier to see. The best are at the beginning and the rest are quite difficult to spot

A short distance away archaeologists have begun to construct a copy of the **Stone Age village** in 1990, originally on the opposite shore, as it might have been (open same times as the power-station).

Researchers are trying to establish the connection between the dwelling-site and the carvings, and are making comparisons with other cold countries such as Russia and Canada. Experiments are being done to discover the technology of daily life. A tent of 15 elk-skins on a frame of pine-saplings is edged with a flap of birch-bark sewn with linen around the bottom as the skins rot on contact with the ground. (Acid rain is unfortunately also a hazard nowadays.) An elk-skin is stretched on a frame and scraped with horn or flint to soften it. It has been found that if it is soaked for a week the fur comes off. Grease from an elk's brain has been tried to treat the skin, one brain to one hide. A dug-out canoe is made from an aspen tree. There was asbestos in the clay pots made here but it is not known how this was achieved. Stone Age sewing and cooking is also practised.

On the way back to the coast you could follow the north-east bank of the river from Sollefteå. **Multrå** has an 18C church, and **Sånga** church is medieval (restored). **Överlännäs** church is medieval, and **Gålsjö**, 9km north of Överlännäs, has an 18C ironworks open to the public, **Boteå** church has a Rococo interior, while the church at **Torsåker** is medieval with paintings by 'Eghil'. **Sandslån** was once a great timber-sorting centre. In the 18C logs began to be floated down the river and in 1874 the first sorting device was installed, with up to 700 men employed in the busy season. In 1952, 23 million logs were sorted, but 1982 saw the end. Many of the old buildings remain, and a **tourist centre** is being developed, with a museum and restaurant.

Back in Lunde **Sandö bridge** (1942) is 2km long and 45m above the water (view). The bridge and the E4 will soon be replaced. On the other side of the Ångermanälv the E4 cuts across an irregular peninsula forming part of the **High Coast** (Höga kusten). Some of the scenery can be appreciated by taking a detour into the peninsula to Nordingrå (12km).

To Nordingrå

At Gallsätter, 13km from the bridge, you can follow the winding road to Nordingrå among hills of 200–300m with rich vegetation, and small lakes.

Nordingrå stands on the shores of Vågsfjärden, once an inlet, now a lake because of the rising of the land. This was an important centre in the Middle Ages, and some ruins of the medieval church remain. In the ruins are seven tombstones of priests of Nordingrå.

The new **church** was consecrated in 1829. The interior is neo-Classical, but items from the old church have been preserved, foremost of which is the Brussels **altar-piece** of about 1510, with a carved Passion scene. The **paintings** on the doors are of particular artistic value. Figures of St. Birgitta and a Madonna, both early 16C, are to either side of the altar. The processional **crucifix** on the altar is also from the early 16C, with the Evangelists pictured on the ends of the arms. There is a glass case with historic **vestments**, with one from the 15C and one from the 17C. In the room at the entrance used for lesser services is a statue of St. Katarina, daughter of St. Birgitta, and eight carved figures from an old pulpit.

Behind the church is a row of wooden huts. These were **stables** for the horses to wait in during the service when the weather was severe. There are about a dozen left out of probably 80, each with room for four horses. Near the church is the tourist bureau, and on the upper floor of the building is a toy museum.

The road round the lake clockwise arrives at (3km) Häggvik where the painter Anders Åberg and his wife have begun to establish a series of small local museums round the Café Mannaminne (Living Memory), also used for exhibitions and concerts. It is hoped to have displays on art, boats, cars, railways, farming, archaeology, technology and ecology.

On the coast to the south-east is **Barsta** (9km) with a 17C chapel which has naive wall-paintings from the late 17C.

You can return to the E4 by going north from Nordingrå and then west, rejoining the road at Ullånger. (The road direct from Häggvik to Gallsätter is very poor.)

From Gallsätter the E4 continues north to (10km) Ullånger and (13km) Vibyggerå where the medieval church has 18C decoration.

Docksta, after 2km, is the nearest harbour to **Ulvön**, actually two islands under one name.

The fishing village on the sheltered south coast of the north island was once Norrland's largest but few fishermen are left. It is claimed the island was the birthplace of *surströmming*, the fermented Baltic herring, or at least closely connected with its early development. The story goes that in the 16C salt, normally used to preserve the herring, became very expensive. When the amount of salt was skimped, the herring fermented. It is now sold in characteristic round tins—1.5 million of them a year. It is definitely an acquired taste—most people advise that the bulging cans should be opened out of doors because of the smell.

The 17C wooden **chapel** in Ulvöhamn has 18C paintings. On the north coast of the north island is Sandviken, an old fishing village which has been restored. The south-east part of the south island is a nature reserve.

After 1km a sign points left to the chair-lift (*linbana*) up *Skuleberget, the isolated 293m hill rising directly from the E4. The view includes lakes, sea and forested hills. The hill is a nature reserve.

After 2km a complex of buildings between the road and the mountain contains a **tourist bureau** and information centre, nature museum (geology, flora, fauna), restaurant, motel, camp-site, showers and changing-rooms.

Skuleberget was once almost covered by sea, and a ten-metre belt at c 280m shows where the coast-line was. The cave near the top was the lair of robbers, about whom many legends are told. They commanded the road and waylaid rich travellers, as well as striking terror into the local farmers.

A special **climbing path** with cables attached to the rock has been arranged, which any fit person over 12 may attempt, with compulsory hire of safety harness and helmet from the Naturum. The climb takes about two hours. There is also a walking path, besides the chair-lift mentioned above.

The **High Coast trail** goes through here and further into **Skuleskogen national park**. This covers an area of 30km^2 and has very varied scenery, including the impressive **Slåttdalsskrevan**, a ravine which is 200m long, 7m wide, and 40m deep. (Information on walking in the park is obtainable from the tourist bureau.)

The road continues through the thick forests of the national park. At (17km) Bjästa a side road runs to Köpmanholmen (7km), the nearest port for the island of **Trysunda**. This is still a centre for fishing, and there is a marina for visiting boats. The island is a nature reserve, with walks, bathing places and viewing points. The 17C chapel has wall-paintings.

Örnsköldsvik (pop. 31,000) is 18km further on. The E4 passes a roundabout from which signs lead to the centre. The **tourist bureau** is on the main square which lies at one end of a long open space. Half of this is Örnpark (Eagle park) with the granite **Eagle monument** by Bruno Liljefors, and the other half is Museum Park, at the end of which the museum stands on a height.

The **museum** is housed in an imposing school building of 1905 (open Tue–Wed 11.00–20.00, Thurs–Mon 11.00–16.00, closed Mon Sept–May). The permanent exhibitions start on the second floor. One display shows how local traders went south to sell linen, fur, reindeer meat and fish. Two rooms have carved and painted **wooden objects** from the locality. On the third floor, there is local archaeology, and Sami objects. To the left of the museum entrance is the **studio** of the sculptor Bror Marklund, with his sketches and models. (Ask for the key in the museum.) In front is his 'Figure in a storm' sculpture.

The **church** is to the north of the centre about 500m along Storgatan from the square. It was finished in 1910. The pulpit was designed by Clarence Blum and there is a carved granite font. The chancel painting was done by Sigurd Möller. The Chapel of Miracles has windows depicting the miracles of Christ.

There is a road to the top of the hill of Varvsberget to the west, with a view of the town and river, and a restaurant. This is the north end of the High Coast walking trail. To get to **Gene pre-historic village** (6km), go back to the roundabout, take the road to the left and follow the signs *Gene Fornby*. The route ends in a forest track. The pre-historic village lies to the right of a group of old houses.

This Iron Age site (open summer 11.00–19.00) dates from the beginning of the Christian era, and was abandoned in about 600 for no obvious reason. Remains of ten houses have been found. Reconstruction of the 'long house' started in 1991. This was a building 38m by 10m, containing dwelling and animal quarters, with a central fireplace, housing 15–25 people. In the year 100 there were four buildings and some time after 350 a new main house was built and buildings for iron-working and bronze-casting. Sheep's wool was woven on an upright loom, and gold was used for ornament.

Beyond the Iron Age site is the 'Pioneer village' where old survival skills are practised. During the summer you can see such crafts as trapping, tar-burning or weaving.

On the way back to Örnsköldsvik there is a view over the inlet. At the roundabout continue on the E4. At 5km the pink and cream Rococo **church of Arnäs** (1782) is a short distance off the road. It was designed by the court architect Carl Fredrik Adelcrantz, and has entrance gates and a funeral chapel in the same style. In the sacristy are two wooden figures from the medieval church, St. Olof and St. Katarina.

Opposite the church the sign *gravfält* leads 500m to a group of **burial mounds** of the period 600–800, the most northerly in Sweden. At 24km there is a left turn to Grundsunda church, begun in the 13C, standing among scattered old wooden houses. It has a handsome wooden bell-tower. The vault is Gothic with paintings, and there is an 18C pulpit. The south door is richly carved (not always open).

Nordmaling, in 30km, was an iron-working centre. The church in the village 1km off the road to the right has a three-storey wooden bell-tower (1739). The church was built in the 15C and the roof in the 18C after a fire. The gallery paintings of the twelve tribes of Israel were done in 1781. The chancel window is by Bo Beskow (1977). A museum nearby shows church exhibits from the 15C to the 19C.

2km off the E4 on the other side is Olofsfors with the restored buildings of the ironworks, which flourished from 1762. The workshops with machinery, manor and workers' homes remain. (Some are open certain days in summer. Guided tours.)

After 52km the E4 reaches **Umeå**.

Umeå (pop. 60,000) was granted its charter in 1522. The Russians burnt it down several times, and there was another great fire in 1888, after which the rebuilt broad streets were lined with birch trees to act as fire-barriers. It has a university, and is the county capital of Västerbotten, which includes the old province of Västerbotten plus the southern third of old Lappland. There are many ferries to and from Finland bringing businessmen and shoppers (for whom Swedish prices are a bargain).

Tourist bureau: Renmarkstorget 15. Tel. (090) 16 16 16.

Post office: Vasaplan.

Bus station: By the station. Travel information: tel. (090) 13 20 70.

Telephone, telegram: Rådhusesplanaden 7. Tel. (090) 90 200.

The E4 crosses the Umeälv and the centre of the town is to the right, with many one-way and barred streets. The **tourist bureau** (open Mon–Fri 08.00–20.00, Sat 10.00–18.00, Sun 12.00–18.00, shorter hours in winter) is in the pedestrian square Renmarkstorget between Kungsgatan (no cars on this section) and Skolgatan. Ask here about parking concessions for tourists.

Rådhusesplanaden (Town Hall Esplanade) is a broad open space to the east of the tourist bureau with the red brick town hall at the south. Walk north and take Väster Norrlandsgatan to the right. A block down on the left is a large old wooden house, yellow-panelled with angled wings and dormer windows. These wooden **mansions** are dotted here and there over the town, but the area along and east of **Östra Kyrkogatan** is particularly rich in them. (Continue along Väster Norrlandsgatan for two blocks and turn right into Östra Kyrkogatan.) Sometimes the panelling alternates between vertical and horizontal on different floors, some have carved balconies or other decoration, and all are painted in pastel colours. As Östra Kyrkogatan meets Storgatan, there are two handsome examples on the left. The one on the corner is the Moritzka house, and just along Storgatan is the Scharinska house. On the right is a small park with bays provided with seats and sculpture by various foreign cities twinned with Umeå, and a globe sculpture to show friendship between Sweden, Norway, Finland, Russia and Canada.

Opposite on a height on the other side of Storgatan is the red brick neo-Gothic church (1894). The modern addition on the south side is used for social events. The choir chapel is used for lesser services and has modern textile hangings showing scenes form the Bible.

Near the church to the east is a monument to Lieutenant-Colonel J.Z. Duncker who died during the Swedish-Russian war in the battle at Hörnefors (south of Umeå) in 1809.

To the east of the church across the road is **Döbelns Park**. After the peace of Tilsit in 1807, Russia invaded Finland, then part of Sweden, and the Swedes had to remove their army. In 1809 the Finns acknowledged Russia as their ruler. After a struggle, peace was signed at Fredrikshavn later in 1809, by which Russia retained Finland and the Swedish boundaries were drawn where they are today. This was the end of the combined Swedish-Finnish army. On 8 October 1809, the commander, Georg Carl von Döbeln, stood on this spot and formally disbanded the army. There is a **monument** and **information board** recording the event.

Return along Storgatan and take Vasagatan to the right. Along the open space of Vasaplan there is a pleasing mixture of old and new, with a pale blue turreted wooden inn contrasting with modern styles.

The museum complex is called **Gammlia** and is on a hill about 1.5km north-east of the centre. Cross the railway line, turn right and follow the signs. The largest building is the **county museum** (Västerbottens museum—open Mon–Fri 09.00–17.00, Sat, Sun 12.00–17.00. Information in English available). On the **first floor** are sections on the pre-history of the area, reindeer-breeding and Sami life,and the life of the Swedish settlers from the 17C. From here you can reach the unique **Swedish Skiing Museum** which shows the history and development of skis and snowshoes through the ages and displays the oldest known ski, 5200 years old. The next floor shows agriculture (mostly cattle), industrialisation (mainly sawmilling) and the **history of Umeå**, with a 20m long model of the river frontage in the 1880s before the fire. In the adjoining building is the **Picture Museum** (*Bildmuseum*—open 12.00—17.00) run by the university. This holds temporary exhibitions, often dealing with media other than than traditional pictorial art.

The open-air museum has about 20 buildings (open 11.00–17.00, demonstrations and activities in summer). These include a windmill, farm buildings, a school, two threshing-floors, one octagonal, a grain-drying kiln, a smoke-house for pork, and an octagonal chapel popular for weddings. In the bakery the making of crispbread is shown. The 18C Burträsk farmhouse is furnished in 19C style. The maritime museum has sections on seal-hunting, fishing and shipping, all important to Västerbotten.

Sävar Manor near the entrance is now a restaurant. The building next to it is called Lars Färgares House, and survived the fire of 1888. On 19 August

1809 it was the Swedish military HQ in the morning, and the Russian in the afternoon.

24

Umeå to Storuman and Tärnaby

Total distance 349km. Umeå—E12 10km Brännland for **Stornorrfors**—15km Vännäsby—98km Lycksele—101km Storuman—125km Tärnaby.

This route forms part of the 'Blue Way', a co-operative tourist promotion by Norway, Sweden, Finland and Russia. It stretches 1760km from the Atlantic islands of Norway, through Mo i Rana into Sweden, along the E12 to Umeå and its port at Holmsund, across the Gulf of Bothnia to Vasa in Finland, thence to Kuopio and into Russia, along Lake Ladoga through Russian Karelia to Petrozavodsk.

The E12 follows the north-east bank of the Umeälv. After 7km there is a turn on the left for Baggböle manor, formerly the centre of a sawmilling business notorious for cheating in its dealings, so that its name became a Swedish word for timber-swindling—*baggböleri* (café in the manor). There is a footbridge to Klabböle (see below). Nearby is an arboretum with trees from countries with a similar climate to Sweden's.

At Brännland in 3km there are four 17C **soldiers' cottages** from the time when villagers had to support troops.

Here there is the turning for **Stornorrfors power-station** (4km) signposted *kraftstation* (guided tours mid June–late Aug 11.00–16.00).

Vattenfall and Water Power. Vattenfall (Waterfall) is the Swedish energy body and produces almost half the country's total electricity. Nearly half of this comes from water and most of the rest is from nuclear power-stations. It owns about 60 hydro-electric power-stations, most of which are in Norrland, the northern half of the country, and on the Göta River. Its nuclear power-stations are at Ringhals and Forsmark. It owns and operates the national electricity grid.

Because its activities have such an effect on the landscape and ecology, it has to put much effort and money into protecting and breeding fish, preserving old buildings, providing tourist facilities, supporting museums, exhibitions and information centres and protecting archaeological sites. The latter is particularly important because pre-historic peoples tended to gather near rivers and waterfalls, using them for trapping large animals, and it is sometimes only because of the power-stations that sites have been discovered, examined or developed.

Stornorrfors power-station, opened in 1958, produces 2 billion kWh per year. It is the largest one which can be visited (Harsprånget is the largest). Because of the nature of the rock hereabouts it was not built close to the dam. Instead, the water is forced by the dam to flow down a 2km channel to the head-race at the power-station. There it drops 75m below ground. Up to 1000m^3 of water pass through the turbines per second.

The guided tour takes visitors 90m below ground. First the great machine hall is shown, below that are the generators, and below again are the deafening turbines. Guides explain the process, from the four intakes via turbines, generators, transformers, switch-gears and cables, to the consumers.

To reach the dam, drive back along the channel, over the bridge and turn left. On this side of the dam is the 240m long **salmon-ladder**, the longest in Sweden, whose 65 steps enable the salmon to ascend 18m.

An Act of 1918 provides that anyone who interferes with the natural cycle of fish life in the river must ensure that the fish population continues as before. It is calculated that 5 million fish are reared annually in Sweden.

The salmon come up the rivers in summer and autumn to spawn. They are caught and the eggs are removed and fertilised. They hatch in April and May and the fry are kept in tanks where they are automatically fed. It takes two more years before they are ready for release, then they will swim down to the sea and will return to the same river to spawn.

At the top of the salmon-ladder the fish are caught in a pool, checked whether they are wild or bred, weighed and released upstream. The process can be watched at 12.30 every day from the end of May to the end of September.

The waters of the dam are released one Sunday in July when a folk-festival with between 10,000 and 20,000 people takes place. ***Fallens dag** (Falls' Day) provides music, displays, entertainment, competitions and games. The events of the day culminate at 15.00 (but check the time locally) when the waters are released to surge along the dry rocks of the old river bed.

On the other side of the dam is the **salmon-breeding centre** (open 11.00–14.00 mid June to end of August). The centre releases thousands of young salmon and sea trout every year, and visitors can see the tanks with fish at various stages of development (guided tours).

Beyond the fish-breeding centre are some Stone Age **rock-carvings** (*hällristningar*). The rocks were an island until the dam was built, when the carvings were discovered.

In the village of Sörfors which lies between the two bridges on the way back to the E12 there is a right turn leading back along the south bank of the river to **Klabböle Energy Centre** (8km). (This can also be reached from Umeå by driving south over the river and taking road 554 to the right. About 8km from the bridge take a right turn.)

The Klabböle hydro-electric power-station was the first on the Umeälv. In 1899 the streets of Umeå were lit by electricity from here, and the station continued until 1958. The red wooden building, looking rather like a private home, has been preserved. Inside, the turbines remain, down on the level of the water, reached by a wooden stair. In the machine-room can be seen the old instruments and machinery. An exhibition in the store-house traces man's efforts to make use of water-power. The elegant house where the staff lived contains the head engineer's home on the upper floor with some original fittings. There is a room for experimenting with electricity, and a café.

Continuing from Brännland the E12 crosses the Vindelälv in 11km, where it joins the Umeälv. The Vindelälv is not used for electric power so the 65 **rapids** along its length attract tourists and rapids-shooting enthusiasts. Road 363 follows the river valley and ends at Ammarnäs. The tourist bureau in **Vindeln** has information about trips on the river ranging from hours to days, with varying degrees of excitement. Vindeln has a museum about timber-floating and a 19C mill in a leisure area by the rapids, and an open-air museum which includes an 18C loft-house.

At (4km) Vännäsby the E12 reaches the junction with road 92. (This runs from Holmsund and Umeå to Borgafjäll under the name of the Road of the Seven Rivers, and passes through Bjurholm, Åsele and Dorotea, offering much in the way of unspoiled nature, outdoor activity and sport. Borgafjäll has a hotel designed by Ralph Eskine.)

Just after Hednäs in 38km a sign *Fångstgropar* to the right leads into the woods where after some minutes' walk there is a series of **Stone Age trapping-pits**. Eleven pits extend in a rough line for 600m. Some of the pits have been reconstructed, with a fence to show the method of trapping. There are about 20,000 such pits in Sweden, the oldest dating from 5300 BC. Here the oldest is from 2000 BC.

The E12 runs here through a pleasant hilly landscape with rivers and forests. After 40km the sign *Tuggengården* points to the home of a local artist Olle Blomberg with a collection of his paintings from the 1930s to the 1980s.

The area contains patches of untouched **primaeval forest** (*urskog*) and one such, on the left 7km further on, has been marked out as a 1km walk. After 13km, on the edge of Lycksele an outsize Sami hut advertises an hotel on the right. The **tourist bureau** is just before this on the same side.

Lycksele (pop. 9000) is the main town in southern Lappland and is in the modern county of Västerbotten. Carl von Linné (Linnaeus) came to the area in 1732 and was not impressed. There were a few Swedish settlers here, enticed by the promise of freedom from conscription, and freedom from tax for 15 years. The town became an important market and meeting-place, known as Lapp-Stockholm. The fells in southern Lappland are more broken up than further north and attract fewer tourists. The few Sami reindeer breeders live either in the mountains in the summer and on the coast in the winter, or are settled in the forests.

The E12 crosses the Umeälv into the town. The zoo (follow the signs *Djurpark*) is the most northerly in Europe and specialises in Nordic animals, bears, muskoxen, elks, Arctic foxes, beavers, deer, reindeer, lynxes, wolverines, wolves and pine-martens. An imaginative running-water aquarium shows the fish species of the area. There are children's amusements, and refreshments.

Turn right at the end of the bridge for the forestry museum and open-air museum. On the way, the white-painted **church** is on the road one block in from the riverside road. Built in 1789, it has ceiling paintings of the 1850s, showing Doubting Thomas, the Ascension and Pentecost with Lazarus over the north door. It has a good organ of 1978.

On the other side of the main road is the museum area. There is a small **hunting museum** (*jaktmuseet*) showing animals in different environments and how they are hunted. This is a very popular hunting area, and information about the different types of licences and conditions is available from the tourist bureau. Big game is hunted in teams, and there are limited quotas for elks.

Skogsmuseet (forestry museum, open Mon–Fri 11.00–17.00, Sat, Sun 12.00–16.00, June–Aug 10.00–18.00, July to 20.00.) presents a picture of working conditions and tools in the forestry industry mainly from the 1920s to the 1960s.

The camaraderie of the loggers was legendary and a romantic aura now surrounds their work and way of life. Transport of logs on horse-drawn sledges is shown, and how tracks were iced to ease hauling. The forest-worker's hut resounds with snores. Old tools show the techniques before the power saw which is also displayed. A log-sorting machine shows how the logs were graded for size. The life of the women and children is also described as they struggled with the croft and animals while the crofters and their horses worked to bring the timber to the rivers. There are sections on flora and fauna, and afforestation. A few exhibits outside the museum give explanations in Swedish on trees and wood.

Beyond is **Gammplatsen**, the open-air museum (open June–Aug 10.00–18.00, café). About 20 old local buildings have explanations in English on them. These include an octagonal barn, a Västerbotten farmhouse, a cobbler's cottage of 1709, a 19C granary and a forestry workers' bunkhouse for 16 men. A 19C bowling-alley has been rebuilt and houses a craft shop. The church is a compressed octagon shape, a copy of one of 1736—the lock on the door is the only original part. It is called the Margareta church because a Sami woman of the 14C who tried to spread Christianity among her people is said to have walked all the way to Lund in the very south of Sweden to ask for help from Queen Margareta. The bell-tower, reconstructed in 1972, is modelled on that of Jokkmokk.

Lycksele has an adventure pool, the 'Ansia badpark'.

The E12 continues north-west now on the south-west bank of the Umeälv. After 54km the confluence of the Umeälv and Juktån creates a large expanse of water spanned by three bridges. An attractive picnic-site is nearby.

Here the rivers are wandering and spreading, creating tortuous bays and inlets. At (12km) Gunnarn there is an extensive lake on the right. **Stensele** after 32km has a very large wooden church of 1886 in the same style as many others of the periods in Lappland, such as Jokkmokk and Arvidsjaur. It has some interesting items in a glass case, including a miniature prayer-book. **Stenseleberget** (Stensele mountain) has a road (3km) leading to a view at the top.

Between Stensele and (3km) Storuman the E12 coincides with the 45. To the left is Umluspen power-station which can be visited (mid June–mid Aug 11.00–16.00).

After Storuman (see Östersund to Storuman, Rte 27) the E12 bears left along the large Storuman lake and after 70km at Forsnacken begins to enter the mountain area.

At 55km **Tärnaby** is a tourist resort. It has a **Sami museum** with an exhibition, craft shop and café (open end June–mid Aug). The view from **Laxfjället** can be reached on foot or by cableway.

Beyond Tärnaby the road continues for 75km through the fells to Norway. On the right is **Norra Storfjället**, through which runs the last section of the King's Trail (see Abisko, Rte 29) which ends at Hemavan, a tourist resort. On the left is a nature reserve which includes a large cave-system. Information on entering the caves, which are not easy, can be had from the tourist bureau.

Tärna Fjällpark in Hemavan is an unusual mountain museum. A mushroom-shaped building has a covered footway leading from its top directly on to a cliff. On the ground floor is a section called the Kingdom of the Senses, with light, sound and smells, with caves, animals and plants, objects from Sami and settler life, plants and animals, snow and water build up an experience of the fells. The head of the mushroom is a restaurant, and the walkway leads on to the fell where there is a botanical garden with mountain plants. Then the visitor can walk out on to the fell itself.

25

Umeå to Luleå

Total distance 265km. **Umeå**—E4 134km **Skellefteå**—82km **Piteå**—49km **Luleå** and turning for Boden.

The E4 leaves Umeå northwards. At (16km) Sävar where an important battle was fought with the Russians in 1809 there is a monument to the fallen Swedish soldiers. A road goes right to Norrfjärden (9km) where there is a ferry to the island of **Holmön**. The group of islands to which Holmön belongs is comparatively young—a few thousand years. They have rich flora and fauna, especially birds. Holmön has a boat museum, daily guided bus tours and ferry links with the other islands.

Bygdeå in 25km has a medieval church with a 16C vault. The former church village now consists of only a few stables. After 12km there is a turn left for **Robertsfors** (4km) with a local iron-works museum and a church with stained glass by Bo Beskow. At (15km) **Nysätra** the wooden church dates from 1710. Nearby is a group of Bronze Age cairns, one of several along this coast. Before the land rose they were all close to the sea.

Lövånger, after 18km, has a medieval church with a pulpit of 1623. The **church village** has over 100 cottages no longer used by distant parishioners, and renovated for tourists to stay in. After 10km a side road goes to **Bjuröklubb** (18km) on the point of a peninsula where there is a lighthouse, nature reserve (interesting geology and flora), weather station, chapel and remains of a fishing village. **Bureå** in 17km has a national romantic style church of 1920. At (6km) **Yttervik** there are more prehistoric cairns. It is 15km to Skellefteå.

The centre of **Skellefteå** (pop. 31,000) is on the other side of the Skellefte River (Skellefteälv). The Viktoriabro (bridge) leads into Viktoriagatan and a few blocks further on S:t Olof church can be seen on the right. This was consecrated in 1927 as the town church, whereas the older church (see below) was for the wider district of Skellefteå. The **tourist bureau** is in the section of Storgatan on the other side of Viktoriagatan.

Nordanå, the open-air museum, is further on in the same direction, entrance from Strandgatan (parallel to Storgatan nearer the river). The largest building is **Skellefteå Museum**, in an old school (open Mon–Thurs 12.00–19.00, Fri–Sun 12.00–16.00). On the ground floor are reception, café and temporary exhibitions. On the first floor are local prehistory, archaeology, money, measures and industrial history. An important exhibit is the Kåge find 4C–5C bronze jewellery. On the top floor are sections on food production and textiles.

The **open-air museum** consists of 13 buildings on the site of the old market centre (detailed notes in English available in the museum reception). From mid June to mid August the 19C shop selling traditional goods, the bake-house demonstrating and selling bread, and the Kåge house are open (Mon–Fri 10.00–17.00, Sat, Sun 12.00–16.00). The Wadmal Press and Wadmal Stamp were buildings used for treating the local cloth, wadmal, for working clothes. There is also a tar-sorting house where tar was inspected and redistributed for export, and a Sami storage hut.

Follow the road round the perimeter of the open-air museum to arrive at the **church village**, *Bonnstan*, also signposted from Brännavägen and other main roads. Most of the cottages have been rebuilt after a fire in the 19C. It is a large and compact village, three to four streets wide, with most buildings of dark heavy logs.

Beyond the village is the white neo-Classical district **church**, finished in 1799, on a Greek cross plan, with temple-like porticoes, and a cupola with lantern. This is partly on the site of the medieval church and the 15C vestry is preserved. It contains many valuable **medieval wood-carvings**. In the vestry are St. John the Baptist, St. John's head on a charger and a processional crucifix. The six statues behind the altar are St. Michael, Virgin and Child, SS. Erik and Katarina, St. Anne with Virgin and Child, and St. Olof. St. George and the Dragon is from the 15C as is the triptych which is North German, and the crucifix. The **Romanesque Madonna** of walnut wood is probably German. The pulpit is dated 1648 and other fittings date from 19C and 20C.

The bridge which crosses the river near the church is the Lejonström bridge, built of wood in 1737, 207m long.

Boliden, 35km from Skellefteå on road 95 (west), was an important mining centre, producing copper, silver, gold and arsenic. It has a mining museum.

Continue north on the E4 towards Piteå through undulating forest. At 50km is the border between the counties of Västerbotten and Norrbotten.

At Jävre after 5km a sign left *arkeologstigan* points to an archaeological walk which starts on a side-road parallel to the main road—the sign is liable to be hidden by foliage. Sketch-maps at the start show the routes, one walk of 7.5km, marked by orange signs on the trees, and two of 2km, marked in white. There are Bronze Age cairns and Iron Age stone-settings of varying kinds, and a maze of uncertain age in the middle of the longest walk.

In 27km you arrive at **Piteå** (pop. 18,000), which was moved here in 1667 after a fire in the original site at Öjebyn. The E4 enters as Sundsgatan and the main square is two blocks to the south, along Storgatan. The buildings on the square are 19C, but the town-planning is from the 17C, with closed corners to the square and access on the sides. The 1830s **town hall** is now the museum with displays about the area, including a local bookbinder's workshop. There is some **tourist information** available here. (The **tourist bureau** is some distance away, in Noliagatan.)

On the right of Sundsgatan is the white **church** of 1686, one of Norrland's oldest wooden churches. The **pulpit** was carved by Nils Fluur, a local craftsman. The Baroque **altar** came from the Maria Magdalena church in Stockholm. The Russians burnt the town in 1721, but spared the church because it was their headquarters. To the east in the triangle between Kyrkbrogatan and Sundsgatan near the harbour is a picturesque area of **wooden houses**.

Rejoin the E4. In **Öjebyn** after 2km the church and church village are at the junction of Affärsgatan, Tingshusgatan and Sockengränd, and the sign *vägkyrka* should point the way in summer. On the way, beside a motel, you may see the sign *Paltzeria*. Here you can sample the the local dumpling, *Pitepalt*, rather solid with a little meat and served with lingon sauce.

The **church** (detailed notes in English available) was begun in the 15C. The stone tower beside it is probably older and may have been used for defence. At the end of the 15C the porch and vaulted roof were built, and the transepts were added in 1750. The **altar** was made by Caspar Schröder

of Stockholm at the beginning of the 18C. The **pulpit** (1706) was carved by
Nils Fluur who also made those in Piteå church and in the church village
near Luleå. There are two plaques in carved frames commemorating Karl
XII's victory at Narva in 1700 over the Danes, Poles and Russians, and the
meeting at Uppsala in 1593 which confirmed the Reformation.

The **church village** consists of a mixture of buildings, some brought here
after the 18C fire in Piteå. There is a small museum and tea-room in the
parish house.

Rejoin the E4 which now runs very close to the coast. In 9km, at **Norrfjärden** off the road to the west, there is a church village and a local museum
in a typical Norrbotten farmhouse.

The road crosses two peninsulas and after 38km arrives at the junction
for Luleå (7km).

Luleå (pop. 43,000) was actually founded upstream at what is now known
as Gammelstad (Old Town), but in 1649 was moved to its present position
9km away, because the rising of the land made the port unusable. The
ravages of the Russians and great fires slowed development until shipbuilding became the foundation of 19C expansion. But the shipyards could not
compete when steamships came in, so Luleå had to wait for the ironworks
in Norrbotten to thrive before it began to prosper again. In 1888 the ore
railway was built linking the great ironfields of Kiruna and Malmberget
with Narvik in Norway and Luleå, making its port essential for iron export.
Now it is a centre for technology, especially metallurgy, and has an important steelworks, a university and an airport. It is the administrative capital
of Norrbotten, the largest and northernmost county of Sweden, now comprising the old province of Norrbotten plus half of the old province of
Lappland. (See Introduction: Lappland and the Sami.)

Norrbotten has nearly a quarter of the area of Sweden and 3 per cent of
the population, roughly two and a half people per km^2, compared with the
national average of about 20 per km^2. The thaw after the last Ice Age did
not start in Norrbotten until seven or eight thousand years ago, four or five
thousand years later than in the southern areas. The land, released from
the pressure of the ice, began to rise and is still rising at the rate of 85cm
per century. One result of this is that ports like Öjebyn and Gammelstad
were stranded and the new towns of Piteå and Luleå had to be established
to take their place on the new coastline.

There are three main regions—the coastal strip, the forest and the mountains. 60 per cent of the population of the county live along the coast. Six
per cent of the land is farmed (half as much as in 1950 due to rationalisation),
40 per cent is productive forest and the rest is unproductive forest, lakes,
marshes and tundra. The coastal towns are frozen in from January to mid
May, and ice-breakers have to be used to keep the ports open. More than
half the county is north of the Arctic Circle—Kiruna, for example, has 70
days of midnight sun.

The mountains, forests and lakes form a wilderness which in some places
has hardly been mapped in detail. The valleys run from north-west to
south-east. Kebnekaise (2111m) is Sweden's highest mountain, first
climbed in 1883.

Iron-ore mining is still important and hydro-electric power has been
highly developed especially on the Luleälv. In the forestry industry, the
number of workers has been cut, but still 10 per cent of Swedish timber
comes from the county, while fish is the fourth large earner of the region.

Despite the earning capacity of the region it needs considerable help from the government, since transport, heating and wages' costs are high, and also special aid is given to the Sami people. The majority of reindeer-breeding Sami live here and most of Norrbotten is designated reindeer-herding land. (See Introduction.)

The central part of Luleå is situated on a peninsula in the mouth of the Luleälv, with several approaches from the E4.

Tourist bureau: Rådstugatan 9. Tel. (0920) 937 46.

Post office: Storgatan 53.

Bus station: Near station. Tel. (0920) 890 85.

Telephone, telegram: Kungsgatan 29. Tel. (0920) 102 80.

The **tourist bureau** is on the corner of Rådstugatan and Köpmangatan, but a small temporary office may be open on the car park at the end of Bodenvägen as it reaches the centre. (One-way and barred streets make it advisable to park and walk.)

Bodenvägen swings right into Skeppsbrogatan and Rådstugatan is a few blocks further on to the left. There are some attractive old **wooden villas** in this area. Köpmangatan will bring you to **Norrbottens museum**, a solid brick building in a park (open Mon–Fri 11.00–16.00 Sat, Sun 12.00–16.00). The museum has been completely refurbished and now on the ground floor are reception, shop and unusual **café** among displays of 20C furniture. Sami culture occupies much of the first floor, while on the second are the permanent displays of **regional history** based on the lives of workers in different trades. The top floor has an exhibition area for temporary displays as do each of the other floors.

Beyond the museum are county administrative buildings, among which is the decorative wooden 19C governor's residence, while to the north-west is **Gultzauudden**, a headland with recreational facilities and a bathing beach. Returning towards the centre you will see the 67m spire of the neo-Gothic cathedral in Kyrkogatan, parallel to Rådstugatan. This was consecrated in 1893. The picture of St. Ansgar the apostle of Scandinavia to the right of the chancel was painted in 1937, and there is a statue of him in the nave, opposite a statue of Olaus Petri. Until 1937 there were wooden galleries to increase the capacity of the church to 1000. Now it holds 500.

The 'Shopping Center' designed in the 1950s by Ralph Erskine aroused much interest at the time. This is in the shopping area east of the centre, on the corner of Storgatan and Timmermansgatan.

Teknikens Hus (House of Technology) is on the university campus. Take Bodenvägen to the roundabout by the Scandic Hotel, take the first right, and follow the signs to the *Högskola* (university). Teknikens Hus is a red building with two yellow chimneys on the right opposite a car park (open mid June–mid Aug 11.00–17.00, closed Mon, rest of the year Tue–Fri 09.00–16.00, Wed to 20.00, Sat, Sun 12.00–17.00, leaflets in English, café).

Here the aim is to let the visitor learn about technology by seeing it in action. The areas covered include geology, mining, energy, steel, industrial technology, hydrodynamics, aerodynamics, forestry and communications—everything which is relevant to Norrbotten. Demonstrations can be worked by the visitor and consist of the practical applications of physics to industry and everyday life. There is also a planetarium and library.

From Luleå you can travel on the ore railway to Narvik in Norway, via Gällivare, Kiruna and Abisko, almost 500km. There are boat-trips into the archipelago from the North and South Harbours. The nearest island is Sandön, with a nature reserve.

*Gammelstad (Old Town), the original Luleå, is on road 97, 2km to the west of the E4. The town arose in the 14C with a market and church. Trade through the busy harbour was in furs, salt and fish so that this was a rich parish for the time.

Gammelstad, the 'church village' of Luleå, with cottages used by distant parishioners when they travelled to church

The stone *church with its decorative brick and plaster gables was built at the end of the 15C. It has a stout defensive wall and an aperture over the south door for pouring boiling oil on unwelcome guests.

The 15C *high altar was made in Antwerp. Each figure is mounted separately (so scenes could be composed to order). In the centre is the Tree of Jesse leading to the Virgin at the top. A row of prophets is along the bottom. The three large scenes are of the Passion and the four smaller of the Infancy of Christ. Notice the figure holding three nails from the Crucifixion. The twelve apostles are painted below.

The medieval **crucifix** has the four Evangelists at the ends of the arms. The *wall-paintings in the chancel are also 15C, probably by Albertus Pictor or one of his pupils. High to the left of the altar is the coat of arms of Archbishop Jakob Ulfson 'Örnfot' (Eagle's Foot) with two eagles' feet. The medieval **choir stalls** have carved ends. By the window behind the altar are **figures** of SS. Birgitta, Katarina, Olof and Erik.

The wood-carver Nils Fluur who was active in this region made the **pulpit** in 1712, as well as the memorial tablets. The one beside the pulpit commemorates the Reformation with Luther on the left and Huss on the right. Another commemorates Karl XI. A glass case holds two valuable **vestments**. The south door is of 1616.

Around the church gather 500 or so **church cottages**, mostly 17C to 19C. The church holds the land, and people may not stay here more than one or two days at a time. Distances and the climate meant church-going was not easy, and these cottages were for church-goers to stay in. In the same way church stables were provided for the horses to wait in. Today you will notice that most Swedish churches have large entrance-halls, with coat-racks, mirrors and toilets, for the same reasons. In the old days, if parish-ioners lived up to 10km away they had to attend church every Sunday, if 20km, every second Sunday and so on. Here one of the cottages is generally open for tourists to look at. Many have in their windows squares or rectangles of lace held on wooden frames. Beside the church is an 18C **tithe barn**.

The local open-air museum, **Hägnan**, is at the end of the village to the north, next to a wetland nature reserve where the old harbour used to be. The museum has nine buildings including a manor-house furnished in 19C style with painted décor on the walls, a bakehouse, stable, cow-shed and fisherman's cottage (open 11.00–17.00, summer demonstrations of old crafts).

Excursion to Boden

On road 97 towards Jokkmokk, 35km from the E4, **Boden** (pop. 20,000) is a predominantly military town where several regiments have their base. On the way in there is a sign to the **Svedje fort** (*Svedjefortet*), on the other side of a long lake (5km). It can also be reached from the centre of town.

The Svedje fort is an example of early 20C defence (open mid June—Aug 11.00–19.00, guided tours, café). At the turn of the century with the opening up of the north with railways and industry, it appeared imperative to defend the area against invasion. The fort was blasted out of Svedje Hill, and was finished in 1913, consisting of the Eastern and Western Batteries. The guns were to fire south-west over the lake as it was assumed an attacker would approach from that direction. In the 1940s cannons were installed in the Eastern Battery. Some of the guns are still in position, with models of gunners in uniform. There is a wide view from the top.

You can continue into town on the same road or follow the 97. From Kungsgatan where it runs along the lake follow the signs for **Björknäs**. Here are the church, church cottages and a group of old farm buildings on part of a leisure area alongside the lake.

First on the right are the 18C church cottages, now renovated for holiday-makers. The **church** is known as Överluleå (Upper Luleå) church, as the church in Gammelstad is known as Nederluleå (Lower Luleå). It dates from 1831. It was originally fitted with three interior galleries to seat over 2000 people. The **crucifix** in the sanctuary is by the sculptor Tore Strindberg, and Bror Marklund carved the **twelve apostles**. Wallpaintings are by Simon Sorman. There is a '*columbarium*', a room with niches for urns with ashes.

Beyond the church to the right is the **court-house** of 1834 and to the left the school of 1848 (English information on brass plates). These two build-ings are on their original sites. On the other side of the road is a group of old local buildings with the **tourist bureau** in an attractive farmhouse which has original wall-decoration. This bureau has a very wide range of infor-mation. Other buildings include a smithy and a bakehouse.

Garnisonsmuseet (the Army Museum) is south-west of the centre on Sveavägen. Take Garnisonsgatan to the west, then Hedenbrovägen on the left and Sveavägen again on the left. The museum is some distance along on the right (open summer Tue–Sat 11.00–16.00, Sun 13.00–16.00). A track leads through the woods and a collection of cannons, to a group of houses round a courtyard. The museum is in the one to the left. It shows defence through 400 years and includes a collection of Swedish **officers' uniforms**, and weapons.

Boden **Power Station and Aquarium** (open mid June–mid Aug 10.00–15.00, guided tours) is situated on the Luleälv. To get to it from the Army Museum continue along Sveavägen to the T-junction, turn right and right again.

26

Luleå to Haparanda

Total distance 126km. Luleå—E4 50km Töre and turning for road E10 to Över-kalix—76km **Haparanda** and turning for road 400 to **Pajala**.

The E4 continues northwards 31km to Råneå, an old ironworking town, where it crosses the Råne river (Råneälven). There is a wooden church of 1857. The road turns eastwards following the coast. Töre, in 19km, has a church designed by Evert Milles (Carl's brother) in 1936, and a local museum.

From Töre you could take the E10 north and then west to Gällivare, Kiruna and Abisko, following the Kalix River valley. At 32km there are the Räktfors rapids. **Överkalix** (19km) is pleasantly situated at the confluence of the Kalixälv and Ängesån, just south of the Arctic Circle. In Nybyn (4km north) there is a preserved 18C house with local fittings and furnishings. From the top of Brännaberget (198m—road all the way up) there is a good view of the valley, and at midsummer of the midnight sun.

Back on the E4 **Kalix** in 26km, lies at the mouth of the Kalix River. The church was built in the 15C and has a late medieval altar and font. There is a local museum. *Ryssgraven* is a mass grave of Swedish, Finnish and Russian soldiers from the 1808–09 war. Filipsborg is a handsome wooden mansion in woods by the shore, now a restaurant and conference centre. On the road out towards Haparanda is Englundsgården, a 19C farmhouse is open to visitors.

At 18km there is a 7m high **Viking burial mound** c 50m from the road. The sword and shield-boss found here, now in the Norrbotten Museum in Luleå, have been dated to c 800 BC.

In 2km Sangis is on the boundary between the Swedish and Finnish-speaking areas. In 16km a road goes right, over a series of bridges to the holiday island of **Seskorö**. **Haparanda**, after 14km, is one half of Provincia Bothniensis, (Province of Bothnia) the other half of which is Tornio in Finland (spelt Torneå in Swedish). In 1987 the two united under one governing council, tactfully choosing a name neither Swedish nor Finnish.

Tornio, on the east bank of the Torne River (Torneälven), was granted its charter by the Swedish king Gustavus Adolphus in 1621 and it became a thriving market centre for the whole area. In 1809 the Swedish-Finnish border was drawn along the Torne which meant that there was no Swedish town at the river mouth, so Haparanda was founded. During the First World War it was a vital border crossing-point since the Baltic was virtually closed.

The architecture of the railway-station (1916) reflects this importance. Spies and black marketeers inevitably haunted the place at that time.

The copper-clad Haparanda **church** (1967) with its very high central portion has remarkable acoustics. There is a mid 19C merchant's house built round a courtyard. The archipelago offers many boat-trips—**Sandskär** island is particularly rich in flora and fauna. There are outdoor activities both summer and winter, for example shooting the rapids and snow-scooter safaris. Playing on the golf-course involves driving off in Sweden and landing in Finland—because of the time difference—an hour later.

To the Torne Valley

Traces of habitation dating from 600 BC have been found in the **Torne valley**. The river used to be one of the great timber-floating highways, and for over 100 years until 1971 logs were floated down 320km of its length. Logging was part of the pattern of crofters' life, fitted in during the summer, leaving the women and children to work the croft. Felling took place in the winter, and from April or May onwards it was the job of the loggers to get the wood down to the sorting depot on the coast.

The Torne valley also had a part to play in the history of the Swedish sauna. The Swedish word for sauna, *bastu*, comes from a word meaning bath-hut and there were communal bathhouses all over Sweden until they were condemned as unhealthy and immoral. This area preserved the Finnish sauna and continued to do so even when Russia took over Finland. In the 1880s Swedish doctors became interested in the sauna as a means to health through improved hygiene. By the 1930s the idea had spread throughout the country, being encouraged particularly by the sporting organisations. The oldest type is the smoke-sauna. In a wooden hut of about 3m by 4m a fire takes several hours to heat stones to glowing. When the fire dies down the smoke is driven out and the sauna is ready for use. It is recommended that the bather sits in dry heat first before throwing water on to the hot stones to obtain steam. Thus the Finnish sauna can be either dry or steamy. It is not necessary to cool down suddenly with a roll in the snow—this can be too great a shock to the system. Another type of sauna had a chimney so the room never became full of smoke and covered in soot, though some maintained the soot was more hygienic as it killed bacteria. Nowadays of course most saunas are electric and are available everywhere in hotels, sports centres and swimming-pools.

The Torne valley has a road each side of the river. On the Swedish side this is road 400. At (14km) **Kukkola** there are rapids (Kukkolaforsarna). Some old local buildings have been preserved and there is a fishing museum, showing fishing from the 13C. Wooden jetties are built into the river and bag-nets are used to catch whitefish from them.

In **Karungi** after 11km, the Karl Gustav church dates from 1796 with a bell-tower of 1745. In (25km) **Hietaniemi** the church was built in 1747, and has an organ from 1781. The bell-tower is from 1773.

Father Christmas lives on (10km) the **Luppio Hill** and has a proper Swedish post code to receive requests by mail. His workshop is open in summer (*Tomteverkstad*) and Mother Christmas has a small café on the hill.

Övertorneå in 8km has a large wooden church of 1617, renovated in the 18C, with **medieval woodcarvings**, the most famous of which is the Madonna in the Mantle, with doors like a cupboard. There is a pulpit of 1737, and an **organ** of 1608, one of the oldest in Sweden, previously in the

German church in Stockholm. The bell-tower was built in 1763. There is a local museum.

After 111km, 4km before Pajala there is a turning to **Kengis bruk**, an iron and copper working centre started in 1646, rebuilt in the 18C and working until 1879. The manor-house dates from 1805.

Pajala in 4km has connections with Lars Levi Laestadius (see Jukkasjärvi, Jokkmokk to Abisko, Rte 29). Laestadius was vicar here from 1849 to his death in 1861, and is buried in the churchyard. His vicarage is open to the public. The church was built in 1871. There is a museum which includes the history of Kengis works.

From Pajala road 400 continues to Karesuando (182km), and road 395 goes to Vittangi (11km) where it meets the 45. (See Jokkmokk to Abisko.) The 395 runs along the Torneälv where there is a rare phenomenon—near Junosuando the Tärendöälv splits off from the Torneälv and flows to join the Kalixälv at Tärendö. At Tärendö there is a tourist complex and a local museum.

27

Östersund to Storuman

Total distance 295km. Östersund—road 45 102km Strömsund—71km Dorotea—54km Vilhelmina turning for (150km) **Stekkenjokk**—68km Storuman.

Leave Östersund by the north road which in 3km splits into the E14 and the 45. After 8km on the 45 a side-road on the right goes to Kyrkås church in 3km. (See Sundsvall to Östersund and Åre, Rte 22.)

After 11km the 45 crosses the Indalälv, one of the great power-producing rivers of the north (see Vattenfall and Water Power, Rte 24). At 10km Häggenäs has a 19C church.

In 38km **Hammerdal** lies by a lake. The church here (1780) was built and furnished by local craftsmen Daniel Hagman (see Borgsjö) and Johan Edler (see Brunflo and Hackås). Nearby are church cottages.

The road continues north through woods, swamps, rivers and lakes. The trees are mainly spruce, while pines grow on the poorer ground. Some woods in this area are untouched 'primeval' forest in the strict sense. There is plentiful natural wild life including foxes (comparatively rare in Sweden), elks and bears. Plants include mosses and lichens which provide grazing for reindeer, and wild raspberries and lingonberries, with orchids in some places.

Strömsund in 32km lies amid extensive and complex water-systems. An example is Ströms Vattudal to the north-west, which illustrates how difficult it is in Lappland to disentangle lakes, rivers and bogs, and determine what is flowing where. This is a centre for skiing in the winter, canoeing and other boat-trips, walking and fishing. Strömsund has an open-air museum on the waterside. The 7m figure of the Giant Jorm, otherwise appropriately known as Dunderklumpen, is a film character. The 19C church has a medieval altar.

At 50km comes Hoting and after 13km is the border of Lappland. In 8km, **Dorotea** bills itself as the gateway to Lappland. It was named Dorotea in 1799 after Gustav IV Adolf's wife, Fredrika Dorotea Vilhelmina, whose other two names were also given to towns. The church was designed by Carl Milles' brother Evert in 1934, with Carl's **sculptures** of Paul on the way to Damascus, and an angel. The mountains to the north-west round Borgafjäll are a centre for skiing, walking and fishing, and are reached by the Road of the Seven Rivers (roads E12 and 92 from Umeå to Borgafjäll).

3km out of Dorotea the 45 goes north and road 92 goes to Umeå. Continue on the 45 for 51km to **Vilhelmina**, also named after Gustav IV Adolf's wife. It was only later in the 18C that Swedish settlers began to drift into the area and scratch a scanty living for themselves and their families. In 1782 there were 10 families but by 1810 there were more Swedes than Sami.

There is a **church village** of 26 wooden cottages which here have been renovated for tourists to stay in.

On the same site is the local **museum** displaying the life of the pioneer settlers, their homes, work and way of life. They fished, hunted and harvested hay from natural meadows until they had tamed the land sufficiently to wrest a living from it. Their cramped quarters, household equipment and decorative handicrafts are shown. There is an archaeological section with objects from the area of which the most important is the 8C Maksjö find of rich grave goods.

The Wilderness Way

The road called the Road of the Sagas, from Örnsköldsvik into Norway, passes through Vilhelmina. Part of this forms a section of a circular tour of 500km called the Wilderness Way (Vildmarksvägen). It goes into the mountains to the west of Vilhelmina, turns south and later east to rejoin the 45 at Strömsund. The most spectacular part of this is the **Stekkenjokk plateau**, c 150km from Vilhelmina. (Start by turning left 10km north of the town. Take a pullover.) The plateau is above the tree-line and the **view** extends over the wild fells into Norway. The highest fell, west of the road is Sipmeke (1424m). There is a mine here, 820m above sea-level, which used to yield copper, zinc, silver and gold. Noteworthy points on or near the circular route include the Sami meeting-place at Fatmomakke, off the road to the right before reaching Stekkenjokk from Vilhelmina, Trappstegsforsen series of rapids 7km east of Saxnäs, and a high waterfall 27km south-east of Gäddede (Hällingsåfallet). Along the way there are hotels, campsites, hostels and cottages for hire, with petrol stations and shops in the larger villages.

It is 68km to **Storuman** the next town, where the E12 crosses the 45 from Umeå to Mo in Norway (the Blue Road). Storuman is a centre for skiing, fishing, hunting, canoeing and walking. The old railway hotel, with panelled and painted interior, is now the library. (For surroundings, see Rte 24.)

28

Storuman to Jokkmokk

Total distance 320km. Storuman—road 45 76km Sorsele turning for Ammarnäs—
83km **Arvidsjaur** turning for **Arjeplog**—161km *__Jokkmokk__ and turning for
Vuollerim.

From Storuman north to Sorsele on road 45 is another 76km of forests and
lakes, which brings you to Sorsele, a resort for fishing, walking and skiing.

To Ammarnäs

From Sorsele the 363 runs north-west for 90km to Ammarnäs, lying
between two rivers as they run into a lake. This is Sami country and the
area with the densest population of reindeer. In autumn the reindeer are
rounded up for ear-notching and slaughtering, an impressive sight, but
tourists are begged not to get in the way. Ammarnäs tourist bureau sells an
Adventure Card which covers riding Icelandic horses, shooting rapids,
canoeing, fishing and more. The King's Trail (Kungsleden—see Rte 29) runs
through here, and the old trading route to Norway has also been turned
into a walking trail. (The local inhabitants used to go to Norway with fish
and game and return with flour and salt.) Near the church is a Sami church
village still in use. Potatoes are actually grown here on a warm slope, near
which there is a local museum. There is a cable car up to Näsberget.

The 45 turns east for 83km to Arvidsjaur. At Slagnäs the road crosses the
Skellefteälv. The terrain alternates between bog, and scrub and forest,
which opens out to reveal distant mountains across a broad plain.

As you approach Arvidsjaur a railway bridge crosses the road. A road to
the right 100m before the bridge doubles back to the old vicarage with a
local **museum** (open mid June–mid Aug). It was the home of the first vicar
Magnus Berlin, built in 1891. It contains furniture and household items from
the late 19C and early 20C, both Sami and Swedish.

Arvidsjaur (pop. 5000) earns its living from forestry and timber, but the
forest Sami (Lapps) were the original inhabitants and there are still 25 Sami
families here who herd reindeer for a living. Around Arvidsjaur there are
several Sami camps which are used a few times a year for herding the
reindeer, marking and slaughtering.

Besides the downhill skiing on Vittjåkk fell 8km outside the town and the
slalom hill 2km away, you can also, depending on season, try shooting
rapids, cross-country skiing, fishing, walking and swimming.

The *__Sami village__ (Lappstaden) is on the north-west edge of town, on the
left opposite the church as you enter on the 45. It is next to modern flats
which provide a piquant contrast. Arvidsjaur was an important market and
church centre, with a transport route (by reindeer) to the silver mines at
Nasafjäll, worked until 1810. Norwegians came to swap dried fish and
groceries for iron goods, game and pelts. The Sami and the Swedish settlers
met for business and festivals. Early settlers found that tar-burning was a
profitable enterprise with the upsurge in shipbuilding in southern Sweden.

Karl IX founded a Sami church village in 1605 to make it easier for them
to attend church. The 83 buildings here date partly from the 18C. The

Sami village in Arvidsjaur, with dwellings in the foreground and raised storage huts behind

rectangular ones on piles are the storage huts, and there are nearly twice as many stores as dwellings. The living-huts are c 4m square, a squat pyramid shape set on low vertical walls. The pyramid has a cut-off top and this is fitted with a double sloping trap-door to let out the smoke. Originally they had beaten earth floors but usually now they have concrete or something similar. There is often a double line of stones from the door showing where you can walk, which widens to surround the fireplace. On either side are rugs and furs. Nowadays modern tools and cooking equipment are used. Here in Arvidsjaur these are private dwellings in current use, but one is usually open for tourists and guided tours are available.

In *Arvas*, the timber house nearby, you can eat Sami food. There are guided tours to Sami settlements, to have coffee round a fire with Sami people, and to see the marking of calves. You can also try your hand at reindeer-herding for a day.

The church (1902) opposite, with its entrance on one corner, is slightly reminiscent of a Victorian conservatory, pale beige and white painted wood, and large windows, similar to others in Norrland of this period.

To Arjeplog

From Arvidsjaur road 95, part of the Silver Road from Skellefteå into Norway, goes north-west reaching **Arjeplog** after 85km. Arjeplog lies amid lakes and bogs—notice how many place-names include 'myr' (bog), or 'heden' (moor). The municipality (*kommun*) of Arjeplog shares with Jokkmokk the distinction of being listed as having a population density of nil—in fact about one-third of a person to the km^2. Europe's largest lead-mine is at Laisvall to the west. (Guided tours.)

The 18C **church** is situated on a point in the lake and possesses some objects saved from a 17C chapel, including a bridal crown. The yellow wooden building near the church is the **Silver Museum**, the creation of Einar Wallquist (died 1985), the 'Lapp doctor'. He came to Arjeplog in 1922 and began to collect Sami objects and also objects typical of the Swedish settlers' homes. This collection developed into the Silver Museum, with silver from the 16C onward, including church silver and silver collars. Other sections relate the history of Arjeplog and the natural history of the fells.

The 45 turns north at Arvidsjaur towards Jokkmokk. It is 48km to Moskosel and another 10km to the bridge over the Pite river. At 30km road 374 towards Älvsbyn goes right (south-east).

To Storforsen

In 28km the 374 comes to *Storforsen (Great Rapids), the largest un-exploited cascade in Scandinavia. Follow the signs to *Storforsen*. (Large car-park, information centre, restaurant.)

Storforsen falls 80m over 5km, but here in the last 2km it falls 60m. About 250m^3 of water surge and crash through per second, which increase to 870m^3 after snow-melting. The best time to go as regards volume is in the second half of June. To make it possible to float timber down, its course was altered, leaving the 'Dead Fall' (Döda Fallet) bare and dry for the most part. Downstream a bog delta and meadows with wild flowers have been formed.

The area has been provided with a comprehensive network of wooden footways, but good footwear is recommended for the many enticing rocky byways and footways slippery with spray. There are barbecue sites and the place is crowded with sunbathers and picnickers in sunny weather. The footways and platforms get to the very edge of the rapids, and over small ravines and waterfalls, pools and streams to the Dead Fall. Large potholes formed by a stone whirled round inside by the force of water above are frequent—some have spirals inside. Most are between 0.5m and 1.5m deep, but some go down 3.5m. Here and there wild flowers flourish.

On the slope to the right of the entrance is a series of wooden buildings, some with old forestry tools, and beyond are huts once used by loggers working on the river and other buildings associated with forestry work. (No information in English.)

At 10km (road 45) Kåbdalis is the starting point for **Kronogård** (15km north-west), a leisure area with 250 lakes, for fishing, hunting orienteering and berry and mushroom-picking. Campsites and cottages to hire are available.

At 55km you cross the **Arctic Circle** (information board), and after 8km arrive in Jokkmokk.

*Jokkmokk like other Lappland towns gives an impression of scattered houses amid wide spaces. The main street is like an elongated park with broad belts of grass and gardens. The 45 comes in on Klockargatan and a right turn into Storgatan brings you to the **tourist bureau**, tucked off the road (open all year, in summer to 21.00).

The name Jokkmokk means 'bend in the stream' in the Sami language. In the 17C Karl IX decreed that this, the Sami winter gathering-place, should have a church and a market. Still today the February fair attracts thousands of visitors who book rooms up to a year in advance. Today only a few hundred Sami in the district are engaged in reindeer breeding, and live in houses or flats in the winter. The town has a college for Sami students. The municipality (*kommun*) of Jokkmokk produces 15 per cent of Sweden's electricity.

Close to the tourist bureau is the **church**, a copy (1972) of the 1753 church which burnt down, and which was on the same site as the one ordered by

Karl IX (open 08.00–20.00). It is surrounded by a double wooden wall about 1m high with a pitched roof. Coffins with bodies were put inside in the winter to wait until graves could be dug in spring. There is a detached wooden bell-tower.

The shape of the church is a compressed octagon with a deep roof. The interior was somewhat adapted in the rebuilding and now the emphasis is on the Sami colours of blue, yellow and red. The candle-sconces on the walls are of brass, the chandeliers of iron and wood. There is a plain cross at the back. The hanging rya rug with four crowns was made by the wife of a local rector with whom Karl X stayed on his visit to Lappland in 1858, in honour of the king.

In the park is a fountain with a large figure of a logger. Here you may see (even in summer) old people whose walking-frames are fitted with snow-runners as well as wheels.

•**Ajtte**, the Sami museum, is or will be the largest and most comprehensive of its kind (open Mon–Fri 09.00–16.00, Sat, Sun 12.00–16.00, to 18.00 in summer, closed Mon Oct–Apr. Shop, restaurant, good book-store, souvenirs. English translation of information available to borrow from reception). It is a few minutes' walk east along Storgatan. Ajtte is thus called because it is the Sami word for storage hut, and the museum is an information-store. The main part is shaped like a reindeer corral a model of which is shown at the entrance with a central circle is surrounded by sections fanning out from it. At the time of visiting some of the planned displays were not yet open, so the following description is necessarily incomplete.

From the entrance hall there is first a room with temporary exhibitions, then a corridor leading into the centre lined with series of figures showing the development of working clothes and equipment. The first section on the left is about the life of Swedish settlers in Lappland. The possibilities of this land were first realised by the Swedes in the 16C. In the 19C and early 20C navvies arrived to work on the railways, and then came forestry workers. Miniature carved wooden scenes show their everyday life, fishing, children picking berries, potato-growing, hay-making. When the museum is complete, there will be sections on the River, the Forest, The Mountains and Geology.

The section on Sami **everyday life** shows items of superb artistry such as a Sami baby's cradle cum sleeping-bag, blue for a boy, red for a girl, knives, boxes, scoops and cheese-moulds, axes and fishing-nets, and ropes of spruce-root. There is the first Bible in the South Sami language (1811). Tools, equipment and clothes intricately ornamented, carved or embroidered, are a delight. A weaving heddle of reindeer horn and an early sewing-machine illustrate contrasting techniques.

The section on Sami **culture** shows how bears were regarded as the messengers of the gods. Their meat was eaten with special ritual. The religious drum, only 70 of which remain after destruction by the missionaries, was used by the Noaidi (holy man) to induce a trance during which he was believed to be able to transfer his soul to the world of the dead and negotiate about the sick on earth. Here too are illustrations from old sagas.

The 17-minute slide show has a Swedish commentary but this is immaterial since it gives simply an impression of Sami life, with barks and grunts of reindeer on the sound-track, and lassooing, use of snow-scooters and modern technology against the Lappland landscape.

A separate section of the museum deals with the fells and fell-walking. Much information is in English, and includes what to see in the national parks, necessary equipment, weather, maps, and flora and fauna. You can look at bark, mosses and fungi under microscopes.

Across the road from the museum is the 1889 church, similar to the one in Arvidsjaur, in cream and green painted wood with decorative carving, and large windows. Inside it is painted cream, pink and gold. The font is of carved wood.

On the outskirts of town there is an open-air museum.

Excursion to Vuollerim

Vuollerim is 43km away to the south-east on road 97, where the Great and Lesser Lule rivers meet. A Stone Age (4000 BC) village was found here in 1983 and there is an exhibition in the town, with buses to take visitors to the archaeological site and to the reconstruction (open mid June–mid Aug 10.00–18.00).

The **information centre** in the town shows some of the thousands of finds from the site, with background information and a slide-show (open mid June–mid Aug 10.00–18.00). Visitors are then ferried to the **sites**. The inhabitants appear to have abandoned the site hastily, leaving everything behind, fortunately for the archaeologists. The actual site of the finds is marked out with the positions of post-holes, cooking-places, storage areas, fireplaces and so on. There are the remains of at least four houses, with cooking and trapping sites. The dwellings were surrounded by a low wall and were c 11m by 4.5m, with tools and other objects of quartz, slate and greenstone. These were a hunting people, eating mainly elk and beaver, but also fish, berries and other plants. This was their winter home and in summer they went some distance up river where archaeologists have found remains of cooking sites.

At the reconstruction site you can see the full-scale reconstruction which researchers made in order to learn the techniques and problems involved. The house has an inverted V framework of branches which is covered with 70 elk-hides sewn together. The central heating system was an ingenious arrangement of a cold air intake being led over hot stones to a fire. One end of the hut was used for sleeping and to one side were the storage pits covered with wooden lids. Food was cooked in holes in the ground. The bottom was filled with 30 or so stones heated by a fire, then the food, wrapped in bark, was laid on top and covered with earth and moss. Groups can order a Stone Age meal in advance, and it may later be possible for the casual visitor also to sample beaver meat prepared in a cooking-hole.

29

Jokkmokk to Abisko

Total distance 316km. Jokkmokk—road 45 7km turning for Kvikkjokk—36km **Porjus**—52km **Gällivare**—75km Svappavaara and turning for road 45 Karesuando—E10 40km turning for **Jukkasjärvi**—8km *Kiruna**—98km *Abisko**.

Just north of Jokkmokk off road 45 is Akkats **power station** and **aquarium** showing specimens of almost every fish in the Lesser Lule River (Lilla Luleälven). (Both open mid June–mid Aug 10.00–16.00.) 7km from Jokkmokk is the turning for Kvikkjokk.

Kvikkjokk (120km) is at the end of road 805 to the north-west of Jokkmokk. In the 17C it was known for its silver working—silver mines were discovered in 1657. Carl von Linné (Linnaeus) visited Kvikkjokk on his Lappland journey in 1732. Vallespiken (15km walk) was the first bare mountain Linné had climbed and he was overwhelmed by the view from 1385m, and the rich flora of the countryside. The Padjelanta Trail starts in Kvikkjokk and the King's Trail passes through—there is a fell station. The wooden church was built in 1906. Guided walking and boat tours are arranged and even trips by plane. (See below under Porjus for information on Padjelanta National Park, and under Abisko for the King's Trail.) A new walking-trail, *Nordkalottleden*, goes through Sweden, Norway and Finland. On the Swedish side it starts here, and passes Treriksröset (where the three countries meet). Information from STF (08) 7903200.

At 17km is a sign for **Muddus National Park**. This area of c 500km^2 consists of bog and forest. In the south are clefts and gorges, and a 40m waterfall. Virgin pine forests are to be found. There are many new pines, grown since the severe fires of the first half of this century, but pines can in fact survive several fires. The marsh and heath vegetation is very rich, with some unusual species. There are lynx, bears, elks, otters and beavers, and over 100 different birds, of which about half breed here, including whooper swans and cranes.

Much of the park is very difficult terrain. Certain areas are closed to visitors from 15 March to 31·July for the breeding season, and this includes a large central section. However, the bird observation tower is always accessible. (Information and car-park near the entrance. Cottages for hire, picnic sites and toilets.)

The 45 continues north to (19km) **Porjus**.

It was in 1910 that the Swedish railways requested a power source in this area and the 2km length of falls at Porjus, where the population at the time was seven people, was chosen to be developed, at the enormous cost of over 10 million kronor. There was no road to the railway at Gällivare, so all materials had to be carried the 50km for the first year until the railway was finished. Each man carried 50kg or more and took 24 hours for the journey. Up to 1500 men worked on the project at a time and living conditions left much to be desired. This, the first state-owned power-station, was opened in 1915. At that time output was 38 megawatts, compared to today's 530 megawatts.

The old power-station building, signposted *G:la Kraftstation* and *Expo*, stands high over the river, and has now been converted into a museum (both old and new power-stations, and the historic photograph exhibition *Expo* are open mid June–mid Aug 09.00–18.00).

The **old power station** is entered by the so-called King's Gate, and upstairs in the control-room you can see the control-system, while the machine-room is 50m under ground. A film is also shown.

Porjus Expo is a permanent exhibition of historic photographs chronicling the early days of the building work in progress, the tools and machinery, the workers and their shanty-town living-conditions, the general shop, and much more.

The new power-station is a couple of hundred metres away and provides guided tours. On one day in summer the waters are released for tourists in the now traditional festival of Fallens dag.

In the small park next to the old power-station is an arresting 400-ton sculpture symbolising power, by Bo Holmlund.

At 7km there is a sign for **Stora Sjöfallets National Park**.

Three great **national parks** lie together, Stora Sjöfallet, Sarek and Padjelanta. Together they cover 5232km^2. There are Sami settlements here, with spring, summer and autumn reindeer pastures. In each of these seasons there are critical times for reindeer-breeding, the calves in spring, the marking in summer, and the autumn slaughtering, so it is important for tourists to keep their distance. Where there is vegetation it is mostly mountain ash and mountain birch, with a flurry of wild flowers in summer. Reindeer of course are common, and bears and elks are seen too.

Sarek National Park has a reputation for being the most difficult and dangerous area of the Swedish mountains with around 100 glaciers, and bears, lynxes, wolverines and artic foxes among the fauna. There are no tourist facilities, shops or telephones, no bridges or marked trails, and there are dangerous fords. It is **essential** to have experience, good equipment and information. (Information from Fjällenheten, Åsgatan 20, 960 40 Jokkmokk.) The highest peak here is Sarekjåkko (2090m).

Padjelanta is easier, there are huts and trails, but certainly demands experience. There are large lakes, and reindeer grazing lands, with rich flora and fauna. **Stora Sjöfallet** consists of high fell with areas of primeval forest, and along the King's Trail (see Abisko) there are overnight huts. The Akka massif reaches 2016m at its highest point.

To the west of these parks lies **Sjaunja Nature Reserve**, 1000km^2 of mainly boggy ground. Some of the pines are 300–400 years old. 25 species of mammals live here, and birds include the golden eagle and the sea-eagle.

The 45 shortly passes the north edge of Muddus National Park. In this district there are frequent signs offering smoked fish (*rökt fisk*) for sale.

At 38km the road passes **Dundret**, an isolated 820m hill criss-crossed with flood-lit ski-slopes, cable railway and ski-lifts. Even in the 19C it was regarded as a good place from which to see the midnight sun, visible here from 5 June to 11 July. You can drive to the top (10km) but not when there is snow on the ground. The **view** includes Sarek fell and Kebnekaise. On a lower slope nearer the town and main road is a village of holiday chalets (stugby). There is a large building constructed of 'dry-pine', that is, 200–300-year-old trees which dry on the root, and acquire a curious lustre. These are found mainly in the Finnish parts of Lappland.

At 7km the 45 loops through **Gällivare** with its pleasant open centre, in summer with fountains, flowers and open-air cafés. In the 18C rich ore deposits were found in the area but could not be exploited until the end of the 19C, when the ore railway to Luleå was built. The Aitik mine nearby produces copper, gold and silver—it is Sweden's largest gold-mine (guided tours). Gällivare is also the terminus of the celebrated Inland Railway (Inlandsbanan) from Östersund, continually threatened with closure. Here you can play golf under the midnight sun, go panning for gold, tour a gold mine. In winter everybody skis on Dundret and snow sculptures turn the streets into an art gallery.

Follow the signs to the **tourist bureau**, in the same building as the museum and a café. Here a wealth of tourist literature is available, not only on the town but Lappland as a whole, with information and advice on the mountains and all activities. Books and Sami handicrafts are also sold. The **museum** (open 10.00–17.00, shorter hours in winter) has Sami objects, with a tent, boats, a sacrificial stone, tools, weapons, with flora and fauna, accompanied by sound effects. Aspects of the life of Swedish settlers are also shown.

The **church** is on the other side of the main road, built in 1882 and painted white, with many small pitched roofs. Inside it is dominated by a tapestry showing the Sermon on the Mount (key at the 'Pastorsexpedition' nearby).

It is worth noting the Viking-style railway-station.

The **old church** stands on the river bank on the other side of the railway. Take the road going south behind the 'new' church. It turns sharp right at the railway line. Where this main road goes left over the river almost immediately, take the narrow road straight ahead over the railway and follow the signs *Gamla Kyrkan* to the right. (The palatial decoratively carved pale green villa on the opposite river bank before the turn was built in 1889 by the manager of the mine—now a children's day centre.)

The old church is also called the 'one-öre church', as every household in the country had to contribute one öre to finance it. It was built in 1747, and the bell-tower in 1768. The original congregation consisted of 850 Sami. The paintings on the pulpit of the Evangelists were completed in 1779, by the same artist who painted the Last Supper and Crucifixion in the new church. The altar has wooden figures of Christ and two kneeling Sami (1963).

On the south-west edge of town on the banks of the Vassara river, there is an **open-air museum** with a windmill (rare here), a Sami camp with reindeer enclosure, and old houses from the area including a shop and bakery. •

A few minutes' drive north on Malmbergsleden brings you to Gällivare's twin town **Malmberget**, which means 'ore mountain'. Follow Malmberg-sleden to the T-junction and directly opposite is the **Mining Museum** (Gruvmuseum, open mid June–mid Aug 10.00–17.00). All mining is under-ground and there are 250km of passages altogether. The museum displays the history of mining over 250 years and has a collection of all the different minerals found in the Malmberget mine.

When the railway to Luleå was finished in 1888 people streamed in to find work in the mines. The British company which developed the railway and the mines did not own the land and so did not build homes for the workers. They were forced to shift for themselves, constructing hovels from dynamite crates, turf, bits of scaffolding, stone and other scrap. The main street of Kåkstan (shanty-town) with shops and cafés has been recon-structed, but more tastefully, with goods to sell and activities to take part in. The cleft in the ground nearby, called Gropen, is becoming larger every year due to the mining.

You can cut down to the 45 from Malmberget or regain it from Gällivare. At 12km it joins the E10 from Töre and turns north to Svappavaara. From here northwards virtually all place-names are either Sami or Finnish (the two are related—see Introduction).

At 34km there is a turning to the left to Fjällåsen (47km), from which a track (drivable) leads to Kaitum (5km) where a chapel has been built to the memory of Dag Hammarskjöld (1964). It is in the shape of a Sami tent, with chancel windows looking out over the fells, and decorated with **Sami art**.

The 45 and E10 split in 29km just before Svappavaara.

To Karesuando

The 45 turns north-east to **Vittangi** (27km) and then north to **Karesuando** (108km). At Vittangi there is a church built by Lars Levi Laestadius in 1854 (see below under Jukkasjärvi) and a museum.

(From Vittangi road 395 goes off east to Pajala and the Finnish frontier. At 30km is **Masugnsbyn** (Blast Furnace Village) where the tale is that a 17C squirrel-hunter discovered his iron-tipped arrows stuck to some black stones—iron ore. This was the first iron-mine in Norrbotten. A blast furnace was accordingly built, and can be visited together with the old ironworks' buildings.)

Northwards on the 45 the forests give way to scrub and the scenery becomes more and more desolate. At 48km there is a turning right for **Lannavaara** (8km) where there is a gold-panning centre just outside the village. There is also an exhibition of minerals found locally.

Towards **Karesuando** (60km) the ground is in the grip of permafrost. Karesuando is 250km north of the Arctic circle and there is midnight sun from 26 May to 18 July. In this inhospitable landscape, distinctions of nationality and frontiers are blurred, and family relationships and commerce with Norway and Finland take precedence.

Here is Sweden's northernmost church (1905). Beside the church is the small wooden **cottage** (open to visitors) of Lars Levi Laestadius, the revivalist preacher who was vicar here 1826–49. Visitors can stay in Sami huts and there is also the preserved settlers' village with cabins, a sauna and cowsheds and a Sami holy spring. A new botanical garden in honour of Laestadius has been planted with Lappland flora. The mountain Kaarevaara (517m) to the south-east (12km) has a **view** which can extend to the tundra at the northernmost extremity of Sweden.

To get to **Treriksröset** (Cairn of the Three Countries) where Sweden, Norway and Finland meet, you have to drive north-west through Finland to Kilpisjärvi (112km), take a ferry and walk 3km to a large ugly concrete cylinder marking the spot (enquire at the tourist bureau about possible bus trips).

The E10 runs through the village of Svappavaara. Raw copper was produced here from the 17C, the copper then being sent to Kengis Bruk near Pajala for refining. The modern ironworks had to be closed down during the mining recession. At 40km there is a turning on the right for Jukkasjärvi (7km).

Drive through the village of **Jukkasjärvi** to where the road ends at the **church** (open Mon–Fri 11.00–20.00 in summer). Its oldest section dates from the 17C and the rest and the bell-tower from the 18C. In 1947, bodies of ministers, Samis and settlers were found under the floor.

The large **altar-piece** (1958) occupying most of the rear wall is by Bror Hjorth. This is a tribute to Lars Levi Laestadius' life among the Sami.

Laestadius (1800–61) was born in Ångermanland and studied theology in Uppsala. In 1826 he became vicar in Karesuando, a poor village of Sami and settlers. During the first years he also managed to become a renowned botanist and took part in a French expedition in Lappland, for which he was made a chevalier of the Légion d'Honneur. But after a crisis of faith he returned to his preaching with renewed conviction and vigour, becoming a fiery revivalist who transformed his parish. His movement spread to Finland and Norway, and even in North America Scandinavian settlers formed Laestadian congregations.

The altar-piece is in three sections, low-relief in wood, brilliantly coloured, mainly in the Sami colours of red, blue and yellow. The style is direct and naive. In the centre is Christ, both Suffering and Reigning. To the left Laestadius is preaching in front of the church. Two sinners confess, a stolen reindeer is returned and alcoholic drink is poured away. On the right is Laestadius's disciple Johan Raattamaa, with Laestadius kneeling. The woman with the halo is Maria, a Sami woman who inspired Laestadius.

There are also in the church two wooden panels left by four French travellers in Lappland. The one shaped like the end of a Sami sledge is from 1681. The one made from half a barrel-lid is dated 1718. Both have Latin inscriptions.

Next door is an **open-air museum** in old farm buildings (open in summer, buildings open only for guided tours: 12.00, 14.00, 16.00, 18.00, café, shop). This shows Sami culture with different types of dwellings, a boat, a place of sacrifice, and a smoke-sauna. The museum collections include sacred drums, objects of worship and a bear-spear.

It is 8km to Kiruna. The forests have thinned, and small birches and scrub take their place. *•**Kiruna**, a municipality of almost 20,000km^2, has a population of 26,000 (the town itself 20,000), and lies 140km north of the Arctic Circle and 950km north of Stockholm. It has midnight sun from 28 May to 18 July. It is dominated by the lowering bulk of the ore mountain Kiirunavaara to the south, with its dramatic edge of steps which former open-cast mining has etched into the silhouette. To the north is Luossavaara mountain, also ore-bearing but no longer worked. It is a popular place for skiing, and admiring the view and the midnight sun.

In 1890 when the geologist Hjalmar Lundbohm came to investigate the iron-ore deposits he found one turf hut. The deposits were known but had never been examined and assessed, and Lundbohm's investigation led to the discovery of a huge iron-ore field. Lundbohm became manager of LKAB, the Luossavaara-Kiirunavaara Aktie-Bolaget, now state-owned. He helped to plan the town of Kiruna, including schools and hospital, and is regarded as the founder and father of the town. By the end of the century mining on a large scale had been started, the railway to the Norwegian border had been built, and there were 15 houses and 100 huts.

The E10 enters at **Malmvägen** and swings round to the right. On the left is the great mass of Kiirunavaara, and soon the distinctive tower of the town hall appears on the left, with an open square and the **tourist bureau** on the right (open summer to 20.00, winter to 16.00).

The **town hall** (open all year, summer to 16.00) was designed by Artur von Schmalensee and finished in 1963. The open spiky iron-work **tower** is by the sculptor Bror Marklund, and the 23 bells play 14 different melodies (12.00 and 18.00).

The reindeer-horn and masur birch door-handles represent the Sami sacred drum. In the light galleried interior court, the bricks are hand-made, the floor is Italian mosaic and the wood-work is Oregon pine. Here there is tourist and municipal information available. The large **wall-hanging** is also inspired by the Sami drum, marked by the white line, and was designed by the artist Sven X:et Erixon, who included the Lapporten, (a distinctive valley near Abisko), (lake) Torneträsk and Swedish autumn colours in the composition. Other rooms are the Council Chamber, the Library and the Court-room.

Returning across the square, passing the tourist bureau and places offering rafting trips, take Gruvvägen up the hill to the **church** (1912) among ash and birch trees (open all year 11.00–17.00). The **bell-tower** was built in 1907 of wooden props from Russia, with an onion-dome.

Hjalmar Lundbohm told the architect to build a church like a Sami tent, and the dark walls with light from above, as well as the beam construction show this source of inspiration. The gilt-bronze **figures** on the roof of the church by Christian Eriksson represent various states of mind, Despair, Devotion and so on. The **relief** with Sami people over the door is by the same artist.

Above the altar is a **painting** by Prince Eugen representing Paradise, actually completed in 1897 as a Tuscan landscape. On the altar is the only cross in the church. Lundbohm wanted a church with no reference to any specific religion, but the bishop insisted, so this plain cross with Sami people was placed on the altar. To the right is Christian Eriksson's St. George and the Dragon made of scrap materials. Many details in the church are of wrought-iron as befits the situation.

Return down Gruvvägen, turn left and then right into Ingeniörsgatan, and then first left to reach **Lundbohmsgården**, Lundbohm's house which is now a museum. This shows the history of Kiruna, and Lundbohm's study as he left it (open all year, summer to 20.00, café).

Out in the other direction (north) is **Samegården**, a Sami centre where Samis stay when they come to town, with a museum, shop and small café open to tourists (June–Aug 10.00–18.00.) Take Hjalmar Lundbohmsvägen north from the town hall, turn left after about 500m into Adolf Hedinsvägen, and it is on the corner of the third road on the right (Brytaregatan 14).

In the **museum** English notes can be borrowed from reception. The displays include a tent, sacrificial stones, a baby's reindeer-skin 'container', weaving-techniques and clothes, and exquisite silver, reindeer-leather and reindeer-horn items. The shop also sells Sami work. They hope to build a new museum in the near future.

The tourist bureau, Lundbohmsgården and the mine itself all run **·tours of the mine**. (Tourist bureau tours mid June–end Aug 10.00, 12.00, 14.00, 16.00 multilingual. 1½ hours.)

From 1900 to 1950 open-cast mining was carried on, creating the present characteristic outline of the mountain. Now the 1km deep underground mine has been developed into the largest in the world. The tower on top is a lift for waste products. Below ground there are 400km of roads and 40km of railways. 400 people work underground, of whom 10 per cent are women (most in the restaurant). There are morning and afternoon shifts, and blasting takes place at night.

The method used here is called sub-level caving. Tunnels are drilled, then the rock is sliced ready for blasting in sections, and finally retrieved. LKAB produces both high and low phosphorus ores and pellets. 85 per cent goes for export, mostly to Europe but also to the Middle and Far East. The ore railway with open trucks which you can see waiting at the lakeside goes to Narvik (Norway) or Luleå.

The bus takes tourists through the extensive ground-level complex of electrical and mechanical workshops and offices, before travelling 3km into the mountain to a depth of 370m. A drilling-machine is switched on and shown working. It produces 100 decibels of noise and drills a metre in 1–2 minutes using compressed air and water. A mechanical shovel then shows how 14 tons of broken ore can be picked up at a time. A 10-minute film is shown in various languages.

The tourist bureau organises trips to **Esrange**, 45km to the east (June–Sept Mon, Wed, Thurs, Fri 13.00. 3 hours). Esrange is Europe's only civilian rocket base, owned by the European Space Research Organisation. It was founded in 1966 and its first job was to investigate the aurora borealis. Now they conduct experiments with rockets and balloons, monitor satellites from many different countries, and log and process data from satellites. The latest task is to monitor the ozone layer.

From Kiruna a road, first south, then west, to Nikkaluokta (60km) provides the nearest approach by car to **Kebnekaise**, Sweden's highest mountain (2117m). From Nikkaluokta it is a 19km walk to the Kebnekaise fell station (1940m). The massif is the most concentrated high-alpine area in the country with 20 peaks of about 2000m, and 50 glaciers. In another 14km the trail joins the King's Trail from Abisko.

The E10 continues north-west from Kiruna to Abisko. The landscape becomes more bare and wild. After c 55km the road turns more westerly when it meets **Torneträsk lake**. The scenery here is very beautiful, with the mountains now close on both sides of the 70km long lake.

* **Abisko**, in 43km, has midnight sun from 13 June to 14 July, and lies in a favoured rain-shadow with the lowest annual precipitation in the country, and more sunshine than other places nearby. **Lapporten** (Lapp Gate), a great U-shaped valley between two peaks formed by glacier action is a dramatic feature of the landscape.

Beyond the small village is STF's largest fell station which is a village in itself, with its own railway station. It functions as a youth hostel, holiday chalet village and camp-site, with a food-shop and sports equipment for hire.

The **Naturum**, á small natural history museum, has sections on the geology, glaciers, the Sami, birds, flora and fauna of the region (English translation of the information can be borrowed). They arrange walks, tours and evening events to study the landscape, birds, flowers and the Sami.

A couple of hundred metres to the north-west is the little Abiskojåkk **canyon** reached by a footpath parallel to the main road. (Jåkk means river, and is a North Sami revised spelling of Jokk. The pronunciation is the same.) This was the site of an old power station used during the construction of the railway (1899–1900).

Cross the road opposite the tourist station and take the tunnel under the railway. To the left behind the railway station a sign points into the woods *Lapplägret 0.3km*. This is an autumn-spring **Sami camp** reconstructed by Samis, of two turf dwelling huts and storage huts on piles.

To the right behind the station is a small road along which on the left is an inviting wooden gateway marked Kungsleden, revealing a well-trodden path beyond. This is the beginning (or end) of the celebrated King's Trail. In the gateway are leaflets (also in English) with suggestions for walks, sketch-maps, information and advice, and a book to record where you go in case of accidents.

The **King's Trail** stretches 500km from here south to Hemavan. Between Abisko and Kvikkjokk, and between Ammarnäs and Hemavan there are overnight huts 8–21km apart but none on the middle section. The trail is well-marked, with bridges over rivers and boggy areas, and boats across larger stretches of water. There are emergency telephones here and there. The huts have cooking facilities and beds. (You need a sleeping-bag, and you have to clean up and replenish the wood and water.) At the fell stations there are the usual hostel facilities including saunas and some food for sale.

This is the easiest trail for beginners and therefore is very popular, especially this northern part with good communications to Abisko. The approximately one-week walk to Kebnekaise has become something of a classic and accommodation is crowded between mid July and mid August.

Between Abisko and Kvikkjokk there is varied terrain, mostly above the tree-line, in broad valleys and on plateaux, with some steep climbs. The highest point is the Tjäkta pass at 1150m. The trail passes through Stora Sjöfallet National Park. Then there are forests before you get to Kvikkjokk. The middle section crosses the Piteälven, and road 95 from Arjeplog at Jakkvik, after which it goes through Pieljekaise National Park. The southern section from Ammarnäs to Hemavan is easy to walk, over low fells, but passing fell massifs, the highest point of which is Sytertoppen (1767m). The path then goes through Vindelfjällen Nature Reserve and the terrain is varied, with bare fells, moor, birch woods and boggy areas, rapids and waterfalls.

The area surrounding the north end of the King's Trail is **Abisko National Park** where Lappland animals, birds and plants can be observed. Reindeer and lemmings are common, and bears and wolverines may be seen. In the forests there are blue hares, ermine, elks, martens and lynxes. Birds include the dotterel, long-tailed skuas and ptarmigan in the mountain regions. The part round the mouth of the river is closed between 1 May and 31 July for the breeding season.

Continuing past the gateway to the King's Trail brings you to the Abisko-jåkk river with a trail along the river and remains of the old dam to the left, ahead a road to the cable railway up **Njulla mountain**, and to the right back to the tourist station.

The E10 continues towards Norway. The railway disappears into a 2km long tunnel. Problems for road-builders here are many. Traffic is melting the permafrost in the ground under the road, avalanches can travel at 100km an hour and have to be diverted, and Torneträsk lake can produce 2m high waves. Besides all this, there are the waterways—on the 9km between Abisko and Björkliden there are 25 bridges.

Björkliden has views, caves which can be visited and a nine-hole golf-course open for play 24 hours a day in summer. There are one or two special problems—over one hole the height difference is 60m, and extra rules have had to be made to cover reindeer eating or moving the balls. *Silverfallet* is a waterfall on the edge of the lake.

At 5km in **Tornehamn** the old railway navvies' graveyard with simple white crosses is in a grove of birches. One of the inscriptions reads 'Anna, Norge' and is thought to be the grave of a legendary navvies' cook, also known as the Black Bear.

It is 20km to the border with Norway. Some distance to the north of the road is Vadvetjåkka National Park which has very difficult terrain, bogs, precipices, unusually bad weather and no facilities or communications.

Riksgränsen (Kingdom's Frontier) the border town, has a tourist station. It holds the Swedish record for high annual precipitation, while Abisko 34km away has the lowest.

Index

Swedish speakers should note that in this index the letters Å, å, Ä, ä, Ö and ö are incorporated within A and O. People are indexed in *italic*.

If you would like more information about
Blue Guides please complete the form below and
return it to

Blue Guides
A&C Black (Publishers) Ltd
Freepost
Howard Road
Eaton Socon
Huntingdon
Cambridgeshire
PE19 3BR
or fax it to us on
0171-831 8478

Name...

....

Address...

....

....

....

....

....